Queen Victoria is one of the great subjects of biography; yet this is the first life to be published for quarter of a century. Many new disclosures have come to light in the last twenty-five years, and these illuminate her story as never before.

The stuff of high drama is everywhere in these pages. Fatherless at eight months, ignored at best by her royal uncles, and confined at home by her mother, Princess Alexandrina Victoria survived to become Queen at eighteen. An arranged betrothal became a love match as well as a tempestuous marriage, yet ended tragically when she was still a comparatively young woman. A 'soldier's daughter', as she called herself, she was more belligerent than her generals or her prime ministers, insisting that wars should be fought only when a compelling national interest arose, but then should be fought to win.

Queen during the dynamic years when England grew from island nation to the largest colonial and industrial empire on earth, she had to alternate between the conflicting roles of wife, mother and sovereign, and then reconcile the inner compulsions of widowhood with the responsibilities of the throne. Throughout her eventful reign, tragedy stalked amid the triumphs – not only the deaths of loved ones but a nearly fatal illness of her own, little examined until now, and seven failed assassination attempts. Brutally attacked in the press in Albert's time – once she and the Prince Consort were widely believed to have been imprisoned in the Tower of London – and maligned as a widow for allegedly taking a servant as lover, and for malingering rather than reigning, she returned from rumour-ridden seclusion to become the beloved symbol of the era that bears her name.

Stanley Weintraub is Evan Pugh Professor and Director of the Institute for the Arts and Humanistic Studies in Pennsylvania State University. He is the author of numerous previous books, including biographies of Whistler, Beardsley and Shaw, a group biography of the Rossettis; and an account of the end of the First World War *A Stillness Heard Round the World*.

FOR HARRY P. CLARK, BOOKMAN AND BIBLIOPHILE

Illustration credits: page 26, National Portrait Gallery; page 142, collection of the author; page 176, British Museum; pages 95, 151, 616, and 627, Pattee Library, The Pennsylvania State University.

Royal Archives photos in photo gallery reproduced by gracious permission of Her Majesty Queen Elizabeth II. Copyright reserved.

VICTORIA
BIOGRAPHY
OF A QUEEN

STANLEY WEINTRAUB

UNWIN
PAPERBACKS

LONDON SYDNEY WELLINGTON

First published in Great Britain by Unwin Hyman, an imprint of
Unwin Hyman Limited, 1987

Published in the United States by Truman Talley Books,
E. P. Dutton a division of New American Library in 1987

First published in paperback by Unwin® Paperbacks, an imprint of
Unwin Hyman Limited, in 1988

UNWIN HYMAN LIMITED
15/17 Broadwick Street, London WIV 1FP

Allen & Unwin Australia Pty Ltd
8 Napier Street, North Sydney, NSW 2060, Australia

Allen & Unwin New Zealand Ltd with the Port Nicholson Press,
60 Cambridge Terrace, Wellington, New Zealand

British Library Cataloguing in Publication Data

Weintraub, Stanley
    Victoria: biography of a queen.
1. Victoria, *Queen of Great Britain*
2. Great Britain – Kings and rulers –
Biography
I. Title
941.081'092'4   DA554
ISBN 0-04-440187-6

Printed in Finland by Werner Söderström Oy

"I don't know what you mean by *your* way," said
the Queen; "all the ways about here belong to *me*. . . ."
—Lewis Carroll
Through the Looking Glass

Contents

CONTENTS

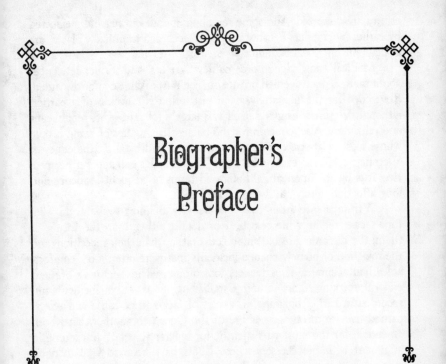

Biographer's Preface

It has often been said that someone really worth writing about deserves reappraisal every twenty years. A quarter of a century has now passed since the last full-length biography of Queen Victoria was sent to the publisher. In our data-ravenous contemporary world, new lives of some figures—even trivial individuals by any historic measure—emerge nearly every year, often for no other reason than a ready market. Meanwhile, other potential subjects intimidate biographers into writing around their edges, or into silence.

Our sources of information about Queen Victoria have been considerably enriched since the early 1960s. New material has become accessible, such as Victoria's own *album consolatium;* and we now know that she was not her father's first child, nor even his first Victoria. Vivid and colorful diaries, journals, and letters of her relatives and her social and political confidants and acquaintances keep surfacing as scholars dig and estates are dispersed. And some revealing episodes in her life, neglected by earlier biographers because they were recorded in unlikely places, are available if one locates them.

Medical knowledge affords us new insights, and former reticences about matters once deemed private or even unspeakable can be discarded. Reverence for the monarchy as an institution is now less of a barrier, although Victorian England itself was largely tolerant of its republicans and reformers. Also, concern for the pained sensitivities of living people whose close relatives, even a generation ago, had lived on the edges of Victoria's orbit, has eased with time. This life adds still another perspective: it is by an American, although, in terms of frequent residence and long affection, almost a "London Yankee."

Writing a life from the documentary richness available in Victoria's case requires the selection of details rather than the listing of them; the discarding of old shibboleths rather than their repetition; and the rejection of homely chance incidents that were often more comfortable than accurate. Thus readers long immersed in Victoria's life and era will encounter here some unfamiliar names as well as incidents unrecorded in earlier biographies. Errors of fact and of cause and effect, carried over from one earlier life of the Queen to another, have been amended, for the most part silently, for biography is not an exercise in argument with predecessors whose labors have been so vital to one's own work. It is an attempt to inch ever closer to that elusive concept so lightly called *truth*.

One can find different Victorias in many earlier lives, where the girl and the woman, the wife and the widow, the mother and the matriarch are concealed rather than revealed by the oft-told myths and legends that offer popular perception rather than private reality. Victoria was pleasant and unpleasant, selfish and selfless, democratic and dictatorial, heroic and humble, sophisticated and naïve, energetic and slothful, passionate and passive, queenly yet middle-class at heart. As a poet put it less accurately about himself, she contained multitudes.

It is now a century and a half since a girl christened Alexandrina Victoria, eighteen years old and not quite five feet tall, became Queen of her country, and one hundred years since her Golden Jubilee on the Throne celebrated what seemed likely to be lasting imperial greatness, and the Queen's translation into almost mythic status. The Victorian age requires a library rather than a book. Nevertheless, this volume explores the complex individual behind the statues, coins, stamps, place names and portraits—behind even the adjective *Victorian*. Queen Victoria was one of the most scrupulously honest of humans. I would like to think that she would find herself fairly returned to life in these pages.

STANLEY WEINTRAUB
University Park, Pennsylvania
July 1986

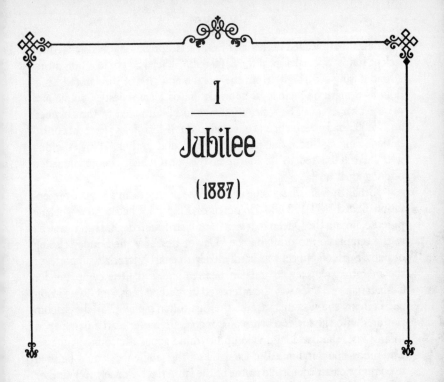

1

Jubilee

(1887)

The Queen detested Buckingham Palace. Yet in December 1886 she had returned to the fogs and fumes of a London she loathed to receive a delegation of two hundred peeresses of the realm, on business related to her Jubilee. Little about Victoria resembled the engaging young girl of eighteen whose accession nearly fifty years earlier would be celebrated across the breadth of the empire throughout 1887, and for which the visit of the ladies was preparation. Dressed in black, and in the fashion of 1861, as she had been since the death of the Prince Consort twenty-five years before, needing a walking stick to support her ample yet tiny frame, she might have been anyone's elderly, well-to-do grandmother. Only Buckingham Palace itself, and the small army of guards in bearskins and courtiers in velvet, suggested the Queen-Empress.

Some of the peeresses, on their way to the palace, may have seen hoardings that pleaded on behalf of Guy's Hospital, "200 beds closed for lack of funds. Special appeal for £100,000." They had come representing a fund-raising campaign "from the women and girls of the United Kingdom as a mark of their loyal appreciation of Her Majesty's public and private character." The solicitation was to be extended to the colonies, as £75,000 had already been collected in the British Isles alone, in contributions ranging "from one penny to one pound sterling." Now Victoria was "herself invited to decide upon the form which the accumulated offering shall take."

Other British ladies, some of them also peeresses, in a Jubilee presentation signed by 1,132,608 "Women of England," had a more specific purpose, urging the Queen to lessen "want, strife and degradation" as well as the temptation to drink on the "Day of Rest" by the Sunday closing of pubs. Such an appeal was hardly likely to enlist Victoria's support, for she preferred whiskey to milk in her tea and had little sympathy for Sabbatarian zeal. Nor was she interested in funding beds for Guy's Hospital. Perhaps she was unaware of the institution's plight, as she seldom ventured into the lower reaches of London, and never read a newspaper. In any case, she had long made up her mind about the Jubilee largesse. The funds, she announced to the ladies at her audience, would be used to commission an equestrian statue of the late Prince Consort in Windsor Park.

The number of statues of Prince Albert in every conceivable posture, from recumbent to equestrian, was already dismaying to those who perceived more urgent national needs. Much of the kingdom failed to reflect a Golden Jubilee aura. Unemployment and poverty gripped the richest nation in the world; unrest in the colonial reaches upon which the sun never set belied the beneficence of what was called civilization. Yet the British press reported the Queen's recommendation to the peeresses without suggesting that she had confused her priorities, and without urging either abdication or revolution. As much myth as monarch after half a century, she could do little wrong except in the eyes of the extremists, to whom few paid any attention. Even the once-feisty Algernon Swinburne, who earlier had poetically praised regicide and republicanism, and had composed scurrilous, even obscene, verses about Victoria, now wrote to "praise a blameless queen" of an "empire that no seas confine."

Britain had buzzed with rumors that Victoria would use the occasion to announce her retirement in favor of her eldest son, Albert Edward, an aging playboy to whom she had given little to do. She had privately confided more than once, to people likely to gossip to "Bertie," that she hoped to outlive him—that he was unfit to be king. Moreover, his eldest son, Prince Eddy (officially Albert Victor, Duke of Clarence), was even less fit to reign. Backward and almost uneducable, allegedly bisexual, cosseted by bands of tutors and equerries he wanted only to elude, he was the best contemporary argument for a monarchy shorn of responsibility. The portly Prince of Wales, at least, knew how to handle people, his mother excepted; but even there he managed a small triumph. His New Year present to her was a Jubilee inkstand (commemorative trinkets were already flooding London shops and stalls). The lid was a royal crown; when it was lifted, one saw the Queen's face and its reflection in a pool of ink. "Very pretty and useful," she confided to her diary.

It has been suggested that only then was "her imagination . . . first stirred" about the Jubilee, but she had been central to the preparations for many months. Already for sale on the Strand were patent automatic musical bustles that played "God Save the Queen" whenever the wearer sat down; teapots that represented Victoria's head, with the lid a crown; and walking sticks with Victoria's head the knob. She had already sat for authorized portraits and statues and, as Empress of India in state robes and wearing the Koh-i-noor Diamond, for a photograph to be enlarged to nine feet by six for the government of the Punjab. A shelf of books on the Jubilee had already appeared. One, *Fifty Years of a Good Queen's Reign,* inspired an anonymous critic in *The Pall Mall Gazette* the month before—a young Socialist named Bernard Shaw—to observe that "if the Royal Jubilee is to be a success, the sooner some competent cynic writes a book about her Majesty's shortcomings the better," as "a few faults are indispensable to a really popular monarch." The world was growing out of passive loyalty, the reviewer suggested, and public fulsomeness paid the Queen, he predicted, "will be pure hypocrisy. . . . Yet there must be much genuine superstitious loyalty among us. . . . Were a gust of wind to blow off our Sovereign's head-gear tomorrow, 'the Queen's bonnet' would crowd Bulgaria out of the papers. Clearly the ideal of Royalty is still with us; and it is as the impersonatrix of that ideal that the Queen is worshipped by us. That feeling is the real support of thrones."

For a monarch who could seem impossible, impenetrable, and even invisible, the words demonstrated how far she had come from the days when her throne seemed to be tottering.

In Signor Raggi's Osnaburgh Street studio, a colossal statue of the Queen, commissioned by loyal colonists for Hong Kong, was taking shape, suggesting a majesty that Victoria demonstrated physically only in her increasing stoutness, as she weighed, in the 1880s, nearly twelve stone (168 pounds)—"rather much for her height," said her once and future Prime Minister, W. E. Gladstone, out of her hearing. ("Everyone grows but me!" she had lamented to her Prime Minister when she was eighteen. "I think you *are* grown," Lord Melbourne had countered, and she was, from the first, elevated beyond her inches by an instinct for dignity.)

To be erected at the edge of the garden at Kensington Palace, where she was born, was a modest marble statue of the young Queen,* modeled but not yet cast by her talented daughter, Princess Louise, and a gift from the citizens of Kensington; while at the studio of Sir Joseph Edgar Boehm, R.A., another statue of the Queen, paid for by subscriptions of the "Inhabitants of Windsor"—servants of Victoria and inhabitants of "grace and favour" dwellings on the castle grounds—was being sculpted for Castle Hill. The standing, unsmiling Queen holding the royal orb and sceptre—a slight frown creasing an otherwise uncharacteristically bland face—would suggest, Boehm hoped, a legendary warrior queen of the Boadicea mold.

Similar statues would emerge, as if sown from Boehm's seed, around the red-tinted areas of the globe, the only differences being whether Victoria's sceptre was lowered, as if laying down the Imperial Law, or raised; whether she was scowling or placid; whether she had the thick torso of age or the slender, youthful one she had lost long before. Even in remote South Africa one would observe the variety of perceptions of the Queen as one traveled from Cape Town to Kimberley, from Port Elizabeth to Durban and Pietermaritzburg.

Everywhere in London one could already purchase more modest replicas of the Queen's person, souvenirs of the Jubilee fired in Staffordshire or engraved in Fleet Street. Whether Victoria reigned or ruled did not seem to matter; what excited her subjects was the uniqueness of a half-century on the throne. Those with the longest memories remembered the embarrassing state of the monarchy when it was represented by mad George III and his largely discreditable progeny, the Royal Dukes.

How much Victoria ruled was observed by Sir John Brunner, Radical M.P. from Cheshire, when he went to the House early in January 1887, "for the ceremony which is called the declaration of the Queen's consent to a Bill." In a sumptuous room in the Lords, he told his constituents,

*The statue lost its nose to vandals in the spring of 1985.

there was a table with a clerk on each side, and at the far end "the Lord Chancellor with a Peer on each side attired in scarlet robes lined and fringed with ermine. The Speaker of the House of Commons, the representative of the people of England, the representative of the majesty and the power of England, stands in the sheep pen, and these . . . three figures, who hardly looked as if they were alive, lifted their hats exactly like waxwork. The clerks at the table went through . . . not much more than a mummery, and we understood that the Queen had given her consent to the Bills passed by the House of Commons and the House of Lords."

The ritual invoking the Queen's name was now as close as she came to the Houses of Parliament, which were opened in her name with a speech written for her, and read in her name by a functionary. Yet she lent legitimacy to power. She symbolized the nation, and much energy was going into marking Victoria's remote representation of the kingdom-by-the-sea. Authors began sending presentation copies of their Jubilee books to the Queen, few of them gaining her admiration. A two-volume *Reign of Queen Victoria,* edited by Humphry Ward, employed experts handling each aspect of the half-century. Thomas Huxley treated Science; Matthew Arnold covered Education; Richard Garnett examined Literature; and William Archer reviewed Drama. The volumes interested the Queen less than did a gossipy biography. "Sir Henry [Ponsonby]," she instructed her hardworking Private Secretary, "must tell this man how erroneous his anecdotes are," she observed of one book. But the anecdotes, fictitious or not, were sentimental, sympathetic, and even flattering, suggesting the rise in her reputation by 1887. Most years past she could have expected an uncomplimentary press at best, a scurrilous one more often than that. Not many years had gone by since the gutter press had called her "Mrs. Brown."

Disrespect as well as distance were largely annihilated by the prospect of Jubilee. Enthusiasm assumed many forms. From the Viceroy of India in February came word "that all the ladies of Calcutta are ordering Jubilee bustles." George Meredith, long a satirist of the Establishment, wrote in exaggerated pessimism from his sickbed that April to the etcher George Stevenson, "To the Lady whose Jubilee of wise Government I shall not live to help celebrate . . . may you [do so] with lustiest lung and a leg that can show a calf. . . ." Swinburne arranged with his publisher, Andrew Chatto, for seats at the festivities for his friends, and young Winston Churchill wrote to his mother from public school, not of the playing fields, but that "I can think of nothing else but Jubilee."

Long before the events, the Queen had approved the designs of Jubilee medals and coinage. Ladies-in-waiting brought her list after list of prospective guests at receptions and ceremonies, and participants in progresses and processions. The number of preliminary public appearances, in all kinds of weather, multiplied for the once-reclusive Queen. By the time she traveled to Birmingham late in March to lay the foundation stone of the new Law Courts, she was already hoarse. Still to come were soirées, symposia, balls, garden parties, commemoration services, presentations of testimonials, royal progresses, dinners with interminable toasts and droning addresses, dedications of buildings and statues, naval reviews, openings of exhibitions. Fortunately the Prince of Wales, who was gregarious and good at such things, could take up some of that burden; but the public preferred the Queen and the pomp that went with her presence. If they received one without the other, there were protests at being shortchanged. Even Joseph Chamberlain, a former republican, Birmingham M.P., and cabinet minister, complained about the absence of the Household Cavalry from the Law Courts cornerstone-laying. Simplicity belonged to republics, he informed Sir Henry Ponsonby: a sovereign should be synonymous with splendor. To Victoria, Chamberlain was a dangerous radical in process of domestication; further ceremonies involving the Queen, she commanded, must be dignified by the Household Cavalry.

Invitations to heads of state, from empires to petty principalities, had to be dispatched. Despite her failing eyesight, Victoria cautiously scanned them for language appropriate to protocol and precedence before signing. Royal Highnesses needed language different from mere Serene Highnesses, and lesser nobility and aristocracy had their own codes and symbols. Honours Lists had to be scrutinized, and Jubilee remissions of sentences had to be signed. Victoria read everything that came to her, rejecting or revising where her powers permitted, even refusing a pardon to a prisoner sentenced for cruelty to animals. It was, she insisted, "one of the worst traits in human nature." Appreciative of such royal sentiments, the Society for the Prevention of Cruelty to Animals would send her a grateful Jubilee Address, mounted on a roller and enclosed in a velvet box. (She also opposed vivisection. "The subject causes her whole nature to boil over against these 'Butchers,' " she observed in a memorandum in 1882.) In another Jubilee-year case she refused to deprive a sergeant of his Victoria Cross after he had been convicted of embezzlement. "The Queen cannot bring herself to sign this," she noted to Ponsonby. "It seems too cruel. She pleads for mercy for the brave man." In April the Poet Laureate, Lord Tennyson, performed his duty with sixty-five lines in *Macmillan's Magazine,* announcing,

> *Fifty times the rose has flower'd and faded,*
> *Fifty times the golden harvest fallen,*
> *Since our Queen assumed the globe, the sceptre. . . .*

The poet much talked about as his likely successor, Lewis Morris, published, in the April *Murray's Magazine,* an Inauguration Ode to be sung under the direction of the composer Sir Arthur Sullivan. Eager to be the next Laureate, Morris spared no compliments in his "Song of Empire," where Victoria was

> *First Lady of our English race,*
> *In Royal dignity and grace*
> *Higher than all in old ancestral blood,*
> *But higher still in love of good. . . .*

The occasion for the ode meant much to Victoria. She was scheduled, on June 20, to lay the foundation stone of the Imperial Institute in South Kensington—the culmination of one of Prince Albert's dreams for the site of the Great Exhibition of 1851.

As the year advanced toward the Jubilee climax in June, thousands of letters and telegrams poured into Buckingham Palace, many of which the Queen had read to her. From Agra came a vast acrostic poem in Hindustani and English from a grateful ex-convict whom her signature had released, and from Madras came a poem in Sanskrit that, Victoria was informed, greeted railways and steamships as "celestial messengers from the Queen-Empress." At Mithi, she was told, the Sind authorities had dedicated "The Queen Victoria Jubilee Burial and Burning Ground." At Mandalay, His Highness Taksingjee of Bhownugger established a fund of thirty thousand rupees for the support of twenty-five widows, to be known as the Victoria Jubilee Pensioners; and at Udaipur the Maharani commissioned C. B. Birch, A.R.A., to execute a large marble statue of the Queen, to be placed in the public gardens. In Rangoon, "The Empress Victoria's Golden Jubilee Anthem," a stirring march played on clarions, bamboo clappers, drums, and silk-stringed harps, was premiered. All appropriate (and some more awkward) gestures had to be acknowledged, with some fended off, raising problems of tact and taste that kept the Household staff up late night after night.

The Queen quickly exhausted herself by taking on every Jubilee problem of which she became aware, even creating some new ones. Although she demonstrated little interest in a Jubilee Address, mounted on silk, from the National Society for Women's Suffrage, she intended to ease the rules for her drawing-room receptions, imposed decades before by the Prince Consort, so that "poor ladies" among her subjects who had been the innocent parties in divorce cases might be permitted at Court. Before long, she told her Prime Minister, the Marquess of Salisbury, she also wanted to lift the ban as well on innocent foreign divorcées. Salisbury warned against the "risk of admitting American women of light character." On March 6, two days after her first drawing-room of the season (with the divorcée rule still unaltered), she noted in her diary that she was unhappy at having fallen asleep in her chair after tea—"a very rare thing for me."

The Jubilee meant gifts received and gifts bestowed. Many already accepted were resplendent in silver and gold and jewels. Victoria's largesse had to be more modest, given the numbers involved, and consisted largely of signed photographs; but saffron Jubilee robes were ordered for Buddhist monks in Mandalay, and extra helpings of rice on Jubilee day for hospital patients in Singapore, including, the Queen commanded, the colony's lepers.

Weary, Victoria stole off to Aix-les-Bains and Cannes under her usual transparent traveling name, the Countess of Kent. (Sometimes she was Madame la Comtesse de Balmoral.) It was already too warm on the Riviera for the Queen, who preferred the temperature, even indoors, to be under sixty degrees Fahrenheit. Late in April she was back, contending with Jubilee problems that had accumulated, among them the disposition of the Women's Jubilee Gift she had accepted in December, with more money to come. Unless the equestrian statue of the Prince Consort were to be cast in silver or gold, there would be many thousands of pounds of surplus funds. Her physician, Sir William Jenner, suggested relieving distress through a Queen's Fund to encourage emigration of the unemployed. Victoria, however, had no desire to call attention to the army of the jobless already demonstrating in Hyde Park and Trafalgar Square. Ponsonby suggested the device of a committee of women to advise the Queen, the group to include the still-formidable Florence Nightingale. As he expected, the committee proposed a Queen's Jubilee Nursing Institute. Victoria gave her assent.

At Windsor Castle on May 4 a deputation of colonial premiers and governors from eighty countries and colonies, led by the Premier of Newfoundland, offered "humble, earnest and united congratulations." The group was colorful in costume, from formal Court attire to native garb. Afterwards they were photographed on the terrace for the Queen's albums. Led by the Lord Mayor, a deputation of one hundred and seventy from the Corporation of London, some in black silk Court suits and others in official robes and gowns, was received on May 9 at Buckingham Palace. The Address, wishing that "all good may continue to your Majesty," was read by the Recorder, then handed to the Lord Mayor, who knelt to deliver it to the Sovereign. Then Victoria, in a musical voice unchanged in clarity over the years, read her reply, recalling how much the prosperity of the realm during her reign had been owed "to the sound sense and good feeling of my subjects and to the sympathy which has united the Throne and the people." That such sympathy was long in coming and had often been absent was something that, on such an occasion, Victoria chose to ignore. Albert, she knew, had seldom experienced it in nearly twenty-two years at her side.

On the ninth, a royal drawing-room at Buckingham Palace was open for the first time to "poor divorced ladies, . . . owing to cruelty, desertion, and misbehaviour, but [who] are in no way to blame themselves." The Queen remained for an hour, sitting down several times because of fatigue, then permitted the Princess of Wales, Alexandra, to take her place. The ceremonial assistance of "Alix" paralleled a gain in status for her husband. The Foreign Office, as the Prime Minister wrote Victoria the same day, was "anxious to obtain your Majesty's permission that H.R.H. the Prince of Wales should have a similar key [to the Queen's]. The dispatches of a highly confidential nature are now by your Majesty's command communicated to the Prince; and the old Cabinet key, which he has, is not quite reliable now." Victoria had long resisted giving her son access to state papers, but the Cabinet, recognizing his need to know, had begun to transmit them to him quietly. The inevitable was being recognized on both sides. However insubstantial his role, he could not be left totally unprepared for his ultimate one.

At the Albert Hall a month later, after a fanfare on silver trumpets, the loyalty of the Freemasons of the United Grand Lodge of England was accepted for the Queen by the Prince of Wales. Again her Majesty was wished "a long and happy continuance of your reign over a loyal and devoted people." The Address was presented to the Prince of Wales for his mother in a royal blue velvet casket, lined with white satin. If, in all such cheers and self-congratulations, the nation offered itself in its "fervent and unabated attachment to your Majesty's Throne and Royal person" (to quote the Masons), Victoria heard fading echoes of earlier cries for her abdication as a recluse who did not reign—an unworn garment of state on an empty throne—she kept such memories to herself.

Organizations of every description offered ceremonious Addresses to the Queen. When James A. McNeill Whistler, the cocky American-born president of the Society of British Artists, discovered that the Royal Academy was preparing one, he rushed out with his own, complete to his personal butterfly signature. The rather fusty group he had taken charge of that year was a poor second to the Academy, but not in presidential originality. Instead of what Whistler called the "illuminated performances" traditional on such occasions,

> I took a dozen sheets of my old Dutch paper. I had them bound by Zaensdorf. . . . You opened it, and on the first page you found a beautiful little drawing of the royal arms that I made myself; the second page, an etching of Windsor, as though, "here's where you live." On the third page, the Address began. I made decorations all around the text in watercolour—at the top, the towers of Windsor, down one side, a great battleship, plunging through the waves, and below the sun that never sets on the British Empire—What? The following pages were not decorated, just the most wonderful Address, explaining the age and dignity of the Society, its devotion to Her Glorious, Gracious Majesty, and suggesting the honour it would be if this could be recognised by a title that would show the Society to belong especially to Her. Then the last page. You turned, and there was a little etching of my house in Chelsea—"And now here's where I live!" And then you closed it, and on the back of the cover was the Butterfly.

Unaware of its president's action, the council of the Society requested a meeting to consult on an appropriate Address to the Queen. Whistler asked what members proposed spending, and shocked them by explaining that the single guinea recommended might not meet a twentieth of the expenses he had already incurred. By the time a stormy protest assemblage convened, Whistler had received an acknowledgment from the Queen "and Her command that the Society should be called Royal." Withholding the news, he permitted complaints of high-handedness in his sending an idiosyncratic message in their names. One artist rose to declare his intention to resign. "You had better make a note of it, Mr. Secretary," Whistler said.

> And then I got up with great solemnity and I announced the honour conferred upon them by Her Gracious Majesty. They jumped and rushed toward me with outstretched hands . . . I waved them all back. . . . But, the meeting over, I sent for champagne.

There seemed no Jubilee matter too trivial for the Queen's attention. As with everything else during her fifty years as Sovereign, she wanted to know about everything and make her views known where, constitutionally, they counted—and even in some cases where they were technically illegal. The "Te Deum" to be sung at Westminster Abbey was to be, at her command, in the late Prince Consort's musical arrangement, and the seating in the Abbey was to reflect her opinions of the guests. (Dour Mr. Gladstone would not have a good pew.) Ticket allotments, *Truth* charged, reflected Victoria's priorities. Fifty went to the Corporation of the City of London—the merchants and financiers. One went to the Royal Society —the representative of Science. Had Albert lived, that allocation would have been different. The Jubilee Honours List had to strike a balance between diplomacy and display, but the most sensitive proposal in it, offered even more discreetly than most titles, leaked into the newspapers anyway. Quietly, Lord Bute was offered a dukedom. Victoria was attempting to make amends to the family for a scandal that had not been forgotten over a half-century and in which her guilt was considerable. Bute declined "in consequence . . . of a written request which was left by his father, who keenly resented the disgraceful harshness and injustice . . . to his sister-in-law Lady Flora Hastings." When the Queen noted in her journal for May 11 that there were "great difficulties" about some honors, but identified none of them, one almost certainly involved the long-dead Lady Flora.*

Taking tea, she then put the problem aside, setting it even further

---

*The second Marquess of Bute (1793–1848) had a posthumous connection with Lady Flora, having married her younger sister, Sophia, in 1845.

aside by the most unusual appearance she would make in the entire Jubilee year. For decades after the Prince Consort's death it was unthinkable for the Queen to enter places of public entertainment. But following tea at Buckingham Palace with Lord Salisbury, she and Princess Beatrice, escorted by equerries and ladies-in-waiting, drove in several carriages to the great exhibition hall at brash and bustling Earl's Court, where—Victoria noted in her journal—"we saw a very extraordinary and interesting sight —a performance of Buffalo Bill's 'Wild West.' " From Earl's Court they returned directly to Paddington Station, and were back at Windsor by half-past seven.

Normally the Queen shut her ears as well as her eyes to urban problems, but on May 14 she made a progress, in an open carriage, to the Mile End Road in the overcrowded East End, to open ceremonially the new People's Palace, a combination of theater, exhibition hall, and community center. The cheers were "damped," she complained to Salisbury, by "a horrid noise" she had seldom if ever heard—"booing and hooting," she labeled it. The Prime Minister explained that the malefactors were only "Socialists and the worst Irish." The incident led her to expect more trouble, for in his best patrician manner, the Prime Minister had added that it was "impossible . . . to prevent such ill-manners; and London contains a much larger number of the worst kinds of roughs than any other great town in the island; for all that is worthless, worn out, or penniless, naturally drifts to London." Victoria was not without a social conscience, but that faculty had long been blunted by prime ministers, beginning with Viscount Melbourne, her first, who blamed all discontent upon a rabble of agitators, most of them Irish, some of them Socialist, some of them both.

At High Holborn, where—as with Temple Bar to the south—the City technically began, the Lord Mayor had greeted the Queen's party, presented her with the official sword (which she immediately returned), and led the way through the crowds to the exhibition hall, which Bertie ceremonially opened for his mother. There was a flourish of trumpets, a singing of the Hundredth Psalm, and cheering and applause. Then the Queen left the dais and walked to the nearby site of the Technical Schools, for which she laid the first stone "with the usual ceremony and prayer." With the Lord Mayor and his family still in attendance, and the Queen's extended family in tow (a prince, two princesses, and their spouses), the party stopped near the Albert Docks to greet sailor-suited orphan boys from the Barnardo Homes, each waving a tiny Union Jack.

Then the royal party were guests for tea at the ceremonial center of the City, the Mansion House, "where, strange to say, I had never been before." After fifty years as Queen, Victoria was becoming sovereign of all the people rather than a remote presence on coins and postage stamps.

Not everything was going so well, especially within the extended family. The Maharajah Duleep Singh, whom for years she had indulged almost as a surrogate son, had "quite gone to the bad," an embarrassment for her as she greeted visiting Indian princelings to present Jubilee honors. In her own family it was taking special legislation to recall Prince Arthur from the Bombay Command in time for the festivities. And from Berlin on May 19 came a telegram from her eldest daughter, Vicky, the Princess Royal and Crown Princess of Germany, desperately imploring that the Queen send Dr. Morell Mackenzie, the eminent London throat specialist, to talk Crown Prince Frederick William's doctors out of conducting a tracheotomy to relieve Fritz's suspected throat cancer. Dubiously (Victoria's own doctors did not trust the flamboyant laryngologist), the Queen dispatched Mackenzie. The Jubilee was a month away and she wanted her son-in-law present. Mackenzie would dispute the diagnosis and pocket his fee. Meanwhile the willful Prince William, impatient to become Kaiser, bombarded his grandmother with telegrams suggesting that it was the old Emperor's command that young Willy take his ailing father's ceremonial place. Victoria wrote to her daughter, "You both must not be absent on this day which will move me deeply." The Crown Prince, now nearly mute, would ride before the Queen's coach, as he had often done on state ceremonies since Albert's death, would look impressive in procession, and would go home to die.

On Saturday, June 18, with the great event close at hand, Viscount Cranbrook (Gathorne Gathorne-Hardy) and other members of the Cabinet gathered for an audience at Windsor. "H.M. was very gracious," he noted in his diary. ". . . She rather dreads the impending ceremonies especially wh. involve much standing as her knee tries her & in hot weather her ankles swell. She is however clearly pleased at the extraordinary demonstrations wh. are indeed remarkable. The scene in London increases in excitement daily & the crowds are great."

Monday, June 20, was the fiftieth anniversary of her accession. "The day has come and I am alone," she wrote in her journal, thinking of Albert; then she added, "though surrounded by many dear children. . . . God has mercifully sustained me through many great trials and sorrows." After breakfast in the park at Frogmore she was driven down the hill from the castle to Windsor Station, where a royal train waited to whisk her to Paddington and on to Buckingham Palace. There, at a luncheon, where a bank of flowers formed the initials *VRI* for her Queen-Empress title, sat fifty royalties at a horseshoe-shaped table, many of the European highnesses her own relatives by blood or marriage. The main courses included, in addition to cold beef, fowl, and tongue, *filet de boeuf au macaroni, quartier d'agneau roti, poulets aux nouilles, cotelettes de veau panées aux pois,* roast fowl, and venison steaks. On the Queen's right was the King of Denmark; on her left was the King of Greece; opposite was the King of the Belgians. It was, she thought, "a large family dinner," despite the Eastern potentates whose jewels and orders gleamed in her "splendid" gold plate. The state dining room, she noted, "I had not used since '61." It had been a strenuous day. "At length, feeling tired, I slipped away."

That evening there was a family dinner party, her nine children (not all of whom had survived to the Jubilee) having given her broods of grandchildren and relatives-in-law. Yet the next morning she was up early to confirm that the day was "beautiful and bright with a fresh air." For her that meant a chill that made others shiver. She was happy to be in an open landau (she had refused the ornate State glass coach), wearing her characteristic bonnet and a black silk dress trimmed with white lace. Lord Salisbury had commented, hoping the observation would reach the Queen, that the Empire should be ruled by a sceptre rather than a bonnet. The Princess of Wales had even been deputed by the children to talk the Queen into wearing the Robes of State and her crown. Victoria's concession was to wear diamonds and white lace on her bonnet, and to gild her setting by having six cream-hued horses draw her carriage, and colorful Indian cavalry escort it. "The scene outside," she noted, "was most animated and reminded me of the opening of the Great Exhibition." Again a memory that included Albert.

In her usual combination of pomp and simplicity, the Queen had decreed that "Ladies [were to be] in Bonnets and Long High Dresses without Mantle." The men, including thirty-two princes related to the Queen (one of them young Willy), who proceeded through garlanded triumphal arches and bowers, were costumed in their gaudiest garb. The most spectacular was her son-in-law, the tall, bearded Crown Prince Frederick William of Germany, silent and drawn, in his white Pomeranian Cuirassier's uniform and silver helmet with the imperial eagle. Riding at her side, next to her carriage, as full of years and dignity as the Queen herself, was the white-plumed and white-whiskered "George Cambridge," Commander-in-Chief of the army and her royal cousin, a few months her elder but unlucky to have been born of a younger Royal Duke. Had Edward, Duke of Kent, not won the race to furnish an heir to the throne, the Duke of Cambridge, as he must have told his mirror every day of his life, might have been in the gilt landau himself. "The crowds from the Palace gates up to the Abbey were enormous," the Queen noted, "and there was such an extraordinary burst of enthusiasm, as I had hardly ever seen in London before. . . . The old Chelsea Pensioners were in a stand near the Arch. The decorations along Piccadilly were quite beautiful, and there were most touching inscriptions. Seats and platforms were arranged up to the tops of the houses, and such waving of hands."

The Queen had not entered Westminster Abbey in nearly forty-nine years—not since June 28, 1838, when she was crowned. Now participants alighted from horses and coaches, and proceeded slowly up the nave to the strains of Handel. The Queen, from her dais, peered into the gloom to pick out familiar faces. To the music of Albert's "Te Deum" and "Chorale," the congregation gave thanks for her long reign, and Victoria recorded afterwards in her journal, "I sat *alone* (oh! without my beloved husband, for whom this would have been such a proud day!)." Impassively she watched from Edward I's venerable coronation chair, while dignitaries droned in the pauses between anthems, until, at the close of the service, members of the royal family filed past the Queen for emotional embraces. Then the pageantry reversed direction for the return to Buckingham Palace, where Victoria distributed Jubilee brooches and tiepins to the family.

It was already four o'clock, time for a late luncheon, after which a guard of honor had to be reviewed from a balcony, Jubilee gifts accepted in the ballroom, and telegrams read. "I felt quite exhausted . . . & ready to faint, so I got into my rolling chair and rolled back to my room."

Still to come was dinner for visiting royalty and the diplomatic corps. Her old dresser, Annie Skerret, who had helped with the coronation robes forty-nine years earlier, was now ninety-four, and so another servant assisted Victoria into her embroidered Jubilee gown, glittering with diamonds and with silver roses, shamrocks, and thistles to represent the three united island kingdoms. Though Albert was never far from her mind, it was no mourning dress, nor—but for a widow's cap or bonnet—did she in fact wear mourning. She was an elderly lady and wore the traditional black of her generation, giving way to display only on rare, great occasions.

"I was half dead with fatigue," she remembered, and had her attendants wheel her into the Chinese Room to watch from her window the fireworks in the Home Park, rocketed off by James Pain & Sons. No account of its most infamous mishap survives in her journal. Item 29 (of 30), a bouquet of flowers to metamorphose into a pyrotechnic portrait of the Queen, 200 feet across and 180 feet high, turned out to have a technical flaw: the right eye of the Queen blinked uncontrollably, as if she were winking at the crowds. It was the only mishap in one of the great pyrotechnic spectacles in history.

The following day was no less exhausting. First there was a visit to St. James's Palace, a courtesy call to her eighty-nine-year-old aunt, the dowager Duchess of Cambridge. Soon the palace—once the royal residence—would house a display of Jubilee gifts, already straining the ingenuity of palace household staff as to where to put them, and in some cases even to determine what they were. More Jubilee medals were awarded to kings and princes at Buckingham Palace, and more gifts received, including a further £75,000, "in a splendid gold coffer," from the Women of the British Empire. Then it was time to go to Hyde Park, where there were tents, military bands, and 26,000 schoolchildren each furnished (by the enterprising *Daily Telegraph*) with a bun, and milk in a Jubilee mug ("an earthenware pot," Victoria described it) decorated with the Queen's portrait. A little girl presented a bouquet tied with a wide ribbon on which was embroidered, "God bless our Queen, not Queen alone, but Mother Queen and Friend." (Victoria disliked children, and had never taken to the vigorous sponsorship of motherhood until her own had begun families.) A balloon with *Victoria* on it was released, and one of the children, newspapers reported, exclaimed, "Oh look! There's the Queen going up to heaven!" "The children sang 'God Save the Queen' somewhat out of tune," Victoria noted in her journal with more honesty than was necessary.

Even her subjects with little faith in royalty made a holiday of it. George Gissing, remembering the day later in a novel, *In the Year of Jubilee* (1894), has Nancy Lord ask her father, a pianoforte salesman of radical persuasion, "You don't think of going to see the Queen tomorrow?"

"Not to see Her Majesty," Mr. Lord insists, much as Gissing himself did. "I care as little about her as you do. But I thought of having a walk in the evening . . . to see the people and the illuminations."

Sydney Cockerell, a disciple of the Socialist William Morris, found it a "perfect" day, and enjoyed the Chinese lanterns festooning Bedford Park, and the rockets and fireworks. William Michael Rossetti, an unreconstructed republican who had written a sonnet praising regicide, took his young son Arthur along Regent Street, Piccadilly, Bond Street, and Oxford Street to see the blaze of lights and to mingle with the throngs, returning home at the unprecedentedly late hour of ten-thirty. By then the Queen had returned by train to Eton and Windsor to unveil her statue by Boehm and to watch a torchlight procession of students singing college songs in the castle Quadrangle and cheering her. "I thank you very much," said Victoria in a bell-like voice ("as loud . . . as I could") after the final loyal Address of the evening. The Round Tower at Windsor was illuminated by electric light, new to the castle and the town. Victoria was too exhausted for more spectacle and retired to her room to write in her diary, "These two days will ever remain indelibly impressed on my mind, with great gratitude to that all-merciful Providence, who has protected me so long, and to my devoted and loyal people. But how painfully do I miss the dear ones I have lost!"

The sentiments would reappear publicly in the Queen's expression of thanks to her people, issued through the Home Secretary. In it Victoria saw her half-century as "twenty-two years of which I spent in unclouded happiness shared and cheered by my beloved husband, while an equal number were full of sorrows and trials, borne without his sheltering arm and wise help." Her country and subjects were "inseparably bound up" with her life, and her "sense of duty" toward them would keep her at her "very difficult and arduous . . . task" for the remainder of her days.

June 23, 1887, was marked by a Jubilee gift to herself that the Queen had long planned. The next best thing to residing in the India she knew she would never visit, but whose Empress she had become after putting great pressure upon a reluctant Disraeli, was to have her own native servants. That touch of the exotic arrived at Windsor in the persons of her subjects Abdul Karim, twenty-four and clearly the more clever of the two, and Mahomet Buxsh, plump and passive. ("They both kissed my feet. . . .") Abdul was not of the servant class, he let it be known; he was the son of a professional, a physician at Agra. Quickly, Victoria engaged an English tutor for him, a young man who expected to be serving an Indian prince but found he was serving a servant. By August 3, Abdul was himself doing the teaching, with his willing pupil the Queen. "I am learning a few words of Hindustani," she wrote in her diary, "to speak to my servants. It is a great interest to me for both the language and the people I have never come into real contact with before." To Sir Henry Ponsonby in September she sent a memorandum expressing pleasure at how handy Abdul had become when she signed documents "by drying the signatures," while Mahomet was "wonderfully quick and intelligent." Sir Henry understood. Their practical usefulness was minimal, but they were a touch of her exotic Empire just as much as were the bowls and rugs and pictures.

The Jubilee meant problems with both gifts and givers. At her Buckingham Palace garden party on June 29, the Queen proceeded about the area of the Royal Pavilion, stick in hand, and with the burly Prince of Wales, by whose side her tiny stout figure was nearly invisible. "I bowed right and left," she remembered, "talking to as many as I could, but I was dreadfully done up by it." The guests with whom she mixed, invited "on strictly democratic principles," from the unwanted Gladstone to the Queen's Watermen, were such that half of them wondered how the other half had got there. Both halves wondered about large, dusky Queen Kapiolani of Hawaii, whose Jubilee present had been a *VR* embroidered in feathers from the islands, in a diamond-studded frame. Prince Willy, no future *Anglophil Kaiser,* as his father was expected to be, complained to his mother's lady-in-waiting, Hedwig von Brühl, of being treated by Victoria "with exquisite coolness, with bare courtesy," even to the placing of his wife, Princess Augusta, "behind the black Queen of Hawaii." At the banquet for heads of state following the Abbey ceremonies, the Prince of Wales had escorted the Hawaiian queen, while her sister-in-law, the future Queen Liliuokalani, was taken in by Prince "Affie," the Duke of Edinburgh. "Ticketed" to the King of the Belgians for the supper procession in the palace garden, Liliuokalani had been left standing, Leopold II rejecting his swarthy partner; and courtiers reassigned her to the King of Saxony, who also refused to escort a "coloured" person. Finally, Prince Alfred was instructed by Victoria to do the correct thing.

The next day at three, "I had a great reception of Indian Princes and Deputations, in the Green Drawing-room," the Queen wrote, always thrilled (to the disgust of Sir Henry Ponsonby) with things exotically Indian. Gifts were offered, and she in turn presented Jubilee decorations. In the group, she noted, was "the handsome young Rao of Kutch, most beautifully dressed; really he and his brother were like a dream." Victoria may have been a long-widowed and long-celibate sixty-eight, but her interest in masculine good looks remained undiminished.

The Jubilee offerings included bejeweled bowls, cups, and boxes of gold and silver, presented by Indian maharajahs who ignored the desperate plight of their people; a silver statuette of the Prince Consort, from the army; ship models in silver, from the Royal Navy and Royal Marines; and a jeweled Saint George and the Dragon pendant, from "Bertie's Household." The simplest gift reported was two new-laid eggs sent for the Queen's breakfast by an Irish farm woman via her bishop, who, she had heard, was going to London for Jubilee week. The bishop carried them across St. George's Channel to Windsor, with a description of the woman's poverty and loyalty. Accepting the eggs, the Queen ordered her aides to make inquiries as to what the most useful present to be offered in return might be.

The gift from her faithful Irish subject would be one of the few not to go on display in September at St. James's Palace. The crowds that queued from ten until four would be urged on by the authorities at such a pace that few would have time to read any of the descriptive labels. The printed catalogue was delivered so late—November 15—by Harrison and Sons of St. Martin's Lane, that most Londoners assumed there was none. Listed were 528 of the first 540 gifts to arrive; Victoria kept twelve for personal use. The place of honor, as number one, went to a silver and silver-gilt *plateau* (an ornamented tray) with a lion-and-unicorn motif, designed by Vicky. The two fresh eggs from Ireland were inappropriate for display, but included were a woolen shawl and hearth rug from the Roman Catholic Blind Asylum at Liverpool, musical instruments from Burma, and a casket made from thirty ounces of gold dug in the Gold Coast.

Progresses, presentations, and ceremonials had continued through the summer months, the Queen's normal interest in foreign affairs taking a lower priority than usual, despite memorials from exotic places among her realms. Illuminated Addresses included one from the B'nai Israel Community of Poona (India), and another wrapped in yellow silk (with translation) from the Emperor of China. One message from Africa had to please the Empire-conscious Victoria more than the courteous effusions that arrived from most countries. What Chief Letsie of Basutoland, seventy-six, had written was a rare indigenous justification of the White Man's Burden:

For us, it is a curious thing that a woman should be a Queen, although we hear out of the Book of God that there was once a Queen of Sheba who paid a visit to the wise King Solomon. If I was not old and infirm, I would have liked to go and see her Majesty with my own eyes, as I hear that many kings and princes from far countries have done.

We hear also that her Majesty's subjects are an immense multitude, numbering more than 300 millions of people, that the sun never goes down on her empire, and that all glory in being her subjects. I am not surprised at this, as we ourselves owe our present peace and our very existence to the deliverance she granted to us in 1868, when we were on the brink of an absolute ruin. And although since then we have gone through troubles and difficulties, still we exist as a people, and we have to thank, after God, her Majesty's Representative in this country for the confidence we have now that better times have dawned upon us and that peace and tranquillity shall henceforth reign in this land, and that, with the continuance of her Majesty's beneficial rule, we shall go on increasing and progressing, and shall prove ourselves worthy of the care and protection granted to us.

Basutoland (now Lesotho) had been saved from the plundering Boers of the Orange Free State, when Chief Moshesh—father of Letsie—had appealed desperately to the Cape governor to protect his country and his people, whom he described humbly as "only lice in the Queen's blanket." Victoria's capacious imperial blanket had many uses.

The great event of July was the naval review off Spithead, on the twenty-seventh, at which one of the few Americans was Jimmy Whistler, the autocratic president of the now-Royal Society of British Artists, who assigned the society's official seat to himself. At the Abbey ceremonies in June he had brought with him a grounded copper plate, and had sat at one side of the triforium, etching *Abbey Jubilee*— probably to whispered imprecations about his Yankee rudeness. At Spithead, from Commodore Vanderbilt's boat, he etched twelve small plates, economically capturing the mood of the day, from the snapping pennants to the melancholy quiet of the aftermath. Presenting a set of the etchings to W. H. Smith, First Lord of the Admiralty, Whistler described them as "notes as I might say of the needle, not the pen, taken at the moment, and from point to point of that imperial, but pacific, and more than Roman Triumph." In the final nine words, Whistler had seized the essence of the Jubilee.

Also on the Isle of Wight, an old gentleman who had been a political radical when Victoria was still a princess was selected to deliver the

Address to the Queen on behalf of the inhabitants of the island. When he finished, the Queen said, "Mr. Seely, you have not always spoken the same way."

"No," he said, having outlived his republicanism, "both you and I, your Majesty, have learned to hold different views from those we formerly held."

In August, before returning to Berlin, Crown Prince Frederick brought Dr. Morell Mackenzie to see the Queen. Quick to advise what he thought Victoria wanted to hear, Mackenzie suggested the bracing climate of Scotland as a suitable restorative setting for the Prince. Mackenzie knew that his patient was beyond bracing air, and Victoria must have guessed as much. Besides, Fritz's aged father, Emperor William I, was reportedly dying—this was no time to be remote from Berlin. Still, grateful for the optimistic diagnosis, the gaunt Prince begged the Queen to knight the controversial physician, whose obtuseness had enraged German specialists in the case. Crown Princess "Vicky" was foremost in the Queen's thoughts. Not to knight Mackenzie would have acknowledged to her daughter and son-in-law that Frederick was under a sentence of death. As Sir Morell, then, in November, the doctor would confirm that the Crown Prince was dying of cancer. "Poor darling Vicky," the Queen wrote in her journal, "the thought of all her trouble makes my heart ache. . . . It is a terrible state of affairs, and I am haunted by the thought of it."

Further weeks were crowded with well-wishers, the birth of another grandchild (the future Queen Victoria Eugénie of Spain), and joyful fuss, but the excitement would ebb after the high tide of Jubilee. The inevitable lethargy and anticlimax were deepened by new disappointments and sorrows, even while another, smaller crest came in October. In her beloved Scotland, a second larger-than-life bronze executed by the busy J. E. Boehm was presented by the tenants and servants on the Queen's estates of Balmoral, Abergeldie, and Birkhall. Victoria would leave a legacy of sculpture that would suggest a giantess of a matriarch, and the newest example would contribute to the calumny. Two hundred yards from the kilted, cairn-pedestaled statue of the Prince Consort, dedicated in 1867 and overlooking the valley of the Dee, the Queen unveiled her gift and thanked the subscribers. She missed from their midst, she added, "the kind faces of old friends no longer among us."

Loyal old Skerret had died in August, with Victoria too busy to see her before the end. Memories of her favorite Highland servant, John

Brown, must have also flooded back, for she had a Boehm statue of Brown erected at Balmoral, to the undisguised disgust of her children. Some faces she worried about not seeing again. Court intrigues led by Prince Willy were undermining Frederick and Vicky even before the German throne became vacant for them: Fritz, she realized, might not survive long enough to become Emperor in Berlin.

In many ways, beneath the pomp and glitter of celebration, little was going right. Closer to home, political divisions over Home Rule for Ireland created anxiety. Down the Mall from Buckingham Palace, unrest had now turned violent. Answering the Queen about "more humane treatment for the casual poor, who are in effect, the unemployed," the Marquess of Salisbury offered little more as solution than to announce the closure of Trafalgar Square to public meetings. Those of the poor who could read had hardly cheered every Jubilee extravagance reported in the newspapers while their bellies rumbled; some may have encountered the report from Balmoral that Madame Emma Albani, the wealthy and famous diva, who had twice gone to sing for the Queen while both were holidaying in Scotland, was given by her Majesty, as a token, "a costly brooch of diamonds, sapphires and pearls . . . and the Jubilee medal."

As a Radical reaction to such perceived inequalities in the year of Jubilee, Socialist groups in London had convened a "Charing Cross Parliament" in the railway hotel a few steps from Trafalgar Square. Opening the event was an official-sounding "Queen's Speech" drafted, as at Westminster, by the ruling party's Ministers. "I have summoned you to meet," it began,

in this, the Jubilee year of my reign, for the transaction of business of great importance, unfortunately delayed these many years, and now become indispensable. The state of my nation is such as must fill the most hopeful with anxiety. Owing to the operation of economic conditions which no application of the existing law can thwart, the vast wealth produced daily by the labour of my people is now distributed not only unequally, but so inequitably that the contrast between the luxury of idle and unprofitable persons, and the poverty of the industrious masses, has become a scandal and reproach to our civilisation, setting class against class, and causing among the helpless and blameless infants of my most hardworking subjects a mortality disgraceful to me as head of the state, and unbearable to me as a woman and mother. And since this is in no wise due to any stint of the natural resources whereby my oppressed people may better themselves if you apply yourselves to their enfranchisement with due diligence and honesty, and without respect to persons; and since, too, every day of avoidable delay is a day of avoidable and unmerited suffering to millions of innocent persons throughout the realm, there will forthwith be submitted to you a series of measures for the redress of their heavy and crying wrongs.

The "Bloody Sunday" riot in November, which grew out of the banning of protest meetings in Trafalgar Square, underlined the dilemma. The problems in the Mile End Road that the Queen had recognized in May could not be solved by bureaucratic dismissals of them or by club-wielding mounted police putting down "free speech" demonstrations. (One of the fleeing heretics was the chief drafter of the mock "Queen's Speech," Bernard Shaw.) The comic magazine *Tit-Bits* commented on the bleak winding down of the Jubilee year with a cover drawing on November 5 showing the Queen rising from a portable throne to address a discontented throng. In the background is St. Paul's. In the foreground a ragged old man holds up a sign reading HELP US OR WE WILL PERISH. Another farther back threatens BREAD OR BLOOD. But Victoria responds by handing out cookbooks and copies of "Guide to the Poorhouse."

Three weeks later a mock-sympathetic letter to the Queen in *Tit-Bits* condoled with her over the "disturbances" at Trafalgar Square, which "must be very discouraging to a peaceable old lady like yourself. . . . Such an occurrence must be a serious interruption to your study of the Hindu-stanee language, and to keeping tally of Princess Beatrice's progeny." The fictitious sympathizer had a solution for dispersing the next "mob" more peaceably—that the Queen appear before the people "clad in your royal robes and an air of superiority, and read aloud some extracts from your own writings. This would act as an anaesthetic, and after the mob had been put to sleep, the bayonet could be introduced with great effect."

Certainly no one dared show such a product of England's free press to Victoria. Still, that protests could be so fierce, yet lawful, augured that the inevitable solutions would themselves be lawful. Victoria, still assum-ing in the manner of her class and time that progress would continue to trickle down from above, saw only "disobedience to the law," but the shocking event further darkened the year's close. On balance, she thought, nevertheless, writing in her journal from Osborne on the last day of 1887, it had been a "brilliant year," one "richly blessed."

"Rags and Royalty"—
Tit-Bits,
November 5, 1887.

Princess Beatrice and her husband "Liko" (Prince Henry) Battenberg came into her room at midnight to wish her a happy new year, after
which Victoria returned to add a final paragraph in her journal. The last
line was "May God help me further!"

II

Alexandrina Victoria

(1817-1820)

On November 6, 1817, Princess Charlotte died, opening a gap in the British royal succession. The high-spirited Princess of Wales had been heiress to the throne after her father, the Prince Regent (and future George IV). At twenty-one she had been the darling of the nation. Suddenly, having given birth to a stillborn son after a labor of fifty hours, she was dead. Sir Richard Croft, the attending physician, committed suicide.

None of the surviving seven sons and five daughters among the intermittently insane George III's fifteen had a legitimate child qualified to reign. Some were unable for one reason or another to have one. The prospect of any of the siblings becoming king or queen was dismaying, as they were eccentric at best, discreditable at worst—"the dregs of their dull race," said Shelley. Even the loyal Duke of Wellington conceded that they were "the damndest millstone about the necks of any Government

25

Charlotte, Princess of Wales, whose death in 1817 precipitated the race for an heir to the throne. Portrait by George Dawe.

that can be imagined." Nevertheless, both Parliament and the Prince Regent wanted an assured succession, and used the debts of the available dukes as a lever to force them to do their duty.

With the Princess's death, William, the unmarried Duke of Clarence, fifty-two, moved up in the succession as did his ailing brother Frederick, the Duke of York. Prince William had already tried to solve the dilemma of his own debts by jettisoning Mrs. Dorothy Jordan, the actress by whom he had ten FitzClarence children, to look unsuccessfully for an heiress. Now he needed a prospective queen. The next unmarried duke was the sturdy, six-foot-two Edward, Duke of Kent, fifty and bald, with whiskers dyed black. He had been in the army and was known as a harsh disciplinarian, but within his own class he was considered warm and humane, with a fondness for making after-dinner speeches and a curious mind that kept several private secretaries busy with correspondence, usually to public departments which dreaded his name on a note. He had lived happily with his middle-aged French mistress for twenty-seven years, unaware that "Julie de St. Laurent"—his name for Thérèse-Bernardine Mongenet of Besançon—was not his own age but seven years his elder. The youngest unmarried duke, Adolphus of Cambridge, was only forty-three, lived seldom in England—he had a shooting lodge and country house in the family's German kingdom of Hanover where he was regent —and kept no women. He preferred his blond wig, his violin, his amateur scientific laboratory, and his investments, and had no interest in governing anything. Like the others, however, he was acquainted with his duty. Before Princess Charlotte had been dead ten days, he had rushed a proposal to Augusta, Princess of Hesse-Cassel.

With the Hanover connection, and the necessity for the succession to be definitively Protestant, the jigsaw puzzle of German dukedoms and principalities was a dynastic treasure trove. It was even more important for the Duke of Clarence to find a wife. If he lived long enough to succeed, he would be William IV. If not, his child might be sovereign of England. Quickly he, too, began shopping for a bride in Germany.

The Duke of Kent had more of a problem. Even before he disposed of the amiable Madame de St. Laurent, he had secretly begun looking for a legitimate wife, for financial rather than dynastic reasons. Princess Charlotte was then still alive and promised, with her consort Prince Leopold of Saxe-Coburg, to furnish continuity for the throne of England. Not, however, continuity for Hanover, the Royal Dukes realized, as Salic Law applied to the German pocket kingdom. Only male heirs could reign there, and if Charlotte became queen, the eldest of her surviving uncles would become King of Hanover.

Edward of Kent's idea of a suitable match was a bride with a bundle of money and the proper blood for an approved royal marriage, but his explorations had led only to ladies beyond a certain age. They stirred in him no impulse to public service. Yet one woman seemed, on paper at least, more interesting. The Duke had been helpful to Leopold—a Prince of Coburg—and Charlotte when the Prince Regent was hostile to their marriage. The pair were eager to match him with Leopold's younger sister, the Dowager Princess of Leiningen, a widow of thirty with two children, Charles and Feodora. Regent for her young son of the tiny principality of Amorbach, with barely fifteen thousand inhabitants, she had few if any real duties. Charles of Leiningen, whom she had married in 1803, and who had died in 1814, had lost his family territory above the River Speyer, notable largely for the Bad of Dürkheim, to Napoleon, and had been given in compensation an impoverished town and some countryside to the east, just below the River Main between Mannheim and Würzburg. (Nothing had improved the family situation after Waterloo.) The Duke went so far as to visit Princess Marie Louise Victoire in Darmstadt, one of the larger

The Race for the Throne

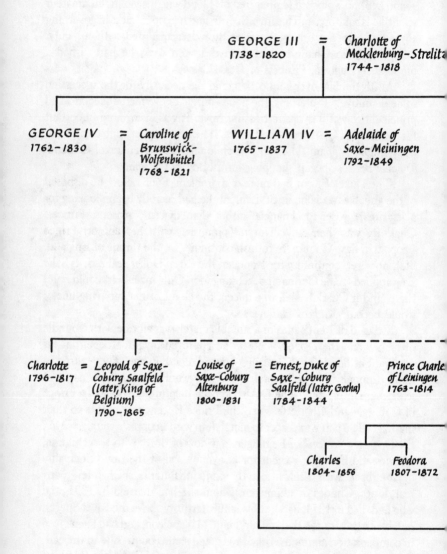

NOTE: 1. Only those children of George III who were important to the succession are included here.
2. The broken line represents siblings from the House of Coburg.

Ernest, Duke of = Frederica of
Cumberland   Mecklenburg-
(later, King of Hanover) Strelitz
1771 - 1851   1778 - 1841

Adolphus, Duke of = Augusta of
Cambridge   Hesse - Cassel
1774 - 1850   1797 - 1889

George V,   =   Mary of Saxe-
King of Hanover   Altenburg
1819 - 1878   1818 - 1907

Louisa   = George, Duke   Mary   = Prince Francis
Fairbrother   of Cambridge   Adelaide   of Teck
(Mrs. FitzGeorge) 1819 - 1904   1833 - 1897 1837 - 1900
1816 - 1890

(1 = Victoire of Saxe- = 2) Edward, Duke
   Coburg Saalfeld   of Kent
   (later, Duchess   1767 - 1820
   of Kent)
   1786 - 1861

Prince Albert = VICTORIA   Adelaide Victoire Dubus
of Saxe-Coburg   1819 - 1901   (illegitimate)
Gotha   1789 - ?
1819 - 1861

cities close to the borders of Amorbach, after which he dispatched a lengthy letter expressing his affection and proposing marriage. She might be an appropriate Queen of Hanover.

Following her husband's death, the widow—and now prospective bride—unused to business, had turned for advice to the Master of the Household, a Captain Schindler, who had added a *von* to his name to suggest his pretensions. Realizing that his position would be undermined, Schindler pointed out to Princess Victoire that she would have to give up the equivalent of £5,000 a year if she married. Besides, the disparity in ages was even greater than when she had become the second wife, at seventeen, of the forty-year-old Prince of Leiningen. There were also the problems of her children—whose future lay in Germany—the Duke of Kent's large debts, and Madame de St. Laurent. For the moment, Schindler prevailed.

Charlotte's death redoubled the Duke's ardor. Furnishing an heir to the British throne would undoubtedly enhance his fortunes, and he foresaw competition in the run for the dynastic sweepstakes not only from the younger Duke of Cambridge, but more crucially from the Duke of Clarence, who was pressing his suit upon the eldest daughter of the Duke of Saxe-Meiningen, Princess Adelaide, a plain young woman in her midtwenties, but ripe for childbearing. However, to secure money, Edward needed money. He had to demonstrate a suitable station in life, and he needed to buy off his loyal mistress. That meant borrowing money from friends who might consider it an investment in future power and perquisites. By January 1818 he could press Victoire for a "positive" response, and from Amorbach on January 25 she wrote prettily that she hoped to find compensation—presumably for loss of home and income—in the Duke's love.

His debts were now unimportant, Edward explained to a friend; the nation would be his debtor. The only one not to see it that way was Madame de St. Laurent, who had been prostrated by reading in a London paper, when the pair were living frugally in Brussels, a leader urging the Royal Dukes to marry for the sake of the succession. It had been a matter of great anxiety for the Duke to keep his negotiations under cover, especially from his cranky brother the Prince Regent, but nothing could be concealed from the London press, the *Morning Chronicle* having written on November 7, 1817, the day after Princess Charlotte's death, that it was now "the earnest prayer of the nation, that an early alliance of one of the unmarried Princes may forthwith be settled." The *Chronicle* had gone on to mention rumors "some time ago" of the marriage of the Duke of Kent with "one of the sisters of Prince Leopold," a union that England "would hail with . . . rapturous delight." By November 24, Madame de St. Laurent had seen the paper over breakfast. Her wretchedness was unconsoled by the Duke's hoping aloud to her that his "naval Brother" Clarence would marry, or that the Regent "may carry thro' *his* plan of Divorce."

His earnest disavowals left both in what Kent called "this sad state of suspense" until he had heard from Amorbach on February 6. After that he cautiously instructed the Master of his Household in England, one of his oldest friends from army service, General Frederick Augustus Wetherall, to write and send him something "shewable" to his "excellent and beloved" Madame, to give him cause to leave for London "to perform some *legal* act" for which his presence was—in his spelling—*"indispensible."*

Wetherall's "shewable" paper arrived on February 20, and Kent communicated it to his undeceived *"poor faithful Partner."* Maintaining their separate pretenses, complete to keeping the lease on their house in Brussels, the Duke set out for London, and for his campaign to raise funds to marry the woman he denied knowing anything about. On the same day, March 19, Thérèse-Bernardine left in a carriage for Paris, where she would be, thanks to a courtesy title from Louis XVIII, the Comtesse de Mongenet, with apartments in the Hotel de St. Aldegonde, supported by painful letters of solicitude from the Duke, and a small pension. He had been paying her £1,000 a year until his financial plight forced a reduction, at her suggestion, to £400.

Now he wanted his "beloved companion" to live in dignity, and the guilt he felt at his desertion was painful. To a mutual friend, the Baron de Mallet, the Duke wrote, hoping the letter would be seen by Julie, "We must *never* lose sight that our unexpected separation arose from the imperative duty I owed to obey the call of my family and my Country to marry, and *not* from the least diminution in an attachment which had stood the test of twenty-eight years and which but for *that* circumstance, would unquestionably have kept up the connexion, until it became the lot of one or other of us to be removed from this world."

Vowing nevertheless that he would make Victoire the first object of his life, the Duke offered her a "double plan" to learn each other's language and intensify their intimacy. His tenderness, he wrote, might make her forget their disparity in age. Then he borrowed £3,000 from Thomas Coutts the banker, optimistically expecting after the marriage an annual £25,000 supplement from Parliament, and even before the marriage £12,000 for an "outfit"—the clothes, presents, staff salaries and paraphernalia with which to go out into the world in his new status.

In the Schloss Ehrenburg in Coburg on May 29, 1818, at nine-thirty in the evening, the Dowager Princess of Leiningen was married, in Lutheran rites, to a man she had seen only once before. The Duke was resplendent in his English field marshal's uniform. The Princess, pretty and plump, was in pale silk lace. Afterwards she wrote in her diary that she hoped in her second marriage to find a happiness she had never enjoyed in the first. The month of May, Victoria would insist years later to her eldest daughter, was unlucky for marriages. "In Scotland nobody would marry in May and you know Uncle Leopold and Princess Charlotte were married in May, [and] Grandmama and my poor Father. . . . I never would let one of our children marry in that month. I have quite a feeling for it."

Four days after the wedding at Amorbach, the Duke and Duchess of Kent left for England, where at Kew Palace on July 13, at four in the afternoon, they were married again, this time according to the Church of England, but in a dual-language ceremony. Not only was the ceremony doubled, but there were also two brides for the Prince Regent to give away, for the Duke of Clarence and Princess Adelaide were united as well. The Archbishop of Canterbury officiated, assisted by the Bishop of London. And in the absence of pathetic George III, blind and insane, the fragile old Queen Charlotte, mother of the dukes, was chief celebrant at the wedding banquet.

The wedding trip, as Edward and Victoire realized even before the knot had been tied, had to be a hurried return journey to less expensive Amorbach. Parliament had offered nothing for an outfit, and nothing approaching what the Duke wanted seemed forthcoming as a marriage grant. There were too many ducal weddings at once, and no public inclination to fund grander royal life-styles. Lord Althorp even rose to agree that it was desirable for some of the dukes to marry and beget, but the country should not have to support sumptuous marriages for all of them. Sir Charles Monck felt that all hope of heirs from the Duke of Clarence's marriage should be exhausted before further expenditures toward the succession were made. One by one, exasperated Members demonstrated that they were in no mood to furnish further money to George III's spendthrift children, especially if they, like Edward of Kent, required a committee to administer their income on behalf of impatient creditors. Eventually some concession was made to the marrying dukes, and each was offered £6,000 to supplement his £25,000 annual grant from Parliament. The Duke of Clarence scornfully rejected his supplement as unworthy of his status and his sacrifice (but withdrew his disdain three years later, even requesting back payments). The Duke of Kent was desperate for the funds, which had to materialize painfully through the bureaucracy; and while they were slow in arriving, his fund of £3,000 from Coutts was already gone. Half of the Coutts loan had been due to his bride outright as part of the marriage contract. Another five hundred went hurriedly to Madame de St. Laurent, who was already very hard up. Wedding presents, gifts to attendants, a new equipage, servants, and the Duchess's fondness for new hats (one cost £108 10 *s.* 0*d.* —a year's wages for many professionals) had used up the rest. The Duke was already so deeply in debt that his mother, Queen Charlotte, urged the couple to leave England forthwith. She was failing rapidly, and was to live only four months longer; but she was not about to dip into her purse for him.

By September 11 the Duke and Duchess of Kent were across the Channel at Valenciennes, just below the present Belgian border, where the Duke of Wellington had his headquarters for the post-Waterloo occupation of the Low Countries. Wellington gave them a dinner and a ball, although privately to Thomas Creevey, a visiting M.P. who quietly kept a detailed diary, he referred to the retired field marshal as "the corporal." Having nothing whatever to do, and preferring in his circumstances to live off the land, the Duke of Kent would have been happy to remain in the area. He visited, with obvious enjoyment, a Belgian military school, asking too many questions and keeping underlings on their feet past their mealtimes. When you travel with the corporal, Wellington advised Creevey, who missed a lunch because of Kent's love of inquiries, always breakfast first.

By then the Duchess was pregnant, a fact confirmed in a letter written by the Duke on November 18 to the Prince Regent's private secretary, Sir Benjamin Bloomfield. Since the child was due in May, the Duke wrote, it would be his duty to bring the Duchess to England early in April, so that the birth could take place "at home," as would be prudent if the child was a potential sovereign. But that would "bear hard upon our limited income," he noted, although he had by then granted his Duchess £3,000 a year as a personal allowance, an amount that must be seen in perspective if we are to understand what he considered pin money. (The $25,000 annual salary of President James Monroe in the United States was the equivalent, then, of £5,000. The annual salary of Lord Liverpool, as Prime Minister and First Lord of the Treasury, was £5,000—and his private secretary received only £500.) Still, the Duke felt he had prospects now, and his committee had in effect agreed by granting him an additional £2,000 a year, retroactive to April. As a last resort there was always Thomas Coutts.

To his brother the Prince Regent, however, the Duke set out his needs as if he were about to deposit on English soil the one and only likely wearer of the crown of England for that next generation. He needed travel funds to come home. He needed a "yatcht" for the crossing. He needed London quarters for the confinement, and suggested "the Princess of Wales's late apartments" in Kensington Palace. He needed "an arrangement for our Table . . . upon a very limited scale." Also, the Duchess's physician had recommended a seaside location for a few weeks' recuperation, perhaps in royal residences at Brighton or Weymouth. That his requests were the economical minimum, he argued, would be clear if they were measured against the expenses of bringing over additional personal attendants. But all accommodations had to be properly fitted up for so auspicious an event—and he gave meticulous instructions for alterations of the suites at Kensington Palace, from the opening and closing of passages to the papering of walls. Fittings and furnishings for the wellborn were not cheap. A settee with silk upholstery might cost £587; a single chair for a dining room as much as £225.

The importance of his gift to the nation, the Duke felt, would guarantee that all his requests would be accepted, especially as he had itemized each and demonstrated its prudence. It was a shock when Sir Benjamin Bloomfield returned a curt refusal from the Prince Regent to all of them. There was "no money" for this "increase of expenditure" from any government department—and thus, implicitly, none from the Royal Household. Further, Sir Benjamin wrote, His Royal Highness had instructed him to refer the matter to the Prime Minister, Lord Liverpool, who "distinctly declared his inability to contribute in the least possible sum . . . as a grant from Parliament. . . ."

Had the Duke of Kent not already known of it, he was further informed that his bride was not alone in expecting a royal infant. Both the Duchess of Clarence and the Duchess of Cambridge were pregnant, and both planned to go through with their confinements in Hanover, where the Duke of Cambridge was regent. The Prince Regent, Bloomfield observed, "could not resist" recommending Hanover for the Duchess of

Kent also, as it would not only avoid "great expenditure" but would relieve her from "the Dangers and fatigues" of travel to England.

At least one of the Duke of Kent's requests, although he cannot have realized it, was certain to raise the Prince Regent's anger: the petition to move into his dead daughter's apartments, to bring into the world a successor to her and her stillborn child. The Prince Regent had disliked Princess Charlotte heartily, and had disapproved of her marriage. His brother had unintentionally reminded him of his failure to manage any other successor on his own. He had abhorred his wife, Princess Caroline, and kept her from their bed after their one and only child had been conceived, closing off any prospect of further legitimate offspring. He had contributed significantly to the likelihood of the extinction of his family's line. And he cared nothing for the technical connection to that line of the possible children of his brothers. Given contemporary child mortality rates, it was likely that none of them, even if born, would live to succeed.

The Duke of Kent was nothing if not stubborn. To James Putnam, a member of the committee overseeing his income, he wrote that he had no choice but to remain for the moment at Amorbach, certain as he was of no cordial reception by his brother. But he had planted in his committee's mind the importance of a birth *in England*. To General Wetherall, the Duke worried that he might be forced into a five-year wait in Germany, in order to pay off his debts. Yet he fully intended to have his child born in England. At the same time, he set out—with money he had not even borrowed yet—to improve the Amorbach property as if he intended to stay there, at least while the Duchess remained regent of the principality.

On New Year's Eve, 1818, the Duke wrote an affectionate letter to his wife even though she was in Amorbach with him. He loved letter-writing, and, sincerely fond of his wife, wanted to put his feelings on record.

> Thursday evening 31st December 1818. This evening will put an end, dear well beloved Victoire, to the year 1818, which saw the birth of my happiness by giving you to me as my guardian angel. I hope that you will always recall this year with the same pleasure as I do, and that each time a new anniversary comes round, you will be as contented with your fate, as you make me hope you are today . . . all my efforts are directed to one end, the preservation of your dear health and the birth of a child who will resemble you, and if

Heaven will give me these two blessings I shall be consoled for all my misfortunes and disappointments, with which my life has been marked.

I would have wished to be at least able to say all this to you in pretty verses but you know that I am an old soldier who has not this talent, and so you must take the good will in accepting this little almanack you will remember that it comes from your very deeply attached husband, for whom you represent all happiness and all consolation. On that [note] I tell you in the language of my country, *God bless you, love me as I love you. . . .*

Such sentiments, seen against the cynicism of the deplorable Royal Dukes, of whom Edward had certainly been one, foreshadow ways of thinking that would replace the chilly Regency values. Victoria's father seems an early Victorian.

Twenty-seven years with Madame de St. Laurent (later legends notwithstanding) had not left him a father. His only experience of that condition had been one he would have preferred to forget. As Prince Edward, a colonel in the Royal Fusiliers (with no apparent duties) at twenty-two, he had been living in Geneva with a young French actress, Adelaide Dubus. On December 15, 1789, she died giving birth to a daughter, whom the Prince christened Adelaide Victoire Auguste. In arranging for the child's care as absentee father, he signed an agreement that the deceased woman's father, and her sister, Victoire, would be pensioned. In return, the child would be brought up as a Protestant and was not to become (the term may have been a euphemism) "an actress." With baby Victoire in the care of her aunt, the Prince returned to London, where he hoped to explain away his embarrassment to his father. But within two days of his return, the escapade was made public in the pages of the *General Evening Post,* and George III ordered Edward out of England.

By the time the baby was brought to him for a visit, in July 1790, the Prince was stationed in lonely Gibraltar. Neither aunt nor little Adelaide Victoire remained for long. Edward may have hoped to inherit Victoire as replacement for her sister, but she had no need to furnish any services beyond her foster care. Money paid to Victoire Dubus, and later to "Madame Barthelmy," would appear regularly in the Prince's accounts with Coutts's bank, and her name occurs in Geneva records until 1832. The child, however, vanishes from history.

By 1819, Victoire (and Adelaide Victoire) had become only items in a ledger that the Duke never saw, entries that added insignificantly to his debts. His hope now was for a child legitimately his, one not to be hidden away but to be presented to the nation. Edward was as excited about the prospect at least as much as he was looking forward to its tangible rewards. And he was as concerned about the unsuitability of the drafty, remote former convent at Amorbach, hours away from the closest real city for a royal confinement, as he was about its political unwisdom. Hanover would have been little better, even if the Duke of Cambridge would have allowed Edward there, no certain thing. Financial embarrassment in any case left him no recourse but to appeal to Hanover, asking that the Duke of Cambridge lend him £8,500, although Edward estimated that only £1,139 11s. 0d. would be needed for the expenses of the "accouchement." The rest was to pay new debts, and possibly to continue improvements at Amorbach, including a stable for his expensive new black mares and carriage horses. Nothing was forthcoming from Hanover, however, perhaps because the Duke of Clarence and his bride —who was carrying the only possible offspring to stand between the Duchess of Kent's child and the throne—were already in the kingdom.

Despite newspaper criticism—the *Morning Herald* declared that the Duke's aim in coming to England was "to transfer his Highness's debts from himself to the public"—the Duke's supporters in England sensed that the gambling odds were good; the chances that the new Duchess's child might reign were, in any event, the only realistic hopes they had of recovering their investments in the Duke. Ignoring the *Herald*'s contention that the birth of a prince or princess "may be attested by sufficient witnesses, just as well in Germany as in England," they preferred to reason that Kent, while only a fourth son, was in line of succession behind a childless Regent, a childless and ailing Duke of York, and a Duke of Clarence well past fifty with a new wife of untested fecundity. From London, one of Kent's committee, Joseph Hume, wrote that it was urgent for the Duke to bring his wife to England, so that the legitimacy of the child to reign would not be challenged "from the circumstances of the birth taking place on foreign soil." It might be said, he pointed out, that "to have a Son and heir born abroad a foreigner, will be thought by the nation to arise from the wish of the Duchess to remain in her own country." The "greatest and most important duty your Country looks for from you," Hume insisted, required making immediate plans to return. Alderman Wood, another member of the committee (and a onetime supporter of the Prince Regent's estranged wife), and Lord Darnley, still another, offered to sign a bond for £10,000 to enable the birth to take place in England, the news of this reaching Amorbach on March 14, 1819 —almost the last possible minute, as the Duchess was going into her eighth month of pregnancy. Further, two others, Lord Dundas and Earl Fitzwilliam, each raised £2,500 for the grand design, turning the funds over to General Wetherall. With nearly twice what he first claimed he needed, the Duke of Kent was elated, writing to the Duke of Bedford the next day that an enormous weight had been taken off his mind, "for, as an *Englishman*, I felt it my first duty to my *Country*, to my family and to my *Child*, to make every possible sacrifice to ensure the Infant being born, *ipso facto*, on British ground."

To Sir Benjamin Bloomfield, for the Prince Regent, the Duke announced the same day that he had been "induced" by friends in England to proceed there for the Duchess's confinement. The Duchess of Kent, her husband wrote, would arrive at Calais on April 18. If the royal yacht could be sent, it would be a great boon, and some accommodation at Kensington Palace would be "an act of kindness," but the Duke wanted the Prince Regent to be assured that no further assistance "of *any* sort" would be expected. A Captain John Conroy, the Duke's equerry, the letter added in a postscript, would be sent ahead to handle all details.

Reluctantly, the Duke's brother gave in as far as the yacht and the temporary quarters in Kensington were concerned, but noted his regrets that such an inexpedient journey was to be undertaken by the Duchess. Both sides knew of the state of the four hundred miles of roads to be traversed, bumpy at best, and the three rough hours of even the shortest crossing of the Channel. Still, the political consequences were such that the Duke was willing to risk a premature and possible fatal birth, and the disfavor of the Prince Regent, who was certain soon to be king in his own right.

On March 28, 1819, the Duke and Duchess set out from Amorbach in a motley convoy of vehicles. First was the Duke's small but comfortably springed phaeton, with himself at the reins, the Duchess at his side. Next came the Duchess's phaeton, with the household's German and English maids. Third was the Duke's barouche, with Baroness Spaeth, the Duchess's lady-in-waiting, and Frau Siebold (who also practiced as Dr. Heidenreich), her *accoucheur*, in facing seats. Then the Duchess's post-chaise, empty (for use in bad weather), young Feodora's post-chaise (with the Princess, her governess, two Russian lapdogs, and cages of songbirds), a cabriolet with the cooks, a wagon for the household plate with an English manservant in charge of it, a low phaeton in case the Duchess required a bed, two gigs with the Duke's valet and footmen, and a curricle for Dr. Wilson, the Duke's personal physician and manager of the Duchess's pregnancy (although his medical experience had been largely as a ship's doctor in the Royal Navy).

Since the party intended to make evening stopovers at inns, the journey often had to be extended beyond their plans in order to find accommodations spacious enough to handle everyone. With good weather holding, there were no problems in transport, and the Duchess held up well—even better, the Duke wrote to Mr. Putnam proudly, than at home. By April 5 they were at Cologne; by April 18, as planned, at Calais. By then there was news that the Duchess of Cambridge had given birth, on March 26, to a son, but the Cambridges were junior in precedence to the Kents. More significantly, the Duchess of Clarence, the next day, had given birth prematurely to a daughter who had survived only seven hours. No Salic Law limited the succession in England to male heirs, and had the baby lived, she might have been queen ahead of any child born to the Duke of Kent. Perhaps the important fact to the Kents was that the Duchess of Clarence had proved capable of bearing children. Whatever might happen to Victoire's child, it faced the possibility of being bypassed by a future Clarence.

The winds to Dover were unfavorable for sailing, and remained so for nearly a week. Victoire was going into her ninth month. On the twenty-fourth the Channel was crossed—a rough but short passage, with the Duchess "certainly very sick," the Duke wrote to her mother, the Dowager Duchess of Coburg. But "All has ended well."

Old, red-brick Kensington Palace, once the country seat of William and Mary, proved unready for occupancy, the late Princess's apartments overlooking the gardens having been vacant and stripped for five years. The Duke had to secure fixtures and furniture, as well as move additional furnishings into the palace from houses he owned in town and in the country. At the time, Kensington was in the London suburbs, and the palace, although renovated by George I, had deteriorated into a less-than-grand residence, divided into apartments for several royal occupants. Whatever the Duke's avowals to his brother about intending to use Kensington only temporarily for the birth, his efforts and expenditures told a different tale. The firm of Elliot and Francis, 104 New Bond Street, would value the furniture in the Duke's rooms in the palace the next year as worth over £6,000. The Duke's library alone had "book cases in 52 parts"—which did not suggest any intentions of returning to Amorbach soon after the confinement.

To Robert Owen, manufacturer and experimenter in practical socialism, whose utopian New Lanark Mills in Scotland the Duke proposed to visit, and whose sympathy he thought he had gained, the Duke detailed his grievances against Parliament for failing to vote him funds to maintain his household. His servants were overworked; he had more than doubled his cost of living by taking on a family; he did not live showily. "I now candidly state," he explained, "that, after viewing the subject in every possible way, I am satisfied that, to continue to live in England, even in the quiet way in which we are going on, *without splendour, and without show, nothing short of doubling the present seven thousand pounds will do,* REDUCTION BEING IMPOSSIBLE." If his value to his nation went unappreciated, despite the "extensive losses and privations" he had experienced in its service, he would not "scruple, in *due* time, to resume my retirement abroad, when the Duchess and myself shall have fulfilled our duties in establishing the *English* birth of my child, and giving it material nutriment on the soil of Old England; and which we shall certainly repeat, if Providence destines to give us any further increase of family."

On May 23, a Sunday, with the work of renovation still proceeding slowly, the Duke sent a message to General Wetherall that the Duchess's labor had begun that evening. His Majesty's Privy Councillors were sent for as observers. Soon, in a room adjoining the Duchess's, and shepherded by the general, were the Archbishop of Canterbury, the Duke of Wellington, the Bishop of London, the Marquess of Lansdowne, Earl Bathurst, George Canning, Nicholas Vansittart (Chancellor of the Exchequer), and the Duke of Sussex (who had married out of the succession and in any event was now childless and separated). Such distinguished cachet for the confinement would have been impossible in Hanover, hardly more than a colony.

With Frau Siebold overseeing the delivery, labor took a little over six hours, and an apparently healthy girl was born at 4:15 on Monday morning, May 24, 1819. Elated, the Duke sent a special courier to Coburg with a message to the Dowager Duchess that the baby girl was "truly a model of strength and beauty combined" and the mother was also "doing marvellously well." An English physician standing by, Dr. David Daniel Davis, had not been needed. Soon the German *accoucheur* would be on her way back to Coburg. She would officiate three months later at the birth of a son to the wife of the Duchess of Kent's brother, the Duke of Coburg, a boy who would be named Albert.

A second royal grandson, christened George after the King and the Regent (as was the Cambridge infant two months earlier), would be born three days after the Princess, this time to the Duke and Duchess of Cumberland, the fourth of the dukes to have been hurriedly married. Ernest of Cumberland was the fifth son of George III, in line to be king if he survived his brothers and the princess. Rumor had him guilty of grisly crimes, ranging from incest with his sister Sophia to murder. Something of that reputation came from his warped face, the result of a battle wound at Tournai in 1794, but his nature was allegedly ugly as well. He had married ahead of the others, in 1815, becoming the third husband of the widowed Princess of Solms-Braunfels (herself alleged to be guilty of dispatching one husband), banking on Salic Law—if Princess Charlotte became queen—to make him and his male progeny kings of Hanover. In 1817 they had a stillborn daughter, but hoped for a son who might be King of England as well—for he would precede Prince George of Cambridge, two months older but born of a younger son. Now another royal daughter stood in the way of that throne, and unfounded but credible rumors for years would suggest that he hatched plots against the life of the princess.

The names for the infant Kent daughter would be a dilemma for the Duke as the likely date of the christening approached. The Prince Regent had let it be known that he alone would fix the time and place for the ceremony, and that he would insist on choosing the names—or at least on having a royal veto. Meanwhile the Duke doted on his daughter, professing no unhappiness at the child's sex. In the absence of Salic Law it made no difference, and with his wife likely to have further children as long as both parents remained healthy, he could foresee sons. Still, the child might be queen, and needed regal names, despite the Duke's fears, as he wrote to the Duke of Orleans early in June, that "the brother before me *will in all human probability yet have a family."* Because of that likelihood, and the long-simmering hostility between the Duke and the Prince Regent, the Regent's plan, the Duke confided, "is evidently *to keep me down."*

One way was to ignore any formal honors or official notification to the ambassadors in London from the courts of Europe. Since the infant Princess was in the direct line of succession, both gestures were appropriate. To the Regent the Princess's father communicated his choice of names, the first to honor the Regent himself, as he was asked to stand as one of the child's godfathers. The other godfather, who had already consented to his role although he could not be present, was Alexander I, Czar of Russia. Thus the Prince Regent was offered the christening names Georgiana Charlotte Augusta Alexandrina Victoria.

Cruelly, the Regent waited almost until the last moment to announce to the baby's parents that the christening would take place at his pleasure at three in the afternoon on June 24, a Monday—only three days later. The only guests permitted were to be the Duke and Duchess of York (next in line for the throne), Princess Augusta (sister to the dukes and one of those honored in the selection of names), the Duke and Duchess of Gloucester (Princess Mary, the Duchess, was Augusta's sister), Prince Leopold (Victoire's brother and Charlotte's widower), and Princess Sophia (another unmarried daughter of George III). Since the ceremony was to be private, dressing up was forbidden (frock coats only), and no members of the diplomatic corps would be present. The Duke of York would stand for the Czar, whether or not the Czar, or Edward, had designated someone else; and the Regent would stand for himself. The names? Almost as afterthought Sir Benjamin Bloomfield added that the "Prince Regent will explain himself to your Royal Highness, previous to the ceremony."

The blow about the names fell the evening before the christening, although the Duke of Kent must have been prepared for it by the pressure put on his brother-in-law Leopold by the Regent to prevent the name of Charlotte from being given to the child. The beneficiary of a huge pension —£50,000 annually—from Parliament, Leopold chose not to risk it. As for the other names, the Regent announced, he would insist (as the Duchess explained it later) "that the name of Georgiana could not be used, as He did not chuse to place the name before the Emperor of Russia's, and He could not allow it to follow."

There were still several names left when the group assembled in the Cupola Room at Kensington Palace. In honor of the occasion the royal baptismal font had been brought from the Tower of London. The Archbishop of Canterbury and the Bishop of London officiated, interrupted soon by the Regent, who forbade, additionally, the names Charlotte and Augusta, thus effectively refusing all names then borne by the Royal Family. Cautiously, the Archbishop, baby in his arms, asked the Regent to pronounce the name by which the child might be baptized. "Alexandrina," the Regent said. The Archbishop waited further, certain that a royal child deserved, at the least, one other name. "Elizabeth," urged the Duke of Kent. The Regent shook his head. "Give her the mother's name also then, but it cannot precede that of the Emperor."

Born fifth in succession to the throne of England, although first in precedence in her own generation, the child would be known during her earliest years as "Drina." At home, the preferred name, Victoria, became *Vickelchen* to her German mother. Once Victoria had learned to write her name, Alexandrina disappeared altogether, yet it remained her official name until much later, when she proclaimed otherwise. (Very likely she never knew of a half-sister who also had Victoria as her second name.)

With the child the Duke's most valuable property, he was determined to remain in England. Fearing that the worst excesses of expenditure and indebtedness were now to come, his committee cautioned him about living within his means and reducing his debts from income. For the creditors, Joseph Hume stressed such economy. The Duke, on the other hand, applied to his trustees for £18,000 to settle "extra claims," and Captain Conroy, the Duke's equerry, reacted loyally to Hume's suggestions "with sentiments of indignation."

The Duke's unused country house at Ealing, replete with mechanically operated waterfalls, had cost £200,000 to build and develop. He had not been able to sell it even at its valuation price of £50,000, and his committee suggested a lottery to raise funds. Such a sale needed Parliamentary approval, and Lord Castlereagh, leader of the House of Commons, refused to entertain the motion. It would set an undignified precedent, he warned. Meanwhile, the Duke piled up new debts, and took his daughter, at two months, to a military review. He intended to flaunt her before England.

"What business has that infant here?" the Regent screamed. Edward pretended not to notice.

"Look at her well," the Duke would say confidently to his friends, "for she will be Queen of England."

The Duke and Duchess entered enthusiastically into London life after the christening, despite continuing signals of disapproval from Windsor. With other people's money, the Duke was an energetic patron of charities. Masked balls were in fashion, the most glittering being given by the Persian ambassador. At another, a charity ball in costume at Carlton House on July 17, the Duchess appeared as a plump Joan of Arc. Following up his interest in Robert Owen's socialist schemes, the Duke chaired a meeting promoting additional "Villages of Co-operation," but despite a model of New Lanark on display, there were few subscriptions from the well-to-do, who preferred to see the working-class surplus emigrate to the colonies.

At ten weeks, Victoria was vaccinated. She was in blooming health, and her parents intended to keep her (and themselves) that way. Snubs from the Regent, who remained convinced that the Clarences would do Victoria out of a place in the succession, proved to have no effect on the Kent's optimism about their prospects, especially when Adelaide, barely four months after the death of the hastily named Charlotte Augusta, miscarried at Calais on the homeward journey. That they had been following the example of the Kents in returning from Germany for the birth was obvious. The strategy had failed.

The Regent's hostility toward Princess Alexandrina Victoria's parents was only raised a degree by the way the succession competition had gone. Realizing that, Princess Mary of Gloucester, sister to the Regent and to Edward, knew what her own position had to be, with the Regent certain to become king in his own right within months, as George III was fast fading. "The Kents passed two nights at Windsor with bag and baggage," she wrote cattily to her brother George on September 10, "I mean by that besides the baby she brought her daughter and Mdlle de Spate and they all *retired to rest* both evenings at 9 o'clock." For the high-living Regency dukes and duchesses, such drab contentment was a scandal, although nine would have been a proper bedtime for the baby, the young Princess Feodora, and their governess, Baroness Spaeth. The Duchess was beside herself with mockery, observing further that "*all* wished them good night at the same time *& actually went to bed* to the very great *amusement* of the whole society at Windsor."

Another memorandum from the Duke of Kent went to his committee that month, outlining his increased needs, this time scaled down to reflect intentions to leave expensive London for a country house in Devonshire. He even went, with Conroy, to look over suitable properties with modest upkeep, and found one, white-painted Woolbrook Cottage, at Sidmouth, which was leased for him by Alderman Wood, of the committee. The winter there, Kent wrote his brother-in-law, the Duke of Coburg, on November 19, was "less severe." The Princess, he added proudly, had already been weaned, and at six months was as advanced as infants of eight. He was himself in a happy mood, having celebrated in London his fifty-second birthday (on November 2) with a family party at which his stepdaughter sang a song, his stepson Prince Charles of Leiningen sent a letter in English from his school in Geneva, and Victoria presented a birthday letter written for her by the Duchess.

Schemes for borrowing money took up much of the Duke's time in December, delaying his move to Devonshire. Coutts declined further advances from his bank, then also from his personal funds. The bankers Bosanquet and Co. were also approached unsuccessfully for the £30,000 for which the Duke claimed urgent need. Spending time at Prince Leopold's estate at Claremont—to save money—the Kents were bombarded with advice to return to Germany now that the purpose of their residence in England had been accomplished. And from the Duke's solicitor, Mr. Karslake, came the estimate that the Ealing property might be divided into large parcels and sold, the furniture auctioned off and the vacant mansion torn down for sale as building material. The lot, he guessed, might fetch perhaps half the Duke's original investment, yet twice what the Kents claimed was necessary for survival. But the season for such activity had to be spring; their present income would have to suffice until May.

With the committee in any case offering, the Duke wrote, "every disposition to do all in their power to make me comfortable," he set off with his entourage toward Sidmouth. Upon reaching Salisbury on December 21, they were the guests of the bishop (Edward's boyhood tutor, Dr. John Fisher) for two days, only arriving at Woolbrook Cottage on the afternoon of Christmas Day, in the midst of a "tremendous snowstorm." The Duke blamed the water on the journey for the "very deuce" of a time he was having with his bowels, and a gastric attack that came on as they arrived. Reporting to Wetherall on the last day of the year, however, he pronounced himself "completely recovered," but weak.

One of the reasons given for the relocation to Devon had been the health of the Princess, but the Duke had not been thinking about assassination attempts. Three days after their arrival, a window in the drawing room, where the Duchess was sitting with Victoria, was shattered by gunfire. No one was hurt, although the Duchess was *"most* exceedingly" alarmed. Retainers rushed out to find a boy shooting erratically at birds with a heavier pellet than necessary—swan shot. Conroy quickly applied to the local magistrate for some measure to prevent a recurrence of the incident—possibly a ban on shooting in the vicinity of Woolbrook Cottage. But punishment of the boy was ruled out at the request of their Royal Highnesses.

As 1820 opened, the milder winter the Duke had been looking for was nowhere to be found. Channel weather was hazardous for shipping; snow, rain and wind pounded inland; the Kents all had colds, and Dr. Wilson made regular visits from his nearby lodgings, supervising the cutting of Victoria's first two teeth. General Wetherall had arrived from London to conduct the Duke's business, and Captain Conroy remained in attendance. While they prepared to winter over, the Duke, struggling with his cold and writing letter after letter, was exploring the possibility of returning to Amorbach. The weather in Devon, he conceded, was "rather Canadian."

After tending the horses with Conroy early in January, the Duke returned wet and chilled, and his cold flared up. A few days later he was feverish and in bed, in a room the Duchess described to her German friend Polyxene von Tubeuf as "inconceivably cold." Beset by problems, and in a strange country the language of which she was not learning very quickly, Victoire appealed to Polyxene for "encouraging sympathy." "Vickelchen," she added, was recovered from her own cold and "a greater darling than ever," but "beginning to show symptoms of wanting to get her own little way."

On January 12, with the Duke's fever unabated, he was moved to a larger and warmer room, but that evening he became delirious, and vomiting weakened him further. In the belief that loss of blood would lessen the Duke's fever, Dr. Wilson applied leeches to his patient's chest, and the tough constitution of the Duke began to give way under the mistaken medical practices of the day. He would outlive his brothers, he once predicted, but the Duchess, now terrified, sent to London for Dr. David Dundas, reputedly the best of the royal physicians. In his place, however, rushed Dr. William Maton, former physician to the late Queen Charlotte, as Dundas could not be spared while George III still struggled for life. Dr. Wilson had already decided on further bleeding, ordering the Duke to be cupped, as a method more efficient than leeches. Cupping meant applying a heated four-ounce cup to an incision in the patient's flesh; blood filled the cup as the vacuum created by the cooling drew it out. To relieve the Duke's headache he was cupped on his forehead as well, and when cupping failed to relieve any of his problems, leeches were reapplied to draw further blood. The Duke's pneumonia intensified.

On January 17, a Monday, the new doctor arrived. He spoke no German and little French, and the Duchess still knew very little English. Further, Dr. Maton was an exponent of bleeding, and in looking over his patient he determined that the already wan and exhausted Duke had been insufficiently bled. When Maton ordered more bleeding, and the Duke was told, he wept. It was probably clear to him that he was not going to survive his treatment, even if he could live through his illness. He had an "unendurable" pain in his side, an undiminished fever, hiccups and a cough, and intermittent delirium. That his mind wandered further was the only useful outcome of the treatment, as he was then less aware of his misery. His wife, however, was fully aware of what was being done in the name of medicine, writing to Polyxene that the Duke's situation was now "too dreadful. . . . There is not a spot on his dear body which has not been touched by cupping, blisters, or bleeding. He was terribly exhausted yesterday after all that had been done to him by those cruel doctors. . . ."

All told, the cupping alone would remove, by the physicians' calculations, 120 fluid ounces of blood from the Duke's wracked body—nearly a gallon. Leeches were applied as the remedy for almost any complaint, and the routine prescription of doses of calomel and other purgatives like James's powder drained further fluid from the Duke's dehydrated tissues. Antibiotics have since reduced the chances of death from pneumonia to a negligible level. In 1820 few survived, and the Duke's treatment ensured that he would not be among that small percentage. "English physicians kill you," the cynical Viscount Melbourne would later tell Victoria; "the French let you die."

On Thursday, the twentieth, Prince Leopold and others with an interest in the Duke's future were sent messages in the Duchess's name to warn them that the outlook was gloomy. Leopold was shooting in Berkshire, and left immediately for Sidmouth, "in bitter cold and damp weather I shall not easily forget," accompanied by his closest adviser (and former physician) Baron Christian Stockmar. To Sir Benjamin Bloomfield, for the Regent, General Wetherall sent a similar preparatory message, eliciting a response expressing the Regent's "anxious solicitude." A paper in the Windsor archives, possibly an invention of Kent's household, which desperately needed good relations with the soon-to-be George IV, quoted the Duke as responding to the Regent's message with a heartfelt "If I could now shake hands with him, I should die in peace."

On January 22, Leopold and Stockmar arrived. After taking the Duke's pulse, Stockmar told the Duchess that "human help could no longer avail." General Wetherall called Stockmar aside and asked "if it would be injurious to speak to the Duke about signing his will." With

Kent's mind wandering, onlookers wondered whether such a document would have any legal force, but the general brought papers in, and his familiar voice, Stockmar recalled, had the effect of bringing the Duke to an awareness of the people around him. He asked for his wife and child, and had the will read to him twice. His emaciated body propped up, he signed "Edward" at the bottom of the page presented to him, gazing at each letter as he made it, and asking afterward whether the signature was legible. "Then," Stockmar wrote, "he sank back exhausted on the pillows." It was an age that coveted last words, and those of the Duke were reportedly, "May the Almighty protect my wife and child, and forgive all the sins I have committed." And to his wife they were, "Do not forget me." Whether they in fact were spoken, the Duchess let them be known, and cherished them.

The next morning, a Sunday, the Duke died. His hand was in the Duchess's, who knelt by his side. "My father," Victoria would insist more than fifty years later, ". . . would have been King had he not been cut off in health and strength!" Instead, he would be borne to Windsor only to be interred in St. George's Chapel, in a huge coffin seven feet five inches long, deep in the iron-gated family vault. "In the centre," Victoria wrote in her journal on May 15, 1873, "quite close to the entrance, on a sort of long stone platform stood my poor dear Father's coffin. It was indeed solemn and moving in the extreme for me, his only child, who had never known him[,] to be standing near his earthly remains." The coffins of the Hanoverian kings were covered with purple; her father's coffin lay under royal crimson.

In the chill of Woolbrook Cottage, dazed by shock and grief, the Duchess left removal arrangements to retainers. She had no idea how precarious her situation was. She knew little English and had no friends in England except Stockmar, and no relations but her brother. The Duke had left nothing but debts, and she did not have enough money of her own to return to London, let alone to Amorbach.

The next day, little Alexandrina Victoria was eight months old.

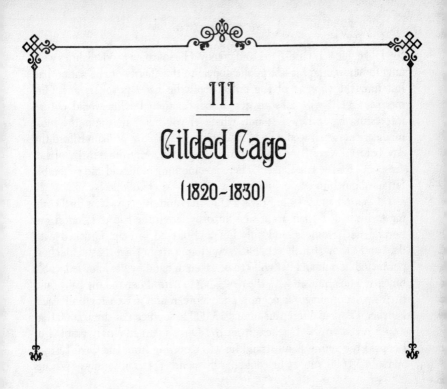

III

Gilded Cage

(1820–1830)

While his father, George III, lay in state—he had died at eighty-two on January 29, 1820—the Duke of Kent was borne from Sidmouth to Windsor with a cavalry escort and the muffled tolling of a funeral bell. The King had died in darkness; Edward of Kent's body would arrive at the Chapel of St. George in darkness, the smoky glare of torches barely piercing the gloom. The Duchess had not followed; social custom still frowned on the attendance of women at funerals. "I am sick at heart and very lonely," she wrote to her friend Polyxene von Tubeuf. But she had "dear, sweet little Vickelchen. . . . God has indeed been good in letting me have such a treasure. . . ."

With Victoria, the Duchess would begin her return journey to London on January 25, amid unfounded rumors that she had been left pregnant. Venomously, the same day, Princess de Lieven, wife of the Russian ambassador, wrote to Prince Metternich, "No one in England will mourn the Duke. He was false, hard, and greedy. His so-called good qualities were only for show, and his last public appeal to the charity of the nation had lost him the support of the only friends he had—prisoners and City men. . . . His wife kills all her husbands, though. She would cut an interesting figure now . . . but, whatever you may say, she is the most mediocre person it would be possible to meet." To Sir William Elford the day before, Mary Russell Mitford had written, very differently, of her "respect" for the late Duke. "There is something of his old and venerable father about him . . . a fine public speaker—a charitable man."

Charitableness from Edward's brothers and sisters was less forthcoming to his widow than insincere sympathy. Even the trip to London was beyond her resources, and only Leopold offered to help. Crushed with debt and sorrow, hardly yet able to communicate in English, the Duchess permitted herself and her child to be taken in hand by her knowledgeable brother, who arranged with the new King to permit her and the baby (and their small entourage) to occupy, once more, rooms in Kensington Palace. Further, Leopold offered an annual £3,000 to supplement the £6,000 that would revert to the Duchess from the Duke's parliamentary grant. For Leopold the sum was no strain; he was receiving from the Civil List an annual £50,000, money he could hardly spend. Yet as niggardly as was his

Edward, Duke of Kent, the Queen's father. Engraving from a portrait by George Dawe.

nobility in the circumstances, it was overwhelmingly generous compared to that of George IV and his brothers. Leopold's life-style was unthreatened by the largesse. He maintained a palatial estate, Claremont, and a mistress, on the remaining £47,000. (His unrepaid "loans" to the Duchess as of 1834 would total only £16,000.)

The Duke's insurance went to his creditors, one of them Thérèse-Bernardine Mongenet, known to her friends as the Comtesse de Montgenet; she had added a *t* to the name for further distinction. The Duchess was "not ignorant" of the long liaison, the former Madame de St. Laurent had written to a friend in 1818, "and gives me every reason to believe that she respects it." If evidence was needed, it came to the Comtesse immediately after the death of Edward via Louis-Philippe, then Duke of Orleans: "Here, my dear Comtesse, is a letter for you from Madame the Duchess of Kent that Prince Leopold sent to me, asking me to pass it on to you with the consideration and care your situation requires. I send it to you, however, without delay, so that you can prepare your reply, for which I will come in about three hours if you can receive me, in order to discuss with you what you would like me to write. . . . Be brave if you can."

Such tact and consideration were luxuries the desperate Duchess soon learned to forgo. She had to live for her child, who might be Queen. Leopold stressed the destiny of the infant, and exhorted Victoire to remain in England with her, despite the indifference, at best, of the new King and the Royal Dukes. All of those with precedence to the child appeared older than their years, ailing and dissipated. They would not live forever. The Duchess might soon be Regent of Britain for a child queen, with Leopold as the power behind the cradle. She would have to relinquish her meaningless title as Regent of Leiningen for her son Charles, now sixteen, and prepare for more ambitious possibilities. And she would have to guard her infant jealously from the wicked uncles, each one of whom had something to gain from Alexandrina Victoria's demise.

In London, condolence calls were paid on the Duchess, who had already established a protective regimen that always kept the child attended by someone above servant class. Her nurse slept in her room.

The Royal Dukes seemed, largely from a distance, pleased with "little Vickelchen." The Duke of Cumberland wondered, from Berlin, to his brother the King, how Edward could have thought of "leaving his comfortable apartments at Kensington" during "such a cold season. . . . I should have thought he would have outlived us all from his regular habits of life. . . . The poor Dss & his little girl go to my soul, for though I never saw her in my life, still I must feel deeply interested for her. . . ." His sister, Princess Augusta, would write spitefully to Lady Harcourt in February 1820, that "dearest William" (the Duke of Clarence) was "so good hearted" that he had instructed Adelaide, his Duchess, "to go to Kensington every day; she is a comfort to the poor Widow; . . . they can read the same *Prayers* and talk the same *Mother Tongue* together." More helpfully, Princess Mary wrote to her brother, George IV, that his sister-in-law was in a "deplorable *reduced* state" requiring "some little immediate assistance." The King, however, hoped that financial desperation would force the Duchess back to Germany, although her debts in Amorbach, as a result of the late Duke's abortive rebuilding extravagances, left nothing to live in, and nothing to live on.

Since her establishment had to befit a future queen, she borrowed £6,000 on Leopold's signature (he could have given her the money outright), at exorbitant interest, to furnish and rehabilitate her dilapidated and drafty segment of Kensington Palace. When, on July 3, 1820, the House of Commons voted to continue allowances made during the reign of the late King, the parsimonious Lord Castlereagh announced that further support for the Duchess and "infant Princess" would be unnecessary "as the Prince Leopold with great liberality, had taken upon himself the charge of the support and education" of the child. In effect he was voicing indirectly the public criticism of Leopold for continuing to accept the huge annuity voted him for life when it was expected that he would be the consort of an English queen.

Whatever was being said in public, the Duchess was accepting less and less advice from her brother, for he was seldom physically present and dithered over decisions. Some former aides to her husband were still actively on the scene. General Wetherall struggled with the late Duke's insolvency, for which his £30,000 insurance in behalf of his creditors was hardly a down payment. In the household the energetic former equerry to the Duke, Captain John Conroy, was establishing himself as indispensable to the Duchess. As the "dear devoted friend of my Edward," she wrote Madame Tubeuf, he "does not desert his Widow, doing all he can by dealing with my affairs. . . . His energy and capability are wonderful." The ambitious Conroy, who saw himself as master of a future queen's establishment, was "invaluable, I don't know what I would do without him."

The prospects of the Princess kept the household from foundering in gloom and kept creditors from the door. When the new King nearly died of pleurisy that winter, the stock of young Vickelchen went up. (She was, her mother announced, perhaps hoping that George IV would hear, the "image" of the King.) When the childless Duchess of York died in August, and the gouty Duke, fifty-seven and next in line for the throne, refused to remarry, again the future of Vickelchen seemed bright. But at about the same time the Duchess of Clarence was observed as once more noticeably pregnant. On December 10, however, after the excitement of a FitzClarence daughter's wedding, the Duchess went into labor six weeks prematurely. Although the child was born "disturbingly small," Vickelchen once more fell back in the succession. The King was delighted with the newest princess, and permitted her to be christened Elizabeth Georgina Adelaide. Londoners began referring to the little Queen Bess, and by New Year's Day 1821 the military band that had played at the mounting of the guard outside St. James's Palace, and had fallen silent in order not to disturb mother and child, resumed its daily schedule.

"Our little woman's nose," confessed the possessive Captain Conroy, "has been put out of joint." That was exactly the attitude of the King, who, when Lord Liverpool asked him in February 1821 about putting the fatherless princess under Royal protection, told the Prime Minister that he damned well would not. The child's uncle "was rich enough to take care of her." Hearing of the remark, the King's son-in-law told Lord Liverpool that he would care for his niece, "but remember it was not I who grasped at this management of the Princess, but that the Princess is by the King in this manner confided to me, and H. Maj. thereby delegated to me a power which belongs to him."

Early in March, newspapers revealed the sudden serious illness of Princess Elizabeth. On the fifth they reported that the child had expired the day before "in a convulsive fit," with the cause of death an "entanglement of the bowels." The afflicted mother—"a poor *wishy-washy* thing" to her doctor, Sir Henry Halford, perhaps because of the weakness of her newborn children—was distraught. Pulling himself together, the Duke of Clarence wrote a note to Mrs. Clayton, the princess's nurse, to assure her that the misfortune was no fault of hers. George IV, hearing the news at his rococo but ramshackle palace in Brighton, appealed to his confidential secretary, Sir William Knighton, "For God's sake come down to me. The melancholy tidings of the sudden death of my poor little niece has just reached me & has overset me beyond all I can express to you."

Although Princess Victoria returned to her former position in the succession, it changed nothing for the King. She remained the daughter of a brother he had disliked. The next month, with no help forthcoming from the King, or even from the dilatory Leopold, the Duchess of Kent went to Thomas Coutts and borrowed a further £6,000 on the signatures of the Duke's executors, General Wetherall and Captain Conroy. The money would not go to repay old debts, but to maintain the Duchess's establishment, which seemed to expand with her prospects.

The possibility of another swing in the succession pendulum arose in August 1821, when Queen Caroline, from whom George IV had been quarrelsomely separated for twenty-five years, unexpectedly died. The King was fifty-nine, and might still marry, his confidants thought. He was going to Hanover and Vienna that autumn, Thomas Creevey wrote in his diary, and "probably will pick up something before his return at Xmas." Their optimism had not reckoned with the King's favorite, the rapacious Lady Conyngham, blowsy wife of the Lord Chamberlain at Windsor. (In Princess Sophia's inverse code she was the "Gazelle.") A change in the King's marital status was not in her interest, and it would not happen. Victoria was to remember her with affection.

At St. James's Palace, Adelaide, the Duchess of Clarence, would commission from the sculptor William Scoular a representation of her baby princess asleep, which she kept in her bedroom the rest of her life. By then she had suffered a further early miscarriage, of twins, and William had written in anguish to the King, his brother, of "these repeated misfortunes to this beloved and superior woman. I am quite broken-hearted." Adelaide was only thirty, but newspaper reports of later pregnancies were probably imaginary. "My children are dead," she wrote to the Duchess of Kent, "but your child lives and she is mine too." To Victoria herself on her second birthday, the Duchess of Clarence wrote, "My dear little heart,—I hope you are well and don't forget Aunt Adelaide, who loves you so fondly. . . . God bless and preserve you is the constant prayer of your most truly affectionate Aunt, Adelaide."

A year later Uncle William and Aunt Adelaide would send "Xandrina Victoria" their best wishes on her third birthday, including surrogate kisses for "Mamma" and "Sissi" and the maiden aunts who shared Kensington Palace—and even for "the *big Doll*," which suggests a relationship warmer than mere form. The Clarences were genuinely fond of Victoria, and the Duke had undergone a humanizing metamorphosis in his early years of belated marriage; but the Duchess of Kent distrusted everyone in the succession, and kept her daughter at a distance. Careful not to affront his brother the King, William had to be cautious in his relations with Victoria's mother. Her wariness made that easy, but compounded her isolation from the Court. How much of that distrust came from the increasing influence of John Conroy can only be guessed. Nearly alone, unsophisticated in business matters and uncertain in the language of the country, she was easy prey to someone influential in her household who intended to exploit the gathering likelihood that the child in his charge would become queen.

At two, Vickelchen knew nothing of the great game being played in her behalf. The elderly Evangelical enthusiast William Wilberforce, an M.P. for a Yorkshire constituency, wrote to Hannah More of visiting the Duchess of Kent and "her fine animated child on the floor by her with its playthings, of which I soon became one." Banking on the child's future, such influential figures in English life made a point of calling on the Duchess. "My earliest recollections," Victoria reminisced in an 1872 autobiographical fragment, "are connected with Kensington Palace, where I can remember crawling on a yellow carpet spread for that purpose —and being told that if I cried and was naughty my 'Uncle Sussex' would hear me and punish me, for which reason I always screamed when I saw him! I had a great horror of *Bishops* on account of their wigs and *aprons*, but recollect this being partially got over in the case of the then Bishop of Salisbury . . . by his kneeling down and letting me play with his badge of Chancellor of the Order of the Garter. . . ."

Her uncle Leopold's estate, Claremont, near the village of Esher, was her contact with the world of opulence and leisure. The "brightest" interludes of her "otherwise rather melancholy childhood" occurred "under the roof of that beloved Uncle." When there were dinner parties she was still too young to attend, she could listen to a chamber orchestra play in the hall, and she could be "doted on" as "too much an idol in the House" by old Mrs. Louis, once Princess Charlotte's dresser, and the other servants. Her own governesses, Victoria recalled, "paid little real attention." She "used to ride a donkey given to me by my Uncle, the Duke of York, who was very kind to me. I remember him well—tall, rather large, very kind but extremely shy. He always gave me beautiful presents. The last time I saw him . . . when he was already very ill . . . he had Punch and Judy in the garden for me." When she rode on the donkey her nurse, Mrs. Brock, and her half-sister, Feodora, would walk alongside and Mrs. Brock would remind her, as gentlemen touched their hats, "Bow your head, Princess."

With her awareness growing that she was somehow perceived as different, Victoria once asked Mrs. Brock, "Why do all the gentlemen raise their hats to me, and not to Feodora?" What answer Mrs. Brock fumbled for is unrecorded.

"Up to my 5th year I had been very much indulged by every one," Victoria remembered, "and set pretty well *all* at defiance. Old Baroness de Späth, the devoted Lady of my Mother, my Nurse Mrs Brock, dear old Mrs Louis—*all* worshipped the poor little fatherless child whose future then was still very uncertain. . . ." The Baroness's devotion, Feodora once recalled to Victoria, was especially excessive: "She used to go on her knees before you when you were a child."

Unless a fatal illness or accident intervened, Victoria would be queen. The deference she began to observe, and then to expect, had come without her awareness of a throne to be occupied. That, and her heritage of Hanoverian obstinacy and willfulness, made her "naturally very passionate, but always most contrite afterwards. I was taught from the first to beg my maid's pardon for any naughtiness or rudeness towards her. . . ."

In the summers the Duchess would take Victoria to Ramsgate or another seaside resort, often with Uncle Leopold, and sometimes they would go to such watering places as Tunbridge Wells. At Ramsgate, their neighbor at East Cliff was Moses Montefiore, who had a London house in Park Lane, and had retired from banking in 1824, at forty, to devote himself to philanthropic causes, at which he would spend sixty-one more years. Montefiore presented her with a little gold key that unlocked his garden gate, and told her to make use of it whenever she pleased. "And indeed we did," Victoria would tell his granddaughter in 1886, "and I still possess the key."

Whatever her relief to be away from London, Victoria was still never left alone, and had to sit through "Fidi's" lessons. Diplomatically, later, Feodora blamed her sister's tantrums on climate rather than claustrophobia. "The sea air always made us both so hot and bilious," she recalled. "You used to torment Lehzen and myself during my French lessons while we were at Ramsgate." (Louise Lehzen, Feodora's governess, would also become Victoria's.)

Wherever she was, Victoria never had a room to herself. When beyond the need for a nurse in her room, she slept in a small bed in her mother's room, a situation she grew to find awkward. "At Claremont, and in the small houses at the bathing-places, I sat and took my lessons in my Governess's bedroom. I was not fond of learning as a little child—and baffled every attempt to teach me my letters up to 5 years old—when I consented to learn them by their being written down before me."

Because Feodora was much older—there was even some concern that George IV had designs on her as a possible new wife—Victoria recalled to her half-sister twenty years later having had "no scope for my very violent feelings of affection—had no brothers or sisters to live with —never had a father—from my unfortunate circumstances was not on a comfortable or at all intimate or confidential footing with my mother . . . and did not know what a happy domestic life was." Victoria had little idea of her mother's anxieties, although she gradually came to know a great deal about, and resented greatly, the increasing authority Captain Conroy exerted in the household. Whether Conroy encouraged the Duchess's insecurities or merely supported them, she seems to have seriously believed that Victoria's life was in constant danger from her wicked uncles, particularly Ernest Augustus, the truculent Duke of Cumberland, who would be king if he survived Victoria, and whose son George would then succeed as well. Rumors were current during Victoria's early childhood that the Princess was chronically ill, and would not live into maturity, "could hardly walk, and was diseased in her feet. . . ." It was "well known," Victoria wrote in 1878, when she was nearly sixty, "that Sir John Conroy's daughter was the cause of this." But Conroy had "traced" the allegations to the Duke of Cumberland, who, the captain claimed, had been heard to confide that "one delicate life only stood between him and the Crown and . . . he should yet be King of England."

Conroy, Victoria added, fed her mother with concerns about the Princess's food being poisoned by unscrupulous servants in Cumberland's pay, and about "accidents" planned. Apparently the fears took hold. Victoria was never permitted even to ascend or descend the stairs without someone holding her hand. That sense of insecurity also explains the Duchess's excessive hostility to the financially unhelpful Hanoverian uncles, all of whom she felt were conspiratorial, and her obsessive treasuring of everything associated with her child. "Such touching relics I have found!" Victoria wrote to her eldest daughter in 1861, after her mother's death. ". . . Not a scrap of my writing or of my hair has ever been thrown away—and such touching notes in a book about my babyhood."

The return to Kensington in early autumn "was generally a day of tears." They lived "in a plain simple manner," Victoria recalled about life in unpalatial suburban Kensington Palace; "breakfast was at half past eight, luncheon at half past one, dinner at seven (to which I came generally when it was no large dinner party) eating my bread and milk out of a small silver basin. Tea was only allowed as a great treat in later years." To her grandmother, the Dowager Duchess of Saxe-Coburg-Saalfeld, who was "a good deal bent and walked with a stick," Vickelchen was "the flower of May," but when Victoria at seven was "crying and naughty" at her lessons, the elderly Duchess stalked into the room and scolded her *"schönes Kind"* severely, which had a "salutary effect." (Victoria traced the quickness of her temper to "Grandmamma.")

In the summer of 1825—Victoria was off a year in this and other memories of 1825—at Claremont, when something resembling dysentery rampaged through nearby Esher, Victoria came down with it, just at the moment when Parliament and the Court were beginning to see her as the inevitable future queen. "The Doctor lost his head, having lost his own child from it, and almost every doctor in London was away." The Duchess's Kensington doctor was summoned, and Victoria recovered, remembering "being very cross and screaming dreadfully at having to wear, for a time, flannel next [to] my skin."

That Victoria's sudden fragility was an intrusion into the Government's game of chance over the succession was clear from the maneuvering begun that May, when George IV had proposed an additional £4,000 annually for "better support and maintenance" of the Princess, and a more generous £6,000 to Prince George, son of the unsavory Duke of Cumberland. Indignantly, the Duchess of Kent refused the sum "lower for the Princess than that assigned to a member of the family who was further removed from the throne." Prince George, if the Duchess's daughter survived, would only be heir to Hanover (after his father). The arrangement, she contended, was "derogatory." Victoria saw none of that in the newspapers, as she was only beginning to read the watered-down moralities of Mrs. Trimmer, considered safe for impressionable young minds. When Louise Lehzen read to her (so that she would not chatter indiscreetly to lowly servants) as she was being dressed or put to bed, again the fare was "improving" and unthreatening. The Princess had no idea that an august future awaited her, and the instructions to all who came into contact with her was that she should not be told. Not only was it too soon to disturb her development as just another child of a family of exceptional status; there was still a chance that she might be checkmated.

In the Commons, meanwhile, the Duchess of Kent's outrage, combined with the affection that the nation was beginning to demonstrate for the Princess, had the effect of raising the grant for the Duchess to £6,000,

Lord Brougham describing Victoria in the debates as the "heiress presumptive to the British throne." Rather than accepting the change as only the end to a particular humiliation, the Duchess, abetted by the ambitious Conroy, began to think more and more of her prospective regency, although the Dukes of York and Clarence were still likely kings, and the Hanoverians, barring such catastrophes as had befallen her husband, were tough and long-lived.

Victoria saw little of George IV not only because he lacked interest in her, but because her mother wanted no undue influence from someone she distrusted. "I remember going to Carlton House [in 1823] when George IV lived there, as quite a little child before a dinner the King gave. . . . In the year '26 (I think)* George IV asked my Mother, my Sister and me down to Windsor for the first time. . . . When we arrived at the Royal Lodge the King took me by the hand, saying, 'Give me your little paw.' He was large and gouty but with a wonderful dignity and charm of manner. . . ." But he was also grossly fat, and wore a wig in the older fashion. When he pulled her up on his swollen thighs so that she could kiss him, it was "too disgusting because his face was covered with greasepaint." Pushing a bunch of flowers at him, she said, "As I shall not see my dear uncle on his birthday, I wish to give him this nosegay now." Reciprocating, he offered her "something for me to wear and that was [a miniature of] his picture set in diamonds, which was worn by the Princesses [his sisters] as an order to a blue ribbon on the left shoulder. I was very proud of this,—and Lady Conyngham pinned it on my shoulder." Several of the parasitic younger Conynghams were directed to take Victoria for a drive. She went with them, as did Miss Lehzen, "in a pony carriage . . . with 4 grey ponies . . . , and was driven about the Park and taken to Sandpit Gate where the King had a Menagerie—with wapitis, gazelles, chamois, etc." The next day she was taken to Virginia Water, where the party encountered the King in his phaeton, "and he said 'Pop her in,' and I was lifted in and placed between him and Aunt Gloucester who held me round the waist. (Mama was much frightened.) I was greatly pleased."

At one dock, the Fishing Temple, were two barges, one for the King's guests to fish from, the other for a band that played while the royal party stroked the water. "The King paid great attention to my Sister, and some people fancied he might marry her! She was very lovely then—about

*Actually 1827.

17—and had charming manners." Sensing danger, the Duchess hurriedly arranged Feodora's betrothal to Prince Ernest Christian Charles of Hohenlohe-Langenburg, and Feodora was glad to escape both her mother and the King. (By order of George IV the marriage was to be private and he would give the bride away himself, but an attack of gout kept him from the wedding altogether.)

Later, in the Royal Lodge, Victoria watched Tyrolean dancers create a "gay uproar" and listened to the band play under colorful Chinese lanterns. It was a rare opportunity to please the royal uncle who the Duchess constantly feared might kidnap the Princess, to do away with her or—what might even be worse—to raise her according to his own recipe for rulers. "What would you like the band to play next?" asked the King.

"Oh, Uncle King," said the artless Victoria, "I should like them to play 'God Save the King.'"

As she was being safely extricated from Windsor, she told him, as Lady Elizabeth Shelley remembered it, "I am coming to bid you adieu, sire, but as I know you do not like fine speeches I shall not trouble you by attempting one."

"Tell me," he asked, "what you enjoyed most of your visit?"

"The drive with you," said Victoria. On returning home she asked her mother to send her "best love and duty" to "dear Uncle King." The Duchess never permitted her to return.

That the belligerence of the King and the Royal Dukes had abated considerably through the 1820s, as Victoria's place seemed more assured, became apparent when George IV advised the Duchess in July 1827 to have Victoria revaccinated. Inoculation against smallpox was still considered a new technique, and compulsory vaccination would only become law in 1841; nevertheless, the Duchess agreed to have "our dear little girl" attended to, an event that took place only a week before the Windsor visit, which may have been the bait. Further evidence of goodwill occurred the next month, when Louise Lehzen and John Conroy, at the Duchess's request—to make them more fit in rank to serve an heiress to the throne —appeared in the Birthday Honours list in August. As King of Hanover, George IV raised one to be a Hanoverian baroness, the other to be a Knight Commander of the Hanoverian order.

The Duchess may have read it as a slight that they were given only Hanoverian rank; she sent her thanks, however, and, as gift, a "resemblance of our little angel." But she warily kept her family distant from the King and accepted few social opportunities to mingle with the Court, although a small court existed in Kensington Palace itself, where the unmarried Hanoverian princesses lived out their strange lives, and where the Duke of Sussex kept apartments as well.

In waiting on the Duke of Sussex, the young Lord Albemarle recalled looking out his window some mornings to watch "the movements of a bright pretty little girl, seven years of age. It was amusing to see how impartially she divided the contents of a watering pot between the flowers and her own little feet." Leigh Hunt, an outspoken republican—he had served time in prison for libeling the Regent—encountered the Princess at about the same time in Kensington Gardens "coming up a cross[ing] path from the Bayswater Gate holding another little girl by the hand. A large footman followed behind them, looking like 'a gigantic fairy.'"

Few children had the opportunity to play with Victoria, an honor largely reserved for Sir John's daughter Victoire, whom the Princess liked less and less as their contacts became forced. She was very likely the girl in Kensington Gardens with Victoria. It was difficult to be a playmate to a princess who had been instructed to insist always on her place. Lady Jane Ellice recalled such a situation when she had been taken to play at Kensington Palace, and immediately chose toys on the floor for herself. "You must not touch those," she was told; "they are mine; and I may call you Jane, but you must not call me Victoria."

When Victoria was nearly eight her uncle the Duke of York succumbed to gout and dropsy, leaving huge debts but saving the nation £26,000 a year. The King had preferred the refined York as successor to the throne over the equally idle, but vulgar, Duke of Clarence. At a dinner, King George looked across the table at him and commented to the catty Dorothea de Lieven, "The Duke of Clarence will be a fine King! They will remember me, if ever he is in my place!" But the likelihood that William would sit on the throne had increased, and he turned to his brother the Duke of Sussex at the funeral, Thomas Creevey noted, to observe, "We shall be treated now, Brother Augustus, very differently from what we have been." And they were, at least by Parliament, which voted to increase its grant to the Clarences by £9,000. More significantly for the Duchess of Kent, it added £10,000 for maintenance of the Princess, and appointed the Duchess regent in the event her daughter succeeded while still a minor. It was a great step upward in status. The

Duchess was now a highly desirable figure in society, giving and attending brilliant dinners, and going in near-state to the opera (sometimes with Victoria).

Until her new eminence, the Duchess's society had been largely that of Kensington Palace, where her chief female friend was Princess Sophia, whose external life had effectively ended decades before when a supposedly secret love affair (there was an illegitimate son) had been suppressed by George III. Lonely and miserable, Sophia had become prey to Conroy, who became her comptroller and confidant, and to whom she reported conversations at Court in faintly veiled code. Sir John's plans to become the power behind the future queen required that he become the chief influence over everyone with a role in directing the Princess's life. The strategy also involved getting rid of those he could not control, one of those being the harmless, middle-aged Baroness Spaeth, who had served the Duchess for twenty-five years. She would be sent as lady-in-waiting to the now-married Princess Feodora. Next on his list was the Baroness Lehzen, but that had to wait. She was liked by the King as well as the future king, the Duke of Clarence.

Each move toward control necessitated bringing subtle pressure upon the Duchess, which for Conroy proved the simplest part of the scheme. They were the same age; he was attractive and she was alone; he hovered over her so smotheringly that observers—from her son Prince Charles to the Duke of Wellington—assumed that they were lovers. If his intrigues required it, Conroy could have employed his masculinity between the sheets; but he was sufficiently cautious to avoid any scandal that would have ended his hopes to rule by proxy. He would manipulate the Duchess and her household for years, often openly, as her position required that someone of rank act *for* her, and often in her name.

More and more completely, Victoria's domestic world was dominated by Sir John or his appointees, with the exception of Louise Lehzen, to whom Victoria turned increasingly as she understood her situation. She still slept in her mother's bedroom, where Lehzen sat each evening until the Duchess decided to retire. She saw no one, not even a child, without an adult of the household present, usually a Conroy spy. At age ten, her life was less one of involvement with companions her own age, or even with people outside Kensington Palace (which she could leave only under supervision), than a life with dolls. Her unreal world began to be populated by small adult dolls, not child figures, often based upon characters from plays and operas she saw in her mother's company, and dressed in clothes that she and Lehzen made. Wooden Dutch dolls with jointed limbs and sharp noses, they were at most nine inches high and lived in a large box in the nursery. A list that Victoria kept recorded 132 by name —including Amy Brocard as the Countess of Leicester and Zoe Beaupré as Queen Elizabeth. Victoria played at teaching them manners, in effect her own well-learned lessons.

"We dined on the 3rd at the Dss of Kent's," Harriet Arbuthnot noted in her journal on May 6, 1828, "and saw the little Princess Victoria, who is the most charming child I ever saw. She is a fine, beautifully made, handsome creature, quite playful & childish, playing with her dolls & in high spirits, but civil & well bred & Princess like to the greatest degree. The Duchess of Kent is a very sensible person & educates her remarkably well." To the pretty and influential Mrs. Arbuthnot, confidant of the Duke of Wellington and wife of a Cabinet official, Victoria's upbringing was exactly right. The Duchess's careful display of the Princess, orchestrated by Conroy, remained a strategic success.

Those who saw Victoria in the park riding her donkey, or playing in the public paths that ran through Kensington Gardens, assumed that her life was a delight, and that she was being brought up not with royal rigidity, but almost like an ordinary child. It was, she wrote in later years, nothing like that, but she remembered that her compensation for the "personal affronts" she suffered from the domineering Sir John was the sympathetic attention of her other father figure, Uncle Leopold. Lacking anything vital to do, he had nevertheless lived on opulently in England after the death of the Princess of Wales. The Prince's maintenance of Claremont occupied some of his time, even to the point of his sending produce from his estate to market in London—behavior that outraged Englishmen who believed he should not compete in trade while accepting Parliament's munificence. He wanted more to do than compete in fashionable society and bed its attractive women. But he himself was less than fashionable, with an ill-fitting black wig and three-inch cork soles on his boots to increase his height, as well as a manner so tentative that he was known as "Monsieur Peu-à-Peu." He had studied the intricacies of statecraft with Baron Stockmar, and although at forty a pensioner of the state, he sounded like a potential king, and through his abortive position as consort to an almost-queen he was considered an eligible candidate for minor vacant thrones. While Victoria was growing up he was actively shopping for a kingdom, even if it meant giving up the German actress

Karoline Bauer, whom—to the Duchess's moral outrage—he had installed in a villa overlooking Regent's Park.

Although Leopold interested himself in the education of Princess Victoria, he saw little of Kensington Palace while the Duchess registered her unhappiness with the Berlin actress in his life. Still, he persisted. The child was his opportunity to be a surrogate consort to an English queen, and he exhorted her in person and by letter about the things she should know. As he wrote to her in April 1829, just before her tenth birthday, he expected in a few days to have the happiness of seeing her and embracing his "dearest little child." More importantly, he added, "I have travelled far over the world and shall be able to give you some curious information about various matters." He was her eyes and ears in the world, beyond the language exercises, lessons in court decorum, readings from moralistically bowdlerized literature, and religious education she received from Lehzen and the tutors at Kensington Palace. Victoria anticipated with delight the visits from, and to, her uncle, and treasured his letters.

Leopold's "curious information"—and a reason for his travels—was that he had lobbied for, and been offered, the throne of Greece, newly independent after centuries of Turkish rule. The British government, which was still disputing Greece's frontiers, wanted no such complication with Turkey, and would force him to decline early in 1830. In 1862, writing her memories of Leopold, Victoria remembered "her joy when this took place, as she adored her Uncle and was in despair at the thought of his departure. . . ." Her supplementary education was to continue a little while longer.

Had Victoria been permitted the London papers, she would have read, about Leopold's forgoing Greece, satirical verses by "Ingoldsby" Barham, which declared that the infant nation, for Leopold's part, "may sink or swim," for he would rather Victoria's "Regent be":

> *Wanted a Sovereign Prince for Greece!*
> *For the recreant Knight*
> *Hath broken his plight,*
> *Some say from policy, some from fright,*
> *Some say in hope to rule for his niece,*
> *He hath refused to be King over Greece.* *

---

*George IV was more than willing to have an English hand in the selection, as long as

In May 1829 the King had the rare opportunity of commanding Victoria's presence at Court, from which the Duchess still kept her distance. A ball was planned for the visiting child queen of Portugal, Maria da Gloria, who, like Victoria, was ten that month. When he mentioned the need to invite Victoria, Lady Conyngham commented maliciously, "Oh do; it will be so nice to see the *two little queens* dancing together." That took too much for granted, and the King, according to Charles Greville's diary, was "beyond measure provoked." Among the Princess's accomplishments was dancing, but Greville, invited as Clerk to the Privy Council, came prepared to take the King's side about Victoria. The young queen, he noted, was "good-looking and has a sensible Austrian countenance," while "our little Princess is a short, plain-looking child, and not near so good-looking as the Portuguese. However, if nature has not done so much, fortune is likely to do a great deal more for her." But Queen Maria, dancing, "fell down and hurt her face, was frightened and bruised, and went away. The King was very kind to her."

King George, Greville added, "looked very well and stayed at the ball until two." It was one of the last public occasions when his health, uneven at best, permitted him to keep late hours. Possibly suffering from porphyria, the same malady that had enfeebled his father, he was losing his sight, his power of locomotion, his control over his bladder functions. Later in 1829 he was in a wheelchair, dulled by painkilling laudanum, visible to few but the Conynghams and—fortunately for the public purse—the only person at Court who could stand up to them, Sir William Knighton.

With the King failing, the Duchess knew she had to make a move to retain control over her daughter. There was no telling how long the King's brother and successor might reign. The formal part of Victoria's education had, by then, established a pattern overseen by her mother. The Reverend George Davys, a liberal Evangelical clergyman, lived at Kensington Palace as the Princess's Principal Master. He had come in 1827, when she was eight. After breakfast, at 9:30, she began two hours of lessons: geography, history, mathematics, and drawing. Then came play, and lunch at one. From three to five o'clock she studied English, French, and German, except on Wednesdays, which were scheduled for religious

the candidate would not exacerbate ties with Turkey, and proposed Duke Charles of Mecklenburg-Strelitz, brother of the Duke of Cumberland's wife. In the end the King of Greece would be Otho, second son of King Louis I of Bavaria, chosen at the Conference of London in 1832. By then Leopold was King of Belgium.

instruction. Thursday mornings were reserved for dancing lessons, and Friday mornings for music lessons—both piano and voice. Saturdays were devoted to a review of the week's lessons, usually with the Duchess observing. Later, Victoria would note that her mother was not present as often as she claimed, but the Duchess was a force in the method, and by the early months of 1830, Victoria could read and speak some German and French. Shrewdly, the Duchess would not speak her native German to Victoria: it was impolitic.

As the Princess's eleventh birthday approached, the Duchess (perhaps at Conroy's suggestion) decided to establish herself publicly as the appropriate person to continue to supervise the education of the future Queen by inviting Church of England officials to validate the results to that stage. The Bishops of London and Lincoln agreed to come to Kensington Palace to question the Princess during the first week in March 1830. The outcome left them "completely satisfied." They reported that she had "displayed an accurate knowledge . . . of Scripture, History and the leading truths and precepts of the Christian religion as taught by the Church of England," and had an acquaintance with the "principal facts of English history" which they found "remarkable in so young a person." She also demonstrated her grasp of geography, arithmetic, English and Latin grammar, modern languages, and drawing. The strategy was vindicated.

The next week the Bishop of London asked for an interview with the Duchess. Did Victoria know, he asked, about her likely future role? When would she be told? The Duchess assured him that the knowledge would come to Victoria "by accident, in pursuing her education." It was evident to her, however, that she was being instructed to arrange for the happy accident, and the next day, March 11, 1839, the Princess learned about her likely destiny.

The recollections differ, but what they agree upon is that Victoria was to discover in a book of English history a page carefully removed earlier that listed the line of succession. According to Lehzen, Victoria observed with surprise that she had never seen that table before. "I see that I am nearer to the Throne than I thought."

"So it is, Madam."

"I will be good," said Victoria, along with much else that suggests Lehzen's sentimental memories of the scene thirty-seven years later, rather than the words of a child not quite eleven.

In the margin of the Baroness's reminiscence Victoria wrote, "I cried much on learning it." After the revelation, Lehzen assured her that it was still possible that her Aunt Adelaide would have children, and spare Victoria the awful contingency. If that were so, Victoria answered, "I should never feel disappointed, for I know by the love Aunt Adelaide bears me, how fond she is of children." Here a marginal note adds, "The Queen perfectly recollects this circumstance. . . ."

The Duchess's tactics had not only been successful but well timed, as George IV was rapidly failing. Quickly she applied to the Archbishop of Canterbury for an interview, and sent him, as the most eminent churchman in the kingdom, a copy of the bishops' report via "my confidential servant Sir John Conroy." He could not otherwise have known how well she had served the nation, she explained modestly, because of her "quiet and unobtrusive life."

The meeting with Dr. William Howley, the Archbishop, took place on April 2, 1830. He also examined the Princess himself, afterwards writing to the King that "from the general correctness and pertinency of her answers, I am perfectly satisfied that Her Highness's education in regard to cultivation of intellect, improvement of talent, and religious and moral principle, is conducted with so much care and success as to render any alteration of the system undesirable."

The King was then beyond any interest in the education or the destiny of his brother's daughter. When he died, on June 26, 1830, Victoria's Uncle William and Aunt Adelaide quietly succeeded. William IV was already sixty-five. No one else stood between the eleven-year-old Princess and the throne.

IV

Royal Pawn

(1830–1837)

Another of the allegedly wicked uncles had become King. Several more waited behind Victoria, two of them with sons who might themselves someday sit on the throne of England. The Duchess maintained her state of aggressive alarm, but as Victoria knew about some of them then, and all of them later, the real wickedness could be credited to the father of the brood, George III. A rigid believer in making his children exemplars for the nation, he insisted that each son have an occupation, and not enough money to encourage extravagance. With the alternatives for service limited for royalty to the army and navy, they were, where possible, put into uniform.

The new King, William, had gone to sea at fourteen. Even the favorite among the sons, Frederick (of York), had endured seven years of military training in Germany. Edward went into the army in Germany at seventeen, and complained afterwards that he never heard from his father. Few of the sons did. Ernest (of Cumberland), severely wounded several times, had to plead to be sent home for treatment, and survived with an ugly crease on the right side of his skull. Not sufficiently robust in health for the military, Augustus (of Sussex) was sent to Göttingen, and then to Italy and France, for an education; the experience resulted in his wanting to marry, and to go into the Church. Neither option was permitted, nor was he allowed to return home. Yet the King's sons could not conceal their birth, and they were expected to live grandly. Each preferred to believe that with so many brothers, another of the seven who had survived into maturity would provide for an heir in the bloodline. They accumulated extravagant debts and, responding to their sexual yearnings, accumulated mistresses (or wives illegal by the Royal Marriages Act); they bred children wholesale, few of whom were eligible for the throne; they accumulated grievances, frustrations, and deplorable life-styles while their royal father reproved them or ignored them. If they all turned sour, it was with some reason.

The daughters fared worse. All six who reached adulthood lived, by royal instructions, lives of cloistered insularity. The Queen had to provide for them out of her personal income, as the King would not. Reading and needlework filled their days. Only three married, two of these in their forties, the other at thirty-one. None had a child who survived infancy. Of the other three, rumor had it that two contracted secret marriages, one resulting in an illegitimate child, according to scandal (rather than fact) by one of the royal princes. The third (and youngest), Amelia, was not permitted to marry an equerry to the King, with whom she had fallen in love, even though her chances of succession were nil. When she died in 1810, leaving him all her little property, her pathetic will proclaimed, "Nothing but the cruel situation I am placed in of being the daughter of the King and the laws made by the King respecting the marriages of the Royal Family prevents me from being married to him, which I consider I am in my heart."

If each was less of an uncle or aunt than the fatherless Victoria needed, a later generation can understand why. Sometimes to Victoria, overhearing Sir John Conroy's gossip or planted rumor, and certainly to the Duchess of Kent, the world encompassed by the Court was a jungle of jealousy, meanness, mental instability, backbiting, bitchery, and intrigue. The Duchess, Lady Elizabeth Grosvenor gossiped in a letter, "hardly ever sleeps, occasioned, I believe, by her constant anxiety as to the future."

King William and Queen Adelaide would have brought Victoria up as a surrogate daughter, but the Duchess would have none of it. Time was on her side, eliminating her adversaries and increasing her purse. Even her predecessor, the Comtesse de Montgenet, died soon after George IV, on August 9, 1830—an event the Duchess may have learned about through her bankers, and through the gossip telegraph from France. The new King, however, was a sturdy sort whose decline might be protracted.

William IV's reign began in a wave of popularity. The gouty and gross George IV had kept to his rooms and, but for Lady Conyngham and her family, saw few people in his last years. William enjoyed prying into the workings of his regime, reviewing the Guards, both horse and foot, and even inspecting the Tower of London. There an observer described him as "a little, old, red-nosed, weather-beaten, jolly-looking person, with an ungraceful air and carriage," while the unpretentious Queen was a "little insignificant person as I ever saw." According to Greville, William's "exaltation" in his mid-sixties after a life of obscurity so excited him that "he nearly went mad, and distinguished himself by a thousand extravagances of language and conduct, to the amusement of all who witnessed his strange freaks." Though he "sobered down," he remained something of a "buffoon." He walked the streets alone, to the concern of his aides, spat out of his carriage windows and, when riding, offered surprised Londoners "lifts." On a royal night at the opera, Thomas Creevey recorded that "Billy 4th"—the onetime-sailor—had quite a *"Wapping* air," complete to "seaman's gold lace cock-and-pinch hat." The King "slept most of the Opera—never spoke to anyone, or took the slightest interest. . . . I was sorry not to see more of Victoria: she was in a box with the Duchess of Kent, opposite, and of course, rather under us. When she looked over the box I saw her, and she looked a very nice little girl indeed."

The key word was *opposite*. There were few occasions when William and Adelaide could place their niece before the people as their legitimate successor. One was the King's first opening of Parliament, when, with Victoria at her side, Adelaide watched the procession from the garden across from St. James's Palace. Noticing her, crowds cried, "The Queen! The Queen!" Adelaide picked up the tiny Princess and sat her on the wall. "God save both Queens!" someone shouted.

The relationship between the King and the Duchess was a morass of misunderstanding. The day after the death of George IV, a letter written by Conroy and signed by the Duchess was submitted to the new Sovereign. In it the Duchess argued that understandings with the late

King were no longer valid. Further, since her daughter was now "more than Heiress Presumptive" to the throne, the Duchess should be legally given new authority as both regent and guardian of the future queen. In addition, she wanted a lady of rank—of her own choosing—to be given the title of official governess to Victoria. And—perhaps more important to Conroy than to his employer—she wanted all moneys due the Princess until she came of age payable directly to her.

The Duke of Wellington, then Prime Minister, suggested to the King that the demands be treated as a private letter or even as one that had never been written, as it was more prudent for initiatives to come from the King or his ministers. Then the Duke assured her that the interests of the Princess would be high in the government's consideration, adding, "I entreat your Royal Highness not to allow any Person to persuade you to the contrary." The Duchess understood the allusion to Conroy, and retorted that all communications with her would have to be made through Sir John, whom Wellington despised.

Reassembling in November, Parliament heard Lord Lyndhurst—ever after a Whig renegade to Victoria—heap encomiums upon the Duchess for "the manner in which Her Royal Highness the Duchess of Kent has . . . discharged her duty in the education of her illustrious offspring." It gave the nation "the best ground on which to hope most favourably of her Royal Highness's future conduct." He spoke, he said, "not from vague report, but from accurate information"—the Duchess's triumphant employment of the bishops. Satisfied, Parliament passed legislation making the Duchess sole regent and guardian for Victoria. Happily, the Duchess permitted Conroy to draw up a memorandum defining her new powers over the Princess so that she could limit any control that the King might attempt to exercise.

The idea of codifying her claims had real justification, as she realized when Earl Grey, taking over as Prime Minister in July, sent her a note expressing the new King's hope that Alexandrina Victoria's foreign-sounding name might be changed to one more befitting an English queen. Uncharacteristically, the Duchess answered with tact and grace. Although her baptismal name was "dear to the Princess," her mother was sure that Victoria would "do whatever would suit the feelings of the country."

When the King failed to respond, the Duchess wrote again, explaining the manner in which the Princess's names were forced on her by George IV, and observing that she would be grieved to have her child "lay aside the name of Victoria, which she alone uses, as being mine. . . . She also has a great attachment to that name." Still, the Duchess again expressed her willingness for Victoria "to do that which is most suitable to Her Station. . . ."

Grey then suggested that an Act of Parliament be passed, or that at the Princess's confirmation some rechristening be made, and the Duchess agreed that legislation be initiated as soon as possible, to get the country used to a new name. William was delighted, and even offered the Duchess a financial reward retroactive to the Duke of Kent's death. Yet, rather than seize it, the Duchess began to have second thoughts, prompted by newspaper speculation about the name. Nothing seemed to escape the London papers, and there the Duchess found support for *Victoria*, which sounded regal to the future queen's subjects. Further, there was some religious feeling against using the act of confirmation to effect a change in the sacrament of baptism, an opinion supported by the Archbishop of Canterbury. By June 25, nearly a year after the exploration of a new name began, the Duchess had changed her mind completely, writing as much to Grey. The King was furious. The name Victoria was not English, he thundered, and not even German in origin, but French. "His Majesty cannot but regret," he wrote her, although his target unmistakably was Conroy, "that Her Royal Highness should have suffered impressions to be made upon her Mind by Representations which do not, in His Judgment, rest upon sufficient foundation."

That even the King's huge financial inducement failed to win the Duchess over is evidence of how much more significant power had become, in relation to money, as the inevitable day of Victoria's accession drew closer. Keeping Victoria out of William's hands was crucial to the Duchess's strategy for control, and an excuse to maintain a protective distance had already come at Windsor, where the Duchess and the Princess had, on a rare occasion, been breakfasting. One of the King's many FitzClarence sons blundered into the room, and the outraged Duchess ordered her carriage. The unsought contact with the illegitimate—and thus tainted—offspring had jeopardized the Princess's purity. As her mother explained to the Duchess of Northumberland, "I never did, neither will I ever, associate Victoria in any way with the illegitimate members of the Royal family; with the King they die. Did I not keep this line, how would it be possible to teach Victoria the difference between vice and virtue?" Still, for a time, the Duchess of Kent permitted her daughter to attend important functions at St. James's and at Windsor. On July 26, 1830, the first of these after the death of George IV, the Princess, her small figure nearly lost in the deep mourning of Court train and floor-length veil, walked behind Queen Adelaide and stood to the left of the throne during the investiture with the Garter of the King of Württemberg.

Explosions of pique on one side or the other would result in a temporary suspension of contacts but, for the most part, appearances were preserved. Another of the outbursts occurred when the Princess appeared at the King's drawing-room reception on February 24, 1831. There, the Countess of Jersey, according to Greville, "made a scene" with Lord Durham, apparently because of his allegations about her virtue. (She had been a mistress of George IV.) The cantankerous Durham—John George Lambton—was one of the Duchess's most sympathetic Whig advisers, and a habitué of Kensington Palace. If Durham saw Lady Jersey as representative of the tone of William's court (which was far more respectable than that of the preceding George), the Duchess professed to want no more of it. The Princess, William complained, looked at him "stonily" that day—apparently on instructions from her mother. It was to William a public affront, but Earl Grey urged him to downplay the "Disunion and Jealousy," which, by then, had become a regular subject of newspaper comment.

The battle over the Princess had been joined in the midst of the bitterest electoral squabbling in more than a century. The legacy of the four Georges had been an arrogant evasion of political reform, the bills for which came due in William's first year. By the summer of 1831 the Tory government he had inherited was out, and a new Parliament elected, with a huge pro-reform, Whig majority. In the very fluid electoral alignments then characterizing parties in Britain, Whigs and Tories operated largely at the local level, seeking parliamentary seats through political connections, patronage, patrimony, and purchase of the few votes cast in each constituency. Traditionally, the Tories (now Conservatives) upheld the principles of land and gentry; the Whigs (from whom emerged the Liberals) represented, along with the aristocracy, more of the rising industrial and mercantile classes, and pressed for social and political reforms. In actuality, both parties were groupings of overlapping special interests. The Whigs were sometimes more reactionary than their opponents. Yet burgeoning within the Whig party was (by contemporary standards) a radical movement that pressed for extension of voting rights to the emerging middle class and to the populous industrial communities that had hardly existed when seats in the House of Commons were last allocated.

Shrewdly, William put off a formal coronation, declaring that, given the current mood of the country, he could save the nation an expensive exercise in antiquarian flummery by putting the crown on his own head. Such royal frugality—described by newspapers in terms of the now-obsolete coin as the "Half-Crownation"—would return to William some of the popularity he had lost in fighting the Reform Bill that was about to pass.

Although the Duchess was popular with the Whigs, whom she had cultivated when they were the "out" party, she found it difficult to achieve her financial ends while the King was preaching public austerity. Yet William made a show of pressing her claims, ostensibly on her behalf but contrary to her strategies, by asking for funds not for the Duchess, but for Princess Alexandrina Victoria. The Chancellor of the Exchequer, Lord Althorp, recommended an additional £10,000 for the Princess, bringing her allowance to £16,000 in addition to her mother's annual £6,000 inherited from the Duke. Henry Hunt, the Radical Member for Preston, proposed an amendment halving the ten thousand pounds, in the interest of opposing "every kind of extravagance." The vote against him —in the end he did not even vote for his own bill—was 223 to 0. At about the same time, a satirical paper, noting that a new Bishop of Derby was to be appointed, at a lavish annual salary of £11,000 a year, suggested wryly that the nation could be saved expense if the Princess, rather than have her maintenance raised, were made the new Bishop of Derby.

On September 6, two days before the frugal coronation of William IV, the money bill for Victoria received the Royal Assent. A cartoon at the same time showed the Duchess, the Princess weeping on her shoulder, declaring, "Say no more about the Coronation, child. I have my *particular reasons* for not going to it." *The Times* was indignant over the boycott, declaring that "she who is ignorant of the respect which is due to the Crown, is unfit to form the mind and superintend the education of the infant who is destined to wear it." A few days later *The Times* reported that Sir John Conroy had informed the Court that if the Duchess attended, she would have her coronet carried by whomever she pleased, not by whomever it pleased the King to assign to her. Further, and somewhat in contradiction, the report added that she was willing to attend as instructed but that it was "inexpedient to interrupt the benefit which the Princess Victoria's health was receiving by her residence near the sea," on the Isle of Wight, and that it was also too expensive to remove "all her establishment to town, so as to appear in state at the Coronation."

In later years Victoria herself would often refuse to leave the Isle of Wight, or to entrain south from Scotland, to conduct governmental business, behaving like a true daughter of the willful Duchess.

The reasons for the absence of the Princess and her mother had, of course, nothing to do with the newspaper stories. William wanted to punish the Duchess for her insistence on royal prerogatives that he felt should come only with his demise, and the Duchess wanted to dramatize her unhappiness at not being awarded Victoria's maintenance money in her own right. The King established his point by declaring that Victoria was not to walk immediately behind him in the procession at Westminster Abbey, but to come after his brothers, the despised Royal Dukes. The Duchess demonstrated her power of withholding, at her prerogative, the person of the Princess. The loser was Victoria, who wrote later that "nothing could console me, not even my dolls." She wept "copious tears." A few days later, Charles Greville, dining with the Duke of Wellington, discussed the absence of the Duchess of Kent and the Princess, Wellington blaming the business on Conroy. "I said I concluded he was her lover," Greville recorded in his diary, "and he said he supposed so."

The first years of William's reign were clouded by the battle over reform of the franchise, the continuing agitation making many of the haves fear that the future would be in the hands of the have-nots. John Wilson Croker, Tory M.P., Admiralty bureaucrat, and diarist, noted in April 1832 that he had dined at the Duchess of Kent's with four dukes and three duchesses, and was "almost the only undecorated guest" of thirty present. "The little princess ceases to be little. She grows tall[er], is very good looking, but not, I think, strong; yet she may live to be plain Miss Guelph. . . ." The reference to one of Victoria's family names (the Hanoverian Welfs) suggested his concern that England would become a republic, much as seemed likely to happen, for the second time, in France. On the other hand, Lady Wharncliffe, dining at Kensington Palace and "delighted with our little future Queen" (and the Duchess's "quite perfect" training of the Princess), looked to Victoria "to save us from Democracy, for it is impossible she should not be popular when she is older and more seen."

Presenting her more often in public was the Duchess's intent, and the dinners and drawing rooms were only a part of the campaign. Conroy was also planning regal progresses, to expose not only the future queen to the nation, but the Duchess as future regent. All the activity, which cost a great deal, was to come out of the prospective Privy Purse, borrowed in advance on Victoria's expectations. At most of the Duchess's entertainments, Victoria was the *pièce de résistance,* to be produced briefly with the dessert.

At the Duchess's dinner for the King on April 1833, signs of a change seemed to appear—although not a thaw in the frosty relations with the Court, as Queen Adelaide was pointedly unwell and absent. After dinner the band of the Grenadier Guards played, and Victoria was permitted to stay up until 11:00 P.M.

A month later she would write, "I am today fourteen years old! How *very old!*" There was a children's ball in her honor at St. James's Palace, which she formally opened by dancing with her cousin, Prince George of Cambridge, also fourteen. William IV had already made it clear to people who had the Duchess's ear that the Prince was his choice for a husband for Victoria, when both were older, but his powers in that sphere were nonexistent.

There was still another cousin named George, also fourteen, the son of the Duke of Cumberland. He and his father would be kings of Hanover if Victoria became queen, and kings of England as well if they outlived her. Prince George was a slim, handsome boy, whom some in England looked upon, if first cousins should marry, as the ideal match for Victoria. It would bring warring factions of the family together, and add some "English" blood to a line almost certain otherwise to become more attenuated. But in 1832 the Prince, at Kew Palace, suddenly lost his sight. His parents, Princess de Lieven wrote Lady Cowper from Richmond, "put him in the sunlight, but he could see nothing at all. . . . He has now been four days in a state of complete blindness." Since English physicians held out no hope, he was taken to Prussia to be examined by a German specialist reputed to have accomplished much where others had failed. Nothing could be done. At the end of 1833 the Duke of Cumberland's sister, Princess Elizabeth, then Landgravine of Hesse-Homburg, was writing sadly of her nephew, "To see that lovely creature led about . . . [and] his good humour, his sweet way of expressing himself, his gratitude for every kindness, is not to be expressed—but he certainly sees nothing, such a *real dear* as he is, it is enough to break one's heart."

Attempting to link Victoria's future with either George was only one skirmish in the battle of wits that William fought with the Duchess, and he would keep trying to press future husbands of his own choosing. Some of the tilting was more trivial, yet symbolic, for both realized that the public perception was reality, and that how Victoria was acclaimed in the

Duchess's provincial progresses would be a signal to the country. He was still King, but already there were disquieting reports of incidents off the Isle of Wight—of regal salutes to the Princess in the Solent. Victoria had taken to sailing there summers, using at William's own invitation the *Emerald*, a tender to his yacht the *Royal George*. The result was a constant popping of respectful salvos from passing vessels. Such signals, William felt, should be reserved for the sovereign, and the Prime Minister was directed to ask the Duchess to waive the right to be saluted. Conroy advised her to refuse, causing the King to issue an order in Council that the Royal Standard would be saluted only when the King or Queen was on board. Such frustrations with the Duchess were out of proportion to the trouble she made, but he had no intention of permitting her to begin her regency while he was still alive.

For Victoria, her life was full of contradictions. She was kept seques- tered and exhorted to behave modestly and demurely, and educated by pious spinsters and cautious clergymen; yet she was also a future queen whose prerogatives were insisted upon and fought for by her guardians, who at their pleasure would push her out into the world to be fawned over. One recorded image of 1833 encapsulates the dissonance—a tourist on the Isle of Wight coming upon the Princess, then fourteen, reading to her mother *The Dairyman's Daughter*, a popular Evangelical tract about a short but devout life written by the Reverend Leigh Richmond, who had once been her father's chaplain. She was seated on the grave of the young girl on whose life the book was based. A duke's daughter, likely to be queen, Victoria was staying at Norris Castle, nearby, and at her mother's insistence receiving the salutes of passing ships when she went out in the King's boat. Yet the homiletic tale was intended to instruct her.

The elaborate progresses of Duchess and Princess began in the sum- mer of 1832. To exasperate the King further, the tour followed a visit by two of the Princess's cousins, Hugo and Alfonso Mensdorff, sons of her mother's sister Sophie. The Duchess's plans included marrying the future queen to one of *her* nephews, not one of William's. (No one worried much about the genetic consequences of first-cousin marriages.) Since Victoria's companions of her own age were largely limited to Conroy's daughter, the Princess was ecstatic at having other young people about, especially young men who, she noted, were "so merry and kind." It was a wrench to have to leave them behind for the journey to Wales, but that event was marked by something new—a notebook with mottled covers and leather binding given to her by the Duchess as a stimulus to writing: "This Book Mamma gave me that I might write the journal of my journey to Wales in it. Victoria. Kensington Palace. July 31st." It would be succeeded by 121 further volumes, but only the journals prior to Victoria's accession—the circumspect ones she knew would be read by her mother—survive. The others were destroyed by Victoria's youngest daughter, Beatrice, who copied out what she, as literary executor, felt should be preserved.

The route by carriage to North Wales taken by what wags called the "Conroyal party" went through the rain-drenched Midlands. For Victoria it was a rare, horrifying look at the England that kept the elegant society of the great houses they would visit prosperous. "The men, women, children, country and houses are all black. . . . The grass is quite blasted and black." A blast furnace they passed was "an extraordinary building flaming with fire," after which everything continued to be "black, engines flaming, coals, in abundance, everywhere, smoking and burning coal heaps, intermingled with wretched huts and carts and little ragged children." But despite the grim conditions, at every stopping place there were crowds shouting with loyal enthusiasm, Addresses offering future devotion, choirs singing patriotic anthems, and salutes fired by celebrants unaware that such anticipations of his death made King William more than unhappy. The historic Welsh castles at Powys and Caernarvon were decorated with bunting and flowers, and the splendid country residences of Lord Grosvenor (Eaton Hall), the Duke of Devonshire (Chatsworth), Lord Shrewsbury (Alton Towers), and the Earl of Liverpool (Pitchford) were the sites of stylish luncheons and dinners and presentations. At Chester, where Eaton Hall was the seat of the Grosvenors (Lord Grosvenor had been made Marquess of Westminster the year before), the Princess was given the honor of naming the new bridge over the Dee. The city authorities hoped to be the first to have a Victoria Bridge, although the Grosvenors seem to have desired a Royal Bridge. According to *The Times*, the mayor "presented himself to their Royal Highnesses to take their pleasure in naming the bridge." In her response the young Princess, possibly coached to be modest, upset local calculations by saying, "I seize the occasion of our being the first persons to pass over this magnificent bridge to lend myself to the feeling that prevails, and to name it Grosvenor Bridge."

In her journal, Victoria recorded eating from gold plates and drinking from gilt cups at Eaton Hall, singing after dinner while Lady Westminster played the organ, and staying up until ten. When the entourage left, the weary hostess wrote to her mother, "The visit has altogether done very well from the public point of view, and nothing can be better or more 'la grande dame' or more kind and considerate than the Duchess' ways in all respects. Sir John Conroy manages it all admirably and the Duchess gives munificently to all [charitable] things."

When the party stayed at Wytham Abbey, with Lord Abingdon, they visited Oxford, where the Duchess received an Address, in queenly fashion, from the town fathers, and Conroy the honorary degree of Doctor of Civil Law—both rewards for bringing, and bringing up, Victoria.

The tour, which, to the King's open disgust, had gone triumphantly, ended on November 9 at Kensington Palace. Victoria was exhausted. Often she had been awakened before dawn for another jolting carriage ride. Overdressed, overfed, and overworked, she had combined a continuation of her lessons with Lehzen with a relentless regimen of public appearances. The pattern would be repeated, as Sir John and the Duchess were certain that, in the pro-Whig wake of the Reform Bill, anti-William reaction would prompt a succession of love feasts for Victoria and the Conroyals.

To William's further exasperation, two additional nephews of the Duchess, the princelings Alexander and Ernst of Württemberg, sons of her sister Antoinette, came to Kensington Palace in June 1833. Victoria's journal described them as *"extremely tall"* and *"amiable,"* with Alexander *"very handsome"* and Ernst *"very kind."* At fourteen she was beginning to understand that there was a purpose behind such visits, but emotionally she was still a child, and her need to offer and respond to affection was better met, in her fishbowl life, by "dear sweet little Dash," a spaniel given to the Duchess by Conroy, and passed on to Victoria, and "dear little Rosa," the Princess's horse, which traveled with their entourage on their progresses. "Dashy" became an animated four-legged doll, as Victoria dressed him "in a scarlet coat and blue trousers."

Despite Dash and Rosa, Victoria could not remain a child. Her lessons took on renewed urgency, and were rounded off with singing instruction and sketching. The Duchess's dinners were now crowded with distinguished people, many of them clever, amusing, powerful, and intimidating, but all were reduced to onlookers when Lehzen brought in Victoria, the reason for the fuss. And there were more splendid provincial establishments to visit, lessons in themselves in history, art, and manners. Their resident aristocrats, wealthy commoners, gaitered churchmen, and country squires, with their ladies and their children, were cross-sections of the ruling classes she would represent. The rounds of public engagements and progresses left Victoria reeling with headaches, backaches, indigestion, and influenza. From Uncle Leopold came warnings to watch her diet, as Hanoverians had a tendency to plumpness, and Victoria's short stature emphasized each ounce. Fortunately, there would be fewer encounters with the public in 1834, as she began the year with an "indisposition," and grandiose plans were put off.

London in the spring afforded a feast of opera-going. Victoria went as often as two or three times a week to Covent Garden, to be thrilled by the latest creations of Bellini, Rossini, Meyerbeer, and Donizetti, or to watch ballets like *La Sylphide*, danced by such favorites of hers as Marie Taglioni, who, she told her journal, was "like a fawn." In the previous role tailored for her talents, *Robert le Diable*, Giacomo Meyerbeer's sensational opera, Taglioni had led a band of spectral dancing nuns from their tombs in a moonlit cloister. (Such scenes could only have reinforced English fears of Roman Catholics.) The same ghostly gaslighting was used in the ballet *La Sylphide*. On the legitimate stage Edmund Kean and Fanny Kemble played Shakespeare, and more modern melodramas, and when Victoria returned to her rooms, she and Lehzen often still collaborated on costuming a tiny Dutch doll—usually three inches high—as some character they had seen, a *Sylphide* Taglioni in muslin and gauze, a Count Almaviva from Rossini's *The Barber of Seville* in blue and white breeches. "I went last night to the Royal Opera," the visiting young American physician Oliver Wendell Holmes wrote in 1834. It was a state occasion, and he had to pay the equivalent of more than two dollars for a pit ticket, even at that hardly having enough room in which to stand. "The Duchess of Kent and the Princess Victoria—a girl of fifteen—came in first on the side opposite the King's box. . . . The Princess is a nice, fresh-looking girl, blonde, and rather pretty. The King looks like a retired butcher. . . . [He] blew his nose twice, and wiped the royal perspiration repeatedly from a face which is probably the largest uncivilised spot in England."

Instead of being pushed again into the provinces, Victoria gratefully received visitors in London, among them Prince Ferdinand of Saxe-Coburg Kohary, her mother's second brother. His presence took the emotional pressure off Victoria, and he relieved her (so it appears) of feeling that her suspicions about her mother and Conroy were unfounded by being "so *extremely clever in seeing through everything,*" she told her journal, cautiously, knowing that the Duchess read every word. When Ferdinand left, at the end of May, Sir John reappeared at the dinner table, and Victoria told her journal, "I do not remember passing *so* sad a day for a *long* time."

A week later her spirits revived with the reappearance, after six years, of Feodora, with her husband Ernest, Prince of Hohenlohe-Langenburg, and their two eldest children. Recapturing as much of the treasured past as they could, the sisters spent hours together, and Feodora, eleven years the elder, used her years and experience to coach Victoria in manners— even to keeping her mouth demurely closed. The visit was the occasion for a rare appearance at Windsor, and a royal excursion to Ascot, where Victoria was cheered by the crowd. The King, caught up in the exuberance, made a bet on a race with Victoria, which she won.

On July 25, 1834, the Princess recorded the departure of Feodora —a *"dreadful"* separation. "I *clasped* her in my arms, and *kissed* her and *cried* as if my heart would break, so did *dearest* Sister. . . . When I came home I was in such a state of grief that . . . I sobbed and cried most violently the whole morning." The emotional release was probably useful. Puberty as well as the tensions of Kensington Palace were, for Victoria, just fifteen, probably at the bottom of many "indispositions" she suffered during the year, which had the benefit of reducing the pressure on her to engage in progresses, or otherwise to be at the center of the tug-of-war between the Duchess's party and the King's. Her uncle Leopold had written to her from Belgium, where he, too, was at the center of conflicting interests. As the new King, he had taken a bride acknowledging his more populous Catholic faction, a daughter of King Louis-Philippe of France. "The position of what is generally called great people has of late become extremely difficult," he explained. "They are more attacked and calumniated, and judged with less indulgence than private individuals." Victoria would learn that few attacks were empty of cause.

More help from Leopold came in mid-1834 when Baron Stockmar was sent to analyze the situation and offer himself as intermediary. "How can my words help," he appealed to the Duchess on July 4, "when nobody wishes to change and nobody wishes to give in?" *She* was not the "main difficulty," he observed courteously; the problem lay in the relationship between the "resentful" Princess and Sir John ("the sole regulator of the whole machine"), whom he praised as "excellent" and "devoted," but described also as "vain, ambitious, most sensitive and most hot tempered." Conroy's ambition to impose himself in a regency as private secretary to a child queen was seen by Stockmar as "dangerous" as well as unrealistic and irresponsible. To get out of such a situation, if forced on her, he predicted, she would marry as soon as she was able, and her husband would jettison Conroy. All that the Duchess and Sir John would gain would be *"coldness and distance"* from the future queen.

The Conroyal strategy that followed employed more softness and subtlety. Rather than endure an autumn tour of the provinces, Victoria enjoyed a trip to Tunbridge Wells and a holiday at St. Leonard's-on-Sea. In addition to the "usual party" of the Conroy family (her way of describing that imposition in her journal), she had a new companion to assist Lehzen, Lady Flora Hastings, who had become lady-in-waiting to the Duchess. Eldest daughter of the Marquess of Hastings, she was in her late twenties, and was attractive and clever—clever enough to know that she owed her new position as companion to the future queen to her loyalty to the Duchess. That possibility was not lost on Victoria, who guessed as well that Lady Flora was really inserted into the household as a replacement for Lehzen, the only person in whom the Princess could rest her confidence. Stockmar had warned that Victoria should be permitted to choose her own young women; not surprisingly, an instant antipathy arose between the Princess and the unwanted and sharp-tongued Flora Hastings. It took no time for Victoria to recognize Conroy's hand in the plot, as he seemed on almost as close terms with Lady Flora as with the Duchess, and her presence coincided with a campaign to make life so miserable for Lehzen as to encourage her to depart. By March 6, 1835, the harshness of her treatment was so visible as to cause the Duchess of Northumberland, Victoria's official governess, to write to Feodora to ask her to "tell the King what he *ought* to do" to forestall Conroy, as it would only "further the plans of that man" to leave Victoria unprotected.

Never at a loss for plans, Conroy had already drafted a letter for the Duchess of Kent's signature, which requested, since Victoria was on the verge of confirmation, the phasing out of her system of education, and with it an end to the governess establishment, which included Lehzen and the Duchess of Northumberland. Instead, he proposed a Lady of the Bedchamber, who was to be Flora Hastings. The rudeness of the Conroyals toward the Duchess of Northumberland had even preceded the letter, and came to the King's attention. Through the Archbishop of Canterbury, William instructed the Duchess of Kent to detail her wishes about the confirmation ceremony through the official channel, Victoria's governess. The Duchess of Kent refused to communicate with the Duchess of Northumberland, who by then was being denied any role in Victoria's education; William refused to accept any other method of communication, and wrote a letter himself to the Bishop of London forbidding the Bishop to confirm Victoria in the Chapel Royal. Temporarily, the Duchess was thwarted.

Outwardly, the Duchess's handling of her daughter appeared impeccable, and the unaware were admiring of her affectionate cultivation of their future queen. What they saw in the spring of 1835 was not the Princess's suppression, but a highly visible (yet private) sixteenth-birthday concert in Victoria's honor, an expensive and dazzling present paid for by loans on the Duchess's expectations. The great Maria Malibran, at twenty-seven the dominating contralto in European opera (she would die suddenly in Manchester the next year), arrived late, "dressed in white satin with a scarlet hat and feathers," Victoria observed in her journal. For range, she had added a strained soprano to her thrilling, impassioned lower register, and Victoria, unawed, noted, "Her low notes are *beautiful,* but her high notes are thick and not clear. I like *Grisi by far* better than her." Giulia Grisi, the soprano, had already sung—Victoria drew her in her notebook as Bellini's Norma, and as Elena in Donizetti's *Marino Faliero.* So also had Victoria's music teacher, the basso Luigi Lablache; Antonio Tamburini, the baritone; and the already legendary tenor, Battista Rubini, who was credited with bringing the vibrato and the sob to sentimental Italian opera. (Victoria had seen him the year before in Rossini's *The Siege of Corinth,* and drawn him in her sketchbook.)

The event was a publicity triumph for the Duchess, but for Victoria only an interlude in the infighting about her; and in that skirmish the victory in arranging for her confirmation would go to King William, who held all the cards. At his command, on July 30, 1835, Victoria was duly confirmed, with William and Adelaide in attendance. When the King observed Conroy entering the chapel with the Duchess, he ordered him out. The public affront reinforced Sir John's enmity. In her journal, Victoria recorded that she was "drowned in tears" at the ceremony, which was as emotionally wrenching as its preliminaries. The aftermath was no less traumatic. The Duchess, who no longer spoke privately to her daughter about anything but trivialities, whatever her public professions of love and intimacy, handed her a long letter informing her that Lehzen had been told (in writing) that the instructress relationship was to cease with confirmation, and that Victoria was to write a letter of dignified thanks in similar terms. Until Victoria was twenty-two, she would be "confided to the guidance of your affectionate mother and friend."

Even into William's seventieth year, and beyond, Victoria's accession remained uncertain, and the Conroyals' expectations shaky. As long as Queen Adelaide possessed the slightest chance of conceiving an heir, Victoria remained only heir presumptive. The uncertainty kept King William—as it had also kept his brother George—from putting the Princess firmly under Court protection or, despite the Bishops' imprimatur, guardianship.

On January 25, 1835, Viscount Melbourne's sister, Lady Cowper, wrote to Dorothea de Lieven, who had returned to Russia, "Our Queen has just announced her pregnancy; this is a tremendous excitement, and a death-blow to the Duchess of Kent. It is sad for the little princess who is so nice, and you know what a country this is for malice and slander. 'Oh Lord *Howe* wonderful are thy works'—this is one of the vulgar jokes going around, a paraphrase of the Psalms." The handsome and happily married Lord Howe was Chamberlain to the dowdy and decorous forty-three-year-old Queen. Although he was devoted to her, that he was her lover was a scurrilous invention—as proved the pregnancy. In St. Petersburg, even before Lady Cowper's letter arrived, the rumor of the pregnancy had reached Princess de Lieven from someone else. As late as William's final illness, Victoria seemed to have had no guarantee of elevation to the throne, the government unsure whether the Princess could be declared Queen if Adelaide were pregnant. Such suspense—although unwarranted, given the Queen's age and childbearing history—added to the anxieties in the Kensington Palace atmosphere.

Royal personages officially came of age at eighteen. The Duchess was striving to prolong her control, assuming that Victoria, without recourse to sophisticated advice, would be miserable, but pliable. Victoria ignored the directive, and Lehzen remained at her side, the Princess continuing to complain, as she had all year, of feeling "very poorly," with a nagging backache one might now assign to menstrual difficulties, or tension, or both. Whatever her complaints, however, she was scheduled to go on an autumn progress into the Midlands, which Conroy had arranged, with scheduled stops at some of the great mansions in the north and east of England. On the eve of the journey, against which Victoria continued to protest, she was handed another long letter from her mother. It made no difference, the Duchess insisted, that the traveling was "disagreeable," or that "the fatigue of it will make you ill," for "it is of the greatest consequence that you should be seen, that you should know your country, and be acquainted with, and be known by all classes." If the King really loved her, she went on, he would not try "to stop our Journey."

The tour commenced, headaches and backaches notwithstanding. At the York Music Festival she sat through Handel's "heavy and tiresome" *Messiah,* conceiving a dislike for it that lasted through her life. Then came Leeds, Wakefield, Barnsley, Wentworth, the races at Doncaster, Belvoir Castle, Lynn, Stamford, Burghley House, and Holkham. At Exeter, where the party arrived from Belvoir in a downpour, the Duchess received the formal Address, which spoke of Victoria as "destined to mount the throne of these realms." According to Greville, who came there from Doncaster, where his horse lost the St. Leger, "Conroy handed the answer [to the Address], just as the Prime Minister does for the King."

Conroy and the Duchess were pleased by the throngs and the enthusiasm; Victoria had difficulty keeping awake at the grand dinners, and at a ball at Burghley House she went to bed after the first dance. On September 25 the tour ended, she noted in her journal. "I was much tired by the long journey & the great crowds we had to encounter. We cannot travel like other people. . . . I could never rest properly."

Her reward was a holiday at Ramsgate, where King Leopold of the Belgians, with Queen Louise, whom she had never seen, and who was only seven years her elder, would be visiting. Leopold himself had not been in England for four years, and was still avoiding London, having had political problems at home and financial ones in England. The price of English support for his ambitions in Belgium had been the relinquishing of his pension, and he had reneged by retaining thousands of pounds annually for the upkeep of his English properties, for which he had little further use. During their years apart, Leopold had corresponded with Victoria over her political judgment and her reading in history, recommending books that had pertinence to her future position. "I am much obliged to you, dear Uncle," she had once written the year before, "for the extract about Queen Anne, but I must beg you, as you have sent me to show what a Queen *ought not* to be, that you will send me what a Queen *ought to be.*"

After one Sunday evening session with Leopold, Victoria noted that her uncle had offered her "very important & valuable advice." With her journal an open book, she had to be circumspect, but one can assume the advice had more to do with handling Conroy than with the statecraft of Queen Anne. Leopold, in fact, while Victoria tried on her young aunt's Parisian clothes, took a walk with Sir John and suggested that if he did not overplay his hand he might achieve "a very good position" for himself.

The same day the royal party—without Louise, a Catholic—had gone to church, where Victoria heard a sermon not untypical of feeling then in England, but the Princess was revolted. "It was all against the Roman Catholic religion. It was a most impious, unchristian-like and shocking affair. I was quite shocked and ashamed."

A few days later, as Leopold and Louise were preparing to sail, Victoria felt ill, but accompanied them to Dover anyway. Back at Ramsgate she collapsed. Since her doctor, James Clark, had been sent back to London, Lehzen (still present because of Victoria's persistence) asked that Clark be urged to return. The Duchess scoffed that such a summons would make a "noise" in London, and was unnecessary. When the Princess became delirious, a local doctor was sent for, although Conroy claimed that to do so was "politically dangerous."

Victoria became worse during the night, and Dr. Clark was hurriedly recalled. According to Lehzen's recollections, "the scales fell from his eyes" about Victoria's condition, and he "succeeded in restoring to her the necessary *peace of mind.*" Later, writing to Baroness Lehzen, Leopold took the credit for managing the situation to prevent further harm to Victoria. "Had I not . . . had the courage, in Ramsgate, to tear apart the whole web of intrigue, Clark would never have learned the true state of affairs, and God knows what would have become of the Princess. . . ." Yet once Leopold set sail for Ostend, Dr. Clark, at Conroy's orders, had gone back meekly to London. Perhaps it took the Princess's collapse to convince Clark that Leopold's tales were true, and that there was an emotional basis for much of her misery.

With the spindly, fiercely protective Louise Lehzen in constant attendance, Victoria remained in her room for nearly five weeks. Clark cautiously called her ailment a "bilious fever." Later biographers suggested everything from typhoid fever to chronic (and severe) tonsillitis, in a pre-tonsillectomy age. She lost weight, and even tufts of hair, and suffered poor circulation, especially cold feet, which Lehzen rubbed every night for months thereafter. To Victoria's half-brother, Charles of Leiningen, Conroy dismissed the illness as "a mere indisposition," but the illness was real, and was at least in part a reaction to the psychological warfare in the household, still far from over. Seeing Victoria's enfeeblement as opportune, Sir John confronted her with a paper in which she appointed him her private secretary. She refused to sign.

Nothing of the episode could appear in her journal. For the last three weeks of October 1835, the pages are blank. Later, Victoria told her Prime Minister, Lord Melbourne, "I resisted in spite of my illness."

"What a blessing!" was his reply as she recorded it. She knew at the time that nothing she signed under duress would have any validity, but she would not give the detested Conroy even the temporary triumph. When the household was able to leave Ramsgate for Kensington Palace early in 1836, she was wan and weak, but—as she wrote about another event some months later—"I can bear more now."

There were other changes. She was under orders from her doctor to exercise more, to work at a standing desk, and to visit open spaces about London, such as Hampstead, for walks in more bracing air. Even the palace had changed. Clark as a young physician had written a thesis, *"De Frigoribus Effectis,"* establishing to his own satisfaction that cold and fresh air were good for people, warmth and heated air debilitating. The windows in Victoria's rooms were to be kept open, even in her absence.

The household had moved to refurbished and more spacious apartments, designed by Sir Jeffry Wyatville, who had restored Windsor Castle for George IV and made it more comfortable. The work at Kensington had been accomplished despite William's expressed disapproval. He never visited the palace, and had he passed in his carriage, he might have seen no changes to the approaches and entrance. The King's refusal had been based on dislike for the Duchess rather than on the adequacy of the accommodations for the heiress presumptive, as the rooms were gloomy, dilapidated, and infested. Victoria bloomed in the bright new quarters, happier than she had been for years. Her lessons with Mr. Davys resumed, and she began to keep up with the London newspapers, which she read with Lehzen. She also had a busy social calendar, including several visits to William and Adelaide, disapproved of by the Duchess. Best of all, Victoria's tedium was lightened by the opera and the theater, not because her mother cared that she enjoyed the lively arts, but because she could be seen there to advantage by the right people.

At the beginning of February 1836, Elizabeth Longford writes in her *Queen Victoria,* Dr. Clark had permitted his patient to visit St. James's Palace "wearing her grey satin *broché* coat trimmed with roses which Aunt Louise had sent from Paris." Victoria "looked so bewitching that young Lord Elphinstone sketched her in church; the Duchess secured his banishment to Madras." The cryptic note ends there, and no source is given; but clearly the suggestion is that the Princess, now recuperating, had inspired an admirer of unsuitable rank and condition, whom the Duchess of Kent had caused to be removed from the scene.

Is there more to the story? John Elphinstone (1807–1860), thirteenth Lord Elphinstone, was in the Royal Horse Guards from 1826 until his appointment as Governor of Madras. Rumors quickly surfaced that Elphinstone's translation to India—to a surprising appointment at twenty-nine—was to quiet talk that he and the Princess were in love. Perhaps Victoria was—or would do almost anything to extricate herself from the grasp of the Conroyals. Court gossip, at least, connected the pair; and Robert Browning remembered, in 1861, "twenty-five years ago," when Victoria, recovering from her long illness, "was lame and unable to stand upright," yet "bent on marrying nobody but Lord Elphinstone."

The evidence for that is hearsay,* but suddenly there were visits scheduled the next month for two more Coburg male cousins, sons of Duke Ferdinand of Saxe-Coburg Kohary. One son, Prince Ferdinand, was on his way to Portugal, to marry Queen Maria da Gloria, whom he had never met. The other, Prince Augustus, "speaks through his nose and in a slow funny way. . . . He is very good looking, I think. It is impossible to see or know him without loving him." Early in April he returned to Germany, and Victoria was grieved at the departure. It meant the end of balls and other entertainments where young people were accessible, and close companionship with young men, for whose attentions she was starved. It was easy to fall a little in love with each of them.

There seemed no end of Coburg cousins, and William would have prevented every one of them from reaching English shores. But he was nearly seventy-one, and Victoria almost seventeen. Both facts encouraged matchmakers, Leopold in particular, who had still another set of nephews in readiness for Kensington Palace. But so did William, who in April 1836 invited the Prince of Orange and his two sons to visit from Holland. One of them, he hoped, would be a husband for Victoria. Leopold had to move quickly. To him, the Netherlanders were particularly unattractive prospects, as Belgium had only recently broken away from the Dutch nation, and there was no love lost between the neighbors on the North Sea. Besides, he had long considered the sons of his brother Ernest, Duke of Saxe-Coburg Gotha, prime candidates for Victoria's hand, especially the younger nephew, Albert, as Ernest would inherit his father's domains.

---

*Nevertheless, a reference to Lord Elphinstone's being in love with Princess Victoria is included in the account of his life in the *Dictionary of National Biography*.

To Lord Palmerston, the Foreign Secretary, William sent instructions to delay, or even prevent, the visit of the Coburg cousins, but he could do nothing about a private visit of the Duchess's brother, with his sons. To the King's satisfaction the Orange aspirants arrived first. On May 13, 1836, he gave a ball in honor of the Princes William and Alexander. As Prince George of Cambridge also attended, three potential suitors were present, and two more were making their way down the Rhine. Early in 1837, after the surfeit of suitors, Viscount Melbourne, then Prime Minister, would tell the King impatiently that an heiress to the crown at seventeen was "a troublesome commodity," and that "we have Coburgs enough. . . . But she must marry somebody. Why not the Prince of Cambridge? After all, he has been educated here and we know him. . . ." Nothing overt was said to Victoria then, or earlier, by the King or his advisers, but the parade of young men was a language of gesture she well understood, and Louise Lehzen could tell her things that could not be put on paper. The pressure on her, she recalled nine years later, was so intense that she felt "extremely crushed and kept under, and hardly dared say a word." Leopold was relieved when she wrote to him, "The [Netherlander] boys are both very plain and have a mixture of Kalmuck and Dutch in their faces, moreover they look heavy, dull and frightened and are not at all prepossessing. So much for the *Oranges,* dear Uncle."

The next day, May 18, 1836, she met Ernest and Albert for the first time. Ernest was sturdier and a year older than Victoria. Albert was several months younger, and still sufficiently immature physically to fall asleep over his supper if it were a late evening. Dinners, balls, and other after-dark entertainments fatigued him to the point of illness. To Victoria he seemed a child.

A formal dinner on May 20, at St. James's Palace, lasted until two in the morning. The next afternoon there was a drawing-room reception with a receiving line of nearly four thousand people, and a lavish dinner and concert followed. On May 23, at a grand dinner at Kensington Palace, Albert, having endured enough, excused himself and went to bed. The next day, Victoria's seventeenth birthday, was the occasion of a state ball given by the King at St. James's Palace. "Poor, dear Albert," Victoria noted, ". . . looked very pale and felt very poorly." After dancing twice he "turned pale as ashes; and we all feared he might faint; he therefore went home."

The weeks that followed before Ernest and Albert returned to Germany were less exhausting. They went to the opera; the princes sat in on

Victoria's music lessons; Albert played piano duets with her, and managed to stay up "until 10 minutes past 10." He told Victoria about his plans to attend the University of Bonn, and to live with his brother in Brussels, Florence, and Rome to learn more about the world. On July 10 they left, and Victoria again lamented to her journal, but this time she "felt the separation more deeply."

More than a month before the brothers left London, Victoria had asked her uncle Ernest for a private meeting, the substance of which became clear in a letter dated June 7, 1836, which she gave to him to hand-carry to Leopold en route to Coburg. Albert, she confided, "possesses every quality that could be desired to render me perfectly happy. He is so sensible, so kind, and so good, and so amiable too. . . . I hope all will go on prosperously and well, on this subject of so much importance to me." The rest of the understanding was unsaid, but its roots were in a letter of May 1 from Leopold to Lehzen beginning, "I talk to you at length and through you speak to Victoria." Any "immediate alliance" was not possible, he realized; "she must reach her 18th birthday. . . ." At that point "the possibility of a Regency vanishes like an evil cloud." He and Stockmar had selected Albert, he explained, for his "pure unspoilt nature" and "excellent intelligence." Of all the available consorts he saw "not a single Prince of riper years to whom we could entrust the dear child, without incurring the gravest risk." Lehzen had accomplished her mission.

The summer passed in a routine of renewed lessons, followed by a country holiday at Claremont. The stay at Claremont gave the Duchess a reason not to attend Queen Adelaide's birthday reception at Windsor. Although the Duchess and Victoria were invited to stay a fortnight, through the King's birthday on August twenty-first—his seventy-first—the Duchess offered to come to Windsor only on the twentieth. Annoyed at the King's snubs to her "gentlemen," she preferred the minimum exposure to William. But when she arrived, the King did not appear; he had gone to London on urgent parliamentary business, and used the opportunity to look in at Kensington Palace on the way back to Windsor, finding for the first time that the Duchess had taken over seventeen rooms that he had refused to let her have the year before.

At ten in the evening, he returned to Windsor, after some hours of seething in his carriage. He went to the drawing room where guests were still assembled, took hold of Victoria's hands, and expressed regret that he did not see more of her. Then he turned to the Duchess, told her loudly he had seen her misappropriation of space in Kensington Palace, and could neither understand nor endure conduct so disrespectful of him. On that chilly note the reception ended.

The next day was William's birthday. There were one hundred to dinner. After a toast to the King—the customary "health and long life" —William arose to respond. "I trust in God," he began, not looking at the Duchess, who sat next to him, "that my life might be spared for nine months longer, after which period, in the event of my death, no Regency would take place. I should then have the satisfaction of leaving the Royal authority to the personal exercise of that Young Lady, the Heiress Presumptive of the Crown, and not in the hands of a person now near me, who is surrounded by evil advisers and who is herself incompetent to act with propriety in the station in which She would be placed." Then he toasted "the youngest member of the Royal Family." Although he had not, he said, *"seen so much of her as I could have wished,* I take no less interest in her, and the more I do see of her, both in public and in private, the greater pleasure it will give me." Recording the King's words, Greville called them "civil and gracious," but the Duchess took note of the deliberate insults, and ordered her carriage. Victoria burst into tears, and it was with difficulty that others at the dinner persuaded the Duchess to remain overnight.

Several weeks later, King Leopold arrived at Claremont, without Louise, who was expecting another child. Victoria was ecstatic over the presence of the closest person she had ever had to a "real father." Their private conversations were crucial for her, as she now realized that her accession would not be long delayed. After some time at the sea, at Ramsgate, they returned to Claremont, the Duchess apprehensive after the King's outburst at their spending much time at Kensington Palace. It was February before they were back in London, barely in time for the opera and ballet season that Victoria longed for, and a renewal of lessons. Yet the first significant lesson of the new year had come unexpectedly before they left Claremont. At Hersham, just to the west, she encountered her first railway train, "& saw the steam carriage pass with surprising quickness, striking sparks as it flew along the railroad, enveloped in clouds of smoke & making a loud noise. It was a curious thing indeed!" The invention would transform Victoria's world and way of life.

At Windsor, William continued to appear spry, and Conroy agonized over the fading hopes of a regency. To Charles of Leiningen, visiting in April, he suggested that although Victoria would be of age to be queen at eighteen, she was still legally a minor under parental control until she became twenty-one, an argument the pliable Prince Charles readily accepted. "God knows," Stockmar exploded to Leopold, "what schemes are being built on this fact. . . ."

Not until the King received guests at a levee on May 18, 1837, sitting in a chair, was it clear that he had failed considerably over the winter. Palmerston wrote that the King was "in a very precarious state," but thought he would again rally. On the same day William wrote a letter to the Princess, informing her that when she came of age on May 24, he intended to apply to Parliament for £10,000 a year to be at her personal disposal, and that she was to appoint her own Keeper of the Privy Purse to administer it. She was also to form her own household if she wished.

The letter had arrived at Kensington Palace via Lord Conyngham, who informed Conroy that he had instructions from the King to place it in Victoria's hands himself. Conyngham was allowed to present it only in the presence of the Duchess, who read it after Victoria. Furiously she told the Marquess that she hoped Parliament would "refuse to vote money for such a purpose." While Victoria wept, the Duchess insisted that she knew her maternal duty, and that her daughter had, "of her own free will, told the King that she desires nothing but to be left as heretofore with her Mother." She and the Princess, she then wrote to the King, "reject the idea, that on such a subject, we could have a separate feeling."

Forced to sign a letter written by the Duchess on Conroy's instructions, Victoria on June 6 dictated a memorandum to Lehzen describing how she had been coerced, as she was afraid to put the details in her journal, which was accessible to her mother. A draft of the letter, which Victoria kept, has a later note in Albert's hand, "Written by the Duchess of Kent on Sir John Conroy's advice." In it the Princess confessed "my youth and inexperience which naturally unfits me to enter into all the details" of the financial settlements. Everything, it went on, "may be given to my dear Mother for my use, who always freely does everything I want on pecuniary matters. . . ."

The King was not well, but he had enough of his wits about him to observe, "Victoria has not written that letter."

Financial arrangements remained unsettled on the day that Victoria came of age, and Lord Melbourne reminded the King's confidential secretary, Sir Herbert Taylor, that Victoria was still legally a minor for all purposes except the succession. Money, Sir Herbert thought, was the problem with "the Duchess and King John." More likely, they craved power and status, both of which Leopold worried they would extract from Victoria. Everyone had a breaking point.

On the Princess's birthday, while ordnance depots about London were firing salutes at dawn, Stockmar set out from Leopold's residence in Belgium. "How old!" Victoria was writing in her journal, "and yet how far am I from being what I should be. I shall from this day take the *firm* resolution . . . to keep my attention always well fixed on whatever I am about, and to strive every day to become less trifling and more fit for what, if Heaven wills it, I'm some day going to be!"

Although the King had arranged a state ball in honor of her coming of age, and there were other celebrations—even London streets were decorated and thronged—William was too ill to participate. (But he had sent to her a magnificent Broadwood grand piano as his personal gift.) En route to the ball at St. James's Palace, Victoria passed through beflagged and illuminated streets crowded with jubilant Londoners, and was "touched" by "the anxiety of the people to see poor stupid me."

Significantly, William had directed that in his absence the chair of state reserved for him at the ball should be occupied by Victoria. It set her apart from her mother, who, observers thought, was "exceptionally ungracious."

Conroy, her escort, appeared happy and confident. He was again putting pressure on Victoria to name him Private Secretary, as it was that possibility of future influence that had been giving him an importance far beyond his technical title of comptroller to the Duchess. But Stockmar, long considered a friend and confidant to the Duchess, had determined to support Victoria's position once he learned from her that the letter in which she had refused money in her own right, and asked that her mother handle her affairs, had been written by Conroy. To counter it, Victoria had Stockmar dictate for the record a memorandum to Lehzen, reiterating her objections to Conroy's interference through her mother. "Sir John Conroy is *Her* private secretary and neither *my* Servant, nor Advisor, nor *ever was.*"

As the condition of the King deteriorated, Victoria noted that fact in her journal and in letters to Leopold. She was now receiving almost daily visits from Stockmar, whose long history of service to the family was such that the Duchess could not order him away, whatever she thought of his intrusion. To Leopold, Stockmar sent by courier reports of Conroy's "impudent and insulting conduct" toward Victoria, which occurred even in the Duchess's presence. "O'Hum" (Conroy), he explained, "continues the system of intimidation with the genius of a madman, and the Duchess carries out all that she is instructed to do with admirable docility and perseverance. . . . The Princess continues to refuse firmly to give her Mama her promise that she will make O'Hum her confidential adviser. Whether she will hold out, Heaven only knows. . . ."

One of Victoria's few friends permitted access to her was Lady Catherine Jenkinson, a lady-in-waiting to the Duchess. (Her father was the Earl of Liverpool, brother of the late Prime Minister.) Through Lady Catherine, Victoria managed to see Lord Liverpool alone on June 15, and explained her dilemmas. Conroy, he agreed, was unsuitable to manage her affairs, but he saw no way she could leave her mother's house until she came to the throne. Her political advisers, as queen, he assured her, had to be her Ministers, particularly Lord Melbourne. Before parting, Victoria asked Lord Liverpool to see Baron Stockmar, "who would tell him many things I like not to name," and also to consult Lady Catherine for further details of Conroy's conspiracies.

The next day Victoria wrote Leopold that "it may all be over" for the King "at any moment." At the same time Stockmar was writing that "the struggle between the Mama and the daughter is still going on," with the Duchess "pressed by Conroy to bring matters to extremities." To Charles of Leiningen, Conroy confided that Victoria *must be coerced,* and Charles, passive until then, rushed to his mother to warn her against doing anything drastic, speaking to her in German to evade Conroy. Meanwhile, all of Victoria's lessons had ceased, social activities had halted, and everyone waited and watched for William's end.

On June 17, Leopold sent, via Stockmar, instructions to the Princess on "what is to be done when the King ceases to live," largely confirming Liverpool's advice. She would have few, if any, enemies in the King's party, he suggested, as "your immediate successor, with the mustaches" —the Duke of Cumberland—"is enough to frighten them into the most violent attachment for you."

In response, on June 19, Victoria wrote, for Leopold's courier, that William might not live until the next day. "Poor old man! I feel sorry for him; he was always personally kind to me, and I should be ungrateful and devoid of feeling if I did not remember this." But she added that she looked forward "with calmness and quietness" to what was to follow. "I

*"The Contrast"—an 1837
cartoon cautioning
Englishmen that the
alternative to the girl queen
was the allegedly malign old
Duke of Cumberland, who
would become instead King
Ernest of Hanover.
Reproduced from the
unsigned memoirs of
G. W. E. Russell.*

am not alarmed at it, and yet I do not suppose myself quite equal to all; I trust, however, that with *good will, honesty,* and *courage* I shall not, at all events, fail." She now knew that she had the will to be what she had to be.

The Duke of Wellington, meanwhile, had held the annual Waterloo banquet on June 18 as usual, at the King's request. William had wanted to see the sun set on Waterloo Day, and had managed that. The next day the Duke took his annual "rent" for his country seat, Stratfield Saye, to Windsor—a small tricolor flag fringed with gold, which was his symbol of gratitude for his honors. The King "buried his face in its folds." Then the Duke went to see the Duke of Cumberland, whose accession to the throne of Hanover was imminent, and who was at Windsor awaiting the end. Leave the castle, and leave the country, Wellington advised. "Go instantly, and take care that *you don't get pelted.*"

A print dated 1837 underlines the alternatives. Headed "The Contrast," it is divided into a pair of vertical panels. On one side is a young woman, her hair coiled in the shape of a small crown. On the other is a hoary-bearded old man, his face twisted into a scowl. The first is labeled "England" and "Victoria." The other is identified as "Hanover" and "Ernest." Adapted from Shakespeare is a caption:

Look here upon this picture, and on this
The counterfeit presentment of "two" sov'reigns.

That evening Prince Ernest of Hohenlohe, who had come to England with Feodora for the birthday festivities, and who was not only Victoria's brother-in-law but also Queen Adelaide's cousin, arrived at Kensington Palace from Windsor to report that the King was slipping into his last hours, propped up in a heavy leather chair to ease his labored breathing. Victoria, who had been suppressing her tangled emotions, wept, leading Prince Ernest to think that William's condition had been kept from her; but the reaction was a natural one for a girl of eighteen who was living under tensions of which the Prince could hardly conceive.

At 2:12 the next morning, the King's life flickered out. At six, the Lord Chamberlain (Lord Conyngham) and the Archbishop of Canterbury arrived at Kensington Palace from Windsor. Victoria was awakened by her mother, in whose bedroom she still slept. "I got out of bed and went into my sitting-room (only in my dressing gown) and *alone*," Victoria wrote in her journal, "and saw them." She underlined *alone*. That decision was her first as Queen.

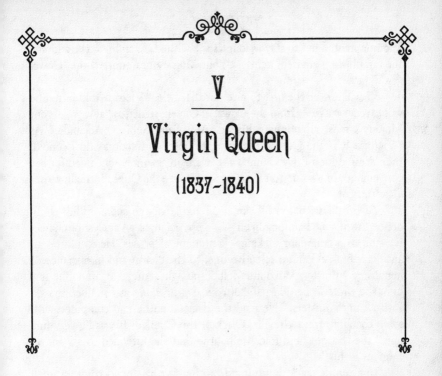

V

Virgin Queen

(1837~1840)

An imprisoned young princess released from confinement on the death of the grumpy king, to become queen of the most sprawling empire on earth—the stuff of a fairy tale, or the essence of a legend. Yet it was the reality Victoria faced on June 20, 1837. Despite occasional parole from the prison of Kensington Palace, she had been under what can be described as house arrest by the Duchess and Sir John—two figures who might have been conceived by the Brothers Grimm. The Lord Chamberlain and the Archbishop of Canterbury set her free.

Despite being awakened at daybreak, Victoria, expecting such a summons, had her wits about her. Pulling on a robe, she went to her writing table and penned a condolence letter to her aunt Adelaide, addressing it to "The Queen." Adelaide had asked, through the Lord Chancellor, to be permitted to remain at Windsor until after the funeral.

Victoria invited her to stay as long as she wished. Examining the address, the Archbishop advised, gently, "Your Majesty has omitted the 'Dowager.'"

"I will not be the first to give her that title," Victoria told him. She would receive a reply from the Dowager Queen, signed as "always . . . your Majesty's most affectionate Friend, Aunt, and Subject, Adelaide." As "Victoria R.," the Queen hastily wrote notes to Feodora and Leopold, then dressed for a Privy Council at eleven, an assembly scheduled for her convenience in Kensington Palace, to introduce the Queen formally to her Government.

At breakfast, Baron Stockmar offered advice to shore up her confidence. At fifty he had long been—as a physician, as an analyst of character, and as a confidant of kings—a student of power. He would be an antidote, but seldom an effective one, to the charm and insouciance of her Prime Minister, Viscount Melbourne, who arrived at nine. She saw him, she wrote in her journal, "of course *quite alone* as I shall *always* do with all my ministers." He read the declaration he had composed with some coaching from Greville, Clerk of the Council. It was "a very fine one," she thought, and told Melbourne that she intended to ask for no changes in his Ministry.

In a simple black mourning dress, her fair hair braided into a small coronet, Victoria went into the Red Saloon for the meeting. In size she was a child. Onlookers expecting Conroy flanking her on one side and the Duchess on the other saw neither. Sir David Wilkie, at her command, would paint the scene, with the eyes of every dignitary focused upon Victoria; but he dressed her in white, probably to emphasize her "virgin queen" qualities. Of the ninety-seven Councillors, many are missing, to relieve the clutter, but Greville, sitting for Wilkie, wondered at the "strange selection" and asked why "ordinary men" were included while "conspicuous men of the time"—like Lords Brougham and Stanley— were not. Wilkie confided "that great anxiety prevailed to be put into the picture, and many pressing applications had been made." And as "only vain and silly men would make them," Greville concluded, "importunity" prevailed. The moment, stiffly frozen, is a perversion of mourning custom as well as a falsification of history. Later the Queen would dismiss the picture scornfully.

The crown was transferred, Greville wrote, "with a tranquillity which is curious and edifying." In the crowd to pay homage to the new queen were the Duke of Sussex and the Duke of Cumberland. Raised in an atmosphere in which she had to keep her feelings under strict discipline, Victoria advanced to meet her uncles, one of whom, Sussex, was infirm, and swore them in together as they knelt before her and kissed her hand. "I saw her," Greville thought, "blush up to the eyes, as if she felt the contrast between their civil and their natural relations [to her], and this was the only sign of emotion which she evinced." The ceremony formally shifted the allegiances of the members of the government from one sovereign to another, Victoria proceeding with a dignity and confidence that, Greville wrote, produced "a chorus of praise and admiration." She was "perfectly composed," an ambitious young M.P., Benjamin Disraeli, wrote to his sister, Sarah, having heard about the Council from Lord Lyndhurst, his leader in Commons. What surprised them both was that she was "alone in the council chamber and attended by no women." Victoria was setting her style.

"She not merely filled her chair," said the Duke of Wellington, "she filled the room." It was not that she had been magically metamorphosed by her new title; the self-possession evinced in a regal bearing and a bell-like voice was the product of long hours alone with her thoughts and the coaching of Lehzen, Leopold, and Stockmar. She knew what she had to do. She also knew that she was a political innocent and had much to learn. As Lord Aberdeen put it to Princess de Lieven, Melbourne's opportunities had no parallel since the days of Edward Seymour, Duke of Somerset, who became Lord Protector of England during the minority of the young son of Henry VIII. "He had a young and inexperienced infant in his hands, whose whole conduct and opinions must necessarily be in complete subservience. . . . I do him the justice to believe that he has some feeling for his situation. . . ." But Edward VI, in 1547, had been only nine, and it had been the propaganda of Conroy, in jockeying for power in a future Victoria court, that the new queen would be helpless as a child.

That was also the fear of *The Times*, which, in a leading article the next day, excoriated Melbourne, whom the paper distrusted, for furnishing the young queen with a speech full of what were seen as Whig catchphrases. "We have seldom heard of any political expedient more unprincipled, more treacherous, or unfeeling than this. It is an actual trepanning of their innocent Sovereign into a course of policy subservient to their own selfish interests." The Queen, so *The Times* predicted, "unless we be much mistaken, will [not] remain long without herself detecting it."

Fears that a girl of eighteen could be manipulated easily were far from groundless. Much depended on Melbourne's sense of his guardian-ship, but much more upon Victoria's own common sense, which led her after the Privy Council to receive in audience, each "in my room alone," she noted, various members of the Government and the Royal Household. "Saw Stockmar." With Stockmar was a paper he had just received from Conroy, dated that day, and confessing that he felt "completely defeated" and was ready to retire from the Duchess's (and thus from Victoria's) life. His price was a peerage, the Grand Cross of the Bath, and £3,000 a year. Melbourne was outraged, but weakly proposed an Irish peerage (when available) and the money.

Without any immediate payoff, Conroy would linger, to the disquiet of the Queen. His continuing influence was apparent the same afternoon, when the Duchess (her powers now drastically reduced) asked permission to have Sir John and Lady Flora Hastings with her the next day at the proclamation of the Queen's accession. Victoria refused. She then saw Stockmar again, and Melbourne. "Went down and said good-night to Mamma, etc." That night Victoria slept alone, at her wish, for the first time in her life.

Early the next morning she again refused her mother's entreaties about Conroy, although the Duchess had warned that people would notice his absence, and talk. "It is Lord M's decided opinion," Victoria scrawled in a penciled note; and the Duchess countered, ineffectively, as the Queen had shut Conroy out of her life forever, "You do not know the world. . . . Take care, Victoria . . . ! take care that Lord Melbourne is not King . . . !"

Perhaps even the Duchess saw something in the relationship that Victoria, in her sheltered innocence, did not. The Queen's feelings, Gre-ville wrote, "are sexual though she does not know it." That she appeared unaware of that dimension in Melbourne's magnetism is clear from the fact that the London gutter press did not seize upon it. The tone of such comment was more like that of Lady de Grey to Creevey: "I hope you are amused at the report of Lord Melbourne being likely to marry the Queen. . . ."

Long isolated and longing for human contacts, yet as an unmarried young queen rigidly limited in her friendships, Victoria needed a father more than a consort. Leopold, then the closest to a father in her life, confided that it was impolitic for him to come to England during the early months of her reign. ("People might fancy I came to enslave you!") Stockmar, his deputy, remained as political confidant, but the wizened and cautious physician from Coburg could respond to none of Victoria's emotional needs. Conroy, however much her mother hung on his arm, was hardly a substitute parent. Melbourne, however, seemed as ideally cast for the part as Conroy had been for wicked stepfather.

William Lamb, Viscount Melbourne, was a handsome and youngish fifty-eight, long a widower after an unhappy marriage. Seven months earlier his only child, Augustus, pathetically backward and epileptic, had died in his twenties. Witty, wealthy, and well-connected, Melbourne had hardly been without society, which he found to his taste in the great London mansions presided over by such sophisticated political hostesses as Lady Elizabeth Holland. The venerable, turreted Holland House in Kensington, where he had dined more evenings than anywhere else, including his own residence, was sparkling, largely in its artificiality, even to the incense burned to mask honest odors. In such settings, Melbourne played to his own image in many-mirrored drawing rooms. With Victoria, his unused reserves of affection could be directed toward a surrogate child. Besides, he would be educating a queen.

On June 21 came the ceremony of the Proclaiming of the Sovereign, at St. James's. The declaration, describing the Queen as Alexandrina Victoria, had to be corrected at her order, *Alexandrina* vanishing from her life forever. The Duchess should have been pleased—the Queen bore her name. Yet the Duchess's own eminence had been extinguished. Victoria would carefully see to it that her mother lived with her, but at a distance. Conroy, who remained technically comptroller of the Duchess's establishment, would never be granted an audience with the Queen.

Almost every day involved another regal procession somewhere, as the Queen ceremonially made appearances to establish her identity as sovereign. She dressed in black, in mourning for the late King, but the public saw only a radiant young woman. For the most formal functions, the Order of the Garter had to be worn, and Victoria had no idea where to put it. The Duke of Norfolk was sent for as the hereditary master of ceremony and protocol. He suggested locating a portrait of Queen Anne, and there the Garter was observed on the left arm. In no other way would Victoria consciously emulate the last Queen Regnant.

At receptions of every sort, the people who really counted in English political, social, and commercial life were offered, over the early months of Victoria's reign, an opportunity for symbolic contact. Thousands of pairs of lips brushed the plump queenly hand, which ministers had already found "soft" and "sweet." Having somehow missed presentation, Greville was ushered in by Conyngham only to find that he was fixed in an awkward position while the Queen struggled to remove her glove, as she wore so many rings. "But she blushed and laughed and pulled, until the thing was done, and I kissed her hand." The rings, she explained to Melbourne, "improved an ugly hand." "Makes them worse," he grumbled. She remained self-conscious about her stubby fingers, and would wear more and more rings, sometimes even on her thumbs, and at cost to the deft handling of knife and fork.

The young Queen was a symbol that her realm seized with enthusiasm. After a king who was pathetically blind and insane as long as most people alive could remember, another who was corpulent and profligate, and a third who was boorish and blustering, the Queen promised much by being herself. As young Alfred Tennyson toasted (in verses he did not publish),

> *The reigns of her fathers were long or were short,*
> *They plagued us in anger or vext us in sport.*
> *Let them sleep in their good or their evil report—*
> *But a health to the Queen of the Isles.*

On June 30, Victoria's Royal Assent was given to forty pieces of legislation—the first bills to become law in the Queen's reign. Parliamentary clerks, since the death of Queen Anne, had written *"Le Roy le veult,"* and referred to *"His"* Majesty. Feminine appellations had to be recalled and revived after 130 years to formalize such Acts as one abolishing the pillory, and after some poring over musty papers the appropriate terminology was located.

Victoria and her entourage moved in mid-July to Buckingham House. It had been bought by George III and ordered rebuilt by George IV, who never lived in it. William IV had ordered the refurbishing hurried, but when Victoria succeeded him she was told that it could not be ready before Christmas. According to Sallie Stevenson, wife of the American Minister to England, who was an early guest in Victoria's new quarters, the Queen called in the functionaries responsible for the alterations and told them that she expected to dine there by a date in July she specified. "I am sorry to inform your Majesty," one said, "that it is impossible."

On July 21, exactly one month after Victoria had been officially proclaimed Queen, Mrs. Stevenson wrote to her "beloved Sisters" in

Virginia that she and her husband had been invited to dine with Victoria at Buckingham House, and a fortnight later she described it as replete with "rich and gorgeous apartments, which reminded me of the descriptions in the Arabian Nights." The "magnificent banqueting room" was brilliantly lighted, "and the table covered with a service of gold so splendid it dazzled one's eyes." What had happened, she reported, was that the "grave old Lords" had received written instructions "from her little Majesty . . . written by her own hand, issuing her commands that the Palace be ready for her on the day named. . . . There was nothing left for them but to put all the workmen that could be hired to work, & she moved to the new Palace on the day & hour appointed. So much for a young Queen!"

Victoria would grow to loathe Buckingham House (soon elevated to Palace), and to abhor the noise and fumes of London, but in her early years as Queen it was a convenient place to live and in which to entertain, and from which to stage forays to the theater and the opera.

Even before the official month of mourning for King William was over, Victoria had begun to entertain at Buckingham House as confidently as if she had been doing so for years. Her first drawing-room was held on July 17, and invitations were coveted. That evening Lady Elizabeth Grosvenor (the Marchioness of Westminster, but better known under her earlier title) put off a dinner she was to give at Grosvenor House to attend a dinner given by the Queen, even though the "order to dine" had come only that morning. The guests included minor German princelings, including Victoria's half-brother Charles of Leiningen and their mother, the Duchess of Kent, two of the Queen's new maids-of-honor, and her mother's ever-present Lady Flora. The postprandial entertainment was unexciting, yet—for the worldly Grosvenors—different: Victoria sang, after which the Duchess found partners for whist. The Grosvenors remained politely until eleven, "and then went to a magnificent supper on the staircase at Stafford House and came home at past 2."

The Prime Minister, rarely absent in those early months of Victoria's reign, was not always at Buckingham House for dinner, occasionally needing the antidote, as one of his biographers put it, of "dalliance with Mrs [Caroline] Norton or racy gossip around the table at Holland House" after evenings of "shilling whist with the Duchess of Kent, [and] six hours a day of *tête-à-tête* with the Queen, a perpetual check on swearing and loose talk."

Evenings with the Queen, Greville reported from his experience the next year, would not change much. He appreciated "her good-nature and thoughtfulness about other people's little vanities, even those of the most insignificant," but there was no gaiety or ease, since social equality was impossible where "some ceremony, and a continual air of deference and respect must be observed." The Queen was good-humored and cheerful, "but still she is Queen, and by her [example] must the social habits and the tone of conversation be regulated, and for this she is too young and inexperienced. She sits at a large round table, and Melbourne always in a chair beside her, where two mortal hours are consumed in such conversation as can be found, which appears to be, and really is, very up-hill work."

Windsor was even more of a strain for the guests than crowded Buckingham Palace. The advantages at Windsor of moving about "as best pleases them" produced "none of the sociability which makes the agree-ableness of an English country house." There was no central room in which guests could relax, and the billiard room was "in such a remote corner of the castle that it might as well be in the town. . . ." The library was well stocked but equally inaccessible, and so cold as to be barely habitable. Nothing but a meal united the company.

To Greville the boredom was less significant than what he saw of the Queen's relationship with the Prime Minister, as "while she . . . does everything that is civil to all the inmates of the Castle, she really has nothing to do with anybody but Melbourne, and with him she passes (if not in *tête-à-tête*, yet in intimate conversation) more hours than any two people, in any relation of life, perhaps ever do pass together. . . . He is at her side for at least six hours every day—an hour in the morning, two on horseback [in midafternoon], one at dinner, and two in the evening." Such a "monopoly" of her time was injudicious and inconsistent with social usage. "But it is more peculiarly inexpedient with reference to her own future . . . , for if Melbourne should be compelled to resign, her privation will be all the more bitter on account of the exclusiveness of her intimacy with him."

Was Victoria in love with her mentor? In Shaw's *Caesar and Cleopatra* (1898), a play with conscious Victorian reverberations, an elderly courtier, Pothinus, accuses the young Cleopatra, sixteen at Caesar's arrival, of having been altered by her intimacy with the fiftyish Roman. "Do you speak with Caesar every day for six months: and you will be changed," she says.

It is "common talk," he goes on, that she is infatuated "with this old man." If by "infatuated" one meant "made foolish," she counters, it was not so. "Now that Caesar has made me wise, it is no use my liking or disliking: I do what must be done. . . . That is not happiness; but it is greatness. If Caesar were gone, I think I could govern the Egyptians; for what Caesar is to me, I am to the fools around me."

"Is Cleopatra then indeed a Queen, and no longer Caesar's prisoner and slave? . . . Does he not love you?"

"Love me! Pothinus: Caesar loves no one. . . . His kindness to me is a wonder: neither mother, father, nor nurse have ever taken so much care of me, or thrown open their thoughts to me so freely."

"Well: is this not love? . . . I should have asked, then, do you love him?"

"Can one love a god?"

The play's Caesar has Melbourne's mannerisms and vanities, his eagerness to instruct and his tendency to coin cynical aphorisms. Shaw's Cleopatra has Victoria's youth, innocence, terrible temper, and ambition to be more than an empty title. Foreign-policy issues deliberately echo a later decade—the English 1870s. Perhaps it was as closely as one could comment on the Victoria-Melbourne relationship in an age when the Lord Chamberlain's Office censored plays for their politics and their allusions to the sovereign.

Educating herself in the business of government was the Queen's highest priority, although she quickly learned also to enjoy the perquisites of her position, especially the devoted—but sometimes only curious— attentions of distinguished and attractive men among her Ministers and lesser functionaries. From a distance, Leopold taught her queenly behavior. "The habits of business" she initiated at the start, he suggested, would organize her life effectively. One rule high on his list was *never to permit* people to speak [to you] on subjects concerning yourself and your affairs, without your having yourself desired them to do so." The solution was to "change the conversation, and make the individual feel that he has made a mistake." She should see her Ministers between eleven and half past one. (It kept the early morning free, and made luncheon a convenient break.) And she should hurry no decision. "Whenever a question is of some importance it should not be decided on the day when it is submitted to you," he advised. "And even when in my mind I am disposed to accede, still I always keep the papers with me some little time before I return them." Both to play for time and to learn what the papers submitted actually were, he recommended having the Minister *explain them to you.*

Then you will keep the papers, either to think yourself upon it or to consult somebody. . . ."

It was a lesson she learned quickly and well, as by August 30 Greville was remarking in his diary that the Queen's practice of "seldom or never" giving an immediate answer but, instead, saying "she will consider it," had been attributed to her consulting Melbourne "about everything." But the Prime Minister told Greville "that such is her habit even with him, and that when he talks to her upon any subject upon which an opinion is expected from her, she tells him she will think it over, and let him know her sentiments the next day." Even Melbourne could not charm her into an immediate response.

The Queen would follow Leopold's advice so rigidly all her life that few but her intimates in the family and Household could speak to her on anything but public business without a sense of superficiality or strain.

To Robert Peel, the diarist John Croker wrote in mid-August that he had been spending a Saturday at White's, his club, talking politics—the forthcoming Parliamentary elections—and the conversation turned to how the young Queen was "overworked, and teased with needless details. They send her all manner of things in the various official boxes for signature, and she, not yet knowing what is *substance* and what *form*, reads all. It is suspected that this is done to give her a disgust for business. I don't suspect any such deep design . . . but Lord Melbourne sees her every day for a couple of hours, and his situation is certainly the most dictatorial, the most despotic, that the world has ever seen." Not a member of the Conservative opposition, George Villiers saw Melbourne's opportunity more benevolently: "It has become his province to educate, instruct, and form the most interesting mind in the world. No occupation was more engrossing or involved greater responsibility."

Whether in London or Windsor, Victoria went at her crimson official boxes with a relish for business. She wanted to see everything and learn everything. As constitutional monarch in a kingdom without a written constitution—a Sovereign with no will, theoretically, other than that of her Ministers—she knew she had much to learn if she was to be more than a figurehead on the prow of the ship of state.

Melbourne's lessons in statecraft were skeptical and unhurried. He believed neither in religion nor in progress: "You had better try to do no good, and then you'll get into no scrapes." Nothing was worth doing, he felt, unless it became urgent to do it. One should not automatically dislike all "bad men," he warned: "that comprises a large number." A believer

"Susannah and the Elders"—the young Queen riding between Lord Melbourne (at left) and Lord John Russell—by John Doyle, October 1837. Contemporary print.

in symbols as substitutes for more substantial action, he encouraged through his own practice an attention to forms and trifles. He cultivated epigrams rather than philosophies, with the exception of his belief that all social change was for the worse. Leader of a weak and divided Whig Ministry, with scarcely enough votes in the Commons for a majority, his own views were more Tory than the traditionalists in his party, and remote from its radicals. The purpose of office, he contended, was to retain it. To retain him in office, Victoria would ignore the ground rules of her position (to her cost), and become a party zealot.

Unacquainted with most royal ceremony, the Queen let Melbourne be her tutor there as well, as his presence enhanced her confidence. When, in July, she drove to the House of Lords for the closing of the Parliamentary session, and donned her "enormously heavy" Robe of State, in which to read her speech (composed by "Lord M"), Melbourne, bearing the Sword of State, stood nearby. He was, Victoria wrote in her journal, "on the left-hand of the Throne, and I feel always a satisfaction to have him near me on such occasions, as he is such an honest, good, kind-hearted man and is my friend, I know it."

Afterwards, despite an initial twinge of nervousness, she felt "quite frisky," she wrote her Uncle Leopold, and ready to conduct the annual review of the Guards in the traditional fashion, on horseback. Although she had not ridden in two years, since her serious illness at Ramsgate, she refused to have a review unless she could do so "on horseback, as Queen Elizabeth did." The review was canceled, and she began, with determination, to regain her proficiency as horsewoman. She also began singing lessons again with Signor Lablache, another activity curtailed two years earlier. The Conroyals had maintained an interest in suggesting her continued invalidism, as it left open another possible avenue to a regency. She had no reason now to abet their charade.

Victoria's chief tutor in external affairs, from etiquette and phraseology to political and commercial relations, was her Foreign Secretary. At fifty-three, Henry John Temple, third Viscount Palmerston, was a man of many boudoirs, although the chief love of his life was Lady Cowper (Melbourne's sister Emily), whom he could not marry until a decent interval followed the death of her husband in the month of Victoria's accession. Elegant, clever, and patient, Palmerston spent time with Victoria over maps and memoranda, niceties and nuances. Stockmar added his fund of worldly advice gathered from years of diplomatic travels, and from encounters with eminences that supplemented Palmerston's knowledge of the international scene. Lehzen furnished her own listening-post store of European gossip about notables in the *Almanach de Gotha,* and acted as social secretary. No one, not even Melbourne, had greater access to Victoria than the Baroness. While the Queen's mother had apartments in a remote section of the new royal residence, and had to write notes asking to see Victoria at times other than those when she was formally invited to dinner (often receiving penciled responses that the Queen was too busy), Lehzen had a bedroom next to Victoria's, with an entrance cut through the wall at the Queen's direction that summer. As Greville gossiped, probably with justification, late in August, when any of the Queen's Ministers came to see her, "the Baroness [Lehzen] retires at one door as they enter at the other, and the audience over she returns to the Queen."

For the maiden Queen, the Duchess was her duenna, and appeared on formal social occasions; but Victoria's interpretation of that function left her free to see men alone when they were her advisers (like Stockmar) or members of her Government. The breach between mother and daughter over Conroy was already the subject of newspaper comment, as the Duchess had reassumed her old role of bereaved and forsaken widow. Yet neither Victoria nor Melbourne seemed able, between them, to use their formidable powers to encourage the exit of the Duchess's "gentleman," as Conroy was called in the polite code of the day. Whatever, too, his extravagances in dissipating the Duchess's money, or that of the elderly Princess Sophia, whose income he still administered, his family neither then nor afterwards lived in particularly lavish style. He would be given £3,000 a year for services to the Queen's mother, as Greville noted, "but he has never once been invited to the Palace or distinguished by the slightest mark of personal favor, so that nothing can be more striking than the contrast between the magnitude of the pecuniary bounty and the complete personal disregard of which he is the object." On the other hand, Victoria remained kind to the Dowager Queen, Adelaide, with whom there had always been a mutual rapport, and would retain various FitzClarence children, all of whom had at first feared losing such perquisites as the rangership of Windsor Park and the captaincy of the royal yacht.

As those who had supped at the royal trough came forward to plead for continued largesse, the Duchess announced, to the Queen's disgust, that despite Conroy's careful ministry of her funds and recent new borrowings from Leopold, she was £70,000 in debt. It appeared that there had been no records kept of Conroy's expenditures or borrowings on her behalf since 1829. Certain that Parliament would not bail her out, whatever their affection for her daughter, Melbourne arranged instead before the year was out to raise the Duchess's annual income so that she could pay her own debts from her Parliamentary grant. Well aware of her long flirtation with the Whigs, and excitable in temperament, Henry Brougham, a Conservative power in the House, opened fire on the proposal, inadvertently calling the Duchess the "Queen-Mother." Melbourne, who had endured enough of the Duchess's regal pretensions during William's reign, corrected Lord Brougham with "Not Queen-Mother—Mother of the Queen." The overly generous measure passed.

From her Privy Purse the Queen was already busy paying off her father's nearly forgotten debts, a task that would take until October 1839. (Each payee would also receive a gift of silver plate from Victoria.) She had renounced all the hereditary revenues of the Crown, except those of the duchies of Lancaster and Cornwall, in exchange for an annuity of £385,000 (£10,000 more than that of William IV). Only £60,000 went to her Privy Purse; almost all the rest was for salaries and expenses of maintaining the Royal Household in all its locations.

The Queen's first state visit to the City of London, on November 9, 1837, was in logistics almost a rehearsal for the coronation. The date was Lord Mayor's Day, and the autonomy of the City was formally recognized by her symbolic pause at Temple Bar, in the Strand, the City's western boundary. There she was greeted by the Lord Mayor, Sir John Cowan, and conducted to the venerable Guildhall to dine with the aldermen and other City dignitaries, all wearing their traditional regalia and symbols of office. Knighted by Victoria on the occasion was her old Ramsgate neighbor Moses Montefiore, who had been elected Sheriff of London and Middlesex that May. (At home in Park Lane, he had, since her accession, drunk to her health every day, fervently saying aloud as he lifted the yarmulka from his head with one hand and raised his glass of claret with the other, "God bless the Queen!") The knighting of a Jew met with some reluctance among her Ministers, but, Victoria wrote in her diary, "I was very glad I was the first to do what I think quite right, as it should be." Observant of his faith's dietary laws, Sir Moses arrived at the Guildhall wearing his robes of office and carrying his own kosher chicken.

The Times had reported that morning that no other women had been invited to the glittering banquet, which proved that it, too, did not yet know Victoria. In any event, Conservative papers and politicians, seeing the Queen only as Melbourne's pawn, hoped to find ways to get at the Whigs through her. "I think the general impression [of the Guildhall affair]," Disraeli wrote his sister hopefully, "is rather flat. There were few ladies; but the Lady Mayoress all agree is a very handsome woman." Among the other ladies was the Duchess, again denied Conroy's company on a grand occasion, and afterwards she complained, in a note partially in Conroy's hand, about proper precedence being ignored in her seating.

Not being seated at all in the gold State Coach rankled the Duchess even more. Victoria insisted on riding *alone,* savoring enthusiastic greetings from onlookers, among them young Charles Dickens and Hablôt Knight Browne, his illustrator, as "Phiz," of the *Pickwick Papers,* then making the twenty-five-year-old Dickens a household word. They sat at the windows of Coutts's counting house and toasted the Queen in claret as she went by.

The Strand still had narrow-fronted houses along it; Londoners hung bunting and green boughs from their roofs and windows, and crowds clustered on the cobbled pavements to cheer. All the houses, Lady Cowper reported, were "scaffolded," with citizens sitting on every platform,

"—and hardly a soldier anywhere; this is the sort of thing that is only seen in England. In France, Austria or Russia there would have been three rows of soldiers to hold back the people—here a few of the New [Metropolitan] Police and one regiment is all that is necessary. After all, it appears that the Reform Act and popular government are not such bad things." The government was not as popular as the Prime Minister's sister liked to believe; but the street clashes that had preceded the Reform Bill were over, and governments succeeded each other after wars of words and battles of ballots (however still limited the franchise), rather than in the violent fashion that had become common across the Channel.

Then came the State Opening of the new Parliament on November 20, at which Victoria, wearing a diamond tiara (even Disraeli thought she "looked admirably"), read a politically vague Speech from the Throne, composed by Melbourne to raise as few problems as possible, as his narrow majority had thinned even further. Only the impending coronation kept Parliament in wary harmony. It even voted £200,000 for the event, four times what had been appropriated for William IV. The royal crown had been carried into the chamber on a velvet cushion by the Duke of Somerset, as Victoria was not entitled to wear it before her coronation. But she could be queenly without a crown, especially when she spoke. From her first morning as Queen, people marveled at the crystalline clarity of her voice, which Sallie Stevenson, listening from the diplomats' gallery, described as "sweet as a Virginia nightingale's," lodging in the memory "like a spell after the sound has passed away. It is sweet, yet soft; powerful, yet melodious. . . ."

Paradoxically, Mrs. Stevenson told her sisters, the Queen's mouth was "her worst feature." Circlets of diamonds did wonders for her brown hair and blue eyes, but Victoria's mouth was "generally a little open; her teeth small and short, and she shows her gums when she laughs, which is rather disfiguring." The Queen's half-sister, Feodora, Mrs. Stevenson gossiped, had warned from Germany when she heard that the Queen had commissioned a portrait, "Do, Victoria, shut your mouth when you sit for your likeness!" But when the Duchess of Kent read her daughter's letter she reportedly said, "No, my dear; let it be as nature made it."

In the waning months of her first year as Queen, Victoria seemed in constant motion, enjoying her status, exhibiting her symbolic self to her people, spending her own money for the first time, and calling attention by her presence to whatever she confronted. Even her first, very modest, intervention in the visual arts aside from portrait commissions caused a flutter (and preceded that royal interest in pictures generally ascribed to the guidance of Prince Albert). At the spring exhibition of the Watercolor Society, Victoria noted in her journal, she bought pictures by Frederick Taylor, Samuel Prout, Peter De Wint, and Copley Fielding. "Lord Melbourne admired and looked at them with the eye of a connoisseur. Taylor's (a group of children and a woman, with fish) he liked. . . . Prout's he much admired. Copley Fielding's he also thought very good. It's a sea-piece, representing *a very rough sea.*" The young John Ruskin had been at the sale, writing to his father, "The Queen bought a Prout a Copley Fielding small sea piece—Taylor a Fish wife piece & another—the last I don't like & luckily the Queen was not Queen last year or my Taylor *Take me up* would have gone, for it is prettier than hers." The reputation of the four artists, he predicted, "shall . . . rise directly for no monarch has lately bought any water colour." His final line on the matter was in the nature of a tongue-in-cheek accolade: "She bo't three of the artists whose pictures I have."

Although Victoria's taste was little involved in the design of coins struck to mark her accession, final approval was still reserved for the Sovereign. The gold £5 piece, known as *Una and the Lion* in the design by William Wyon, and considered one of the finest sculpted coins ever issued, carries on the reverse a full-length portrait of the young Queen guiding a lion. The title, from Spenser's *Faerie Queene,* was a graceful compliment from the artist to a woman he was comparing with Una, Queen Truth, whose protector in the tale is Saint George, the dragon-slaying patron saint of England.

Invitations to the Abbey for June 28, "to make your personal attendance on Us . . . [at] the Solemnity of Our Royal Coronation" were signed by Victoria at the head and by the Earl Marshal, the Duke of Norfolk, at the foot, and dated May 9, 1838. Not only those who were invited came: for Coronation June, four hundred thousand visitors reportedly swelled London's million and a half. Greville described the crush memorably in his June 27 entry:

> There never was anything seen like the state of this town; it is as if the population had been on a sudden quintupled; the uproar, the confusion, the crowd, the noise, are indescribable. Horsemen, footmen, carriages squeezed, jammed, intermingled, the pavement blocked up with timbers, hammering and knocking, and falling frag-

ments stunning the ears and threatening the head; not a mob here and there, but the town all mob, thronging, bustling, gaping, and gazing at everything, at anything, or at nothing; the park one vast encampment, with banners floating on the tops of the tents, and still the roads are covered, the railroads loaded with arriving multitudes. From one end of the route of the Royal procession to the other, from the top of Piccadilly to Westminster Abbey, there is a vast line of scaffolding; the noise, the movement, the restlessness are incessant and universal; in short, it is very curious, but uncommonly tiresome, and the sooner it is over the better.

The procession, from Buckingham Palace via Hyde Park Corner, Piccadilly, St. James's Street, Pall Mall, Charing Cross, and Whitehall to Westminster Abbey, drew people to balconies and housetops. Windows were even lifted out of their frames to furnish more visibility, and streets and sidewalks were "paved with heads." Those alert to the preparations would have seen the Queen first go by a day earlier, on June 27 ("crowds in the streets and all *so* friendly," she wrote), in an open carriage, to try the thrones at the Abbey. Both proved to be too low.

The five-hour ordeal in the Abbey the next day was made more difficult by (in the Queen's words) "remarkably maladroit" clergymen who were seldom aware of what they were doing. Although the procession was not to begin until ten in the morning, Victoria did not sleep well. She was up at four, and out of bed at seven to gaze at the people already massing in Green Park. Dignitaries passing by were greeted effusively by the crowds, and even the staid possessors of seats in the Abbey applauded as the Duke of Wellington and his old Napoleonic rival, Marshal Nicholas-Jean Soult, entered. Lord Melbourne carried the "excessively heavy" Sword of State "like a butcher," Disraeli carped. It was only one of many objects in the antique ceremonial that seemed larger than life as they dwarfed the childlike figure of the Queen. The splendid robes, with their gold and silver thread, and the display of jewels, brightened the dim Abbey as they caught and reflected the lights of candles and made it all the more apparent to Victoria, if not to the congregation, that she had been under-rehearsed. "Pray tell me what I am to do," she pleaded on the dais to Lord John Thynne, the sub-Dean, about the bishops, "for they don't know."

Unexpectedly, she found the Orb put in her hand by the Bishop of Durham.

"What am I to do with it?" she whispered.

"Your Majesty is to carry it, if you please, in your hand."

"Am I? It is very heavy."

In the confusion, it had been handed to her by the wrong person, and when the Archbishop of Canterbury went to fetch it, the Orb was already trembling in her grasp. Suddenly she was also being dressed in a robe of cloth of gold, and offered the Sceptre, ruby ring, and Crown of State. The ring was too small for the fourth finger, having been fitted to the fifth, but the Archbishop of Canterbury screwed it on while Victoria winced in pain. As the crown went on her head, the peers and peeresses donned their coronets, to a crisscrossing of gleams that was a silent fireworks display, and guns boomed in the parks and at the Tower. Inside, trumpets and drums sounded, and crowds outside followed with "God Save the Queen."

To mark the increasing democratization of Britain, the Commons, for the first time, took part in the ceremony, cheering the Sovereign nine times. Yet it was largely a ritual of self-congratulation for an aristocracy that knew how to adapt in order to survive, a practical possibility in a nation where, as Lady Cowper wrote to Princess de Lieven, the Queen "has only to show herself to be adored. Our people are so fundamentally royalist!" It helped, too, when the Sovereign made gestures that touched her people, as she did when elderly Lord Rolle, an infirm eighty-two, stumbled in the procession of peers giving homage. As he made a second attempt at the steps to the throne, Victoria arose and descended to meet him. Frantic cheering burst from the audience at her sensitivity, although a joke inspired by the act suggested that historically the noble lord's family, on demand, had to *roll* before the sovereign.

There had been informalities in the ceremony that, fortunately for its dignity, the congregation did not see. Victoria took the oath to maintain "the Protestant reformed religion as it is established by law," and was anointed with holy oil, after which she retired to St. Edward's Chapel ("a small dark place immediately behind the Altar") to doff her Parliament robes for the grander garb of the crowning. Near the end, after the "Gloria in Excelsis" was sung, the Bishop of Bath and Wells, possibly because he turned over two pages of the Order of Service at once, sent Victoria back into the Confessor's Chapel, as if the service were concluded. The Queen found it, in Melbourne's description, which she quoted in her journal, "more *un*like a Chapel than anything he had ever seen; for what was *called* an *Altar* was covered with sandwiches, bottles of wine, etc." While they waited, puzzled, the Prime Minister drank a glass of the clergy's wine, "for he seemed completely tired." Then the Queen was recalled for the "Hallelujah Chorus," and the close.

Afterwards, Victoria drew a number of illustrations of herself at the coronation, none of them recording the mishaps and hitches in the ceremonies. One pictured her, wearing her circlet of diamonds, exhaustedly prone in prayer before the crowning. Another revealed a small figure from the back, draped in a huge mantle and weighted down with a huge crown. Her own perspective adds poignancy to the observation of Thomas Carlyle, one of the spectators. "Poor little Queen!" he wrote. "She is at an age at which a girl can hardly be trusted to choose a bonnet for herself; yet a task is laid upon her from which an archangel might shrink."

The final delay before Victoria, in purple velvet regalia and wearing the crown, entered the State Coach, was to have the ruby ring removed ("with great pain") from her swollen finger. Ice-water had to be sent for to bathe her hand. Then, at four-thirty, the procession began its way back to the palace, "the crowds if possible having increased." She would remember the day, she predicted, "as the *Proudest* of my life!" "Home at a little after six," she added, "really *not* feeling tired," which she proved by rushing off to her rooms to give Dash his bath.

After the state dinner Victoria confessed, finally, to being "a little tired on my feet," and Melbourne turned to her "with the tears in his eyes"—his eyes often welled with tears when he became sentimental—and told her, "And you did it beautifully—every part of it, with so much taste; it is a thing that you can't give a person advice upon; it must be left to a person." The judgment "from this kind impartial friend" gave her "great and real pleasure."

She remained in the dining room until 11:20, then went to "Mamma's balcony" to watch the fireworks still exploding over Green Park. It was the first reference to the Duchess that was more than an aside in one of the longest journal entries that survives. Those at the coronation who received the designation of "most dear Being"—her highest accolade —were Melbourne and "my dearly beloved angelic Lehzen, whose eyes I caught when on the Throne, and we exchanged smiles."

The laxity of coronation discipline among the clergy did not warm Victoria further toward the Established Church she had just sworn to uphold and defend, and neither her sympathies nor her theology ever remained close to Anglicanism, High Church or Low. No faith that preached exclusivity attracted her, as Lord Normanby, the Home Secretary, discovered when he accompanied the Queen to the Chapel Royal on a sultry Sunday after the coronation. They sat through a sermon attacking, without naming names, Peel and the Tories for allegedly sacrificing their consciences to political expediency in consenting to support Roman Catholic emancipation. Whatever happened to the Throne, the minister went on, the Church would endure. As they left, Normanby asked, "Did not your Majesty find it very hot?"

"Yes," said Victoria, "and the sermon was very hot too."

The Queen's freedom of action in 1838 revealed itself in personal decisions that were an index to her personality. She invited Lady Jersey —the Zenobia of Disraeli's *Endymion*—to dinner at Buckingham Palace, an occasion of enormous satisfaction to the Duchess's old enemy. She began rejecting advice from people she had once leaned upon, when their counsel was at variance with her ideas. Stockmar wrote Leopold that she had become "as passionate as a spoilt child." Leopold himself was discovering that his latest well-meant lessons were being responded to with tangential trivialities. Privately, Victoria noted that "dear Uncle is given to believe that he must rule the roast everywhere." The misspelling suggested how much the Queen had yet to learn, but she was accepting advice only from Melbourne and Lehzen, and the Baroness's was usually predicated on what she thought Victoria wanted. As a result, the Queen airily announced to Melbourne that she was not planning to marry at any time soon, and that her informal cousinly understanding with Prince Albert was of no legal or moral consequence. This was in part pique at the managerial Leopold, but more that she was enjoying all her perquisites, and had no interest in being diminished by a husband or disabled by a pregnancy. She preferred later and later hours, often not dining formally until one in the morning—the band had to wait until she was ready to move toward the supper table to strike up "God Save the Queen" —and not putting her knife and fork down until two.

"I hope that the Coronation will bring us some people to choose from," Lady Cowper had written Dorothea de Lieven, who earlier had observed that the Czarevitch—the future Alexander II—was expected in London for the coronation. "He is a very handsome boy. How dreadful it would be if the Queen were to fall in love with him! For actually he is the only man whom she could not possibly marry." In Coburg the news of Victoria's doubts and delays left Albert feeling compromised and embarrassed.

Late in 1838, and into 1839, Victoria varied her regular visits to the opera at Covent Garden, and to the theater, with a new interest that became a temporary passion. Isaac Van Amburg, a young American lion tamer, was the new sensation of London, first performing at Astley's Amphitheatre, at the foot of Westminster Bridge, and later at Drury Lane Theatre. Before 1838 had run its course there was a biography on sale, *The Life of Van Amburg, the Brute Tamer,* and his portrait by Edwin Landseer was exhibited in the Royal Academy. The Queen *had* to see the show, and did—six times—once it moved to Drury Lane. Enthralled by the spectacle of hungry lions and leopards obeying orders not to devour a lamb set before them, Victoria went to see the tall young man with "receding forehead and very peculiar eyes" after one performance, and was shown the "stick made of Rhinoceros hide" that was Van Amburg's only implement in his cages. Her obvious interest added to his popularity, which cut into the box-office receipts for traditional theater. With disgust, Dickens wrote to his actor friend William Macready, "I hold any society to be valuable which recognizes something of slight interest in the Drama shorn of Lions and Tigers."

Victoria's enthusiasm would have been understandable in an unsophisticated girl of nineteen, but became talked about disparagingly because that young girl was also Queen. "You might as well ask our young Queen," Elizabeth Barrett (later Browning) wrote a friend in April 1839, "to prefer Shakespeare to Mr. Van Amburg." It was something over which Melbourne had no control, but early in 1839 he had more acute problems than burnishing the serious side of the Queen's image.

When Charles Dickens wrote to T. J. Thompson that he had heard "on the Lord Chamberlain's authority" that the Queen "reads my books and is very fond of them," he had no way of knowing that this was as close to a view of the lower reaches of society as she would get under Melbourne's tutelage. On December 30, 1838, she recorded in her journal that she had read *Oliver Twist* and found it "excessively interesting." On New Year's Day 1839, she told Melbourne of her "getting on" in the novel, and of the accounts in it of "squalid vice," and of "starvation in the Workhouses and Schools." Her mother, she added, "admonished me for reading [such] light books," but Victoria suggested to Melbourne that he read it. "It's all among Workhouses, and Coffin Makers, and pickpockets," he said, apparently having heard much about it. "I don't like that low debasing style." She "defended *Oliver* very much," she noted on January 7, "but in vain."

It disturbed Melbourne little, if at all, that the England outside his social and political circle was one in which children under eighteen could be employed legally twelve hours a day, except for those under eleven, whose workday was limited by the law-abiding to nine hours; in which the cheapest popular entertainments were public executions (common until 1836), since their horror was considered a deterrent; in which transportation of convicts, like Dickens's Magwitch in his later *Great Expectations,* to bestial labor in chains, usually in Australia (a system that survived until 1853), was often considered by the condemned as worse than execution; in which jerry-built tenements along grimy alleys—a favorite target of Dickens—housed entire families, deemed human rubbish having little feeling or worth, in a single windowless room, and whose expenditure on food had to be limited to a penny ha'penny per person per day, enough for a few rotten potatoes. Since Divine Providence was responsible for such arrangements, the young Queen knew, she interested herself now and then in individual circumstances rather than in the general alleviation of misery, a condition that it was comforting to think represented God's will as much as did her own well-being. And if she had helped along her own privileged circumstances by force of will, why couldn't others less fortunate similarly add an iota to their lives?

Low behavior in high life was, for Melbourne, more attractive. Daniel Maclise had conducted a notorious affair with Henrietta, Lady Sykes, whose portrait he had painted. Lady Sykes, already Disraeli's mistress, was simultaneously involved with the much older Lord Lyndhurst, the Tory politician, but when Sir Francis Sykes surprised her in bed with a lover in 1837, it was Maclise he found between the sheets. Sykes sued for divorce the next year, and on February 3, 1839, Victoria—she was an indifferent speller—noted in her journal, "Talked of McLise having run away with Lady Sykes; Lord M. said 'They're a bad set; they're granddaughters of Elmore, the horse dealer; old Elmore traficked with his daughters much as he did with his horses.'" Clearly that was something amusing to Melbourne, while the matters raised in *Oliver Twist* were unworthy of his interest.

Little amelioration of the human condition emerged from Whitehall, but Victoria announced a bounty of £1 for each member of a triplet or quadruplet birth—perhaps the first foreshadowing of the British welfare state. (The entitlement survived until 1957.) The gesture suggests Melbourne rather than Victoria.

François Guizot, historian and French premier from 1840 to 1848, characterized Melbourne (after meeting him once) as "a certain mixture of *bonhomie* and of authority, of carelessness and responsibility which is most unusual." The result was a patchwork government surviving by expedients and compromise. Stockmar saw him as "perfectly disinterested, without nepotism, and without vanity," as he maintained the Queen's government and managed her involvement in it. But he also saw "a keen observer of the follies and vices of mankind, taking the world as he found it, and content to extract as much pleasure and diversion as he could from it." Something of that capriciousness which both continentals perceived led Melbourne to what Stockmar called the "two great errors in judgment" into which the Prime Minister was betrayed by his own interest in Victoria's "ease and happiness."

On February 10, 1839, Melbourne described to the Queen a Cabinet meeting so "stormy and unpleasant" as to suggest the disarray of the Whigs and his concern about "being much longer able to hold the Administration together." Only a week had passed since Victoria had noted in her journal that she had informed Melbourne of an "awkward business" concerning Lady Flora Hastings. The affair had arisen at an inopportune time, for he was distracted by what seemed the imminent dissolution of the Government. Victoria had been powerless to prevent the woman she considered Conroy's spy from living in the palace, as her mother had every right to appoint her own household. However, Lehzen had noticed, and Victoria's observation had confirmed, a bulge in Lady Flora's figure that left the Queen "no doubt"—she informed Melbourne —that the despised woman was "with child!"

The Queen's knowledge of the reproductive processes was sketchy, but she knew that impregnation required a man, and that Lady Flora, who was a maidenly twenty-nine, had some months earlier traveled overnight from Scotland in a post-chaise with no other companion than Conroy. Also, Melbourne himself had indiscreetly told Victoria that her mother —twenty years Lady Flora's elder—was jealous of the younger woman's closeness to Sir John. Even the Court physician, Sir James Clark, had been asked to survey, at a distance, Lady Flora's figure, and could not, the Queen excitedly informed Melbourne, "deny the suspicion." The "horrid cause of all this is the Monster and Demon Incarnate, whose name I forbear to mention. . . ."

At first Melbourne suggested quiet watchfulness, and there was watchfulness in great measure, as gossip from Victoria's side of the palace enlivened both households. Soon there were charges and countercharges, while Lady Flora's abdomen seemed to swell further, compelling her to issue a statement that she had been suffering from "bilious illnesses since the beginning of December." She even asked to be placed under the care of Sir James Clark, who gave her a perfunctory examination but was not permitted to look under her clothes. On February 16, her statement continued, he asked her if she were "privately married," as "no one could look at me and doubt it."

The honor of the Court, as well as that of Lady Flora, was at stake, as London society now seethed with rumors about her. Lord William Russell saw the imbroglio as arising from the Queen's "distrust of her mother's virtue" and a desire to emphasize a "superlative chastity" about her; but, he scoffed to his wife about the prudish Lady Flora, "Did the *St. Esprit* operate the miracle?" Forced to agree to the indignity of an examination without clothes, Lady Flora quickly called on Sir Charles Clarke, a doctor who had known her since childhood, and the two, in the presence of a lady of the Household and Lady Flora's maid, conducted their investigation on February 17, after which Sir James was accused of unprofessional indelicacy. Yet their statement cleared Lady Flora, attesting that "although there is an enlargement of the stomach, . . . there are no grounds for suspicion that pregnancy does exist, or ever has existed."

Greville blamed the "disgraceful and mischievous scandal" as much upon Melbourne's mishandling as on the Queen's "youth and inexperience." Melbourne, said Russell, was having "more difficulty to govern the Court than to govern the Nation. He very properly chose the most chaste Whig Ladies to place around our young virgin, but in seeking for chastity he forgot good sense, good feeling & other little virtues which adorn the same character." To her uncle, Hamilton Fitzgerald, who lived in Brussels, where English scandals quickly echoed, Lady Flora complained of the "diabolical conspiracy from which it has pleased God to preserve the Duchess of Kent and myself," engineered by *a certain foreign lady, whose hatred to the Duchess is no secret, [and] who pulled the strings.* The Queen's evil genius, it was clear, without naming names, was Lehzen. Fitzgerald returned to London to validate the story, and rushed off an article to *The Examiner,* after which the "Palace party" was so abused in the press that Victoria refused to read a newspaper.

Later she recalled that the affair occurred when "the old Baron" was away, permitting things "which God knows I did not dream of" to happen. The "terrible story" (in her description thirty years later) remained the scandal of the moment for discussion at fashionable dinners. Lady Flora continued under suspicion although proved to be an intact virgin, and Victoria was dismissed as an easily manipulated child. Agitated and embarrassed, the Queen tried to make her peace with her mother and with Lady Flora. Buffeted between the Duchess and the Queen, distraught and looking ill, Lady Flora came to Victoria's sitting room and declared that for the Duchess's sake, all would be forgotten. But Lady Flora's figure was still ballooning.

In the cynical world of politics, the humiliating Hastings affair was another weapon the Tories could use to discredit the faltering Whig government, which was finally brought down early in May when the sugar planters in Jamaica, backed by the Tories, refused to accept the measures abolishing slavery in 1834 and 1835. That a colonial measure would cause the fall of his Cabinet was not a surprise to Melbourne, who expected that almost any bill during the session of 1839 might be so used. But the Queen was unprepared, even though on April 26 Melbourne had warned her that the Jamaica issue would spark a confidence vote. After the division, at two in the morning on May 7, he wrote to her again, suggesting that he expected her to "meet this crisis with that firmness which belongs to your character, and with that rectitude and sincerity which will carry your Majesty through all difficulties. It will also be greatly painful to Lord Melbourne to quit the service of a Mistress who has treated him with such unvarying kindness and unlimited confidence. . . ."

A self-styled Whig born of a Whig father, Victoria had known no other Prime Minister at her side but Melbourne, who realized that she would find it difficult to face the necessity of a new Ministry. He had no idea how that firmness of character—which he had praised—would, after her first emotional response of "agony, grief and despair," turn the unwritten British constitution upside down. For a day, she was unable to control her emotions, weeping through every interview, able to eat nothing despite her well-remarked and hearty appetite. Finally, as she noted in her journal, she "wrote one line to the Duke of Wellington to request him to come. Till nine, I sobbed and cried convulsively . . . and went to bed calmer at 12."

The next morning Melbourne called, as he remained in office until his successor accepted the position. Having cautioned her, first, not to show "great dislikes" for her inevitable new Ministers, he added, more dangerously than he realized, that the Tory government would not "touch your ladies." A morning later, Wellington spent twenty minutes with Victoria, gently turning down her request that he replace Melbourne. He was too old and deaf, he told her; besides, he had no influence in the

Commons—"if he was to say black was white," the Queen quoted to Melbourne, "they would say it was not." He advised her to send for Sir Robert Peel, "who was a gentleman and a man of honour and integrity."

Peel arrived at two, "put out," Victoria told Melbourne, at being passed over in the consultations. They discussed the composition of the proposed new government, Peel agreeing that Wellington should be offered a major post. "One of the marks" of her confidence in any new government, the Queen added, was "my Household." The atmosphere of the interview was stiff and formal, Peel having had none of Melbourne's long and familiar access to Victoria. He was, in her journal, "such a cold, odd man [that] she can't make out what he means." On May 9, the next day, she wrote to Melbourne to warn him that something unexpected "*may* happen in a very few hours. Sir Robert has behaved very ill, and has insisted on my giving up my Ladies, to which I replied that I would never consent, and I never saw a man so frightened."

"Now, dear Peel," his friend Lady de Grey had cautioned him, "the first impression on so young a girl's mind is of immense consequence, accustomed as she has been to the open and affectionate manner of Lord M, who . . . treats her like a father, and, with all his faults, feels for her as such." Despite Peel's "noble character" she felt that he might fail to gain Victoria's confidence, "as I think your bearing [is] too reserved and too cautious." Part of that caution was a natural stiffness— he came from the newly rich factory-owner class and not from the relaxed wealth and easy status of landed aristocracy. Further caution came from his political dilemma. The Melbourne Ministry had fallen because it could not command its thin majority in the Commons; Peel had to form a minority government, which meant dealing in offices. He could not leave the Court populated with titled ladies whose husbands and fathers were his political opponents. Yet when Victoria taunted him, "Is Sir Robert so weak that even the Ladies must be of his opinion?" he could come up with no appropriate response except, deferentially, to take his leave.

That Melbourne's laxity should have permitted a Court so narrowly partisan in the first place was not Peel's fault. At Victoria's accession, as Greville explained it, "The Queen knew nobody, and was ready to take any Ladies that Melbourne recommended to her. He should have taken care that . . . her household should not have a political complexion, instead of making it exclusively Whig. . . ." Croker noted a constitutional matter —that the sovereign's minister had a right to deny an appointment in the case of someone in a statutory position whom he "might *know* to be perfectly unfit to be about the person of the Queen," and that this was a "great public principle."

Victoria saw her Ladies of the Household as personal, rather than political, attendants. Peel's political needs were interpreted as "trickery" and she would have none of it. He had quickly explained that he planned to change only the important and ceremonial posts, such as that of the Mistress of the Robes, but Victoria insisted that she would not part with *any* of her ladies. In particular, she would not part with her Mistress of the Robes, the graceful, statuesque Harriet, Duchess of Sutherland, "who moves like a goddess, and who looks like a queen," according to admiring courtiers. The Duchess had become far more than a mere representative of her husband's party in the Household. Although of an earlier generation than Victoria's, she had become the Queen's closest confidante. In headstrong fashion the Queen wrote to Melbourne that the interference in her Court "was an attempt to see whether she could be led and managed like a child." Her ladies, she insisted, "are *entirely* her own affair." By custom, however, they were not, and Court appointments reflected the power balance in Parliament. If the Queen recognized this, her refusal to permit tradition to take its course was only a pretext to force Peel to withdraw and Melbourne to fill the vacuum. If she did not have such designs, the political effect was the same.

As far as Victoria was concerned, Peel had been offered his legitimate due. "Sir Robert told the Queen," she informed Melbourne on the tenth, "[that] if the Ladies were not removed, his party would fall directly, and could not go on, and that he only awaited the Queen's decision." Her choice was to call for the return of Melbourne, who had mixed feelings about staying on, which, as Victoria realized, skirted the thin edge of constitutionality. "The Queen fears Lord Melbourne has much trouble in consequence of all this; but the Queen has fully prepared, and fully intended to give these people a fair trial. . . ." Was it a fair opportunity to form a government? Sixty years later, during a conversation with Sir Arthur Bigge (later Lord Stamfordham), her Private Secretary, she thought differently about Peel, whom she had later come to revere. "I was very young then, and perhaps I should act differently if it was all to be done again." But Peel had removed himself with a graceful letter expressing his hope that her Majesty's next government would be conducive to her "personal comfort and happiness, and to the promotion of the general welfare."

In the press and in Parliament there was indignation at Victoria's "caprice" in overturning "national institutions," and sharp comment that the only solution for her childish inexperience was a husband who could rein in her improprieties. None of it had any effect. Melbourne's unstable government was to hold together for two more years, and Victoria would continue to hold out against matrimony, irritated by letters from Stockmar about Albert's Grand Tour, designed to provide a patina of worldly knowledge to serve him as Consort. Victoria was acutely conscious that while Albert was going through his schoolboy exercises at Bonn, and gazing at ancient monuments in Rome, she was dismissing and recalling governments. Does Albert know, she asked Leopold in a message sent by special courier, "that there is *no agreement* between us? . . . I can make *no final promise this year,* for, at the *very earliest,* any such event could not take place till two or three years hence." Frankly, she gave her *"great* repugnance to change my present position" as her reason for the delay. Her candor appalled Leopold and Stockmar, and left Albert with the feeling that he had been left to twist slowly in the wind.

Victoria was seeing in herself signs of queenliness that, after the Household affair and the Lady Flora fiasco, were not so visible to eyes less loyal that those of Lehzen and Melbourne. The Flora Hastings embarrassment, at Lady Flora's initiative, had even made the pages of the *Morning Post,* where she rashly published her correspondence with Melbourne. The ventilating of the dispute, Victoria wrote that April, was "infamous" and "wicked"—and the Duchess's continued support of Lady Flora, she told Melbourne, made her an "enemy in the house." Only her mother's insistence that she would never leave her daughter while she was unmarried kept Victoria from dismissing entirely the idea of a husband. Sensing her increasing isolation, she reveled self-consciously in balls and dinners, dancing with abandon with the visiting Grand Duke Alexander of Russia, and in other visible ways showing the world beyond Buckingham Palace that she did not feel embattled.

One piece of news, at least, suggested to her that events at last were turning her way—and that she had accelerated their pace. When it became clear to Sir John Conroy that Melbourne was to remain in office, he asked for an interview early in June and announced to the Prime Minister that he was resigning his position with the Duchess of Kent and going to live in Italy. His situation had become more and more uncomfortable; even his visits to the Duchess on business were considered affronts by the Queen, who still refused to see him. On his Privy Purse income he could live very well on the Continent, where he would be an important foreigner rather than the object of gossip and bad jokes. Also, the Duchess was now shorn of glamour by increasing years and decreasing influence; and Lady Flora was dying.

The Queen at first refused to believe the sobering news about Flora Hastings. When the subject came up in a meeting with Melbourne on June 12, Victoria responded by asking the Prime Minister how he liked her hair in curls. Four days later—a Sunday—the Duchess stressed the seriousness of Lady Flora's condition. Her fever had not abated, and she could keep nothing in her stomach. Victoria told Lord Melbourne. "Then she'll die," he said, and commented disparagingly on Sir James Clark's failure to recognize serious disease when he saw it.

Since Lady Flora lived in the Duchess's apartments at the palace, the pall that fell over that wing permeated the Queen's own quarters, but as the dying woman's condition deteriorated, there was no visible change in the royal schedule until a ball that was to follow the day after a visit to the opera at Covent Garden on June 25 was abruptly canceled. (But not the visit to the opera.) People invited to the palace were relieved to escape the prospect of a grim gaiety; Victoria used the cancellation to suggest a visit to Lady Flora, but she was too sedated to see anyone. The next day, June 27, Victoria hurriedly left a meeting with Melbourne on word that Lady Flora was awake and able to see her. "I went in alone; I found poor Lady Flora stretched on a couch looking as thin as anybody can be who is still alive; literally a skeleton, but the body *very* much swollen like a person who is with child; a searching look in her eyes, a look rather like a person who is dying. . . ."

Lady Flora declared that she was comfortable, and was grateful for the care she had received. When Victoria suggested that she would visit again when Lady Flora was "better," the dying woman grasped her hand in a manner that was as if to say, Victoria wrote, "I shall not see you again."

When there was word, on June 29, that Lady Flora had rallied a little, Victoria went once more to the opera. Two days later it was clear that there was no hope, and Victoria gave way, in conversation with Melbourne, to feeling that it was "disagreeable and painful" to know that there was a dying person in the house.

In the first hours of July 5, that discomfort ceased for Victoria. Lady Flora had succumbed to cancer of the liver. "The poor thing," Victoria was told, "died without a struggle and only just raised her hands and gave one gasp." However quiet her end, that calm acceptance was not reflected in the Tory press. Signs of what the Lady Flora scandal and the Bedchamber imbroglio had done to the Queen's reputation had been clear weeks before, although the warning signals went unheeded. At the Sheldonian Theatre in Oxford, where Robert Southey, William Wordsworth, and Thomas Campbell were present for the awarding of honorary degrees, *Jackson's Oxford Journal* reported, "Before the procession entered, the younger members of the University indulged themselves in the license usually given on this occasion for the expression of their feelings. . . . We regretted to observe that when our Queen's name was given the cheering was very faint. . . . On the other hand, the Dowager Queen Adelaide was rapturously cheered; and the Duke of Wellington, Sir Robert Peel . . . and other Conservative names were loudly applauded."

"The *Morning Post,* ignoring the fact of mortal disease, took up Lady Flora's case as if she had been hounded to death. At Ascot, where Victoria went to the races accompanied by her Prime Minister, she was hissed by two women and called "Mrs. Melbourne." It was an act of obstinate imprudence to go to Ascot immediately after Lady Flora's well-publicized death, but Victoria's private reaction to Melbourne was that she wished the two women could be flogged. She saw no reason for remorse, she insisted: "I felt *I* had done nothing to kill her."

Diplomatically, Melbourne urged that the Queen send a carriage with her representatives to the funeral. She did, despite fears of a demonstration. The innocent but worried occupants were neither hissed nor stoned.

Further amends were in order, and Victoria sent fifty pounds to Lady Flora's maid. The Hastings family directed that the money be returned. Lady Flora's brother even tried to challenge Melbourne to a duel on grounds of insult to old Lady Hastings. Rectifying slightly her other major blunder, Victoria used the retirement of one of the ladies of her Household to appoint the wife of a friendly Tory peer, Lady Sandwich, to the Bedchamber, ending its Whig exclusivity, although not Tory ire over the affair that had cost them the government. There was even difficulty over the Royal Marriages Act, as the elderly Duke of Sussex, whom she liked, had illegally married a wealthy widow, Lady Cecelia Buggin, who wanted to be recognized as a duchess and as a member of the Royal Family. Cross about many things, Victoria told Melbourne that if she were a private person she would leave England, as she was "so disgusted at the perpetual opposition." She was tired of everything—even "tired of riding."

"Tired of riding?" Melbourne asked in disbelief. Riding had become the Queen's chief pleasure, even more than the opera, dancing, or food. To her "horror," Victoria now weighed eight stone thirteen (125 pounds): "an incredible weight for my size." She had already demonstrated a tendency to plumpness that no number of hours on horseback could counteract, and brought her problems to Melbourne, who discouraged Spartan efforts for which she had insufficient self-discipline. Hanoverians had a tendency to heaviness, he told her; besides, the best figure for a woman was "full with a fine bust." She had tried forgoing luncheon, limiting her consumption of beer, and reducing her dinner intake, but nothing had helped, and her Parisian dresses had to be ordered from embarrassingly larger measurements. She began to dislike dressing, and even getting up in the morning, possibly as much to avoid new (or continuing) problems as to postpone seeing herself in the mirror.

Depression was not easily shaken off. Bathing was put off as late as possible in the day, often until bedtime. She disliked her hair, which was turning darker, and she even found brushing her teeth a struggle. Wellington quoted to her Mrs. Sheridan's injunction to her daughters: "Fear God. Honour the King. Obey your Parents. Brush your Teeth." When she found walking inferior as exercise because she got stones in her shoes, his advice was "Have them made tighter."

Being on a horse was still her greatest pleasure. She thought she looked her best in riding clothes, especially when mounted on Comus, the white horse on which she was painted by Landseer. Riding was also vigorous, placed her in public view, and helped her to throw off anxieties. When in London she rode in the large suburban spaces, accompanied by Melbourne, another Minister, or members of the Household. It was the Queen's custom, Lady Cowper once wrote to Princess de Lieven, "to cross the town by going up Regent Street and Portland Place as far as Hampstead, where she gallops and canters to her heart's content." Sometimes, Lady Cowper added in another letter, Victoria "remains three hours in the saddle, and goes as far as Richmond Park." It was better than shouting at her maids—she had already dismissed one of her dressers, and was making do with only two.

Minor ailments accompanied her disenchantment with Court life and queenly responsibilities. Symptoms of emotional stress included a series of sick headaches, a rash, a sallow complexion, bouts of nausea, and a general listlessness that caused her to write in her journal honestly about some days as "Dawdled." The result was a renewal of pressure to marry.

The Duke of Cambridge and his wife were particularly unsubtle in putting forward the claims of their son George, whose bad complexion was being hidden by whiskers. Even Victoria's mother seemed part of the conspiracy; but when she pressed for an invitation to Windsor for Prince George, Melbourne advised against it. When the Duchess of Cambridge (the former Princess Augusta of Hesse-Cassel) next caught sight of Melbourne in a Windsor corridor, she exclaimed, in the Queen's hearing, *"Da geht mein grösster Feind"*—There goes my greatest enemy. "Infamous woman," Victoria told her journal.

On August 6, 1839, Victoria discussed with Melbourne the forthcoming visit of her Coburg uncles, and possibly of Ernest and Albert, speculation about which had already been published in London papers. To Leopold on August 26 she tried to put the visit off. "I do not *feel* well," she wrote him; "I feel *thoroughly* exhausted from all I have gone through this [Parliamentary] Session. . . ." Still, she expected the uncles, and at the end of August they arrived: the penurious Prince Ferdinand of Saxe-Coburg-Kohary and the difficult Duke Ernest of Saxe-Coburg Gotha, father of Ernest and Albert. On September 6 a third uncle arrived, Leopold of Belgium, with Queen Louise. Despite many misgivings, Victoria agreed to dates in October for another inspection of the Coburg princes.

The visit of Ernest and Albert began inauspiciously. On the evening of October 10 they arrived at Windsor, after a rough Channel crossing, without their baggage, which had gone astray. "Having no clothes," Victoria wrote Leopold on October 12, "they could not appear at dinner, but nevertheless *débutéd* after dinner in their *négligé*. Ernest is grown quite handsome; Albert's *beauty* is *most striking*, and he is so amiable and unaffected—in short, very *fascinating;* he is excessively admired here. . . . We rode out yesterday and danced after dinner. The young men are very amiable, delightful companions, and I am very happy to have them here; they are playing some [four-hand piano arrangements of] Haydn Symphonies *under* me at this very moment; they are passionately fond of music." The cautious language could not have been misunderstood by Leopold, who waited impatiently for the next message. Victoria had fallen in love.

Had Leopold been privy to the Queen's journal, he would have had his hopes confirmed. "It was with some emotion that I beheld Albert—who is *beautiful,"* she wrote. Suddenly, attractive father figures had lost their appeal. "Albert," she further confided to her journal, "really is quite charming, and so excessively handsome, such beautiful blue eyes, an exquisite nose, and such pretty mouth with delicate mustachios and slight but very slight whiskers; a beautiful figure, broad in the shoulders and a fine waist; my heart is quite *going*. . . ." On October 14 the Queen told Melbourne that she had changed her mind about marrying, and Melbourne wrote Lord John Russell, "I do not know that anything better could be done. He seems a very agreeable young man, he is certainly a very good looking one, and as to character, that, we must always take our chance of. . . ." The same day she let Albert know through a message from Lehzen to his equerry, Baron von Alvensleben, that a personal declaration from the Queen was forthcoming. That evening, when saying good night, the Prince, forbidden by etiquette even to dance valses with Victoria, because he would have had to hold her waist, and forbidden as well to speak his mind before spoken to, reacted by pressing her hand in more than perfunctory fashion. It was the only body language available.

Soon after noon the next day, Victoria summoned Albert to a private audience. "I said to him," she wrote, "that I thought he must be aware *why* I wished them to come here, and that it would make me *too happy* if he would consent to what I wished (to marry me); we embraced each other over and over again, and he was *so* kind, *so* affectionate; Oh! to *feel* I was, and am, loved by such an *Angel* as Albert was *too great a delight to describe!* he is *perfection;* perfection in every way—in beauty—in everything! I told him I was quite unworthy of him and kissed his dear hand—he said he would be very happy *'das Leben mit dir zu zubringen'* and was so kind and seemed so happy, that I really felt it was the happiest brightest moment of my life, which made up for all I had suffered and endured. Oh! *how* I adore and love him, I cannot say!! *how* I will strive to make him feel as little as possible the great sacrifice he has made; I told him it was a great sacrifice,—which he wouldn't allow. . . ."

It was no sacrifice, Albert knew, to permit himself to be extricated from the claustrophobic court of Coburg, where he was a superfluous son, as his brother Ernest was heir to the humble principality of three hundred thousand people to the north of Bamberg and Bayreuth. The flesh market of marriageable princelings and princesses was a product of both scarcity and surplus in the forty-odd states of fragmented Germany. With all European nations (but for Switzerland) still monarchies, the principalities east of the Rhine were a shopping mart for spouses, even when the available Highnesses were Serene rather than Royal. For England the Hanover connection had meant special ties to German ruling families, but the key attraction was that most ministates could guarantee a Protestant marriage partner. Prince Francis Charles Augustus Albert Emmanuel of Saxe-Coburg Gotha had little choice but to make a good marriage or to go into someone's army. There was no prospect of money; his father was known for sexual and financial profligacy, and had abandoned the wife he had married when she was sixteen (and he was thirty-three) after she had borne him two sons. Albert was four. He never saw his mother again.

With her husband flagrantly unfaithful, Louise had turned for consolation to a young army officer, Lieutenant Alexander von Hanstein. She left Coburg with him in 1824, and became Countess von Polzig when she married him after the Duke had divorced her and remarried. Louise died of cancer in 1831, when she was thirty. Only in 1921 did an allegation appear, in an anti-Semitic tract published in Berlin, that Albert may have been fathered by someone other than Duke Ernest—not the romantic lieutenant, but the Jewish court chamberlain, Baron von Meyern. The following year Lytton Strachey seized the baseless calumny, suggesting bitchily that the young Duchess followed her husband's scandalous example, and that the Jewish court chamberlain had been "talked of." The Duke had indeed charged his wife with infidelity long before her flight from Coburg with Hanstein, even naming the guilty party as a Count Solms, but the Duke was only deflecting more serious allegations about his own morals.

Albert had realized when he came to England to be looked over for a second time that the experience was demeaning, yet desperately necessary. He knew that he was handsome and purchasable. He did not know that Victoria's fascination with male beauty was such that for years she had noted exceptional faces and figures of men at Court in her journal, and candidly discussed attractive courtiers with her ladies. As for herself, she knew that when one peeled away Court flattery, her feminine charms were less than overwhelming. Albert was not unaware of that, but she was Queen, and seen through that lens there was a special radiance to her petite person. If a match could not be arranged, he would have to withdraw rather than accept vague postponements. As he wrote to a student friend from his days at Bonn, Prince William of Löwenstein, if negotiations dragged on and then fell through, "he would be known to have failed." Other marriageable princesses would look elsewhere, and he would be left "an object of ridicule." Now he had been offered the career for which he had been groomed. "I think I shall be *very* happy," he wrote Prince William.

"My feelings are a *little* changed, I must say, since last Spring," Victoria wrote King Leopold, who returned a letter advising her, *"If you love him, and are kind to him,* he will easily bear the burden of the position."

It would be a burden; the career of consort to a reigning queen at any time or place had seldom, if ever, been a source of satisfaction. For the next few weeks, however, as Ernest and Albert lingered on at Windsor at Victoria's request, the couple were in a state of complete bliss. Alone, they kissed "again and again," and Albert called her *"vortrefflichste"*—superb one. Still, Albert was uneasy in England. He was uncomfortable with the language, the climate, the food, the prospect of alienation, the likely frustrations of his occupation. To Stockmar he wrote that the announcement was to be withheld until Parliament met in mid-November. What particularly grieved him, he confided, was that Victoria's mother—his own aunt—"is not to know of it. But as everyone says, she cannot keep her mouth shut and might even make bad use of the secret if it were entrusted to her."

The fleeting days before the public notice of the engagement were spent in work and play. Between kisses in the Queen's blue sitting room one day, Victoria signed a sheaf of papers and warrants, with Albert at her side, "and he was so kind as to dry them with blotting paper for me." It would be symbolic of his official role. Consultations on wedding precedents and Albert's future establishment were made, and a date fixed—February 10, 1840. With much to do before the ceremonies to wind up his affairs in Germany, Albert left England with his brother on November 14, traveling via Belgium, and Leopold's residence, but not before Victoria called in the Duchess, telling her on November 10 of the betrothal. She wept with happiness, and seemed well satisfied; the next day, however, she began urging upon Albert appointments of her friends, and declaring that she would live with the couple after their marriage—"which we agreed *never* to do," Victoria noted. For days thereafter the Duchess grumbled and wept about the imminent separation from her daughter, who offered no consolation. Instead, Victoria consulted with Melbourne to confirm his support, as the matter was certain to make the newspapers. Of more concern to her was her sudden physical loneliness. She wrote letter after letter to Albert, partly in English, partly in German, the first when his carriage had hardly cleared the gates of Windsor.

The formalities in England were her next business. On November 18 she invited the Cambridges—including Prince George—to give them the still-confidential news. Her cousin, she told Melbourne, was "evidently happy to be *clear* of me." Melbourne's sister, Lady Cowper—to be married to Palmerston in a month, which amused Victoria, since the elderly lovers were in their fifties—had also been to Windsor, even before Albert had left. Not told of the engagement, Lady Cowper had easily guessed as much. "Nothing openly stated," she wrote to Dorothea de Lieven, but "with a good figure and well built," Albert had "everything which is likely to engage a young girl's affections." Marriage, Lady Cowper assumed, would come "sooner or later, and I do not think she could find anyone more suitable. They say that he is as sensible as his uncle [Leopold] and has great learning."

The Privy Council met at two in the afternoon on November 23. When the folding doors were swung open, the Queen entered alone, wearing a simple morning gown. Her only jewelry was a bracelet containing Albert's picture in profile—a miniature by Sir William Charles Ross. "I had to read the Declaration," Victoria wrote Albert. *"It was rather an awful moment, to be obliged to announce this to so many people, many of whom were quite strangers."* Greville, as Clerk of the Council, saw her hand tremble as she held the folded sheet with the statement composed by Melbourne, but, Croker wrote to Lady Hardwicke, "I cannot describe to you with what a mixture of self-possession and feminine delicacy she read the paper. Her voice, which is naturally beautiful, was clear and untroubled; and her eye was bright and calm, neither bold nor downcast, but firm and soft." The next steps were Stockmar's arrival as Albert's agent, and the fixing of Albert's position. The public was delighted with the betrothal, but Parliament was already less than enthusiastic about providing a purse for another penniless German prince, especially in the midst of political agitation that in some areas had reached the stage of mob violence. Poorly paid, and unemployed, industrial laborers not enfranchised by the new Reform Bill had swelled the ranks of Chartists seeking a modern Magna Charta of extended rights. Albert had nothing to do with riots from that quarter, but religious uproar about his allegedly suspect Protestantism had added to Parliamentary concerns about public unrest.

Melbourne's natural caution led to a vaguer betrothal announcement than Victoria wanted. She immediately pressed for recognition of Albert as "King Consort," using the precedent of Albert's cousin Ferdinand in Portugal. Melbourne told her that England was not Portugal. But while he understood what was unacceptable to the nation on that score, in his search for elegant phrasing he had ignored the political necessity to declare Albert a Protestant prince. Rumors immediately flew that he was a Papist, or at least had Roman Catholic leanings. (Coburg had Catholic Bavaria as neighbor.)

Whether on religious or national grounds, the undercurrent of hostility towards another imported sovereign or consort was real. England had endured five Hanoverian kings and their German brides. It had not forgotten Leopold, the Coburger husband of a Princess of Wales who did not survive to reign. That consort, although remarried (to a Catholic!) and now king of another country, was still collecting a Parliamentary pension. One could understand why a malicious broadsheet declared of Albert, the Coburger's Coburg nephew,

> *He comes the bridegroom of Victoria's choice,*
> *The nominee of Lehzen's vulgar voice;*
> *He comes to take "for better or worse"*
> *England's fat Queen and England's fatter purse.*

Albert's annuity was fixed at £30,000, little more than half that voted Leopold. (When one added to Albert's proposed grant what Leopold still retained from his—a matter that rankled many in Parliament—the sum approached the customary £50,000.) Melbourne, unable to carry his party with him, lost the annuity motion by 104 votes. Even more embarrassing was that a bill to grant Albert naturalization failed until it was amended to remove life precedence for him above Princes of the Royal Blood, for Cambridge and Cumberland had objected. In effect, even Victoria and Albert's hypothetical sons would have precedence over their father, but after Greville did some research he reported to Melbourne that the Queen, through Letters Patent, could remove much of Parliament's meanness.

Lord Shaftesbury recalled nearly forty years later being told by Melbourne that the Queen was eager to have Albert made, by Parliament, King Consort upon his marriage. Cautiously evading a direct answer, he was very pressed for one, and determined that it was his duty to be "very plain" about it. "For God's sake," he said, "let's hear no more of it, ma'am; for if you once get the English people in the way of making kings, you will get them into the way of unmaking them." To Victoria's further indignation, Albert was to receive no title whatever. "Everything will be very easily arranged," she had promised him on November 21. Instead, since Parliament was determined that Albert should play no political role, he was also to have no rank in the army, and no English peerage. "It needs but the stroke of your pen to make me a peer and to give me an English name," Albert had written from Wiesbaden en route home. He had no idea what an unpopular and even illegal act that would have been. From status-conscious Vienna, Prince Metternich would scoff that one could no more make a man royal who was not so than make him eight feet tall. Victoria was furious at the outcry. Parliament was not merely legislating, mean-spiritedly, the lives of two twenty-year-olds about to be married; it was attempting to diminish the powers of the Sovereign. She blamed the "abominable infamous Tories," especially "this wicked old foolish Duke [of Wellington]." They were "ill-using" Albert, she screamed into her journal. "Monsters! You Tories shall be punished. Revenge! Revenge!" Was Albert, she asked Melbourne, worth less than Queen Anne's consort, "stupid old George of Denmark"?

The votes against comparable arrangements for Albert were actually less a rebuff to Victoria than to the weak Melbourne Ministry that she had, through her own willfulness, kept too long. Albert was paying the price. It did not augur well that his only legal position in England was to be that of a minor foreign princeling who happened to be the Queen's husband. He could continue to wield the blotting paper. The functions for which he was imported from Coburg would have to be performed in bed.

VI

Royal Husband

(1840-1843)

Having gone to England to settle his future occupation, Albert found himself in love with his employer. He also found himself trapped in unexpected ways. "My future lot is high and brilliant," he wrote to Löwenstein, "but also plentifully strewn with thorns." That seemed realistic; nevertheless, he expected to be more than a husband. "While I shall be untiring in my efforts to labour for the country to which I shall in future belong, and where I am called to so high a position," he added, "I shall never cease to be a true German, and true Coburg and Gotha man." Before he had any opportunity to put that idealism into practice, he was taxed by the English for his German origins. They had endured enough of imported Germans who took their lands and money, and seemed glad that Salic Law had separated them from Hanover and, they hoped, from the Duke of Cumberland, now its king. Albert of Saxe-Coburg Gotha gave Londoners a chance to sing in the streets, in a mock-German accent, a ballad that purported to be Victoria's marriage song:

> So let 'em say, whate'er they may,
> Or do whate'er thay can;
> Prince Hallbert he vill always be
> My own dear Fancy Man.

At the moment the song was accurate; what Victoria saw in Albert was his charm and attractiveness. She already enjoyed being Queen. What she thought she wanted was simply a consort; her Ministers, who knew England and the English, would handle the business of government. Thus, when she wrote to him early in December, mentioning that at Windsor she had knighted the mayor of Newport, Thomas Phillips, for his coolness in facing a Chartist riot—Melbourne thought it would set a good law-and-order example—she added, "I am plaguing you already with tiresome politics." Politics was *not* to be Albert's province.

What the Prince's formal occupation was to be remained uncertain. He had hoped to bring with him a corps of public-spirited advisers who would help him carve out a sphere of usefulness—perhaps in patronage of art, music, literature, and science—but the funds for that staff ("German Sassages fresh imported from Saxe Humbug" to the man in the street) had already been stripped by Parliament. Further, Victoria had written to him, explaining why a peerage was out of the question—it would entitle him to a seat in the House of Lords—that *"the English are very jealous of any foreigner interfering in the government of this country, and have already in some of the papers . . . expressed a hope that you would not interfere. Now, though I know you never would, still, if you were a Peer, they would all say, the Prince meant to play a political part.* I am certain you will understand this." Those, Victoria added, were the *friendly* newspapers—as would have been obvious to Albert had he seen those indices to English opinion, the satiric cartoon-and-caption Twelfth Night character cards sold at Christmas by street vendors and in shops. One asked, "Why is Prince Albert liable to a military flogging from Victoria?" The blunt answer: "Because he's subject to her."

What little potential authority that had been left for Albert also was taken away. He was not even permitted to name his own private secretary. George Anson, private secretary to Melbourne, was seconded to the Prince. His resentment would be so marked in that case—imposing upon

him as his most confidential servant the Prime Minister's lieutenant—
that he managed to have Anson detached entirely from Melbourne's
employ as the price of acceptance. Albert would not be sorry. Anson
would be a shrewd and devoted adjutant. But even this negotiation, largely
left to Lehzen, let the Queen's husband-to-be know where he fit in the
power structure. *"No one could feel more for you in the very trying position
you will be placed in than I do,"* Victoria insisted, even as she blocked
every independent move he wanted to make. Albert was to be permitted
only personal attendants, which meant a demotion for his secretary, Dr.
Schenck, who had to serve under Anson, as would Dr. Emil Praetorius,
Albert's librarian. He would also have his loyal *Stallmeister*, Wilhelm
Meyer, to look after his horses, and a valet and dresser. Otherwise his
entire establishment was chosen by the Queen and Melbourne.

Albert left Gotha in a melancholy mood on January 28, 1840. His
grandmother, the Dowager Duchess of Coburg, screamed and cried as he
entered his carriage. There was a hard frost; the fields and forests were
covered with snow and a bitter northeast wind was blowing. He was going
to a country of fog and rain and smoky cities, where he knew he was not
welcome.

The Queen had opened Parliament with the traditional speech,
rendered devoid of content by Melbourne, who wanted nothing controversial in it. Before long, however, the Duke of Wellington had raised the
matter of Albert's Protestantism, and insisted on an amendment to legislation authorizing Albert's income in which the word *Protestant* appeared
—"a sop to the silly," Greville called it. The Queen had even been
attacked for going in person to Parliament, as her aunt Elizabeth, Landgravine of Hesse-Homburg, and a daughter of George III, had died. With
a show of mourning on a grand scale the custom—it had not come in with
Victoria but more likely with John Wesley—she was concerned that there
might be Evangelical agitation to postpone the wedding. On the premise
that the duties of one's station supersede everything else, Victoria made
her speech. Further, she arranged to have mourning "taken off" the day
of the wedding and "for two or three days after," then resumed to run
its course.

As the bridegroom traveled to Brussels (and Leopold) en route to
London, Victoria continued what must have seemed to Albert (as he read
letters posted to him in Belgium) a campaign to downgrade his dignity
as well as his duties. Even the Royal Arms for his seal were quartered
above his own, as if he were a woman; and his suggestions for a post-

wedding idyll were reduced by Victoria to a carriage ride from London to Windsor. *"You forget, my dearest Love,"* she admonished, *"that I am the sovereign, and that business can stop and wait for nothing. Parliament is sitting, and something occurs almost every day, for which I may be required, and it is quite impossible for me to be absent from London; therefore two or three days is already a long time to be absent."*

As Albert's emissary, Stockmar was already in London. To Leopold he reported, "The ultra-Tories are filled with prejudices against the Prince, in which I can clearly trace the influence of Ernest Augustus of Hanover. They give out that he is a Radical and an infidel, and say that George of Cambridge, or a Prince of Orange, ought to have been the Consort of the Queen." But Stockmar found that "the mere determination of the Queen to marry, and the satisfaction thereby given to what was a very universal desire (for the idea that the King of Hanover and his line might succeed to the throne was very distasteful to the people) has raised the Queen's popularity, and will for a while lend some strength to a very weak ministry. The public is tolerably indifferent as to the person of the bridegroom; but I hear it generally complained that he is too young." On the wedding day itself, *The Times* was to editorialize sourly, "If the thing were not finally settled, one might, without being unreasonable, express the wish that the consort selected for a Princess so educated and hitherto so unfairly guided, as Queen Victoria, should have been a person of riper years, and likely to form more sound and circumspect opinions. . . ."

Because Victoria and Albert were so young, and the Queen's mother so ill-equipped to be of any use, Leopold attempted, as the wedding day drew close and Albert was expected in England, to offer heartfelt advice about how the Queen would have to control her quick temper and never let any misunderstanding with Albert persist into the next day, thus adding new problems to the old. When Albert arrived in Brussels, Leopold further warned, "He was rather exasperated about various things, and pretty full of grievances. . . . You will best treat these questions. . . . Albert is quick, not obstinate. . . ."

Talking about Albert with her Prime Minister as the wedding day approached, Victoria responded to all she had heard about the bridegroom's youth and inexperience by announcing that she could never marry a man who had loved another woman. Melbourne scoffed that one affair before marriage was nothing, and should be permitted to any man. Then Victoria confided that one thing about Albert that pleased her most was that he paid no attention to other women. According to the Earl of Clarendon, to whom Melbourne related the incident, he shrugged the comment off in Regency fashion with a "No, that sort of thing is apt to come later," and the Queen answered angrily, "I shan't forgive you that!" Victoria would have nothing to worry about, whether because such behavior was not in Albert's nature or because he had observed enough of his father's habits to find promiscuity repellent.

When at last they met again, Victoria's romantic memories were confirmed. Albert was trim and handsome, not very tall in fact (at five feet seven inches), but statuesque beside her own diminutive figure. His slight sidewhiskers and mustache, and longish blond hair, were in the contemporary Continental fashion, and he could wear a uniform with regal dignity. Reunion awakened a wave of passion that Victoria admitted "put me at rest about everything." Large, friendly crowds had lined his route from the Dover docks to Buckingham Palace, where he arrived late on the afternoon of February 8. There the Lord Chancellor administered the oath of naturalization to a prince who was visibly uneasy, it seemed, at giving up his birthright, but his bearing may have been affected by the nightmare of seasickness that had left him helpless during the voyage. When he settled down for the night and the next day at the palace, the impropriety in prenuptial etiquette scandalized the Duchess and even surprised Melbourne. The Queen dismissed such concerns as "nonsense."

On the morning of the tenth, Victoria's confidence surfaced in a note she sent to Albert's bedroom regretting the rain but predicting that it would cease in time for the wedding. "Send one word when you, my most dearly beloved bridegroom, will be ready," she added romantically. Albert's last note was to his grandmother in Coburg, asking her blessing, which would be his "safeguard" and "future joy." Not a particularly pious person, he ended nevertheless with a fervent "May God help me!"

The ceremony took place in the Chapel Royal at St. James's Palace, with an almost total absence of Tories—Greville counted five out of three hundred guests. One Tory, however, was the Duke of Wellington, whom the Queen had invited only after pleading from Melbourne. According to Florence Nightingale, only a sightseer outside (her family despised Albert as a penniless fortune hunter), the Prince's clothes looked "borrowed to be married in." According to gossip recorded by the malicious Miss Nightingale, Lord Melbourne had pressed the Queen to invite more, she claimed, but Victoria had said, "It is MY marriage and I will have only those who sympathize with me." John James Ruskin, a prosperous Tory wine merchant (and father of the critic), thought that the social level of the wedding guests was low because the Queen was "wholly abandoned . . . by all the high families. . . . We are a King & Queen loving people but they must keep up their own dignity & keep the higher classes around them—else we may grow tired of paying for pomp. The Queen is but a silly child & seems to have no character." To him, Albert augured badly. "I wish the Boy may grow into something better. It is a poor prospect for the Country."

To Albert it made no difference whether the dignitaries in the Chapel were Whig or Tory. He knew only his aunt—the Duchess of Kent —and his father and brother, both dressed in green Coburg military uniforms. (Albert was in a British field marshal's uniform, without insignia, since he had no rank, but with the Ribbon of the Garter across his breast.) For political reasons as well as domestic religious ones, Leopold did not attend. The Duke of Sussex, her uncle, gave the bride away.

Victoria had driven from Buckingham Palace separately, with her mother, and entered in a white satin dress trimmed with lace and jeweled with a royal diamond necklace and a sapphire brooch that had been Albert's wedding present. In the procession herself, Sarah, Lady Lyttleton, saw Victoria's eyes "much swoln with tears, but great happiness in her face." Victoria recorded little of the event, but called it "imposing, fine and simple. . . . I felt so happy when the ring was put on. . . ." Since Albert had no property, Sallie Stevenson wrote to a niece in Virginia, "the only comic part of the whole affair was when the poor German prince 'endowed her with all his worldly goods.' "

The ceremony had technically altered Victoria's family name to Wettin, but historical practice authorized a reigning queen to retain her family name rather than adopt that of her husband—a tradition followed by Elizabeth II. During the 1914–1918 war, however, the wave of hostility in Britain to all things German would lead the Royal Family to change its name legally—after which William II, the Kaiser and Victoria's grandson, was reported to have said that he was going to the theater to see *The Merry Wives of Saxe-Coburg Gotha.*

At the close of the ceremony, Victoria kissed her aunt, Dowager Queen Adelaide, but only shook hands with her mother. Then the couple went alone in the rain to Buckingham Palace, where they had half an hour alone, to change clothes. Victoria put on a silk gown and a deep bonnet —a bonnet, whatever external fashion, would become her symbolic garb. Since a bridegroom's ring was not included in the wedding, Victoria gave

Albert his ring while they sat together on a sofa, and he told her solemnly that there must never be a secret that they did not share. (Much later Victoria added marginally to her journal, "There never was.")

At two-thirty they joined the guests for a wedding breakfast, then left at four for Windsor, in "one of the old travelling coaches," Greville complained, "the postillions in undress liveries, in a very poor and shabby style." Three other coaches from the palace followed as escort, and well-wishers on horseback and in a motley assortment of carriages and gigs galloped beside them, scattering happy throngs in the road all the way to Windsor.

To his friend John Forster, Charles Dickens parodied Robert Burns about the wedding journey,

> *My heart is at Windsor,*
> *My heart isn't here;*
> *My heart is at Windsor,*
> *A following my dear.*

At Windsor, the Queen recalled, she ordered dinner to be brought to their suite, but had "such a sick headache" that she could eat nothing. The lusty cheering all the way had left her "quite deaf." Albert took her in his arms and caressed her. She spent the evening on the sofa, with Albert on a footstool by her side, "and his excessive love and affection gave me feelings of heavenly love and happiness I could never have *hoped* to have felt before. He clasped me in his arms, and we kissed each other again and again. His beauty, his sweetness and gentleness—really how can I ever be thankful enough to have such a *Husband!* . . . to be called by names of tenderness, I have never yet heard used to me before—was bliss beyond belief!"

A London cartoonist, in a broadside sold on the streets, showed the newly wed couple "Counting the Chickens" at their dining table. "I have decidedly made up my mind, Al," says Victoria, "to have our first Boy named after my much respected Uncle Leopold, the next in honour of my Uncle Cambridge, Adolphus Frederick; then we must have one [named] Augustus Fred for Uncle Sussex; and then, Al, in case of twins, Albert and Edward, we will call them; there's my cousins of Hanover and Cambridge [both named George]; we mustn't forget them, you know. . . ." In case of girls, she adds, they might use Mary, Caroline, Sophia, Wilhelmina, Louisa, and Adelaide. Albert is given no response.

"Counting the Chickens"—broadside cartoon, 1840, in which Victoria and Albert discuss possible names for their future children, largely compliments for the uncles and aunts, from Leopold to Sophia.

"It was much remarked," Greville wrote, that the Queen and the Prince ". . . were up very early on Tuesday morning walking about, which is very contrary to her former habits. Strange that a bridal night should be so short; and I told Lady Palmerston that this was not the way to provide us with a Prince of Wales." To Melbourne the morning after, Victoria scribbled an ecstatic message about her "most gratifying and bewildering night." She never thought she "could be so loved." In her journal she noted only that "we did not sleep much."

From the start, two tables were set up in the Queen's room so that they could work side by side, but the work was Victoria's. Albert could make small talk or write personal letters. Sometimes she involved him enough to record a journal entry like "Rested and read Despatches—some of which I read to Albert." What she wanted during the first days of marriage was closeness to Albert. She would watch him shave—an occasion dramatized with great charm by Laurence Housman in his play *Victoria Regina* (1934). "How strange it looks!" he has his Victoria exclaim, ". . . and how interesting! —fascinating! . . . Is it dangerous?"

"Not if you don't talk to me," says Albert.

When Victoria dressed, in those first idyllic days, Albert would help her put on her stockings—assistance unstageable in days when the Lord

Chamberlain's censor guarded theatrical propriety so rigidly that even Housman's most circumspect scenes were first forbidden because "her near kin" were alive.

Victoria's own reaction is clear enough from a letter she would write to their cousin "Victo" (Victoria Augusta Antoinetta), daughter of Uncle Ferdinand. The young Saxe-Coburg duchess was about to marry the Duc de Nemours, son of King Louis-Philippe of France. Only weeks after her own wedding, Victoria rushed to offer such advice as "Love him with all your heart always and then you will be happy. YOU CANNOT IMAGINE HOW DELIGHTFUL IT IS TO BE MARRIED. I COULD NOT HAVE DREAMED THAT ANYONE COULD BE SO HAPPY IN THIS WORLD AS I AM."

Eager to show Albert off to her contemporaries, Victoria ordered Lord Clarence Paget to organize a dance for her second evening at Windsor, and had high-spirited young people in for galoppes and quadrilles. After three days, as she had warned Albert, the royal couple were back in London. Buckingham Palace had been newly decorated for Victoria when she became Queen, and early in 1840 many of the rooms were equipped with gaslight. The modern lighting eased paperwork, but there was still no work for Albert to do. At first Melbourne, characteristically cynical, approved. "The Prince is indolent," George Anson noted Lord Melbourne as saying, "& it would be better if he was more so, for in his position we want no activity."

Already loyally taking the Prince's side, Anson countered that there was "no scope" for Albert's energy. "If you required a cypher in the difficult position of Consort of the Queen you ought not to have selected the Prince; having got him you must make the most of him, & when he saw the power of being useful to the Queen he will act." Not until December would Albert have his own key to the dispatch boxes, and in the early months of the marriage the Queen still confided in him only after she had consulted with Melbourne and Lehzen. Lehzen even retained her private passage into the couple's bedroom, and controlled the Queen's personal expenditures, no bill being authorized for payment until the Baroness had signed.

It did not appear that way at the start, but Melbourne predicted to Greville that the Prince would acquire "boundless influence." Possibly because he did not want the next—almost certainly Tory—Prime Minister to have his own influence with the Queen, he urged Victoria to show her husband all the state papers he wished to see. Albert, he knew, would be above party. The Prince, in fact, had already argued about that, before the wedding, in pressing for a personal Household without a political bias.

To help the process along, Melbourne quickly began discussing public matters with Albert, and since Albert's background suggested that his interests might lie in foreign affairs, the Prime Minister urged that the Prince forward his views. "He seldom answers me," Albert would write his father, "but I have often had the satisfaction of seeing him act entirely in accordance with what I have said." For Albert, any discussion with someone as easy with words as Melbourne was painful, as his own English was awkward, and that realization, combined with his natural shyness, left the impression of a frigid reserve. Newspapers made the most of it. Victoria corrected his spelling in drafts of his letters, but even there his prose retained a rigidity that paralleled his public persona.

On March 21 the Queen awoke feeling unwell; recognizing the symptoms as possibly the first signs of pregnancy, she cried bitterly. Two months before the wedding she had confided to her journal how much she looked forward to marriage, and how little to childbearing—"the ONLY thing I *dread.*" Years later she would describe pregnancy to her firstborn as "an unhappy condition" that replaced "happy enjoyment." She was then, she confessed, "furious."

The disappointment as well as the discomfort were brief, and since she appeared to be in radiant health, the news surfaced slowly. Lord Melbourne's advice, when the Queen confirmed that she was expecting, was to eat and drink heartily, for which she needed little prompting. Albert tried to restrain her involvement in public business, but she insisted she was Queen, and had her responsibilities. Still largely shut out of her working routine, he looked for things to do on the fringes of official life. He joined organizations, accepted honorary posts.

In May 1840, Albert wrote to Löwenstein that in his home life he was "very happy and contented," but that he had difficulty in finding any dignified role for himself. "I am only the husband, and not the master in the house." Later that month, Anson recorded a conversation between the Queen and Melbourne, about Albert's frustrated desire to be more involved with political affairs. She confided—since Melbourne had already advised her differently—that she knew she was wrong, but when she was with Albert she preferred to avoid state matters. Melbourne suggested that she worry less about possible differences of opinion, and "by degrees impart everything to him." He suspected that the difficulty arose from Lehzen's desire to retain her influence. He had "spoken most seriously" to the Baroness, Melbourne told Victoria, warning Lehzen that if she created dissension "between husband and wife," she would "draw down ruin on herself."

The subject had come up in a meeting between Melbourne and Stockmar, the Count placing the blame on Lehzen, already then in a power struggle with Albert that she could not win. Biology was against her. The Queen's pregnancy not only drew husband and wife together emotionally, but threw more responsibility onto the husband. That would happen gradually, as Victoria relinquished more of the day-to-day details she had always insisted upon knowing. The dispatch boxes arrived anyway, whether or not the Queen was up to them, and Albert read the contents, often to Victoria. As pregnancy induced indolence on the Queen's part, and the selection from the red boxes became his, Albert's informal authority and influence grew.

Without official status—he was only a naturalized British subject of the Queen, although married to her—he had to become useful in other ways. One of his first attempts was to accept the presidency of the Anti-Slavery Society. Since it was not only international-minded but above party—slavery was already illegal in the Empire—Albert found the role in keeping with the public posture he wanted to display. He wrote his own brief address—only about two hundred words—first in German, then translated it with Victoria's help. Nervously he memorized it, trying out on Victoria his ringing phrases about the slave trade as "repugnant to the spirit of Christianity" and "the blackest stain upon civilized Europe." Then, on June 1, 1840, he delivered it before "five or six thousand people" (in his estimate), at Exeter Hall in the Strand, to "great applause"—a courageous achievement for a twenty-year-old who had never spoken publicly in English before.

Ten days later, as the Queen and Prince drove up Constitution Hill early in the evening, beginning an outing in the long summer light, "a little mean-looking man" (in Albert's description), a pistol in each hand, fired a shot at them from about six paces away. The open phaeton made them an easy mark, but the gunman missed. When he fired again, Albert drew Victoria down out of view. His reaction would have been too late for an accurate marksman, but young Edward Oxford, a waiter in a "low inn," was slow-witted and equally slow of foot. (He would be judged guilty but insane.) Onlookers who had cheered the Queen and Consort seized him, and the royal couple called to the postillions to go on. They visited

"Aunt Kent"—who had moved briefly to Ingestre House, Belgrave Square —and took a drive through Hyde Park, Albert wrote, "to show the public we had not . . . lost all confidence in them."

The attack had no adverse effect on Victoria's pregnancy, then four months along, and common knowledge. As the news of the attempted shooting spread across London, crowds massed at the palace, on horseback, in carriages and on foot, to cheer the Queen as her carriage made its way back through the gates. For days afterwards, wherever the couple went they were applauded enthusiastically, with special cheers for Albert, whose coolness was much admired in the newspapers. Spontaneous choruses of "God Save the Queen" were common, even at the opera, where formality usually prevailed.

With Albert devoted to music, Victoria had begun going to concerts of more serious fare than heretofore. Her first hearing of Mozart's *The Magic Flute* was on June 12, 1840, when excerpts were performed at an amateur palace concert arranged by the Prince, at which he and Victoria sang a duet from Luigi Ricci's opera *Il disertore de amore*, "Non funestar, crudele" ("Don't afflict me, cruel one!"). Luigi Lablache also took part —Albert knew he was one of the Queen's favorites—as did Battista Rubini and a lesser-known singer, Michael Costa, whom Victoria later knighted for his eminence as a conductor; and other roles were taken by the ladies and gentlemen of the Court. A year later, Victoria heard her first full-length *Magic Flute* at Covent Garden. Even earlier, in March 1840, Albert had become a director of the Ancient Concerts, which attempted to keep alive such neglected composers as Handel, but Victoria began to balk at attendance when the public discovered that these were good opportunities to see the Queen close up, and thronged the concert hall. A royal box at the theater or opera, where darkness during the performance added further privacy, was more to her taste.

Albert was only twenty-one that August, and still too inexperienced to promote his ambitions. Nevertheless, he was making good use of the cultural opportunities that came his way, and Parliament registered its confidence when his birthday came, and with it his legal majority. He was designated Regent in the event of Victoria's death while their child was still a minor. (It would take the birth of the child, however, to keep the King of Hanover from the throne. Stubbornly, the old Duke of Sussex, the King's brother, cast the only negative vote in the Upper House.)

Stockmar's political efforts had made the Regency Bill possible, even over Lehzen's protests, and on that success he quietly returned to Coburg (where he spent his summers with his family), briefing Anson before departure. His concerns about the royal couple's immaturity were still acute, but he realized that there were too many Germans at Court, and that he and Lehzen both had to go. (He kept a low profile and would disappear for months at a time.) A fiery partisan in her own interest and in what she conceived as Victoria's—Albert's term for her was "the House Dragon"—Lehzen would have to be removed from her lair in the palace by someone else.

That August, however, the impetuousness of both Victoria and Albert led them into unnecessary embarrassment. The issue of precedence, which had provoked the Duke of Sussex's lone *nay*, had been handled just as ungraciously by the Duchess of Cambridge. At a dinner given by Dowager Queen Adelaide, the Duchess remained seated when Albert's health was toasted. The Queen retaliated by giving a ball to which no Cambridge was invited, a marked public snub. Then Albert found occasion for his own youthful folly. He had been invited to receive the Freedom of the City of London, the ceremony to be followed by a banquet at the Guildhall. The venison and turtle soup, the Lord Mayor promised, "would be such as to startle the company." But the Duke of Cambridge was present, and rather than sit next to him, Albert announced that he could not remain for dinner because of the illness of the Queen's aunt, the Princess Augusta. (She died on September 22, a month later.) Augusta, the Duke observed loudly, was his own sister, and he had heard no news so urgent. If he could stay, the Prince could also. But Albert left anyway, which meant that the Duke had to reply to the toast to Albert, a halfhearted gesture to the absentee that the company had assembled to honor. That the illustrious Prince could not remain, the Duke declared, was everyone's disappointment, but he thought that all would understand the validity of His Royal Highness's excuse. "The Prince had lately married a very fine girl, and they were somehow or other very fond of each other's society." There was loud cheering. Then the Duke added broadly that he thought no one present would deny the Prince credit for his "performances" to date—a smirking reference to Victoria's pregnancy that provoked more laughter and cheers.

The Queen was shocked to read an account of her uncle's response in the newspapers the next day. She wrote to her aunt, the Duchess of Gloucester—another Hanoverian sister—asking that she scold the Duke.

Problems with the Cambridges continued, largely of the royal couple's own making; they should have risen above petty family spite. Two years later, rumors reached the newspapers that Prince George of Cambridge—already known as "The Royal Boy"—had made Lady Augusta Somerset, a duke's daughter, pregnant—an allegation then publicly denied. To further silence the scandal, when the Duchess of Cambridge was invited to Windsor several months later, she brought Lady Augusta with her, demonstrating that the young woman appeared unviolated. The Queen was outraged that her drawing-room should be used as imprimatur of purity, especially since she believed that the Prince was often carelessly immoral. "I know the stories are true," she insisted to the Duchess of Gloucester. The old Duke of Cambridge complained to Prince Albert, who replied ungraciously, "As Prince George has given his word of honour that the story is untrue, I suppose we *must* believe *it is so.*"

Greville thought that the affair was a result of the young Queen's "heartless" love of gossip and her young Consort's rigid morals. Lehzen's hold on Victoria lay, in part, in her genius for gathering gossip to pass on to the Queen; when the Baroness was finally evicted from the palace by Albert, Victoria became less susceptible to tales of scandal. As her own emotional life became richer, she also had less need of them. The Prince's prudery was another matter, one that had nothing to do with his own impulses. He and Victoria had quickly discovered a compatibility between the sheets that would last. The works of art they bought for each other, and displayed in their private chambers, reflected their delight in the nude form, male and female. Yet Albert was fiercely protective of the public's perception of the Court. He knew what it had been like during the raffish atmosphere of the Regency, and after. And he knew the sleazy sexuality of the Coburg court under his own father, not to mention Albert's brother, already a victim of venereal disease, and likely to produce, Albert warned him, a "sick heir."

Albert had only to look around him every day for evidence of what he had escaped. With him from Coburg had come his Swiss valet, Cart, who had been with him since childhood, and a second personal attendant, Rudolf Löhlein. The Queen later described Löhlein as the son of a forester of Füllbach, near Coburg, but her courtiers were convinced that he was a by-blow of Duke Ernest, whom he closely resembled. If so, Albert had brought with him his unacknowledged half-brother.

Victoria and Albert's first heir arrived in midafternoon on November 21, after an uneventful pregnancy. The Queen remembered, forty-four years later, "a dark, dull, windy, rainy day with smoking chimneys, and . . . Papa's great kindness and anxiety." If Dr. Locock—later Sir Charles

—had not miscounted, labor came three weeks early; and it lasted twelve hours. When he first examined Victoria, he asked about her need for sedatives. "I can bear pain as well as other people," she insisted. On his way out he asked Albert, who scoffed at the claim. He expected that she "would make a great *Rompos.*" Writing to the Duke of Wellington before the birth, Charles Arbuthnot, repeating the confidences, said, "Locock seems to tell Lady Mahon everything." Locock's first impression, he told her imprudently, was a certainty that the Queen "will be[come] very ugly & enormously fat," and that her figure without stays was "most extraordinary. . . . She is more like a barrel than anything else." To help Victoria sleep in the last uncomfortable weeks, Locock gave her camphor, which she continued to use occasionally; later he prescribed chloral in doses so minute that they often did not work.

In the next room during the Queen's labor was a shifting population of Cabinet ministers and bishops. At Victoria's side were Locock, a midwife, and Albert. "Oh, Madam," the dignitaries could hear Locock say before the naked baby was brought out for their inspection, "it is a Princess."

"Never mind," said the Queen, "the next will be a Prince." Both parents, Lord Clarendon wrote to Lord Granville in Paris, "were much disappointed at not having a son . . . but what the country cares about is to have a life more, whether male or female, interposed between the succession and the King of Hanover." For making that possible, Dr. Locock was paid a fee of £1,000. Two other physicians not even present received £800 and £500.

On one of Locock's visits after the delivery, the Queen asked whether Prince Albert might read to her. When the doctor objected that a novel would be too exciting in her condition, she explained, "No, he would read to me the lessons for the day, and as he has done so ever since we were married, it would be particularly gratifying to me now." In an age when religion permeated the home, from morning prayers to bedtime, Locock found no way to refuse.

The Princess Royal was named Victoria. From the beginning, Albert was as devoted to her as he was to the Queen, and a rapport would grow between them unlike that with any of the later children. But Albert's solicitude for his wife was tender beyond anything she could have expected, and as she indulged in the lassitude of postnatal recovery, which physicians then preferred to prolong, she became more and more dependent upon him than she had intended. As her pregnancy had progressed, she had approved setting up side-by-side writing tables in Buckingham Palace, like those in use at Windsor, and from there Albert began sending almost daily notes to Melbourne, usually on foreign questions. Mehmet Ali, Turkish viceroy in Egypt, had used the death of the Sultan and the succession of his sixteen-year-old son, Abdul Mejid, to attempt to break away from Turkey, reawakening the seldom-dormant great power rivalries in the Middle East. Albert pressed for the politics of conciliation rather than confrontation with France and Russia. Melbourne and Palmerston did much as they wished, but were pulled back into more temperate language by the Prince's intervention. Carefully, however, Melbourne's messages went to Victoria, with reference to "the Prince's observations." More and more, even the letters in Victoria's hand would be based on Albert's "observations."

The Court returned to Windsor for Christmas, which was celebrated in German fashion. Gifts were placed on tables under small Christmas trees, with each table and tree, decorated with candles, sweetmeats, and cakes hung by ribbons and paper chains, intended for a different recipient. Introduced from Germany earlier in the century, credit for their popularity is sometimes given to Queen Adelaide, and even to George III's Queen Charlotte, who had set up a Christmas tree of yew branches at Windsor. But Albert imported small trees from Coburg, and turned the Royal Family's Christmases into semipublic events. The fashion caught on, popularized by the new illustrated papers.

Not intended as a Christmas present to Albert, but timed almost as such, was Albert's key to the Cabinet boxes. During the last weeks of Victoria's pregnancy he had handled all her business, and become, as Anson put it, "in fact, tho' not in name, Her Majesty's Private Secretary."

Even in the first months of the new Princess's life, the Queen was little inconvenienced by the child's existence, having only to consent to an arrangement for her day-to-day care. A wet nurse was engaged from the Isle of Wight, and twice a day "Pussy" was brought in by the new Superintendent of the Nursery, Mrs. Southey, for inspection. Victoria would always insist that babies were "mere little plants for the first six months," as she would explain to her daughter when the Princess would herself become a mother. To the Queen, "baby-worship" was an evil, as at best each was a "nasty object." Frankly, she would tell the Princess Royal that she preferred babies only after "they have become a little human." Even "the prettiest is frightful when undressed . . . as long as they have their big body and little limbs and that terrible froglike action."

An 1840s lithograph showing Albert's contribution to English festival tradition—the Christmas tree. Victoria and her mother are to the left.

To Leopold she would write, on January 5, 1841, "I think, dearest Uncle, you cannot *really* wish me to be the 'mamma d'une *nombreuse* famille.'" A large family would be "a hardship and inconvenience" not only to herself but to the country; besides, "men never think, at least seldom think, what a hard task it is for us women to go through this very often."

Two minor but significant events had closed the old year for Victoria. In his tenth year her spaniel, Dash, had died at Windsor. Impulsively, on the day of her coronation two years before, she had given Dash a bath, reaching out to him in the frightening loneliness of that crowded day. Albert had brought his greyhound, Eos, with him from Germany, for similar reasons, and he and Victoria would have other dogs; but the beginning of a family had reduced the importance of resident pets. The lithe, loyal Eos meant enough to Albert that when he experimented with sculpting he used his greyhound as model, then going to a professional to have the work cast.

Early in the month of Dash's death, in the predawn hours of December 3, 1840, "the Boy Jones" was discovered lolling about in Buckingham Palace. Edmund Jones had climbed a wall and crept through a window, "sat upon the throne," he said, "saw the Queen and heard the Princess Royal squall." Home Office interrogation revealed that he was seventeen, stunted in growth, and the son of a poor tailor in Cannon Row. A chronic intruder, he had been declared insane the first time, and discharged; this time he was sentenced to three months for vagabondage, after which he returned once more, and following three more months on the treadmill at Tothill Street he was sent to sea.

The royal couple had known little about the lax security that had encouraged the curiosity of "Boy Jones" and an even earlier "Boy Cotton." Now, Albert had a reason to reform the slipshod administration of the palace. To accomplish that meant removing the stewardship reins that Lehzen had been accumulating in her hands, but Albert was determined to end the palace inefficiencies as well as the Baroness's powers. For both he needed some further pretext, and he began to look for one.

One area of the Queen's life he could begin to organize was the business of the Duchy of Cornwall, which furnished hereditary income in 1840 of £36,000 a year. One-third of that, Albert discovered, disappeared in administrative costs. He began cutting costs and raising revenues, to furnish the royal couple with more discretionary funds. He also began organizing the Queen's day, which before marriage had begun so late that much of it was wasted. They began to breakfast regularly at nine, then took a walk, and worked on incoming and outgoing correspondence immediately after. Relaxing after their business, they drew or etched together. Albert was eager to pull Victoria out of a postpartum depression that grew worse when she discovered, before the end of the winter, that she was again pregnant. Since the only respectable method of birth control was abstinence, the passionately fond young couple, both only twenty-one and even more ignorant of contraception than their doctors, had to take for granted that biological roulette was the mandate of Divine Providence. Artificial methods of birth control were condemned by the Church; and most nineteenth-century physicians who had the temerity to recommend the semi-abstinence of a rhythm method (would a Queen's gynecologist have had the courage?) were confused about the menstrual cycle. Assuming that women were like animals in heat, they recommended against intercourse immediately after the menses and considered it safe in mid-month.

The early months of the new pregnancy required no alteration in the royal routine, although later Albert would take some trips without the Queen, enjoying his first opportunities to try out a railway carriage, new technology that was still considered risky.

When at Windsor or at Buckingham Palace, they would lunch

together at two, after which Victoria, often now accompanied by Albert, would meet with one or more of her Ministers, usually Melbourne. (When the Queen was at Windsor, Lord M. usually lived there unless Parliament was sitting.) Then the royal couple would drive in the park in a pony phaeton, the Prince at the reins. (If the Prince was away on his own or the Queen's affairs, as became increasingly frequent, she went for a drive with her ladies-in-waiting, or the Duchess.) Dinner was at eight, usually with guests. Before or after dinner one often read to the other, Albert reading "serious" works, Victoria reading fiction.

Sometimes they went over albums of their own drawings, or of engravings and etchings they had begun to purchase. The Prince's interest had been quickly recognized in London, and Peel would appoint him chairman of a royal commission (at first a select committee) "to take into consideration the Promotion of the Fine Arts of this Country, in connexion with the Rebuilding of the Houses of Parliament." At the studio of John Lucas, a portrait painter and engraver for whom Albert would sit, Elizabeth Barrett visited and talked, she wrote to her friend Miss Mitford, "of Prince Albert & his talents," quoting Lucas as saying, "If he had studied five years under Raffael, his remarks could not have been acuter." Lucas, she added cattily, thought the Prince "very handsome, & the Queen charmless if you except the pleasant countenance & youthful freshness."

Just after the New Year, Victoria and Albert had returned to Buckingham Palace, to be closer to government business. The weather continued cold in February, and Albert, who took pride in his ice skating, tried out the palace pond. Victoria intended only to look on, but the ice cracked, and Albert fell in, the water closing over his head. "Luckily," Lady Palmerston wrote, "he can swim, . . . the Queen showed much presence of mind and courage. . . ." While her lady-in-waiting screamed, Victoria reached out for him as he came up, and pulled him to safety.

Foreseeing the change in government that the Bedchamber Crisis had only postponed, Albert attempted to keep the Court above party disputes. Absurdly, Melbourne had been blaming declining revenues on the popular new Penny Post, the new postal service, one of the more successful innovations of his unpopular administration. With political change imminent, the Duke of Wellington, so recently considered by Victoria as her bitter enemy, was asked to stand in at the christening of her firstborn, on February 10, 1841, for the designated godfather, Albert's absent brother Ernest. "The Duke is the best friend we have," Victoria assured herself in her journal, an indication of her acceptance of the likely political change. Even a series of small strokes that the Duke suffered five days before the christening failed to keep him from serving, although his health was now increasingly frail. Whatever the Queen's earlier hostility to him, it had never been reciprocal. As early as August 1840 he had been invited (with some reluctance on her part) to the palace, and seated next to Victoria at dinner. "She drank wine repeatedly with me," he noted; "in short if I was not a milksop, I should become her Bottle Companion." At the christening dinner he was limited to nothing stronger than ice water.

To Peel on May 17, 1841, Wellington would write, expecting a change of the guard, "The truth is that all I desire is to be as useful as possible to the Queen's service—to do anything, go anywhere, and hold any office, or no office, as may be thought most desirable. . . . I don't desire even to have a voice in deciding upon it." It was a tribute to the Queen's continuing metamorphosis from Whig partisan to sovereign above party, and evidence of Albert's growing influence. When Melbourne arrived to discuss the dissolution of Parliament, "Albert was present and joined in," the Queen's journal notes—the first recorded presence of the Prince at a Ministerial meeting. Legally, he had no claim to be there.

Nine days before Wellington's approach to Peel, the Prince had sent Anson to Peel to consult about the Queen's ladies. Sir Robert's "doggedness," Melbourne had suggested to Anson, might cause the Bedchamber once more to become a matter of principle, and Albert felt that both sides had to yield. Without telling Victoria, he had Anson recommend a compromise whereby the Queen would announce the "resignations" of her three most politically visible ladies. Division after division in the Commons that May went against Melbourne, with a vote of no confidence failing on June 4 by only one vote. But he would not resign, banking on new elections.

An antidote to the Queen's sagging popularity at the time—she was identified as a Whig because of her Melbourne connection—was another failed assassination attempt. On May 29, she and Albert had been shot at again while out in an open carriage near Buckingham Palace. When the gunman, John Francis, was not apprehended, Victoria worried over being "shut up for days" because of the threat of a renewed attempt. Such fears were not empty. Peel's private secretary, Edmund Drummond, would be shot and killed early in 1843 by a gunman who thought he had hit Peel. Attacks on political figures had been a hazard of office since Spencer Perceval, the Prime Minister who was the younger William Pitt's successor, was assassinated in 1812. As if nothing had happened, the royal couple drove out again the next afternoon, this time without a lady-in-waiting but with their usual "gentlemen," to try to draw the man's fire. "You may imagine," Albert wrote to his father, "that our minds were not very easy. We looked behind every tree, and I cast my eyes round in search of the rascal's face." From five paces, Francis fired again, and missed; this time he was arrested. (John Francis was condemned to death; then, on July 1, 1841, hardly a month after the incidents, he was reprieved. Two days later, John William Bean, a stunted young man barely four feet tall, fired a pistol at the Queen. When it proved to be loaded more with tobacco than gunpowder, he was released as insane.) The public applauded the royal couple's courage. A later age may marvel at their youthful folly. The Queen's birthday had just passed. She had already reigned for nearly five years, and was just twenty-three.

As elections approached, Victoria and Albert went to Oxford, where he was awarded an honorary doctorate. In the Sheldonian Theatre the Queen was cheered, as was Albert, but, Greville wrote, "her Ministers, individually and collectively, were hissed and hooted with all the vehemence of Oxonian Toryism. Her Majesty said she thought it very disrespectful to the Prince to hiss her Ministers in his presence; but she must learn to bear with such manifestations of sentiment, and not fancy that these *Academici* will refrain from expressing their political opinions in any presence, even her own."

Unused to the electoral system, Albert observed the turmoil with amusement. He heard the arguments about Free Trade versus Protection, and realized that seats in the House of Commons were being won less on the price of bread than on the price of a vote. He was less amused when he learned that Lehzen, an outspoken Whig, had given £15,000 of the Queen's money to the party coffers. When Albert confided his horror to Melbourne, the Prime Minister shrugged the complaint off, observing that the few thousands were nothing compared to what George III used to spend on elections. Bribery and corruption were casual; the Reform Bill had increased the number of ballots for purchase, and many nonvoters also expected something for their vocal support, something that Albert—and the Queen—did not realize when they were greeted at Ascot with loud cheers and cries of "Melbourne forever!" Even so, it was clear that the Whigs were unpopular and that the Tories would get their chance.

Victoria dissolved Parliament on June 29. Whether or not she perceived it, a summer round of visits to several great Whig country houses, including Melbourne's own estate, Brocket, suggested a political bias rather than a social predilection for people she knew. It made no difference. The Whigs were smashed, and despite second thoughts about her resignation by the Duchess of Bedford, she and two other ladies were replaced. Victoria's initial feeling (according to Anson) "that she had been hurried and compromised by the Prince and Lord Melbourne," was quickly over, but not before a scene that Anson watched with dismay. "The Q[ueen] . . . burst into tears which could not be stopped for some time—& said that she could Not force the Duchess [of Bedford] to resign —they could not make her do that & she would never appoint any Tories. . . .

"The P[rince] said, in this moment all shd be done to quiet you & get you over difficulties & it was shameful on the part of those who attempted to convert her mind. . . ."

Albert was clearly accusing Lehzen, behind the scenes, as Melbourne in his usual manner was only indifferent and unhelpful. With Anson's help, the Prince, still new to the nuances of English politics, prepared Victoria's mind for the inevitable, and as part of the transition to a Conservative government she gave up the right to appoint three officers of the Household—Lord Steward, Lord Chamberlain, and Master of the Horse—as well as male courtiers who held Parliamentary seats.

In her seventh month of pregnancy, in September, when the shift occurred, Victoria was still prone to depression, but handled the ceremonial changes with composure. The Privy Council was summoned to Claremont, where the Queen rarely now went, for the appointment of the new Ministers. The Tory Cabinet, realizing her burden, praised her dignity and fairness. "This struck me," Greville wrote, "as a great effort of self-control, and remarkable in so young a woman. Taking leave is always a melancholy ceremony, and [those] whom she thinks are attached to her, together with all the reminiscences and reflections which the occasion was calculated to excite, might well have elicited uncontrollable emotions." Peel told Greville that she had behaved "perfectly," and that he had told her he would put forward no person "who could be disagreeable to her."

What Peel did not know at the time was that at her emotional parting with Melbourne she had asked him, unwisely, to continue contacts. Their emotional bonds were too great to be wrenched apart at once, and it would take both Anson and Stockmar to make Melbourne keep his political distance. Sensing his opening, Albert also urged Melbourne, through Anson, to suggest to the Queen that her husband be her future guide on political questions. Melbourne wrote that he had "formed the highest opinion of H.R.H.'s judgment, temper and discretion," and that the Queen "cannot do better than have recourse to it." That, too, was a changing of the guard as great as the Ministerial one, and it would be even longer-lasting. While the Queen was lying-in for the birth of her second child, Peel sent Albert nightly reports of debates in the Commons and discussions in the Cabinet. A year earlier, Albert had not even had his own key to the Cabinet boxes.

With that victory of the Prince's came another, equally crucial. The Queen was discovering that she could live without Lehzen, but felt guilty about sending her away. The visits to the Whig country houses in June had been Victoria's first travels since she was a child of five on which Lehzen was not present. She confessed to "feeling a little low." Albert noted in his own, more sketchy diary that "the moon was on the wane." Yet the moon waned slowly.

Problems in the Household grew more acute as Victoria's second confinement approached. Lehzen still oversaw that aspect of the Queen's life. The baby Princess Royal was reacting poorly to her post-weaning diet, and losing weight. She had difficulty cutting her first teeth. There was constant confusion in the nursery, especially as preparations began to be made for the new baby. The Queen felt "wretched" about going through the ordeal of labor again in that pre-anesthesia age, and was having nearly daily "false alarms."

Finally, on November 9, 1841, early in the morning, labor began in earnest, and Dr. Locock—whose attendance on Victoria would make him the most fashionable obstetrician of the day—was sent for. "My sufferings were really very severe," she recorded, "and I don't know what I should have done, but for the great comfort and support my beloved Albert was to me." Just before eleven that morning an heir to the throne emerged —a large, healthy boy. Because of earlier false alarms, the new summons was not taken seriously by the Archbishop of Canterbury and the Lord President of the Council, and both missed the birth. Later children would be born also without an official audience.

On December 4, the new Prince Albert Edward was created, by Letters Patent from the Queen, Prince of Wales. His christening the next month would provide a London cartoonist, recalling Albert's Household economies and Victoria's fecundity, with a double-pronged opportunity. In "The Royal Christening Cake" Sir Robert Peel advises Victoria and Albert to keep the cake uncut "for next year." (A cartoon with a horticultural motif on a similar theme would refer to the couple's "tender annuals.")

The Prince's regimen was to be strict and efficient, which meant releasing Mrs. Southey. The appointment was offered to Lady Lyttleton in April. Born Lady Sarah Spencer, she was well connected and a widowed mother of five. Her appointment marked the beginning of the end of Lehzen's domination, which the Baroness herself hurried on by proposing that she take charge of the Duchy of Cornwall revenues, usually linked with the Prince of Wales, and that nursery expenses be drawn from them. Since Anson's authority came in part from being comptroller of the Duchy's revenues, he and Albert perceived Lehzen's bid as a test of strength.

Whatever the Baroness's credits with the Queen, and they were many and well-earned, she had outlived her usefulness at Court. Victoria, in her inexperience, had depended upon Lehzen. Although the Baroness had no official title, and was innocent of administrative detail, she had been given a proliferation of duties and responsibilities. Beneath her sightless gaze, sinecures and wasteful perquisites flourished. Courtiers, from titled officials to humble attendants, lived and dined on the Queen's purse; tradesmen furnished supplies that went elsewhere than Buckingham Palace, or Windsor; and horses and carriages were ordered by anyone willing to sign someone else's name. Few of the figures presented for inspection were verifiable, but no one had ever been concerned about that before.

Unsophisticated about the costs of anything, Victoria entertained often and lavishly, and gave expensive gifts. In 1839 alone—her last year without Albert—she spent £34,000 from her Privy Purse on pensions and charities, and £600 on her box at the opera. In the first three months of 1840, when royal guests had come for the wedding, inflating normal expenditures, 24,600 dinners were served at Buckingham Palace. At Windsor Castle the year before, 113,000 dinners were served, not including the grand ball suppers, and even when the Court was not in residence, more than a dozen large joints of meat were roasted daily for the servants permanently present. The statistics also included people who elected to dine at the Queen's expense because it was easy to do. Many meals may have never been served, with someone pocketing the funds. The christening of the Prince of Wales cost the Queen's purse £4,991 16s. 5d. And this was an age when the pound sterling was so sturdy and inflation so low that a shilling—a twentieth of a pound—could purchase a dinner, and a penny—a twelfth of a shilling—could post a letter.

Laurence Housman's stage Albert explains to Victoria, "One of the things I discovered was that anything once ordered always goes on being ordered. The thing is sent in and paid for, but it is not used." It was very nearly like that. In the palaces, Albert observed, hundreds of candles were placed in chandeliers and candelabras daily, then discarded even if never lighted. He discovered—the Queen had never noticed—that since Queen Anne's day the privilege of selling "Palace ends" for pocket money had been that of the servants. Similar sinecures existed at Windsor Castle, such as the thirty-five shillings that a half-pay officer received annually for "Red Room wine" meant for a captain of the guard last on duty in the reign of George III. Too many absentee authorities officially oversaw such matters, and it would be a long time until Albert could get Court administration under control; but in Lehzen he had someone to blame for at least part of the chaos. He had already enlisted Stockmar to do research on the problems and possible solutions, all of which would make many more people unhappy in addition to the Baroness. Still, consolidating administrative functions and powers, as much as he could within existing traditions and regulations, in his own hands and those of George Anson as his deputy, meant that Albert had to push Lehzen aside. Since all her powers were informal, he needed only Victoria's acquiescence. Albert confronted her with a litany of Household waste and inefficiency detailed in Stockmar's memorandum. When Victoria refused to see Lehzen as obsolete, or the relationship with the Baroness as dangerous, Albert explained to Stockmar, Victoria "has never been away from her, and like every good pupil, [she] is accustomed to regard her governess as an oracle. Besides this, the unfortunate experience they went through together at Kensington has bound them still closer, and Lehzen, in her madness, has made Victoria believe that whatever good qualities she possesses are due to her." He saw "the welfare of my children and Victoria's existence as sovereign" at stake if Lehzen remained, and through the first weeks of 1842 there were bitter words exchanged between husband and wife, each writing to Stockmar in Coburg as intermediary.

"Victoria is too hasty and passionate . . . ," Albert explained. "She will not hear me out but flies into a rage and overwhelms me with reproaches of . . . want of trust, ambition, envy, etc. etc. There are, therefore, two ways open to me: (1) to keep silence and go away (in which case I am like a schoolboy who has had a dressing down from his mother and goes off snubbed); (2) I can be still more violent (and then we have scenes . . . , which I hate, because I am sorry for Victoria in her misery, besides which it undermines the peace of the home). . . ."

Lehzen was no longer her confidante, Victoria insisted to Stockmar; Albert made too much of the Baroness's presence. "I have often heard Albert own that everybody recognized Lehzen's services to me and my only wish is that she should have a quiet home in my house and see me sometimes . . . about papers and *toilette* for which she is the greatest use to me. . . . Dearest Angel Albert, God only knows how I love him. His position is difficult, heaven knows, and we must do everything to make it easier." In a later letter to Stockmar, on January 20, 1842, Victoria acknowledged that she was "so passionate when spoken to," an impulse she feared was "irremediable," and made her say "cross and odious things which I don't myself believe and which I fear hurt A., but which he should not believe." Their position was "very different to any other married couples. A. is in my house and not I in his. —But I am ready to submit to his wishes as I love him so dearly."

Submission came melodramatically, when the Princess Royal became seriously ill and Albert blamed "Pussy's" condition on Victoria's toleration of Lehzen's handling of the nursery and Sir James Clark's continuing incompetence. Dr. Clark, he told the Queen in a note, "has mismanaged the child and poisoned her with calomel, and you have starved her. I shall have nothing more to do with it; take the child away and do as you like, and if she dies you will have it on your conscience."

The war was over, although more battles would be fought—delaying actions by Lehzen. Had she made any conciliatory gestures toward Albert, her place in the Palace might have remained as Victoria claimed she wished it. Instead, the Baroness discovered that her departure was the price of the Queen's future happiness. As with Peel and the ladies of the Court, Albert took the initiative when he saw his opportunity. Lehzen had known it was coming. Her help with Victoria's papers had been to make copies in a letter-press, a responsibility she quietly passed on to the Queen's loyal dresser, Annie Skerret. The niece of Queen Charlotte's sub-treasurer, she had entered Victoria's service in 1837, and would remain into 1862, largely writing letters to tradespeople.

On July 25, Albert informed Victoria that Lehzen had decided to retire because of her health. Since the Baroness was a vigorous fifty-six, Victoria understood that it was a move "for our & her best." Lehzen was presented with a carriage and a pension of £800, an annual income which would enable her to live in comfort in Germany. At the end of September she slipped out of London without any farewells—her last gesture to spare Victoria's tears—and went to Bückeburg, a quiet town west of Hanover. Although Lehzen's intention had been to live with her sister, the sister died three months later, leaving the Baroness alone. She remained anyway, in a house she filled with pictures of Victoria, until her death at eighty-six, in 1870.

It was Lehzen, Albert confided to Anson, literally his only intimate when Stockmar was not in residence, who was responsible for the Queen's sense of intellectual inadequacy. She had been responsible for Victoria's education, he exaggerated, and had kept it at an inferior level. From the standpoint of content, it was probably true that Victoria knew little about science and technology, Albert's chief passions, and was reluctant to bring them into her conversation. She knew somewhat more about art and music, also his passions, but her tastes were more conventional. She knew still more about history and politics, and understood their direct importance to her; but Albert saw that as only a beginning, and had set to work to become her Stockmar as well as her university. Statecraft was a subject about which her instincts were good, but where Albert saw evidences of laziness. Some of her passivity came from Melbourne; when she began to lean more and more on Albert's competencies, and later, when she would have to work alone, her Ministers would confront a shrewd mind and a sharp writing style. The Baroness had not done her job badly. Victoria, at twenty-three, did not have some of the sophistication that might have been useful during country-house weekends, but she had survived her upbringing well. Few people would dominate her intellectually, if only because as Queen she could select her subject or dismiss it.

Whatever the external frustrations in his own position, Albert could see growth in Victoria's grasp of her role, and could preen himself on adding a dimension to it. When Victoria was having her hair done, she read *Cornwallis on the Sacrament* or Guizot's *Révolution de l'Angleterre.* When Felix Mendelssohn came to England in June 1842 to conduct a performance of his new A-Minor Symphony (later called the *Scottish* Symphony), Victoria was eager to invite him and his wife Cécile to Buckingham Palace. On June 20, the composer, thirty-three but small and boyish under a mass of curly black hair, arrived to play for the royal couple, giving them a recital of his *Songs Without Words.* Afterwards, he and Cécile were taken to tea in the Grand Gallery. Before they left, Albert invited the Mendelssohns back the following Saturday, so that Felix could try out the palace organ; and he returned to play "How Lovely Are the Messengers" from his *St. Paul,* with Albert assisting with the stops.

The musical capacities of Victoria and Albert, Mendelssohn discovered, went beyond any social requirements. First, Albert played a chorale, "by heart, with the pedals, so charmingly, clearly and correctly, that it would have done credit to any professional . . . , and then all the music sheets going all over the floor, and being picked up by the Queen."

Finding the pages she wanted, Victoria sang the composer's lyrical "Italien," from his first set of songs, which embarrassed Mendelssohn into a confession. As he wrote his mother, he could not let the Queen be unaware that his sister Fanny had written "Italien" although he had published it under his own name. (A woman could become a sovereign more easily than a recognized composer.) "I was obliged to confess that Fanny had written the song, which was very hard, but pride must have a fall, and to beg her to sing one of my own also. If I would give her plenty of help she would gladly try, she said, and then [with Mendelssohn at the piano] she sang the *Pilgerspruch,* 'Lass dich nur,' really quite faultlessly, and with charming feeling and expression."

When the composer thanked her, Victoria said shyly, "Oh, if only I had not been so frightened! Generally I have a long breath." To his mother, Mendelssohn observed what he could not insist to the Queen—that she had indeed sung well, "as one seldom hears it done."

Then the Prince sang the *Ernteleid* from the same set, and finally Mendelssohn improvised happily on the piano, introducing themes from the musical pieces that had been sung. It seems likely that in conversation Victoria mentioned her forthcoming trip to Scotland, for, once back in Germany, he wrote to the Queen to obtain her permission to dedicate his *Scottish* Symphony to her.

The final weaning of Victoria away from Lehzen came in August and September, when the Baroness did not accompany the Royal Family on their first visit to Scotland. Preparations by the Lord Chamberlain's office for the first long trip by the Queen away from London took weeks, and covered every scrap of minutiae that cautious bureaucrats could conceive. Every possible solecism had to be avoided; every sensitivity had to be anticipated. Since presentations to the Queen were always made by someone who had previously been presented, that detail agonized the Scots officials who realized that there would be a dearth of presentees at such places as Holyrood Palace in Edinburgh. (The answer was "yes, under [the] circumstances, but not letting it too loose.") There was the question of the suitability of "Highland garb." ("Answered not aware of any objection.") And there were rumors of recent scarlet fever at Holyrood, and of bad drains.

The Great Western Railway Company had constructed a state carriage for the Queen, short (by modern standards) and ornate, with a small crown on the roof, the interior suggesting a small but opulent parlor. On June 14, 1841, the Queen and Prince made their first journey in it, on the new Great Western line from Slough, near Windsor, to Paddington Station in London. The Queen announced herself "quite charmed" but Albert worried that the speed was dangerously excessive—fifty miles an hour.

For the trip to Scotland the Court proceeded on August 29, in a convoy of carriages, to Slough, where they boarded a special train of engine, luggage tender, royal saloon, and two carriages for attendants and railway officials. Before their successful experiment, Victoria had been worried about railway accidents, especially the crumbling of embankments on which trackage had been laid, and Melbourne earlier had dismissed such concerns as the price of progress in a rainy climate. Ahead of the party by ship went twenty-seven royal horses and five carriages, and the party itself would change to carriages at Paddington Station in London, crossing the city to Woolwich, where they embarked on the antiquated yacht *Royal George*.

The voyage was unpleasant. The *Royal George*—the very ship that had ferried the eight-months-pregnant Duchess of Kent from Calais to Dover in 1819—was a cumbersome sailing ship in the new age of steam. Lurching to Scotland it was towed by two steamers, and the uneven strain on the tow ropes, combined with the North Sea swells, left the royal party severely seasick. In addition, the inefficient transport made them half a day late arriving at Inchkeith, near Edinburgh. Lying at anchor through the night further aggravated everyone's motion sickness, and before eight, Victoria insisted on going ashore.

The Edinburgh welcoming committee, which had waited all the previous day, and then gone home, had not yet returned, and officials pleaded with the Queen to wait. She had waited too long already, however, and disembarked. Uniformed escorts, and the Lord Provost of Edinburgh, with the Keys to the City, raced back, finally inserting themselves into the procession before it arrived at Dalkeith, where the Queen was to be the guest of the Duke of Buccleuch. Although the planning had been meticulous, there had been one exception—the unrealized obsolescence of the *Royal George*.

At Perth the worried Lord Provost, due to present the Keys to the City to the Queen, wrote ahead to inquire which knee to bend, and whether to present the Keys while kneeling. ("It is better kneeling. Right knee.") With protocol the most weighty problem, the royal tour went well. "The Highlands and the mountains are too beautiful," Victoria wrote to Melbourne from Taymouth on September 10, "and we *must* come back for longer another time." (She was still corresponding with Melbourne, but neither Peel nor the Prince was concerned anymore, as the letters now exchanged felicities and trivialities.) Besides, Sir Robert Peel, now the Prime Minister, had accompanied her on the voyage, and was working at winning her confidence. He was "very nervous," Peel later told Greville, for the tour went through "disturbed districts" where there had been unrest among the working class, but the outpouring of loyalty to the Queen impressed both Peel and Victoria. "Her chief fault, in little things and great," Greville recorded from Peel and from Lord Adolphus FitzClarence, her cousin and the yacht's captain, "seems to be impatience; . . . she can't bear contradiction nor to be thwarted. . . . She insisted on landing as soon as it was possible, and would not wait till the authorities were ready and the people assembled to receive her. . . . There was . . . much discontent among the crowds who had come from distant parts, and who had paid large sums for seats and windows to see her go by." FitzClarence, long a sailor, could not imagine seasickness-induced impatience.

There was never a time on the tour when Victoria was not impatient, but Scottish devotion to her remained high for the full fourteen days. As she told Melbourne, she would come back. She refused to return on the heaving *Royal George,* however, and embarked for London on the steamship *Trident.* A royal steam yacht would be ordered for future progresses by sea.

Once back with her red dispatch boxes of government business, the Queen was faced again with the realization that domestic concerns could not shut out external ones. She remained alert to her own conception of English interests after the Tory Earl of Aberdeen had replaced Palmerston as Foreign Secretary, but her primary channel of communication remained Sir Robert Peel. At the start, both had felt uncomfortable about it. Victoria refused to forget the Bedchamber Crisis, which she blamed unfairly on Peel, and also the Conservative Party's vocal opposition to Albert. She cautioned her husband about seeing too much of the new Ministers. Albert, on the other hand, admired Peel and appreciated the quality of his mind. With Victoria, Peel was at first ill at ease. "She would like him better," Greville confided to his diary, "if he could keep his legs still."

Uncomfortable in the Queen's presence, he was there much less than Melbourne, who had made a second home of Windsor. Eager to take on the business of his Ministry, he soon found himself tangled in the trivia of status and precedence, which he had hoped were closed issues. For example, the Prince of Wales appeared to need a coat of arms, although it would be years until he would notice that matter himself. The Queen wanted to quarter the arms of Saxony with those of England, claiming imaginatively that Albert was a Duke of Saxony. The reference in the Liturgy to the Royal Family had to be altered to accommodate Prince Albert Edward, and it became a matter of renewed dispute whether His Royal Highness—the Queen's husband—should be inserted before the Prince of Wales—the Queen's heir.

Of more importance were such foreign-policy matters as disputes with the United States over Canada's border with Maine, and over the right to search ships suspected of slave trading; interventions in Afghanistan, India, and China, with the seizure of Hong Kong as a base for trade. France's grudging entente with England had been interpreted by many Frenchmen as having Palmerston as their own foreign minister. Now he was gone, and the government of the bourgeois monarch, Louis-Philippe, was intriguing in Spain, where England supported the weak regency for an *infanta.* The Regent of Spain, Victoria wrote Aberdeen, "is thoroughly attached to England." That would always be the index to her policies. After reading a draft of a message to her ambassador in Portugal, she returned it to Aberdeen with the suggestion "to *soften* the words under which she has drawn a pencil line." The matter was not as important as the conciliatory intent and the intervention with her Ministers. It made no difference that Albert may have drafted the original of a memorandum that Victoria then rewrote in her own hand. It was the Queen who would always insist on being informed, and on making her views known. Melbourne had suggested to Peel that he convey information to the Queen *"elementarily,"* by which he meant with the support of explanatory detail. He had already seen that predilection in questions he was asked. Victoria's authority in matters constitutionally those of her Ministers would always emanate from her continuity as Sovereign and their discontinuity in government. The Queen survived the electoral processes. That she would have a continuing moral mandate was in large measure due to the Prince's instilling in her a detached view of parties, which was to prevail even when she, as Sovereign, took a stand on a particular policy or person.

As all rulers discover, even the most high-minded, nonpartisan intentions can have contrary results. The Queen and Prince would regularly have to wonder to each other whether they were naïvely expecting too much. A painful example in 1842 had been the Plantagenet Ball, on May 12. Since Sir Robert Peel had emerged from a successful cotton-spinning family in the Midlands, his background had helped focus Victoria's mind on the vast and crucial English textile industry, then beset by foreign competition and falling demand. Why not, she and Albert thought, create what would be described more than a century later as a "media event" to focus attention upon English goods? Specifically, they had the Spitalfields silk-weaving industry in mind in planning a ball in fourteenth-century costume, and after some research they determined to come themselves as Edward III and Queen Philippa, in costumes copied from their effigies in Westminster Abbey. Intended as a tribute to English history as well as to domestic industry, the ball fell victim to a practical joke.

Richard Monckton Milnes (later Lord Houghton) sent the *Morning Chronicle* what he purported was the text of a debate in the Chamber of Deputies in Paris about the intentions of the *bal masqué* to reawaken "the long-buried griefs of France" about their defeats by the English at Crécy and Poitiers and Calais. The Home Secretary rushed to Sir Robert Peel, crying, "There's the devil to pay in France about this foolish ball!" And in Paris a newspaper suggested holding a similar ball at which the Duke of Orleans should attend, costumed as William the Conqueror.

Controversy increased interest in the ball but twisted its focus. The display of the Queen's gown in Hanover Square drew crowds to gaze at its magnificence, but also caused London newspapers to decry the extravagance at a time when the unemployed were starving. *Punch* published verses in which aristocratic "revellers" in "purple dress'd" were contrasted with the poor, whose "only swathing was / The cere-cloth of the dead." Instead of promoting the weaving industry, the Plantagenet Ball promoted discord, but the Queen stubbornly commissioned Edwin Landseer to paint her and Albert in their regalia. By a stroke of good luck it was only days later that John Francis tried to assassinate them; the attempt stirred a new wave of public good feeling. The royal pair would regularly ride such tides of rejection and acclaim.

Albert's responsibilities were staggering for a young and inexperienced man, and his status was only what he could make of it. Fortunately for Victoria, he submerged much of his ego in tireless work behind the scenes to extricate her from the trough of despair and disappointment that had followed her euphoric first years as Queen. The Bedchamber imbroglio, the battles over Conroy, the Lady Flora embarrassment, the defeats over Albert's status and stipend, the loss of Melbourne, the expulsion of Lehzen, the unwanted pregnancies (with fear of more) had proved Victoria less than she seemed. With her Ministers she was assured; in her correspondence she was confident; at Court ceremonials she was queenly. Yet Anson had already written at Christmas 1841 that "Her Majesty interests herself less and less about politics"—because, he knew, Albert was discreetly maintaining the monarchy's business until Victoria struggled through a prolonged depression about which few were aware.

Albert bore the matrimonial trials this involved with patience and grace, but he realized that if he did not assert himself as husband, Victoria's Hanoverian hauteur could unravel the monarchy as well as their marriage. Sallie Stevenson recalled a social evening at Buckingham Palace when, after she complimented Albert on his English, and he said, realistically, "Oh, no; it is just tolerable. I hope to improve," a group sat down at tables with the Queen to play whist, as usual. The Prince, who despised cards, sat separately with several others over four-handed chess, a curious nineteenth-century version of the game, played with partners and two sets of chessmen of different colors on a board of 160 squares. After some hours of tedium the whist players rose, at the Queen's lead, to retire. Since the Prince "was still intent on his game," the Queen "leaned over to him and said in the softest, sweetest tones, 'Albert!' But as His Royal Highness was too much employed to hear these soft and silvery accents, she repeated his name again and again, each time modulating her voice to greater earnestness, without losing any of its sweetness or tenderness. They do say, however, that, Queen though she be, he will not allow himself to be, in matrimonial phrase, 'managed,'—that when it is necessary, he resists her firmly, though kindly, and I think it is the best security for their future happiness."

The painter E. M. Ward remembered one such moment when the Prince had gone to dine with the Council of the Royal Academy. Before dinner had proceeded very far, a messenger arrived to announce that the Queen desired Albert's presence at Buckingham Palace. The Prince nodded, and sent the messenger off. Half an hour later a second messenger turned up with a message that the Queen was still waiting. Albert again nodded and waved the emissary off, only to find a third messenger soon at the door with a peremptory "The Queen *commands* your Royal Highness's immediate return to the Palace."

The Prince dismissed the messenger and remained with the company the rest of the evening, and when Ward escorted him to his carriage he heard the coachman instructed to drive to Claremont, where, undoubtedly, Albert slept soundly while Victoria learned once more that even sovereigns made up only half of a marriage.

Albert's assertiveness and Lehzen's departure combined to bring a semblance of stability to the marriage. It did not take Victoria long to recognize that. The night following Lehzen's exit, Victoria dreamed that the Baroness had come back to say good-bye, and the Queen awakened only to the reality of her loss. But the next day she pulled down some of her old diaries to examine, perhaps to remind her of Lehzen's part in her life, and came to a passage in 1839 where she had written of her "happiness" with Melbourne. The reference was to the confidence-vote defeat that had threatened to deprive "a poor helpless girl" of her Prime Minister, an outcome she had frustrated. Now, with both Melbourne and Lehzen gone, she wrote in her journal, "1st October. Wrote & looked over & corrected my old journals, which do not now awake very pleasant feelings. The life I led then was so artificial & superficial, & yet I thought I was happy. Thank God! I now know what real happiness means."

On December 13, 1842, Victoria and Albert, musing over the departure from their lives of Melbourne and Lehzen, wondered what had caused her "unbounded admiration and affection" for Melbourne, which already was beginning to seem puzzling, given their satisfaction with each other and the rapid emergence of their confidence in Peel. In her journal, Victoria blamed her "very warm feelings," which had nowhere else to go, but, she added, "Albert thinks I worked myself up to what really became at last, quite foolish." Equally foolish, she realized, as she listened to Albert's recital of what he had put up with under Lehzen, was her stubborn unwillingness to close that chapter of her history.

After the discordant notes recorded by Anson at the close of 1841, the ending of 1842 echoed with harmonies that Victoria and Albert hardly dared anticipate only a few months earlier. Even the Queen's less than welcome new pregnancy caused no alarm, and she could respond to Leopold's congratulations, "My poor nerves, tho' thank God! nearly *quite* well *now* were so battered last time that I suffered a *whole year* from it. . . . Still those nerves were incidentals and I am otherwise so strong and well, that if only my happiness continues I can bear anything else with pleasure."

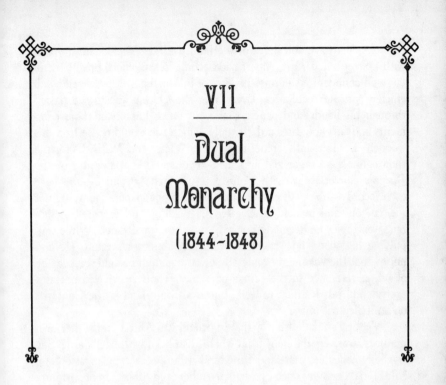

VII

Dual Monarchy

(1844–1848)

"I wish you joy of the Prince of Wales's walking alone," Feodora wrote to Victoria in the first days of 1843. ". . . I think children ought to have walked from the first, as all the little animals can when they are born." Her sister's sentiments reflected Victoria's own impatience with infants, although for once the Queen was reacting buoyantly to her pregnancy. To Princess de Lieven, Lady Palmerston wrote that Victoria was "in excellent health, and her pregnancy does not trouble her, for she remains on her feet like a young girl. It is impossible to be kinder than she is to old friends. So please do not believe the false rumours spread by the Tories to blacken her character."

Only twenty-three, the Queen was still a very young woman, and was increasingly comfortable with herself. Her routine enabled her to be as much a Queen as she could constitutionally be, while allowing her to enjoy her marriage and her growing family. Under Peel's Ministry and with Lehzen's departure, Albert had become her unofficial private secretary and confidant, acquiring the kind of informal power possessed by all efficient private secretaries. Everything the Queen was to see passed through his hands, and papers that went on to her usually bore comments and in some cases a draft reply, which she would revise from his wooden English into something more Victorian. With Germanic thoroughness he organized and filed documents, kept minutes of the Queen's conversations with Ministers—which he attended—and gave each record a subject title in red ink. He read newspapers she would not see, cut out and marked articles for her reading, and prepared memoranda on topics he deemed of current or future importance. While simplifying her work, he was carefully forming Victoria's mind. He also hoped that the volumes of material he was compiling would someday be of use as reference to the Prince of Wales, whom he viewed not as a pretty child just learning to walk, but as a future king in the Consort's own intellectual image.

Victoria's relationship with Peel, thanks to Albert and to her own maturity, was very different from what it had been with Melbourne. She was less malleable, more inquiring, and willing to accept, or assent to, Ministerial decisions once Peel had given her (and Albert) an opportunity to register their impressions. Theoretically unfettered by a written constitution, the Queen was nevertheless bound by the increasing restraints of Cabinet democracy. She had the right to be informed—a right that she and Albert insisted upon—and to be heard. The sovereign, as the continuing instrument of government, possessed moral authority beyond that of elected officeholders, and technically, royal assent was needed for a host of government appointments and operations; however, an expanding electorate had left few initiatives to the monarch and little more than what Walter Bagehot would call, in the later years of Victoria's reign, the right to be consulted, the right to encourage, and the right to warn. Used shrewdly and cautiously, these "rights" remained powers that could make the sovereign more than a symbol. And not only the sovereign but, in Victoria's case, her Consort. However he effaced his traces from her official actions, she knew how much of her authority emanated from Albert's preparation and from his reshaping of her personality. She recorded in her journal how she once told the Prince, "It is you who have entirely formed me." The sweeping adverb was far from accurate, as she was too strong a personality to be so diminished, but Lord Brougham, then of the Whig opposition, understood, and called her privately "Queen Albertine." More reasonable observers might have recognized the development, in the mid-1840s, of an informal dual monarchy.

In the early years of her reign, Victoria had enjoyed the fishbowl of public attention in which she lived from morning to night. Royal levees and drawing-rooms remained the formal entrée into Society, levees held on an occasional morning to introduce gentlemen to Court, drawing-rooms in the afternoon for ladies. Rigid in dress and in protocol, emotionally arid and only momentary in contact, the opportunities to brush one's lips upon the Sovereign's hand and to exchange fleeting words with the Queen and the Prince were, nevertheless, essential credentials for the privileged. Yet the first years with Albert saw a gradual withdrawal by the Queen, as much as was possible, into some reserved hours of privacy. Since Albert was uncomfortable with the demands and preoccupations, as well as the denizens, of upper-class society, Victoria soon disappeared as the focal point of high life in London. The tendency to be socially self-sufficient accelerated when she and Albert began exploring the possibilities of a country home in which to escape London and capture a semblance of family life. As the monarchy became more bourgeois, in public as well as in private, it would lose much of its attractiveness to the aristocracy, traditionally a counterweight to the fickle public mood. Although peerages and perquisites remained in the Sovereign's gift, in the diminished modern monarchy these were far more often her Prime Minister's selection than her own.

Change came at first imperceptibly. The most private part of their lives, apart from the large bed in which Victoria and Albert slept, was their morning. The romantic pair of writing tables, side by side in the same room, had soon given way to the more efficient practice of using separate rooms. At the close of the morning's work the Prince would come to the Queen's room. There they would discuss business, or read to each other from books as various as Hallam's *Constitutional History* and Scott's *The Lay of the Last Minstrel.*

After a luncheon usually with guests, appointments often filled their afternoons. When there was leisure time, they still played piano duets, sketched, or painted. Despite Albert's seriousness in public, a result of his continued grappling with English language and manners, when with Victoria, as with his young children, he was playful and eager to shed restraints, crawling about the floor with Pussy and Bertie, delighting Victoria by making her an "April Fool." But her self-portrait, drawn on

May 19, 1843, reveals how seriously she thought of herself after six years on the throne. Her lips are set, her large eyes broadly spaced, her hair trimly parted in the middle and braided at the sides. It is a portrait of a sovereign who had left fun behind.

All of Princess de Lieven's visitors, the Princess wrote to Lady Palmerston from Paris, told her "that Prince Albert is exceedingly unpopular, the Queen also, and that both of them are extremely rude." They were both not so much rude as ungracious—the acquired arrogance that often came with elevated position. Whatever small courtesies Victoria had been taught as a child, protocol, even among the most privileged, limited her intimacies as Queen. Albert bore himself stiffly and shook hands awkwardly—more, perhaps, a sign of insecurity of position (he still had no legal status in England other than as the Queen's husband) than Germanic hauteur. It was said that he did not even sit on horseback in the English manner. At Court there were murmurs of resentment that the pair, for privacy, often exchanged comments in German. Albert even made comments in English that suggested unweaned loyalty to Germany. His "No tailor in England can make a coat" caused as much outrage on one island as his "The Poles are as little deserving of sympathy as the Irish" did on the other.

The public prudery by which they protected the Court caused additional difficulties. A repetition of Palmerston's escapade—Victoria knew nothing of it until she married—of breaking into a bedroom at Windsor and trying to violate its screaming occupant because he mistook one room for another, would not be permitted to recur. Caution required that ladies-in-waiting not receive men in their rooms, neither husbands, brothers, nor fathers. "On the Queen's accession," Albert noted in a memorandum in 1852, "Lord Melbourne had been very careless in his appointments, and great harm had resulted in the Court therefrom. Since her marriage I had insisted upon a closer line being drawn, and though Lord Melbourne had declared that 'damned morality would undo us all,' we had found great advantage in it and were determined to adhere to it." Albert recorded an instance that year when Lord Derby, as Prime Minister, appealed unsuccessfully to have the wife of the new Lord Chancellor, Lord St. Leonards, presented at Court "although she had run away with him when he was still at school, and was now nearly seventy years old." The transgression had occurred a half-century earlier, and the couple had since lived respectable lives, but the Queen "said it would not do to receive her now . . . although society might do in that respect what it pleased; it was a principle at Court not to receive ladies whose characters are under stigma."

With the most succulent gossip barred from conversation, Victoria ran out of things to say after family talk and empty pleasantries, even with her closest friend in the Household, the Duchess of Sutherland. Almost the only time the Prince came alive at dinner was when he could discuss problems of drainage and heating, or the royal farm animals.

Dinner for Victoria and Albert, whether in London or at Windsor, was often solemn and seldom private. With rare exceptions, courtiers, however much they dreaded the duty, were present, even when no formal evening entertainment was scheduled. The cycle of ladies-in-waiting and gentlemen-in-waiting might change the names of the company at the table, but each was expected to remain in nominal attendance until the Queen and Consort elected to retire for the night. The Queen was, by protocol, last to arrive at dinner, Albert preceding her but first looking in at her preparations and paying her some small compliment. Then came Victoria, often a quarter of an hour later, her doors opened by two courtiers who bowed deeply as the bejeweled Queen made her entrance with a nod or a smile at the Prince.

Dinner was over when the Queen finished her portion. Since she was served first, and never toyed with her food, small talk could leave a guest hungry. The knowledgeable kept their remarks animated but brief. An intimate family meal with a rare Coburg visitor was more relaxed, Victoria noting how her husband was "always so merry" on such occasions.

After dinner, if no guests outside the Court were present, Albert in the earlier years of marriage would try to settle down to a game of chess —with an opponent, if available, or playing both sides himself. When he wanted to relieve the boredom of "chess evenings" by an invitation to men in scientific or literary life, Victoria resisted. Her fund of conversation was limited, and she saw herself as having the choice of keeping silent or having her educational deficiencies exposed. Albert would have to meet men in English intellectual life elsewhere than Windsor or Buckingham Palace. And he did.

Often, during domestic evenings, Albert was even diverted from chess to cards, one of his many intellectual sacrifices to keep the Queen content. Where they agreed, however, was in their hostility to the practice of permitting gentlemen to remain at table for hours over brandy, coffee, and cigars, while the women had to leave. The tradition emphasized that though the Queen might be sovereign, she was a woman, and as such remained in second-class status to the men. *She* had to leave her own table.

The Prince's practice was to leave the men a quarter of an hour before the others, this a signal, then going to join the ladies. Often he sang duets with Victoria, who preferred not to perform before gentlemen (although she sometimes did). But unless there were family members visiting, or a period of formal mourning intruded, evenings were lost to other pursuits, and Albert, who loved reading, had to catch up late into the night or very early in the morning.

One residence that the Queen acquired at her accession remained low on her list as a place to live. Much as Victoria enjoyed the seaside, the Royal Pavilion at Brighton, so loved by George IV, was uncomfortable by her standards and orientally ornate—"a strange Chinese looking thing, haunted by ghosts best forgotten." The town had grown around it, leaving little privacy. "I only see a little morsel of sea from one of my sitting room windows," she objected. And when she and the Prince walked along the crowded seafront, they were "mobbed by all the shopboys in the town, who ran and looked under my bonnet, treating us just as they do the Band, when it goes on parade." Before the year had ended, she and Albert had determined to investigate alternative places by the sea.

Other changes in life-style, including the Admiralty's ordering a paddlewheeled steam yacht for the Queen, had been assured by the trip to Scotland. In April 1843 the 1,049-ton *Victoria and Albert* was launched, to be manned by the crew of the obsolete *Royal George,* complete to Lord Adolphus FitzClarence as captain. Railway travel would be another fixture in Victoria's future movements. New trackage not only enlarged the range of accessibility for the Queen's visits, it also made it possible for her to think beyond the London suburbs for that seaside residence to replace the Brighton Pavilion.

The Queen's travels, however brief, were limited by what she thought appropriate to her position. Thus she would not go to Hampstead to see what was reputedly Cardinal Wolsey's bed, according to Elizabeth Barrett "a splendid fabric of tortoise shell & ivory, presented to the little prince of Wales by its proprietor, Mr. [John] Thompson, and waiting in his cottage . . . [at] the queen's pleasure for its removal to Windsor." Thompson, a wealthy antique collector, would have given the Queen more of his collection—part of his present was an ivory chair "in which a Pope had sate"—but, said the disappointed donor, "Her Majesty was too proud to come herself and inspect it." Finally she sent Albert, who spent two hours there, but too late, as Thompson died soon after at ninety-six, leaving "everything over & above his presents to Victoria" to a relative, the editor of a gossip sheet.

Whether the Queen agreed or refused to attend an event had much to do with whether it materialized as scheduled. The famed actor William Macready postponed his farewell from the stage for Victoria, who attended a Drury Lane command performance of *As You Like It* (with J. M. Morton's *A Thumping Legacy* as curtain-raiser) on June 12, 1843, the date he had set for his retirement. Macready put *Macbeth*—and his farewell address—off until the fourteenth. Even at that, in the tradition of grand opera and the grand style of acting, he would go on making farewell performances, Victoria paying a state visit for a benefit to the actor as late as July 10, 1848. It was unprecedented for a command performance to benefit the actor also, but the Queen made it an event by bringing with her not only the Prince, but Dowager Queen Adelaide and the Duchess of Kent. (Macready kept on retiring publicly, doing his last *Macbeth* at fifty-eight, again at Drury Lane, on February 26, 1851.)

Princess Alice had been born on April 25, 1843, expectation of the confinement having furnished Victoria with excuses for not doing such things as visiting the venerable Mr. Thompson. The christening, in early June, signaled a new round of activities, among them the unpleasant duty of entertaining the King of Hanover. Bent and thin, using his deafness to advantage where he could, Uncle Ernest deliberately materialized at the christening, Victoria wrote Leopold, *"just in time* to be *too late."* He also made a fuss over the rights to the late Queen Charlotte's jewels, which Victoria wore, although he claimed they belonged to the Crown of Hanover. She was "loaded with my diamonds," he complained to a friend, adding that they made "a very fine show." The wedding in July of Princess Augusta of Cambridge to the Grand Duke of Mecklenburg-Strelitz, a duchy hardly larger than its name, found the King of Hanover still in England, looking for ways of airing his rancor. He took his controversial seat in the House of Lords, an act that Sir Robert Peel downplayed, and at the wedding he pushed his way to the register to try to sign after Victoria, as a claim of precedence over the Prince. The Queen and Albert had just recovered from influenza, and were unsteady on their legs; nevertheless, after some discreet pushing and shoving, she managed to get the pen and the book to the Prince before her uncle could snatch them.

The next month he was still in England, threatening to remain until he retrieved Queen Charlotte's baubles. Worried about the potential

"John Bull's Connubial Vision for 1850"—sketch by John Doyle, July 1843. By 1850 the prophecy was well on the way to realization. Albert is the much-abused father to the far right, buried under the weight of his family.

embarrassment, Peel queried Victoria for advice. "The Queen is desirous that whatever is right should be done," she responded on August 13, 1843, "but [she] is strongly of opinion that the King of Hanover's threat (for such as it must be regarded) not to leave this country, till the affair is decided upon should in *no way* influence the transaction, as it is quite immaterial whether the King stays here longer or not." It was clearly a letter in which Albert had no hand.

A commission consisting of Lord Lyndhurst, Lord Langdale, and Chief Justice Tindal was appointed to review the dispute. All three died before deciding the award. Only in 1857 was a settlement made, substantially in favor of Hanover. By then Victoria, who had come to the throne with little jewelry of her own, had acquired more than she needed.

In the final days of the King of Hanover's visit, he proposed, according to Greville, that Albert take a walk with him. The Prince made some excuses that walking in city streets would expose them to inconvenience from the London crowds. "Oh, never mind that," said King Ernest. "I was still more unpopular than you are now, and used to walk about with perfect impunity." With that story about, he could return to Hanover feeling that he had got back some of his own.

On August 24 the Queen ceremonially closed the Parliamentary session and readied herself for her state visit to King Louis-Philippe of France. The voyage across the Channel was the first major test of the royal yacht, which Greville had inspected a few days before and pronounced "luxuriously fitted up, but everything is sacrificed to the comfort of the Court, the whole ship's company being crammed into wretched dog-holes, officers included." No one called the Queen's attention to any such problems, and the *Victoria and Albert* would be heavily used.

The royal houses of Europe treated Louis-Philippe coldly because he was considered a usurper and because he had initially courted popularity as a bourgeois king, thus becoming a traitor to the class into which he had forced himself. Since the Queen's visit to France early in September 1843 was the first by an English sovereign since that of Henry VIII to a country often considered its hereditary enemy, the encounter had more signifi-cance than a social visit to a favorite uncle's father-in-law. Enthusiastic receptions were worked up for Victoria at Tréport, en route to the Cha-teau d'Eu, and she was not displeased at having conveyed some semblance of respectability to the King. "The Emperor of Russia will be very much annoyed," she wrote in her journal, "but that is neither here nor there."

Then came autumn visits to great country houses like Chatsworth and Belvoir, and Peel's own Drayton Manor, with a day for an honorary degree for the Prince at Cambridge. There is a tale told of the young Queen, still innocent about much of the world's ills, being taken then to Trinity College, where she was shown about by the stern, massive-browed Master, William Whewell—her appointment, at the suggestion of both Albert and Peel. Looking down at the raw sewage floating along the Cam under the bridge, she asked, "What are those pieces of paper floating down the river?"

"Those, ma'am," said the quick-witted Whewell, "are notices that bathing is forbidden."

While Victoria remained at Drayton Manor, Albert visited the Radi-cal stronghold of Birmingham, where the mayor—a hosier—was an out-spoken Chartist. It was considered too hazardous a setting for the Queen, but the Prince was charmed by his cheering reception, the mayor assuring him of "the devoted loyalty of the whole Chartist body." It almost put out of mind Albert's awe at William Paxton's grand conservatory at Chatsworth. He would remember it later, but at the time it was Victoria who would write to Leopold that the structure designed by the Duke of Devonshire's efficient superintendent of gardens was "out and out the finest thing imaginable of its kind. It is one mass of glass, 64 feet high,

300 feet long, and 134 wide. The grounds, with all the woods and cascades and fountains, are so beautiful too." The facts she marshaled demonstrate what the Queen had picked up in interests from Albert, who seven years later would commission Paxton to plan a structure in that manner to house the Great Exhibition.

With Pussy already "learning her letters," Bertie struggling with sentences, and Alice leaving the "froglike" stage, Victoria learned to switch frames of reference back and forth from nation to nursery. As the year ended she wrote to her half-sister in Langenburg to ask Feodora how her children said their prayers. Feodora's answer suggests another family source of the questioning spirit associated with the Princess Royal, soon to be the more grown-up "Vicky." "They say it when in their beds, but not kneeling," "Feo" wrote; "how absurd to find *that* necessary, as if it could have anything to do with making our prayers more acceptable to the Almighty or more holy. How really clever people can have these notions I don't understand."

The only concern that preoccupied Victoria more than foreign affairs in the first months of 1844 was the need for a more private life than she could manage with the children in London, at Windsor, or in unloved Brighton. After retreating to Claremont, where they would not be, as she explained to Leopold, "the constant object of observation, and of newspaper articles," she was more determined than ever to have a place of her own. But plans to conduct a search went awry when Albert's father died on January 29. Duke Ernest, in his sixtieth year, was a victim of his dissipations. Nevertheless, Victoria and Albert mourned as if he had been a paragon cut off in his prime. "Here we sit together, poor Mama, Victoria, and myself, and weep," Albert wrote to Stockmar from Windsor, "with a great cold public around us, insensible as stone." Victoria was a "consoling angel," he added, and indeed her desolation was excessive in the manner of the time, which exploited the event to create a *frisson* of grief. More revealingly than she understood, Victoria wrote to Leopold, the dead duke's younger brother, "One loves to *cling* to one's grief." Although she hardly knew her father-in-law, he was "our dearest Papa," and the Court was commanded into deep mourning. The royal notepaper was heavily bordered in black; courtiers dressed in black; official gloom pervaded royal residences already known for a surfeit of solemnity.

Most appalling of all to Victoria—the reality of what was otherwise a distant and overdramatized death—was that it forced Albert into planning a return to Coburg. In part it was to pay his respects at his father's grave; more significantly it was to caution the new Duke Ernest, his brother, about his unashamed excesses, and to secure insincere pledges of good behavior. Besides, Albert ached for the sights and smells of what Victoria called his *"dearly beloved Vaterhaus."*

The thought of the empty bed (although she was again pregnant) filled the Queen with alarm. "I have *never* been separated from him for even *one night,"* she confided to Leopold, "and the *thought* of *such* separation is quite dreadful." That she meant it, and more, is evident from her later letter to Vicky, recalling being "clasped and held tight in the sacred Hours at Night when the world seemed only to be ourselves."

Even before his Channel crossing had begun, Albert wrote to her from Dover, expressing his hope that although his place at table would be vacant, his place in her heart would not be. By the time she received his note, he assured her, one of the fourteen days he would be away would already have passed—"thirteen more, and I am again within your arms."

With Albert's return from Coburg, Court mourning again became selective, as Victoria was eager to see the suddenly famous "General" Tom Thumb. The thirty-seven-inch entertainer had been filling Egyptian Hall in Piccadilly, as well as Phineas T. Barnum's pockets, but the American showman—who cut a foot from the General's height for publicity—knew a coup when he saw one, and hung a placard on the darkened door reading, *Closed this evening, General Tom Thumb being at Buckingham Palace by command of Her Majesty.* The Queen had asked that "the General appear before her, as he would appear anywhere else, without training in the use of the titles of royalty, as the Queen desired to see him act naturally and without restraint."

Despite that injunction, Barnum—six feet two—and his tiny charge arrived in velvet Court dress, and were solemnly briefed about bowing upon introduction, responding to the Queen indirectly through her lord-in-waiting, and retiring on command by backing smoothly out. In the Waterloo Gallery, Barnum recalled, "The Queen was modestly attired in plain black, and wore no ornaments. Indeed, surrounded as she was by ladies arrayed in the highest style of magnificence, their dresses sparkling with diamonds, she was the last person whom a stranger would have pointed out in that circle as the Queen of England." Barnum did not know that her simple costume was a concession to mourning.

The General made a graceful bow, and in a wavering treble he greeted Victoria and her guests with "Good evening, ladies and gentlemen!" After some laughter, he was invited to take the Queen's hand. He chatted volubly on the "first rate" pictures, and asked to see the Prince of Wales, then three years old. The Prince was in bed, asleep, said Victoria, and invited Tom to come again when Bertie was awake. Then the General sang and danced and did his repertoire of imitations for an hour, concluding with a dialogue with Prince Albert.

Discovering that their audience would receive notice in the *Court Circular,* Barnum asked whether it would be a favorable comment or only a brief mention. Whatever he wanted, he was told—and so Barnum wrote his own review, in which Tom Thumb's "personation of the Emperor Napoleon elicited great mirth and this was followed by a representation of the Grecian Statues after which the General danced a nautical horn-pipe and sang several of his favorite songs."

A lord-in-waiting led the way for Barnum and Tom Thumb to exit from the royal presence, and the long-legged impresario found retirement in Court fashion easier than did the tiny General. "We had a considerable distance to travel in that long gallery . . . , and whenever the General found he was losing ground, he turned around and ran a few steps, then resumed the position of 'backing out,' then turned around and ran, and so continued to alternate his methods of getting to the door, until the gallery fairly rang with the merriment of the royal spectators." The curious behavior finally excited Victoria's favorite poodle. It went barking after the midget, who "with his little cane commenced an attack on the poodle, and a funny fight ensued, which renewed and increased the merriment of the royal party. . . . We had scarcely passed into the ante-room, when one of the Queen's attendants came to us with the expressed hope of Her Majesty that the General had sustained no damage. . . ."

At a second audience, Tom Thumb met the Princess Royal and the Prince of Wales. "The Prince is taller than I am," said Tom, "but I *feel* as big as anybody." As for the Yellow Drawing Room in which he was received, he thought it was "a prettier room than the picture gallery; that chandelier is very fine."

At a third visit, the General sang "Yankee Doodle" and received for his pains a gold pencil case, having earned earlier an enameled coat of arms set with emeralds. At each visit Barnum came away with a purse that made up for closing Egyptian Hall. Payment was hardly necessary. The royal sponsorship had made Tom Thumb the rage of London. It also said something about the Queen's lowbrow tastes. She liked lion tamers and midgets, waxworks and French farces, melodramatic operas and paintings of animals, sentimental novels and moralistic sermons. In a few years she would patronize Barnum's next sensation, the "Swedish nightingale," Jenny Lind. In such tastes, Victoria mirrored her people far better than did her imported husband, and in later years she would make that perception one of the strengths of her reign.

News of an imminent state visitor soon pushed aside all thoughts of restoring the mourning for Albert's father, and put the Court and Cabinet into a frenzy of preparation. Nicholas I, the Russian Czar, had become interested in England as a result of Victoria's own visit to his longtime enemy, France. This time the French were unhappy at the possible rapprochement with Russia, and Victoria told Leopold, her informal conduit to Louis-Philippe, "If the French are angry at this visit, let their dear King and their Princes come [here]."

When Nicholas arrived in June, Victoria was seven months pregnant; yet she went to Ascot with the Czar, and to the opera, held a review of troops for him in Windsor Great Park, gave huge dinners for him every evening in Buckingham Palace's Waterloo Room, and listened to his undiplomatic bellowing, carefully directed toward the Prince and Prime Minister—since she was a woman—on European politics, particularly his loathing of France and his contempt for Turkey. Autocratic and severe at home, he was unversed in the niceties of Court behavior abroad, but Victoria was charmed by his rough handsomeness (at forty-eight he was six feet two), his "melancholy" eyes, his stern honesty, and his declaration on arrival at Windsor that he needed some straw from the stables on which to sleep. Besides, she wrote to Leopold, the Czar "spoke in the highest praise of dearest Albert."

With little warning of the visit, Court officials had to improvise each event, yet everything went grandly except the military review. The Duke of Wellington (attired as a Russian field marshal) had ordered that no guns go off until the Queen was at a distance, as she abhorred cannonfire. By mistake, the order to fire was given as the Queen approached. The Duke swore lustily and ordered the artillery out of sight. Victoria professed unconcern. The Czar was content.

When the King of France rushed to London afterwards, following a suitable period for Victoria's recovery from the birth of Prince Alfred on August 26, he had words to describe Albert that Victoria relished— that *"le Prince Albert, c'est pour moi le Roi."* Such nomenclature was far from possible in reality, where an M.P., Peter Borthwick, early in 1845 upset any plans Victoria might have had for renewing the attempt to give

Albert an English title. A paragraph had appeared in the *Daily Chronicle* in February rumoring that the Prince would be named King Consort, and Borthwick, in the Commons, raised the question with Peel. When the Prime Minister correctly denied that any title was being considered, Victoria, embarrassed by the speculation, quickly picked up by provincial papers, wrote to Peel that she was "positive that something must at once be done to place the Prince's position on a constitutionally recognized footing, and to give him a title adequate to that position."

Again, nothing happened, but a happy distraction had already come along to divert the Queen. Some months before, Peel had discovered a potential royal seaside residence for sale, in one of Victoria's favorite places, the Isle of Wight. Negotiations faltered when the Prince went to Coburg; they dragged on during the Queen's confinement. The asking price for the two hundred acres at Osborne was £30,000, later reduced to £28,000, including furniture, but that figure was reasonable only if the purchaser planned to use the existing structure. For the Royal Family the house was far too small, and the furniture of little but temporary use. Whatever was there would have to be replaced or substantially enlarged.

Peel had warned Victoria and Albert that no Parliamentary grant could be expected, and that there would even be resistance—the times were hard—to the renovation and repair of Buckingham Palace. Expecting no help with Osborne House, they planned to sell the obsolete Pavilion at Brighton, and use the proceeds to compensate the government for any expenditures to improve Buckingham Palace.*

The Privy Purse, in which Albert and Anson had made substantial economies, would pay for Osborne, which became private property, as Victoria put it to Leopold, "a place of *one's own,* quiet and retired, and free from all Woods and Forests, and other charming Departments who really are the plague of one's life." She offered £26,000 and Lady Isabella Blatchford accepted that amount if her furniture was a separate valuation. When settlement was made on May 1, the final account came to £27,814

---

*The Queen ordered the stripping of the Pavilion begun in 1846, and through 1848 143 vanloads of furniture, decorations, porcelain, pictures, clocks, and carpets were removed to Buckingham Palace, Kensington Palace, and Windsor Castle. In 1847 a sale of part of the objects was held; in mid-1848 the remaining items were sold. On June 7, 1848, the doors of the Pavilion were locked and the keys given to the Lord Chamberlain. However, demolition by the government met with opposition from the town councillors of Brighton, who bought it in 1850 (for £60,000—but not before the fixtures had been removed by the Board of Woods and Forests, which wantonly destroyed much of the interior in the process).

18s. 5d. When the Prince decided that for privacy and guest accommodations, more land was required, a further £18,000 arranged that. It was impossible to imagine a prettier spot, Victoria wrote enthusiastically to Lord Melbourne. It reminded the Prince of the bay at Naples.

Even before settlement, Albert sent for his proposed builder—*his*, because Victoria was quite willing to leave renovations of the existing property to him. Albert's intention was to enlarge and repair the mansion, which already had sixteen bedrooms, but not nearly enough service area. He consulted not an architect, but an imaginative and successful London builder, Thomas Cubitt, who had made a fortune out of developing the district now called Belgravia. Cubitt, then in his late fifties, had first been called upon at Christmas 1844 and asked for a survey of the house. His report recommended a new structure as "less expensive in the end than the repair of the present one." Victoria and Albert had agreed, but wanted to live there as soon as possible, and directed that the old house be repapered and painted for occupation while plans went ahead to design and build a new house. Architects grumbled at the slight to their calling, but the self-taught Cubitt went ahead with the Italianate structure Albert outlined. After Easter, Cubitt walked around the property with the couple, explaining his ideas for the new house as well as his plans for immediate improvements to the existing one. He would become a friend, one of Albert's few real friends in England.

The next year, once Victoria and Albert moved into Osborne House, Cubitt was also given the task of rehabilitating Buckingham Palace, most parts of which, the Queen had told Peel in February 1845, "are in a sad state." A large sewer had been discovered under the forecourt, which explained why substantial portions of the palace were, in her words, hardly "*decent* for the occupation of the Royal Family or any visitors." There were also too few rooms for formal or family use. A study commission representing the rival bureaucracies was appointed, and the Commons, on receiving its report, voted to add £150,000 to funds available for what was called the enlargement of the palace; but not until 1847 were plans even unveiled for the project. In the meantime, the Queen determined to live away from London as much as possible.

One official function performed at Buckingham Palace before the Royal Family left for Osborne in the spring of 1845 brought William Wordsworth, the elderly Poet Laureate, to London. For the Queen's Ball he had neither Court suit nor ceremonial sword, at seventy-five never having needed such accoutrements before. An even more venerable poet, the eighty-two-year-old Samuel Rogers, lent Wordsworth what was needed, including buckle and stockings, and he was presented to the Queen after his publisher, Samuel Moxon (so Benjamin Haydon reported), "had hard work to make the dress fit." According to Elizabeth Barrett's secondhand report, Victoria told him that she was quite "fluttered" but "was glad to see him & had never seen him before." At Court afterwards she confided that she had never read Wordsworth's poems—upon which a maid-of-honor (according to another, Amelia Murray) answered more earnestly than decorously, "That is a great pity—they would do your Majesty good."

To mark the move to Osborne, the Privy Council met there in May, the first of hundreds of voyages across the Solent that members of the government would have to make over the years. A more important problem involving officials accompanying the Queen was the forthcoming journey to Coburg that she and Albert had planned. So that no regency need be declared in the Queen's absence, a Minister of State would join the party. The arrangement was a sign of the revolution in communications in Victoria's lifetime. The steamship and the railway had been followed, in the year of her accession, by the first practical electric telegraph. By 1845, telegraphy was operational in America and England, and on the Continent. If necessary, an Act of State could now be performed abroad.

Since Victoria's mother was a Coburger, as was Albert, anticipation of the August journey to the cradle of her family excited the Queen. Her first impression, as she crossed into the conglomeration of states east of the Rhine, was of the singularity of hearing "the *people* speak German." The royal party's first overnight stopping place was the Schloss Brühl, between Cologne and Bonn, a stately castle belonging to the King of Prussia. From there they traveled to Bonn, where Albert had been a university student, and where the seventy-fifth anniversary of the birth of Ludwig van Beethoven was being celebrated on August 12 by the unveiling of a statue, and by a concert conducted by Franz Liszt. Because the King and Queen of Prussia had promised to take part, and to bring with them Queen Victoria and Prince Albert, huge crowds began to mass in the early hours of the morning. By noon, as people became agitated and unruly in the sweltering sun, there was still no sign of the heads of state.

At last the shriek of a train whistle was heard, and peals of bells began to announce the arrival of their Majesties Wilhelm IV and Victoria, with their retinues, who took places on a balcony overlooking the shrouded

statue. Then Professor H. K. Breidenstein stepped forward to the monument, delivered his delayed oration, and—to the roar of cannon—pulled
on a cord. "Unfortunately," Victoria wrote in her journal, "when the
statue was uncovered, it turned its back." Beethoven had been placed with
his posterior to the assemblage, which was perfectly in character for the
irascible composer but inappropriate for the occasion.

Several of the musical celebrities there—one was Hector Berlioz—
shuttled back and forth between Bonn and the castle at Brühl to give
command performances. Liszt's was the most memorable. Finding his
playing interrupted by royal chattering, he hammered more stridently at
the piano; when the chattering continued, he stopped in mid-measure. A
second attempt produced no more silence than the first, and he again
lifted his hands from the keys. None of the eminences took it amiss, and
the concert was abruptly over.

The last morning of the festival began with a great memorial concert
in the *Festhalle,* featuring Marie Pleyel, Jenny Lind, and Liszt himself.
The program began without the exalted guests. When Liszt approached
the rostrum to conduct the cantata he had composed for the occasion, the
royal party was still absent. He held his baton until the restlessness of the
crowd forced him to begin, and was at the closing bars of the long,
lugubrious work when the royal guests finally arrived. For them, Liszt
conducted a second full performance, although the audience made unmistakable signs that once had been enough.

Victoria was less concerned about the King of Prussia's lack of
interest in music than about his failure to accord Albert the precedence
at official functions "which common civility required," she recalled in a
memorandum in 1856, "because of the presence of an Archduke, the
third son of an uncle of the then reigning Emperor of Austria, . . . whom
the King would not offend." (Albert's only legal position was that of the
younger brother of the Duke of Saxe-Coburg. English law, Victoria continued to complain, "does not know of him.") For years thereafter she
refused invitations from the Prussian Court.

Though insignificant in Victoria's scale of values, a more serious
problem, causing widespread indignation in England, was the participation of the Queen and Prince in a Prussian massacre of deer. The continental custom was to herd them into an enclosure to be shot. To the
London press, that was murder rather than sport. In his diary Greville
dismissed the "clumsy (and false) attempt to persuade people that she was
shocked and annoyed. But the truth is, her sensibilities are not acute, and

though she is not at all ill-natured, perhaps the reverse, she is hard-hearted, selfish and self-willed." If any corroboration were needed for Greville, it came at Coburg, where Victoria and Albert were guests on an elevated stand in an enclosure where thirty wild boar were let loose to be speared, or shot. According to her journal the platform for the audience was "charmingly arranged"—curious words in the aftermath of a butchery. "After this," she concluded, without indicating any lacerated feelings, "we walked away & then got into our carriage & drove home."

How much may captive guests be excused? Were English "hunting" parties more sporting when a pack of hounds was loosed to torment a fox, or when the Prince was applauded for shooting one hundred pheasants beaten toward him between breakfast and *Mittagessen?* Whatever one called hunting, the slaughter was a matter of degree, and for Victoria and Albert a public relations fiasco at home. Unknowing, they gloried in the *Gemütlichkeit* of their sentimental journey to Coburg. Uncle Leopold and Aunt Louise had arrived ahead of them for the family reunion, as had Victoria's mother and Albert's stepmother ("Mama Marie"), and Feodora. At the palace on August 19, Victoria's journal records, "the staircase was full of cousins." At the Rosenau, a mock-medieval structure set high in the Thüringer Wald four miles from Coburg, where Albert had spent the happiest days of his boyhood, the couple used three rooms atop a winding staircase. "I felt," she wrote, "as if I should like always to live here with my dearest Albert, and if I was not what I am—this would have been my real home . . . it is like a beautiful dream."

The presence of Lord Aberdeen and Lord Liverpool were constant reminders of the Queen's world outside the fairy-tale atmosphere, but the days passed largely in sightseeing, levees, balls, concerts, theatricals, family mealtimes, and in a pervasive feeling that time had bypassed Duke Ernest's ministate. More German than usual crept into Victoria's account as she slipped into the Coburg ambience. On a quiet Saturday afternoon she "sent for *Bratwürste* which is the national dish of Coburg—from the Markt & ate them & drank some of the excellent Coburg beer—they were so good."

On August 26, Albert's twenty-sixth birthday was celebrated at his birthplace—*"more than I ever hoped for,"* Victoria wrote. Her gift, carried from London, was a painting by Thomas Uwins (1782–1857), *Cupid and Psyche,* which she knew he liked, and a walking stick and a snuffbox. (At Osborne, reflecting the Queen's distaste for tobacco, the only room not monogrammed above the doorway with a *V & A* was Albert's smoking room. It was denied the *V.*) "From Mama," she added, scrupulously, "he got trifles, and from Ernest a beautiful chessboard." Albert's health was drunk at dinner, after which the family went to a concert at the *Marmorsaal* (Marble Hall), where two of the pieces performed were compositions by Albert and Ernest.

"God grant that we may come here again ere long!" she wrote. The next morning they left in carriages for the long ride to the nearest railway station. Fifteen years later, when finally they were able to return, there were tracks laid all the way. Time would creep up even on Coburg.

As 1845 wound down, it was clear to officialdom, as Greville noted in his diary, that Albert had become "so identified" with the Queen "that they are one person, and as he likes and she dislikes business, it is obvious that while she has the title, he is really discharging the functions of the Sovereign. He is King to all intents and purposes." His memoranda of meetings with Ministers carefully used "we" rather than "I," but Peel usually brought his problems to Albert. Among them, when the couple returned from Coburg, was the Government's inability to repeal the Corn Laws in order to import cheaper grain into Ireland. The failure of the potato crop had caused widespread famine, but protectionists in Peel's party refused any compromise. Not even the Duke of Wellington, who often saw beyond party lines, would support Peel, who reluctantly announced his resignation early in December, while the Royal Family was at Osborne.

"We were, of course, in great consternation," Albert noted in a memorandum written at Osborne when Peel's message arrived. Since public opinion opposed the protectionist policy, they could not understand, the memorandum went on, why measures similar to those adopted by other European countries hit by the potato blight could not be enacted in England—opening the harbors and otherwise taking "energetic means" to replace the "usual food" of the "poorer class." Parliament, however, reflected the landed interest, and the "poorer class" had few votes. When even the revered and godlike Duke of Wellington would go no further than to deprecate the "fright" given to Peel over some "rotten potatoes," the Sovereign could only privately deplore rather than publicly lead. All that Victoria could do—and only then, a year later, when the founding of the organization made it possible—was to contribute to the British Association for the Relief of the Extreme Distress in the Remote Parishes of Ireland and Scotland, created by Lionel de Rothschild and

Abel Smith. Legend has it that the Queen subscribed a mere five pounds; in fact, in the subscription list preserved in Dublin the first three names are "H.M. The Queen, £2,000, Rothschild's, £1,000, Duke of Devonshire, £1,000."

It had been easy for Victoria and Albert to believe, confident as they were of Peel's efficiency and integrity, that he would go on forever. The imminent reorganization of government further demonstrated the instability of electoral office and the continuity of the sovereign, political realities that Victoria would not allow herself to forget. Less concerned about distress in Ireland than about relations with France if the Francophile Lord Palmerston, as seemed inevitable, returned as Foreign Minister, Victoria hoped that Lord John Russell—the heir apparent as Prime Minister—would be unable to form a government. After a fortnight he did indeed fail to piece a Cabinet together from his split party, and Peel was asked to continue. Meeting with Victoria and Albert at Windsor, according to the Prince's minutes, Peel was "much moved" by their desire to have him return to office. "There is no sacrifice that I will not make for your Majesty," Peel assured the Queen, "except that of my honour."

Peel's patched-up Cabinet promised only a temporary delay of the inevitable. Attempting to help him, Albert went to the Commons on January 27, 1846, to lend moral support at a Corn Laws debate. On the floor, Lord George Bentinck described the Prince's presence as giving "the semblance of a personal sanction of her Majesty to a measure which, be it for good or for evil, a great majority, at least of the landed aristocracy of England, of Scotland, and of Ireland, imagine fraught with deep injury, if not ruin, to them."

Albert would never again go to the House of Commons. Yet more and more, as Peel struggled through the tumultuous last months of his Ministry, Albert was King without a crown. Victoria, again pregnant, left nearly everything but the most ceremonial functions to her husband. "When politics are chaotic," Lady Palmerston complained to Dorothea de Lieven, "evening parties become duller. The Queen is in good health, but her pregnancy is the despair of her dressmakers. . . ." Albert's memoranda of conversations with the embattled Prime Minister more often read, "I saw this day R. Peel" than the more circumspect but misleading "We." Victoria's letters suggest more involvement with affairs than was the case, because she routinely commented in writing on matters brought to her; but it was only after the birth of her third daughter, Princess Helena, on May 25, 1846, and Peel's final departure from office early in

July, that she returned to full activity, again prompted by foreign-policy concerns. As Greville put it on July 4, and as she realized, "Small as is the direct authority of the Sovereign, it is by no means inconvenient or unimportant to have her preference and good will. It is a source of strength, and it may often turn a balance; in short, it is a very good thing and may possibly hereafter be turned to great account."

The authority of the sovereign manifested itself in many ways, and heedful that any cession of authority relinquished it forever, and led to new erosion, Victoria gently vetoed the suggestion from Sir George Grey that commissions for army officers be stamped with her seal rather than be sent to her for signature. "The Queen does not at all object to the amount of trouble which the signature of so many Commissions has hitherto entailed upon her, as she feels amply compensated by the advantage of keeping up a personal connection between the Sovereign and the Army." She understood the relationship between symbolism and authority.

It was a wrench for Victoria to release the seals of office to Lord John Russell, a weak Prime Minister, and to Viscount Palmerston, his domineering Foreign Minister, in place of Peel and Aberdeen; but there were no alternatives. Overstepping the niceties of protocol, she declared to Viscount Hardinge, in asking him to remain in charge of affairs in India, that the Ministry that had fallen had been "one of the most brilliant Governments this Country ever had." But she had learned much since the last political changing of the guard. "The Queen is very kind and gentle, and shows no regrets," Lady Palmerston observed. "How things change in this world!" The regrets were there, but not on public view. And to make certain of that, Victoria returned to the privacy of Osborne, where her chief external interest became the long-running affair of the Spanish royal marriages and succession, in which the French intervened in September with an announcement from Queen Marie Amélie that her son had married the Infanta Louisa.

Victoria's icy response, which she could send as a private letter in return to a private letter, was clearly her own. The Government's response was another matter, and Russell sent Palmerston's proposed instructions to his ambassador in Madrid to the Queen for review. She kept the draft two days, then returned it with her own comments and objections. "Her letter," Greville noted, "was remarkably well written, and all the objections concisely but ably put, and it exhibited a very correct knowledge of the state of [political] parties in Spain. The consequence of the Queen's letter was that Russell assembled Palmerston, Lansdowne, and Clarendon at his house, where they discussed the matter for two hours, and finally agreed on a letter to be written in place of that which Palmerston had first composed."

The next morning the revised instructions were sent to Victoria, who gave her approval. "Nothing can exceed her indignation and that of the Prince at the conduct of the King of the French," continued Greville, "and she spoke of it to Clarendon in the most unmeasured terms. 'He did not write to me himself,' she said [of Louis-Philippe], 'but made the Queen write. I don't think they will be much pleased with my answer.' " The affair quickly validated Greville's assessment of the foreign-policy influence an activist sovereign could have.

To Leopold, whose wife was acquiring a Spanish sister-in-law, Victoria called the cynical arrangement *"infamous."* In the long run the machinations proved useless for France, and soured the *entente cordiale* that Victoria had been encouraging.

On September 14, 1846, the Royal Family moved into the new Osborne House. Lady Lyttleton, remaining in charge of the Royal Nursery, wrote of the children scampering about, each attended by a scarlet-clad footman, and Victoria called the occasion "like a dream to be here now in our own house, of which we laid the first stone only fifteen months ago." Cubitt and the Prince had meticulously planned everything down to the height of the furniture. The Queen's private sitting room had twin writing tables of the same elevation, but the Prince's had three-quarters of an inch more knee room. The dining room table and chairs were an inch lower than normal height to compensate for the Queen's small stature.

At the close of their first dinner in the house, everyone rose to drink to the royal couple's health, and Albert responded with a house-warming hymn of Luther's, from the 128th Psalm:

> *So shall thy wife be in thy house*
> *Like vine with clusters plenteous,*
> *Thy children sit thy table round*
> *Like olive plants all fresh and sound.*

"The windows," Lady Lyttleton wrote, "lighted by the brilliant lamps in the rooms, must have been seen far out at sea."

"When one is so happy & blessed in one's home life, as I am,"

Victoria had written in her journal a few months earlier, "Politics (provided my Country is safe) must only take a 2nd place." Home life meant the proximity of Albert rather than the presence of her children, as she confided to Stockmar when, in July 1846, the Prince had gone off on one of his many ceremonial journeys, this time to dedicate the Albert Dock at Liverpool. "I feel lonely without my dear Master," she wrote, "and though I know other people are often separated for a few days I feel habit could not make me get accustomed to it. Without him everything loses its interest. It will always be a terrible pang for me to separate from him even for two days; and I pray God never to let me survive him."

In December, when the family returned, Cubitt arrived with plans for Household and Main Wings to replace the old house, which continued to be a service structure until the next stages were constructed. (By the time Victoria and Albert were finished building and furnishing Osborne, it had cost them £200,000, all of which they were paying for out of their own income, now efficiently managed.) The plaster walls were nearly dry, furnaces having been run while the family was away, and more of Victoria's and Albert's personal pictures could be hung. For the dining room's largest wall, Franz-Xavier Winterhalter was painting a large group portrait of the Royal Family, the Queen and Prince seated, the children around them.

It may have been the Italianate quality of structure and setting that suggested to Victoria and Albert commissioning statues of themselves in Roman dress. Albert's, by the German sculptor Emil Wolff, shows the Prince in a warrior's short skirted tunic, and barefoot, shield at his side, left arm resting on his belted scabbard. Victoria's, by John Gibson, is a Roman queen, crowned and sandaled, in bare-shouldered dress and cloak, scroll in one hand, wreath in the other. Both are at Osborne House still, where the Queen and Prince accumulated a long corridor of classic reproductions as well as new works in Roman style. One, bought at the Great Exhibition of 1851 and given by Albert to the Queen as a Christmas gift, was William Geefs's heroic and half-nude *Paul et Virginie*. Another would be John Bell's neoclassical nude and erotically posed Andromeda, exhibited by the sculptor ostensibly as an example of modern bronze casting, and bought by Victoria in 1851 for Albert. Still another was William Theed's neoclassical *Narcissus*, totally nude in the original but fig-leafed in Victoria's copy. Perhaps this was done because the exposure of male genitals would have made guests uneasy: Victoria and Albert demonstrated few qualms about flesh in art.

Possibly the most intriguing painting to be hung at Osborne House was one not publicly visible—a startling, sensual *Hercules and Omphale*, by Anton von Gegenbaur, well over life size, that covered much of the wall opposite Albert's bathtub in the couple's private apartments. The canvas, which would be astonishing in the household of a truly prudish pair, suggests that Victoria and Albert were not. But perhaps *Hercules and Omphale* is also an index to Albert's subconscious. The nubile young woman, dandled on the broad knee of the muscular god and clad only in alabaster flesh and a head scarf, is in Greek myth the Queen of Lydia, who once kept Hercules as her slave. Dated Rome, 1830, it was bought by the Prince in 1844, when furnishings were being acquired for Osborne. It hangs there still.

Painting remained important to Victoria and Albert. They regularly commissioned pictures. The year before, each had had Sir Charles East-lake do a painting as a birthday present for the other, with Eastlake having to keep the secret. Maclise was also kept busy. "He is in great favour with the Queen," Dickens gossiped to Cornelius Felton, "and paints secret pictures for her to put on her husband's table on the morning of his birthday, and the like." The Queen and Prince also enjoyed receiving lessons from artists they admired, like Edwin Landseer, recognizing that they could improve their standard of competence and make a pleasant avocation more rewarding.

Having seen a volume of lithographs by Edward Lear on the Abruzzi, and another on Rome and its environs, Victoria asked Lear, author also that year of *The Book of Nonsense,* whether he would consider giving her lessons. Lear, then a scholarly-looking thirty-four, with small round eye-glasses and a thin mustache, traveled to Osborne in July 1846. Victoria noted in her journal for the fifteenth of that month, "Had a drawing lesson from Mr Lear, who sketched before me and teaches remarkably well, in landscape painting in watercolours." Later, the instruction was resumed at Buckingham Palace, where Victoria gratefully took Lear about to show him the art treasures on the walls and the cases containing the royal collection of miniatures. Completely carried away, and as usual forgetful of his surroundings, Lear exclaimed, "Oh! how *did* you get all these beautiful things?"

"I inherited them, Mr. Lear," said Victoria.

Two landscapes that the Queen did under Lear's tutelage have survived, and are in the Royal Library at Windsor—*Pavilion Wing at Osborne,* and *View of Portland from the Isle of Wight.*

On one stay in Buckingham Palace the next year—these became fewer and shorter as the family expanded—Victoria and Albert sat in the greenhouse (for the best light) for the photographer William Edward Kilburn. The new art attracted them—their first daguerreotypes had been taken several years before—and they would soon possess their own cameras and equipment. "Mine was really very successful," Victoria noted in her journal. "Those of the children are unfortunately failures." Children could not sit still long enough for the cumbersome time exposures required in 1847. She would capture her family better in her sketchbook.

Early in December 1848, the Queen was drawn to a more popular art form—Madame Tussaud's waxworks. As Princess, she had visited the exhibition in Baker Street, already then England's quasi-Pantheon, and as Queen she would make an annual visit to the cattle show held in the large hall beneath Madame Tussaud's. She might then have also gone upstairs, as did a Norfolk farmer.

On paying his fee and entering, the farmer appeared to be the only spectator there, but as he gazed at the effigies of authentically costumed murderers and monarchs, he encountered "some ladies and children," and commented to one woman, "What ugly, grim-looking people some of these kings and queens are!"

The woman smiled. "I perfectly agree with you; they are!"

Someone in the party, pointing to a waxwork, identified Lord Nelson, and the farmer, proud of his coming from the same county as the illustrious admiral, exclaimed, "Ah! He was from my neighborhood!"

"Then you are from Norfolk?" one of the ladies asked. "Pray can you tell me anything about poor Mrs. Jermy, with whose melancholy fate I so deeply sympathize? Have you any information different from that which has appeared in the public papers?"

Mrs. Jermy was the widow of Isaac Jermy, the Town Recorder of Norwich, who had been murdered, with his son, a fortnight earlier, at Stanfield Hall, Wymondham, by a local auctioneer, James Rush. The farmer knew of the affair, but confessed, "No, madame, for I have been some days from home."

At that point Madame Tussaud herself entered, and quietly asked the farmer how he had got in, as she had forbidden paying visitors until the party he had seen had left. He had put down his money and walked in, he protested.

"Judge of my surprise," he recalled, "when she informed me I had had the honour of speaking to no other than our good and gracious Queen, and that the lady whose tender anxiety had been so warmly expressed for the injured widow of Stanfield Hall was the same illustrious person whose exalted rank does not, however, so elevate her but that the misfortunes and afflictions of others can reach her heart and excite her generous commiseration."

The group with Victoria had been her children and her attendants.

Foreign-policy matters continued to dominate the attention of the Queen into 1847, with Spain and Portugal resisting solution. Portugal seemed on the verge of civil war, with the unhelpful Queen Donna Maria, as Victoria put it in her journal, "as foolish as ever." Albert sent one of his equerries to Lisbon to help both sides negotiate, while Palmerston, separating himself from such efforts, showed unmistakable support for the anti-Queen "Junta." On Portugal, Albert acted alone, using the first-person-singular pronoun when writing to Palmerston and receiving responses directly. On a second level, Victoria dealt with the Prime Minister, writing to Russell at one point, about English foreign policy in general, how much she wanted to see England on the side of "integrity, morality, and honour"—elements she saw by implication as lacking in many of Palmerston's underhanded approaches. Her language, almost certainly reflecting Albert's as well, was a model for any nation at any time. "The Queen entreats Lord John Russell not to underrate the importance of keeping our foreign policy beyond reproach. Public opinion is recognized as a ruling power in our domestic affairs; it is not of less importance in the society of Europe with reference to the conduct of an individual state. To possess the *confidence* of Europe is of the utmost importance to this country."

With the winter of 1847 too vile for the family to be at Osborne, the Irish in another year of famine with little government effort at relief, foreign policy reverses abroad, and a section of scaffolding collapsing at Osborne on March 10, killing one of Cubitt's men and injuring several others, Albert was sunk in gloom. "We betook ourselves here," he wrote to his stepmother that March from the Isle of Wight, "in the hope of getting a breath of spring . . . but have found nothing but frost and a parching east wind; the day before yesterday for a change we had a foot of snow." Finally, April brought real spring; Albert busied himself with Cubitt's construction work, and Victoria received dispatch boxes from London and planned another trip to Scotland. Their savings from Privy Purse income and other sources were such that she saw the possibilities of leasing or buying property in Scotland, which reminded her of Coburg.

Still, spring and summer in the seclusion of Osborne were compensations enough, and the family looked forward to regular visits. Albert was planning formal gardens to emphasize the Italianate nature of the structure, the work involving patios, balustrades, stairways, topiaries, pathways, lawns, parks, statues, and urns. He was ecstatically busy. The Queen even took her first sea bath, in the privacy of her own beach. A bathing machine —a dressing cubicle on wheels—could be moved on rails to the water. Victoria entered through a rear door, put on a bathing garment inside (and a broad hat) and went down the steps from the forward platform, which led into the water. When she reached a foothold, her dresser rang a bell, and the bathing attendant led the horse drawing the machine out of the water until it had to be recalled. The Queen splashed about until she was ready to emerge, then went back into the machine. It was not a method to encourage swimming, but at the least it was contact with the new reality of sea water. Bathing machines would survive into the 1930s.

On August 11 they left Osborne Pier in the *Victoria and Albert* with the Queen's half-brother Prince Charles of Leiningen and the two oldest royal children, in a convoy including four warships and the tender *Fairy*. The trip took them up the Welsh coast and past the Isle of Man, to the Clyde and Glasgow. While the steam yacht continued on around Scotland to the Sound of Jura, they visited sparsely populated and wild country, undisturbed by the incessant rain, or by the fact that the Queen was pregnant. Sir James Clark remained convinced of the tonic properties of mountain air, and suggested for a residence that Deeside, in the east, near Aberdeen, provided the best of both worlds—a drier climate and a Highland location. The Prince wrote to Stockmar, "Whenever we stir out we come home almost frozen and always wet to the skin. . . . The grouse are wild, and the deer very hard to get at, despite all of which we are still very happy." What particularly made them happy was the sense of remoteness from crowds and business. When, just after they returned from Scotland, Sir Robert Gordon, tenant of Balmoral, died, the Queen and Prince became interested in acquiring the lease. It was a place of mountain solitude in the sunnier Deeside area. James Giles, an Aberdeen artist, was asked to send sketches of the property to Osborne.

The Russell Ministry, which the Queen had temporarily escaped in Scotland, had been piling up frustrations for her at home. Appointments were being made by Russell without consultation—even that of a Court physician—and dispatches from Palmerston were leaving the Foreign Office before Victoria had seen a draft. Her absences were no excuse: a Minister was always at hand as liaison. Late in December 1847, she noted her "shock" to the Prime Minister that a member of his Government, Sir Charles Wood—he was Chancellor of the Exchequer—had made a speech in which he named people destined to hold "high offices" in the "next Government." To do that without consultation was bad enough, but one of the names he had suggested was "Mr. Disraeli(!)"—whom Victoria privately viewed as a bounder.

The external upheavals of 1848 only brushed England. France was about to go through another convulsion. From neighboring Belgium, Leopold, who had much to fear, wrote to Victoria, "The human race is a *sad* creation, and I trust the other planets are better organised and that we may get there hereafter." One of the sadder creations was Louis-Philippe, his portly and pompous father-in-law, who had disappointed French expectations of the early 1830s, yet smugly assumed that he could hang on and even create a dynasty. In Greece, popular risings threatened to depose King Otho, named when Leopold was forced to give up his ambitions there. Otho had long flouted the liberal constitution under which he was crowned, and few had any sympathy for him. In Spain and Portugal, civil wars loomed. In the ramshackle Hapsburg empire, Austria was finding it difficult to restrain the smoldering national aspirations of Magyars, Czechs, Serbs, and Italians, among others, while in fragmented peninsular Italy there were renewed outbreaks of unity movements.

To a friend, on February 29, Charles Dickens wrote, "If the Queen should be marked in her attentions to old Papa Philippe, I think there will be great discontent and dissatisfaction expressed throughout the country. Meantime, we are in a queer position ourselves, with great distress in the manufacturing towns, and all sorts of public bedevilments." Overthrown on February 24, the seventy-four-year-old Louis-Philippe had fled from Paris in disguise with his family, managing, with the connivance of the British consul, to sail from Honfleur. When the refugees arrived in New-haven, the King appealed to Victoria for asylum. Since she had already been cautioned by Russell to offer no help that might give the appearance of assistance in recovering the French crown, she sent Louis-Philippe to Claremont; it belonged to his son-in-law. For temporary living expenses, funds were advanced from a secret Intelligence account. By the end of the year the new French regime, glad to be rid of the monarchy, restored the King's property, but not Louis-Philippe.

Political turmoil on the Continent would continue in the intervening months. In Germany early in March the Prince of Prussia, afterwards Emperor William I, highly unpopular in his own country, fled for his life, also in disguise. Belgium appeared safe enough as refuge for him to wait out what would be only temporary exile.

In England, Victoria, more careworn than ever before in her adult life, worried about uprisings and about the imminent birth of her sixth child. The assessment of Mary Ann Evans—"George Eliot"—was that Victoria had nothing to worry about. "Our little humbug of a queen is more endurable than the rest of her race," she wrote to the preacher John Sibree, "because she calls forth a chivalrous feeling, and [because] there is nothing in our constitution to obstruct the slow progress of political reform." Yet there had been financial panic in England; speculators had caused huge losses in inflated railway stock; wheat had sunk to new price lows, although the starving Irish could not afford it and would not eat it; unemployment and poverty had given new impetus to Chartism; and in the late winter the homeless and the hungry thronged London and other industrial cities. On March 18, 1848, another daughter was born to Victoria, to be named, after Albert's mother, Louise.

Chartist demonstrations in London had been growing larger and noisier since the revolution in Paris. To prevent the disaffected from rallying around symbolic martyrs, those radical leaders in prison for alleged sedition were released. As quid pro quo, the Chartists announced a nonviolent mass meeting on Kennington Common, in South London. From there a procession would convey a petition to the House of Commons, demanding the six points of liberalized enfranchisement spelled out in their charter, and signed by over a million people. The date set for what promised to be a peaceable revolution was April 10.

Alarmed, the Government called up reserve troops to patrol the streets, and 150,000 special constables were enlisted. "Every gentleman in London was sworn," Greville wrote. (Among them was a French exile, Prince Louis Napoleon Bonaparte.) Choosing prudence over political theater, Victoria, her child of three weeks with her, elected to go with Albert to Osborne, and, for security, Waterloo Station was cleared for her departure to Gosport on the morning of April 8. To Greville, Sir James Graham deplored the Queen's departure, "which he thinks will look like cowardice in her personally, and as indicative of a sense of danger which ought not to be manifested." On the night of the ninth, Colonel Charles Phipps, Equerry to Prince Albert, quietly walked the streets listening for any disparagement of the Queen's flight from London. He heard none, and reported to Albert, "Her reputation for personal courage stands so high, I never heard one person express a belief that her departure was due to personal alarm."

Before the tenth of April dawned, the Government seized the telegraph system to prevent any false reports from being spread. Gunboats patrolled the Thames, and soldiers guarded all bridges. Government offices were locked and guarded. Shops were shut. Chartists converging on Kennington Common began arriving at dawn; later, Metropolitan Police Commissioner Sir Richard Mayne told their leaders in a nearby public house that although no attempt to break up the meeting would be made, no procession would be permitted across the Thames bridges. They shook hands warmly; then Feargus O'Connor addressed his disappointingly small turnout of twenty thousand supporters, advising them to disperse. Hailing a cab, he took his petition to Sir George Grey at the Home Office. It was a very English demonstration.

The fear of upheaval would not be forgotten easily. Victoria now felt, she wrote Leopold, "an uncertainty in everything existing, which (uncertain as all human affairs must be) one never felt before. When one thinks of one's children, their education, their future—and prays for them—I always think and say to myself, 'Let them grow up fit for *whatever station* they may be placed in—*high or low.*' This one never thought of before, but I *do* always now." Yet she remained convinced, having seen a destiny in her birth and in that of Albert, that the Chartists had it all wrong except in the final outcome of their demonstration. "I maintain," she told Lord John Russell, "that Revolutions are always bad for the country, and the cause of untold misery to the people. Obedience to the laws & to the Sovereign, is obedience to a higher Power, divinely instituted for the good of the *people,* not the Sovereign, who has equally duties and obligations." It was a concept which she saw at work in the pocket principality of Coburg, but it now worked badly in the larger world. She would have to adapt herself, if not her ideas.

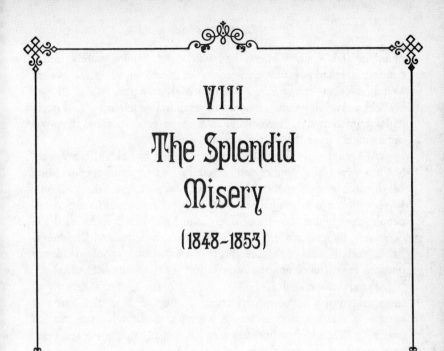

VIII

The Splendid Misery

(1848-1853)

That politics was the art of the possible was something that Victoria, despite her growing sophistication about people, never quite learned. The willful young princess who had had no reasonable expectation of success when she defied the Conroyals would now and then reemerge in the experienced Queen. In 1848, for example, she decreed that every person who appeared at her drawing-rooms wear British-made clothes. British manufactures meant British jobs. But the edict was unenforceable, and people who counted—at least on the distaff side—had a predilection for Paris fashions that would survive the Queen's idealism.

So it was, too, with larger issues, which meant acquiring a tolerance for frustration. Victoria managed this by immersing herself in the management of her family and its new homes. Osborne meant peace of mind; its furnishings, scaled down to her size and state-of-the-art in lighting and plumbing (few country houses had toilets and running water), meant comforts she had never experienced in the overblown sumptuousness of Windsor, or in the bedraggled luxury of Kensington Palace. "I was brought up very differently," she would recall to Disraeli in 1875. "I never had a room to myself; I never had a sofa, not an easy chair; and there was not a single carpet that was not threadbare."

At Osborne the Queen had a residence that met almost every need. She was away from Windsor and London, yet a steam packet could bring her dispatch boxes from the rail terminus at Gosport, which itself was only two hours from Whitehall. There were no impertinent tourists and townspeople; the children ran about freely, and Lady Lyttleton handled the "accounts, tradesmen's letters, maids' quarrels, bad fitting of [children's] frocks, desirableness of rhubarb and magnesia, and by way of intellectual pursuits, false French genders and elements of the multiplication table."

What exasperated Lady Lyttleton was the Queen's lament, in the sparkling if windblown perfection of Osborne, that they were not amidst "Scotch air, Scotch people, Scotch hills, Scotch rivers, Scotch woods. . . . The chief support to my spirits is that I shall never see, hear, or witness these various charms." To the Queen these charms were not merely aesthetic. A home in Scotland meant additional escape—further retreat from politics (despite what would be the inevitable bone-chilled Minister-in-Residence) and the ultimate in privacy from the public gaze. When James Giles's sketches of Balmoral arrived, and then Giles himself with more details, which Dr. Clark followed with confirmation that upper Deeside was exactly right for the Queen's health, the lease was taken up sight unseen.

Victoria and Albert saw Balmoral for the first time on September 8, 1848, after a voyage north to Aberdeen. Although the Queen in her journal called it "a pretty little castle in scotch style," it was hardly larger than an ordinary country house, and had been completed only nine years earlier. With mullioned windows, gables, turrets, and round towers with cone-shaped roofs, it had some aspects of a miniature castle. Victoria found the situation "solitary" and the mountain air "refreshing"—by which she meant cold. Her Household would dread its chill and loneliness, on both of which the Queen thrived. "All seemed to breathe freedom and peace, and to make one forget the world and its sad turmoils."

As with Osborne, the structure was too small for the necessary retinue, and at first much of the adjacent land could be leased but not purchased. Eventually the royal estate would encompass 24,000 acres, and miles along the Dee. All farmers and cottagers on the estate would be forbidden to let their houses or to receive lodgers—a drastic protection of the Queen's privacy. The acquisition would take much money, which came unexpectedly in 1852 in the form of a fairy godfather, "Miser Nield." Even by English standards, James Camden Nield of 5 Cheyne Walk, Chelsea, was an eccentric, the uncharitable child of a wealthy amateur sociologist who had visited English and Scottish prisons in fifty-nine counties, gathering material for a book, *The State of the Prisons* (1812). His son inherited only the elder Nield's frugality and his fortune in Home Counties real estate. When he died in a nearly empty, cob-webbed house that might have excited the admiration of Dickens's Miss Havisham, there was little more to tally of his possessions than a bed made of a board, a few old sticks of furniture, a tallow candle, and a cat. But he also had properties that would realize more than £250,000, and with no family, he left it all to the Queen. Nield knew, Victoria observed, that she "would not waste it." Leased lands could be purchased, and a grander Balmoral built. Stockmar wished Nield "a joyful resurrection."

Nield's largesse also went into the improvement and expansion of Osborne. Additional land was purchased, as was an importation from Switzerland, in prefabricated sections—one of the earliest uses of the scheme—of a two-story cottage intended as a playhouse in which the princes could learn carpentry and gardening, and the princesses the rudiments of housekeeping and cookery. Although the children sometimes entertained their parents at "tea" there, the location, a half-mile from Osborne House, suggests that the royal brood was to amuse itself (under Household supervision) remote from parental eyes and ears. Equipped with small-scale furniture and a working kitchen, it remains on the estate, as does the adjacent garden shed with tools marked—perhaps to forestall bickering—with the names of the children.

Seldom seen or heard by visiting dignitaries, the royal children were aware nevertheless of the constant water traffic on the Solent, which Osborne House had created, and could recognize the arrival of someone interesting and new. Before the landing of a peer whose deformed foot and limp made his presence obvious, Victoria and Albert debated the usefulness of informing the older children in order to ensure that the guest was not embarrassed. It seemed better to ignore the problem, which appeared to them to be the proper solution when the day passed with some anxiety but no crisis. Then the next day the Princess Royal asked the whereabouts of the visitor. "He's gone back to London, dear," said the Queen.

"Oh, what a pity," said Vicky, who, with her brother, had trapped the noble lord in a corridor. "He promised to show Bertie and me his foot!"

On the Queen's 1848 visit to Balmoral, her party, in a convoy of carriages, progressed in stages from Aberdeen, making each stop a signal day in the life of the excited community. At Aboyne, for example, village committees met almost daily to plan what to do in her honor, and debated a triumphal arch and platform for dignitaries even while a local carpenter was hurriedly assembling it. On September 5, just before noon on a bright, sunny morning, the entourage arrived, and Lord Aboyne signaled a cheer from the population, most of whom had gathered for the event. The Queen emerged from her carriage with Albert and the three oldest children, onto a strip of tartan spread for the purpose. A table was laid at Lord Aboyne's for the party, but the Queen and Prince permitted only the children to have a snack. Napkins were pinned tidily under their chins and they sampled some broth, pudding, and oatcake—"the bread of the country," Albert told them. Outside, Victoria spent a great deal of time taking off and then putting on her cloak, Lady Charlotte Guest assuming that it was to enable the assemblage to have a better look at her; meanwhile, Albert announced his admiration for the local scenery.

Twenty minutes after the party arrived, they were off again, to the next town, and the carriages were hardly out of sight when the Gordon tartan on which the Queen had stepped was "cut up into pieces of an inch in size and kept by the people as relicks."

Before the expansion of Osborne (which was accomplished quickly) and the rebuilding of Balmoral, family life for Victoria's brood in both settings was *gemütlich* in the extreme. Limited as the facilities were, especially at Balmoral, Victoria preferred being away, in conditions far from royal, to the gloomy grandeur of Windsor and the city seediness of Buckingham Palace. Charles Greville, who visited Balmoral with Lord John Russell before the new castle was begun, a trip by rail and carriage of nearly twenty-four hours, was amazed at the smallness of the house and the lack of "any state whatever":

They live not merely like private gentlefolks, but like very small gentlefolks, small house, small rooms, small establishment. There are

no soldiers, and the whole guard of the Sovereign and the whole
Royal Family is a single policeman, who walks about the grounds to
keep off impertinent intruders or improper characters. Their attendants consisted of Lady Douro and Miss Dawson, Lady and Maid
of Honour; George Anson and Gordon; Birch, the Prince of Wales's
tutor; and Miss Hildyard, the governess of the children. They live
with the greatest simplicity and ease. The Prince shoots every morning, returns to luncheon, and then they walk and drive. The Queen
is running in and out of the house all day long, and often goes about
alone, walks into the cottages, and sits down and chats with the old
women. . . . We were only nine people, and it was all very easy and
really agreeable, the Queen in very good humour and talkative; the
Prince still more so, and talking very well; no form, and everybody
seemed at their ease. In the evening we withdrew to the only room
there is besides the dining-room, which serves for billiards, library
(hardly any books in it), and drawing-room. The Queen and Prince
and her ladies and Gordon soon went back to the dining-room, where
they had a Highland dancing-master, who gave them lessons in reels.
We (John Russell and I) were not admitted to this exercise, so we
played at billiards. In the process of time they came back, when there
was a little talk, and soon after they went to bed. . . .

Because Victoria thought that a property tie with Ireland might bind
the loyalties of her unhappiest subjects, she also contemplated exploring
for a residence there. Fortunately nothing came of it, as such a showplace
would have been only the most conspicuous example of Irish landlordism.
Ireland, after all, was an anomaly—legally part of the United Kingdom,
with representation in Parliament, yet treated in many respects like a
colony. Propaganda advantages could accrue from a Royal Progress, but
no one expected measures relieving the population's plight to follow. The
Queen had no such authority and her Government had no such intention.
A ceremonial visit, nevertheless, seemed carried along on its own momentum.

After more realistic observers described the prospect of bunting and
banquets as an affront to desperately poor and hungry Irishmen, some
reconsideration followed. The Government declared that the visit was still
on, but that "State" formalities that would cause "ill-timed expenditure
and inconvenience to her subjects" would be dispensed with. Even at that,
officialdom in Ireland continued to deplore the trip, and the press sarcasti-

cally suggested showing to the Queen "miserable emaciated inhabitants" perishing in unroofed cabins, rather than the tourist attractions of Killarney. Victoria sought "any demonstrations of loyalty" from her Irish subjects, and worried less about whether that would be forthcoming than did her representatives.

The Queen's own officials in Ireland deplored the "wretched display of wealth" inevitable on such occasions, but Lord Clarendon, Lord Lieutenant of Ireland, was ordered to go ahead with plans that would have no appearance of excess. For Clarendon, that meant that he and others would be out of pocket. The Chancellor of the Exchequer, Sir Charles Wood, was horrified at such estimates as £500 for erecting a tent at the dock for a reception. "The Prince's idea," he insisted, "was some £500 to cover everything beyond eating and drinking."

As a temporary stimulus to the Irish economy, the visit had a positive aspect even before the Queen arrived. If nothing else, the preparations put armies of unemployed to work erecting scaffolding, face-lifting buildings, tailoring presentation dress. Most of the funds, other than a reimbursement bill for £2,000 submitted by the desperate Clarendon, came from the private means of local businessmen and the landed gentry.

Arrival at Cove (now Cobh), the port of Cork, on August 2, 1849, came early, to the consternation of the town fathers. Victoria intended to stick to a tight schedule, and would keep it. If the decision seemed to presage a difficult visit, it did not work out that way at all. She toured the harbor in the *Fairy* tender, to salutes from surrounding vessels and cheers onshore. Then, landing at Cove at a hastily erected pavilion, she announced that she had given her "sanction" to the new name of the port, Queenstown, at the request of the inhabitants. (After independence, the Irish *Cobh* erased the memory of Victoria.) Then the Queen returned to her ship and steamed up the bay to Cork, where, on the deck of the *Fairy*, the mayor of Cork was knighted. To enthusiastic cheers, Victoria toured the city for two hours, in what she described as heat and dust, in an open landau, characterizing the crowds as foreign-looking and good-humored —"running and pushing about, and laughing, talking and shrieking." She thought Irish women were remarkably pretty—"such beautiful dark eyes and hair, and such fine teeth."

The next morning they weighed anchor for Kingstown (now Dun Laoghaire), on the south edge of Dublin Bay, but with the weather rough and the Queen seasick, the *Victoria and Albert* put in at Waterford for the night. Although the sea was still rough at daybreak, Victoria, still "giddy and tired," ordered the vessel under way, "as it could not be helped and we might have remained some days for no use." The Queen would remain prone to seasickness all her life, but refused—usually—to give in to it. Once when she and Albert were crossing to Osborne, Colonel Francis Seymour (afterwards Lord Hertford) was surprised to find the Prince on deck during the rough crossing, and Victoria—apparently ill— below. Seymour confessed surprise, as he thought that Albert was the "bad sailor."

"I know the English laugh so much at seasickness," the Prince confided, "that I am quite willing it should be so, and that the laugh should be directed against me rather than against the Queen."

Some years later, discussing seasickness with the old sailor who was master of the *Fairy*, Victoria advised the elixir that was also to ease her last bouts of labor agony. "Why don't you take my remedy, Mr. Welsh, a few drops of chloroform?"

"May I advise you, Madam," he countered with the license that only special servants possessed, "to take *my* remedy, a pipe. You would find it much more to the purpose."

The first three hours out once more in the Irish Sea were the worst, with Victoria and the children all sick, but they recovered by the time the Wicklow Hills and Dublin were in sight. It was seven on a Sunday evening, "and the setting sun lit up the country, the fine buildings and the whole scene with a flowing light which was truly beautiful." Again the enthusiasm, Victoria added, was "extreme." Until then, to the Irish, she had been the picture on the parlor wall, in nearly every house above the status of hovel, of a young woman decked out in her coronation robes. The next morning, as she stepped ashore with her children, an old woman shouted, "Ah, Queen, dear, make one of them Prince Patrick and Ireland will die for you!"

Victoria found that the crowds responded in lively, un-English fashion, jumping and shrieking and "excitable beyond belief." Many appeared "ragged and wretched," but she saw no hostility, and enjoyed everything but what she described as "heat"—a relative term, since she abhorred anything warmer than a bracing chill, and Ireland was seldom warmer than that at any season. Despite the years of famine and despair, the Irish were ready to respond happily to the Queen, in part because they were starved, too, for diversion; in part, perhaps, because they hoped that the visit meant more attention to their concerns.

Reports of plots to kidnap her, and of planned insurrections, were shrugged off. In Dublin she visited the Bank of Ireland with the Prince and two ladies-in-waiting, and no other escort. At Trinity College she inspected the *Book of Kells;* at a home for old soldiers she again visited without escort. She drove about Dublin with Lord Clarendon in his carriage, the Prince behind in another, and several mounted police ahead to clear a path, as she was not on a planned route. Still, eager crowds gathered, happy but for one excited man who ran alongside the carriage shouting, "Mighty Monarch, pardon Smith O'Brien!" The worried coachman quickened the pace—for William Smith O'Brien had been sentenced to be hanged, drawn, and quartered for high treason. Although the law did not give the Queen power to commute in a case of high treason, she stayed the sentence until special legislation was passed permitting her to alter the punishment to transportation for life.*

Quickly, the Queen's evident simplicity and appreciation of Irish hospitality won over even the aggressively hostile *Freeman's Journal,* which confessed that she had won its own affections for her "frank and confiding manner." At a grand levee at Dublin Castle, more than four thousand people were presented—"without intermission," Victoria noted. Then the tireless Queen returned to the Vice-Regal Lodge for a dinner, an evening party, and a concert, yet was fresh the next morning for the popular event of the visit, a military review in Phoenix Park, which seemed to draw, for three hours (plus additional hours for securing a viewing position), nearly everyone in Dublin.

To rest, the Queen dined alone; then she presided at a drawing-room reception at the Castle, which ended only after midnight, 1,700 more people having been presented (and each with a presenter). Victoria wore Irish poplin or Irish linen, decorated with shamrocks or other Irish symbols, and when she wore non-Irish silk, it was decorated with "Limerick lace."

The final visit on her schedule was to Ireland's ranking peer, the Duke of Leinster, at Carton, his estate just beyond the Catholic seminary of Maynooth, whose students cheered her as she passed. For the occasion the Duke opened his grounds, and as the Queen's carriage, with its scarlet outriders and lancer escort, bounded along the valley of the Liffey and through the gates of Carton, crowds on motley conveyances followed. The people "were riding, running and driving with us," Victoria noted, and were "extremely well behaved."

*O'Brien was released in 1854 on grounds of poor health.

The Duke gave the Queen a tour of his demesne in a jaunting-car —a two-wheeled carriage that carried four people, two on each side. The experience charmed Victoria, and was even recalled in a popular song in which she said, "Be me sowl, I like the joultin' of yer Irish jauntin' car." The Duke had one made for her, and shipped to England.

The return from Carton, Victoria recorded, was filled with "every possible demonstration of affection and respect." So would be her re-embarkation on the *Victoria and Albert.* The cheers along the route to the station at Westland Row were deafening, and Dubliners crowded every viewing surface, from roofs to windowsills and bridge girders. At Kingstown, the harbor in early evening was jammed with jostling boats filled with spectators. The *Dublin Evening Mail* reported that as the Royal Yacht moved off, her Majesty, seeing how many people had gathered at the quays, "ran along the deck and, with the sprightliness of a young girl and with the agility of a sailor, ascended the paddlebox." There, atop the arch of the paddlewheel housing, she was joined by the Prince, and holding his arm, she waved to the people on the piers. It seemed to the *Mail* that she then gave an order to the ship's captain, for "immediately the paddles ceased to move and the vessel floated on with the impetus it had already received. Her Majesty remained in this position (the vessel moving very slowly and as near the pier as was compatible with safety), waving her handkerchief and receiving the plaudits of the thousands who crowded the extremity of the pier. An occasional revolution of the paddles kept the vessel in motion. . . ." Only a half-mile down harbor did the Queen leave her perch on the paddle box, permitting the *Victoria and Albert* to pick up speed.

Lord Lansdowne, on the dock, found the departure "quite affecting." The Radical M.P. John Bright was so moved as to "defy any man to have felt otherwise." But the moment for reconciliation it created was not seized by the Queen's Ministers. Succeeding visits, in 1853, 1861, and 1900, could not recapture what had been possible earlier, and even emphasized the sense of abandonment that would lead to further "troubles" and to separation.

Only weeks after the return from Ireland came the second of what would be three deaths in a two-year period that closed a chapter in Victoria's reign. The first had been that of Viscount Melbourne, who had died in November 1848 at sixty-nine. In his decline he had brooded over imaginary financial difficulties, and Victoria had lent him money he did not need. He was "good natured," she now recalled, and she owed him much, but he had not been, she now understood, an effective Prime Minister. In October 1849, George Anson died of a stroke at thirty-seven. He had been having severe headaches for a year, and was clearly failing. Albert had already given some of Anson's responsibilities to Colonel Charles Grey and Colonel Charles Phipps. Anson had been, Victoria wrote, "almost the only intimate friend" Albert had. He and Victoria mourned for Anson (whose wife was expecting what would be a posthumous baby) "as for a brother."

At the end of June, the next year, Sir Robert Peel's horse slipped on Constitution Hill, slick after rain, and fell on the former prime minister. In great pain, three days later, Peel, at sixty-two, died. Albert "felt and feels Sir Robert's loss *dreadfully,*" Victoria wrote Leopold. "He feels he has lost a second father." Peel had been as much a surrogate father to Albert as Melbourne, earlier, had been to Victoria.

Peel's accident had occurred only a day after the greatest triumph of a politician whose lack of integrity Victoria and Albert had despised as much as they had respected the sense of honor represented for them by Peel. Viscount Palmerston had been pursuing a personal foreign policy independent of his Prime Minister and his Sovereign. That the Queen was to be consulted, or at least informed, meant only to him that sometime after the fact he would let her know what he had done. Outrage and anger at Court grew into the certainty that something had to be done to dismiss the belligerent Palmerston, whose power, lodged in his popular appeal, seemed to grow with the years. As Victoria told Lord John Russell, Palmerston "knows when the mails go, he has only to write in time for them, and he must recollect that the 28,000 despatches in the year come to you and to the Queen as well as to himself." In his sixty-seventh year, "an old painted Pantaloon" to Disraeli because he dyed his sidewhiskers, Palmerston was more dexterous and decisive than ever.

The "Don Pacifico" affair in 1849 first appeared to be a serious blunder for Palmerston. A Gibraltar-born Jewish businessman living in Athens, Don David Pacifico had suffered the sacking and burning of his house by an anti-Semitic mob. When his claim for damages was rejected by the Greek government, he applied for help—as a British subject—to the Foreign Office. Palmerston acted only after twenty months of fruitless negotiation, but to the Court it was overreaction, for he had ordered British gunboats to seize Greek shipping to satisfy the claim.

When the French and Russian governments objected, and foreign protests continued, the Queen warned him "that for the sake of one man the welfare of the country must not be exposed." She insisted to him and to Lord John Russell, ostensibly his superior, that she expected to be forewarned, and to be given opportunity to give "her Royal sanction." If that was then "arbitrarily altered or modified," she would see a "failing in sincerity towards the Crown, . . . justly to be visited by the exercise of her Constitutional right of dismissing that Minister."

Palmerston waited for an opportune moment to respond, and in the House of Commons, on June 24, 1850, during a debate on the Pacifico affair, he spoke for nearly five hours, rejecting allegations of heavy-handedness with one of the most memorable speeches ever to be delivered in the Commons. He saw as a principle of foreign policy of her Majesty's government the duty "to afford protection to our fellow subjects abroad," so that, "as the Roman, in days of old, held himself free from indignity when he could say *'Civis Romanus sum'* [I am a Roman citizen], so also a British subject, in whatever land he may be, shall feel confident that the watchful eye and the strong arm of England will protect him against injustice and wrong."

The cheers to which he sat down were as nothing compared to his hero status in the press the next day. After that he could do little wrong. When, despite his condemnation of General Haynau, known as "General Hyaena" for his Hungarian atrocities, the Austrian butcher came to England anyway, and was roughed up by workmen at a brewery he visited, the Queen felt embarrassed. She instructed Palmerston to convey apologies to the Austrian Minister in London. Since Palmerston felt no sympathy, his perfunctory letter suggested as much, Victoria receiving a copy only after the fact. Feeling that visitors to England deserved as much respect as her own subjects in foreign parts, she perceived a glaring political inconsistency on her Minister's part that—aside from his having flouted instructions—made him unsuitable as her representative. She asked Lord John Russell to discipline him.

Palmerston ("Pilgerstein" to the hostile Queen and Prince, who privately Germanized his name) demonstrated his contempt for placing manners over morals by a further outrage. Not long before, he had protected the Hungarian revolutionary Lajos Kossuth when, in the aftermath of a failed uprising, the Austrians had demanded his extradition by Turkey. Now the Hungarian patriot landed in England—fast becoming, for its protection of personal freedoms, the European haven for political exiles*—and began making speeches denouncing the reactionary regimes of Russia and Austria. Uneasy that Palmerston might exacerbate relations with both countries by a show of sympathy for Kossuth, both the Court and the Cabinet tried to head their Foreign Minister off. "There are limits to all things," he wrote angrily to Russell on October 30, 1851. "I do not choose to be dictated to as to whom I may or may not receive in my own house. . . . I shall use my own discretion. You will, of course, use yours as to the composition of your Government." It was a direct challenge to dismiss him, which would have gratified the Queen and Prince; but Palmerston evaded the inevitable by quietly canceling Kossuth's personal visit. ("The Queen has *every reason to believe* that he has seen him after all," Victoria wrote Russell skeptically.) Unrepentant in any case, Palmerston lost no opportunity to brand the emperors of Russia and Austria "merciless tyrants and despots." The Queen vainly urged Russell to find a new Foreign Minister.

With Palmerston the most popular person in the Cabinet, and gaining in public support while the rest of the Government appeared fumbling and futile, Russell could cling to office only if Palmerston stayed. Victoria seethed, finding a new cause for objection when, in December 1851, Louis Napoleon overthrew the French government and established himself in power. The politics of the "Prince-President" should have alienated Palmerston, yet he told the French ambassador, Count Walewski, that Louis Napoleon "could not have acted otherwise." In effect he had granted recognition, on his own authority, to a dictatorship that had supplanted a constitutional government—perhaps doing so because he understood Napoleon's external enemies to be his own as well. Russell, unconsulted, was as furious as were Victoria and Albert. Realizing that he and Palmerston could no longer sit in the same Cabinet, Russell gambled that he could survive his Foreign Minister's exit. He asked the Queen to appoint a successor in the Foreign Office.

Later, in his *Notes on England,* Hippolyte Taine would write that Victoria and Albert "have no party of their own in Parliament, and never intrigue against a Minister, not even against one whose person and ideas are displeasing to them; they accept their [constitutional] position favourably." It may have appeared that way to a Frenchman used to violent

---

*Karl Marx and Friedrich Engels, authors of the *Communist Manifesto* in 1848, had settled quietly in England after expulsion from Prussia and France.

governmental change, and to overt interference with his ministers by a sovereign. As Palmerston knew, in Victoria's case the "never" would be less accurate than "hardly ever." "It is a miserable thing," she once complained in her journal, "to be a constitutional Queen and to be unable to do what is right."

The younger Lord Granville, who had succeeded his father in 1846 and had briefly been an Under-Secretary for Foreign Affairs, was given Palmerston's post. He was persona grata with Victoria and Albert, but the victor in the struggle proved to be Palmerston, who "crossed the floor" of the House with his supporters to leave the Tories for the Whigs, who were now calling themselves Liberals. Within weeks, Russell's government (the Tories now called themselves Conservatives) fell, and in February 1852 the Earl of Derby (who had been Lord Stanley) became Prime Minister, and Lord Malmesbury—one of Victoria's favorites—became Foreign Minister.

Derby's shaky Ministry would not last out the year, and was replaced by one led by the Earl of Aberdeen. (Palmerston had to take the post of Home Secretary because the Queen would not have him again as Foreign Minister.) As Derby prepared to leave office with his Cabinet, he took the train and packet to Osborne on December 17 to settle his Cabinet's resignation. His description of the scene to his son mirrors many such audiences in Albert's time—the Queen ostensibly in charge, the Prince outlining royal policies. The Queen received Derby cordially, but

> she seemed grave and anxious; the Prince entered into confidential discussions on many subjects, appearing desirous to take . . . the last opinion that he could receive from his ex-minister. He spoke often of Disraeli, extolled his talent, his energy, but expressed a fear that he was not in his heart favourable to the existing order of things. My Father defended his colleague: said he had been unnaturally kept down for several years, and then suddenly raised to the highest position. "He has better reason than anyone to be attached to our constitutional system since he has experienced how easily under it a man may rise." The Prince was glad to hear it, but still thought Disraeli had democratic tendencies "and if that is the case, he may become one of the most dangerous men in Europe."

There was "a strong feeling" against Disraeli at Court, Derby thought, because the Queen and Prince feared Disraeli's inevitable rise to the top. Only a few heartbeats, at most, kept him from that already —partly, Derby thought, because of "the mingled dread and contempt with which persons in high places are apt to look on satirists." He had heard the Prince predict that Disraeli's example would "raise up a host of inferior imitations," Albert mentioning as example Ralph Osborne, an M.P. known for his wit. Victoria would have nothing to fear from Osborne, who would rise only to Secretary at the Admiralty; but satirists abounded in Parliament, and made life uncomfortable in the glass house that was the Court.

One of the recurring problems that had weakened each unstable government of the early 1850s had been the disputes in Parliament over the place of religion—and which religion—in the life of the nation. Although no one seriously questioned the status of an Established Church, the Oxford Movement had created antagonism between laissez faire clerics and ritualists. There were added strains within Protestantism by the growth of what was called Dissent, in that it was not Anglican. As Defender of the Faith, the Queen was the sponsor of Presbyterianism as well as Anglicanism, an anomaly she found more intriguing as her acquaintance with Scotland, through Balmoral, grew. Victoria would write in her journal, in 1855, of a sermon delivered at the kirk near Balmoral by the Reverend James Caird, "which lasted nearly an hour, but which kept everyone's attention riveted" with its text from the twelfth chapter of Romans: "Not slothful in business; fervent in spirit; serving the Lord." The lesson was not theological hairsplitting, which was preoccupying the Anglicans, but one of "being and doing good" in what she saw as the British manner. And it was "not a thing only for Sundays"—she and Albert deplored rigid Sabbatarianism—but "for every action of our lives." The Queen liked Scottish religion in her life as much as she enjoyed whiskey in her tea.

When it came to religious faith, Victoria was an instinctive believer in a Higher Power in the heavens, and in some form of posthumous spiritual existence, but she could not accept barren self-denial as a pious impulse that would bring one into harmony with the ineffable. In June 1850, when Lord Ashley, later the seventh Earl of Shaftesbury, was campaigning against the delivery of letters on Sunday, she wrote to Lord John Russell that she thought it was "a very false notion of obeying God's will, to do what will be the cause of much annoyance and possibly of great distress to private families." (The Cabinet ducked the issue by appointing a committee to study the problem, and Sunday mail survived.) When

Victoria's daughter Vicky asked her later about the propriety of going to the theater on Sundays, she suggested local custom as a guide. "You know," she added, "I am not at all an admirer or approver of our very dull Sunday, for I think the absence of innocent amusement for the poor people, a misfortune and an encouragement of vice."

Church of England appointments, ostensibly the Queen's, were the focus for opposed factions of Anglican religious feeling. Books and tracts by the dozens exercised emotions over conflicting doctrines of baptism or biblical infallibility. Into the ecclesiastical swamp of controversies, affecting the Queen at every level, however tiresome she found them, came a new one when on September 24, 1850, Pope Leo IX issued without consultation with the Queen—who after all was head of her Church— a decree dividing England into twelve sees to be presided over by his bishops and archbishops.

Roman Catholics were in England and Wales in increasing numbers, as famine had caused Irish Catholics to flee into the industrial cities across the water, such as Liverpool, in search of work and food. The Pope's pronouncement was his recognition of a need to exercise spiritual authority over people belonging to his Church. In the process he elevated Dr. Nicholas Wiseman to Cardinal—the first in England since the Reformation—and made him Archbishop of Westminster. Wiseman's first pastoral letter infuriated the Queen. Lord John Russell, then Prime Minister, advised her coolly, "The persons to be affected by this change must be already Roman Catholics before it can touch them." The Queen did not see it that way. "The Cardinal has desired the Pope to be prayed for before me," she objected. It was "a *direct* infringement of my prerogative. . . ." She was not joining what Greville called the "No Popery hubbub," but claiming her sovereign rights, as she would all her life; and she opposed the punitive Ecclesiastical Titles Bill, aimed at repelling "Papal Aggression." When the bill passed, after many disputes and modifications that made nonsense of it, she gave her Royal Assent on July 29, 1851. The bill would never be enforced, and was repealed in 1871. "Sincerely Protestant as I have always been and always shall be," she wrote to her elderly aunt, the Duchess of Gloucester, "and indignant as I am at those who call themselves Protestants, while they are in fact quite the contrary . . . , I cannot bear to hear the violent abuse of the Catholic religion, which is so painful and so cruel towards the many good and innocent Roman Catholics."

While "Popery" was being excoriated, some of its noisiest detractors found nothing objectionable in the fashionable new preoccupation with table-turning, seances, and other forms of spiritualism. Making a table move merely by placing one's hands upon it and calling for spirit messages left a few participants concerned when something happened, but most considered it a harmless parlor game not at odds with their churchgoing. At least once the Queen was teased into trying it, on a spring evening at Osborne in 1853. The table spun, and Victoria regarded it as "peculiar," but she was not interested enough to repeat the experiment, although when she met Louis Napoleon he told her "some certainly extraordinary things" about the American spiritualist Daniel Home, who lived in England but had a following in Paris. Victoria would never bother with Home, and when, nearly a decade later, she had what she considered to be a personal spiritual experience unexplainable by rational means, she merely accepted it. It profoundly affected her life, but not her religious practice.

In part the "No Popery" excitement masked anti-Irish feeling; also, it reflected a feeling that England's enemies in Europe were the nations that had never turned away from some form of Catholicism, whether Greek or Roman. Since religious furor also offered assistance to a variety of domestic causes, ecclesiastical, social, and political, it would not fade easily. Victoria would have to contend with it as long as she was Queen.

While the Ecclesiastical Titles Bill was exercising some anxious Englishmen, others had been turning their anxieties toward a scheme that the Prince had been promoting and that had the potential to be a greater embarrassment for the nation than suffering a Cardinal in its midst. Long interested in encouraging science and industry, Albert had observed exhibitions elsewhere, and he had been involved with exhibitions by the newly founded Royal Society of Arts. Now he wanted to organize a trade show that would be international in scope, yet would be an advertisement for British arts, crafts, and industries.

Since the financing of the scheme had to quiet skeptics at the start, the Queen gave £1,000 and the Prince £500; public subscriptions followed, largely from industry, which had the most to gain—or lose. At a banquet at the Mansion House on March 21, 1850, at which the Prince solicited City luminaries, he declared that they were living "at a period of most wonderful transition," the progress of invention now inevitably leading to *"the realisation of the unity of mankind."* The Exhibition of 1851 would be "a true test and a living picture of the point of development at which the whole of mankind has arrived in this great task. . . ."

An existing site would cost the exhibition commissioners less than new construction, and Somerset House, a handsome warren of government offices extending along the Thames at Waterloo Bridge, was offered. But it was too small a space to accommodate Albert's concept. Henry Cole of the Public Records Office in Somerset House, who, with Thomas Cubitt, was advising the Prince, proposed an outdoor site. Leicester Square, Albert suggested. Too small, said Cole. What about Hyde Park? Hyde Park, however, was sacrosanct. On June 25, 1850, *The Times* warned that the exhibition would turn the Park into "the bivouac of all the vagabonds of London," and that the exhibition building itself would be "a vast pile of masonry" that would forever destroy the character of "our pleasant Park, nearly the only place where Londoners can get a breath of fresh air."

Attacks came from every quarter. Protectionists saw the exhibition as propaganda for Free Trade. Politicians attacked the likely destruction of natural beauty. Embattled, Albert saw his grand dream fading, since with no start on a physical site, there could be no exhibition on the announced date the next year. Other controversies also diverted his energies. The Popery debates had begun in the Commons, and there was running warfare with Palmerston. Also, the Queen was again pregnant, and the overworked Albert had more than the usual demands on his time as her confinement approached.

A year to the day before the planned opening of what then appeared to be a misnamed Great Exhibition, May 1, 1850, Victoria was delivered of her third son, and seventh child. The date was also the eighty-first birthday of the Duke of Wellington, and the child was named Arthur, after him, with the Duke standing as godfather. The delivery went well, and the Queen was soon up, but hardly had she been out again in public when William Hamilton, a visiting Irishman, fired his pistol at her as she drove up Constitution Hill. Although the gun proved to be loaded only with blanks, the shock was no less. Eight days later, on May 27, Robert Pate, an ex-officer, who was in the crowd watching the Queen leave Cambridge House, where her elderly uncle was seriously ill, struck her viciously on the forehead with the brass knob of his cane. The brim of her bonnet absorbed some of the force of the blow, but she was badly bruised. Nonetheless, she went with visiting christening guests to a production of Meyerbeer's *Le Prophète*, as scheduled, and pronounced the opera beautiful, dramatic, and "very touching." Giovanni Matteo Mario, then forty and at the peak of his powers as a singer and a stage lover, she told Leopold, "is the finest tenor I have ever heard."

Leopold's interests could not be distracted by Victoria's reports of failed assassination attempts or successful new operas. After ignoring his wife's tuberculosis for many months, and pretending that she could go on as usual, he now knew that Queen Louise, only thirty-eight, was dying. She would not survive the year. The old Duke of Cambridge, whom Victoria had been visiting when struck by Pate, had died on July 8, the day before the burial of Peel.

Despite her outward calm, the second attempt on her life in hardly more than a week had left the Queen badly shaken, and had left the Prince, beset by other worries, far more agitated than he confided to Victoria. "All this does not help," he wrote Baron Stockmar, appealing to him to return from Coburg. On July 2, 1850, Albert wrote again that it appeared that the Exhibition would have to be abandoned. There no longer seemed to be sufficient lead time to construct exhibit space and secure exhibits. "If you can come," he pleaded, "pray do so, as we have need of you."

Victoria wrote to Stockmar also, worried about Albert's decline into depression, usually an outlet reserved for her. Then, suddenly, Peel met with his accident and died, leaving both the Queen and Prince with a terrible sense of loss. Yet Peel's legacy would, in effect, be the Great Exhibition. Many in Parliament knew that Peel had wanted the Exhibition to succeed, and that he favored the Hyde Park site. Opposition began to fade, although money difficulties remained. Subscriptions were insufficient, forcing Albert to raise a guarantee fund. Even so, opposition to a huge masonry edifice was substantial. Those who wished to save the park had no expectation that a building to be as large as or larger than St. Paul's would be torn down after a season's occupancy. On that reasonable suspicion, plans again stagnated, although 13,937 applications for exhibit space had been received, and financing had been assured.

Then, in June 1850, only ten months before the scheduled opening, Joseph Paxton, designer of the Duke of Devonshire's conservatory at Chatsworth, which had entranced Victoria, came to London with an M.P. friend to look over the rebuilt House of Commons, the earlier structure having burned to the ground in 1834. Discovering the Exhibition Committee's dilemma, Paxton translated his Chatsworth experience into a drawing of a "palace of glass," in effect a long, elegant, enormous greenhouse that promised rapidity in erection and equal dispatch in disassembly. Since to the committee his drawings suggested something too flimsy to work, he shrewdly offered his exterior design to the *Illustrated London News*, which published it on July 6, 1850. Admiration for it was instant, and on July 15 the committee authorized Paxton to draw detailed plans that would require the enclosure, rather than the cutting down, of any trees on the site.

With the aesthetics of Hyde Park thus protected, the contracting firm of Fox and Henderson was given the task of erection, with Henry Cole as official overseer of the project for the committee. The actual overseer proved to be the embattled Prince, as he was concerned with the exhibits as well as with the exhibit space. Doubts were soon raised in the press and in Parliament about the ability of a structure of ribbed glass to withstand wind and storm. Then *Punch,* which earlier had satirized building ideas for the Exhibition with a drawing that resembled the much ridiculed (and rejected) "Albert helmet" that the Prince had designed for the army, christened Paxton's concept a "Crystal Palace." The name caught on, quickening the excitement caused that November by the bridging of the great transept with huge wooden ribs, painted to look like steel, rising high above the great elms. Crowds gathered daily to watch, the Queen and Prince among them, although the presence of Victoria and Albert was a distraction that cost work time.

More than two thousand workmen labored daily at the site, with exhibits arranged in four categories: raw materials, machinery and inventions, manufactures, and sculpture and plastic art. No rent was charged, but exhibitors had to deliver and remove their exhibits as well as maintain them at their own expense. In scale, nothing like the Crystal Palace had ever been built. The structure was 1,848 feet long—more than a third of a mile—and 408 feet wide, one of the greatest engineering achievements of the century.

The ever-malicious uncle of the Queen, the King of Hanover, now becoming dotty, warned Frederick William IV that it would be unsafe to attend "this rubbishy Exhibition" because "the excommunicated of all lands" were in London and constituted a threat to visiting eminences. According to his informants, "Ministers will not allow the Queen and the great originator of this folly, Prince Albert, to be in London while the Exhibition is on." Other forecasts, that the mammoth structure would collapse in a gale, or cause epidemics because of the masses of people spreading contagion, or, as Albert put it to the worried King of Prussia, "that this second Tower of Babel would draw upon it the vengeance of an offended God," kept few of the curious away. As the opening drew near, and concerns about further attempts on Victoria's life mounted, plans were made for a private ceremony. *The Times* was indignant: "Where most Englishmen are gathered together, there the Queen of England is most secure." The Queen intervened to assure a public opening to which all season-ticket holders were welcome. The result was a burgeoning of ticket sales to more than 25,000.

Problems ranging from security to protocol went to the Prince when no one else had a solution. "I am more dead than alive from overwork," he wrote to his grandmother in Coburg. "My poor Albert," Victoria wrote in her journal the day before the opening, when she visited the site for a preview, "is terribly fagged. *All* day some question or other, or some difficulty, all of which my beloved one takes with the greatest quiet & good temper." Even the Exhibition's motto, at the head of the catalogue, was chosen by the Prince—*"The earth is the Lord's and all that therein is."* That too would inspire controversy, as the president of the Bible Society complained that Albert had used the Prayer Book version of the line rather than that of the King James Bible. Victoria would have had good reason, as she entered, to recall what she had written in her journal more than a year earlier: "I *do* feel proud at the thought of what my beloved Albert's great mind has conceived."

Nothing went awry—except that a curious Chinese man in traditional robes, actually the proprietor of a junk moored in the Thames, was assumed to be an emissary from the Celestial Kingdom and was placed in the procession between the Archbishop of Canterbury and the Duke of Wellington. Ecstatically, the Queen recorded in her journal one of its longest and most vivid entries. The bustle, the crowds, the excitement— even her own anxiety—reminded her of her coronation day. With Vicky and Bertie and the Prince in her carriage—one of nine state coaches— they arrived in "Queen's weather," the light rain that fell as they started having stopped. "The sun shone & gleamed upon the gigantic edifice, upon which the flags of every nation were flying. . . . The glimpse through the iron gates of the Transept, the moving palms & flowers, the myriads of people filling their galleries & the seats around, together with the flourish of trumpets, as we entered the building, gave a sensation I shall never forget, & I felt much moved."

The spectacle was "magic and impressive" as light danced about the dazzling interior, sunlight streaming through its 293,655 panes of glass and reflecting off the thousands of facets of a twenty-seven-foot crystal fountain that was the structure's centerpiece and that had been concealed from public view until that morning. The four faces of the clocks on the building were about to record noon when Albert escorted Victoria in, Vicky at his hand, Bertie (in Highland dress) holding his mother's hand. "The tremendous cheering, the joy expressed in every face, the vastness of the building, with all its decorations & exhibits, the sound of the organ (with 200 instruments & 600 voices), & my beloved Husband the creator of this great 'Peace Festival,' uniting the industry & art of *all* nations of the earth, *all* this, was indeed moving, & a day to live forever. God bless my dearest Albert, & my dear Country which has shown itself so great today. . . ." Tennyson echoed the national enthusiasm in lines that evidenced nothing of the strains in Victoria's life:

> Her court was pure; her life serene:
> God gave her peace; her land reposed;
> A thousand claims to reverence closed
> In her as Mother, Wife, and Queen.

To Leopold, Victoria called the Crystal Palace "astonishing, a fairy scene. Many cried, and all felt touched and impressed with devotional feelings." It was a reaction that united onlookers. The historian and politician Thomas Macaulay, careful with his words, in his diary called the interior "a most gorgeous sight; vast; graceful; beyond the dreams of the Arabian romances." Greville marveled at "no soldiers, hardly any police-men to be seen, and yet all so orderly and good humoured"—and although 6,063,986 visitors, equal to a third of the kingdom, poured through the Crystal Palace over 140 days (no Sundays), there would be no damage and no violence. "The *frondeurs* are all come round," Greville wrote on May 10, "and those who abused it most vehemently now praise it as much."

In June, *Punch* would even print a cartoon of a shipwrecked Lord John Russell government saved by a steamer labeled "Exhibition," which was substantially true, in that the marvels of the Crystal Palace were a distraction for both Parliament and the press. Excursion trains brought tens of thousands of sightseers (the word *sightseer* itself dates only to 1847) to the Exhibition, and tens of thousands more came by boat from the Continent and from America. The Queen herself came several times a week until the formal closing on October 15, 1851. She was inquisitive about everything, and one day, according to a possibly apocryphal story, she was found in the hall of American manufactures examining some fine carved soaps that looked so much like marble that, doubting that one was really white castile, she decided to test it with her shawl pin. "Pardon, Your Majesty," said the worried Yankee exhibitor, "it is the head of George Washington!"

"It was such a time," she wrote in her journal (July 18, 1851), "of pleasure, of pride, of satisfaction & of deep thankfulness, it is the triumph of peace & good will towards all,—of art, of commerce,—of my beloved Husband—& of triumph for my country." For many who came, it was their first glimpse of the new realities of mechanical invention and accomplishment in arts and crafts, a revelation of the technological future. Victoria was not the only one who would come again and again. "A very fine thing," said Flaubert, "despite being admired by everyone."

Enthusiasm for the Exhibition ran high, spilling over into popular feeling that the Queen might have employed to realize her thwarted desire to confer English royal rank on her husband. When the couple attended a ball at the Guildhall given by the Corporation of London to celebrate the success of the Great Exhibition, on July 9, 1851, flood stage seemed to have been reached. The royal party left Buckingham Palace at nine, traveling through the city in state carriages to swelling acclaim from Londoners lining the streets. Then, no one left; the crowds, rather than

Victoria and Albert viewing the Koh-i-noor ("Mountain of Light") diamond in the Crystal Palace. Contemporary print.

dispersing, continued to grow, awaiting the return of the Queen's carriage. The ball was a brilliant extravaganza, and the Queen stayed late; but so did the crowds waiting outside. As Albert wrote to Stockmar, "A million of people remained till three in the morning in the streets, and were full of enthusiasm towards us." It was an occasion without precedent.

At her final visit to the Crystal Palace, Victoria found the building, still filled with the last visitors, in the process of being dismantled. A huge brass organ, labeled a Sommerophone, was playing, and the booming notes, she wrote, "nearly upset me." The glass fountain was already removed, and exhibits being taken down. "The canvas is very dirty, the red curtains are faded, and many things are very much soiled, still the effect is fresh and new as ever, and most beautiful." So much remained beautiful, she noted, "I could not believe it was the last time I was to see it. . . . It made us all very melancholy." There at the close, in the crowd, was an old Cornishwoman, Mary Kerlynack, "who had walked hundreds of miles to see the Exhibition." A "most hale old woman," she was "at the door to see me," and was "near crying at my looking at her."

The next day saw the official closing, and the Queen regretted not being there. (It was "not to be in state.") Albert left at ten for the ceremonies, where an estimated fifty thousand people crowded inside. "Albert was right," she recorded. ". . . I could hardly have been there as a spectator. . . . How sad and strange to think that this great and bright time has passed away like a dream. . . . I feel as if it were doing my dearest Albert an injury that it should be gone by. . . ."

In the season of the Great Exhibition, Victoria celebrated her thirty-second birthday and her fourteenth year as Queen. A grand family concert was held, with scenes enacted from Racine's melodramatic *Athalie* (in French) and Kotzebue's comic *Das Hahnenschlag* (in German), and a concluding "Scale in C" by Princess Louise, then three. Victoria could not imagine any higher point in her reign in the future, and lavishly credited the Prince, in public and in private. Yet although she carefully recorded family events in her sketchbook, from birthdays to Christmas and New Year's Day, and even her birthday party just a few weeks after the opening of the Crystal Palace, what astonishes the spectator today (in the words of the editor of the sketchbooks, Marina Warner) "is that its motive force and inspiration, Prince Albert, is invisible. The Queen never drew or painted her husband with her children. He is absent. The unflagging work he undertook, both on his own account and on the Queen's, passed unrecorded . . . it is surprising not to find Albert the paterfamilias at all in her albums." It is especially surprising, since Victoria doted physically on Albert, and took advantage of the new age of photography (which became practical in the 1840s) to fill her photo albums with his portraits, as well as those of herself and their children.

The new science and art of photography recorded much of the Crystal Palace and its interior, as well as its dismantling and reerection, and the new opening ceremonies at which Victoria and her family participated amid choruses, orchestras, and audiences of thousands became history's most populous daguerreotype. The Exhibition commissioners had solved one of their twin problems that the closing had created when the London, Brighton & South Coast Railway bought Paxton's structure for £70,000 and moved it to a hill in the Kent countryside at Sydenham. Shortened and slightly heightened by a barrel-like roof, it prospered as a concert and exhibition center until it was destroyed by fire in 1936.

Sale of the building in 1852 added to the commissioners' parallel problem by supplementing a surplus that had already reached £200,000. Disposing of the largesse was a politically sensitive matter. The Prince's scheme was to purchase property in South Kensington to continue the goals of the Great Exhibition. Skeptics would label the idea "Albertopolis," but the educational, cultural, and scientific institutions initiated by Albert's energy and foresight would materialize into a great South Kensington complex of museums, colleges, and concert halls, keeping Victoria busy at dedications for decades.

The Great Exhibition would be the summit of Albert's public career, but at a cost. He had regularly complained of a "weak stomach," and was subject increasingly to severe stomach cramps blamed by Albert on the tension of his crush of activities and by his biographers on his conscientiousness about detail. On October 10, 1851, when he was involved with planning the closing ceremonies at the Crystal Palace, he was ill through the night with what Victoria described as another stomach "attack." He was only thirty-two, yet, balding and paunchy, he looked prematurely old. But not to "George Eliot," who, at Covent Garden to hear *La Juive,* "fell in love with Prince Albert who was unusually animated and prominent. He has a noble, genial, intelligent expression and is altogether a man to be proud of. As for the Queen, she is deplorable—worse and worse the more one looks at her—so utterly mean in contour and expression."

However ill he felt, Albert's crowded schedule kept him going. His work load had not been reduced significantly by the close of the exhibition. He was now deeply concerned with exploiting the energy it had released and the favorable mood in the country for related enterprises. And he was busy designing and supervising the building of a new Balmoral structure, and purchasing neighboring freeholds (with Victoria's Nield inheritance) to enlarge the estate into a vast royal retreat. There were also problems of domestic and foreign politics, about which the Queen was content to let the Prince be her buffer. Then on September 14, 1852, at eighty-three, the Duke of Wellington died, the Royal Family learning the news by telegram in Scotland. Princess Feo, the Queen's niece, was there, and asked, hearing of the Duke's end, "What will become of Aunt Victoria?"

While the Duke's obsequies were being arranged in London, the Royal Family remained at Balmoral. Wellington was refrigerated as well as circumstances permitted. A two months' delay of burial was highly extraordinary, but the plans afoot, with Albert contributing, were grandiose, as were the Queen's and Prince's schemes for their Scottish retreat. To mark Balmoral's possession, the Queen noted in her diary for October 11, 1852, most of the Household set off at midmorning to climb to the top of Craig Gowan to build the traditional cairn setting claim to the site, the former pile having been pulled down by the servants. "I then placed the first stone, after which Albert laid one, then the children according to their ages." Then, in turn, the ladies, gentlemen, servants, and tenants, including spouses and children, each placed stones on the cairn, while a piper played and whiskey was "given to all," and "some merry reels were danced."

When the cairn reached its final height—about eight feet, Victoria guessed—"Albert climbed to the top of it, and placed the last stone, after which three cheers were given." She was touched by the event and the setting, and "felt almost inclined to cry. The view was so beautiful over the dear hills; the day so fine; the whole so *gemütlich*. May God bless this place, and allow us yet to see it and enjoy it many a long year."

Reluctantly they left for London. Once, Victoria had wanted to exclude the Duke of Wellington from her wedding. Now he was, she announced, "Britain's pride, her glory, her hero." The mourning period had already reached royal dimensions, and the lying-in-state had become one of legendary length, 65,073 persons filling by the sable catafalque surrounded by rows of colossal candelabras.

For the final procession the Prince designed a huge funeral car so awkward and heavy as to give the horses and men dragging it extraordinary difficulty. Prevented by protocol, the Queen was not present at the final ceremonies at St. Paul's, but the orgies of sentimental mourning, all at her own insistence, exhausted her emotionally anyway. Besides, she was again pregnant, and distracted, too, by Albert's ill health—in the winter of 1853 he suffered a prolonged, heavy cold—which she began to interpret as lack of attention to her. On April 7, 1853, her fourth son and eighth child, Prince Leopold, was born, with the assistance of "blessed chloroform" administered by Dr. John Snow. Two weeks later, in her journal, she recalled its effect as "soothing, quieting and delightful beyond measure." Yet she had not been quieted long by its application, for there were problems with the new baby, who was diagnosed as hemophiliac. Victoria was also suffering again from postpartum hysterical crises, which went on to become intermittent intervals of depression and recrimination embittering her relationship with Albert.

It was a matter of class and rank as well as of sheer disinterest that the Queen and Prince quickly turned over to their attendants all parental involvement with their infants, short of formal social occasions. They had often seen Vicky and Bertie bathed and put to bed. Now that they had less time for that, the Queen confessed, she saw the "younger ones" on such occasions "once in three months perhaps." But she was able to tell her uncle, after whom Leopold was named, that he seemed "a jolly fat little fellow," belying his diagnosis as a hemophiliac, which added to Victoria's anxieties. She sent vicious, accusing notes to Albert, usually about alleged affronts too trivial to suggest anything but emotional breakdown, and her surviving official correspondence of the period is so slight as to suggest unusual inattention on her part.

Albert would respond in notes addressed to "Dear Child," once calling attention to a "distressing scene" caused by a "miserable trifle," yet realizing that he only increased her distress by referring to the "groundlessness and injustice of the accusations." Pregnancy always increased her hostility to her husband because she brooded over the injustice of woman's lot in suffering all of the disfigurement and discomfort. The baby's poor health—Albert blamed the difficulties on her insistence upon a wet nurse from the Scottish Highlands whose milk seemed to disagree with the child—aggravated her feelings about the futility of repeated pregnancies. The Queen's testiness—a recurring agony to Albert—would continue off and on for years, into and beyond her ninth and last pregnancy in 1857. When she told her eldest daughter in 1859 that too many pregnancies too soon had made life "wretched" for years—"one becomes so worn out and one's nerves so miserable"—the lesson was from painful experience still fresh.

Few husbands in history can have tried as hard as Albert to maintain the equilibrium as well as the professional effectiveness of a wife. Leonard Woolf's self-abnegating and diplomatic handling of the suicidal Virginia —a far more extreme case—comes to mind in the century after Victoria. Albert's love survived the trials of his inferior position and his continued unacceptability as an alien, and it survived the pendulum swings of Victoria's almost helpless doting upon him and her using him to vent frustrations of which he was victim rather than cause. He thought constantly of her emotional and physical needs, once writing her from Chobham, where he visited military maneuvers in June 1853, that he was happy that she had got through her day without needing him, and signing off with the familiar German love song,

> Du, Du liegst mir in Herzen,
> Du, Du liegst mir im Sinn,
> Du, Du machst mir viel Schmerzen,
> Weisst nicht wie gut ich Dir bin.

One matter that continued to mar their domestic happiness, and remained a matter for mutual accusation, was the apparent backwardness of the Prince of Wales. While Vicky was rapidly growing into a miniature of Albert—at three, the Princess, so the Queen told Leopold, thought and spoke "like a person of twenty"—all that Bertie seemed to have in common with Vicky was Hanoverian obstinacy. At three he was already a master of the social graces—"most exemplary in politeness and manner," said Victoria. But no study regimen, however meticulously devised by Albert, made any impression upon the Prince of Wales. Whether he would have been a better scholar had the pressure upon him been less intense is idle speculation. At eight he was considered by his father as "too backward" even to begin to learn his catechism; yet even earlier, Victoria sensed that Albert was requiring too much of the child and asked Lady Lyttleton to see that Bertie was not "overworked." But Bertie remained overworked for his capacities. He would take out his frustrations in Hanoverian blind rages at his tutors, and occasionally at his parents, who perceived nothing of the potentially effective ceremonial sovereign in the amiable young man already at ease with adults. With their hopes for the future of the monarchy invested in him, they saw only a vacuous future King of England. The other children were unimportant. The girls would have to be found appropriately arranged marriages, perhaps with a diplomatic intent; the other sons were only insurance.

Such attitudes suggest an insensitivity to their children that flies in the face of the *gemütlich* image that has come down to us of family picnics and outings, Albert on a sledge in the snow with a child, or crawling about on the hearth rug at Osborne playing children's games, Victoria sketching outdoors with the girls. At Osborne and Balmoral there was more togetherness, but the royal parents were like other rich parents of their time and place except that they had a far busier social and official life. The doting, devoted, and cozy family of the illustrated papers and the gossipy articles was largely legendary, yet positive, public relations. Windsor Castle would have denied none of it. Still, when the royal children were small, they seldom appeared at the table, or anywhere else where their parents happened to be in the servant-saturated households. Except on holiday or ceremonial occasions, they were overseen rather than seen.

Even later, Victoria could seldom separate being a queen from being a mother, and Albert wrote one of his admonitory letters meant to evade a painful scene. "It is indeed a pity," he confessed, "that you find no consolation in the company of your children. The root of the trouble lies in the mistaken notion that the function of a mother is to be always correcting, scolding, ordering them about and organising their activities. It is not possible to be on happy friendly terms with people you have just been scolding."

It had been difficult, in the exhilarating months of the Great Exhibition, for Victoria to think about anything else. Its aftermath was akin to postpartum depression, and everything and everyone was somehow found wanting. The new litany of problems was as nothing, however, to the fall in the Prince's popularity after the high tide of the Crystal Palace. It was almost as if its removal from London lifted the lid off years of simmering suspicions and hostilities. On foreign-policy questions the Queen and Prince, in the most jaundiced English view, seemed always to come down on the side of Prussia, and of a future unified Germany (almost certainly under Prussia), which frightened Englishmen. It was enough to make the Queen's subjects yearn for further rapprochement with the historic enemy, France, even under the Bonapartist nephew who, by the end of 1852, was calling himself Napoleon III. There seemed something symbolic in the death of the first Napoleon's nemesis, the Duke of Wellington, in the year of the new Napoleon's rise to power.

To many Englishmen, Louis Napoleon was a charismatic figure. He was not only the nephew of a legend, but a man who had lived by his wits and accomplished the impossible. He had lived in conspiratorial exile in England, had English friends in high places, and even had a wealthy English mistress, a Miss Elizabeth Howard. Victoria despised him as a usurper, a vulgarian, an immoralist. In the popular mind, however physically unhandsome he was, he was more dashing and attractive than the cramped foreign intellectual who was Victoria's consort. What made matters even worse was the Queen's discovery that the self-designated Emperor of the French, seeking to found a dynasty and in need of an appropriate bride, was interested in Her Serene Highness Princess Adelaide of Hohenlohe, seventeen, daughter of Victoria's half-sister. The Queen had only to recall the disgust of her own mother at the possibility that Feodora—Adelaide's mother—might have been taken as wife by the wicked and gross George IV.

Feodora might have looked on the match as a way out of the difficulties that had dogged her since 1848. Although her husband had rescued his principality when revolutionary fervor receded, they had been living "a new existence of privations" (as she wrote to Victoria) that was alleviated largely by "loans" from her sister and mother, and frequent residence for her daughters in England. "Ada" was even with Victoria when the marriage offer was transmitted to the Queen through Count Walewski, the Emperor's ambassador in London. Indirectly through her Ministers, Victoria replied that the proposal was a matter for the girl and her parents; informally she made it clear that she disapproved of both Napoleon III and the proposal. Feodora considered the bargain "disagreeable," not because of the religious *mésalliance,* but because of her daughter's immaturity and the Emperor's morals. Yet she thought that Ada would "rather like" the dazzling marriage, a misunderstanding of her daughter, who refused on her own "a position as elevated as it is perilous."

By the time Princess Adelaide of Hohenlohe had written her refusal, the question was moot. Expecting otherwise, the Queen had said frankly to Lord Derby, "You know *our* family [the Coburgs] have always been accused of being too ready to pick up any crown that had tumbled in the dirt." Anticipating a rebuff, however, the Emperor remained susceptible to signals from other marriageable women, even those only on the fringes of acceptability. On December 31, 1852, Count Walewski arrived from

London to report on the state of his mission, and was greeted to his surprise with *"Mon cher, je suis pris!"* Louis Napoleon had met and been captivated by the beautiful, ambitious Eugénie di Montijo, who was appropriately Catholic, a mature twenty-seven, and ostensibly the daughter of a Spanish count. The ambassador reminded him that his engagement announcement was premature; he could not jilt Queen Victoria's niece. He would not have to. Ada's letter would arrive the next day.

The sordid business of government, from political marriages to cynical foreign-policy machinations, left Victoria feeling very different from the way she had when she stood on the dais in the Crystal Palace and felt at one with what she visualized as the aspirations of humankind. With such a person as Louis Napoleon able to manipulate nations, she reflected ambivalently to her uncle, "One can never be for one instant safe. It makes me very melancholy; I love peace and quiet—in fact I hate politics and turmoil, and I grieve to think that a spark may plunge us into the midst of war. . . . Albert grows daily fonder and fonder of politics and business, and is so wonderfully *fit* for both . . . and I grow daily to dislike them both more and more. We women are not *made* for governing—and if we are good women we must *dislike* these masculine occupations; but there are times which force one to take *interest* in them and . . . *I* do, of course, *intensely.*" And she excused herself to dress for the opening of Parliament.

IX

The Woman
Warrior

(1853–1858)

Late in 1853 Thomas Challis, a hide-and-skin merchant and Lord Mayor of London, proposed that it was time for a statue of Prince Albert to be erected in the City. The outcry in the press embarrassed Victoria and Albert, and they quashed the idea. No amount of exposure to English ways seemed to make Albert more acceptable; if anything, the Queen was becoming more German. Blindness to the symbolism of small things did not help. Albert, for example, had brought small green German table lamps with him when he first arrived in England, and he still used their successors in his study, whether from nostalgia or a feeling that they were more efficient than domestic counterparts. Whatever the reason, such objects called attention to his origins. He kept his diary in German. He spoke German within the family—when he would wake Victoria at eight, it would be with *"Es ist Zeit, steh' auf!"* ("It is time, get up!")—and he would always feel insecure with his English correspondence, giving much of his mail to Victoria or his secretaries to read, to reassure himself about his understanding. To Anson, earlier, Victoria had explained, "The Prince and Queen speak English . . . quite as much as we speak German." That was hardly enough.

The Queen and Prince seemed often to side informally with Prussia, which had long been perceived by Englishmen as bullying smaller and weaker German states. Further, Prussia had ties of mutual self-interest with a larger and even more autocratic bully, Russia, connections further cemented by a tradition of dynastic marriages. Additional suspicions about the Eastern sympathies of Victoria and Albert arose when Napoleon III, seeking an external crisis with which to distract his people, found one with Russia. He had been irritated by the Czar's refusal to recognize his dynastic title, although a secret protocol signed in London in December 1852 by Britain, Prussia, Austria, and Russia accepted the obvious and acknowledged Napoleon as emperor.

To provoke the Czar and to validate his own claim as protector of Roman Catholicism, Napoleon III arranged for monks under French armed escort to take over the church in Bethlehem. Professions of protection for Holy Land sites reflected political struggles elsewhere. France was, in effect, siding with Turkey, which was struggling to maintain its restless provinces in the Balkans. Claims from Russia to represent the interests of Christians of the Orthodox Church in Ottoman provinces, and pieties from elsewhere about religious rights, masked rivalries for control of crumbling segments of Turkey, each one of which might add to the power in Europe of an autocratic Russia that was already history's most massive empire.

Because of ambitions in eastern Europe of their own, and rivalries for supremacy among the hodgepodge of German states, Prussia and Austria remained aloof. To Englishmen, this was akin to taking the Czar's side at a time when war fever to join France and Turkey was growing. England had little to gain except what it could by curtailing Russian encroachments in Danubian Europe. Victoria (very likely in Albert's language) warned Lord Clarendon, then Foreign Secretary in the Earl of Aberdeen's Ministry (there had been several unstable governments in the early 1850s), that England was risking war only to defend Turkish territory, and doing so without Parliamentary authority or that of the Crown. Islamic Turkey, curiously, was regarded as the defender of Christianity; and what was even more curious in England was that Albert's efforts to prevent a war were seen as pro-German and as contrary to his constitutional nonexistence. When the Czar's ships, in a preemptive strike, destroyed an obsolete Turkish Black Sea fleet at anchor in Sinope (now Sinop), the island nation that assumed that Britannia ruled the waves felt, at a distance, threatened. If Albert acted otherwise, he had to be guilty of some form of treason.

Toward the close of 1853, stories surfaced about how Albert was allegedly manipulating the Queen—that he appeared at all meetings Victoria held with her Ministers, and was in effect her ventriloquist; that he wrote all the letters and memoranda to which she signed her name; that he interfered with governmental departments, including the army and navy; that he had aspired to take the Duke of Wellington's place as Commander-in-Chief; that he was a Prussian spy and a Russian dupe.

Another charge, which his official biographer more than a generation later thought still kept a "hold upon the public mind," was "that he had amassed large sums of money out of the income allowed him by the nation, part of which had been invested in the purchase of land at South Kensington, adjoining the property of the Exhibition Commissioners. The Prince never purchased any land at South Kensington. . . ."

Some political charges were reasonably accurate, although the allegations that they constituted criminal behavior were imaginative. Albert did, without legal position other than as the Queen's husband, accompany her when she met with her Ministers, and offered his own opinions; indeed, Ministers often sought him separately as a conduit to Victoria, or for his own acumen. He did draft responses for the Queen, who was grateful to have the most loyal and knowledgeable of private secretaries. He did intervene with governmental departments in attempts to promote efficiency and reduce waste; but he also ventured into military affairs by deploring—despite his German origin—duels, and by attempting to foist his equipment ideas on the army. As for his seeking to replace Wellington —the old Duke himself had suggested that, but Albert had declined the offer as impolitic and because he felt it would restrict his usefulness to the Queen.*

Even with little news to feed upon but the threatening international situation, rumors multiplied, nourished by the continued suspicion of the

---

*The Prince wrote to Wellington (April 6, 1850) that his "most peculiar and delicate" position as consort to the Queen required "that the husband should entirely sink his *own individual* existence in[to] that of his wife—that he should aim at no 'power by himself or for himself—should shun all contention—assume no separate responsibility before the public, but make his position entirely a part of hers. . . ."

Prince as foreigner and interloper. Some mischief, the Queen and Prince were certain, came from pro-Palmerston papers, whether or not the dismissed Foreign Minister had anything to do with generating malice. In a letter to Stockmar on January 7, 1854, Albert put some of the blame on "protectionist papers," which "now vie with each other in . . . unscrupulous falsehoods and vehemence. . . ." Some charges would have been funny had they not hurt. One that Albert sent to Stockmar, a cutting from the *Daily News* of January 11, 1854, was skeptical that the Prince could ever "feel and act" like an Englishman, since he had allegedly "breathed from childhood the air of Courts tainted by the imaginative servility of Goethe. . . ."

"In attacking the Prince," Victoria complained to Lord Aberdeen, "who is one and the same with the Queen herself, the throne is assailed." Aberdeen promised to raise the issue in Parliament when it reconvened, but dismissed the accusations as only "contemptible exhibitions of malevolence and faction." With exactly the wrong instincts, Victoria appealed to Baron Stockmar to return as adviser. She and Albert, she explained, had to counter the "Ultras of both parties," especially since the country was "on the verge of war and anything but prepared for it." It would have been a boon to conspiratorial theories had the wounded Queen and Prince kept a German *éminence grise* in residence. Stockmar wisely remained in Coburg.

On January 15, 1854, Greville observed that "the extraordinary run" in the press "for some weeks past against the Court, more particularly [against] the Prince," had "undoubtedly produced a considerable effect across the country." In Greville's view, the attacks were spearheaded by the *Daily News* and the *Morning Advertiser,* then followed up by the Tory *Morning Herald* and *Standard.* Both in articles and in letters to the editors, they were "full of the bitterest abuse and all sort of lies," the charges principally that Albert "has been in the habit of meddling improperly in public affairs, and has used his influence to promote objects of his own and the interests of his family at the expense of the interests of this country; that he is German and not English in his sentiments and principles; that he corresponds with foreign princes and with British Ministers abroad without the knowledge of the Government, and that he thwarts the foreign policy of the Ministers when it does not coincide with his own ideas and purposes."

"One word more about the credulity of the public," Albert wrote to Stockmar on January 24. "You will scarcely credit that my being committed to the Tower [of London] was believed all over the country—nay, even 'that the Queen has been arrested!' People surrounded the Tower in thousands to see us brought to it!" Laurence Housman dramatized the episode in *Victoria Regina* by having the Prince read to the Queen from one of the more circumspect newspapers:

"We learn on what we believe to be good authority, that at a late hour last night two Personages of the highest rank"—("Personages of the highest rank" can only be you and me, Vicky)—"were secretly conveyed to the Tower, under a military guard, by order of the Government, and have there been lodged in safe custody to await their trial on a charge of high treason for conspiring against the safety of the Realm." There, Vicky, what do you think of that? "This news, which it was not intended should at present be made public, will be received with the greatest satisfaction by all who have been aware of the danger to which our Country has lately and increasingly been exposed by the machinations of a certain powerful foreign influence behind the Throne." (That means me, Vicky.)

The suggestion that Albert was a Russian agent (since Prussia supported the Czar) seemed logical enough to Englishmen of anti-German persuasion, and that he had somehow given cause to be marched off through the Traitor's Gate into the Tower, appeared, if not logical, at least as appropriate poetic justice. The inevitable ballads giving spice to the rumor were sung in London streets, one of them suggesting that an impatient Queen had ceased to tolerate Albert's treason:

> *Last Monday night, all in a fright,*
>   *Al out of bed did tumble.*
> *The German lad was raving mad.*
>   *How he did groan and grumble!*
>
> *He cried to Vic, "I've cut my stick:*
>   *To St. Petersburg go right flap."*
> *When Vic, 'tis said, jumped out of bed,*
>   *And whopped him with her night-cap.*

You jolly Turk, now go to work
And show the Bear your power.
It is rumoured over Britain's isle
That A—— is in the Tower.

When a Scots paper circulated the treason charges, and papers farther south repeated the accusations, Lord Aberdeen was finally prompted to put a stop to the rumors by arranging, rather than merely promising, at the end of January, to deflate them in both the Lords and the Commons. There were allegations, he declared on behalf of the Government, that had drawn "thousands" of Londoners to "attend at the doors of the Tower to see His Royal Highness go in." Further, the gullible and the curious who had rushed to Tower Hill also had expected to see the Queen imprisoned, as they had heard that she had "announced her intentions to go with him." Yet, Aberdeen scoffed, the Prince's "unimpeachable loyalty to the Crown and to the Country" should be sufficiently clear to put to rest such falsehoods "at once and for ever."

The refutation, Victoria wrote with relief to Stockmar the next day, was "triumphant." She and Albert had gone to the House of Lords for the event, and had been greeted by "an immense concourse of people" eager to see for themselves whether the rumors were true. The crowds, she thought, were "very friendly." John T. Delane, editor of *The Times*, had already gone to Aberdeen with an offer to counteract the "immense mischief," but Aberdeen first consulted the Prince, who suggested waiting until the vindication in Parliament. Even so, Delane rushed into print a letter signed "Juvenal" (written by Greville), attacking the calumnies of the *Morning Advertiser;* the *Standard* published a defense of the Prince's role as adviser to the Queen by "D.C.L." (A. J. Hope, later Beresford-Hope); and the *Morning Chronicle* printed an anonymous article praising the Prince's loyalty and respect for legality. Victoria was so impressed by the *Chronicle*'s piece that she inquired of her Prime Minister whether he had any idea who wrote it. Aberdeen identified the author as W. E. Gladstone, "although he would not wish it to be known." After the airing in Parliament, the attacks subsided. Only the *Advertiser* took an immoderate time to wind down. It is now difficult to imagine that, midway through the enlightened nineteenth century, a month could have existed when citizens of one of the freest and most just nations believed that its sovereign and its sovereign's spouse had been committed to the Tower.

Greville speculated, as had the Queen and Prince, that some of the virulence had been abetted by Palmerston, with whom the Queen and Prince had long been at odds. The *Morning Post* was "notoriously his paper"—which was all Greville had as evidence. He had also heard that some of the attacks "were paid for by the Emperor Louis Napoleon," to weaken English pro-Germanism. When they ceased, it was not because the public was satisfied that the accusations were false, but because people had been diverted by war fever. No one, Greville wrote early in February, "now thinks of anything but of the coming war [with Russia] and its vigorous prosecution. The national blood is up, and those who most earnestly deprecated war are all for hitting as hard as we can now that it is forced upon us."

War had not yet been declared, but the Russian ambassador left London on February 7, and his British counterpart in St. Petersburg left the next day. In the new age of telegraphy it was possible—where there were wires strung—to communicate more quickly, but not to prepare for war or to prosecute it at long distance. There was no direct wire link to Constantinople.

If the national blood was indeed up, it was not because Victoria and Albert had encouraged the tensions as diversion from their own problems. Still, her ambassador at Constantinople because Czar Nicholas would not have him at St. Petersburg, the unscrupulous Stratford Canning, Viscount Stratford de Redcliffe, was a pro-Turk legacy of Lord John Russell's Ministry kept in his post by Aberdeen (with Russell in the Foreign Office). At the Sublime Porte, Stratford de Redcliffe had taken advantage of the semi-primitive communications with Turkey by conducting personal diplomacy, which meant reading the worst intentions into any Russian communication—an easy enough task—and frowning at his own instructions. If there were any hopes for compromise, he ignored them.

It would take weeks to find that out in London, and to send him fresh dispatches. The Cabinet was full of excuses. To her Foreign Secretary, the Queen (almost certainly in conjunction with Albert) had written a candid warning that Stratford's actions in Constantinople "exhibit clearly a *desire* for war, and to drag us into it," and she wondered how long he should be permitted "to remain in a situation which gives him the means of frustrating all our efforts for peace."

Had her Government wanted the ambassador to do otherwise, Stratford long before would have been ordered home. As with most wars, popular expectation was for a short and victorious affair. It was easy to ignore the reality that Britain had fought no war for forty years and was not ready now to fight one. In concert with France, the British government issued an ultimatum to Russia to evacuate the Danubian principalities (now Rumania) in which the Czar claimed to be protecting Christians under Turkish hegemony. As expected, Czar Nicholas did not even take notice.

As the self-proclaimed policeman of the seas, Britain had no desire to see Russia break out of the Black Sea (through Turkey) into the Mediterranean, or to dominate, in the north, the Baltic. The first thought in London, then, was to get what quickly proved to be an inadequate fleet to Turkish Black Sea ports. Sevastopol, in the Crimea, was proclaimed "the eye tooth of the Bear which must be drawn."

It took little military acumen to realize that a small, isolated war, with theoretically narrow objectives, could metamorphose into something else, and Victoria used her prerogative as Sovereign to urge the King of Prussia, brother-in-law of the Czar, to remain neutral if not friendly. The year before, the dismemberment of Turkey had been a prospect of little concern to the Queen, and she even wondered, with little sophistication in geopolitics, who would gain Constantinople when the collapse finally came. Any difference between feudal, autocratic Russia and feudal, autocratic Turkey seemed imperceptible to her, although to Palmerston's party the difference was that the future Russia constituted a grave threat to the Empire, while Turkey had no future.

Since Russia had few rail lines, its military movement was largely by water, with the naval base at Sevastopol in the Crimea the key to attacks on Turkey and Turkish Europe across the Black Sea. An Anglo-French staging area to counter the threat was fixed at Varna, chief Black Sea port of Turkish Bulgaria. From Constantinople, where he had gone as an army general and as special emissary of the Queen, her cousin George, Duke of Cambridge, wrote frankly of the "wretched" state of the Turkish military—and of the still-feudal Turkish people. The Sultan was friendly and civil, he observed, but the "unvarnished truth" was that the Western allies would have to furnish the resources and do the fighting, and that even so the future of Turkey in Europe seemed nil. But letters took a month in transit from Constantinople to London; even the electric telegraph, because of gaps in transmission lines, took ten days. While diplomats read obsolete dispatches, events found their own momentum. Napoleon III as well as Nicholas I, autocrats relying on large armies and alleged external threats to maintain power, found it useful to stir up foreign tensions even when none existed, creating what Albert would call "spectacles" to divert a fickle public. Both coveted already indefensible segments of the Ottoman Empire. The government in London wanted neither nation to wax too powerful on Turkish spoils, which meant protecting them for Turkey as well as moving into position to claim some reward itself.

With the expiration of the last ultimatum, war officially began on March 28, 1854. While Britain and France emphasized their unity of purpose, pre-Waterloo animosities persisted, making cooperation awkward and ineffective. Further, generals ferried to the war zone on the Black Sea, preparing to land their poorly equipped soldiers on the Crimean peninsula, were baffled and helpless in the local squalor, heat, and disease; cholera and dysentery traveled with the army to the Russian coast even when modern ammunition and guns did not. Mismanagement of sanitation, supplies, and soldiers by the Allies was easy to perceive on the spot, but the bad news became less bad as it was filtered through a haze of slow and inadequate communications and deliberate obfuscation.

The Queen had much to learn. On March 10, 1854, she had left with the Prince for Osborne, to view the battle fleet assembled at Spithead under the command of Sir Charles Napier. In her journal she called it a "solemn moment." She knew that many of the troops aboard, even in victory, would not come home. Then she returned to London for the official pronouncement of a state of war, and for a formal acceptance of a Parliamentary Address of loyalty in response to her message. To emphasize the gravity of the occasion, the Prince of Wales, now twelve, took his place for the first time beside the Queen and Prince in the House of Lords.

To underline the justness of the sacrifice, Lord Aberdeen proposed in the Lords to set aside a Day of Humiliation and Prayer for the success of British arms. Victoria was outraged. She felt "strongly," she informed her Prime Minister, that Humiliation was inapplicable to the situation. "Moreover, to say (as we probably should) that *the great sinfulness of the nation* has brought about this war, when it is the selfishness and ambition and want of honesty of *one* man and his servants which has done it, while our conduct throughout has been actuated by unselfishness and honesty, would be too manifestly repulsive to the feelings of every one, and would be a mere act of hypocrisy."

While war preparations went on, and hastily gathered troops vanished onto ships bound for Black Sea ports, at home the war—largely a skirling of pipes and a flashing of uniforms on parade grounds—was, in

Victoria's words to Leopold, "popular beyond belief." She could only watch it unfold—and later unravel—as she put her energies into her family, her burgeoning estate at Balmoral, and a new interest that would radically alter her focus upon the world—a fixation with the subcontinent of India, which she would never see in person, and with some of its colorful denizens in whose welfare she would become entangled.

On July 26, 1854, she thanked the Marquis of Dalhousie for helping her make the acquaintance of the ousted young Sikh maharajah Duleep Singh, then sixteen. When the Punjab, which his father had nominally ruled, had been annexed to India in 1849, and Victoria bought the family's Koh-i-noor Diamond, which she wore at the Crystal Palace opening, young Duleep Singh was given a pension conditional on his loyalty—which he demonstrated by becoming a Christian and going to England. On both counts Victoria thought the young man was worth cultivating; besides, he had "striking good looks" and brought out her "maternal interest." Seeing him at a royal ball, Benjamin Moran, Second Secretary at the American legation, described Duleep Singh as "small, lithe, and very handsome," with eyes "large, black and liquid" under a turban "literally flashing with diamonds. . . . His complexion is a pure olive, . . . & he looks like an opening tulip." Before the year was out, she was considering marrying him to an Indian princess, having seen that he was "most anxious to improve himself." There would be more young Indians in her life, none of whom would rise to her formidable expectations.

Male beauty had been an obsession with the young Victoria, and life with Albert, however satisfying physically, had not changed that. Her eye still caught striking examples, in life and in art, and she would continue their cultivation. At a time when nudity in pictures was denounced, from some pulpits, as morally corrupt, when the virile Thackeray thought that William Etty's nudes should be hidden by a "great, large curtain of fig-leaves," and the prudish, pontifical Ruskin judged William Mulready's nude drawings "degraded and bestial," Victoria bought nudes. A century later, when the novelist Compton Mackenzie trod the corridors of Buckingham Palace en route to be knighted, he passed an "almost nude" canvas of Diana, and asked himself what Victoria would have thought of it. Then he read the inscription—that it was one of the young Queen's wedding presents to Albert. She even bought a black and red Mulready drawing for her husband, in which a muscular young man is seen at full length wearing nothing but a beard and an anxious expression. It was apparently a birthday present for Albert in August 1854.*

Three years later, Victoria's birthday gift to Albert, designed by Emile Jeannest, was a gilded silver statuette of a nude Lady Godiva, sidesaddle on her horse. In art, at least, Victoria offered Albert access to fleshly attractions, and at a time when her own physical appeal, never great, was diminishing with poundage and pregnancies. She knew that her own beauty was less than overwhelming; she had been made more and more aware of that by the ungenerous eye of the camera lens. She had aged badly and become plainer of face and chunkier of figure; and perhaps because of both unhappy facts, when she posed for the camera in the necessary time exposure, there was often a frown creasing her face. The Court painter could improve on life and discover a more radiant Queen; and so could the sculptor. Contemporary practice, however, was to get the measurements, where possible, from life. When the great Antonio Canova's pupil John Gibson was commanded by the Queen to execute a statue of her, he worried about the propriety of his measuring the features of his sitter, as he usually did, with compasses. Turning to Albert, he suggested that the Prince do the measuring. Albert assured him that "the Queen would permit everything he might think necessary," and Gibson's clay soon took shape. However, when the Oxford sculptor Joseph Durham made a bust of Victoria, he was at first put off by the Queen's practice of not addressing him directly, but only through her lady-in-waiting. After a while both sitter and sculptor began breaking through the awkward etiquette. When the bust was nearly finished, "the Queen proposed that a considerable thickness of clay should be removed from the shoulders of the model," Durham recalled, "thereby improving the bust, though injuring the likeness." Victoria was interested less in likeness than in queenliness, and had her way.

Shortly after his birthday—he was thirty-five—Albert left for France to see whether Napoleon III's forces were more fit for war than the British were. The French, at least, could not fight on nostalgia, since Napoleon I had, finally, lost, but they were nursed on something even more pernicious, labeled *la gloire.* Warily, Albert recorded about his tour of the Boulogne naval base with the Emperor that "on the whole" he found

*Victoria also bought William Powell Frith's panorama of seaside life, *Ramsgate Sands,* which was exhibited at the Royal Academy in 1854. A popular success, it was seen by tens of thousands before being bought by a dealer who sold it for one thousand guineas to the Queen, who once—as a girl—was a regular visitor to Ramsgate.

himself greatly pleased with him (*im Ganzen recht zufrieden mit ihm*). But a royal reception was not a war, and optimistic reports would soon be followed by grim ones.

The 27,000 men shipped from England to the Black Sea in 1854 had almost no reserves behind them, and carried weapons that Wellington's soldiers had used decades before. There was almost no system for the care of sick and wounded, and it took a letter to *The Times* from Sir Robert Peel, the late Prime Minister's son, to raise £25,462 for medicines by popular subscription. As there was no provision for widows and orphans of war dead, Albert put himself at the head of a royal commission, soon known as the Patriotic Fund, for such war relief. It would raise more than a million pounds. Parliament had voted little support for military chaplains—who were often more nurses, and then undertakers. Soon another subscription drive was begun to send more men of the cloth to the Crimea. Finally, a lady with a bent for nursing and a genius for organization, Florence Nightingale, recruited thirty-seven lady nurses for service, and, with several chaperones of appropriate dignity, embarked for Scutari (now Shkoder), on the Albanian coast, reaching there on November 5, in time to receive the surviving wounded from the battle at Balaclava.

The chief woman warrior, however, had little but time on her hands, and put them to work, recruiting also the elder Princesses and her Majesty's ladies to knit woolen scarves, mittens, "and other warm coverings," to be distributed among the soldiers. (The Queen's own handiwork was carefully unidentified.) Her letters of condolence went to many war widows. Writing them, Victoria noted, was "a relief to me, as I can express all I *feel.*" Stories of suffering from sickness and wounds, and of inadequacy of supplies and general mismanagement, moved Victoria to write a New Year's Day (1855) letter to the commander in the field admonishing him that "the Queen trusts that Lord Raglan will be *very* strict in seeing that no *unnecessary* privations are incurred by any negligence of those whose duty it is to watch over their wants. . . ." There had been outcries in the press, particularly from *The Times,* which had a correspondent, William Howard Russell, on the scene—at least near the action, as he was forbidden by Raglan to be in the fighting lines. Reduced to stopping every officer and soldier who looked as if he might know something, and asking what had happened, Russell learned more than Raglan may have. Thus the Queen could warn her army chief that she had heard that the troops had their coffee "given them green, rather than roasted, and some other things of this kind, which have distressed her. . . ."

Governmental stinginess, inflexibility, and absence of compassion were not partisan matters. Whigs and Tories had been of one penurious mind for decades, happily accepting a military policy that made generals of gentlemen from good families who liked colorful parades, dashing uniforms, champagne with lunch, and remoteness from action. Inadequate coffee was the least of the hardships of hastily trained soldiers who had no fires in winter, huddled in wet blankets when they had any at all, died of pneumonia and dysentery by the thousands, had no ammunition for their obsolete weapons, and, if able-bodied, were thrown into combat in textbook drill formations that were little short of suicidal. Only the enemy's equal incompetence kept the war going.

As the news continued bad, and was received at home with indignation, especially the disaster of Lord Cardigan's Light Brigade, committees of inquiry were called for in the Commons, and there were private investigations by the Queen. Her cousin, the Duke of Cambridge, less than distinguished as First Division commander, had been horrified by the bloody field at Inkerman, declared himself sick, and fled to Malta. Soon he received a letter from the Queen expressing her hope that he would return to the Crimea. "Forgive my telling you frankly that I hope you will not let your low spirits and desponding feelings be known to others; you cannot think how ill-natured people are here, and I can assure you that the Clubs have not been slow in circulating the most shameful lies about you."

The Queen knew that the "lies" were fact. In 1863, when Alexander Kinglake had published his *Invasion of the Crimea*, which embarrassed the British military, Disraeli noted in his diary that the Duke of Cambridge had "taken the extraordinary course of sending for Kinglake" to discuss the "alleged misconduct at the Alma. He admits [that] the charge, whatever may be its importance, is in substance true: . . . that at one moment in the advance he consulted Sir C. Campbell and other officers as to whether it would not be expedient to fall back: which drew from Sir Colin an indignant rebuke. It is not even imputed that his hesitation came from personal fear: and seeing that a momentary indecision in an officer who had never seen fire, is no grave fault, society thinks the Duke had better have left the matter where it stood. But this, to a man of his excitable nervous disposition, was simply impossible. The Duke's excitement after Inkerman was so great that he had to be sent home lest he should go mad." Cousin George, clearly, was a Hanoverian. Victoria understood.

The American consul in Liverpool, a sometime novelist named Nathaniel Hawthorne, had occasion to be in London once during the Crimean War when, in conversation with the American Minister to Great Britain, James Buchanan, the subject of the Queen came up. She was, confided the Minister, who would become President in 1857, "a fiery little devil." She was seldom more fiery than when describing the misdeeds of the press in reporting the war. The "boastings" by politicians "of victories not yet achieved [were] in very bad taste and unworthy of this great country," she wrote to Lord John Russell on March 15, 1854. The opposite side of the coin, however—the damaging details about defeatism and incompetence—seemed to her even worse. "The Queen entirely agrees in Lord John's observation respecting the information obtained by *The Times* which she thinks he and the Cabinet ought positively not to tolerate any longer."

The Queen's ire would continue through the war, and into the next Ministry, a draft from Balmoral in the Prince's hand, to the Prime Minister, declaring that the Queen was "much disgusted with the late atrocious articles in *The Times* on the Army in the Crimea. . . ." The Prince's own opinion was that "soon there will not be room enough in the same country for both the Monarchy and *The Times.*" The Queen's feeling was that "repressive laws" against the press would only "aggravate the evil," but she wondered to her Prime Minister "whether it is right that the Editor, the Proprietor and the Writers of such execrable publications ought to be the honoured and constant guests of the Ministers of the Crown."

Delane, at *The Times,* paid no attention to threats and social disapproval. "Continue as you have done, to tell the truth," he wrote to Russell, "and leave such comment as may be dangerous to us, who are out of danger."

Russell did exactly that, although Albert was unrepentant about condemning what he described to Clarendon as "mischief which the gaining of three pitched battles could not repair." Victoria saw some good in war reporting. In her journal on May 28, 1855, she described a talk with Colonel Jeffrys of the Connaught Rangers about conditions in the Crimea. "He described the misery, the suffering, the total lack of everything, the sickness etc., and in no way exaggerated by other accounts I have seen. He knew Mr. Russell of *The Times,* and many things were *not* put down by him, as they would not have been believed here. I told Col. Jeffrys that the misfortune was that by publishing these [accounts of] mismanagements and sufferings, the Russians get encouraged and became aware of everything. He admitted that this was a great misfortune, but that on the other hand they felt certain things *ought* to be made known, else they would not be remedied, and the country must understand what has been going on."

The Queen identified with the army as "a soldier's daughter," but after hearing more about the Crimea, and then seeing her cousin George in London, looking "ill and much broken," she did not hold his failures against him. When Lord Hardinge resigned as Commander-in-Chief in 1856, he was succeeded, at Victoria's suggestion, by the Duke of Cambridge. But while her cousin's reputation did not suffer from the faltering fashion in which the war was prosecuted, her Prime Minister paid the price of mismanagement and incompetence in the lower echelons. After a motion for an inquiry into the condition of the army passed overwhelmingly in the House, Lord Aberdeen resigned.

"I could not confide the Govt. to Ld. Palmerston," Victoria noted in her journal, "(though I may yet have to do so)." To avoid that, she first sent for Lord Derby; then Lord Lansdowne, feeble and seventy-five; and finally for Lord John Russell. On February 2 she returned from Windsor to Buckingham Palace, even for her "like an ice cellar" that day, to meet with Russell, who offered to try. The key was Lord Clarendon, as Foreign Minister, who refused to serve under anyone but Palmerston. Back and forth Victoria shuttled between Windsor and London, "on our *eternal Govt hunting* errand." Russell had told her what she least wanted to hear (as she wrote in her journal), that "there was the most ample cause for [Parliamentary] enquiry, & that the whole country . . . cried for Ld. Palmerston, as the only man fitted to carry on the war with success." Palmerston had been dismissed three years earlier, making any future association awkward. He was seventy-one; his sight was failing; he walked only with the aid of two sticks; and he was more stubborn than ever. However the Queen had exhausted her alternatives.

One face-saving gesture was left. Palmerston, she knew, wanted to put the lawyer-archeologist Austen Henry Layard, discoverer of Nineveh and onetime attaché at Constantinople, into the War Office as undersecretary. He knew the Middle East as did few others in England. But he was a radical, and not a gentleman, having indulged in "ill-conditioned abuse" of Lord Raglan and Admiral Dundas. Palmerston could have the government if Layard were kept from the War Office. It was a cheap price to pay, and "Pilgerstein" became Prime Minister. Victoria thought he would be "somewhat of a trial," but he gained her respect, assisted both by events and by his shrewdness. And in a turnabout in 1878, she would knight Layard.

With the war highly unpopular in France, Napoleon III could not dominate his ally as he wished, and since winter was fast ending in the Crimea, improved organization could be brought to the British war effort. Most important of all, two months after Palmerston moved to Downing Street, Czar Nicholas I suddenly died. Less than half the original British force in the Crimea then survived. With enlistments not filling the Army's needs, Albert suggested hiring mercenaries from Switzerland, Germany, and Italy. Palmerston was on the verge of employing the idea when the King of Sardinia came forward. Eager to unite Italy under him, and seeing an opportunity to put a world power in debt to him, he offered 15,000 troops. With the chance for personal glory slipping, Napoleon rushed in with an offer of his own soldiers, if British ships could transport them. And he offered to accompany them in person to the Crimea.

The French, under Louis Napoleon, were at first more efficient at politicizing the war than prosecuting it. Although the situation at the front seemed stalemated, the Emperor's aides were busy nevertheless formulating postwar allocations of territory they had not won. "The French," Victoria once wrote in exasperation to Clarendon, "show their usual vivacity in pressing so hard for decision upon what is to be done with Sebastopol when taken. Surely we ought to have taken it first before we can dispose of it, and everything as to the decision about it must depend upon the state in which we receive it, and the opinion of the Military and Naval Commanders after they find themselves in possession of it. The Queen hopes, therefore, that Lord Clarendon will succeed in restraining French impatience as he has often done before."

Since British generalship had been incompetent, protests from London about Napoleon's eagerness to settle the war himself remained inappropriate. Instead, Lord Clarendon, and then Lord Granville, suggested that since all necessary vessels to carry French troops were not ready, for many were already engaged to transport Sardinians, the Emperor should pay a state visit to Windsor, at which time the entire situation could be discussed. Then, to add their imprimatur to his reign, the Queen and Prince would return the compliment by visiting Paris. Preparations were quickly made to receive the Emperor in England. By that time he was approaching the very logical conclusion that a regime such as his might not survive his long absence from France, and that it certainly would not survive if he did not, or if his armies won no brilliant victories.

Anti-French feeling continued strong in England, as a broadsheet ballad (including some bad French) suggested, but so was curiosity:

> *The Emperor and Empress are coming so keen*
> *To England, to visit our sweet little Queen.* . . .
> *Thro' the West-end of London so nicely they'll prance,*
> *With all the fine ladies of England and France,*
> *Such wonderful things they are going to do,*
> *Clear the road and get out of the way,* parle veaux. . . .
> *The Emperor of France and his lady so gay,*
> *Are coming to England—get out of the way.* . . .
> *There'll be baked frogs, & fried frogs, & frogs in a stew,*
> *And all the young ladies shall sing* parle veaux!

On April 16, 1855, Prince Albert greeted the Emperor and Empress at Dover, and escorted them to London by special train to the Bricklayers' Arms Station off the Old Kent Road. There they transferred to Paddington, and on to Windsor, greeted everywhere by bands and large crowds. Victoria was ready to be charmed by the Emperor, and indeed was. "I cannot say what indescribable emotions filled me," she wrote breathlessly in her journal, "how much all seemed like a wonderful dream. These great meetings of sovereigns, surrounded by very exciting accompaniments, are always very agitating. I advanced and embraced the Emperor, who received two salutes on either cheek from me, having first kissed my hand. I next embraced the very gentle, graceful, and evidently very nervous Empress."

Louis Napoleon was forty-seven, short, swarthy, and goateed. He was also engaging, and more than that, he had the magic of his connection with the legendary Bonaparte, the most formidable foe ever to confront England. At dinner, in a voice "low and soft," the Emperor confessed admiring her as a young Queen when he was an exile in London. "He also mentioned his having been a special constable on the 10th of April, 1848, and wondered whether I had known it. The war, and the news, which arrived just as he did, of the opening of fire from 400 guns, were a subject of conversation also." Dramatically, there had been a message awaiting the Emperor in Dover—the announcement of the opening, by French artillery, of the siege of Sevastopol. He gave the telegram to Albert, who preserved it among his papers.

A devoted Orleanist, largely because of her uncle's marriage to Louis-

Philippe's daughter Louise, Victoria was an unlikely conquest for the Emperor, but through the succession of state ceremonies, including Louis Napoleon's investment with the Order of the Garter, she became his devoted admirer. "That he *is* an extraordinary man with great qualities there can be no doubt—I might almost say a mysterious man. He is evidently possessed of *indomitable courage, unflinching firmness of purpose, self-reliance, perseverance and great secrecy;* to which should be added a great reliance on what he calls his *star* and a belief in omens and incidents as connected with his future destiny." She also saw him as "endowed with a wonderful *self-control,* great *calmness,* even *gentleness* and with a power of *fascination,* the effect of which upon those who become more intimately acquainted with him is most sensibly felt." The Empress Eugénie, she noted after a supper followed by a ball in the Waterloo Room (renamed for the occasion the "Picture Gallery"), was equally impressive. "Her manner is that most perfect thing I have ever seen—so gentle and graceful, and kind, the courtesy so charming, and so modest and retiring withal."

On April 18, at the end of a day of Anglo-French military discussions that Victoria attended, she described the war council as "one of the *most interesting* things I ever was present at. . . ." Early in February she had confessed to her journal that her heart was not in "this unsatisfactory war." By the end of February she was lamenting instead that "in these stirring times" she was a woman, and unable to participate. Now she felt involved, if only at a distance from the real events.

The long day ended with a concert at the Castle. Victoria closed her record with the feeling that the Emperor was easy in his role—"as if he had been born a king's son, and brought up for the place." The next day they left Windsor for London, which made the Queen "melancholy" ("quite *wehmütig,*" she repeated in German)—an emotion she ascribed to hearing "the very melancholy" Imperial anthem, *"Partant pour la Syrie,"* played.* She heard, Victoria added, "that the Empress was equally sad at going away from Windsor. . . . Altogether I am delighted to see how much Albert likes and admires her, as it is so seldom I see him do so with any woman." It may have assuaged the Queen's sense of having been charmed too easily by Louis Napoleon to feel that Albert had been smitten with the beautiful Eugénie.

---

*The anthem—words and music—was ascribed to Hortense de Beauharnais, mother of Napoleon III.

After the City had given the Imperial couple a formal luncheon at the Guildhall, a state visit followed to Her Majesty's Theatre. The production was Beethoven's *Fidelio,* a worrisome choice since the Emperor might have found the plot subversive. The Queen's party arrived that evening at the first interval, greeted by enormous applause, by the playing of the inevitable *"Partant pour la Syrie,"* and by special new verses sung to an anthem long familiar to Victoria:

> *Emperor and Empress,*
> *O Lord, be pleased to bless;*
> *Look on this scene.*
> *And may we ever find,*
> *With bonds of peace entwin'd,*
> *England and France combined.*
> *God save the Queen!*

In the royal box, the Emperor confided to Victoria that just after her marriage, when she went in state to the opera at Covent Garden, "he had with great difficulty obtained a box, and afterwards they made him pay £40 for it, *'que je trouvais pourtant beaucoup!'* " There were reports now of people paying £100 for a box to see Napoleon with Victoria.

The next day, April 20, under a magnificent sunny sky, they visited the Crystal Palace in Sydenham, which was of great interest to the Emperor, who was planning the first of the Paris International Expositions. "We discovered," the Queen wrote in her journal, "that this was his birthday—his forty-seventh—and though not . . . taken notice of publicly, we felt we could not do otherwise than take private notice of it. . . . I wished him joy. He seemed for a moment not to know to what I alluded, then smiled, and kissed my hand, and thanked me, and I gave him a pencil-case. . . . The Emperor was also pleased at [Prince] Arthur's giving him two violets—the flower of the Bonapartes'."

At departure the next day, the Emperor inscribed his name in Her Majesty's Album with *"tendre amitié."* With some tears, Victoria said her farewells, and immediately began planning the return visit to Paris. She had permitted herself to be wooed in a fashion she had never before experienced, and was ready for more. It had all been, she wrote in her journal, like "a dream, a brilliant, successful, pleasant dream." Further, at the meeting of the monarchs and their entourages, the Emperor had been persuaded to leave the prosecution of the war to the generals. His eagerness to lead troops into battle had been blunted by the continuing news from the Crimea that the Russian batteries defending Sevastopol were numerous and effective, with every sign developing of a long and indecisive siege. Confirmation came in a letter to the Queen dated April 25, 1855, in which he reluctantly conceded that he could not leave France, and closed with appreciation for hospitality and sympathy that had left him "henceforth, bound to Your Majesty."

That there were problems at home for him became quickly obvious when an Italian revolutionary, on April 28, fired at him in the Bois de Boulogne, and missed. Unruffled, the Emperor announced that "there are beings who are the instruments of the decrees of Providence; until I have fulfilled my mission I shall be in no danger." And he went off as scheduled, with Eugénie, to the Opéra-Comique that evening, to tremendous ovations from crowds on the boulevards. Victoria understood, but was nonetheless upset, writing to King Leopold, "It shocked me *the more,* as we had *watched over* him with such anxiety while he was with us."

One way in which the Queen could keep her hand in the war was to present medals personally, which she did for the first time on May 22, at the Horse Guards, perched on a dais with a brass railing, in an unmilitary lilac dress, a green mantilla, and the inevitable white bonnet. At her side was the Minister for War, Lord Panmure, who dipped into a basket of silver medals dangling from blue and yellow ribbons, handing them to her to give to each soldier as he passed by, some pushed in chairs, some hobbling on crutches. Meanwhile, a military band played, and no one noticed how often her hand trembled as she presented the medals, which each man was supposed to return quietly afterwards so that the reverse could be engraved with the name of the awardee and the date. "Many of the Privates smiled," Victoria confided to her journal, "others hardly dared look up. . . ." But "all touched my hand, the 1st time that a simple Private has touched the hand of the Sovereign. . . . I am proud of it— proud of this tie which links the lowly brave soldier to his Sovereign."

So proud were the soldiers of the contact with the Queen that many refused to relinquish their medals for engraving: they wanted to keep the very ones put into their hands by Victoria, who was moved on hearing of it. When the story went around, Melbourne's old friend Caroline Norton asked Lord Panmure whether the Queen had indeed been touched. "Bless my soul, no!" Panmure, misunderstanding, insisted to Mrs. Norton. "She had a brass railing before her and no one could touch her." For the Minister for War it had just been another dull ceremony.

"You never saw anybody so entirely taken up with military affairs as she is," he wrote to Lord Raglan.

Anticipation of Louis Napoleon's visit, and its stylish reality, had—in addition to the war itself—taken the edge off the heralded spring concert series conducted by another onetime revolutionary of 1848, Richard Wagner. The arrogant and argumentative composer, then forty-two, was still proscribed in his own country, making England's opening its doors to him almost a diplomatic affront. Finally, with the Emperor gone, the Queen, with Albert, attended the seventh of Wagner's eight Old Philharmonic Society concerts, on June 11, 1855, and led the applause, of which he had heard little before, for his *Tannhäuser* overture. At the interval the royal couple received Wagner, who affected white kid gloves, with which he pulled at the sidewhiskers that met, in the old-fashioned German manner, under his large, combative, clean-shaven chin. Afterwards the composer wrote to his first wife, Minna, that the Queen and Prince were "amiable and good-natured" but that Victoria was "very short and far from pretty, with a regrettably reddish nose." Despite an anti-Jewish pamphlet he had just published, attacking, among others, their favorite composers, Mendelssohn and Meyerbeer, they were courteous beyond his expectations. In German, Victoria inquired affably whether he might arrange such of his works as *Lohengrin* for Covent Garden, largely a home for Italian opera. Albert objected that Wagner's libretti were unsuited for such a company, and before the composer could respond, Victoria observed that most singers of Italian opera in London were German anyway, and needed only to sing in their mother tongue to sing Wagner. Happily, if tangentially, the composer remarked that German singers were spoiled by being made too much of in England. Although the Queen would not see Wagner again for twenty years, she followed his work and imported new scores from Germany as he produced new operas.

Victoria kept her hand in the war in any way she could, and when noisy, flashy Cremorne Gardens, on the Thames at Chelsea Reach, advertised early in August a "Grand Military Fete for the Benefit of Wellington College for the Education of Orphan Sons of Officers in the Army," the spectacle was presented as "Under the Immediate Patronage of Her Majesty the Queen and His Royal Highness the Prince Albert." The entertainment, at twopence, included "A Colossal Panorama of Sebastopol," and "The Storming of the Mamelon Vert & the Rifle Pits" by five hundred soldiers and three battering rams. After the opening on

August 13, the Queen readied herself for France, where, to fashion-conscious Parisians, the dowdiness of her wardrobe, especially her predilection for bonnets, would become legendary. It had become more necessary than ever for Napoleon to maintain his position through external distractions and internal spectacles, and both happily coincided when, on August 16, 1855, just as the Queen was due to arrive, French troops in the Crimea were victorious at the river Tchernaya in beating back sixty thousand Russians struggling to relieve Sevastopol.

The Emperor had a genius for sumptuous surfaces. Mary Ponsonby, one of Victoria's ladies-in-waiting, was overwhelmed by the transformation of the iron-ribbed vault of Strasbourg Station, where the royal train arrived in Paris. It was "fitted up and brilliantly lighted like a theatre, with thousands of magnificently dressed people. The floor of the platform was covered with thick crimson velvet; the same crimson velvet with a golden fringe was used for *portieres* to those enormous arches." Of course none of the luggage arrived, but "the *coup d'oeil* was something beyond. . . ."

Having been put up at Windsor in a suite full of valuable paintings, Eugénie was determined not to be outdone. Bowing to the privilege of French sovereigns to decorate their palaces with borrowings from state galleries, Comte Alfred Nieuwerkerke, director of the Louvre, nevertheless waited until the last possible moment to comply. At three—the royal party was due to arrive at five—he sent over sufficient masterpieces for Victoria's rooms. The Queen, according to the malicious diaries of Edmond and Jules de Goncourt, must have been doing her homework on Parisian museums she might be visiting. "Ah," they reported her as exclaiming, "that picture comes from the Salon Carre, and that one over there. . . ." Later, when Eugénie escorted Victoria to the Louvre, they found notices on the walls where the paintings had been, announcing boldly, REMOVED BY ORDER AND TAKEN TEMPORARILY TO THE TUILERIES. The French knew how to protest safely against Imperial caprice.

Whatever the truth of the episode, it would have no adverse repercussions. The nine days in Paris captivated the French crowds, who turned out by the hundreds of thousands. The *Préfet* "asked whether they might call the new street leading to the Hotel de Ville after me," Victoria wrote, "on which I said—*'Je serai bien flattee de cela—si l'Empereur le permet,'* on which he cordially gave his assent." On the arm of one Napoleon, the Queen visited the tomb of the earlier Napoleon at the Invalides; the palace at Saint-Germain-en-Laye, where James II lived and died in exile; the Grand Trianon and the Petit Trianon at Versailles, with their associations with Marie Antoinette. At the Trianon, Eugénie appeared in a cloud of Valenciennes lace, a single rose in her hair. Victoria, her embarrassed maid-of-honor recalled, wore an out-of-fashion lilac gown, a bonnet, and her dignity. At the Grand Opéra in the Rue Lepelletier, there was a special program of extracts from French opera, and "a long, too long, ballet, in three acts," which included a scene with a view of Windsor, at which "God Save the Queen" was sung splendidly, and "most enthusiastically cheered; there could not have been more enthusiasm in England." After the performance they returned "home," and the Emperor (who had been a student in Germany) and the Prince sang "all sorts of old German songs."

One afternoon was utilized for a shopping trip incognito, the Queen and Mary Ponsonby hidden behind ordinary bonnets from the Magazin du Louvre, while driven in a common *fiacre* that was sent to the back door of the Tuileries. Victoria "took an immense interest and delight in ordinary circumstances"—people eating outside the cafés, the arrangements of goods in shop windows—and as they were returning through the crowded streets, Albert with his back to the cabman, Victoria and Mary Ponsonby opposite, a woman shouted, *"Celle-la ressemble bien a la Reine d'Angleterre!"* The Queen "bridled," as she enjoyed being recognized when technically *inconnu.* When no one else made the same observation, she complained, "They do not seem to know who I *am!"*

There were few such disappointments. Lord Clarendon, who was with the royal party, described Napoleon's "making love" to Victoria in Paris; however short of sexual intimacy, the Emperor did accomplish the emotional seduction of the Queen. As the glorious visit, complete to perfect weather, came to a close on August 27, and the last of the "endless" farewell fireworks sprayed the sky over the royal yacht at Boulogne, Victoria confided to her diary how "attached" she had become to the appealing Emperor. Albert, she conceded, was "much less taken by people, much less under *personal* influence, than I am." Still, even he "quite admits that it is extraordinary, how very much attached one becomes to the Emperor, when one lives with him quite at one's ease and intimately, as we have done. . . . I know few people, whom I have felt involuntarily more inclined to confide in and speak unreservedly to—I should not fear saying anything to him. I felt—I do not know how to express it—safe with him. . . . I like his face. He undoubtedly has a most extraordinary power of attaching people to him!"

Vicky and Bertie had been with their parents in Paris, and the Queen added to her journal that the children had grown "very fond" of the Emperor too. How much so would have disconcerted her. When Louis Napoleon, taking the carriage reins himself, had driven the Prince of Wales about Paris, Bertie told him, "I wish I were your son!"

A disappointment to both his mother and his father because he had failed to become a miniature Albert, Bertie did not have to be very astute to sense their rejection. By default rather than desire, Albert was the overseer of the children's education and discipline; all but the eldest, Vicky, were afraid of him, failing to realize how much he cared for them. The Queen, who seldom saw the younger children except when she was to be seen publicly with them, confessed to Princess Augusta of Prussia in October 1856 that even when Albert was away she found "no especial pleasure or compensation" in the company of her elder children, and only occasionally did she find "rather intimate intercourse" with them "easy or agreeable." She was only happy, she confided, when with Albert. Having grown up alone, without the company of other children, she was ill at ease with them, even when they were her own. "I cannot get used to the fact that Vicky is almost grown up. To me she still seems the same child who had to be kept in order and therefore must not become too intimate." That intimacy would come, as—of necessity—it came with the younger daughters, but rarely with her sons.

One story emanating from Balmoral suggests the rare other side of Victoria in her relationship with her children. John Ruskin, in a letter to his father, told of hearing from Mrs. Alexander John Scott about "the simplicity and good housewifery of the Queen at Balmoral"—that "some time ago, one of the little princesses having in rough play torn the frock of one of her companions (a private gentleman's daughter) the Queen did not present the young lady with a new frock, but made the princess *darn* the torn one. I would not at first believe that the princesses had learned to 'darn'—but Miss [Margaret Alexis] Bell was able at once to refer me to a notice of one of their exclamations at the Great Exhibition about the sewing-machine, which showed—being an expression of an earnest wish to have one, 'for it would save *so* much trouble'—that they had real experience of what sewing meant." Victoria remembered that as a girl she had been taught to apologize when she had done wrong—even to her maids. Her daughters were being shown that there were ways to apologize that went beyond words.

The world to which the Queen returned from France was very

different from the one she had left. Sevastopol was about to fall, and an uneasy truce would follow until peace terms could be settled. By then Victoria was at Balmoral, where the news of the breaking of the siege came on September 10. A bonfire "prepared," Victoria confessed, "when the false report of the fall of the town arrived last year," was finally lit, and people rushed to the blaze "in every species of attire." There was much drinking of whiskey, and "a wonderful state of excitement." The boys were awakened, and went to the top of the cairn nearby to watch the "ecstacy." Just before midnight the Queen returned, "and, just as I was undressing, all the people came down under the windows, the pipes playing, the people singing, firing off guns, and cheering—first for me, then for Albert, the Emperor of the French, and the 'downfall of *Sebastopol.'* "

The Queen visited such wounded as had been returned to English hospitals, invited ambulatory convalescents to the palace, and reviewed troops to bestow medals. The Victoria Cross would emerge from the war, her idea being that some medal for extraordinary bravery in battle was needed that could be awarded regardless of rank. (The Royal Warrant, largely composed by Albert, referred to "officers or men who have served Us in the presence of the Enemy and shall then have performed some signal act of valour or devotion to their country.") According to Lady Augusta Bruce, who often accompanied the Queen on her hospital rounds, Victoria knew the names and histories of each of the patients she visited, and had a strong stomach for stump-saluting amputees and casualties with "churchyard coughs." Pages of her journal were devoted to graphic descriptions of paths that bullets had taken, but also of her intention to be "of use" to the wounded, "to try and get some employment for those who are maimed for life." Their pensions, she knew, would not be enough to live on.

Even at Balmoral there was no forgetting the wounded, as a stream of inquiring letters went south to worry officials about their care. Returning from Balaclava and Scutari, Florence Nightingale visited. "I envy her being able to do so much good & look after the noble brave heroes whose behaviour is admirable," Victoria had written earlier. Now, Lady Augusta noted in her diary for October 5, 1855, the Queen showed Miss Nightingale "a whole book of photographs she has done of the wounded and the most distinguished soldiers, with a notice of each, *little* required by the Royal memory! One without arms the Queen [personally] pensions and looks after, and [she] is in despair because his friends help him to the brandy bottle which he is unable to handle for himself, and the results are sad! The Prince found he was incorrigible, but the Queen *knows* he has *now* taken the pledge, and 'will not give him up.' "

Miss Nightingale was asked "how many times she went round at night" at the hospital. Three, she said, as there were two thousand patients.

"Then when did you sleep?"

"Oh, that first winter we did not feel as if we needed much sleep."

Even the two eldest princes went with the Queen to the military hospitals at Chatham. A strong letter from her to Lord Panmure followed, praising the attention the wounded were receiving, but deploring in her bluntest language the inadequate physical facilities. The buildings were "bad," she charged, "the wards more like prisons than hospitals, with the windows so high that no one can look out of them,—and most of the wards are small, with hardly [any] space to walk between the beds. There is no dining-room or hall, so that the poor men must have their dinners in the same room in which they sleep, and in which some may be dying, and at any rate suffering, while others are at their meals." She had heard of a proposal to utilize old, no-longer-seaworthy ships to house convalescents, an idea she sniped at by declaring such a hulk "a very gloomy place, and these poor men require their spirits to be cheered as much as to have their physical sufferings attended to." Such matters, she declared, were "constantly in her thought, as indeed is everything connected with her beloved troops, who have fought so bravely, and borne so heroically all their sufferings and privations." When she warned Panmure that she also intended to visit the facilities at Portsmouth, the result was a large new Royal Military Hospital constructed at Netley, near Southampton. The Queen laid the first stone.

International matters preoccupied Victoria well into the next year. Before the close of 1855 she had entertained the King of Sardinia and his foreign minister, Count Cavour, both soon to govern a nearly united Italy. On a cold, dark, wet day—December 4, 1855—Victor Emmanuel II went to the Guildhall for a welcome by the City of London, and the next day, at Windsor, he was invested with the Garter. He was both rough and shy, Victoria wrote to Leopold—"more like a Knight or King of the Middle Ages than anything one knows nowadays." Impatient of ceremony, he confided to Victoria that he disliked "the business of king," and would retire to a monastery if there were no wars to fight. Kings had to be sure that wars were *just,* she warned, for they would have to answer for men's lives before God. The burly, red-haired, un-monkish king agreed that just wars were to be preferred—but that God would forgive a mistake. "Not always," said Victoria.

The final day's schedule had to be shortened because the King was leaving at four in the morning. Well before that hour the Queen and Prince were up to take leave of him, in the early-morning darkness, with a heavy snow falling. Victor Emmanuel had sent needed troops to the Crimea, and the Sovereign's duty was to demonstrate that gratitude.

On his deathbed, the stern Nicholas II had insisted, "My successor must do as he will; for myself I cannot change." The new and reputedly more liberal Czar was his son, Alexander II, with whom Victoria had danced when a young queen; but negotiations with his representatives at Vienna at first led nowhere, despite the huge manpower losses of the Russians, who had no rail link to the Crimea and had to move men and materiel, in winter snow, the final 230 miles by animal and human transport. Only one soldier in ten was said to have arrived in fighting condition; hundreds of thousands had died. Finally, Austrian and Prussian diplomatic moves led to a settlement that, as with all military and territorial compromises, no one liked, and the Queen received the still-secret news on the night of January 16, 1856, by the unlikeliest of means—a telegram, *en clair*, from the secretive and reticent King of Prussia. Although the message came by commercial telegraph, uncoded, the excited King begged that his name be concealed. Albert sent the "telegraphic curiosity" on to Lord Clarendon, noting that the Queen wanted him to be aware of the sender as well as the message, since "the whole line of the telegraph" already knew.

Actual signing of an agreement would take time, and Russia would soon flout it anyway, but when the moment came in April, Victoria wrote to Palmerston that she wished "to delay no longer the expression of her satisfaction as to the manner in which both the War has been brought to a conclusion, and the honour and interests of this country have been maintained by the Treaty of Peace, under the zealous and able guidance of Lord Palmerston. She wishes as a public token of her approval to bestow the Order of the Garter upon him." The gesture was to her credit. She still disliked the old curmudgeon, and would do her best when his Government finally fell, early in 1858, to keep him out of office further. Yet she knew he had earned his ribbon.

For the Queen, the cessation of hostilities meant her presence at return parades and welcoming inspections, which reached their climax in

July at Aldershot, Woolwich, and London. At Aldershot on July 8, 1856, a steady rain pelted down as the Queen watched (in a closed carriage) the Crimean regiments march into a pattern forming three sides of a square around her. The rain happily stopped—"Queen's weather" again—as officers from each regiment that had been under fire, with four men from each company, stepped forward. The Queen then opened her carriage door to offer a symbolic welcome that, in a later era, could have been conveyed by electronic inventions then unborn to the entire mass of troops assembled. "Tell the others for me," she said, in a voice *The Times* described as of silvery sweetness, "that I have watched anxiously over the difficulties and hardships which they have so nobly borne, that I have mourned with deep sorrow for the brave men who have fallen. . . . I thank God, that your dangers are over."

En masse, the troops shouted "God save the Queen!" Helmets, bearskins, and shakos were thrown into the air. There was an appearance of finality to it all, but the next day, as they marched through London, the Queen would greet them again from the central balcony at Buckingham Palace.

These were stirring moments for her, but they were marred at Aldershot by a dramatic audience with Field Marshal Viscount Hardinge, the army chief, who had brought to Victoria the report of the Military Commission on the Crimea. As he began discussing the findings with her, only a watered-down rebuke to the military, he fell forward onto the table with a paralytic stroke. Albert assisted him to a sofa, where (the Prince wrote to Stockmar) Hardinge "at once resumed what he was saying with the greatest clearness and calmness, merely apologizing 'that he had made such a disturbance.' " But his right leg and arm were useless, and he then had to be lifted into his carriage.

Two days later the Queen received his resignation of his command, "the duties of which his sudden and severe illness has rendered him incapable of performing." He would not be the last casualty of the Crimea.

Since the war had solved very little, largely postponing at heavy cost recognition of unsettled ethnic aspirations in the Balkans, Victoria confessed to the Earl of Clarendon, her Foreign Minister, "Much as the Queen disliked the idea of *Peace,* she has become reconciled to it. . . ." Her pride in British arms had been wounded by the French capture of Sevastopol at a time when her own forces had failed at Redan. It had been an "unsatisfactory" war even in its resolution. The heralds who ceremonially proclaimed the Peace of Paris on March 30, 1856, at Temple Bar were hissed by the crowd. Victoria knew, as they did not, that France would not have continued the costly war. Peace, in any case, was relative. British troops were also busy in India, Persia, Africa, and China.

On June 26, 1857, at a review in Hyde Park, the Queen decorated Crimean veterans with the first Victoria Crosses. Even at ten that morning the weather was stifling. With no breeze stirring, men in the seats reserved for the elite fanned themselves with the tails of their coats, and their ladies improvised fans from newspapers and handkerchiefs. While the Royal Standard above the Queen's dais drooped, Victoria, bonneted and implacable under the broiling sun, distributed sixty-two medals to the men on parade, including one in the uniform of a police constable and another in the dress of park keeper, once heroes at Inkerman and Redan. As for the medal itself, *The Times* complained, "Never did we see such a dull, heavy, tasteless affair. . . . There is a cross, and a lion, and a scroll worked up into the most shapeless mass that the size admits of." Valor, it concluded, would have to be its own reward; had the medals been on sale at a penny, "hardly a dozen would be sold in a twelve-month." Victoria liked it.

The christening of what would be her ninth and last child, Princess Beatrice (born April 14), had taken place ten days earlier, and she had just returned to formal activity after her lying-in and recuperation at Osborne. Surfeited with the discomforts and distractions of pregnancy and babies, the Queen was aware more than ever that each one grown to maturity meant money-grubbing from Parliament and matchmaking on her part (an activity that would consume her later years). She and Albert, Victoria told Vicky twenty years later, considered "many Princes a great misfortune—for they are in one another's and almost everybody's way. . . . Papa felt this so much that he was always talking of establishing if possible one or two of your brothers and eventual grandchildren . . . in the colonies." Thirty-eight when Beatrice was born, and possibly embarrassed by the prospects of further motherhood—she had called even more fecund women "rabbits"—Victoria raised the issue delicately with her *accoucheur*. Even more discreetly, he apparently suggested that the only legal and moral solution was abstinence. "Oh, doctor," she is reputed to have exclaimed, "can I have no more fun in bed?" The remark seems too unqueenly to be literally Victorian, but in substance may have represented something of her sexual innocence, even after nine children and seventeen years of marriage.

Victoria distributing Crimean War medals, May 21, 1856. Contemporary engraving.

On the same day as the Hyde Park review, the Queen had learned of the Sepoy Mutiny in India. The news from India, with the "cruel suspense" (as she put it) of weeks of delay in getting information, had come just as she was pressing Lord Palmerston and Lord Panmure to do something about the "defenceless state" of England itself in the aftermath of post-Crimea military retrenchments. Suddenly, penny-pinching seemed abandoned. The Commander-in-Chief of forces in India, General George Anson, was reported dead. Palmerston had to rush a replacement, Sir Colin Campbell, who left the next day, on the long voyage around the Cape to a situation bound to be very different when he arrived from anything he knew as he embarked.

With a confident grasp of the military situation, in part because of lessons learned from the Crimean experience, Victoria pressed upon her suddenly timid Prime Minister a realistically strategic view. After sweeping across the map from the original localities of the mutiny to the large population centers into which it had spread, she concluded, "Our troops are sure to remain victorious against the Sepoys in the open field, if numbers be not too disproportionate, if they be not badly led, or physically reduced by sickness or fatigue." (She expected, at the least, the last, and possibly all three.) The difficulty for the leadership, she suggested, would be "to get a proper 'ensemble' into the military movements, and this will hardly be the case unless an army be formed at Calcutta strong enough to operate from thence with certainty upon the parts of the country in revolt. . . . Our reinforcements, dropping in one by one, run the risk of being cut up by being sent on to relieve the different stray columns in distress." Then she went on to puncture Palmerston's complacency about reinforcements already en route "which are to give a favourable turn to affairs." Had he considered, she asked, "that the first [reinforcements] which were dispatched by the Government to India (exclusive of the Chinese expedition of 5,000 men diverted to it) and now there [in China] will arrive only in October? The time lost in the arrangements, in taking up shipping, &c., brought their departure to July. There will be, therefore, two whole months, August and September, when the Indian Government will get no relief whatever, while fighting, marching, &c., lose . . . often as much as 500 men in a day."

Impatiently she insisted that "early decisions" were necessary, not temporizing "in the vain *hope* that matters will mend." A few weeks later she felt compelled to "repeat" that the measures taken were "not commensurate with the magnitude of the crisis." There was no excuse, she warned, for false economies. "Financial difficulties don't exist; . . . and this appears hardly the moment to make savings on the Army [budget] estimates." To the long history of mismanagement, incompetence, penuriousness, confused responsibility, and indifference, already the source of embarrassment in the Crimea, were added, in India, guilt on the scale of the subcontinent. Ever since the reign of Elizabeth I, under the transparent cloak of a merchant company, Britain had exploited teeming subject races occupying vast tracts of southern Asia. The East India Company, prospering under a feudal royal charter, was gradually relinquishing its political powers to the Crown; nevertheless, it was still landlord and tax collector, and paid the bills for the British-officered army that maintained order. Overseeing the directors of the Company by the 1850s was a Cabinet minister in London, and the Governor General, ostensibly its appointee, was in fact designated by the Government.

Beneath the unrelenting sun, Indians toiled for a few farthings a day, under Company and civil-servant employers for whom India was largely the safety valve for British excess population, from younger sons to superfluous daughters. Sepoys—Indian infantrymen serving under British officers in regiments supported by Company funds—represented five-sixths of the quarter-million troops in India. The rest were in Queen's regiments,

British in origin but in effect hired out to serve an Indian tour of duty.

Early in 1857 a rumor raced among sepoy troops that the new rifles, lighter-weight Enfields, required greased cartridges, for which the manufacturer had used beef fat or—even worse—pork fat. Contact with either meant defilement for Moslems as well as Hindus—even rejection from the marital bed. (A related rumor—one that surfaced in Calcutta—was that at Queen Victoria's command, all sepoys would be baptized.) The concern about pollution with unclean grease was real; to save a few pennies, some British weapons manufacturers had substituted for the prescribed mutton fat (acceptable to Indians of any religion or caste but the strictest vegetarians) bullock's or hog's fat.

When, in April, some troops began to reject the defiled cartridges, eighty-five sepoys at the Meerut encampment near Calcutta were court-martialed for insubordination. Their sentences were ten years' hard labor —in chains—on roadbuilding crews. In the heat and dust of India it was, in effect, a death sentence, but there was never any doubt that General Anson would confirm the verdicts. When the men were publicly fettered to warn off further dissidents, mutiny was certain. Once it flamed up— first as an attempt to free the prisoners—the violence spread across India.

In what seemed poetic justice, from the Indian standpoint, one of the first deaths—albeit from cholera—had been that of General Anson. Epidemics and massacres would take more lives on both sides than conventional skirmishes, but at the start the British were losing the shooting war as well as the silent one. Through the early months of the uprising, as all the belated news from India remained bad, and Victoria feared for the lives of her subjects (Palmerston had once preached that the killing of a single British subject was *casus belli*), she vented her fury on her Prime Minister. "The Queen must say," she wrote him in exasperation on August 25, 1857, "that the Government incur a fearful responsibility towards their country by their apparent indifference. God grant that no unforeseen European complication fall upon this country—but we are really tempting Providence." To Leopold she confided that the affair was "so much more distressing than the Crimea—where there was *glory* and honourable warfare, and where the poor women and children were safe. . . . There is not a family hardly who is not in sorrow and anxiety about their children, and in all [social] ranks—India being *the* place where everyone was anxious to place a son!"

With the raising of the last vital siege in December, Victoria wrote to her former Lady of the Bedchamber, Lady Canning, wife of the

Viceroy, "Thank God! Lucknow is saved!" Charlotte Canning had been commanded to send the Queen full reports every six weeks. Reporting on everything but her husband's infidelities, Lady Canning's informal letters and drawings were, Victoria told her, the most useful information from India. After Lucknow the mutiny began to dissipate, although as late as May 1859, thousands of rebels still held out on the borders of Nepal. What had become clear long before, however, even to the most laissez faire politicians in London, was that the Company had outlived its usefulness. Legislation to take royal control of India received Victoria's signature on August 2, 1858, the Queen afterwards writing to Lord Canning, the Governor-General who became the first Viceroy, that direct responsibility for "that enormous Empire which is so bright a jewel of her Crown" was "a source of great satisfaction and pride."

Of those who survived the mutiny with distinction, one was reputedly an old admirer of Victoria. To Lord Stanley, the Queen would write early in 1859, "Lord Elphinstone also ought not to be left unrewarded, and a step in the Peerage . . . does not appear too high an honour for him, for he also has greatly contributed to the saving of the Indian Empire." Allegedly because of his attentions to Princess Victoria, he had been sent to India, as Governor of Madras. At the time of the mutiny he had been Governor of Bombay, and had demonstrated courage and resourcefulness when panic was more common.

For six years, from 1847 to 1853, he served in London as lord-in-waiting to the Queen, an appointment that Victoria had to approve, and that may have been meant as an implicit reversal of his banishment. Another return to England followed the mutiny, after which the Queen wrote to Canning, now raised to Earl for his own leadership in India, "Alas! another most valuable public servant and friend of ours, Lord Elphinstone, only returned to die!" The word *friend* was rarely used by the Queen, and the two references to John Elphinstone were as close as she would get to intimating anything about the romantic episode. That the handsome guardsman of 1836 died unmarried, his venerable peerage becoming extinct, may suggest something of his feelings as we attempt to read between the lines of history.

Still another British war had been going on in Asia, as a result of attempts to defend commercial traffic into Chinese waters from Hong Kong, a British colony since 1841, when it was pried from China as a port for opium traders from India. Continuing British intrusions into China were protested by Conservatives and Peelites, but when the dispute ended, in 1856, with the dissolution of Parliament and new elections, Palmerston's pro-business forces had enlarged their majority. By the end of the year, British gunboats had bombarded Nanking and Canton, and French and British troops occupied Canton. There were also troops in Persia, ostensibly to protect India, Palmerston explaining to Victoria early in 1857 "that whatever belongs nominally to Persia must be considered as belonging practically to Russia, whenever Russia may want to use it for her own purposes."

The Queen's attitude may have been summed up for her by Sir Theodore Martin in his official biography of the Prince Consort, which Victoria oversaw. There Martin noted that such wars "have never been very popular at home," but resulted from "misdeeds" of foreign rulers who stood in the way of "commercial intercourse." Victoria's practical concern at the time, if British interests were involved, was whether her Government understood the military upshot of an aggressive posture. As she responded to the Earl of Clarendon on July 13, 1856, "The Queen wishes to ask, before she sanctions this draft, whether the Cabinet have fully considered the consequences of this declaration to the Persians, which may be war; and if so, whether they are prepared to go to war with Persia, and have provided the means of carrying it on?" In the communications from Court on military and foreign-policy matters, the hand was usually not that of the constrained and conciliatory Prince, but that of the "soldier's daughter."

Even at Osborne the military preoccupations of the decade had their echo in the interests of Victoria's younger offspring. Behind the Swiss Cottage is a miniature fortress with a boy-size brick barracks, earthwork fortifications, and wooden cannon. It was built largely by Prince Arthur, much later Field Marshal the Duke of Connaught. He was not yet ten. It was the favorite playground of the royal children.

X

Albert
the Good

(1858–1861)

Being Queen Regnant was something that Vicky would be spared, Victoria wrote to her daughter after the Princess Royal's marriage. "Though dear Papa, God knows, does everything—it is a reversal of the right order of things which distresses me much and which no one, but such a perfection, such an angel as he is—could bear and carry through." The Princess Royal had been married at seventeen, on January 25, 1858, to Prince Frederick William, ten years her elder, and son of the heir to the throne of Prussia. That Vicky had married so young troubled her mother and father, but the betrothal had been a love match. The couple had been made to wait since the bride was fourteen.

Both Queen and Prince were devoted to their eldest child, who had all the intellectual qualities they could not perceive in the heir apparent. The Prince of Wales would be bored by the earnest tutors and professors and preachers who were mandated as his companions at Oxford, Edinburgh, and Cambridge. What he wanted were cronies of his own age from the fast-living set of socially prominent students; he knew they existed and, as he could not be manipulated to become what he was not, he would somehow get to know them. Albert had told his son-in-law that Vicky had "a man's head and a child's heart." She was bookish, artistic, and inquiring, always at ease among her elders. She adored her father, and the affection was returned, but he now had to make way for her husband. With a drooping mustache to which he would later add a beard, Fritz was a head taller than his bride, who, at five feet two, was taller and prettier than her mother at the same age. The courtship had already lasted so long that to Victoria and Albert, Fritz had long been like a son.

Both sets of parents accompanied the couple to Gravesend, where they boarded the *Victoria and Albert* to cross the North Sea. On the royal yacht, parting was painful. Everyone in the bride's family cried. "I am not of a demonstrative nature," Albert wrote to Vicky afterwards, "and therefore you can hardly know . . . what a void you have left behind in my heart."

By the time the wedding took place, Albert finally could appear in his new official dignity. The previous June he had written to his stepmother in Coburg, "I now present myself before you as an entire stranger, 'Prince Consort.' " Infuriated by repeated frustration of her attempts to have the title granted by Parliament, the last withdrawn because her Ministers thought that the inevitable squabbling might jeopardize the vote on Vicky's dowry, the Queen issued Letters Patent making Albert something more than a Coburg prince. *The Times*, the Prince Consort wrote to Baron Stockmar, had a "sneeringly approving" article announcing the news. "In spite of the poet," it read, "there is much in a name, and if there be increased homage rendered to the new title on the banks of the Spree or the Danube, the English people will be happy to sanction and adopt it."

Albert had long been king in all but name, Victoria had confessed to Vicky. As the Queen had withdrawn from public view during her pregnancies, he had so completely become ceremonial sovereign outside London that no one any longer expected to see Victoria when a royal presence was necessary to open an art exhibition in Manchester, to launch a ship at Liverpool, to inspect the naval base at Portsmouth or the army barracks at Aldershot, or to visit a factory in Leeds. Still, the Queen acted like one when she wanted to, as when she insisted that although Britain was alone among civilized nations in the sale and purchase of army commissions, the practice should continue. Wealth guaranteed that officers' slots were filled by the right people. "If purchase be removed," she insisted to Palmerston, ". . . seniority with all its baneful effects" would control the system. (Not until 1871 was the anachronism abolished.) And Victoria had been her stubborn self when a proposal emanated from Berlin that, since the bridegroom was a future sovereign, Vicky and Fritz be married at the Prussian Court. "Whatever may be the usual practice of Prussian Princes," she instructed Lord Clarendon, "it is not *every* day that one marries the eldest daughter of the Queen of England. The question therefore must be considered as settled and closed."

In London, enthusiasm for the match was warm, as people hoped it would lead to a reduction in Prussia's ingrained suspicion of outsiders. Only tepid joy manifested itself in Berlin. No one could remember another occasion when an heir to the throne sought beyond Germany for a future queen. Formal primacy of the German confederation still belonged to Austria; it was no secret in Europe that Prussia intended to wrest that away while Austria was busy contending with the non-Germanic appendages of its empire. With the historic enemy, France, now waxing as militaristic as Prussia always viewed itself, and England seemingly on friendly terms with Napoleon III, paranoia—never far from the surface of Prussian consciousness—was on the increase, especially as political rivalries reflected rising industrial and commercial competition. Vicky as a loyal Prussian was seen in Berlin as an impossibility.

Rumors in London already had Victoria's next daughter, Alice, betrothed to a Prince of Orange, the public's explanation for a visit by the Queen of Holland. Pinched and anxious-looking, too young at fifteen, Alice was aware that dynastic marriages were expected in an age when they still represented friendship treaties, and the public approved of ties that were not exclusively German. But the rumor had no basis in fact. The few real candidates remained German, and additional German connections only made the French more wary. Nor did the English appreciate anything German, which also doomed from the start the petitions to Parliament circulating among West End tradesmen that Albert now be made King Consort, and called "His Majesty." Since the Great Exhibition, businessmen saw Albert as on their side, but only the newspapers effectively moved public opinion, and there the Prince Consort seemed forever un-English, if not actually German. In public he appeared tense and cramped; observers preferred their royalty to be like the uninhibited

Princess Mary of Cambridge, whom Benjamin Moran saw at a state ball turning even a quadrille into something broadly British. With 250 pounds to thrash about, she was easy to find in a crowd, he noted. "Her breast was bare, & heaved like the canvas waves in a theatrical sea after the exertion of dancing. The Queen dances badly." The Prince Consort was not worth mentioning. In any case, Albert preferred quieter occasions.

In August 1857 the Emperor of the French, with Eugénie, paid a private four-day visit to Osborne. "Albert said to me the first evening as he came out of the dining-room and saw them standing there," Victoria wrote artlessly to Augusta, the Princess of Prussia (and Vicky's mother-in-law), "I must look very carefully so as to make certain I'm not dreaming!" To Prussians, it was an unpleasant dream, even more so because the visit was kept out of the reach of newspapermen. The Berlin government knew that beneath the social veneer, ministerial meetings were going on, an outgrowth of Crimean War cooperation. Prussian officials also realized that Napoleon would work his personal charm on the Queen, and that he was planning to meet soon after with the new Russian Czar, Alexander II, in Stuttgart, under the auspices of the King of Württemberg. Such moves fed Prussia's fears about encirclement. Any pacific behavior toward a neighbor seemed an unfriendly act.

The return visit by Victoria and Albert to Cherbourg in August 1858 took place in a climate of deep distrust. Napoleon was eager to show off his new fortifications, yet the only possible enemy toward which they could be of any use was England. He was also eager to have the Queen countenance his open liaison with the wife of his Foreign Minister, but Victoria refused to kiss Madame Walewska, who (as Lord Clarendon put it) "was *living in that way with the Emp[ero]r.*" The warmth on both sides was forced and artificial. When the Emperor asked Victoria to silence London newspapers that were publishing speculations about French designs against England and in Europe, the Queen replied that the press in her country was free, and she lacked the power. The implications about Napoleon's cynical strategies were clear. Even if the fortifications were largely busywork, and the large standing army only kept men employed, some use might be found for both if remaining in power required a crisis to rally around.

The only good news came secretly, when a British packet slipped into port with news that the joint Anglo-American effort to lay a transatlantic telegraph cable had succeeded, and that the Queen's prepared message to President James Buchanan was being transmitted. The cable would soon break, and it was 1866 before a new expedition restored the link, but Victoria felt less isolated, although to Vicky she wrote only of family matters and of perfunctory speeches by Napoleon and Albert, the Prince's painfully prepared in French, and of migraine headaches she and Albert suffered.

Vicky often became the repository for confidences not entrusted to Victoria's own journal. From the Queen to the Princess Royal, 3,777 letters survive; more than four thousand exist from daughter to mother. Victoria's were full of the trivia of everyday life: the books she and Albert read together or to each other (*Jane Eyre* the month after the wedding), the plays they saw, the change of seasons at Osborne or Balmoral. The Queen told her of the "yoke of a married woman"— the "sufferings and miseries and plagues—which you must struggle against—and enjoyments etc. to give up—constant precautions to take. . . ." But "with a husband one worships" the married state was a "foretaste of heaven." The price, she went on, was that she had "9 times for 8 months to bear with those above-named enemies . . . and I own it tried me sorely. . . . I think our sex a most unenviable one." Cautionary words, however, had little impact in Vicky's bedroom, and she was soon pregnant. "I hope Fritz would not bear for a minute what we poor slaves have to endure," the Queen wrote unhappily.

At home, none of the children but Bertie was considered old enough to be told the news—not even "Affie," who was fourteen and already in training for the navy. To Vicky's contention that she was giving life to an immortal soul, the Queen responded that the condition was more like that of a cow or a dog, and that she shuddered to think of her daughters as victims of such humiliations. The Queen's letters also included searching questions about Vicky's everyday life, and injunctions on remaining steadfast to her English upbringing and loyalties. "You . . . should go to the English Church some time also, to show the English that you do not forget the Church in which you have been brought up," Victoria instructed. Sending some Osborne ivy for her daughter's hair, she added, "I am sure you would like to wear some of your own dear native ivy—from the woods here." It was very bad advice; the Princess would be distrusted in Prussia.

The constant nagging came to Baron Stockmar's attention because his son, Ernest, had a post in Prince Frederick William's household. While in Berlin in October 1858, the elder Stockmar saw the visiting Lord

Clarendon (who was then out of office) and, according to Greville, revealed that the Queen had been "behaving abominably" to her frightened child, worrying the Princess by attempting "to exercise the same authority and control over her that she did before her marriage," and that her letters, full of "reproaches, desiring all sorts of things to be done that it is neither right nor desirable that she should do," were dangerous. Albert was the only one, Stockmar said, who might be able to stop the harassment.

When Stockmar wrote to Albert, delicately raising the matter, Victoria discovered how the question had come up and, the Prince told Clarendon, was "in a towering passion with the Baron."

She was in an even more elevated passion with Albert, as an undated note from him reveals:

> You have again lost your self-control quite unnecessarily. I did not say a word which could wound you, and I did not begin the conversation, but you have followed me about and continued it from room to room. There is no need for me to promise to *trust* you, for it was not a question of trust, but of your fidgety nature, which makes you insist on entering, with feverish eagerness, into details about orders and wishes which, in the case of a Queen, are commands, to whomever they may be given. This is your nature; it is not against Vicky, but is the same with everyone and has been the cause of much unpleasantness for you. It is the dearest wish of my heart to save you from these and worse consequences, but the only result of my efforts is that I am accused of want of feeling, hard heartedness, injustice, hatred, jealousy, distrust, etc. etc. I do my duty towards you even though it means that life is embittered by "scenes" when it should be governed by love and harmony. I look upon this with patience as a test which has to be undergone, but you hurt me desperately and at the same time do not help yourself.

The badgering quality disappeared from the Queen's letters.

Meanwhile, there was always Bertie to belittle. "I own I think him very dull," Victoria confided to Vicky in December 1858. The next June she was complaining to Vicky not only about his laziness but that his nose had begun "to hang a little," which went poorly with his "want of chin" and "very large lips." Even later, compared to the ruddy Prince Louis of

Hesse, suitor for Princess Alice's hand, the Prince of Wales looked "sallow
—dull, blasé."

Looking poorly for other reasons was the Prince Consort, who appeared more like a man of sixty than one only approaching forty. He no
longer went shooting or even deer-stalking, and was paunchy and overweight, seemingly from lack of exercise. His hair had receded from his
forehead, and his mustache and sidewhiskers had become heavier. He
blamed his pale and exhausted appearance on overwork, and he suffered
from the Queen's zealous policing of fireplaces to make sure that none she
might possibly encounter was ablaze. There were even some angry words
exchanged on the subject, as Albert suffered, in and out of season, from
chills, and needed his fire. Early on September 1, 1858, the Prince wrote
to Vicky of the death of Cart, his Swiss valet for twenty-nine years
(Victoria noted that they had to "choke down" their grief), and added
that he had taken to wearing a wig on chilly mornings. "Osborne is green
and beautiful, but the weather cold and stormy. Mama will be much hurt
when she gets up and finds I have had a fire lit."

Albert was also prone to aching gums, and told Stockmar, "My
sufferings are frightful." Yet he loved his work, even when comparing
himself, in a letter to Vicky, to the mill donkey near Osborne turning his
wheel round and round. He knew he was doing his job well, the job he
had created for himself, and lavished his hours on it. *"Lese recht aufmerk-
sam, und sage wenn irgend ein Fehler da ist!"* he would instruct the Queen
about draft memoranda—"Read carefully, and tell me if there is any fault
in this!" Or *"Ich hab' Dir hier ein Draft gemacht, lese es mal! Ich dächte
es wäre recht so"*—"Here is a draft for you; read it. I should think this
will do."

Her "beloved and perfect Albert," the Queen wrote to Leopold,
forgetting her occasional rages at her husband, "had raised monarchy to
the *highest* pinnacle of respect, and rendered it popular beyond what it
ever was in this country." That was not history, but it was a reflection of
the upward swing in the pendulum of popular appeal. The Crimean War,
the Sepoy Mutiny, and the popular marriage of the Princess Royal had
created a sense of patriotism that masked the political divisions still
rotating governments in and out of Whitehall.

Even Palmerston was turned out early in 1859, only to find the
Queen urgently asking him to find some way to remain. Victoria was no
less suspicious of the old man than before, but he had a hold on the

people, and she trusted Lord Clarendon, his Foreign Secretary. When, however, Palmerston returned to power five months later, after an interim Derby ministry, it was with Russell as Foreign Secretary, Clarendon having declined to serve.

Foreign affairs remained much on the Queen's mind in the months after Vicky's marriage, and she used the marriage as a reason to visit an ambitious Prussia fast becoming a threat to European stability. Her friendship with Fritz's mother (soon Queen of Prussia), largely conducted by letters, seemed some leverage, but Augusta's husband, who had appeared more liberal than his eccentric older brother, proved easily dominated by reactionaries and militarists. Even Vicky's husband had taken happily to soldiering, and Victoria and Albert left with the feeling of having been befriended in all the correct ways, but with no warmth other than the oppressive heat of Potsdam and Berlin.

Also disturbing was Vicky's pregnancy. Victoria worried that she was too young to be tied down to a life of annual pregnancies; and the Queen saw little capacity for rapport between the socially arrogant Prussians and the intellectually arrogant young Princess. On August 28, 1858, tears flowed as Vicky and her parents parted with a mutual sense of abandonment but with an *"Auf baldiges Wiedersehn!"*

The next month, Vicky suffered a fall—catching a foot in a chair leg —and blamed her agonizing delivery on the baby's having shifted position because of the accident. Whatever the reason, the prolonged labor had to be ended with forceps. Mother and child survived, but Prince Frederick William Victor Albert, born on January 27, 1859, would have a withered and nearly useless left arm, attributed by some to birth injury, and by his doctor to nerve damage resulting from an abnormal prenatal position. "It is far more dreadful," the Queen would write to Vicky, "to be born into this world than into the next!"

All her grandchildren, the Queen decreed, would carry her name or that of Albert. Few were to use either. (Nor would the future Emperor William II use his father's name, although it had been placed first.) Feodora rushed a letter to her half-sister, sympathizing, with the long experience of a grandmother, over Victoria's anxiety and Vicky's agony. "It is so dreadful to know what a young creature has to go through—one's own child we have protected from every ill, guarded against every evil, now we must see them in danger and tortured by pain." Newspapers in both countries were full of good feeling about the event, she added. "Oh, if only on all subjects the two nations would feel and act together!"

Victoria could not attend the christening. Governmental business could not be put off, and the Prussian Court would not postpone the ceremony. The Queen was furious with the rigidity at Berlin. She did not see her first grandchild, or Vicky, until an informal visit at Osborne, and that only after a second grandchild, Princess Charlotte, was born.

At home the serious concerns seemed external. Sardinian efforts to unite Italy by wresting from Austria its peninsular provinces were pushing Europe closer to war. With some external distraction needed to replace the Crimea, and a chance for safe territorial expansion beckoning, France was offering military assistance to Victor Emmanuel—for a price. Napoleonic grandeur was a façade of Imperial buildings and boulevards and bravado sustained by borrowed money and borrowed time. Widening the conflict would only further Bonapartist absolutism, yet Victoria's Ministers were not torn as she was between backing her new friends and supporting legitimate existing regimes and frontiers. She admired Victor Emmanuel and she felt warmly (if less comfortably so) toward Louis Napoleon, but Victoria understood that promoting Italian unity meant dismembering Austria.

In her Speech from the Throne prepared by the cautious Earl of Derby—no Francophile Palmerston—in June 1859, any possibility of English involvement on the Continent was evaded. Victoria thought that so opting out in advance was a dubious strategy to retain any control whatever over events. Since friendship with France was as fragile as the unreliability of its Emperor, Victoria donned her mantle as woman warrior, and objected to conveying "the determination on the Queen's part of maintaining a neutrality . . . whatever circumstances may arise, which would do harm, and be inconvenient at home. What the Queen may express is her wish to remain neutral, and her hope that circumstances will allow her to do so. The paragraph about the Navy as it stands makes our position still more humble, as it contains a public apology for arming. . . ." She (or the Prince) suggested stronger passages, and the rare event occurred of a sovereign's Speech from the Throne being rewritten in policy matters by the sovereign.

Derby's government expired quickly. The Queen sent for Earl Granville, hoping to avoid both Palmerston and Russell. Tactlessly, Granville detailed his conversation with her in a letter to John T. Delane of *The Times*, but cautioned him to "wrap it up" in a discreet way. Delane published all the details, which, beyond Victoria and Albert, could have been known only to Granville. He was duly admonished by the Queen, who asked him how she could speak with "unreserved confidence" with her Ministers in such circumstances. Although his apology came quickly, he was offered only a minor post in a new Palmerston government. Lord John Russell would be Foreign Secretary, the other part of the pair of "dreadful old men," in the Queen's description. Age was not the problem, as infirmity had not blunted their effectiveness. They were Liberals, and actively promoted Italian independence, which meant undermining Austria, the occupier of northern Italy—"odious," in Palmerston's words, "to all liberal and enlightened men throughout the world."

Concerning Austria or Germany, the Queen and Prince were less than enlightened. Ties of blood made them tenacious about the security of the Germanic states; however, they were even more concerned about buildup of French forces along the Channel coast, which seemed without cause. When Napoleon III demanded of Sardinia as the price of his help the Italian provinces of Nice and Savoy, and received them, Russell and Palmerston became less Francophile. Finding something on which to agree with her Ministers, the Queen signed an order creating a volunteer coastal defense force. She held levees for volunteer officers, and reviews in Hyde Park for their men.

In the summer of 1860, when the National Rifle Association had been formed, she even fired the first ceremonial shot on Wimbledon Common. The Whitworth rifle was fixed on a stand for her to score a bull's-eye from four hundred yards. From Balmoral she reviewed the Scottish Volunteers. The march past, Victoria recorded, took an hour and ten minutes. "Very good, very fine men, the Highlanders splendid. . . . The only drawback was the dust, which came at times in such clouds, as to prevent the men from seeing anything. . . ." In her open carriage on the hillside, where she sat with her mother—the first time in twenty-six years that the Duchess had witnessed a review—the Queen wiped the dust from her eyes and accepted salutes and cheers.

From Balmoral on October 7, 1859, the year before, Victoria and Albert, with Bertie and Alice in a supporting party, had climbed Ben Muich-Dhui, 4,297 feet high, and the highest elevation in the British Isles. It was a formidable expedition. Both must have been feeling fit. The Queen was also fit enough to dance, as usual, at the annual gillies' ball, where she saw no cost to her dignity in taking a turn with the servants. But Bertram Mitford, the future Lord Redesdale, then a young Foreign Office official, remembered watching "a certain gentleman . . . dressed in gorgeous Highland array," who after having his own turn and making a bow to her Majesty, "cheated, and instead of taking his proper place, tried to win the chance of dancing up to her a second time. The Queen saw through the trick at once, . . . stopped dead short and very quietly drawing herself up, pointed to his proper place, and beckoned up the gentleman whose turn it was."

Before leaving Scotland, Victoria and Albert went to Loch Katrine, in the western Highlands, for the opening—in heavy rain—of the great new waterworks supplying Glasgow. With them were several of the younger children, as the public had an intense curiosity about the Princes and Princesses. Little Arthur, the Prince Consort wrote to Stockmar, was "amiable and full of promise." With Bertie a disappointment, Affie shipped off early to the navy because he promised to be little better, and with the very young Leopold a likely invalid, the Queen and Prince looked to Arthur with desperate hope.

They returned to Windsor by way of Chester and Bangor, then went off again to Oxford to see Bertie at college. The Prince of Wales had first been sent to the University of Edinburgh, as the initial stage of his austere higher education, when he was seventeen. He was not to mingle with students except where necessary at lectures, and was to give dinners to his tutors and to local worthies, as designated by his governor, Colonel Robert

"Best Rest for the Queen's Rifle"—Punch, *July 7, 1860, referring to the Queen's using a rifle fixed to score a bull's eye. The obedient soldier is Mr. Punch.*

Bruce. Then, in October 1858, still not yet eighteen, he had been transferred from Edinburgh to Oxford, where he was technically attached to Christ Church but actually lived out of college in a private house with Bruce, now a major general, and his assistant, Major Christopher Teesdale. Bertie would almost never hear from his mother, but Albert, with good—but misguided—intentions, would write, "I hope you have begun your little dinner parties again and are seeing the chief men of the University at your table . . ." and, about Bertie's study habits, "This is the only road to happiness and I want to see you happy." With no thoughts to exchange with dons and dignitaries, and with access to anyone his own age barred by the ubiquitous Major Teesdale, the Prince of Wales a year later was the most miserable student at Oxford.

To Vicky the Queen explained that her brother was not devoid of brains, but was more adept at cultivating his social talents, which were "remarkable." Bertie was "lively, quick and sharp when his mind is set on anything, which is seldom. . . . Usually his intellect is of no more use than a pistol packed at the bottom of a trunk if one were attacked in the robber-infested Appenines."

By the end of October, what had been a glorious autumn had turned into an early and severe winter, and Albert, having complained for days of a severe chill, took to bed, the first such episode since his marriage, apart from his sharing the children's measles. Stockmar knew of Albert's stomach pains; on a visit to Coburg the year before, the Prince had what he described in a letter to Victoria as "headache and general *malaise,*" and his usual cramps. "I have eaten nothing all the day," he added, attempting to make light of the problem, "to rob my stomach of the shadow of a pretext for behaving ill." To the Baron he wrote, on November 3, 1859, claiming as his reason the need to damp down any exaggerated reports, that he was "rallying from a gastric attack, under which I have been suffering for the last fourteen days, and which kept me two days in bed. . . . The only new symptom I had was a violent cramp at the pit of the stomach, which lasted very sharply for two hours at noon, several days running. . . . I am able to-day to move about the house."

Writing to Vicky on October 29, the Queen had characterized the return of Albert's ailment as, "Dear Papa was a little indisposed with his old enemy, but it was not a very bad attack[,] without sickness or shivering." A onetime physician himself, Stockmar did not dismiss the "old enemy" that easily—and Victoria may have revealed less than she feared, so as not to alarm the Princess Royal. Shaking off the apathy about responding to letters that had been exasperating Victoria for years, the elderly, rheumatic Stockmar wrote to Albert that the description of his illness "has disquieted me, and made me very sad." Among its causes, he suggested, were the physical and mental pressures upon the Prince, but he saw little way that Albert could avoid "all disturbing agencies, and in everything he does be governed by prophylactic rules: for under certain circumstances it is possible for the physician to *prevent*, but under all it is difficult to *cure.*"

On December 8, answering Count Stockmar, Albert wrote from Osborne of the irony of English suspicions of France. "Throughout the country people think of nothing but measures of protection against our Ally; Volunteer Corps are being formed in all the towns. The lawyers of the Temple go through regular drill. Lords Spencer, Abercorn, Elcho, &c., are put through their paces in Westminster Hall by gaslight in the same rank and file with shopkeepers." He also added that his stomach was "decidedly *not* better."

Osborne was choked with snow in December, but it was there that the family—without Prince Alfred, whose ship was at Corfu—celebrated Christmas. Among Albert's New Year letters was one to Stockmar, telling him of the completion of a rail link from Cologne to Mayence, which now made it possible to travel from London to Coburg in thirty-one hours. The Prince hoped that meant he could see Stockmar again. "We are all quite well," he added, "all except my stomach, which is in a state truly pitiable, and is responsible for my waking early in the morning, and being unable to sleep again—'a shocking bore,' as the popular phrase here says." Exhaustion was to plague him through the next two years. He minimized his sleeplessness and pain, and drove himself harder.

Although the Victoria-Vicky correspondence had quickly become voluminous and intense, little passed between mother and daughter that did more than dismiss Albert's complaints. After all, women were the suffering sex, as Victoria had already explained to Vicky. Further, the Princess Royal's concerns had instantly broadened far beyond domestic ones when she became part of the strict Prussian Court. The example of Albert had been poor preparation for an exposed public life in Berlin or Potsdam. Discipline, ceremony, stuffiness, stoicism, conservatism—these were, allegedly, virtues that Vicky, as a very young liberal intellectual, had not taken seriously before.

Sunday observance was puritanical hypocrisy to both women, and at Osborne the Queen often had Sunday dances in a tent, while at Balmoral, churchgoing never interfered with other amusements. Now, to Vicky, the Queen wrote ambivalently that it was prudent "not to go generally to the theatre on a Sunday," yet "to do so is equally right, if Fritz wishes it."

Sensitive about public perceptions, Vicky was concerned, too, about what she should read, or see on stage. The Queen confessed that she had never seen *The Merry Wives of Windsor*, as it was reputed to be "very coarse." Vicky responded that Shakespeare's coarseness in general was not suited to the tastes of German court ladies, as "he gives the worst names to the worst things and makes every improper thing revolting." French drama was even more rude because "they make improper things interesting and gloss the wickedness over." One German play in particular, Vicky confided, she lacked the courage to see—*Faust*. Yet Fritz had read portions to her, and she found it magnificent.

The discussions over books and plays awakened the contradictions in both their minds, as the puritan sides of their natures clashed with their livelier impulses, and both with their need to maintain acceptable public postures for their fishbowl lives. As for *Faust*, said the less intellectual— but more secure—Victoria, "you need not be afraid" of seeing it; and as for French plays, "you should go," for "there are many—indeed quantities of charming little plays," and "Papa . . . used to delight in going to the French plays . . . when we had a good company."

Overdoing one's piety left Victoria with a feeling of contempt, although like many of her time—an age when "sermon tasting" was a Sunday entertainment—she enjoyed an eloquent sermon as an elevated form of theatrical performance. Chief among the suspect pious, once she knew of his habits, was W. E. Gladstone, by then a fixture of Liberal Cabinets. Victoria had watched him with less than admiration when he exposed qualms of religious conscience that to her were absurd. As early as 1845, when she had pressed for a grant to maintain the Roman Catholic college at Maynooth, in Ireland, Gladstone had opposed his own party and voted against it, on the grounds that he had once written a pamphlet attacking the principle of "subsidizing Papists." A vote the other way, he had claimed, would appear insincere. Lord Aberdeen, then Foreign Secretary, had assured Gladstone, "No one reads your book and those who do, don't understand it." Victoria took the controversy less lightly, writing in her journal, "I blush for the form of religion we profess, that it should be so void of all right feeling, & so wanting in Charity."

More than ever a power in his party, and talked of—to Victoria's concern—as a future Prime Minister, Gladstone was admired by many, including the Queen's friend the Duchess of Sutherland, Mistress of the Robes in 1859 for the fourth time. Writing in August 1859 to the Duchess of Manchester, Lord Granville told her of seeing the Queen at the races at Goodwood, where Victoria "mimicked" the Duchess of Sutherland "when she talked of her adoration for Gladstone." A few months later, also writing to the Duchess of Manchester, Lord Clarendon referred to "our Jesuit," who had "got his throat sore (perhaps in some benevolent nocturnal ramble) & can't perform [in Parliament]." Such gossip cannot have escaped the Queen. Gladstone's religious—or other—impulses had caused him to spend many nights seeking out London streetwalkers, whom he would follow to their rooms to urge them to give up prostitution and live a more spiritual life. He would offer them money, religious tracts, and his renowned eloquence—and receive in turn some prospects of future redemption, and the delectable *frisson* of physical encounter with temptation. He had long battled against the flesh. In 1828, at nineteen, he began struggling with his urge to masturbate, a practice that contemporary medicine warned would lead to blindness and insanity. By 1848, neither his marriage that year nor the sensual pleasures found in the attractive but degraded souls he professed to save proved satisfactory. He began following up his encounters with self-flagellation. Sublimation spurred Gladstone's energies in other directions, none of them to the Queen's liking. She found it easy to disapprove of him and despised his politics even more because *he* represented them. To her, he was "cracked," and a "madman," and always "terribly excited." She would have to see much of him.

When Parliament was opened by the Queen in January 1860, Gladstone was Chancellor of the Exchequer, the third most powerful man in his party, after Palmerston and Russell. In the House of Commons, attention remained focused on Italy. Exasperated by Palmerston's undisguised pro-Italian (and therefore pro-French) policies, Victoria preferred (as did Disraeli) rigid neutrality, which was as close as she could position herself to any support for Austria. Russell's response, as Foreign Secretary, was blunt and brutally disrespectful. "Lord John Russell," he explained, "unfortunately does not partake your Majesty's opinions in regard to Italy, and he is unwilling to obtrude on your Majesty unnecessary statements of his views. . . . Whatever may be the consequence, the liberation of the Italian people from a foreign yoke is, in the eyes of Lord Palmerston and Lord John Russell, an increase of freedom and happiness at which . . . they cannot but rejoice."

Since Palmerston and Russell were also, in effect, rejoicing at the forced annexation of Nice and Savoy to France, the Queen saw hypocrisy not only in such views, but in the letter itself, which, as she wrote furiously to Palmerston, was "deficient" in "that respect which is due from a Minister to his Sovereign." Both Lord Granville and Prince Albert intervened to calm the atmosphere, but Napoleon III made the crucial contribution by a display of arrogance to Palmerston's Minister to France, Lord Cowley. The official British line moderated, but it made no difference to the accomplished facts.

That February, at Windsor, the Queen and Prince observed their twentieth wedding anniversary, Albert writing to Stockmar, "I see you still standing in the pew not far from the chancel, as the negotiator of the marriage treaty, when I made my entry in the Chapel. . . . We have gone through much since then, and striven after much that is *good;* if we have not always succeeded, the will was at least good. . . ." To Albert's letter, Victoria added a postscript. "I wish I could think I *had made* one as happy as he has made me. But this is not for want of *love and devotion.*"

The change in the political atmosphere at home, now less Francophile, became obvious in the spring of 1860 when Victoria, writing to her uncle in Belgium, spoke of affairs as being in "a most bewildered state," but added that "Lord Palmerston is *very stout and right* about our neighbor." (Somehow, Palmerston always managed to become *right.*) She ended her letter as "ever your devoted *Daughter* (I *wrote* by mistake *but* will leave, as it *only* expresses what *my feelings* are) and Niece, Victoria."

For Leopold, as well as for Victoria, the season had been saddened by the death at Baden-Baden of the Prince of Hohenlohe-Langenburg, Feodora's husband. There was one good and noble man less in the world, she wrote, in German, to Leopold: *"Es ist ein braver und ehrlicher Mann weniger in der Welt."* In his last years the Prince had been the highly respected President of the Upper Chamber of the Kingdom of Württemberg. Still, the Queen and her mother had been sending Feodora money. She had been unable to manage on mere esteem.

Although Victoria seldom saw him, Feo's husband had meant more to her than Feo's brother (the Queen's half-brother), Charles of Leiningen, who had died in November 1857. Victoria had been sisterly in her sentiments, and gracious when Charles visited, but she never forgot that he had supported the Conroyals when she was on the verge of becoming Queen. (She recalled it to Vicky in 1861 as a time of "brouillée with my poor mother" and "my own brother acting against me.") Yet she was permitting herself to forget her mother's central role. The Duchess, fast fading, had become a wan, grandmotherly symbol in the background of the Queen's life and that of her children. With the birth of little Willy in Germany, she was now a great-grandmother. Some wondered what she had been doing with her £30,000 annual income, as she now bought few clothes and gave only two or three dinners a year. Perhaps Feodora knew. Chronically hard up, Charles may have been a silent beneficiary as well.

While in Scotland in September 1860, Victoria went on one of the earliest and most successful of her incognito journeys. Later her traveling names would be open secrets, and her face and figure and entourage (however reduced) too familiar for anything but faint pretense on both sides. In the late summer she and Albert and a small party—it was meant as psychological therapy for Victoria—rode up the River Geldie to Loch Inch, crossed the Spey in a ferry, and bounced in "very rough vehicles" to Grantown, over sixty miles from Balmoral. "*No* one knew us," she bubbled to Leopold—"anywhere or at the little inn. We went under the names of Lord and Lady Churchill, and Lady Churchill and General Grey who went with us, under the names of Miss Spencer and Dr Grey! Two maids *only* went with us (whom we had sent round with our things), and *no* servants but our two excellent Highlanders, viz. Albert's first stalker or head keeper, and *my own Highland servant* and factotum—*both* excellent, intelligent, devoted people. *Only* when we had *left* was it found out." Her Highland servant was John Brown, then thirty-four. On the journey he nearly gave the game away by calling Victoria "Your Majesty" as she was getting into a carriage, and John Grant, head keeper at Balmoral, who was acting as Albert's servant, once called him "Your Royal Highness." The slips set the others tittering, and increased the deliciousness of the masquerade.

At the inn in the *toun*, Grant and Brown were to have waited on them, not an unusual procedure when a wealthy couple arrived with their own servants, but as Victoria and Albert tidied up in their room, the Highlanders made themselves "wishful" (the Queen's word in her journal —Scots for *drunk*). A ringleted local woman waited on the royal couple and served them their bottle of wine, brought from Balmoral. The next day, permissive as usual about the tippling of her Highlanders, the Queen was up and ready early to complete the expedition without a word of scolding. "To my dear Albert," she recorded, they owed the lark, "for he always thought it would be delightful, having gone on many similar expeditions in former days himself."

The secret had been less than perfectly kept, as the dog cart in which they had begun the journey carried the Balmoral crest, and someone in the street recognized Albert. "The lady must be terrible rich," one woman observed of Victoria, whose fingers remained covered with rings. The Queen retorted that Lady Churchill wore even more rings. The sense of freedom in Scotland to play at not being Queen enraptured Victoria. When, some months earlier, Vicky had written of longing for "dear, dear Windsor," her mother had responded that the wish meant little to someone struggling with "homesickness for my beloved Highlands, the air—the life, the liberty." She could feel no affection for "fine, old dull" Windsor—"which please God shall never hold my bones!"

With Stockmar over seventy, and fading; Vicky already the mother of two, and also in Germany; and Albert's stepmother, Dowager Duchess Marie, in failing health, the Queen and Prince decided to visit Coburg in early autumn, and to meet Vicky there. Cavour, Garibaldi, and the confusion in Italy could wait, especially as the Queen had little influence on events. Still, Lord John Russell accompanied the party to represent the government, as any matters that were likely to come up were expected to be in his province as Foreign Secretary. The royal yacht took the Queen and Prince, with Alice and attendants, to Antwerp. There they met King Leopold and his sons, who accompanied them to the railway station at Verviers. Leopold had a telegram with him from Albert's brother, Ernest: "Mama" Marie was dying. The journey should be put off for a day. Albert telegraphed back that it was impossible, and that he hoped for the best. At Frankfurt a further telegram awaited them. Duchess Marie had died.

"To our regret," Victoria wrote in her journal, "we were received by a guard of honour and a band." Only just in possession of the sad news, they were already in technical mourning. The next day, after staying overnight at the Hotel d'Angleterre, as they had done fifteen years earlier, they continued on by rail, along the valley of the Main to Lichtenfels, where they transferred to the Thuringian railway to Coburg, arriving at five in the evening. The quiet welcome, as befit bereavement, left Albert and Victoria even more agitated than any traditional greeting, in the brightest gala style, would have done. With Alexandrine, the Duchess of Coburg, at the Palace, was Vicky, "in the deepest German mourning, long black veils . . . ," the Queen wrote. "A tender embrace, and then we walked up the staircase. . . . Could hardly speak, I felt so moved, and quite trembled."

Stockmar, whom they had not seen since his farewell visit to England in 1856, was there, looking "a little weak," and little Willy, "a fine fat child" with "very fair curly hair."

Two days later was the Duchess's funeral, which left Albert shaken, but not nearly as much as he would be four days later, after quiet, nostalgic visits to familiar places. The Queen's journal for October 1 opens, "Before proceeding, I must thank God for having preserved my adored one! I tremble now on thinking of it. . . . The escape is very wonderful, *most merciful!*" Albert had been riding alone in a carriage drawn by four horses from the castle at Kalenberg to Coburg. About three miles from the chateau the horses took fright and galloped off uncontrollably. Two miles farther down was a railway level crossing with a bar across the road, and a wagon waiting. With a collision inevitable, Albert jumped for his life. Cut and bruised, but conscious, he rushed to the aid of the coachman into whose wagon his carriage had crashed, while the surviving horses (one had been killed) raced on to Coburg.

In the town the runaway horses were recognized, and Colonel Ponsonby, the Prince's equerry, rushed to the scene of the accident with the party's young doctor, William Baly, and Carl Florschütz, the Duke's physician. Ponsonby then went on to summon the Queen, who found Albert lying on the bed of his valet, Löhlein, with lint compresses on his nose, mouth and chin. Victoria veered between horror and gratitude. "I sent off many telegrams to England, &c., fearing wrong messages."

The next day the Prince kept to his room, but claimed to feel better. "Good Stockmar [was] there. He had been half distracted all night, thinking of what might have happened. . . . Many dispatches and letters; Emperor and Empress of the French inquiring after dear Albert. . . . My heart very full, but would not give way." Among the letters forwarded from London, unrelated to the accident, was one from the Prince of Wales. On a tour of Canada and the United States—a highly successful venture that proved that whatever his failings with books, he had the social graces—Bertie had reached Niagara Falls.

On October 4, the Queen drove with Princess Alice to Baron Stockmar's house in the Weber-Gasse, and met his *"zuvorkommende frau"* (affable wife) for the first time. In none of his stays in England, the months adding up to many years, had she ever accompanied him. Although Victoria and Albert would not leave until the tenth, every day for the Prince was a leave-taking, reliving sights and sounds and smells he sensed he might never experience again. The weather, which had been gloriously autumnal, turned cold and wet, and made the process of drawing away somewhat easier. "Had a last visit," Victoria wrote, "from dear Stockmar, and talked over many things with him. Towards the end of his stay, dear little William came in and played about the room, and we got over the leave-taking without its upsetting Stockmar too much."

In the last days, happily for Albert's peace of mind, there were diplomatic distractions from London—"constant dispatches from Italy and about Italy," Victoria's journal notes. "Matters become more and more complicated. The Emperor [of France] declares he shall protect the Pope in Rome. . . . Albert too busy to go out." The next morning he was also busy with diplomatic papers, but on Albert's last afternoon in Coburg, Ernest took his brother for a walk. Afterwards he remembered Stockmar's words. Having perceived Albert's despondency and melancholy—unrelated to the accident, Stockmar knew, as he had been in constant correspondence with Albert—he confided to Ernest, "God have mercy on us! If anything serious should ever happen to him, he will die."

Very likely something serious had already happened, and both Stockmar and Albert knew it. The Prince, at least, thought that he was slowly but surely dying. "At one of the most beautiful spots," Ernest recalled, "Albert stood still, and suddenly felt for his pocket handkerchief." The Duke assumed that Albert's facial wounds had begun to bleed afresh, and went to him to help, but discovered instead "that tears were trickling down his cheeks . . . [and] he persisted in declaring that he was well aware that he had been here for the last time in his life." The brothers turned back to the chateau in silence.

The slow return journey to London, in persistent cold rain, was a prolonged misery alleviated only by the continued presence of Vicky, who —though married to a German prince—had never traveled the Rhine. Victoria had a heavy cold, with a sore throat and fever. Albert, sicker than she knew, attempted to conceal his continuing headaches and stomach problems, his cramps and chills, until he was on home soil again, and in the privacy of Balmoral.

At the railway station in Coblenz, Vicky's mother-in-law, the Princess of Prussia, joined the party, with Prince Frederick of Baden, expecting the Queen and Prince to sightsee along the Rhine and Moselle. In rain and hail, wobbly on their feet, they did what was expected of them, and remained overnight, but eager for their beds. After two days in Coblenz, on October 13, they left for Cologne, where the Prussian party was joined by the Prince Regent, Vicky's father-in-law, who talked in the train with Victoria and Albert until Aix-la-Chapelle (Aachen), where the Prussians, "little William" included, took their final leaves.

Leopold met the train at Verviers, shocked at the appearance of the royal couple. "I could hardly walk when we got out," Victoria confessed in her journal, "and with difficulty got up stairs. . . . Dr. Baly found my throat very bad, that I had much fever; so I was ordered to remain lying down in my room and to see no one." The dinner in Brussels that Leopold had scheduled in her honor was held without the Queen the next day, October 24. By leaving her door open she could hear the "fine band" play, then Lady Jane Churchill came in and read to her from George Eliot's *The Mill on the Floss*.

Even the final farewells in Belgium were delayed by weather. Before the yacht had gone very far from Antwerp, the sky turned black and a deluge of rain forced the ship to drop anchor. Finally, at six in the evening on October 17, a week after leaving Coburg, they reached Gravesend.

Shaken by her illness, and grateful for what she considered Albert's deliverance at Coburg, Victoria wrote to Sir Charles Phipps, the administrator of Her Majesty's Privy Purse, to explore the possibility of endowing a permanent charity at Coburg, to be distributed on each October 1— the anniversary of Albert's escape. A modest trust, the *Victoria-Stift* (Victoria Foundation) was established for little over £1,000. The interest was to enable men and women "of exemplary character belonging to the humbler ranks of life" to pay small sums for apprenticeships, for purchasing tools and equipment needed for work, or, in the case of women, to secure a small marriage dowry. It would become, in effect, the first Albert Memorial.

The Queen recovered more quickly than Albert. "My attack," he wrote to Vicky on December 11, once he was able to work again, "was the real English cholera." "English cholera," also called "summer cholera," is a diarrheal disease usually lasting two to seven days, and accompanied by severe stomach cramps. Albert had such symptoms, but had been ill for two months. Now he had to act as if he were fit, as Empress Eugénie, staying in London at Claridge's without her philandering husband, was expected on a private visit ("there was not the slightest allusion to politics"); and in residence at Windsor was Alice's future husband, the amiable but empty Prince Louis of Hesse, for whom the Queen found a dentist for his bad teeth, and arranged a military show at Aldershot that had to be canceled because of a sudden snow.

Christmas 1860 was celebrated at Windsor, with both the Prince of Wales and Prince Alfred at home. George Byng, seventh Viscount Torrington, "in waiting" at the time, sent J. T. Delane of *The Times* an intimate account of what was to be the last family Christmas with the Prince Consort. Something of a skeptic and a wit, Torrington (signing his letter "Your Windsor Special") was "agreeably surprised and pleased" by the royal Christmas Eve:

> The Queen's private sitting-rooms, three in number, were lighted up with Christmas trees hung from the ceiling, the chandeliers being taken down. These trees, of immense size, besides others on the tables, were covered with bonbons and coloured wax lights. Some of the trees were made to appear as if partially covered with snow. These rooms contained all the presents for the royal family the one to the other. Each member gave a present to one another, so that, including the Prince of Hesse and the Duchess of Kent, every person had to receive or give thirteen presents. . . .
>
> I have never seen a much more agreeable sight. It was royalty putting aside its state and becoming in words, acts, and deeds one of ourselves—no forms and not a vestige of ceremony. Even as in a public bazaar, where people jostle one another, so lords, grooms, Queen, and princes laughed and talked, forgot to bow, and freely turned their backs on one another. Little princesses, who on ordinary occasions dare hardly to look at a gentleman-in-waiting, in the happiest manner showed each person they could lay hands on the treasures they had received. . . . Prince Arthur (the flower of the flock) speedily got into a volunteer uniform, which, with endless other things, including a little rifle, fell to his lot, took a pot-shot at his papa, and then presented arms.
>
> Some of the presents were beautiful in taste and suited to the receiver, and even the presents of children to their parents were selected so that even the Queen might find use for them. I saw no jewellery of any sort except that given by the Queen to the Household, and all that was done in another room. I received a supply of studs, sleeve buttons, and waistcoat ditto—handsome, plain gold; a pocket-book, and every one of us a large cake of Nuremberg gingerbread. Whether the Prince Consort had a quiet joke in his mind

when he selected certain presents for Phipps, Biddulph, Grey, and Bruce,* I don't know, but Phipps had salt cellars resting on little fish with their *mouths open*, Biddulph a *bread* basket, Grey a sugar basket, and Bruce a claret jug. . . .

I never saw more real happiness than the scene of the mother and all her children: The Prince Consort lost his stiffness, and your *Windsor Special* had much cheerful and friendly conversation with them both. Altogether, it was a sight I should have liked you to have seen. . . .

On Christmas Day the windows at Windsor were clouded by frost, although a cold sun shone. The Duchess came to luncheon, and Leopold and Beatrice ("Baby") were permitted to join the family for dessert. Albert swung Baby in a large dinner napkin.

Christmas dinner was for adults only. Lord Torrington went to the kitchen to watch the roasting of turkeys, geese, and beef—"a mighty sight: at least fifty turkeys before one fire." By custom, he reported, the Lord Lieutenant of Ireland sent the sovereign at Christmas a large woodcock pie. Victoria's had one hundred birds in it—"a worthy dish to set before a Queen."

The dinner "was really wonderful. How I live to tell the tale I don't know. I took some of the baron of beef, the boar's head, and the Lord Lieutenant's pie. Fortunately, I did not go to bed till near three o'clock, as we finished the evening with some pool and billiards, and Captain Du Plat and self cleared the remainder out of every silver coin they possessed. Altogether a jolly Christmas Day. . . ."

Whether Louis of Hesse-Darmstadt could afford his small losses was no matter. Although the Grand Duke of Hesse refused him a Hessian palace, he would be taken care of by Victoria. When, after Alice's confirmation in 1859, Louis had been sent for, and had found it difficult to come to the point, Victoria worried that Alice might be too plain to take chances on an alternative suitor. Still, after a harsh exchange with Victoria, Albert sent Louis away, telling him to return when and if he was ready. In the autumn of 1860 he had returned, and the Queen immedi-

*Sir Charles Phipps, Private Secretary to the Prince Consort and Keeper of Her Majesty's Privy Purse; Colonel Thomas Biddulph, Master of the Queen's Household; General Charles Grey, Private Secretary to the Prince Consort and later to the Queen; General Robert Bruce, Governor to the Prince of Wales.

ately insisted on his learning to speak English at all times, although she and Albert spoke German to one another. Only seventeen, and carefully insulated from marriageable males, Alice was quite willing to believe that the young man earmarked for her by the Queen was an ideal mate. Once the engagement was announced and a wedding date in 1862 set, Victoria began to press for a Parliamentary grant.

Another family betrothal pleased the Queen much less. Feo's son, Victor, an English naval officer, had announced that he would marry Laura Seymour, the beautiful daughter of Admiral Sir George Seymour. Since she was without title or fortune, the Queen considered the match a misalliance. "It is the height of folly and very reckless," she informed Vicky in Berlin. "Of course I shall ignore it." She summoned her nephew to Buckingham Palace for some sharp words, and—Lord Clarendon reported to the Duchess of Manchester—"the youth behaved very well. . . . He said that his family had been mediatized* and that if the Queen ever did him the honour to invite him he hoped it would be with others of his rank in Her Majesty's navy, but he must respectfully decline ever to come to the Palace without his wife."

The Queen quickly had second thoughts. The bride, she announced to Victor a few days later, would be given the courtesy title of Countess Gleichen, after the county in Coburg. Count and Countess Gleichen were married at St. Peter's, Eaton Square, without the unrelenting royal presence, on January 26, 1861; but the Duchess of Kent sent a friend to report in detail, and Feodora received an account of the ceremony.

At Windsor, Victoria railed in public and in private about the French Emperor's hunger for power and glory. The Francophile Lord Clarendon, a frequent visitor, deplored to the Duchess of Manchester the Queen's mixing morality with foreign policy. Commenting on a January party at Windsor Castle, where the stark amenities remained little changed since the young Queen had Melbourne to dinner, he wrote, "If the most agreeable people in the world are invited one hardly sees them as there is no common room for meeting & the *chacun chez soi* system is the fashion of the place. I like it far better than playing company, & the talks with The Q: & The P: are always pleasant & often instructive. I wish they were not so *acharnés* [relentless] agst: The Empr: for it

---

*Mediatizing, a practice common in the German confederation, was the term used for the absorption of a small, weak state into a larger and more powerful one, which left the ruler of the annexed state with his title and some of his perquisites, but little if anything of his former authority.

embitters their lives & their conversation & The Q: is tormented by a succession of Imperial Nightmares of the Anglo-Germanic breed."

That an Imperial Nightmare was brewing could be sensed in both Prussia and France, but it appeared still far away, and perhaps avoidable, when early in 1861 the long-insane Frederick William IV died. To the English Court the accession of Fritz's father, long the actual ruler of Prussia, was an event to celebrate despite the official bereavement. Vicky's husband was now the Crown Prince, and the new King seemed liberal in outlook—although he would quickly succumb to his bellicose "Iron Chancellor," Otto von Bismarck, whom he named Prime Minister the next year. In the first dawn of the elderly King William's regime, the dream of Victoria and Albert that their daughter might soon be queen of a progressive, united Germany seemed to be approaching fulfillment.

Despite such prospects, letters from Vicky were filled with deathbeds and mourning, and the mail she received from England was in a similar vein. At just the time when enlightened medical help was needed in Victoria's Household, William Baly, the Queen's new Physician-in-Ordinary, was the victim of a gruesome railway accident. He had arrived at Wimbledon Station, en route to Osborne, only to see the train steaming away. When he explained to the stationmaster that he was the Queen's doctor, the train was stopped and Baly climbed aboard. Soon afterward, the floor of his carriage collapsed, and he fell to his death on the tracks. He was the only passenger killed. *"Sehr traurig,"* Albert wrote in his diary.

For the Prince, Baly's death was especially sad, as the doctor had been treating him for continuing woes, including gum inflammations that had persisted for two years, and had become worse. "Papa never allows he is any better or will try to get over it," the Queen wrote lightly to Vicky, "but makes such a miserable face that people always think he's very ill. It is quite the contrary with me always; I . . . never show it, so people never believe I am ill or ever suffer. His nervous system is easily excited and irritated, and he's so completely overpowered by everything." Albert indeed felt wretched, although he persisted in his activities, which expanded with the new Parliamentary session.

With the less-than-competent Sir James Clark now semiretired, a new physician was appointed, William Jenner—"a great friend of our poor Dr. Baly," the Queen wrote to Vicky. "He is extremely clever, and has a pleasing clever manner."

As the King of Prussia lay dying earlier in January, Victoria had confided to her daughter, about to confront a grim new experience, "I have never even yet witnessed a death bed." That would soon change. Dr. Jenner had hardly assumed his duties when the Duchess of Kent began to fail. The Queen's priorities altered. She had been concerned with Albert's health, but not so much as to divert her from a continuing preoccupation with matchmaking, this time with the intention of settling the future of the Prince of Wales, whose shallowness had not been reversed by the ceremonial success of his trip to North America. Since Victoria was distracted by her mother's decline, the assignment to find Bertie a bride—almost certainly the future Queen—had fallen to Vicky. Although she was in a place where prospective candidates were likely to originate, there were also Danish and Dutch possibilities. (The princess had to be Protestant.) Victoria, however, thought that Dutch princesses looked unpromising; and the Danish princess, though beautiful, seemed politically unacceptable, given the simmering Danish-Prussian dispute over Schleswig and Holstein.

Vicky had sent the Queen photographs, and Victoria responded, about the Danish candidate, "Princess Alexandra is indeed lovely! . . . What a pity she is who she is!" Albert's response to Victoria was more enthusiastic, although he might have been expected to be even more pro-German. "From that photograph," he said, "I would marry her at once."

As Victoria, with Albert, had watched the final minutes of 1860 tick away, she had worried aloud about war on the Continent and was anxious for England. "My precious husband," she wrote in her journal, "cheered me & held me in his dear arms saying 'We must have trust, & we have trust that God will protect us.' " February 10, however, was the real beginning of each year for her—that date in 1861 was the twenty-first anniversary of her wedding to "that most perfect of human beings my adored Husband!" It was also her opportunity to record her guilt about her "foolish sensitivity & irritability," which continued to mar relations with Albert. A woman whose instincts were so queenly that she never looked behind her when she sat down could not separate her husband from her other subjects when the royal temper was aroused. She resolved again to be calmer.

Although the Queen was agitated over the deterioration of her mother's condition, as late as mid-March there seemed no occasion for immediate alarm. She busied herself over brides and such minor business as offering the royal yacht to take the Empress of Austria, who had suffered a nervous collapse, to recuperate at Madeira.

The Empress's breakdown mirrored the political instability in

Austria, and with Victoria interested in maintaining the status quo in central Europe, she pressed her Government to refrain from encouraging Italian revolutionaries in Austrian Italy. Maintaining the balance of power also meant maintaining deterrent military strength. Having seen at Christmas a picture of the new French ironclad *La Gloire,* brought to Windsor by Lord Torrington, and having heard further about the naval plans of Napoleon from Lord Cowley in Paris, Victoria and Albert pressed for action at home. The Queen was "very anxious," she prodded Palmerston, "to have an exact report of our state of preparations with regard to iron-cased ships and the steps taken to meet our deficiency. We must be superior in numbers to the French and greatly superior from our general position, if we are not to expose ourselves to disasters."

Though rushing from meeting to meeting, and overseeing the Queen's correspondence, the Prince was working at less than his usual efficiency. Well into February he was still suffering through nights sleepless because of swollen glands and gums, and was seldom able to eat his dinner. Then he found himself forced to handle even more responsibilities. On February 28, Sir George Couper, comptroller of the Duchess of Kent's household since Conroy's ouster, died suddenly. Albert had to take those affairs in hand, a matter made more difficult by the weakened condition of the Duchess. At seventy-five, she was painfully crippled by erysipelas. An operation on her swollen right arm did nothing but hasten the end.

As March 15 waned into the next morning, Victoria returned again and again to watch her mother expire. The only sounds in the room were labored breathing and the striking, at each quarter-hour, of the Duke of Kent's large repeater watch, in its tortoiseshell case. At seven-thirty in the morning, Victoria went to the Duchess's room for the last time, to witness her first deathbed. "I sat on a foot stool, holding her dear hand. . . . I felt the end was fast approaching, as Clark went out to call Albert. . . . Fainter and fainter grew the breathing. At last it ceased. . . . The clock struck half-past nine at the very moment."

Victoria was seized by paroxysms of grief that were in large measure feelings of guilt and remorse, and when she began sorting her mother's papers after the funeral, her emotions gave way entirely. Her mother had saved every scrap of childhood memorabilia. She had really loved Victoria. All the villainy was transferred to Lehzen and to Conroy.

The Queen's mourning became so excessive that her family and the Court recognized that the hysterical indulgence in sorrow was a sign of serious nervous collapse. She was now a "poor orphan child," she wrote to Vicky. To Leopold she wrote frankly of "The blank—the desolation—the fearful and awful *Sehnsucht und Wehmuth* * come back with redoubled force, and the *weeping,* which day after day is my welcome friend, is my greatest relief." The Queen, said Lord Clarendon, "was determined to cherish her grief & not be consoled." For three weeks she took all her meals alone (her children were "a disturbance"), and left Albert (in his words) "well nigh overcome" with the Queen's business, the settlement of the Duchess's affairs, and the difficulties of the children.

Often more of a problem than the fragile Leopold, now eight, was his youngest sister. Princess Beatrice Mary Victoria Feodore, born in April 1857, could intrude into the Queen's privacy when no one else could, not even Albert. When Victoria would scold her with "Baby mustn't have that; it's not good for Baby," Beatrice would respond, "But she likes it, my dear," and help herself to whatever had been forbidden. The Prince, according to Lady Augusta Bruce, warned his daughter, "You are very troublesome." "No, Baby's not," Beatrice insisted, "she's a little girl."

At the Royal Horticultural Show in South Kensington in June, a pale, exhausted Prince Consort presided over the opening ceremonies. The Queen was still unequal to public appearances, and remained at Osborne. "Am ill, feverish, with pains in my limbs, and feel very miserable," was a typical entry in Albert's diary at the time. The American Civil War had begun, and there were anxieties about England's being drawn into the conflict, as English textile mills needed the South's cotton. Also, then, Albert and the Queen were resisting efforts by Lord John Russell to provide security guarantees to Denmark, which opposed Prussian claims to Holstein—"a part of Germany" (the Confederation), as a letter over the Queen's signature reminded her Foreign Minister.

Near physical breakdown, Albert found himself nevertheless planning a trip to Ireland with the Queen, which had been arranged to coincide with the Prince of Wales's ten weeks of army service there. An ambitious program had been worked out to put Bertie through the competency requirements of every officer grade—promoting him one rank every fortnight—until he could command a full battalion in view of the Queen and Prince when they visited the Curragh military grounds near Dublin in August. The reports from General Bruce, the Prince's governor, were, one after another, discouraging. Meanwhile, Albert had to pull Victoria further out of her malaise so that royal guests could be met and enter-

*Yearning and melancholy: an echo of Goethe's *The Sorrows of Young Werther.*

tained—the King of Sweden, the King of Belgium, her own son-in-law the Crown Prince of Prussia (and Vicky). These became more than mere protocol matters; European capitals were echoing with rumors that Victoria had suffered a breakdown so violent that she had to be restrained in a padded cell. Even Vicky had reported it—to her father—from Berlin. It was vital that Victoria be seen behaving like a Queen.

That Bertie was unfit to command a company, let alone a battalion, was insufficient reason to cancel the Irish visit. The Queen had not been there since 1849. Cancellation would give credence to the rumors of madness. The Queen and Prince came, visited the encampment at the Curragh on August 24, and watched Bertie march past with a mere company of Grenadier Guards, his command a public airing of his non-progress. But Victoria's mind still dwelled self-indulgently only on her sorrows. In Ireland she was "weak and very nervous," she wrote to Leopold; with her mother gone she felt (at forty-two!) "as if we were no longer cared for."

One member of the family thoroughly cared for was Bertie, who was overseen to absurdity. The other young officers, with whom he was ordered to have little to do, felt challenged to extract him from the royal cocoon. At a party before he left the Curragh, Bertie's brother subalterns conveyed into his bed Nellie Clifden, a young woman with a talent to amuse. The Prince of Wales saw to it that Nellie continued to amuse him. But no news of Nellie followed to Victoria.

Only Scotland was perceived to have the healing qualities that the Queen felt she still needed. Albert carefully planned therapeutic expeditions away from Balmoral, including an incognito stay at the Ramsay Arms, in Fettercairn, where the landlord and his wife—but no one else —were told in advance who their guests would be. Another exploration took them to the inn at Dalwhinnie—where a maid recognized them. They went on daily walking tours, Victoria writing to Leopold about the "invaluable Highland servant" who invariably carried the basket with lunch and refreshment. John Brown (she did not mention his name) "is my factotum here," she went on, "and takes the most wonderful care of me, combining the offices of groom, footman, page and maid, I might almost say, as he is so handy about cloaks and shawls. . . . He always leads my pony, and always attends me out of doors, and such a good, handy, faithful attached servant I have nowhere. . . ."

Soon after she confided to Vicky that "Johnny Brown," in picking up Jane Churchill, who had fallen while scurrying down Craig Nordie, had commented, "Your Ladyship is not so heavy as Her Majesty!" The ladies had all laughed, and the Queen asked, "Am I grown heavier, do you think?"

"Well, I think you are," said Brown, with a servant's license and the authority of one who had often lifted the Queen onto her saddle.

Victoria resolved to be weighed.

On their last expedition, they lunched on the Cairngorm heights, "on a precipitous place, which made one dread anyone's moving backwards." As they packed to leave, "Albert wrote on a bit of paper that we had lunched there, put it into a Seltzer-water bottle, and buried it there, or rather stuck it in the ground." John Brown wished them well as they left, and added the hope that "above all, you may have no deaths in the family." The Queen took the bluff farewell as a reference to the Duchess of Kent. Later, she wondered about second sight. Yet she had forgotten her own remark to Vicky, on October 7, after she and Albert had heard an Edinburgh minister preach a sermon that "touched and enchanted us all," on a text from the Book of Amos, "Prepare to meet thy God, O Israel." The subject now affected her greatly, she wrote Vicky. "I feel now to be so acquainted with death—and to be so much nearer that unseen world."

Concerned about Prince Leopold's susceptibility to seasonal illnesses, Victoria and Albert, on returning to Windsor, shipped off their hemophiliac son to the French Riviera for the winter. That put at least one worry at a distance. A backlog of postponed paperwork confronted the Prince, and he had hardly begun attacking it when a telegram arrived from Lisbon, on November 6, that his cousin Prince Ferdinand had died suddenly in a typhoid fever epidemic. Then came two further telegrams reporting the illness and death of King Pedro V. Both Ferdinand and Pedro were Coburg cousins. The Queen and Prince were stunned.

Several days later, through Lord Torrington, Albert learned of the Nellie Clifden affair. After checking that the story was indeed accurate, he sent Bertie on November 16 a letter written "with a heavy heart upon a subject which has caused me the greatest pain I have yet felt in this life." He went on to draw, hysterically, a picture of a future king compromised by blackmail, scandal, and paternity suits. "Oh horrible prospect, which this person has in her power, any day to realize! and to break your poor parents' hearts!" Bertie would have to be rushed into an early marriage, Albert warned, to channel such dangerous impulses.

Three days before the letter was written, Victoria had been told some of the circumstances, but not "the disgusting details." She confided to her journal that she would never again be able to look on her son "without a shudder." Albert might not have written as he did, or even told the Queen, had his head not reeled with illness, exhaustion, and agony over many other problems. Given his caution, and his feelings about sheltering the monarchy from scandal, he would have railed at his son in any case, although perhaps with less self-pity. He was at a low ebb physically, made worse by sleeplessness, and told Victoria, *"Ich hänge gar nicht am Leben; du hängst sehr daran. . . .* ["I do not cling to life; you do; but I set no store by it."] I am sure that if I had a severe illness I should give up at once, I should not struggle for life. I have no tenacity of life."

In retrospect, his fatalism appears more like a diagnosis than a prophecy. He was in no condition, physically or mentally, to fulfill a commitment to inspect the new buildings for the Staff College and Royal Military Academy at Sandhurst, long one of his goals, but he went anyway, on November 22, despite a drenching rain—*"entsetzlicher Regen"* in his diary. It was no surprise that he returned to Windsor wet, weak, and exhausted, and complaining of rheumatic pains. In his diary on the twenty-fourth he described himself as "thoroughly unwell" and as having scarcely closed his eyes for a fortnight. Still, he pushed himself further. Bertie was then in his mockery of a college stint at Cambridge, and despite cold, stormy weather, the Prince left by train to have it out with his son. When Albert returned the next day, he was so weak that when Dr. Jenner saw him before dinner, Jenner decided to stay the night.

While Albert's condition deteriorated, external events he had ignored were causing distress in the Foreign Office. The Government was blatantly pro-South in the American Civil War, not because it favored slavery, but to protect Lancashire sources of cotton. In the first year of the war, the North's prospects for reunification looked poor, and Victoria, to Palmerston, even referred to "that remnant of the United States." Supporters of English goods could not be unhappy at such reduction of a rival, and formal recognition of the South seemed likely. Americans were lightly regarded by the Court. They were pushy types of little breeding and questionable ancestry, who indulged in promotion of their business interests or in petty frontier disputes with British dependencies. When George Mifflin Dallas, the American Minister to England, received a long-coveted invitation to Windsor for a Saturday-to-Monday in November 1860, it was the first tendered to the head of the American mission in more than twenty years. On the Friday before the Minister was due at the Castle, Mrs. Dallas rushed out to buy $500 worth of new dresses

—a fortune in clothes at that time—and arrived in what must have seemed crass vulgarity.

American envoys themselves were long considered to have confused Court dress with undertaker's garb, and when the sophisticated Charles Francis Adams, replacing Dallas, presented his credentials on May 19, 1861, wearing more traditional diplomatic costume, the Queen is said to have remarked acidly, "I am thankful we shall have no more American funerals."

On the day that the Queen learned from Albert of Bertie's escapades, she also learned from Palmerston that a Union warship docked in Southampton was expected to go to sea to intercept the English mail packet *Trent*, from the West Indies, in order to remove two Confederate envoys, James Mason and John Slidell. The Prime Minister's legal experts had determined that the United States, as a belligerent, could stop and search a neutral merchantman. Nevertheless, two weeks later, when the Federal vessel steamed off with Mason and Slidell as captives, there was indignation in the English press about the insult to the flag and the breach of international law. John Russell (now Earl Russell) drafted a bellicose message for Palmerston to the American Secretary of State, demanding release of the men and an apology. A threat to withdraw their diplomatic mission from Washington was implicit. Intelligence from France suggested that the seizure was a pretext for war with England in order to secure France as an American ally, with France promised restoration of Quebec.

When Victoria brought the draft from Russell to the Prince as he lay on the sofa, he read it quickly and exclaimed, "This means war!" The strident tone of the message reflected a Palmerston-Russell desire to confront the burgeoning power of the United States, but not the views of Victoria. Three weeks earlier she had written to Vicky, "We are somewhat shocked at your speaking of 'those horrid Yankees'—when Bertie was received in the United States as no one has ever been received anywhere, principally from the (to me incredible) liking they have for my unworthy self. . . . Don't therefore abuse the 'Yankees' for their natural defects. . . ." The United States may have been crude and vulgar, but to her it was not the enemy.

In the early morning light of December 1, 1861, Albert tottered to his study and redrafted the ultimatum to give Washington a way out without loss of pride, suggesting a concession that the American warship's captain had acted on his own, without higher-level instructions. At eight o'clock he brought it to the Queen, observing, as he handed it to her, *"Ich bin so schwach, ich habe kaum die Feder halten können"*—"I am so weak, I have hardly been able to hold the pen." But his conciliatory strategy would work.

In the margin of Albert's manuscript the Queen wrote, afterwards, "This draft was the last the beloved Prince ever wrote. . . ."

In the early days of December, Albert continued to deteriorate. His sleeplessness aggravated his fatigue. Food nauseated him; even soup with a bit of brown bread caused vomiting. Dr. Jenner examined him and saw no cause for concern, although he thought "a long feverish indisposition" would be dangerous. Still, the chills and general discomfort had not been followed by fever, which prompted Victoria to downplay the illness when Palmerston, sincerely worried, asked to have another physician called in. In a few days it will "pass off," she told him. "In addition to Sir James Clark, the Queen has the advantage of the constant advice of Dr. Jenner, a most skillful Physician, and Her Majesty would be very unwilling to cause unnecessary alarm, where no cause exists for it, by calling in a Medical Man who does not upon ordinary occasions attend. . . ." Only months before, the Queen had read Wilkie Collins's thriller *The Woman in White,* which General Grey had recommended to the Princess Royal, and Vicky in turn to her mother. Its heroine, Marian Halcombe, is felled by "typhus fever," and is near death because of her "ignorant" doctor's "imbecile treatment." In the inadequate medical language of the day, someone asks the surgeon-apothecary, Mr. Dawson, "Has the fever turned to infection?" He confesses, having misdiagnosed the case, "I'm afraid it has," but on the tenth day—the traditional point of crisis—"merciful Providence" intervenes and the fever passes. All that is needed thereafter, the doctor says confidently, is "careful watching and nursing."

If Victoria remembered the novel—her closest confrontation with typhoid—she must have clutched at the likelihood of life following art. At the least, careful watching and casual nursing were available. At Windsor, the lack of alarm showed in the casualness of Albert's treatment— or lack of it. When he could, he paced about his dressing room, and sometimes changed bedrooms. He could keep little food down, even tea, and alternated between wild incoherence and playing host to his children, who came to talk or to read to him. In an age when nurses functioned only in hospitals, the Prince was tended by such personal servants as Rudolf Löhlein, Court attendants, and Princess Alice. Eighteen, with never a responsibility of any sort before, she filled the vacuum as informal head nurse with instinctive authority, and except when asleep, she remained at his side, following him when he padded restlessly about.

On the eighth, a Sunday, because he had seemed to be no worse, the doctors even told the Queen that Albert appeared somewhat better, a verdict apparently sustained when he asked to hear some music. Alice played, as he requested, the Lutheran chorale "A Mighty Fortress Is Our God," but he could take very little music, and soon murmured, *"Das reicht hin."* Later Alice was permitted to play some German songs that she knew were his favorites, and he asked to have the sofa moved closer to the window so that he could watch the clouds drift across the sky. As Alice thought he had dozed off, she covered him with a blanket, and he opened his eyes. "Were you asleep?" she asked.

"No," he said, with a wan smile, "but my thoughts were so happy that I did not want to drive them away by moving."

In the evening, Victoria read to him from Walter Scott's *Peveril of the Peak,* but he had her stop when he decided to change bedrooms again, and walked from his own to the "King's Room"—the Blue Room, in which both George IV and William IV had died. He was apparently preparing for his own death, yet everything that the attending physicians could possibly conceive as an improvement was declared so, and his renewed activity appeared positive and welcome.

The next day, the two envoys who had been on a visit of condolence to Lisbon, Lord Methuen and General Seymour (Albert's companion in Italy in 1839), arrived, and Albert insisted on seeing them. If they were carrying typhoid from Portugal, he may have thought, it could hardly hurt him now. Also at Windsor was elderly, gout-crippled Lord Palmerston, leaning on canes, to urge again that other medical opinions be sought. Again the Queen refused, although she was increasingly anxious because Albert's mind was wandering and he insisted on calling her *"gutes Weibchen"*—good little wife—and holding her hand.

Since a low fever had now been diagnosed, doctors now remained in attendance day and night. Jenner possessed considerable clinical experience of typhoid fever—often euphemistically referred to as "gastric fever"—and finally thought he saw evidence of the characteristic pink rash of the disease. That it should have taken Jenner so long to identify Albert's ailment remains a mystery, as Jenner, now forty-six, as a young man in 1845 had published a famous paper establishing the clinico-pathologic distinction between typhus and typhoid fever. In any case, whatever he identified as typhoid, given his special reputation, was almost certain to be accepted as such by other physicians—and by the Queen, who later knighted him. To her, he explained the implications of the disease in a dismissive manner. It would run its course in a month, and there were no "bad symptoms," as Victoria put it in her journal. The Prince was not to know any more than that he had a "feverish cold."

As the fever increased, Jenner and Clark felt that their diagnosis had been established, perhaps because it was indeed typhoid, or perhaps because of the deaths of the Coburg cousins in Portugal, which had been on the minds of many since early November. There was, however, no other identifiable typhoid at Windsor, and suggestions that the Prince contracted the disease at Sandhurst seemed without foundation, as Albert had arrived there too ill to have luncheon, and drank nothing. Nor was there any typhoid case identified at Sandhurst.

Tuesday, December 10, was the first day on which Albert was too weak and listless to make any attempt to dress. To the Prince's aides, his condition was beginning to appear sufficiently grave to recall Palmerston's repeated appeals. The Prince and the Prime Minister had long been at odds, but the elderly politician had come to respect Albert's abilities, and was sincerely concerned about losing him. Recalling the Lady Flora Hastings embarrassment twenty-two years earlier, and the persistence at Court of the medical authority of that era, Sir James Clark, now seventy-three, Palmerston had earlier urged on Sir Charles Phipps the necessity of forestalling an even more tragic misdiagnosis. "If it is unavoidable that the highest interests of the nation be sacrificed to personal and professional jealousy," he warned, "there is no help for it and so it must be. I could say much about the past, but my thoughts are wholly engrossed with the future." Now, with some resentment from the attending doctors, Thomas Watson, one of the Physicians Extraordinary to the Queen, and the veteran Sir Henry Holland, were called in, but both quickly supported the therapy in progress. (Holland, another septuagenarian, and Clark, Lord Clarendon said, were "not fit to attend a sick cat.") Once physician to George IV's estranged Queen Caroline, Holland dismissed the Prince's wandering mind as "of no consequence, though very distressing." Neither saw any new medication as necessary, but Watson stayed the night. On the morning of the eleventh, Albert sat up in bed to drink beef tea. When his aide, General Charles Grey, brought him a glass of unwelcome medicine, he managed a wry joke, raising the glass wanly and saying, "Your very good health, Grey." The gesture did not deceive the Queen, who was more frank than usual with Vicky, perhaps preparing herself as well as her daughter for the worst. The doctors were satisfied with Albert's condition, she wrote—"though he gets sadly thin. It is a dreadful trial to witness this, and requires all my strength of mind and courage not to be overcome—when I look at him. . . ." They were so "fortunate in the doctors," she added, but it was necessary "to satisfy the public to have another eminent doctor to come and see him, which I own distressed me much, . . . however I submitted."

The eminent Dr. Watson, later Sir Thomas Watson, author of a textbook on medicine, was, as Victoria suggested, superfluous, but only because the Prince was beyond new medicines. Had Victoria recalled Melbourne's remark that "English physicians kill you; the French let you die," she might have understood that Albert's doctors were applying the more humane French method. Sedated with brandy and given little else, Albert was failing rapidly.

On the twelfth he coughed up a large quantity of mucus, and shuddered with chills and with quickened breathing, although he was still able, briefly, to lay his head affectionately on his wife's shoulder. His temperature had risen, and he was often delirious. He thought he heard the birds singing at the Rosenau, and was consumed with absurd worries, even about cousins he had not seen for years. More lucidly, he asked Alice, now almost constantly by his side, whether Vicky, in Berlin, knew about his illness. "Yes," said Alice, truthfully. "I told her you were very ill."

"You did wrong. You should have told her that I am dying. Yes, I am dying."

Alice had seen her father try to say the same thing to the Queen, who resisted by breaking into sobs and forcing him into silence. Now he appeared to want to confide something to his daughter, and she pulled a chair close to the bed. He struggled to say something, but she could not understand the words.

The thirteenth was a Friday. Jenner told the Queen that the Prince's condition was stable, and that she could take a morning walk, but by late afternoon it seemed essential for the family to gather—a step that Alice had anticipated the day before by summoning Bertie. "The breathing was the alarming thing," Victoria recorded, "it was so rapid. There was what they call a dusky hue about the face and hands, which I knew was not good." She told Jenner, who was alarmed. Then she saw Albert begin to arrange his hair and fold his arms, "just as he used to do when well and dressing. . . . Strange! as though he were preparing for another and greater journey."

The public knew almost nothing, other than that the Prince Consort was ill with a fever. Finally, at five o'clock, the third bulletin of his illness —and the first suggesting any grave consequences—was issued by Clark, stating that "the symptoms have assumed an unfavourable character during the day." The Queen was told that Albert was sinking fast.

When alone with Lady Augusta Bruce that evening, Victoria collapsed into hysterical tears and prayer. When she recovered, she called for Sir Charles Phipps and collapsed again into uncontrollable grief. Then she went to sit calmly by Albert's bed. He seemed warm and comfortable, and managed to recognize her, kiss her, press her hand, and weakly call her *"gutes Fraüchen."* Waiting only for the inevitable pneumonia, Albert's doctors continued drugging him with brandy every half hour. He had taken no solid food for many days.

Phipps was instructed to send a messenger to Palmerston with the warning, "I deeply grieve to say that the Prince's disease has taken a very unfavourable turn, and that the Doctors are in the *greatest anxiety*—they have even fears for the night." When the Prince of Wales arrived, there was concern that his presence might upset his father, but Albert's eyes, when open, now stared fixedly. Once Victoria and the younger children had left for the night, Generals Biddulph, Grey, and Bruce, with Household servants, shifted Albert's bed from the window prospect that had pleased him to the center of the room, in preparation for the end. To their surprise, he was able to get up while the move was in progress, but he had to be helped back into bed.

On the bright early morning of the fourteenth, the doctors permitted themselves some renewed optimism. In the first sunlight, Albert's gaunt face looked younger, and even radiant. Dr. Henry Brown, who had been the Duchess of Kent's physician, even suggested to the Queen that "there was ground to hope the crisis was over," leading her to telegraph as much to Vicky. If the illness was typhoid, that was at least possible. If Albert's affliction, however, was a long, slow, debilitating one—something on the order of stomach cancer, which fits many of his symptoms over at least four years before December 14, 1861—he had no resources left to fight the terminal episode of pneumonia, typhoid, or whatever. Had the physicians—even the obtuse Dr. Clark—fathomed this earlier, they also knew that medicine in 1861 offered no remedies. Victoria, too, seemed earlier to have sensed something potentially catastrophic and to have pushed it away, uncertain as to whether her fragile equilibrium could stand that much reality.*

As the morning wore on, the doctors seemed less sure that the Prince was rallying. "Alas!" Phipps messaged to Palmerston, "the hopes of the morning are fading away. . . ." At midday the Prince was given a spoonful of brandy, but no attempt was made to raise his head. "He is not worse," Dr. Watson told Victoria without conviction, "the pulse keeps up." Then he confessed to being "very much frightened, but [I] don't and won't give up hope."

In the darkened room, a dozen members of the Household had gathered. Now and then one of the physicians checked Albert's weakened pulse, but did little else. Alice remained at one side of the bed, where she had posted herself, when awake, for days. At the foot of the bed were Bertie and Helena and, as the day wore on, Louise and Arthur. Alfred was at sea; Leopold was in France; and Beatrice, at four, was too young for such scenes. The Prince's rapid breathing had become alarming. Victoria hastened to the side of the bed across from Alice and whispered, *"Es ist Fraüchen."* Then she bent toward him and asked for *"einen Kuss,"* and he kissed her. Then he dozed again. Victoria, with a terrible calm, held his thin cold hand until her misery again became overwhelming. She burst from the room and broke down.

The Queen's notes, written later when she could bear the recollec-

---

*One of the clues in the Prince's medical history is his long siege of painful gum inflammation. Three ailments with related symptoms create an oversecretion of hydrochloric acid in the stomach: peptic ulcer, Crohn's disease (regional enteritis)—although the latter was not labeled as such until decades later—and carcinoma of the stomach. The fumes arising from the increased acidity often severely irritate the gums. Regional enteritis, a severe nonbacterial inflammation of the small bowel, has its origins, as does peptic ulcer, in nervous tension, worry, and emotional conflict—a disease of lives lived at high pressure. Migratory arthritis is often present—perhaps Albert's chronic and untreated "rheumatism." The symptoms produce a sense of profound illness in the patient, with mental and physical fatigue, leading to malnutrition and invalidism; mid-abdominal cramps often occur, although not with the persistence of an ulcer; sometimes there is nausea and vomiting, and often a low fever. Albert's mother died of cancer at thirty, suggesting the possibility of a predisposition to the disease. Cancer of the stomach is usually well established before it is identified, but in Albert's time it was less well known and even less treatable than today, when the recovery rate after surgery is minimal. Benign gastric disturbances resembling regional enteritis often mask the disease. Surgery even to relieve regional enteritis was unknown then, and is today considered less helpful than a drastic change of living patterns. For Albert, none of the alternatives was available, even if the doctors knew what was wrong with him. What they did seem to know was that he was beyond their ministrations.

tion, suggest a somewhat quieter scene than that described immediately afterwards by Lady Augusta Bruce. At a quarter to eleven, when the Prince's breathing began to change, Alice whispered to Lady Augusta, "That is the death rattle." Calmly she went for her mother.

"Oh, yes, this is death!" Victoria cried on seeing Albert. "I know it. I have seen it before." She fell upon the still, cold body, and called him by every endearing name she could recall from their life together. Then she allowed herself to be led away.

XI

Victorian Mourning

(1861–1866)

"**W**hy has the earth not swallowed me up?" Vicky mourned when the dreaded news came.

"Oh, my poor child," the Queen returned, " 'Why may the earth not swallow *us* up?' . . . How am I alive after witnessing what I have done? Oh! I who prayed daily that we might die together and I never survive Him! I who felt, when in those blessed Arms clasped and held tight in the sacred Hours of the night, when the world seemed only to be ourselves, that nothing could part us. I felt so v[er]y secure." She would, she insisted, live to do her duty and to follow Albert's wishes. "But how I, who leant on him for all and everything—without whom I did nothing, moved not a finger, arranged not a print or photograph, didn't put on a gown or bonnet if he didn't approve it[,] shall go on, to live, to move, to help myself in difficult moments?"

The children, Albert's staff, Victoria's Ministers, her Household officials, had all come forward in the Red Room once the Prince had breathed his last, to offer not only sympathy but pledges of support in the transition from dependence upon Albert to a reign without him. "You will not leave or desert me now?" she had asked pathetically. Exhausted by lack of sleep and numb with grief, she permitted herself to be led away, first to Beatrice, who was asleep, then to her own room and to bed. In shock, but unable to sleep, and given no sedative, she dozed off only in the early hours of the morning. With Victoria out of the room and unlikely to return for some hours, a death mask of the Prince was made, for the record and to facilitate the work of later sculptors. Albert had been staunchly against the practice, but the handling of a body in the absence of any legal injunctions to the contrary is always the option of the survivors. Told about the mask later, Victoria refused to look at it and would not "allow that sacred cast . . . to go out of the house."

As midnight approached, the dull boom of the great bell atop St. Paul's announced that the Royal Family had been struck by death, and throughout Sunday the bells of London tolled. At Buckingham Palace, people queued quietly to sign a condolence book. Next to it, on a table in the reception room, was a message that although she was in great tribulation, her Majesty bore her affliction with as much calmness and fortitude as could be expected, and, given her bereavement, was as well as could be supposed. On Monday morning the war-scare newspaper placards about the *Trent* affair largely disappeared, replaced by particulars of the Prince Consort's death. While the bells still tolled, newspaper hawkers did a record business, and readers discovered a posthumous and sweeping concession in the press to Albert's value to the Kingdom. Less than a decade after rumors had put him in the Tower for treason, the turnabout would have pleased the Prince's shade. "Placed in a difficult position," said the *Observer*, "Prince Albert knew how to deport himself so discreetly and so well, that he has died without leaving a single enemy, while his friends were a host. . . . He was a man of elegant mind, of cultivated tastes, of a clear understanding, and of high and lofty aspirations for the public good. . . . Peace to his ashes! A good husband, a good father, a wise prince, and a safe counsellor, England will not soon 'look upon his like again.' "

Similar feelings were common among ordinary Londoners. The novelist Elizabeth Gaskell wrote that her friend Mary Ewart had passed through London on the Monday after the Prince's death—the sixteenth —and found that "all the little shops in Shoreditch were shut up—all blinds down—up to Buckingham Palace." With crowds of others she went to Buckingham Palace to put her name down in the mourning book, and found "a room hung with black, & lighted with wax." The fashionable shops, unlike those in the East End, were open, but "people could not give their orders at Lewis' & Allonbys for crying."

These were insignificant consolations for the Queen—if she knew about them—for beneath her initial surface equilibrium, after the first convulsive grief, was a dazed shock not uncommon to sorrowing spouses. Only on the Monday evening after—an interval of two days—could she begin her first letter to Vicky. And not until the twentieth could she write to her uncle, addressing him as "Dearest, kindest Father," and describing herself as the "poor fatherless baby of eight months" (as she had been), now "the utterly broken and crushed widow of forty-two"—as she indeed was:

> My *life* as a *happy* one is *ended!* the world is gone for *me!* If I *must* live on (and I will do nothing to make me worse than I am), it is henceforth for our poor fatherless children—for my unhappy country, which has lost *all* in losing him—and in *only* doing what I know and *feel* he would wish, for he *is* near me—his spirit will guide and inspire me! But oh! To be cut off in the prime of life . . . is too awful, too cruel! And yet it *must* be for *his* good, his happiness! His purity was too great, his aspiration *too high* for this poor, miserable world! His great soul is now only enjoying *that* for which it *was* worthy!

Without instructions, the Lord Chamberlain's Department nevertheless began the necessary preparations, moving the Prince's body to the extra bedstead in the room where he had died. Löhlein and Albert's dresser, Macdonald, assisted. The Prince of Wales, next in authority to the Queen but only nineteen and never called on before for advice, had to fix the date of the funeral. Consulting his uncle, the Duke of Cambridge, he chose Monday, December 23, nine days away. It was a brief span in which to organize a state ceremony, but it was crucial to keep the obsequies from colliding with Christmas—even with Christmas Eve, more important to many than the day itself.

The Lord Chamberlain's staff began with the assumption that the funeral of the Duchess of Kent, only months before, represented the wishes of the Queen as well as those of the Prince, and used that precedent for the arrangements. Although no equivalent panoply was called for, because Messrs. Banting had been the undertakers at the Duke of Wellington's funeral, they were called in as appropriate for Albert. Dr. Jenner filed a death certificate on December 21, fixing the cause as "typhoid fever; duration 21 days," the first time that the label was publicly applied; and although questions were raised in the *Lancet* and in the *British Medical Journal* about the discrepancies between the medical bulletins and the belated diagnosis, there was no autopsy. Instead, Jenner suggested to the Queen that death was "due to the heart being over-strained by the Prince's heavy frame," and Clark added that three things had proved fatal —overwork, worry about the Prince of Wales's love affair, and "exposure to chill when already sick." In 1877 Jenner added further that *"no one can diagnose typhoid at first."* Victoria underlined "no one" in her memo of the conversation. Clark's "when already sick" spoke further volumes.

Calling the handling of Albert's illness, and his death, "a national calamity of far greater importance than the public dream of," Lord Clarendon maintained to the Duchess of Manchester that the doctors had been contributing factors. "Holland and Clark are not even average old women, and nobody who is really ill would think of sending for either of them. Jenner has had little [experience of] practice. . . . Watson (who is no specialist in fever cases) at once saw that he had come too late to do any good."

Early on Sunday morning, having rested only a few hours, the Queen took the Duchess of Sutherland, Mistress of the Robes, into the Blue Room. Her doctors cautioned Victoria, citing the risk of infection, not to touch the body—a bit of nonsense, since she had embraced the dying Prince over and over again during his illness. She obeyed meekly, and instead embraced the clothes in which he was to be dressed. For years she would sleep with his nightshirt in her arms. Every night thereafter, she knelt at Albert's side of their bed before she put her head on her own pillow.

To keep the somber image of the Blue Room from affecting her further, the Queen ordered that the room be cleaned and restored to usefulness, but not until the "sad but lovely image" was photographed. She did not want it to remain as a *Sterbezimmer*—a death chamber—but intended to turn it into a room for her use that would nevertheless be a memorial. The "sacred room," she wrote to Vicky, would have pictures and busts and china. Her precious cast of Albert's hand, made in happier days, would be kept in their bedroom, near her. In each of their homes, his dressing room or study would be kept as it had been, even to the changing of linens, the daily replacement of towels and nightclothes, and —in the dressing rooms—the bringing of hot water for shaving each morning, and a scouring of the unused chamber pot. Yet each room would continue to be used in some way by Victoria. At first her audiences in Albert's silent study or dressing room were disconcerting in the extreme to her Ministers.

In his diary on the sixteenth, Disraeli, having heard of the Curragh incident and its aftermath, wondered how the Prince of Wales would now fare. The matter was "not seriously discreditable," Disraeli thought, "but undignified." The question about Bertie now was "into whose hands he may fall." More crucial, with Albert gone, were the future influences upon the Queen, for she had "long shown indications of a nervous and excitable disposition." He recalled of Albert that "nothing small or great was done but by his advice. . . . I have myself . . . heard him at dinner, suggest to her in German to enquire about this, that, and the other: and the questions never failed to follow. . . . The worst consequence possible is one, unluckily, not unlikely: that without being absolutely incapacitated for affairs, she may fall into a state of mind in which it will be difficult to do business with her, and impossible to anticipate what she will approve or disapprove." The "trying" situation he prophesied would quickly come about. Victoria's sole interest would be to embrace her grief.

Although the Queen, wearing her widow's cap, was hastened off to Osborne on the nineteenth, to be as far away from the funeral as was practical, her instructions for mourning fittings everywhere quickly exhausted supplies of black drapery throughout the kingdom. Dyeing establishments rushed to meet fresh orders. Christmas, following so soon after the funeral in Wolsey's Chapel, was darkened everywhere by official mourning. A grim extravaganza to parallel the Duke of Wellington's farewell, however, did not materialize. The Queen did not want it, and time was too short for ambitious preparations to proceed, or for many sovereigns or other state visitors to attend. From Osborne, Victoria sent word afterwards through Sir Charles Phipps that from reports she had received about the obsequies, everything had been conducted "as she could have wished, with due solemnity and every mark of profound respect, and yet without any unnecessary form or state."

Despite the insouciance he usually affected, Lord Torrington agreed with the assessment, writing to Delane, whose *Times* had set circulation records (an unprecedented 89,000 copies) on the Monday after the

Prince's death, that the obsequies had been "in every respect singularly well conducted—no confusion and no hurry. The music as fine as could be. . . . I am inclined to think that more real sorrow was evinced at this funeral than at any that has taken place *there* [at Windsor] for a vast number of years." Reverting to form, he added that "the champagne went briskly; but then the company had suffered extreme cold for at least an hour and a half. . . . Phipps looked his position, and ate a most excellent luncheon." Disraeli's own private comment seemed not unreasonable in the circumstances: "With Prince Albert we have buried our Sovereign. This German Prince has governed England for twenty-one years with a wisdom and energy such as none of our Kings have ever shown."

On the dreariest Christmas Eve of her life, Victoria wrote again to her uncle from Osborne. She had been considering her future conduct as Queen.

> I am . . . anxious to repeat *one* thing, and *that one* is *my firm* resolve, my *irrevocable decision*, . . . that *his* wishes—*his* plans—about everything, *his* views about *every* thing are to be *my law!* And *no human power* will make me swerve from *what he* decided and wished . . . I am *also determined* that *no one* person, may *he* be ever so good, ever so devoted among my servants—is to lead or guide or dictate *to me.* I know *how he* would disapprove of it. And I live *on* with him, for him; in fact I am only *outwardly* separated from him, and only for a *time.*

The Prince of Wales had also been pondering appropriate responses. Albert had rejected the idea of a statue of himself in South Kensington to mark the Great Exhibition, and plans had been changed to make the principal figure that of the Queen. It had always been her wish, announced Albert Edward, that the figure of the Prince Consort top the monument, and he would bear the cost. Executed by Joseph Durham and unveiled with great ceremony in June 1863, it fronts, appropriately, the later Albert Hall.

Victoria would henceforth see everything through the lens of her bereavement. In that, she contributed nothing new to the vocabulary or the symbolism of mourning. Oxford Street shops already existed that were devoted solely to a trade in black ostrich feathers for women's hats, and sashed crêpe "weepers" for men's tall hats, black armbands, deep purple clothes, black plumes for horses, and funereal accoutrements of every description. In Prussia or in Russia, the attention paid to the body of the deceased was greater; in France or Italy, peasant women who became widowed, at whatever age, would wear black the rest of their lives; in England and Scotland, setting aside a room associated with the dead child or spouse, to keep it undisturbed as a documentation of the beloved's life, was fashionable.

Few looked on such demonstrations as morbid sentiment. One indulged in what grief one could afford. Even Victoria's allegedly vicious Uncle Ernest—King of Hanover after her accession—left the rooms of his Queen, when she died in 1841, exactly as they had been. Night candles were lit, pages and dressers remained in attendance, and the King, who venerated her "sweet and amiable character," went regularly to pray at the side of what had been her bed. The English poor could not afford the luxury of prolonged grief, and, after the obsequies, had to substitute the stiff upper lip. Still, in *David Copperfield*, Charles Dickens inveighed against the grotesque mummeries and extravagant expense of nineteenth-century lower-class funerals, and in 1903, Bernard Shaw wrote in the Devil's great speech in *Don Juan in Hell*, "I saw a man die: he was a London bricklayer's laborer with seven children. He left seventeen pounds club money; and his wife spent it all on his funeral and went into the workhouse with the children the next day. . . . On death she spent all she had." As late as 1914, Hilaire Belloc locked the door of his dead wife's bedroom and left it that way until his own death, forty years later, kissing the door each time he passed it, although he had largely ignored the living Elodie. In the wide black edges on her handkerchiefs and writing paper, and in her widow's weeds, in the planned memorials to Albert and in his portrait in a locket around her neck or in the bracelet around her plump wrist, the Queen was not turning her back on life any more than other widows of her time. She was, however, not merely another grieving survivor.

The "easing of that violent grief," Victoria wrote in 1867, "those paroxysms of despair and yearning and longing and of daily, nightly longing to die, . . . for the first three years never left me. . . ." When Lord Canning, her Viceroy in India, died only six months after his wife (he was suddenly inconsolable, and had a nervous breakdown), Victoria wrote to his sister as if Canning had not been a flagrantly erring husband throughout the marriage, "How enviable to follow so soon the partner of your life! How I pray that it be God's will to let me follow mine soon." But she was Queen: there was civil war in America, into which her country might be drawn; there were conflicts brewing on the Continent nearby; there was social and political and religious agitation in England, and there were Fenian outbreaks in Ireland. Nothing of such external events emerges in Victoria's journal in early January, as she begins again to record her "sad and solitary life."

Mirroring her mourning, the Household, at the Queen's instruction, went about in black crêpe, broadcloth, and bombazine, underscoring the gloom. For a year after Albert's death, no member of her Household could appear in public except in mourning garb, a practice that might have continued indefinitely had her ladies not sunk so much in morale that Victoria relented sufficiently to permit "semi-mourning" colors of white, mauve, and grey. Even royal servants were obliged to wear a black crêpe band on the left arm until 1869. At Windsor, Disraeli noted, the two guest books that existed, for the Queen and the Prince, were not discontinued—"visitors write their names . . . as before—calling on a dead man."

At her instructions the booming of gunnery practice at the naval base of Portsmouth, across the Solent from Osborne, was stilled. The echoes, however faint, throbbed painfully for the Queen. In that quietude on January 1, 1862, she scrutinized sketches of Albert, in Highland dress, for a statue, one of many to be planned because it was difficult to say no to the Queen. Her efforts to recall him and memorialize him would be constant, although the cult of the Prince Consort was imposed rather than real. For many Englishmen he had been too German in his ways—too interested in science and education, in good works, in efficiency and energy.

Once at Osborne, Victoria began an *album consolatium,* a popular contemporary device for self-solace through the recording of extracts from poems, sermons, prayers, and other expressions relevant to the mourner's mood. The Queen's pocket-sized, gold-tooled brown album, with a metal clasp, would have its 182 pages filled by June 27, 1862, the last entry a Charles Kingsley verse beginning, "Shrink not from grief. . . ." A table of contents neatly calligraphed by a lady-in-waiting included poems by Tennyson, Coleridge, Goethe, Heine, Longfellow, Justinius Kerner, and "Novalis" (Friedrich von Hardenberg). There were also extracts from letters from the Countess Blücher and the Reverend Norman Macleod; snippets from sermons; and from the *Book of Common Prayer,* the "Commemoration of the Faithful Departed." Several pages collected such observations on "Widowhood" as

O God, this grief is more than I can bear alone. . . .

Where is the Heart on which my life has leant . . . ?

Lord, why such cruel Wrath
Hard to understand?

Some entries are in the Queen's bold hand; others, made by her ladies, are often marked by Victoria, the most underlined passages those from Tennyson's *In Memoriam,* her favorite work by the Laureate. A matching album would be begun in 1872, the Queen penning an extract from Elizabeth Barrett Browning; most of the book remained blank although added to irregularly. It may have been out of England, possibly in the possession of Vicky.

Even in the relative seclusion of Osborne, potential callers had to be diplomatically warded off. Responses to a flood of official and personal messages kept her ladies-in-waiting busy. Sacks of sympathy letters arrived from the obscure, one from a pious preacher who consoled her, "Henceforth you must remember that Christ himself will be your husband." With indignation the Queen would quote the line and object, "That is what I would call twaddle. The man must have known that he was talking nonsense. How can people like that comfort others or teach anybody?"

One of the earliest to be permitted to pay his condolences was the Duke of Newcastle, whom Victoria received "in dear Albert's room, where *all* remains the same." They talked at length of the Prince, "of his great goodness and purity, quite unlike anyone else." Among the callers Victoria did not see then were the Poet Laureate and his wife and sons, who lived fifteen miles away on the island. They signed their names in the condolence book and returned home. A few days later, on January 7, Tennyson sent a poem—dedicatory verses to his *Idylls of the King*— which, he wrote to Victoria, Albert "himself had told me was valued by him." The Queen replied through Princess Alice, "who desired to tell Mr. Tennyson, with her warmest thanks, how much she was moved by his lines," a blank verse tribute to "my own Ideal knight," who would be "hereafter, thro' all times, Albert the Good." The next month a new edition of the *Idylls* was published that incorporated his words about the "Prince indeed,/Beyond all titles. . . ." The "Dedication" always since has been printed at the head of the cycle.

Meanwhile, the Queen had again turned for consolation to her well-thumbed copy of Tennyson's *In Memoriam,* marking the margins with comments relevant to her experience. In the twenty-ninth stanza, for example, next to "How dare we keep our Christmas-eve . . . ?" she wrote, "We did not keep it in 1861."

Through the Duke of Argyll, the Queen conveyed her desire to meet the poet. Tennyson responded to the Duke that he was shy and had no idea how to greet—or withdraw from—a Queen. The Duke suggested "natural signs of devotion and sympathy. . . . All formality and mere ceremony breaks down in the presence of real sorrow."

The visit took place on April 14, the shy poet taking with him for support his two sons and his closest friend, the Greek scholar and Master of Balliol, Benjamin Jowett. Tennyson, the Queen thought, was "very peculiar looking, tall, dark, with a fine head, long black flowing hair and a beard—oddly dressed, but there is no affectation about him. I told him how much I admired his glorious lines to my precious Albert and how much comfort I found in his 'In Memoriam.' He was full of unbounded appreciation of beloved Albert. When he spoke of my own loss, of that to the Nation, his eyes quite filled with tears." And Victoria replied, "The country has been kind to me and I am thankful." Tennyson had written in his "Dedication" to the *Idylls* of the Prince's devotion to literature, science, and art, and meant it; and, standing by the fireplace, in the presence of the tiny, plump Queen, who seemed to him like a pale statue with a sweet, sad voice, he heard her introduce herself with, "I am like your Mariana now." "Mariana," one of Tennyson's earliest poems, described a lamenting widow whose life alone was predictably desolate and whose final utterance in every lugubrious stanza was "I would that I were dead!"

Later in the year, recalling Tennyson, Victoria wrote to her daughter, revealingly, "For me my very misery is now a necessity and I could not exist without it." Quoting *In Memoriam* (LIX) she added, "Like Tennyson says,

> O Sorrow, wilt thou live with me
> No casual mistress, but a wife,
> My bosom-friend and half of life,
> As I confess it needs must be. . . .

This is what I feel; yes, I long for my suffering almost—as it is blinded with him!"

Talking of Arthur Henry Hallam, the friend about whom Tennyson had written *In Memoriam,* Victoria unpersuasively compared Albert to the dead poet in physical appearance, and Tennyson observed that Albert "would have made a great King." Sensitive to the problem of Albert's title, the Queen quickly agreed. "He always said it did not signify whether he did the right thing or not, so long as the right thing was done." They talked of Macaulay, Goethe, and Schiller, and at parting she asked him whether there was anything she could do for him. "Nothing, Madam," he said, "but shake my two boys by the hand. It may keep them loyal in the troublous times to come."

The times *were* "troublous," and where it was not necessary for the Sovereign to act, the Queen's staff attempted to keep as much of the trouble as possible from her. One such calamity was the cutting off of the Prince's income of nearly £40,000 a year, yet a continuing moral obligation remained to provide for the Prince's staff. The expenses of her own establishment, and those of her children, were increasing, as she maintained private estates at Osborne and Balmoral not covered in Privy Purse allocations, and would soon have titled but unpropertied sons-in-law for whom to provide. Rumors in London suggested that Albert had left large sums, but he had left scarcely enough to cover outstanding liabilities, for his income was spent on the salaries of his servants and his staff, his contributions to public charities, and his purchases of works of art for Osborne and Balmoral. Victoria would find that she could not commission personally all the memorials she wanted, but one she authorized immediately was the publication of a collection of Albert's speeches, edited by Arthur Helps, the new Clerk of the Privy Council.

Since a Privy Council meeting had become urgent to approve necessary business, Helps had been brought in by the Queen earlier to assist in a quiet conspiracy by which she intended to circumvent public business during her official mourning. As she described it in her diary on January 6, "Lord Granville and others, with Mr. Helps, were in dear Albert's room, and I in mine, with the door open. The business was all summed up in two paragraphs, and Mr. Helps read 'approved' for me. This was unlike anything which had been done before."

What obsessed the Queen was grief, and late in January she entered into the Hartley colliery catastrophe, where miners had been entombed, with telegrams of inquiry to the rescue party at the pits. When hope was gone she issued a statement "that her tenderest sympathy is with the poor widows and mothers, and that her own misery makes her feel all the more for them."

When Victoria visited Balmoral for the first time since Albert's death, she made haste to call on a cottager she knew whose own husband, long bedridden, had died during the winter. "And we both cried: she cried and I cried," the woman recalled. "I controlled myself as soon as I could, and asked her pardon for crying."

"But, oh!" said the Queen, "I am so thankful to cry with someone who knows exactly how I feel." Then, thinking about it further, she added, "You saw your husband's death coming, but I—I did not see— it was so sudden!"

Seeking explanations that satisfied her emotional needs, she told Colonel Francis Seymour, who had been close to the Prince and was one of the first visitors she permitted, that Albert had caught a fever from having gone too close to the excavation of "old earth" at the Crystal Palace site, and then she revised her diagnosis to blame also "that dreadful business in the Curragh."

"Oh, no, Madame!" exclaimed Seymour.

Not until the end of the month would Victoria meet with her Prime Minister, who had been too enfeebled by gout to join the Privy Council session. In the interim he did allow the real world to intrude upon Victoria just long enough to recall bitter memories. The United States, Palmerston informed her, had agreed to release the Confederate agents Mason and Slidell, and conceded that its warship had acted without "any orders or authority" in removing the men. Albert's last official act had made the peaceable solution possible.

Palmerston himself would not have an audience with the Queen until January 29, when he crossed the Solent (where the guns had been permitted to fire again) in a gale. "He could in fact hardly speak for emotion," Victoria wrote. To talk of government business was, he understood, still largely inappropriate. After his words of condolence, he came to the point of his visit, urging on the Queen the necessity of seeing to it that the Prince of Wales was betrothed and married soon, for the continuity of the monarchy. Both knew that he sought the possibility, at least, of stability in her son's life. Palmerston also pressed for further official traveling by the Prince, to give him more of the experience that the Queen would not permit him at home. They seemed agreed on what the Queen called "*the* difficulty of the moment," namely Bertie. "I . . . would hardly have given Lord Palmerston credit for entering so entirely into my anxieties."

Victoria would apply her ample energy to matchmaking in many directions, but also in keeping Bertie distant from any official responsibilities. As for public business handled by Albert, that had already devolved upon her late husband's private secretaries, General Grey and Sir Charles Phipps. Probably hearing from Palmerston through the Prime Minister's stepson, Lord Clarendon wrote to the Duchess of Manchester the next day that the Queen "does not seem to improve & her only relief in thinking of her desolate future is Her conviction that She shall & must die soon. She is worse off than ordinary persons with relations & friends who in time bring change & comfort—but She is isolated & the best thing for her is the responsibility of her position & the mass of business wh: She cannot escape from & wh: during a certain portion of the day compels her to think of something other than the all embracing sorrow." There was also the problem, he added, of the "P of W"—a "monomania & nothing can move her upon it."

On her wedding anniversary, February 10, Victoria wrote to Charles Grey, on mourning paper with borders nearly three-quarters of an inch deep, "She feels her Darling Husband very, very near today! But she knows not *where* He is! She lives in a dream! *All* dreams *here* are so unreal!" The only reality was to memorialize "that pure angel," as Clarendon discovered when he was handed the "disagreeable task" of being on a committee with the Earl of Derby and Sir Charles Eastlake, president of the Royal Academy, to decide upon an appropriate memorial to the Prince Consort. He had no qualifications, Clarendon thought, to prevent the money from being misspent and "a disgraceful Monument erected." He could not make himself any more fit for the task "than for leading the orchestra at the Opera House." But the Queen had expressed a desire for some form of obelisk, and that restricted the committee from the start. Another limitation came quickly when cities and towns began to withhold all or part of the funds raised locally for their own artistic uses. As for memorials of the bronze, marble, and granite variety, Clarendon thought, the Queen had "no more notion of what is right & pure in art than she has of the Chinese grammar," and he grimly looked forward in outlying cities and towns to "the late Consort in robes of The Garter upon some curious and non-descript animal that will be called a horse, & Albert Baths & Washhouses. . . ."

On March 15 the first stone of what was to the Queen the real memorial was laid at Frogmore, Windsor—the mausoleum in which Victoria intended to sleep side by side with Albert, in death, as she had done in life. Otherwise, to her, Windsor was "a *living grave*" to which she dreaded returning. Yet doing something she wanted to do energized her, and the foundation stone, containing coins and pictures of the Prince Consort and his family, was duly laid by the Queen. According to Lord Torrington, again in waiting, "The Queen looked very nice; to my eye she looked like a *young girl* and showed great nerve."

Victoria could have entrusted the ceremony to the Prince of Wales, but she was determined to give him as little to do as possible. His purchase of the Norfolk estate of Sandringham was one result, as overseeing the farms and cover for game was an ostensible occupation for a gentleman. The income from the estates of the Duchy of Cornwall had been only £16,000 a year when Albert began administering the properties traditionally assigned to the heir apparent. Efficiencies had increased that amount to almost £60,000, and much of that had been allowed to accumulate. Bertie was now a wealthy young man. He could not only afford the property, but needed it to furnish his private life with some screen from his prying mother. What he had been allowed to do was to travel, as a means of seasoning him and to keep him as far away as possible as much as possible. His trip to Egypt and the Holy Land gave Delane an opportunity to float a trial balloon in *The Times* on the Prince's behalf—that his performance as guest of foreign sovereigns gave him the credentials "to greet the friends of England in his own country," and to perform "many public or semi-public duties" that came the way of the sovereign. It was delicately put, and there was no earthquake at Windsor, but also little result. Victoria remained in seclusion, and the sovereign as symbol disappeared except from currency, coinage, postage stamps, and the *Court Circular* by which newspapers strained to see some meaningful activity by the Queen. "No one," Torrington confided to Delane, "dares to tell her the truth."

To the Earl of Derby she wrote poignantly on February 17, 1862, of herself: "She sees the trees budding, the days lengthening, the primroses coming out, but she *thinks* herself still in the month of December." Victoria's desolation may have included a dimension of culpability—a result of a long and unconfessed realization of the presence of mortal illness, an unspoken secret she may have shared with her husband. Certainly Albert knew, and had attempted to make it known, although to deliberately deaf ears, and he had at times acted openly with a fatalistic acceptance. A denial of that reality during Albert's decline could only have added afterwards to Victoria's sense of complicity, a shameful thing sometimes put aside by blaming the deceased for the desolation in the survivor. Derby, after seeing the Queen, told his son that Victoria "talked freely" of Albert, who *"would* die—he seemed not to care to live. Then she used the words, 'He died from want of what they call pluck.' " That excused her failure to face his obvious decline: he had failed to fight it. Yet her indulgence in so public a private grief had practical advantages. As Disraeli had observed, the nation had buried its uncrowned sovereign. In many ways, Victoria had seldom been called upon to do more than ceremonially reign, interposing herself only when she felt particularly strongly about an issue. Now she could claim physical and emotional breakdown in the aftermath of Albert's death to avoid coming to grips with matters of state. (Her feeling about her own capacities can be judged from her comment to Vicky in 1863, "I know you always had a very poor idea of old Mama's wits, . . . which was natural enough when our blessed oracle was with us.")

When Lord Clarendon visited the Queen at Osborne in March 1862, the Queen raised a variety of subjects as usual, and referred to the sayings and doings of the Prince as if he were in the next room. "It was difficult to believe that he was not, but in his own room where she received me everything was set out on his table and the pen and his blotting-book, his handkerchief on the sofa, his watch going, fresh flowers in the glass . . . as I had always been accustomed to see them, and as if he might have come in at any moment."

What Clarendon also knew was that every evening Albert's clothes were laid out, and other toilet preparations made, as if he were alive. Also, in each of the Queen's residences, hung over the Prince's side of the royal double bed (he had slept at her right hand), was a tinted deathbed photograph, juxtaposing the grim reality with the continuing fantasy. (At Albert's pillows now are photographs of his effigy in the mausoleum at Frogmore.)

When, as Chancellor of the Exchequer, Gladstone saw her, also in March, the Queen was on a rare visit to Windsor. He was uneasy about facing her in her bereavement, and stood through the long interview while she sat and asked him questions about the economic distress caused by the shortage of American cotton, and about Church matters, a special interest of Gladstone's. Finally she shifted the subject to the dead Prince. Her mind, she confided, was not "gifted with . . . elasticity." It was not easy for her to go on without Albert, she added, for "if ever woman had fondly loved a man, she had fondly loved the Prince." She went on about his many attributes, and Gladstone was surprised to hear her list "personal beauty" among them, as she was talking to one of her Ministers, not to a confidant. She intended to do her best as Queen alone, she said, "but she had no confidence in herself."

Cautiously, he sympathized with her attitude. "Over-confidence was a vice; and lack of it was often a virtue." It might have been better to have professed confidence in her abilities and judgment, and Gladstone later blamed himself for not having "gone a little further in the language of hope." Still, she noted in her journal that he had been "kind and feeling," and after Gladstone made a speech at Manchester praising the dead Prince, she wrote to him, on April 28—hardly in the manner of Sovereign to Minister—that her chief desire in life was to leave it. "Her *only* wish is to get soon to her own darling again. Every day seems to increase the intensity of a sorrow which *nothing, nothing* can alleviate, as there never was *love* and devotion like hers! Every source of interest or pleasure causes now the acutest pain. *Mrs.* Gladstone, who the Queen knows is a *most* tender wife, may, in a faint manner, picture to herself what the Queen suffers."

In response, Gladstone suggested that she leave the solution of her eventual reunion with the Prince to a Higher Power. "Unable to see into the future, we believe, Madam, that He can choose for You the best of these [alternatives]; and that He will."

The Queen was no less in mournful seclusion a year later (April 25, 1863), when Disraeli responded, in his very different fashion, about Albert. "The Prince," he wrote to her, "is the only person, whom Mr. Disraeli has ever known, who realized the Ideal. None, with whom he is acquainted, have ever approached it. There was in him a union of the manly grace and the sublime simplicity of chivalry, with the intellectual splendour of the Attic Academe." In time, Disraeli prophesied, Albert's "plans will become systems, his suggestions dogmas, and the name of Albert will be accepted as the master type of a generation of profounder feeling, and vaster range, than that which he formed and guided. . . ." The sweeping flattery enchanted her, but what may have caught her attention more immediately was the present tense in which the opening was couched, the living presence suggested. Gladstone's dutiful sincerity, by comparison, was cramped and incapable of uplift.

The Queen's desire to dwell within her grief continued to be made easy by the willingness of her Government to defer to it, a price willingly paid as long as it meant less interference from her about Cabinet matters in which she had normally taken an interest. As a guest at Windsor in

June 1862, Lord Clarendon had the opportunity to bring up Government business, and she referred to an attack on Palmerston by Lord Derby, leader of the Opposition. Suddenly, then, her manner changed, and she pressed her hands against her forehead excitedly, crying, "My reason! My reason!" The message to him was clear. She was to be spared political crises. Victoria knew of the fears of Hanoverian madness, and may have been playing on them. Rumors of her insanity would intrigue journalists for years. Whatever its pathology, the Queen's deliciously sorrowful self-punishment had its desired effects.

For a while, too, mourning by a genuinely shocked public supported the Queen's response to her catastrophe, and memorial tributes in arts and music and poetry followed the large sales of black sashes and ribbons, and other expressions of sympathy. When these waned, and the Queen still remained inconsolable, attitudes began to shift, a fact noticeable as soon as she decreed a wedding for Alice and Prince Louis that was as funereal and joyless as possible. The occasion was even celebrated in the inconvenience, for everyone but the Queen, of Osborne.

For the marriage, on July 1, 1862, Victoria arranged that the dining room at Osborne House be used, with the ceremony set under the huge Winterhalter family portrait, thus ensuring Albert's benign presence. She herself sat, in what "Baby" called her mother's "sad cap," in an armchair apart from the ceremony, flanked by her eldest sons. Fortunately for the bride and groom, who were much less the focus of attention than the huddled figure in black, the Archbishop of York kept the service short.

The ceremony, Vicky told her aunt Feodora, was "like a funeral." The bride (in mourning for her father) was even required to secure a black trousseau. Whether she used it beyond London is unknown. The newly-weds quickly left for a house in Hesse—unpalatial, but remote from Windsor. With £25,000 from the Queen they would build New Schloss in Darmstadt, with Dutch terraces and Italian gardens.

Next on the Queen's agenda was the safeguarding of Bertie from further temptation and sin by pairing him with a suitable bride. Albert had arranged the previous year that the Prince of Wales would visit the Holy Land; Bertie, a good traveler, had thrived on the experience and returned "much improved" (the Queen thought) just before Alice's wedding. He was now nearly twenty-one. With the Danish princess, Alexandra, apparently the most suitable choice, Vicky was asked to perform the delicate mission of telling something approaching the truth about Bertie to Alexandra's mother. The Queen's recommended story was that *"wicked wretches"* had led the "poor innocent Boy into a scrape" but that he had been forgiven by "both of us." He would make a "steady Husband" and a wife like "Alix" would be his "SALVATION."

For the impecunious Danish house, eager to swap their pretty daughters for status and security, Bertie seemed indeed their salvation, and arrangements were made to have Victoria and Bertie meet Alix and her family at Laeken, under the benign auspices of King Leopold. Ostensibly the Queen was stopping in Belgium en route to Coburg, to pay her respects to Albert's birthplace. Early in September, both parties to the negotiations arrived, and it fell to Victoria for the first time since Albert's death to conduct a major piece of business.

The Queen was impressed by Alix's good looks, and the ravaged beauty—and utter deafness—of her mother. The princess was a few months short of eighteen, with blond curls atop "a beautiful refined profile," and was "quiet [and] ladylike." For Victoria it was a "trying" moment. *"I* had *alone* to say and do what, under other, former happy circumstances, had devolved on us both together." Alix would enter a "sad house," the Queen told her, but the unperturbed princess was not about to throw away her chances to be Queen of England. When Victoria left, and Bertie remained behind to propose formally, he was not surprised to be accepted. The Queen received the news in Germany.

Feodora had joined her sister in Belgium to examine Alexandra. The next day, both left for Gotha, traveling by night train from Cologne. The widowed sisters had not spent much time together during their marriages; with both now alone, Victoria thought they might share their lives at least part of each year—obviously in England, since one reigned and the other was without formal duties. Victoria's preliminary strategy might best have been to prove herself desirable as a companion. Instead, when Feodora broached the subject of having Victoria attend the wedding of her son Hermann three weeks away at Karlsruhe, the Queen stubbornly declined to be present at any festivity whatever. After that, she could hardly bring her subject up; but after ten days at Coburg, including a visit from the loyal Lehzen, then in her eightieth year and still at Bückeburg, Victoria pressed a letter into the hands of her departing sister.

At Liebenstein, her first night's stop en route home to Baden, Feodora quickly but cautiously replied. She thought it would be best "not to fix a certain time, but let me come and stay when you want me, and when my health will permit. I think three or four months in spring or autumn . . . if you will allow me to return to Germany when I feel too unwell. . . . I cannot give up my house nor my independence at my age. At the same time, my life is so bound up with yours, and we sisters, left alone, belong to each other so entirely. . . . I see you before me in tears, unhappy, forlorn. . . . May God give you strength and patience, my beloved Victoria." She did visit in November 1863, a year later, Victoria writing to their uncle, Leopold, that Feodora was "a great resource and comfort."

After Coburg, Victoria returned to the Isle of Wight for the planned visit of Alix to Osborne and the proclamation of Bertie's forthcoming marriage. It became a season of family preoccupations and their European ramifications, as the Prussians were unhappy with a Danish future queen across the Channel, and the vacant and tottery throne of Greece was being offered about—to Alexandra's brother, to Ernest of Coburg, and to Victoria's son Alfred. She "could not spare" a prince, Victoria asserted; after all, in Portugal "three had been swept away in two months" just before Albert's death. Besides, she did not want Alfred's children (he was still unmarried) "brought up Greeks," and he was too young. She also knew that he was in line to succeed Ernest, who was childless, at Coburg. Then Ernest decided that he wanted to be King of Greece himself, and that he would make Alfred his deputy in Coburg. Since that would immediately involve Greece in a succession problem, or push Alfred onto its throne after all, Victoria put a stop to the game of musical chairs, while fruitlessly recommending some alternative choices. In the end a Danish prince accepted the throne, and related the kingdom to Victoria's family in another way.

On December 14 came the first "dreadful day" on which to remember the Consort's passing. In the "dear room" at Windsor, banked with flowers, a family prayer service comforted the Queen. Several nights later, on the seventeenth, she was unable to sleep, as early the next morning Albert's remains were to be moved to the new mausoleum at Frogmore, with Bertie, Arthur, and even Leopold participating, as well as Albert's former aides and his valets Löhlein and Maget. At one in the afternoon, Victoria, with Alice and "Baby," went to kneel at the tomb below the recumbent effigy of the Prince. Victoria would visit often, as a restorative.

One way in which the Queen continued to follow Albert's ways was to insist upon a German component in her life. She was grieved, she wrote to Vicky in November 1862, that Bertie never wrote to Alix "in anything but English." The "German element," she insisted, "is the one I wish to be cherished and kept up in our beloved home." After the Prince of Wales visited Vicky in Berlin, the Queen wrote to her, "I hope you have Germanised Bertie as much as possible." It would have been more important to Anglicize him, but she preferred that he remain away from England as much as possible, and when Lord Granville attempted to initiate the Prince of Wales into the world that Albert had enjoyed by asking the Prince to preside over a Literary Fund dinner, the Queen was outraged. Bertie was "too young and inexperienced." Further, she warned, he was "upon no account [to] be put at the head of any of those Societies or Commissions, or preside at any of those scientific proceedings, in which his beloved great Father took so prominent a part."

Victoria's reasons were that it would be an unfair embarrassment to the Prince of Wales, whose interests were different and whose education was sketchy. Behind her concern to protect Bertie, however, may have been her desire to keep him in a state of unreadiness for responsibility. (She was not even sure he was ready for marriage, and she hardly trusted Alix, only eighteen, to turn him into a husband and father of future sovereigns. "Are you aware," she queried Vicky, "that Alix has the smallest head ever seen? I dread that—with his small empty brain—very much for future children.") Victoria was satisfied that Alexandra could do nothing to turn her future spouse into a plausible king. She knew very well that he was not guilty of his father's death, but neither morally nor intellectually did he mirror the Prince Consort, to her a king without a crown. Yet rumors were already creeping into London newspapers that she would step down in Bertie's favor after the marriage, and her behavior seems to have been calculated in part to smother such speculation. "Disraeli has a story," Lord Stanley noted in his diary, "which comes from the King of the Belgians, that the Queen will abdicate when her son and daughter-in-law have shown themselves fit to take her place: intending to fix her residence for the rest of her life at Coburg."

To suitably inspire Bertie and Alix, the day before the wedding Victoria took them to the mausoleum at Frogmore. Standing before the tomb of Aberdeen granite, on which rested the white marble likeness of Albert executed by Baron Carlo Marochetti in 1862, Victoria joined their hands and said, *"He* gives you his blessing!" (Her own parallel effigy, under which she intended to rest next to Albert until the Resurrection, had already been carved to her measurements and was in storage nearby, a fact that gave her great comfort.)

The marriage, on May 10, 1863, at Windsor, could have been a grand state occasion had the Queen not worn her widow's weeds, and the lack of rehearsal and of accommodations created confusion that she never noticed. The Prime Minister, Lord Palmerston, had to return to London in a third-class seat, as did the Duchess of Westminster, despite the fortune in diamonds she wore. The Queen, determined to play down the marriage of the future king, had resisted all efforts to have her appear out of mourning, and had delayed decisions about cards, tickets, and other paraphernalia until, as Lord Torrington complained to John Delane, "preparations are all in a mess." *Punch* suggested that since the guest list was to be small, and the wedding held in an obscure Berkshire village, noted only for a castle with no sanitary arrangements, the optimum solution was a notice in the marriage column of *The Times:* "On the tenth, inst., at Windsor, by Dr. Longley, assisted by Dr. Thomson, Albert Edward England, K.G., to Alexandra Denmark. No cards."

Every show of enthusiasm the Queen could control was stifled; only the Princess's progress from Southwark Station (after landing at Gravesend) to Paddington on March 7, through enthusiastic crowds that surged through the streets, remained beyond Victoria's powers.

Ostensibly she approved of the demonstrations, writing to Palmerston of the "joy" and "pride" that her "great and good husband" would have felt "had he gone with his son this day and brought him and his lovely bride through the crowded streets to Windsor. . . . Now he looks down, freed from the cares . . . which bow the Queen to the earth, unaided and unsupported and lonely and desolate in joy as in sorrow. . . . The Queen wishes Lord Palmerston would take an opportunity of stating the Queen's feeling on this great demonstration, but also to say that those err who think that the wound can be healed by the marriage of our child!"

At Windsor the lid on celebration was shut tight, and high above St. George's Chapel, in the Royal Closet, Victoria sat out of the ceremony but visible to everyone, casting a pall over the proceedings. Over her black silk and crêpe she wore Albert's own Garter badge with blue ribbon, and a miniature of Albert set with diamonds, which she had worn as a brooch since 1840. When she watched from her window, Albert watched with her. Lord Granville told the Duchess of Manchester that when the chorale composed by Prince Albert—and sung by Jenny Lind—began, "[Victoria] gave a look upwards, which spoke volumes."

The places in the chapel were limited, and Disraeli liked to think that his and Mary Anne's seats were a result of the Queen's increasing regard for him, although they had been issued to him as Leader of the Opposition (in the Commons) at Palmerston's request. "Dizzy" savored the occasion and dined out afterwards on his descriptions of it, even his venturing to observe Victoria better through his monocle. Her Majesty caught him staring, and scolded him with her famous frown. "I did not venture to use my glass again," he confessed happily to society hostess Mrs. Brydges Williams.

Although the wedding arrangements were carried out as the Queen wanted them, she took no part, other than to embrace the couple on their return to the palace, on the Grand Staircase. At the family luncheon for thirty-eight, the Queen was not present. ("I lunched alone with Baby.") When the couple departed, on their way to Osborne, Victoria saw them leave from the Corridor, then from her bedroom window. Once the guests left, she and Louise went to the Mausoleum to pray in Albert's presence.

Even the birth of a daughter to Alice the next month, the first of the grandchildren to be given the Queen's name, required some mournfulness about it to savor, and Victoria used the event to write to Vicky about how grieved she had been that none of the daughters of Vicky and Frederick William had been "called after either of us." Prussian dynastic and diplomatic niceties, the Queen knew, had required the primacy of other names, but happiness of any sort had to be rigorously eschewed.

Nor were Bertie and Alexandra to enjoy themselves, or to disport themselves in any manner the Queen felt was inappropriate. As Lord Stanley reported it on June 16, 1863, "Much talk in London about the extraordinary way in which the Queen undertakes to direct the Prince and Princess of Wales in every detail of their lives. They may not dine out, except at houses named by her: nor ask anyone to dine with them, except with previous approval or unless the name of the person invited is on a list previously prepared: and the Princess, after riding once or twice in the Park, was forbidden to do so again. In addition, a daily and minute report of what passes at Marlborough House is sent to the Queen. The parties most concerned make no complaint, but others do for them, and the whole proceeding is ill-judged." The restrictions paralleled the Prince's miseducation, and invited evasion. In her certainty that Bertie was bound to go wrong, whatever her efforts to guard against it, the Queen mourned to Vicky, "I fear [that Alix] will never be what she would be had she a clever, sensible and well-informed husband, instead of a very weak and terribly frivolous one! Oh! what will become of the poor country if I die! I foresee, if B. succeeds, nothing but misery. . . ."

On the surface, the Queen appeared supportive of the young couple, even holding a rare drawing-room reception on May 16 to introduce Alexandra to the right people in London. Nearly three thousand ladies were presented, and the frail Princess became so exhausted that at one point the doors had to be closed to give her some rest. The Danish Minister, Forben de Bille, commented to the American diplomat Benjamin Moran that Alexandra needed "some of the roast beef and ale of England to give her more flesh and development," but the chief problem, the Queen confided to Vicky, was that Alix had inherited her mother's deafness, which "everyone observes, [and] which is a sad misfortune."

Other than on such few occasions in one of her own residences, Victoria did not appear in public after her bereavement for nearly two years. Only on October 13, 1863, did she show herself outside family ceremonials, traveling to Aberdeen to unveil a statue of the Prince Consort. In what had to be a response to her wishes, Aberdonians were instructed to refrain from cheering, from employing musical instruments, and from decorating the houses and streets with welcoming banners and floral arches. The teeming rain in which the unfestive affair took place seemed appropriate to Victoria, who described the day as "sad & trying & painful." The wide coverage given by the press emphasized the Queen's continued seclusion, as she seemed to emerge in the next few years only to unveil statues of Albert. Even at Aberdeen, the first such occasion, *The Times* observed that two years was a long enough time to spend "in unavailing regrets and in dwelling upon days which cannot be recalled." A year later, when she traveled to Coburg with her family for another unveiling, *The Times* found it increasingly difficult to "awaken sympathetic respect" when it considered the continued "danger of indulging in the luxury of sorrow." The loss of Albert was heartfelt nearly everywhere in her domains, but the insistence on a national preoccupation with memorials rather than upon Albertine ideas of progress* awakened revulsion in the most understanding of her subjects. "If you should meet with an inaccessible cave anywhere," Dickens joked to his friend and illustrator John Leech in September 1864, "to which a hermit could retire from the memory of Prince Albert and testimonials to the same, pray let me know of it. We have nothing solitary and deep enough in this part of England."

*Actually, Victoria had not limited herself to a concern for memorial sculpture. She was lobbying strenuously to have her Government purchase the South Kensington exhibition buildings and land, and transfer to them all the national collections of science and art, to create what skeptics called an "Albertopolis." The first votes in the Commons went against it as impractical.

That prolonging her bereavement was a form of queenly selfishness cannot have escaped Victoria. Her ladies, living as if in a mausoleum, emerged only when in an "out of waiting" cycle. One favorite, Lady Augusta Bruce, sister of General Robert Bruce, who had been Bertie's governor until his death in 1862, escaped altogether by marrying—"most unnecessarily," Victoria complained to Leopold. In November 1863, Augusta was forty-one and her husband, the Dean at Windsor, the Reverend Arthur Stanley, was forty-five. "It has been my greatest sorrow and trial since my misfortune!" the Queen wrote. "I thought she would never leave me!" Dr. Stanley had waited cautiously until after being elevated by the Queen to be Dean of Westminster, and Lady Augusta lived in the certainty of royal reproaches once the news became public. Yet after Victoria had mailed her outburst to Leopold, she thought better of it, going herself to Lady Augusta's sitting room and discussing the sudden change, confessing that she had not suspected a romance even when she saw two photographs of Dr. Stanley in Lady Augusta's collection the previous summer. She would be even more insensitive later, when she managed to delay for three years the marriage of Henry Ponsonby's son Frederick, an equerry, on the ground that a man "always tells his own wife everything," and the Queen's "private affairs would get known all over London."

On November 18, 1863, Gladstone wrote hopefully to his wife after seeing the Queen that he thought he had detected "the old voice of business." But Victoria would not focus on business very long, and the Chancellor of the Exchequer had forgotten his wife's warning in October 1862, as he was about to set off for Windsor, "Now, contrary to your ways, do *pet* the Queen, and for once believe you can, you dear old thing." He could not or would not, and managed to separate himself from her view of the world on every occasion. A Liberal Member's proposal to lower the voting qualification in towns came up in the House in May 1864, after Gladstone had been forewarned by his Prime Minister, Palmerston, not to commit the Government, since the bill had little chance. The impulsive Gladstone did so anyway, feeling that it was time to enfranchise the better educated of the working class. "I venture to say," he told the Commons sweepingly, "that every man who is not presumably incapacitated by some consideration of personal unfitness or of political danger, is mortally entitled to come within the pale of the Constitution." The bill (a highly reasonable one in retrospect) lost by 272 votes to 56, but it added to the Queen's reasons for not trusting Gladstone.

With her entrance into a third year of mourning, in December 1863, newspapers in London began a campaign to draw Victoria back into public life. She had long before exhausted her Hanoverian exemption from traditional English stoicism and reserve. Censuring her conduct more boldly than ever, the press observed that one may be grief-stricken, but that did not mean that one must not get on with one's job, and do it as well and as conscientiously as ever.

There were many matters that, but for her insistence upon sorrow, might have claimed her public or private attention. Affairs in Austrian Italy and along the Prussian-Danish border were precarious, civil war in America continued its impact upon English textile unemployment, and Cabinet divisions were regularly aired in the press, creating an impression of drift. The opening of Parliament was again approaching, and seemed the natural occasion for the Queen to reappear. To make it clear that she had no intention of doing so, the Queen instructed Sir Charles Phipps to write to the Prime Minister explaining that her Majesty's physicians, "after consultation, are very decidedly of opinion that, with a due regard to the preservation of her Majesty's health, it would be undesirable that her Majesty should undertake such duties."

On that unhelpful note, the old year of 1863 effectively closed for the Queen, but the new year had hardly begun when she found herself forced to warn the Foreign Minister, Earl Russell, not to support Denmark over the Schleswig-Holstein issue. The duchies, one of which, Holstein, was a member of the German Confederation although under Danish rule, were largely German in population, although part of Schleswig was Danish. The succession of Christian IX—Alexandra's father—complicated a settlement. There were too many parties, too many treaties, too many interpretations. In Palmerston's epigram (there were several versions) only three men in England had ever understood the Schleswig-Holstein question: the Prince Consort, who was dead; Mellish, a clerk in the Foreign Office who had gone mad; and Palmerston himself, who had forgotten it.

With tiny Denmark suicidally stubborn and apparently unwilling to compromise, war became certain. Pro-German as always, Victoria hardly wanted to be drawn into a war on the other side, yet she was now at odds with the public as well as with Marlborough House. Amidst the anxiety, Alexandra, pregnant with her first child, gave birth prematurely on January 8, at Frogmore. The Queen, years later, recalled hurrying across from Osborne to find "that poor little bit of a thing, wrapped in cotton!"

To the nation's happiness, the "bit of a thing" was a boy; but what he would be called immediately became a political question. One name he would bear was that of his embattled grandfather, King Christian of Denmark; however, his first names were announced as Albert Victor. From the beginning he was "Eddy," although the Queen tried to remind his parents at every opportunity of his legitimate name. At his baptism on March 10, the chorale by Prince Albert, to words by Thomas Oliphant, "Praise the Lord with heart and voice," was sung at Victoria's request.

The business of names prompted the Queen to lecture Bertie on his own future name as king. It had been his father's wish, she reminded him, that he be called by both his names, as Albert Edward, "and it would be *impossible* for you to *drop* your Father's." Bertie observed pointedly that no English sovereign had ever borne two names, and he found that Louis Napoleon and Victor Emmanuel were unpleasant contemporary combinations; yet he saw "no absolute reason" to preclude the use of a double name. The Queen must have known that she had already lost.

"Oh!" the Queen wrote to Vicky in February 1864, after Prussian and Austrian troops had crossed into the duchies, "if Bertie's wife was only a good German and not a Dane!" The "harmony in the family" had further disappeared. "It is terrible to have the poor boy on the wrong side, and aggravates my sufferings greatly." At Marlborough House, the Princess of Wales wept as her country was overrun, and Denmark was forced to give up claims to Schleswig and Holstein.

With fears in England high that underdog Denmark itself, however guilty of illegally annexing Schleswig, might be swallowed up by Prussia, Palmerston and Russell were ready to go with public opinion and send the navy to protect Copenhagen. Victoria had to use all her resources as Queen to keep her country neutral—which, in effect, meant condoning the absorption of the duchies by the victors. Whatever her reasons or her sympathies, her commonsense logic as expressed to John Russell in February 1864 was that a government's first interest is the nation it represents. "Lord Russell knows," she lectured him, "that she will *never,* if she can prevent it, allow this country to be involved in a war in which *no English* interests are concerned." Obstinately she pressed her Ministers to moderate their language, to return the fleet to home ports, and to deplore the conflict passively while offering only to mediate. Beyond her pro-Prussian stance she saw as a parallel Albert's holding back war with America in 1861. "I am glad darling Papa is spared this worry and annoyance," she told Vicky serenely, "for he could have done even less than I can."

Despite her withdrawal from public view, she was functioning now as Queen because she wanted to take sides. She might still mourn Albert, but she had proved to herself that she could do without him, and had upheld her activist view of the sovereign's role. There was one other thing of value she found in the brief war, as she explained to Vicky. It might have been "useful for the Emperor Napoleon to see how very well and rapidly the [German and Austrian] Allies have conducted the campaign."

With anti-German feeling running strong in England, Feodora, still then on her first long visit to her sister, and increasingly uneasy, made much of her rheumatic complaints in the damp English winter to support her decision to return home. She could not face going to breakfast with Victoria on February 10, the anniversary of her sister's wedding, and when she left after four months, she confessed in a letter, "I have not the moral strength to see you and hear you so unhappy constantly." Baden was less luxurious, but a small price to pay for being free of Victoria's self-imposed gloom.

In what seemed a deliberate affront to English feelings about the heavyhandedness of Prussia, the Queen in May permitted her son Alfred to receive the Order of the Black Eagle from King William, and was then furious at attacks on her pro-Germanism in the press. Lord Torrington, known to General Grey as a conduit to *The Times,* received a remonstrance, and replied that Prince Alfred was "aiding and approving of the King of Prussia's conduct" and "injuring" the family into which the Prince of Wales had married.

"Her Majesty sent for me this morning," Torrington wrote to Delane on May 10 on completing his last day in waiting. ". . . I never saw her in better health, spirits or looks. . . ." In a half hour's conversation she defended her relationship with Prussia as a necessity "to keep well with the adopted country of her daughter," insisted that Prussia *"will take nothing"* (which proved not to be the case), and claimed that she was "furious" about the "questionable honour" accepted by Alfred. As for going out in public, Victoria volunteered that she had gone quietly—in an unusual early-spring snow—to a flower show at the Horticultural Gardens, and had become nervous and ill from "the crowd pressing on her." Then she presented Torrington with her photograph, and expressed her regret that his current cycle as a lord-in-waiting was ending.

Since she had found the Horticultural Gardens experience too much for her, and was impatient with the clamor that she show herself more, and involve herself more in state affairs, the Queen had written a letter to *The Times* herself early in April, as most Londoners who could read quickly learned. Addressed "To the Editor of *The Times*," the writing was recognized by Delane as unmistakably that of Victoria, and not a hoax, but he prudently dropped the heading and printed it without signature on April 6 as a paragraph headed "The Court."

"An erroneous idea seems generally to prevail," it began, "and has latterly found frequent expression in the newspapers, that the Queen is about to resume the place in society which she occupied before her great affliction; that is, that she is about again to hold levees and drawing-rooms in person, and to appear as before at Court balls, concerts, &c. This idea cannot be too explicitly contradicted." The statement went on that the Queen would appear in public whenever "any real object is to be attained" by her doing so. She "will not shrink, as she has not shrunk, from any personal sacrifice or exertion, however painful," but there were "higher duties" than those of "mere representation," which would only overwhelm her with "work and anxiety"—presumably the day-to-day business of the sovereign. "More the Queen *cannot* do," she closed (anonymously, despite herself), "and more the kindness and good feeling of her people will surely not exact from her."

Clarendon (writing to his wife) contended that publication "produced a very painful impression, and is considered very *infra dig.*" Lady Palmerston told him, he added, "that Pam has made up his mind to speak to [the Queen] on the subject; but I am sure he won't." Still, she wrote no further letters to the editor, although she needed all the help she could get to arrest the shift from sympathy with her bereavement to hostility toward her refusal to be an active sovereign except in ways that went against the grain of English public opinion. Another case in the first months of 1864 had been the visit of the Italian patriot Giuseppe Garibaldi. Victoria's pro-Austrian bias set her seething privately while English aristocracy, like Palmerston, long pro-Italian, fussed over him, and even her great friend, the Duchess of Sutherland, had him as guest. Conceding that Garibaldi was "honest, disinterested & brave," she nevertheless wrote to Vicky that in London the general had associated with the "worst refugees" and most unreliable politicians, and "the whole [was] crowned by the incredible folly and impudence of your thoughtless elder brother going to see him without my knowledge!"

Unaware of the Queen's resolute role behind the scenes in manipulating her Government's reaction to the war over Schleswig-Holstein, the English public saw her still as remote and ineffective. Rather, as she told

Vicky, she had "the eyes of Argus" and was using them. Innocent of that, a London wag posted on a Buckingham Palace wall a handbill reading, "These extensive premises to be let or sold, the late occupant having retired from business." Amused, Lord Stanley wrote in his diary, "The London papers suppressed it, but there is no doubt of its having been seen. General discontent of the London tradesmen: they believe the Queen to be insane, and that she will never live in London again." A few weeks later he added that he heard it said that, largely because of her Prussian sympathies, "she does right not to show herself in public."

If one accepts the premise that intelligent people are responsible for their actions, one must concede that even in an age when ordinary privilege seemed to entitle one to a degree of selfishness, Victoria's vision of her world was pathologically limited in the years immediately following Albert's death. A measure of design may be seen in her evasion of any test of her queenly capacities. Some self-indulgent grief was easily understood, and accepted. But the refusal to reign, while accepting every regal perquisite, became unacceptable to the Queen's subjects, and her outraged reaction to that was a blindness that overwhelmed reason.

Only a few days after her letter to *The Times* was written (and soon, too, after the facetious handbill had been posted), the Queen held a reception for the diplomatic corps at Buckingham Palace. It was "a great effort for which I am very unfit," she told Vicky, writing from "beloved Papa's dressing-room—his dear dressing-table! I could not bear the silent room near me out of which he always came looking so beautiful to take me to Drawing-rooms and levees. . . ."

Later in the year *The Times* published a satiric piece, suggesting that what England needed in the usual absence of the Queen was some Court official corresponding to the *Proxenos* among the ancient Greeks, whose duty it was to entertain illustrious guests of the state. Pressed to do more, Victoria would only write her uncle in Brussels, "Pilgerstein is gouty, and extremely impertinent in his communications with me." If Leopold's memory were still acute, he would have heard echoes in her outburst of the young Victoria.

With her relations with her eldest son also strained, Victoria confided to Queen Augusta of Prussia on November 8, 1864, "Tomorrow is another bitter day: Bertie's birthday!" More than the tensions of Schleswig-Holstein were involved. The impatience of Albert Edward with his mother emerged at the time in a piece of gossip that had the mourning-garbed Queen objecting to the Prince of Wales about his continual smoking. "When Her Majesty left off her weeds," he was reported to have told a friend, "he would leave off his."

Problems with her adult children were as numerous as the children themselves. Unwilling to rely upon her elder sons—Alfred she considered immoral, selfish, and rude, while Arthur was still a boy and Leopold a semi-invalid—she felt forced to lean upon her daughters. Having made a dynastic marriage, Vicky was unavailable. Alice had gone into disfavor for enjoying society when in London and preferring Germany as a way to escape her mother's demands. Helena—"Lenchen"—wanted to be married, while Victoria wanted her at hand, a solution the Queen thought earlier she had found for Alice with Louis of Hesse. For Helena she found the impecunious and bald Christian of Schleswig-Holstein, younger brother of the unsuccessful claimant to the duchies. At thirty-nine he was, to the Queen, the "young, sensible Prince" she had in mind. Having no place to call his own, he was content to live in England, and was offered Frogmore House on his engagement to Helena in September 1865.

Affie's affairs were in disarray. He wanted to marry the daughter of his mother's cousin, King George of Hanover. "Three generations of blindness and double relationships" were enough, the Queen thought, and sent him looking further. With other minor German princesses unattractive, she pondered non-Protestant brides—the Greek church was marginally possible, but not the Roman. But Affie had his own ideas, and marriage of a sort was acceptable if it did not interfere with his affair with Constance Grosvenor—wife of the Duke of Westminster and a dozen years Affie's elder. What gave Victoria special pain was that the woman was the daughter of her good friend the Duchess of Sutherland.

Events were forcing Victoria out of utter seclusion, and in the winter of 1864–1865 some changes seemed in process, although she again refused to be present at the opening of Parliament, pleading "shattered nerves" and "great fatigue." Without a husband to guide and comfort her, she told Lord Russell, she had become "weaker and weaker." But at Windsor she had begun riding again, on a pony, and—she explained to her uncle Leopold—she had "appointed that excellent Highland servant of mine to attend me always and everywhere out of doors, whether riding or driving or on foot; and it is a real comfort, for he is so devoted to me—so simple, so intelligent, so unlike an ordinary servant, and so cheerful and attentive. . . ." If John Brown's translation from Balmoral had been a Court conspiracy to draw her out, it was at least partially successful. Brown had a way with her, and was forceful and positive. His role would enlarge. But

"Queen Hermione"—
Punch's *caption has Paulina
(Britannia) urge Victoria,
from* The Winter's Tale,
*" 'Tis time! Descend; be
stone no more." September
23, 1865.*

even as she reopened her windows wider into the world, she sought reasons to keep the wound from healing over. "I have been daily on my pony," she wrote to Vicky from Osborne in the spring of 1865, "wandering quietly among the splendid fresh, green foliage which is now very forward, . . . the birds singing—all lovely but all bereft of joy, for he is not on earth to enjoy it with me as he once did. . . . It is the return home with that silent room nearby, and fagged to death with work, which is fearful indeed!"

Again, early in 1865, the Queen held her Buckingham Palace reception for the diplomatic corps—"a hundred of them, with attachés," she wrote Queen Augusta. It was "a great bore." The Queen had appeared as usual in the simple widow's black that would keep her frozen in the fashion of 1861. "My dress is always the same," she told Vicky. "as it is the dress which I have adopted for ever, for mine. The only difference was that I had a train to the dress and a very long veil to my cap, which was trimmed with large diamonds. . . ."

The next month saw the end of the civil war in America, and the death by assassination of President Abraham Lincoln, after which the Queen wrote a letter of sympathy to Mrs. Lincoln. Still withdrawn into her own private grief, Victoria is unlikely to have written without prompting, however much one might like to think so, and indeed the letter followed a message from the Foreign Minister, Earl Russell, urging "that a very good effect would be produced in conciliating the feelings of the United States" if the Queen sent a private letter to Mary Todd Lincoln. For Victoria, the sentiments were easy to describe. "No one can better appreciate than I can, who am myself utterly broken-hearted by the loss of my own beloved husband, who was the light of my life, . . . what your sufferings must be."

That June, Alexandra again gave birth prematurely to a boy, to be christened George Frederick Ernest Albert, and Victoria was unhappy, she told Bertie, with the Hanoverian name *George*. "However if the dear child grows up good and wise, I shall not mind what his name is." The significance of the shift in temperament was enormous. The Queen was indeed coming out, if ever so slowly, from the consequences of the self-imposed long mourning.

Other factors were to push her further. On the Prince Consort's birthday in 1865 she returned to Coburg for the unveiling of a ten-foot-high gilded bronze statue by William Theed in the *Markt.* Rather than do so in a drab ceremony, as earlier ones had been, the Queen went in procession, and the horses and postillions of her four carriages wore the scarlet and gold Ascot livery for the first time since Albert's death. "I was anxious for *this* day," she wrote in her journal, "to do all possible honour to my beloved's memory. The guns were fired from the fortress, and the bells rung, in the peculiar German way, so different from ours. . . . The Ober Bürgomeister read an Address, the signal was given, and . . . the drapery fell away from the statue, which stood there, in all its beauty, so sad and grand. Another salute was fired, and again [the] beating of drums and ringing of bells. An indescribable moment. . . ."

Later, Victoria told Gathorne-Hardy that the feats of the notorious "boy Jones" at Buckingham Palace in her early years as Queen would have been easy in the rustic backwardness of Coburg, as there "a petitioner from the streets" was able to knock at her dressing-room door. As private as she insisted on being in England, the incident amused her; yet she stage-managed her return to avoid being seen. The press objected, and a column in the *Pall Mall Gazette* on the secrecy was reprinted in *The Times* next to a paragraph on the public landing of the Prince of Wales, under the joint heading, "A Contrast." For the Queen, Sir Charles Grey fired off a protest. She would reemerge in her own fashion, and in her own time; but events were pressing her. Refusing to publish it, Delane wrote,

"It is only as a loyal subject, not as a journalist, that I make this suggestion, for of course such a communication would be very acceptable to any newspaper." The next month, on October 18, Lord Palmerston died— "that strong determined man," Victoria noted in her journal. "He had often worried and distressed us, though as Prime Minister he had behaved very well. To think that he is removed from this world, and I alone, without dearest Albert to talk to or consult with!"

Despite her differences with him, she had confidence in Palmerston's decisiveness. His inevitable replacement was Earl Russell, who carried on the titular direction of the new administration from the Lords, while the able Clarendon returned to the Foreign Office. In the Commons, Gladstone and the more elitist Sir Robert Lowe contended for power. Victoria knew that the Russell regime could not last, and that she would have to be more involved. "Poor Lord Russell," she wrote to Leopold; "to begin at his age afresh, after thirteen years . . . is very trying."

Very soon after this, it was Leopold's turn to follow Palmerston out of her history. When he died, early in December, all the old props were gone, and she knew it was time to return to life herself. She had already completed a further act of exorcism by compiling from her journals, to be printed privately, *Leaves from the Journal of Our Life in the Highlands,* her way of reliving the happiest years with Albert. In the month of Leopold's death she sent copies to her children, who were uniformly appalled by its artless candor. The Queen could not understand their failure to applaud it. Yet it had done its job. Although Russell appealed to her in his own weakness that he needed her now to open Parliament in February, she described what he asked her to "go through" as akin to an "execution." Did he really want, she questioned, to have the public "witness the spectacle of a poor, broken-hearted widow, nervous and shrinking, dragged in deep mourning, alone in State as a Show . . . ?" If she disliked a subject, Clarendon told Lord Stanley on December 8, 1865, she would say "it made her ill" to talk about it, or only that she "did not wish to have it discussed." It was not insanity, he concluded, but only "extreme wilfulness and want of self-restraint." Stanley asked whether she had grown better or worse, and Clarendon concluded that there had been little change. Albert had once said to him, he recalled, "It is my business to watch that mind every hour and minute—to watch as a cat watches at a mousehole." Now there was no one to do that, Clarendon thought, and "the constant effort had worn Albert out." Sometimes the Queen received more sympathy than that, and from unexpected quarters. Radical commoners, she discovered, could be gentlemen. At a Reform meeting in 1866, John Bright, the Radical M.P., declared, "I am not accustomed to stand up in defence of those who are possessors of crowns; but I could not sit here and hear that observation [disparaging the Queen] without a sensation of wonder and pain. I think there has been . . . a great injustice done . . . in reference to her desolate and widowed position. And I venture to say this, that a woman—be she the Queen of a great realm, or be she the wife of one of your labouring men—who can keep alive in her heart a great sorrow for the lost object of her life and affection, is not at all likely to be wanting in a great and generous sympathy with you." Victoria never forgot his courtly intervention at a time when "ignorant and unfeeling people attacked her for not going out in the world."

For the first three years, the Queen had confessed to the Princess Royal, the longing to be reunited in death with Albert never left her. Then she told Vicky many years later, when her daughter had herself been widowed and felt death preferable to further life, she had her only experience of "visitation" and was profoundly moved. "I too wanted once to put an end to my life *here,* but a voice told me for *His* sake—no, 'Still Endure.'" As she had confided to Vicky in 1867, "God in mercy willed it so! I was to live. . . ." "Still Endure" became her motto. There is no clue in the journals as they survive as to when the episode occurred, but it seems clear that it had already happened before she chose to make the painful effort, for her, of opening Parliament.

On February 6, 1866, wearing her widow's cap, but with a small diamond-and-sapphire coronet at the back, and a long flowing tulle veil, she set out in her carriage "alone"—a "fearful moment" even though bands played and crowds cheered. "Alone" meant without the Prince; opposite her in the carriage—she had refused the State Coach—were Princesses Helena and Louise. Despite a high wind and the February chill, she stubbornly insisted on having the windows on both sides open: she would be seen. When she entered the crowded House in her widow's black, she felt faint, but took her seat, now truly alone, over a throne draped with the Robes of State she refused to wear, and stared rigidly ahead while the Lord Chancellor read "her" speech. When the "ordeal" —exacerbated in every way by her handling of it—was over, she professed thanks for having been able to get through it, and felt "terribly shaken, exhausted, and unwell from the violent *nervous* shock." Her virtual seclusion was far from over, but she had passed a personal test.

XII

Victoria Adrift

(1866–1872)

Despite acts of apparent exorcism, Victoria seemed determined to keep Albert's loss an unhealed and suppurating wound. However much family matters and affairs of state intruded, nothing diverted her from memorializing the Prince Consort and relentlessly invoking his name. There would be pictures and busts and statues, and a book of his public addresses. Further, there would be an "Albertopolis" of sorts in Kensington to continue his interests in science and industry and the arts. Also, there had to be a biography, and she understood that the first to appear would set a pattern for others. What, then, but to write it herself?

She had her own journals as well as Albert's, and copies as well as originals of many of his letters. While she felt that she could not write about their married lives, why not an *Early Years of the Prince Consort?* At first her assistant was Princess Helena, who translated all the German letters. Then Victoria brought her manuscript to General Sir Charles Grey, her principal secretary, and asked him to see it through to publication. Once Albert's private secretary, Grey would become officially the Queen's, having operated in that capacity under subterfuge titles because Palmerston's government had refused to recognize Victoria's needs in the vacuum left by Albert. Sir Charles found it difficult to refuse; yet when he read her memoir, he found it so candid and guileless that he worried about letting it loose. Although the Queen was artless in the sense of writing without artifice, she was also artless in her simplicity and innocence. Cautiously, then, Grey suggested restricting readership to intimates. "As I believe your Majesty intends to limit the circulation of this volume to your Majesty's own children and family or, if it goes beyond them, to a very small circle of intimate friends, I have not thought it necessary to omit any of the very interesting and private details contained in your Majesty's memoranda, or to withhold the touching expressions of your Majesty's feelings as given in your Majesty's own words. Some of these details, particularly those relating to your Majesty's marriage, it might seem unusual to include in a work intended for more general perusal, though even in that case, judging of others' feelings by my own, I cannot doubt that they would meet with the warmest and most heartfelt sympathy."

Grey's preface to the private printing suggested that he had received only "Letters and Memoranda" which he had "arranged and connected" for the Queen. Yet his specifics hinted that he had been more editor than writer, but for connective tissue; and his request to have a higher historical authority review the contents—Professor Adam Sedgwick, who had been secretary to Albert as Chancellor of Cambridge University—adds weight to the likelihood that his substantive role was small. Protecting his flanks, Grey published Sedgwick's letter to him along with his own preface for the edition released by Smith, Elder in the summer of 1867. The book, if made public, Sedgwick wrote, intimating further Victoria's central role in its writing, "would exalt the love and loyalty of all true-hearted Englishmen. Where everything is so lovely, and so true, why should not our honoured and beloved Queen lay open the innermost recesses of her heart, and thereby fix for ever the loyal sympathy of all who have faith in what is good?" Such a work was clearly not General Grey's, but the title page identified it as "compiled" by him "under the direction of Her Majesty the Queen," with only explanatory footnotes credited to Victoria.

No sovereign had so communicated with the public. The Highlands extracts were still circulating privately, as Grey also wanted to limit the Albert book, but both would escape into a wider readership. Spurred to do even more for Albert's reputation, and her own needs, Victoria called in Theodore Martin, a Tory journalist recommended to her by Sir Arthur Helps, and commissioned a multivolume official biography. With her usual innocent honesty, she offered him all of Albert's and her own correspondence with each other, and both of their journals, with the result that we have, in the extracts published from the Queen's own diaries, almost the only assuredly genuine text to survive the holocaust arranged by her executrix. However accurate Princess Beatrice's text or the pre-1862 typescript arranged for by Edward VII, only the material furnished to Martin (and a later 1892 pair of extracts that Victoria copied herself) preserved words that are unquestionably the Queen's own.

A morocco-bound presentation copy went to Duleep Singh, now thirty-one, "in recollection of former days from his affectionate and faithful friend." "Former days" suggested Albertine times, but also that his extravagance and misconduct had separated him from his surrogate mother. She had sufficient wayward children of her own.

Cherishing her mourning, Victoria commissioned art by which she could reflect further upon her widowhood. She had a photograph taken of all her children and herself, gathered about a bust of the Prince Consort; she then had Albert Graefle paint her, in 1864, sitting, chin in hand, contemplating the "dear, dear, protecting head" of Albert. Five years later she tried to buy the first successful picture of the social realist painter Frank Holl, *The Lord Gave and the Lord Hath Taken Away*, portraying a bereaved fisherman's family praying at the cottage table. She was too late, but in 1870, the next year, he exhibited *No Tidings from the Sea*, in which the central figure is a kneeling Northumberland widow, her bewildered children clutching at a black-clad older woman, apparently their grandmother and the dead fisherman's mother. Its emotional appeal was even stronger for the Queen. She bought it.

The Queen's opening Parliament for the first time since Albert's death had little to do with her emergence from mourning or any revived interest in reigning. With Prince Alfred about to come of age, and two daughters soon to be married, Victoria needed Parliamentary majorities for Alfred's annuity and her daughters' dowries. The mood in the Commons would be surly, as her perverse manner of executing the traditional duties suggested no prospect of change. When it came to performing her family duties, however, a tough matriarch emerged in place of the shattered widow. At the request of the Queen, Princess Helena wrote to Lady Augusta, now the wife of Dean Stanley, to inquire indirectly of the dean whether there was any "actual *bar* against" Victoria's walking to the altar with her and giving the bride away. "She says she is the Sovereign and does the work of a man . . . , she does not see why she cd. not do it as well as she sits on the throne and does so many things wh. a man does. . . ."

In other respects, the Queen's enthusiasm for public appearances was minimal, but political pressures required a visit to Aldershot, from whence Albert had returned to take to his bed for the last time. She had once vowed "never" to go there again. She also held two spring garden parties at Buckingham Palace, finding the crowds "alarming," and she went on inspections of the London Zoo, the Royal Academy annual, and the South Kensington Museum. With unemployment and electoral reform likely to bring down Russell's Liberals, Victoria could not chance her usual May escape to Balmoral. Instead she accepted the loan of Cliveden, "within easy reach of my Ministers." She took with her an entourage of ninety-one, including three doctors, but pined for Balmoral, and after rationalizing to herself that it had never been an "inconvenience" to the Government to have her in the Highlands, she ordered the royal train north on June 14. It was as if she were trying to put more distance between herself and the war between Prussia and Austria that she had long feared, and that had now materialized.

Under the guise of national unification, and emboldened by his easy Danish success, Otto von Bismarck had been plotting the absorption of the minor German states into Prussia. Austria's removal as nominal head of the German Confederation was a prerequisite, and the Prussian chancellor was willing to hasten that by bullying, or to compel it by war. It was an inopportune time for Princess Louise, who seldom held her tongue, to respond with what she thought was wit to her sister Vicky's request from Potsdam for wedding-gift ideas for Helena. "Lenchen" was to marry the portionless Prince Christian of Schleswig-Holstein-Sonderburg-Augustenburg on July 5. "Bismarck's head on a charger" (platter), Louise suggested. Paranoid Prussia was swollen with spies and sellers of information, and Bismarck's agents at Court arranged that he see Louise's tart reply, thereby prejudicing Victoria's appeals to the King. "Beloved Brother," she had written to him in the approved style on April 10, "at this fearful moment I cannot be silent. . . . You are deceived . . . by *one man. . . .*" That one man, however, guided a royal reply that gave Victoria no comfort.

Had the Queen received, rather than written, the letter to William, she might have resented the meddling in her nation's internal affairs, but war in Europe loomed as a personal agony. She had already watched her children take opposing sides in the Prussian-Danish conflict. Now her beloved Albert's dreams of German union under a peaceable Prussia seemed dead. When war came, Victoria proved helpless. Her cousin, the blind George V of Hanover, Cumberland's son, was forced to choose between his throne and his life. Married to a German prince and a German princeling, Victoria's daughters across the North Sea found themselves each other's enemies. The Princess Royal saw her husband go off to command troops for the detested Bismarck. Alice, just delivered of a third daughter at Darmstadt, had no idea where her husband, with a pro-Austrian regiment from Hesse, had gone.

English public opinion labeled Victoria a Prussian sympathizer, and other troubles followed her to Scotland. While Fritz was away, putting Austrians and their allies to rout, Vicky's favorite son, Sigismund, died. At home, Earl Russell withdrew after an eleven-vote defeat in the Commons. In a futile gesture, the Queen refused to accept his resignation on grounds of the closeness of the division. Declining to come south on grounds of ill health, she dictated to Jenner a message of dubious medical sense, which he supinely sent to London. (Sometimes he used his Harley Street letterhead for statements about the Queen's condition that were her own self-diagnoses; sometimes Victoria used General Grey to claim less technical disabilities, such as her being "entirely prostrated by one of her worst headaches.") Even so, the Queen had to return to Windsor late in June while the Earl of Derby struggled to form, with Disraeli, a Tory Ministry.

By then the seven weeks' war was establishing Prussian mastery in central Europe, and adding to its domains Hanover, parts of Hesse, and other principalities that had taken Austria's side or imprudently remained neutral. In Prussia, Fritz was a hero, and Vicky's emotions were mixed. In England, a refugee from defeated Hesse, Alice had established herself at Windsor with her daughters. Victoria told her journal that she wanted no more warring sons-in-law, but husbands for royal princesses were in short supply.

Popular attention in England returned to electoral reform, and a protest mob flooded Hyde Park. Soon the Queen was recommending "wretched Reform" to the Tories. What she wanted was less trouble, and another flight out of the London heat. The swearing-in of the new Government, with Disraeli as Chancellor of the Exchequer and Leader in the Commons, took place on July 5, 1866, at Windsor, the same day that news came that Austria, its army shattered at Sadowa, had asked for an armistice, and the wedding day, as well, of Helena and the balding—but available—Prince Christian.

Curiously, given Victoria's distrust of her elder sons, the Prince of Wales and the Duke of Edinburgh, on hand for the wedding, were also at the swearing-in, perhaps as queenly window dressing. An extra dash of royal decor, however, was her usual preface to asking Parliament for something, and to the new Ministry she quickly dispatched a request for supplementary funds to the £50,000 voted in 1863 for gunmetal (bronze) for Albert's statue—the Albert Memorial—in Kensington Gardens. To Gladstone, now the key member of the Opposition, Grey conveyed the Queen's request for support from the Liberals, and Gladstone tactlessly responded that his principle was never "to ask money . . . for a particular work without intimating that more will be required, and then to ask for more for the same purpose." On principle, and for a cheeseparing sum, he preferred to vex the Queen, and his grizzling sidewhiskers shook with moral indignation in the House debate. Yet he knew he would someday be her First Minister and have to work with her. Disraeli had no difficulty finding the votes, and on July 26, the day after approval in the Commons, he received a warm letter from the Queen thanking him for his appreciation of "her dear, great husband." In his diary, Disraeli's associate Lord Stanley—Derby's son—had written, "Like all women, [Victoria] has a kind of instinct that tells her who are the persons on whom she can exercise a personal influence."

The new Government's position began eroding almost as soon as it took office, its paper-thin majority losing twenty-six seats in the next Commons. Heedless of the volatility of politics, the Queen had left immediately for Osborne, and in August had gone on at her usual time to Balmoral. She saw Gladstone, however, the day after the Liberals had posted their gain, and appeared strained in confronting him. With more electoral erosion, he would be her Prime Minister, and Gladstone assumed that it was the inevitability of clashing with his rigid politics that was disturbing her. If so, that attitude would have been apparent earlier, and regularly, in their relations. "She looked very well, and was kind," Gladstone wrote, "but in all her conversations with me she is evidently hemmed in, stops at a certain point, & keeps back the thought which occurs." There is no way of knowing when, if ever, the Queen became aware of Gladstone's sexual obsessions, which, even in an age of repressed yet rampant sexuality, scandalized those of his contemporaries in high places who knew of them, including her confidant, Lord Clarendon. It seems inescapable that Gladstone's "prophylactic office of accosting prostitutes" contributed to the permanent chill in his relations with Victoria, and to her increasing reliance upon his political and emotional opposite, Disraeli.

As 1867 began, it was obvious that the ailing Derby, increasingly incapacitated by gout, could not continue much longer as Prime Minister, and that only his reluctance to depart was delaying the elevation of Disraeli. One of Derby's last personal decisions was to give to the Queen, officially, a Private Secretary, and to General Grey a title recognizing his functions, which also included the Privy Purse. Ironically, one of Grey's first messages to Victoria in his titular office was to inform her, "Mr. D'Israeli is evidently the directing mind of the Ministry."

Even on good days, the often bedridden Derby had to be carried up and down the stairs in London and at his country seat at Knowsley. As his deputy, Disraeli began to contend with letters from Dr. Jenner warning of the state of the Queen's nerves, which precluded almost everything except what she wanted to do. Thus, the previous November she had gone to Wolverhampton, accompanied by Helena and Louise, to unveil an equestrian statue of the Prince Consort by Thomas Thornycroft. Since Wolverhampton was the first English community to honor Albert's memory, Victoria decided, to the surprise of its mayor, John Morris, to confer upon him a knighthood. Other cities might take notice. Given the reason, it was no surprise when, on May 20, 1867, the Queen went to London to lay the first stone of the Royal Albert Hall, on the southern edge of Hyde Park—on land, she reminded the audience, purchased out of the profits of the Great Exhibition. "I have been sustained," she said, "by the thought that I should assist by my presence in promoting the accomplishment of his great designs." A performance of "L'Invocazione all'Armonia" for chorus and orchestra, by Prince Albert, followed the lowering of the block of granite into place.

At Windsor on June 30, 1867, Lord Stanley found the Queen, at dinner, "in the best of humours, very large, ruddy, and fat (the tendency increases rapidly) but complaining of her health, saying the work she has to do is too much for her, that she is almost knocked up—and so forth."

The Duchess of Kent and the Princess Victoria *(1821). Engraving from a painting by William Beechey.*

The Queen's First Council. *Engraving of inset from the painting by David Wilkie.*
Although Victoria was in mourning black, Wilkie chose white to contrast her with the
men.

The Queen's Coronation *(1838). Engraving from a painting by Sir George Hayter at Windsor.*

OPPOSITE: The Marriage of the Queen to Prince Albert *(1840). Engraving from a painting by Sir George Hayter.*

LEFT: The Queen and the Prince of Wales *(ca. 1844). Engraving from the miniature by Robert Thorburn at Windsor.* COLLECTION OF THE AUTHOR

BELOW: *Queen Victoria with Victoria, Princess Royal (ca. 1844–1845). Early photograph.*

RIGHT: *Queen Victoria and Prince Albert, 1861. Photographed by John Mayall.*

BELOW: *Queen Victoria and Prince Albert, Buckingham Palace, June 30, 1854. Photographed by Roger Fenton.*

OPPOSITE TOP: *The Royal Family at Osborne, May 1857. Photographed by Caldesi & Co. With the birth of Princess Beatrice, in the Queen's arms, the family was now complete.*

OPPOSITE BOTTOM RIGHT: *"I go skating every day on the pond at Frogmore." Colored lithograph, 1840.*

OPPOSITE BOTTOM LEFT: The Royal Family at Home. *Lithograph, 1843.*

ROYAL ARCHIVES, WINDSOR

ROYAL ARCHIVES, WINDSOR

The Queen and Her Family. *Engraving from* The Marriage of the Princess Royal *(1858), by John Philip, at Windsor. Albert is on the far left, the Princess Royal on the far right. Prominent in the background is the Duchess of Kent.*

ABOVE LEFT: *Victoria with Princess Louise and John Brown at Osborne House, 1865. Photographed by C. Jabez Hughes.*

ABOVE RIGHT: *Queen Victoria with John Brown, 1863. Photograph taken at Balmoral by George Wilson.*

An artist's conception of the death of Prince Albert, December 1861. The artist may have been Octavius Oakley, but attribution is uncertain. Photograph of a reproduction of the original.

ABOVE: *Four Victorian prime ministers. Clockwise, from top left: William Ewart Gladstone, painted by John Millais; William Lamb, second Viscount Melbourne, painted by John Partridge; Benjamin Disraeli, Earl of Beaconsfield, painted by John Millais; Sir Robert Peel, painted by John Linnell.* NATIONAL PORTRAIT GALLERY

OPPOSITE: *Queen Victoria, in 1885. Photographed by Alexander Bassano.*

RIGHT: *The future Kaiser Wilhelm II as a prince in his early twenties (ca. 1880–1881). His useless left arm is shorter, and the hand discreetly gloved.*

BELOW: *Lower Regent Street at Piccadilly Circus, decorated for the Golden Jubilee, June 1887. Photo by Yorke & Co., London.*

OPPOSITE: The Diamond Jubilee Procession. *Victoria arriving at St. Paul's. Painting by A. J. Gow, 1897.*

VICTORIA
ALL NATIONS SALUTE YOU

LEFT: *The Queen on the Riviera: "A Cimiez. Promenade matinale. Her Majesty the Queen Empress." Guth in the Diamond Jubilee number of* Vanity Fair, *June 17, 1897.*

BELOW: *The Queen and her* Munshi *listening to a dispatch being read by Sir Arthur Bigge, 1896. The* Munshi, *who was far more corpulent by then, is idealized. From an engraving of a watercolor by J. Begg, Windsor Castle.*

OPPOSITE: *Four generations of monarchs: Victoria; the future Edward VII, at left; the future George V, Edward's surviving son, at right; and the future Edward VIII in Victoria's arms (1894).*

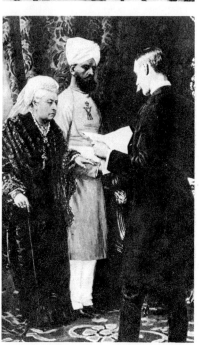

L'ULTIMATUM DU TRANSVAAL.

Président Krüger. — Non, je ne me laisserai pas embobiner.

Le seul vrai Bitter anglais est celui que l'Angleterre reçoit d'Afrique.

ABOVE: *Queen Victoria in old age, wearing glasses and reading a document.* ROYAL ARCHIVES, WINDSOR

OPPOSITE TOP: *The ultimatum from the Transvaal. The Queen is about to have a bomb—the Boer War—set off in her face by "Oom Paul" Kruger. From* Rumoristische Blätter, *Vienna, October 15, 1899.*

OPPOSITE BOTTOM: *The Queen drinks "Ladysmith" bitter after reading a sad account of her nation's military exploits in South Africa. From* Kikerik, *Vienna, November 30, 1899.*

RIGHT: *The funeral procession of the Queen in the Windsor streets, February 2, 1901. Sailors draw the gun carriage with Victoria's small coffin. Behind walk King Edward VII (center), Kaiser Wilhelm II (on Edward's right), and the Duke of Connaught (to Edward's left). Photo by Bender and Lewis, Croydon.*

BELOW: *Effigy of the Queen by Baron Carlo Marochetti for the Royal Mausoleum, Frogmore, Windsor.*

The royal robes on the empty throne, in a contemporary engraving.

WHERE IS BRITANNIA ?

She did work at her red boxes of state and personal business, and may have thought that what she saw was the actual volume of government paperwork. More likely she knew better, but, even so, saw such complaints as useful strategy. Dr. Jenner cautioned regularly that "any strong excitement" produced (as Lord Stanley quoted him) "fits of bilious sickness" —attacks of nervous vomiting—"and if Nature did not provide this relief the effect on her mind might be dangerous." Victoria had found a dramatic way to evade the unwanted.

That summer the Queen resisted the visit of the Sultan of Turkey, Abdul Aziz, then grudgingly agreed to receive him at Windsor (it meant delaying her holiday at Osborne), and again aboard the *Victoria and Albert* at a naval review arranged for him at Spithead. To Derby she complained once more of "the want of consideration shown . . . for her health and strength," which she foresaw would lead "ere long" to a *"complete breakdown* of her nervous system." Empty ceremony was expendable, she reminded him, since she conducted all the necessary business of her office, "working and drudging . . . from *morning* till *night,* and weighed down by the responsibility and cares of her most unenviable position, and with the anxieties consequent upon being the widowed mother of so large a family. Often has she wished that the time might come when she could go to that world 'where the wicked cease from troubling and the weary are at rest.' "

In the heavy swells off Spithead, the seasick Sultan, Victoria wrote, "was continually retiring below, and can have seen very little." But she did invest him with the Garter, borrowing the insignia from Prince Arthur and Prince Louis of Hesse, after which Abdul Aziz returned to Turkey, having cost the government £8,922 14s. 10s., his entourage having been very hard on the Buckingham Palace furniture.

Her next visitor, more willingly received, was Empress Eugénie, whom the Queen had not seen since Albert's death. The Empress, whose relationship with her husband was now only a public one, was as much in need of consolation as the Queen. "Greatly relieved the visit was over," Victoria wrote afterwards.

Balmoral in August was a different matter. She would not have her seclusion there marred by any foreign dignitary, however elevated. The Czar, who had entertained the Prince of Wales the previous autumn, and was then in Paris awaiting an expected invitation from Victoria, was not welcome. Derby suggested that at least she send the Czar the Garter, with a graceful letter in her own hand regretting that her absence from London made an invitation impossible. "The Queen," she replied, rejecting in advance any ideas for further ceremonial visits, "is UTTERLY *incapable* of entertaining any Royal personage as she would *wish* to do, except those who are very nearly related to her, and for whom she need not alter her mode of life." Then she entrained north, and Gathorne-Hardy found her at Balmoral "looking very well and exceedingly merry." She had arrived after stopovers in the Border Country, and found new cause for sadness in having made the visits (her daughters notwithstanding) "alone." As guest of the Duke of Roxburghe on August 21 she had been shown to her rooms by the Duchess, and found her sitting room, dressing room, and bedroom "elegant, nice and comfortable. . . . But the feeling of loneliness when I saw no room for my darling, and felt I was indeed alone and a widow, overcame me very sadly! It was the first time I had gone in this way on a visit (like as in former times), and I thought so much of all dearest Albert would have done and said and how he would have wandered about everywhere, admired everything, looked at everything—and now! Oh! must it ever, ever be so?"

Reports arriving at Balmoral early in September warned that Fenians were plotting to seize or murder the Queen. In the isolated Valley of the Dee, such warnings were not taken seriously. Victoria went off on her usual expeditions, roughing it in her comfortable style, but taking a day to unveil Theed's bronze statue of Albert in Balmoral attire, one hand holding a gun, the other on the head of a hunting dog. In "pelting rain," the prayers and speeches were abbreviated.

On September 18 came news of the capture of Thomas Kelly, the Fenian leader, at Manchester. By evening, as Gathorne-Hardy was planning to tell Victoria the good news at dinner, a telegram arrived with news that an armed Irish mob (actually five men) had shot Kelly's captors and rescued him. "The Queen took it calmly." The next day came another inaccurate telegram: "I sent [it] in to the Queen. They had arrested 29 of the rescuers at Manchester & one [was the man] who shot the police-man who was killed. . . . No news of the reapprehension of Kelly." On September 22, a Sunday, after lunch with Victoria, he had a long talk with her about her safety. She was "very gracious & cheerful. She spoke of Fenians—(did not approve of more mercy) more care in [selecting] detec-tives . . . and the attacks upon her [,] dwelling most on the blow on her head the mark of which she said remained for ten years. Firearms she had not minded as if they missed there was nothing to trouble you & a moving carriage prevented a good aim."

It was "too foolish!" to ring Balmoral with troops, she told General Grey. Nevertheless she consented, although to her it implied distrust of her Highlanders. That the Scots were "so loyal" under English rule while the Irish remained irreconcilable baffled the Queen, but she would not be soft. Three of the suspects captured at Manchester were hanged on November 29 for complicity in the murder of the policeman. Although the radical press had labeled them "Manchester Martyrs," the Queen had written to Vicky, "We shall have to hang some, & it ought to have been done before." Yet on the day of their execution, Victoria "prayed for these poor men."

Despite the concerns of the Home Secretary, when the Queen was driven about by John Brown at Balmoral and later at Osborne, she refused to permit an equerry to be in attendance. Since a Fenian attack remained a possibility, Lord Stanley noted in his diary, "she is followed in these drives by two of the suite, who keep at a distance, and are armed with revolvers." With Derby ailing and away, Disraeli and the Cabinet met in December to review stories and rumors received from informers about Irish plots, Stanley reported wildly on the seventeenth. "One informant speaks of 155 Fenian and republican clubs in London alone, all unknown to the police. Several announce projects for blowing up the Houses of Parlt, and assassinating the Queen. Another reported plan is to seize the P. of W. on his way to or from Sandringham." Another reported a Fenian group in a "privateer" sailing from New York to murder the Queen. After a Cabinet meeting two days later he noted, "The Queen, it appears, is alarmed and angry: she wants Habeas Corpus suspended, militia embodied, in short preparation made to meet an armed insurrection: notwithstanding which, she resists obstinately all suggestions that she should allow herself to be attended when driving about, especially after dark."

A Fenian attempt on December 13 to extricate Irishmen from Clerkenwell Prison resulted in the dynamiting of a wall, and innocent casualties, but no escapes. With Osborne House on an island easy to penetrate, Grey urged the Queen to leave for the safety of Windsor Castle, but she preferred Osborne for Christmas, and the Government had to settle for extra police, and ships to patrol the coast. Even a Fenian attempt to assassinate the Duke of Edinburgh, visiting in Australia, failed to convince Victoria that precautions for her were not a "bore." Alfred, shot in the ribs, recovered, and the agitation ebbed.

Early in the new year, it became obvious that Derby had ceased to function as Prime Minister. For months the Queen had been entertained by daily reports from his deputy. Despite her earlier dislike of Disraeli, she looked forward to his red boxes and extravagant language, whether on a new Reform Bill, on Disestablishment of the Anglican Church in Ireland (a Gladstone preoccupation), or on Russian designs in eastern Europe. Late in February 1868, Derby at seventy-five relinquished what had become little more than a title, and Disraeli crossed the Solent to Osborne to kiss hands, sending a preparatory letter ahead to the Queen that he could "only offer devotion." It would be, he added, "his delight and duty, to render the transaction of affairs as easy to your Majesty as possible; . . . but he ventures to trust that, in the great affairs of state, your Majesty will deign not to withhold from him the benefit of your Majesty's guidance." Any worries about her relations with a Jew—he had been baptized as a boy, but public perception counted more than religious profession— had already been defused during the months of prologue to his Ministry. Wrinkled and goateed, courtly and captivating, he brought a sense of romance and drama to the Queen's business. She looked forward to his visits as she had to his memoranda. "The present Man will do well," she wrote to Vicky on February 29, 1868, "and [he] will be particularly loyal and anxious to please me in every way. He is v^y peculiar, but v^y clever and sensible and v^y conciliatory." On March 4, she added, "He is full of poetry, romance & chivalry. When he knelt down to kiss my hand w^h he took in both his—he said: 'In loving loyalty & faith.' "

Derby, on the other hand, felt peeved at the lack of "sympathy or regret" in her messages accepting his retirement. "He talked to me," his son wrote, "of the Queen's way of writing to him, about which he was at first very sore: but I think he now understands her nature. She is civil to persons in power under her, whose good will contributes to her comfort (and not always to them): but [she] sees no reason for wasting civility on those who can no longer be of use to her."

Disraeli had hardly replaced Derby when Gladstone saw his chance to bring down the new Ministry. On March 16, in the Commons, he proposed the dissolution of the state-supported Church of Ireland. At one stroke he won for the Liberals a considerable Catholic vote, and forced the Prime Minister into opposing the measure more strenuously than was politic. To make a gesture toward Ireland, Disraeli entreated the Queen to permit her unemployed eldest son to visit the unhappy island as her surrogate. In the past two centuries, Disraeli observed, the sovereign had passed only twenty-one days in Ireland, most of those visits having been made by Victoria herself, and he suggested that her Irish subjects "yearned for the occasional presence and inspiration of Royalty."

Although Disraeli extracted her consent, she remained hostile to the idea of Bertie's attending even more races (the Prime Minister had recommended Punchestown), and that he take a house in Ireland for a month's hunting each year, to establish a regular presence. Even in Disraeli's persuasive prose, such suggestions did not go down. What was all right for rustic Scotland was not acceptable for backward Ireland. Further, *"any encouragement"* of the Prince of Wales's "constant love of running about, and not keeping at home or near the Queen, is *most earnestly* and *seriously* to be deprecated."

Ignoring such rebuffs, Disraeli continued his wooing of the Queen, although he knew that the days of his Government were numbered, and that he would have to go to the electorate for a new mandate, which was unlikely to be forthcoming. Since he expected someday to be back, in his communications with Victoria she was his "gracious Mistress," and the leaders of the Opposition were "a *troupe,* like one of those bands of minstrels one encounters in the sauntering of a summer street . . . but with visages not so fair and radiant as the countenances of your Majesty's subjects at Balmoral."

Despite imminent defeat, Disraeli would not resign his minority government to the Liberals. "On great political occasions," he suggested to Victoria, skirting the edge of constitutionality, "it is wise, that the visible influence, as it were, of the Sovereign, should be felt and recognized by the nation, and that Parliament should practically comprehend, that the course of a Ministry depends upon the will of the Queen." What Disraeli intended was a delaying action, in hope that the public could be turned around. Victoria attempted to help through personal appearances, holding two drawing-rooms on March 12 and April 1, and laying the foundation stone at St. Thomas's Hospital, wearing as usual her widow's black, set off by a long veil of white crêpe and a diamond necklace from which hung a miniature of the Prince Consort. Taking Disraeli's side on Disestablishment, she wrote to him that "Mr. Gladstone must be aware that the chief difficulty in governing Ireland has always been to restrain the mutual violence of the old Orange Party on the one hand, and of the Roman Catholics on the other, and he might, the Queen thinks, have well paused before he made a declaration of which the effect will certainly be to revive and inflame the old sectarian feuds. . . ."

At Windsor on April 17, Gathorne-Hardy listened at dinner to the Queen's "anti Gladstonian" religious views. "Scotch Protestantism suits her evidently," he wrote. The Anglican extremes of "High & Low" were distasteful to her, "the latter so very narrow minded." The next day—it may have had more to do with her views than with her seclusion—a "seditious placard" (in Lord Stanley's description) calling upon Victoria to abdicate in favor of the Prince of Wales was posted in Pall Mall, where it became the talk of the clubs. Anticipating a Liberal landslide, the new Marquess of Salisbury, a Conservative who then saw Disraeli as a dangerous radical, wrote to a friend that the Queen had become the pawn of "the Jew," who would only offer a sham resignation to her, having arranged in advance to stay on at her request. "Matters seem very critical —a woman on the throne, & a Jew adventurer [who] has found out the secret of getting around her."

Early in May, Disraeli was again defeated in the Commons. As predicted, he stayed on as Prime Minister, while offering to submit to a general election. It was what the Queen wanted. Reflecting the Cabinet, however, Gathorne-Hardy observed in his diary, "Our opponents are very nasty & in fact insinuate falsehood & faithlessness. I wish Disraeli were more bold & outspoken. . . . I am sick of my position." Under attack as a supporter of the Tories as well as a do-nothing Queen, Victoria sent

William Jenner to visit the Home Secretary on June 4 to explain to Gathorne-Hardy "the state of agitation in which at times he found her in her private room, & the violent headaches & sickness to which she is subject. . . . The late articles in newspapers &c have disturbed her peace at Balmoral. One ought to be very considerate under such circumstances."

Between her spring holiday at Balmoral and her return in the autumn, Victoria took a further holiday, this time in Switzerland. "Carrying on the Government of the Country six hundred miles from the metropolis doubles the labour," Disraeli wrote from Scotland. He was beset as well by the Queen's interest in Church patronage rather than in matters of more moment. It wasted his time, but he wrote to his secretary from Balmoral for a Crockford's directory of the ministry, saying, "I must be armed." Before he arrived, Victoria sent him primroses from Scotland, which she would continue to do all his life. Effusively as always, he responded through his wife, Mary Anne, in what seems pure Disraelian dictation: "Mr. Disraeli is passionately fond of flowers, and their lustre and perfume were enhanced by the condescending hand which had showered upon him all the treasures of spring." Taking more seriously the Queen's personal preferences than any points of Anglican doctrine, he made a show of indefatigable research and then appointed as deans and bishops the very people whom Victoria wanted, one baldly identified as an "eloquent, learned and commanding" advocate of "the Royal supremacy."

Disraeli was lucky on his last visit to Balmoral. It was warm. Usually, whatever the season, the cold was as unrelieved as the tedium. Under the Queen's unremitting discipline, all activity was rigidly controlled, from conversation at table to permission to leave the house. Only the most hardy in her Government sought to be a Minister-in-Attendance, but the Prime Minister was treated differently. Although he told his wife that his health remained "unsatisfactory," and that he drank nothing but sherry (which was bad for him, but not as bad as the Queen's whiskey), he dined with Victoria in her library, and took walks and rustic expeditions with her. From Braemar he wrote to Mary Anne, "I was glad there were no Games."

When he left, it was with Victoria's gifts of two volumes of views of Balmoral, a box of family photographs, a full-length portrait of the Prince Consort, and a shawl for Mrs. Disraeli. His adroit letter of thanks observed that he could now "live, as it were, in your Majesty's favourite scenes," and that Albert was "a gifted being" whose memory he could not recall without emotion. In November, when the Tories were defeated at the polls and Disraeli took his official leave of the Queen, he turned down the traditional peerage for himself, requesting instead that one be conferred upon his wife in her own right. General Grey thought that the "very embarrassing" request could not be refused, but that it would subject the eccentric seventy-six-year-old Mary Anne (Disraeli was sixty-four) to "endless ridicule." Conferring the title of Viscountess Beaconsfield, the Queen wrote to Disraeli that she "can truly sympathize with his devotion." Although society and the London press were predictably rude, Mary Anne had a bauble to brighten her last years. Disraeli owed her much, and the Queen had helped to pay his debt, while permitting him to remain in the Commons.

Before Victoria returned to Windsor for the election and its aftermath, she had a housewarming party, complete to whiskey toddies and reels, to open her fifteen-room "bothy," which she named Glassalt Shiel. At the edge of Loch Muich, it was remote even from the fastness of Balmoral, and had little connection to her life with Albert, a fact symbolized by her single bed. Prince Arthur, Princess Louise, and Lady Churchill were there, as well as servants and soldiers from the unit guarding Balmoral. "I thought of my happy past," the Queen wrote in her journal, "and my darling husband whom I fancied I must see, and who always wished to build here in this favourite wild spot, quite in amongst the hills." Glassalt Shiel was evidence of her retreating further from any visible presence as Sovereign. If anything, the prospect of a Gladstone as Prime Minister made her even less eager to be near London.

The outgoing Government gave up its seals of office on December 9, 1868. "At one," Lord Torrington wrote to Delane from the equerries' room at Windsor, "the old Ministers come; deliver up their seals, eat, drink, and cut out before the new parties arrive." She was sorry to take the seals back, the Queen said indiscreetly; "they had never been in better hands." Clarendon and Stanley were relieved to go. The Queen, they thought, remained "indifferent to business, except where pressed on by relations: jealous lest anything be kept back from her, but interferes little, and only where Germany is concerned, or Belgium." Liberal politicians prepared the Queen's speech for the new Parliament, "and a Cabinet was held on the staircase," Torrington wrote, "to agree to it."

Early in 1869 a country estate in Ireland was made available to the Queen, so that she could establish a residence in "John Bull's other island." Conveying the offer of the Dublin banker John La Touche, Gladstone urged that she accept. Calling the gesture "noble," Victoria nonetheless turned it down, explaining that Balmoral alone was essential to her health. Undeterred, Gladstone pressed another Irish subject upon which his predecessor had burned his fingers. Instead of a Lord Lieutenant at Dublin Castle, he envisaged the Prince of Wales as Viceroy, assisted by a Secretary of State for Ireland. Neither recommendation was welcome. The Queen hardly wanted another visible and official establishment for Bertie, in which he could further cultivate the rich and urbane sybarites—let alone the unspeakable women—who had become fashionable through his friendship. "If you ever become King," she had warned the Prince of Wales in 1868, "you will find all these friends most inconvenient, and you will have to break with *all.*" His cronies were betting people and banking people, often blackballed by the best clubs. They would even be in trade—a millionaire grocer named Lipton, a millionaire furniture-shop proprietor named Maple, a millionaire newspaper proprietor named Lawson, a millionaire merchant named Sassoon, who was also inconveniently Jewish, as was a Hungarian banker and horse-fancier named Hirsch.

The Prince of Wales, the Queen let it be known through Dr. Jenner, gave her a severe headache, and was best unmentioned. To Gladstone on February 3, 1869, she stressed her health, as well as her desire on other grounds not to open Parliament. She wanted no personal association with the Irish Church question, or any of his other ideas involving Ireland. "Eliza is roaring well," Clarendon reported, "and can do everything she likes and nothing she doesn't." Gladstone's government understood that as well, but could not budge her to cooperate. The Irish Disestablishment Bill finally became law on July 26. Six weeks earlier, Gladstone had thanked the Queen for conciliatory efforts—largely fictional, and invented by him to urge her toward further involvement in the duties of her office.

Gladstone's pressure had been prompted by frank advice from General Grey, whose politics were Liberal although he served Victoria above party. Grey had confided that he was "persuaded that *nothing* will have any effect but a strong—even a peremptory—tone. In spite of Sir William Jenner I believe that neither health and strength are wanting, were [her] inclination what it should be. It is simply the long, unchecked habit of self-indulgence that now makes it impossible for her, without some degree of nervous agitation, to give up, even for ten minutes, the gratification of a single inclination, or even *whim.*" A second letter warned that postponement of the struggle to get the Queen to do her duty would make "the fight, which *must* come, . . . more painful and difficult."

Gladstone promptly agreed, blaming the Queen's "fanciful ideas . . . about her own health" as resulting from encouragement "by a feeble-minded doctor . . . , producing in a considerable degree the incapacity which but for him would not exist." Without a Disraeli to draw her out, even Disraeli saw a dangerous drift in the monarchy, which could become irreversible. At dinner on March 15, Stanley found him "out of spirits, says he thinks the monarchy in danger, which he never did before: not from immediate causes, nor from any feeling against it of a strongly hostile character, but from gradual loss of prestige; the Queen has thrown away her chances, people find out that they can do without a Court, etc."

Attempts to draw the Queen out came from many directions, and were seldom successful. One had come on March 4, through Dean Stanley's wife, Lady Augusta, who lured Victoria to the Deanery at Westminster at teatime to meet a group of intellectuals with whom Albert would have felt more at ease. The Queen's journal identified them as "Mr. Carlyle, the historian, a strange-looking eccentric old Scotchman, who holds forth, in a drawling melancholy voice, with a broad Scotch accent, upon Scotland and upon the utter degeneration of everything; Mr. and Mrs. Grote, old acquaintances of mine from Kensington, unaltered, she very peculiar, clever and masculine, he also an historian, of the old school; Sir C. and Lady Lyell, he an old acquaintance, most agreeable, and she very pleasing; Mr. Browning, the poet, a very agreeable man. It was, at first, very shy work speaking to them, when they were all drawn up; but afterwards, when tea was being drunk, Augusta got them to come and sit near me, and they were very agreeable and talked very entertainingly." Of the white-bearded Browning, who had just published his *The Ring and the Book,* acclaimed as a masterpiece, the Queen inquired, "Are you writing anything now?" Carlyle had politely insisted upon sitting in deference to his age and ailments, and they all then sat at Victoria's urging. "Sacred Majesty was very good," Carlyle recorded in his cranky way; "[the] thing altogether decidedly insignificant, ditto *tiresome.*" But she still looked "plump and almost young . . . and sailed out as if moving on skates, and bending her head towards us with a smile."

A year later, her old admirer (from afar), Charles Dickens, now fifty-eight and seriously ailing, visited Buckingham Palace at her request, the Queen going to London largely because the ashen-faced, ashen-bearded novelist was not up to the trip to Windsor.

Arthur Helps, who brought and introduced Dickens, briefed her—little realizing how many Dickens novels she had read—that her guest was "the author whose name will hereafter be closely associated with the Victorian era," and that "he, too, has the most anxious desire to raise what we call 'the lower classes,' and would sympathize with Your Majesty in many of the Queen's views and aspirations."

Instead of inviting Dickens to sit during his ninety minutes with her, Victoria paid him the dubious compliment of remaining standing herself, and "He talked of his latest works, of America, the strangeness of the people there, of the division of classes in England, which he hoped would get better in time." Before Helps ushered Dickens out, the Queen gave him a copy of her Highlands book, inscribed "From the humblest of writers to one of the greatest."

Three months later, on June 9, 1870, Helps telegraphed to Balmoral the news of Dickens's death. "He had a large loving mind," the Queen wrote in her journal, "and the strongest sympathy with the poorer classes. He felt sure that a better feeling, and much greater union of classes would take place. . . . And I pray earnestly it may."

From Osborne in the early spring of 1869, Victoria appealed to her sister to visit, but Feodora declined, blaming her age and ailments, and the harsh English weather. A letter later in the year suggested other reasons—living in close proximity to Victoria remained unpleasant. Feodora diplomatically chided her sister for her inactivity, for the "want of being able to enjoy anything, at times, or to undertake and look forward to those things which formerly used to interest and please us. This comes with growing older and not feeling so strong and well as when young, nor so light-hearted. . . . Occupation, and having the satisfaction to feel that one is of use to others, is the only help. . . ."

Beyond reading over the contents of her red boxes and insisting upon her perquisites, Victoria's occasional bursts of queenliness remained few. In June, on the thirty-second anniversary of her accession—she was one month past fifty—she confided to her journal that God had given her "a very difficult task, one for which I feel myself in many ways unfit, from inclination and want of power." By "power" she seemed to mean personal strength, although the powers of the position had ebbed because she had not used them as earlier. God, she added, "gave me happiness and He took it away, no doubt for a wise purpose and for the happiness of my beloved one, leaving me alone to bear the heavy burden in trying and troubled times."

That June, Gladstone had attempted once more to energize the Queen, whom the exasperated General Grey had been describing bluntly to the Prime Minister as "the royal malingerer." Victoria found a variety of reasons for not doing what she did not want to do. Gladstone reminded her that the Khedive Ismail had entertained the Prince and Princess of Wales in Egypt for two months. Would the Queen, on his visit to England, offer him rooms in Buckingham Palace? A grumbling assent came from Scotland, although she used Buckingham Palace for only a few ceremonial days each year. She would even permit the Khedive a night at Windsor, if his entourage was small; but Victoria, whose frugality had already become legendary, felt that she had to "strongly *protest against* the pretension raised that she should at her *own expense,* in the *only Palace* of her own . . . , entertain all Foreign Potentates WHO *chose* to come here for their own amusement." The agitated handwriting registered her emotions as dramatically as did her emphases and capitalizations —and inaccuracy.

However effective with the electorate, Gladstone's persuasiveness was lost on the Queen, who seemed unmoved by what the Prime Minister regarded as dangerously burgeoning republican agitation. In the completion in midsummer of the new Blackfriars Bridge over the Thames he saw a possibility of drawing her into public view. Would she preside at the opening? Since she was seldom in the City, her progress might also include the new Holborn Viaduct, an additional stretch of Embankment, and the new Underground Railway. Such a public spectacle would require a delay of only a few days in the Queen's return to Balmoral (where she still was that June).

Mr. Gladstone, the Queen replied, had no idea how fatiguing the London heat in August would be to her. She would set back her return to Scotland only if urgent public business demanded it. Gladstone regularly addressed her, Victoria once said, as if she were a "public meeting." In that vein, the Prime Minister returned to his exhortations, reminding the Queen of the difficulty in conducting the Government's business while six hundred miles away, and of the importance of her appearing publicly to "maintain the full influence of the Monarchy." In return she reminded him that she had, in the first five months of 1869, gone to the Royal Academy opening, held drawing-rooms and a levee, and was going to London to give a tea (described as breakfast) to the Khedive at Buckingham Palace, apparently to keep him away from Windsor. Unwilling to acknowledge defeat, Gladstone urged her to remain at Windsor for the week in mid-July when the most urgent Parliamentary business would be debated, so that her Ministers might consult her between sittings.

Only a *"very* uncommon crisis in public affairs" would warrant "so serious a trial of her strength," the Queen warned, "as a longer residence away from the sea [at Osborne] at this time of year." Her concession *"must* be regarded as an *entirely* isolated case, and that it must NEVER be made a *precedent* for any similar representation on the part of her Ministers to her in succeeding years." Her departure dates to and from Osborne and Balmoral were fixed, as was her mind about other matters inconveniently raised by Gladstone. Visiting the new public works in the City— she agreed to that, if put off until November—seemed an opportune time to the Prime Minister to raise to the peerage Sir Lionel Rothschild, who had represented the City of London with distinction for twenty-two years, and was celebrated for his philanthropies. Here she could only remind herself of Bertie's relationships with the Rothschilds and others—many of them Jews—in banking and in brokerage, in betting and in horse racing. Sir Lionel, she contended, had made his money as a gambler "on a gigantic scale . . . far removed from that legitimate trading w^h she *delights* to honour. . . ." Further, her social toleration had its limits, as she explained to Earl Granville for Gladstone—that "she cannot consent to a Jew being made a Peer—tho' she will not object to a *Jew* baronet— and she is quite certain that it w^d do the Govt harm instead of good." Since her interest in propping up the Liberal ministry was less than minimal, as Gladstone knew, he understood which argument was paramount in her mind. The Rothschilds would have to wait for their peerages.

Since the Queen's autumn residence at Balmoral lasted until November 3, the openings of the Holborn Viaduct and the Blackfriars Bridge were scheduled for the first Sunday of her return, November 6. No thought was given to Sabbatarian objections. At the Viaduct, where Delane of *The Times* stood among the crowds in "Queen's weather," he described the scene laconically in his diary as "The cold intense, the show poor, but the loyalty great." The show was even poorer at Blackfriars, although hundreds of thousands lined the route on both sides of the Thames. "Not a window empty," Victoria noted, "and people up to the very top of the houses, flags, and here and there inscriptions, everyone with most friendly faces." At noon, as scheduled, she reached the south side of the new bridge. "Here on a platform with raised seats and many people, stood the Lord Mayor, who presented the sword, which I merely touched, and he introduced the engineer, Mr. [William] Cubitt (son of the eminent engineer Sir Thomas Cubitt, well known to my dearest Albert) and another gentleman. I was presented with an Address and a fine illuminated book describing the whole [history of the bridge]. The Bridge was then considered opened, but neither I nor the Lord Mayor said so. This however has not been found out." According to the program, it was she who had forgotten. Her experience of ceremonials had long been in disuse.

Victoria's experience of entertaining had not been so completely in disuse, but the reaction of others at her table suggested that all was not right. Earl Granville, at Osborne in late December, again as Minister in Residence, arrived with the veteran Radical John Bright, whom he considered less than respectable. The Queen, however, had taken to Bright because he approved of her behavior as the mourning widow. Largely innocent of royal hospitality, Bright ate and drank unstintingly, and, enlivened by the Queen's claret, was boisterously merry. Victoria had come to dinner announcing a "sick headache," but for anyone to talk to Charles Grey, now old and deaf, Granville wrote to Gladstone, shouting into the Private Secretary's "impenetrable receptacle of sound" was necessary. The picture was comic—a shy Princess Louise whispering to Granville while Lady Clifden screamed at General Grey; and Bright, imagining himself an "old roué," telling jokes to the allegedly ailing Victoria, and touching (in Granville's description) "some feminine chord" that caused her to enjoy herself in spite of herself.

Earlier, visiting Balmoral, Granville had a session with the Queen that was awkward in a different manner. He was acting as intermediary for Gladstone, and had been taken aside by Dr. Jenner to be lectured on the Queen's fragile health. Jenner often described Victoria's health in language put into his mouth by his employer, and may have again done so to Granville. "And now I have a queer message to give you," Granville wrote to Gladstone. "Jenner had told the Queen, that the best precaution you can take before seeing her, is to send a suit of clothes which have not been used by you, to Her residence, to put on when you see her." Did Jenner think that the Prime Minister was carrying some contagion? The Queen may have thought so, if only because of his practice of accosting, for whatever reasons, London ladies of the evening.

It could not have helped Gladstone warm his relations with the

Queen that in the first year of his Ministry, political circles buzzed with stories about his friendship with a Mrs. Laura Eliza Thistlethwaite, who was as constant a companion as a busy man in public life could have. According to the former Lord Stanley (the fifteenth Earl of Derby since his father's death in October), the lady was "a kept woman in her youth, who induced a foolish person with a large fortune to marry her." She had "taken to religion, and preaches. . . . This, with her beauty, is the attraction to G., and it is characteristic of him to be indifferent to scandal." The alluring Scotswoman from County Antrim, in her middle thirties when Gladstone first met her in 1865, remained so demimondaine in style as to put his political associates (Lord Salisbury confided) into "a respectable frenzy." His life, Gladstone confessed to her, was "a battle between inclination and duty." Duty always won, but the tension provided Gladstone with an exhilaration as well as a sense of moral earnestness that energized him even beyond politics.

Nothing kept the indefatigable Prime Minister from doing his various duties as he saw them, and he persisted in pressing the Queen to do her own. Still, she would not assist his policies in any way by opening Parliament in February 1870; and she made certain that Gladstone received regular reports on the fragile state of her health, especially a new concern with neuralgia. At the end of January she dashed any hopes of her attendance with the conclusive *"out of the question"* and *"madness."* Not only did she disapprove of Gladstone's reforms; she did not like him. His appeals to Christian principles for legislative change smacked to her of hypocrisy (although he was in fact sincere), and she was largely indifferent—where she was not hostile—to his brand of Christianity.

Victoria's own Christianity was a highly personal and untheological collection of beliefs and practices. Later in 1870, for example, when affairs in France and Prussia were dominating newspapers, conversations, and the Queen's dispatch boxes, she seemed at least as concerned with the impropriety of the genealogical lines in the revised St. Matthew Gospel, where the indirection of the words "David begat Solomon of her of Uriah" was clarified, from Authorized Version to revised text, to read "David begat Solomon of the wife of Uriah." This, Victoria complained, suggested Solomon's illegitimacy, although his parents, David and Bathsheba, had married after Bathsheba became a widow. "The Queen," Colonel Ponsonby wrote for her (Grey had died in March) to Dean Stanley, "is rather scandalized by the proposed alteration."

"This I believe," he added, "is nearly the only subject we have had much discourse on for the last three weeks, except the war which entirely absorbs our . . . faculties." The war between France and Prussia in the summer of 1870 was a trap set by Bismarck to destroy Napoleon III. Unprepared, ill-equipped, and riddled by corruption, the French army was lured, by squabbles over the succession in Spain, into battle with the highly professional and experienced Prussians. It appeared in June 1870, as Bismarck intended, to be unprovoked aggression, and to Victoria it validated Albert's distrust of Napoleon as vainglorious and the French nation as immoral. In a few weeks the war assured the unity of the Fatherland under Prussia—Albert's dream—but Bismarck's Prussia was not the idealized state that the Prince Consort had visualized for Frederick and Vicky. "Words are too weak to say all I feel for you," the Queen wrote to Vicky, "or what I think of my neighbours. We must be neutral *as long as* we can, but no one here conceals their opinion as to the extreme iniquity of the war. Still, *more publicly*, we cannot say, but the feeling of the people and the country is all with you, which it was not *before*. And need I say what I feel?"

Unforgiving of the Prussian bullying of Denmark, the Prince and Princess of Wales declared themselves neutral, but not pro-French, and Vicky, whose husband led divisions into battle, wrote to her mother, "I am sure dear Bertie must envy Fritz who has such a trying, but such a useful life." Such divided loyalties in royal families, the Queen felt, were "quite unbearable. Human nature is not made for such fearful trials, especially not mothers' and wives' hearts." Determined after Princess Louise came of age in 1869 to find for her a spouse free of such foreign entanglements, she encouraged, in 1870, the suit of the Duke of Argyll's son, the Marquess of Lorne. A royal princess had not married a subject since 1515, but Victoria saw political as well as eugenic virtues ("healthy blood") in the match.

As Napoleon III surrendered at Sedan on September 2, Eugénie fled to asylum in England. A republic was proclaimed in Paris, and while France lost its emperor, the victors gained one. At Versailles on January 18, 1871, while Paris still reeled under bombardment and siege, King William of Prussia was proclaimed Emperor of Germany in a ceremony stage-managed by Bismarck. Victoria's immediate reaction was to see nothing but good in a powerful and united Germany, because she saw her son-in-law and daughter as its future heads of state. The new Kaiser was elderly, and he and Bismarck might soon be gone. But Prussian arrogance and vindictiveness in victory, exacting huge monetary and territorial indemnities from France, were already altering the political climate in England. Eugénie and her son in suburban London exile, and the seriously ill Louis Napoleon a prisoner of war in Germany, extracted sympathy and generosity in humiliation that they had failed to secure in times of glory.

With a lady-in-waiting, Jane Ely, and a lord-in-waiting, Charles Fitzroy, the Queen and Beatrice visited Camden Place, a bow-windowed house in Chislehurst, on November 30 and found Eugénie melancholy but dignified, "dressed in the plainest possible way, without any jewels or ornaments, and her hair simply done, in a net, at the back." The Prince Imperial, fourteen and Eugénie's only child, was "a nice little boy, but rather short and stumpy. . . . We stayed about half an hour and then left. The Empress again most kindly came to the door. It was a sad visit and seemed like a strange dream." The Queen invited Eugénie to Windsor the next month, and, on a rainy December day, took her to the hallowed place that Victoria shared only with a favored few—the "dear Mausoleum" across Castle Hill at Frogmore. "What a fearful contrast to her visit here in '55," the Queen observed in her diary.

Late the next March, she received the defeated and disgraced ex-Emperor at Windsor. "I went to the door with Louise and embraced the Emperor 'comme de rigueur.' It was a moving moment, when I thought of the last time he came here . . . , in perfect triumph, dearest Albert bringing him from Dover, the whole country mad to receive him, and now! He seemed much depressed and had tears in his eyes, but he controlled himself and said, 'Il y a bien longtemps que je n'ai vu votre Majesté.'. . . He is grown very stout and grey and his moustaches are no longer curled or waxed as formerly, but there was the same pleasing, gentle, and gracious manner." After exchanges of greetings, Victoria took him to her Audience Room, where they sat alone and talked about the war and its aftermath for half an hour, Napoleon—full of news of the Commune—"dreadfully shocked at 'tout se qui se passe à Paris.' "

Gladstone had no difficulty inducing the Queen to open Parliament in person in 1871. She was even eager. Prince Arthur came of age that year, and she wanted an annuity of £15,000 for him. Princess Louise was to marry in March, and despite the considerable Argyll family wealth, she was recommended by Victoria for a dowry of £30,000 and an annuity of £6,000. It was not an auspicious time for her children. Not many months before, the high-living Prince of Wales had been called into the divorce court to give testimony in the Lady Mordaunt case, and the private life of his "Marlborough House Set," composed largely of his mistresses and their complaisant husbands, received publicity that the Queen found disagreeable and that the public found more interesting than the *Court Circular*. In the Lady Mordaunt episode, at least, Bertie had been innocent, if indiscreet; but his gambling and his womanizing were dredged up once more, and English men were made dramatically aware that his life-style was funded by them through his Parliamentary annuity, the six-figure revenues of the Duchy of Cornwall, and his moneyed friends.

The new French Republic across the Channel had reawakened republican agitation in England, and the Queen's position was further undermined by her inactivity, her alleged pro-Germanism during the war with France, the unpopularity of her children, and the increasing cost of a seemingly vacant throne. That she should choose to emerge to do her duty as Queen only when she sought public largesse struck some of her statistically minded subjects as outrageously mercenary. Since Windsor Castle and Buckingham Palace, and her yacht, were maintained by the nation, and she had £385,000 a year from Parliament as well as what remained of the Nield inheritance of 1852, and seemed in seclusion to spend nothing, a pamphlet published late in 1870, *What Does She Do With It?*, quickly drew a wide readership.

Gladstone called it the "Royalty question" in a blunt letter to Lord Granville on December 3, 1870. "To speak in rude and general terms," he explained, "the Queen is invisible and the Prince of Wales is not respected." The Prime Minister believed in monarchy no less fervently than he believed in the Liberal Party, but Republican Clubs had sprung up in Aberdeen, Birmingham, Cardiff, Norwich, Plymouth, and several London boroughs. A demonstration in Trafalgar Square condemned "princely paupers," and Parliamentary inquiries into the Queen's finances were demanded. The attacks became unpleasant. The marriage of Princess Louise, not a popular favorite, became an occasion for deriding Lord Lorne, whose future position the *Daily Telegraph* saw as "trying" at best, describing him as "apprehensive," and "pale and plainly *ému*"* at the wedding in March.

Far more vicious was the radical *Reynolds' Newspaper*, which, on a Sunday in April 1871, announced the birth of the Prince of Wales's third son, Alexander, under the heading "Another Inauspicious Event," and the death of the infant the next day as "A Happy Release." "We have much satisfaction," it gibed, "in announcing that the newly-born child of

*ému: agitated.

the Prince and Princess of Wales died shortly after its birth, thus relieving the working classes of England from having to support hereafter another addition to the long roll of State beggars they at present maintain." When the crusading *Pall Mall Gazette* reprinted the birth notice (and heading) in its "Occasional Notes" columns, Victoria ordered the paper out of her residences.

The *Pall Mall Gazette* had already given offense in March by ridiculing the Queen's new spate of drawing-room receptions, usually held when she wanted to claim visibility. These were one of the few uses to which Buckingham Palace was put, and "pitiable scenes" occurred outside, the *PMG* reported, as women sat trembling in carriages for an hour or more in the early-spring chill in low-cut dresses, waiting for permission to queue for a further hour inside, and finally emerging, "many of them half-dead, and probably having sown the seeds of consumption." In the ebb of the Queen's popularity, nothing was going right. Even the ladies themselves were suspect. The Lord Chamberlain's office inquired of the Countess of Sheffield, who was scheduled to present Lady Stanley of Alderley, whether there was any truth to reports that Lady Stanley "had lived with Lord Stanley for some years before her marriage." Although the Queen's two eldest sons were notorious for the looseness of their lives and for their entanglements with married noblewomen (and others), Viscount Sydney had the "painful" task of asking her Ladyship if she was "prepared to certify that Lady Stanley's antecedents are such as would enable you to recommend that she should be received by Her Majesty." The matter was resolved, but such apparent hypocrisies did not endear even the Queen's most loyal constituencies to her Court.

With her children more of a problem than ever, Victoria began to look past them at the next generation. What she then discovered, when a tutor, John Neale Dalton, was finally chosen for her eldest grandson in line of succession, Prince Albert Victor, was that "Eddy" was so backward and lethargic as to be nearly ineducable. As for his father, the Queen was almost resigned to giving him Irish employment. Yet she could not decide whether she could better keep him out of trouble by having him near or by posting him away. Bertie gravitated toward pleasure wherever he was. Rejecting the Irish plan, Victoria rationalized that "as years go on I strongly feel that to lift up my son and heir and keep him in his place near me, is only what is right." That had been far from easy. He had his own income, his own residences remote from her, and friends willing to bank-roll his extravagances in order to pursue pleasure in his increasingly substantial shadow. Royal heirs inevitably drew about them an alternative Court. The Queen had made that even easier for Bertie by maintaining little public ceremony about her. She had already admonished the Prince of Wales that at Ascot it would be prudent for him to be seen at the races only on Tuesday and Thursday. "Your example can do *much* for good and may do an immense deal for evil, in the present day." Bertie had done as he pleased then, and in a memorandum about his "wasting time" in Ireland, on June 25, 1871, Victoria noted that she had brushed off Gladstone's proposal for him. She blamed the "bad climate" and saw her son's possible removal from some of the London social season as the only merit in the plan.

The opening of the Royal Albert Hall on March 29, 1871, two days after Victoria's audience with the fallen Napoleon III, demonstrated to her satisfaction that all of the alleged discontent with her post-Albert style of reigning, or with the Prince of Wales's style of living, went little deeper than the leader pages of some newspapers, and that there was no chance whatever of her following the ex-Emperor. Enthusiastic crowds gathered along the route to Kensington; inside, the eight thousand invited guests applauded her entrance, and Bertie's welcoming Address. She felt "quite giddy" at confronting such large numbers after so many years, and limited herself to a single sentence of response, expressing her "great admiration of this beautiful Hall." There were cheers, shouts, and whistles, which faded only when the Bishop of London offered a prayer. The Queen was then to declare the Hall open, but instead called the Prince of Wales to her side and whispered to him that she could not do it. He strode to the front of the stage and announced, "Her Majesty declares this Hall now open."

While Victoria may have thought that the crowds lining the streets were registering loyalty (and many people were), there was a strong component of curiosity involved. The Queen had rarely appeared in public since 1861. As for the enthusiasm inside the Hall, almost all of it was voiced by representatives of the *Red Book*, the street directory of socially acceptable Londoners. As a cross-section of Britain they left something to be desired, yet Gladstone was confident that more royal appearances would draw upon the deep springs of loyalty to the institution of monarchy. He put his prestige behind passage of Prince Arthur's annuity, and managed Princess Louise's dowry through Parliament as well, hoping, he wrote to the Queen, that as an act of "grace and condescension" to her people, the Queen would make herself more visible. She was annoyed, but she had the artistic and bossy Louise off her hands. All of her daughters,

Vicky excepted, disliked each other and battled for dominance. Louise would not even get along with her husband, and the match that the Queen had believed to be the soundest in blood proved to be the opposite. Even in the years before she and Lord Lorne lived apart, there were no children, and there were reports that Louise had menstrual difficulties and was barren. Also, the good son, Arthur, had his difficulties, inexplicably falling out of the billiard room window at Buckingham Palace one evening, luckily upon two policemen below. His concussion was not serious, and he was sent to Windsor to recuperate under Dr. Jenner's supervision.

At Osborne House in early summer, Victoria had children and grandchildren about her, including the Princess Royal's Willy, Henry, Charlotte and Waldemar. Her interest in remaining at Osborne or at Windsor while Parliament completed its business was nonexistent. Her calendar had her due back at Balmoral, where in the spring she had belied her own claims of frailty by climbing the steepest face of Craig Gowan for the first time in ten years. Yet she tore off a tirade to Gladstone, who had asked her to remain several days more, that she was (at fifty-two) "a woman no longer young" who refused "to be driven and abused till her nerves and health will give way with the worry and agitation and interference in her private life." And she threatened to abdicate rather than submit to the "overwork and worry" that "killed her Beloved Husband. . . ." The "heavy burden" would be given up "to other hands." With republican agitation escalating, the last thing that Gladstone wanted was King Bertie.

"Although I do not care about the individual," Lord Granville complained to Gladstone, referring to Victoria, "I doubt whether some remonstrance should not be made either by you or by me, . . . as to the principle which the Queen lays down that it is too fatiguing for her to see Foreign Princes for ten minutes." Gladstone wrote to Ponsonby, on receiving no responses to two further letters to the Queen, "Smaller and meaner cause for the decay of thrones cannot be conceived. It is like the worm which bores the bark of a noble oak tree and so breaks the channel of its life." Vicky wrote a letter signed by the other children warning "our adored Mama and our Sovereign" that she seemed unaware of the threats to the entire fabric of monarchy "which are daily spreading." After second thoughts, they let their timidity get the better of them, and never showed her the manifesto.

The vote on Prince Arthur's annuity passed on August 1, but with fifty-four negative votes cast, and much recrimination aired in the Commons. On the fourth, the Queen recorded awakening to the pain of what she thought was an insect sting under her right arm. When the inflammation subsided, she assumed she was better, but for an attack of rheumatism and a general malaise that affected her usually hearty appetite. Possibly blaming the political pressures on her, she left on August 17 gratefully for Balmoral.

In Scotland, a *Court Circular* was issued on August 20 that the Queen "bore her journey to the north well, but continues indisposed." Her planned visit to the Duke and Duchess of Argyll was described as indefinitely postponed, and the matter of her health largely disappeared from the *Circular,* until an August 30 report, almost certainly an invention of Jenner's, that the Queen had taken a Sunday drive to the Ballochie Forest to call upon an invalid lady who was the sister of a gamekeeper at Balmoral. Now and then the *Circular* would report that the Queen "drove out" with Princess Beatrice and Lady Churchill. In truth, Victoria was very sick. What her doctor lightly described as an inflammation of the left tonsil had left her bedridden.

Because the Queen had suggested an insect sting, a remote possibility exists that she had suffered a nearly fatal systemic anaphylactic reaction. But the effects disappeared quickly, and there was no further reference to a sting. Given the severity of her complications—for one reason or another, she was incapacitated for nearly three months—the record is puzzlingly thin, with much evidence of cover-up. Yet what becomes evident is that she had undergone the most serious illness of her years as Queen.

As her throat seemed to improve, according to the *Lancet*'s circumspect report, apparently written by Jenner, "the Queen began to suffer pain a little below the right arm, at which part a swelling, that subsequently suppurated, made its appearance. Her Majesty's health was again gravely disturbed at the time, in connexion with the formation of the abscess, and for days Her Majesty was unable to take any food." (She lost two stone—nearly thirty pounds—during her illness.) The combination of severe throat inflammation and an underarm abscess suggests a staphylococcus infection that spread to the soft tissue behind the throat. Whatever the cause, her doctors evaded use of the term *quinsy,* the label at the time for peritonsillar abscess. It would have been a frightening diagnosis, as quinsy was regarded as a medical emergency, with severe pain, massive swelling in the throat that could prevent swallowing, and inflammation radiating to the lymph nodes. In Victoria's case, the infection seems to have traveled in the opposite direction, from lymph nodes to throat, but as with conventional quinsy cases, she was toxic, with a high temperature. In pre-antibiotic days the illness was life-threatening.

Eventually the throat abscess ruptured and drained into the back of the esophagus, relieving not only Victoria but her physicians, who still worried about the infection moving backward into the brain, or ending fatally in septicemia—blood poisoning. Knowing nothing of her condition, and assuming that Victoria was malingering, Granville wrote to Gladstone from Balmoral, where he had been Minister-in-Residence but unable to see her, "The Queen is better today. Jenner came to my room this morning, and I had it out with him—so much so that he said my habits of Diplomatic controversy gave me an unfair advantage. . . ." But he would tell the Queen's Foreign Minister no genuine fact that would permit him to assume anything but her evasion of her duties.

Granville's letter was written on the nineteenth. The worst day for Victoria was Sunday, August 20—until, she wrote afterwards, "something seemed to give way in the throat & the choking sensation with violent spasms ceased."

The *Lancet* report insisted that she was "never in any immediate danger, [but] she has been really very ill." Privately, Jenner thought at the time, as he later told Ponsonby, that she might have only twenty-four hours to live. "Never, since a girl, when I had typhoid fever at Ramsgate in '35, have I felt so ill," she wrote in her journal on August 22. Which of the worst days she was referring to remains unclear, but she would write to Vicky later (October 27) of being "fed like a baby which lasted three days and a half—the food being put into your mouth, your nose blown and everything done for you."

Lady Churchill, wanting to do the proper thing, asked Sir Thomas Biddulph why the Queen's children had not been summoned. "Good heavens!" he said. "That would have killed her at once." Ponsonby, who had not seen Victoria since her arrival at Balmoral, agreed. "Other people have relations, but these relations seem to be the very people the Queen is least inclined to send for." Nor had she sent for Ponsonby, who would not see her again for nearly a month.

Intending to be helpful while the public was being fed reports that the Queen was only somewhat more unwell than usual, Jenner had already planted an anonymous paragraph in the *Lancet* of August 19, answering critics of Victoria's seclusion, as if her dereliction from duty had been little more than the failure to be hostess at Buckingham Palace balls. "We have seen with regret," the piece began, "the attacks on the Queen, based on Her Majesty's absence from evening entertainments and on her brief residence in London. . . . Her Majesty is not physically capable of bearing the effects of crowded or overheated rooms, or of prolonged residence in London. . . ." And Jenner went on to describe the consequences—severe headaches, sleeplessness, loss of appetite, and general "discomfort." Writing to his fellow physicians, he concluded, "The profession will readily, without our entering more fully into so delicate a subject, understand the necessity for Her Majesty's medical advisers exercising the greatest diligence. . . ." The report only added to speculation that she might abdicate. It was impolitic, Ponsonby told him—and Jenner, without conviction, denied authorship. "I suppose it was written at the Queen's desire," Ponsonby went on. Jenner only shook his head and refused to meet the Secretary's eyes.

"If not," said Ponsonby, "I may say I think it most unfortunate, as it will enable the abdicationists to say at once, 'Why should we wait any longer—she promises not to do more, but positively to do less.' "

"It is far better that the truth be known," Jenner confessed finally. "As to there being any feeling on the subject, I don't believe it. There is no feeling against the Queen."

Even Gladstone, Ponsonby countered, was talking publicly about some "alteration of our form of government."

A few days later, as the Queen's abscess continued to suppurate, and the pain persisted, Dr. Joseph Lister, Regius Professor of Clinical Surgery at the University of Edinburgh, and already at forty-four the recognized pioneer in antisepsis, was sent for. Jenner continued to blame the Queen's breakdown in health on Gladstone and his Ministers, who had tried to keep her near Parliament until the sitting ended. "By heavens," he swore to Ponsonby, "if she had died I would have borne testimony that they had killed her!" If she had been a man, he concluded, the Government would not have dared to treat her in so "outrageous" a manner. "No," said Ponsonby, "they would simply have turned her off the throne." And he pointed to the increasing disenchantment with her inactivity.

"Nonsense!" said Jenner. The problem was not the Queen but "the advancing democracy of the age, and it is absurd to think that it will be checked by her driving about London and giving balls for the frivolous classes of society."

Lister arrived on September 4, and saw the Queen in her bedroom with the two doctors in regular attendance, Jenner and John Marshall, a new man from Crathie, nearby. "Mr. Lister thought the swelling ought to be cut," she wrote later; "he could wait twenty-four hours, but it would be better not. I felt dreadfully nervous, as I bear pain so badly."

While Marshall held her arm, Jenner administered enough chloroform to make her drowsy. Then Lister froze the abscess, described by Victoria as about six inches in diameter, and lanced it. "In an instant there was relief. I was then tightly bandaged and rested on my bed. . . . Felt very shaken and exhausted."

Lister remained at Balmoral for a further week to observe the Queen's progress. When he left, it was considered time to inform the nation of the Queen's recovery. An account that left out more than it revealed appeared in the *British Medical Journal,* and newspapers expressed anxious concern. At Balmoral, Ponsonby saw the Queen on September 13 looking "rather pulled down, thinner and paler." She was rolled in her wheelchair into her sitting room to see Princess Alice, and carried downstairs by Brown to go for a short drive. The Prime Minister arrived as Minister-in-Attendance—a sign of the Government's anxiety. By note, Gladstone entreated the Queen "after so serious a derangement of health on no account to make any effort for the purpose of seeing him during his stay." With no information to go on but what he saw at Balmoral, he knew that Victoria was far from better.

Although her doctors told no one, her newest problem was what they called rheumatic gout, and her feet had swollen painfully. She was drugged with chloral to help her sleep, and remained too feeble to maintain her journal without assistance. Beatrice continued to take her dictation, as she had for most of August and September.

A delicious confusion reigned in the press and among the public. A decade of post-Albert malaise became intertwined with her sudden need for the ministrations of the already legendary Dr. Lister, soon to be Sir Joseph. She was perceived as having broken in health almost completely as a result of the innumerable pressures upon her, which her subjects had seen fit until then to undervalue. *The Times* on September 18 apologized for having accused her of shamming. *The Daily News* on September 15 had already confessed that the nation was "ashamed" of its complaints that she had been denying "proper splendour to her Queenly position," and "rebukes itself for uttering them." Leaping at the political opportunity, Disraeli toasted the Queen's health at a harvest festival in his home district of Hughenden on September 26, conceding that one could not conceal the seriousness of her condition, and the fact that she had been "morally and physically incapacitated" from doing her duties for a long time. But, he added, her role went beyond mere ceremony, and her other state duties continued to be performed "with a punctuality and a precision which have certainly never been surpassed, and rarely equalled, by any monarch of these realms." His peroration idealized Victoria as a head of state whose signature "has never been put to any public document of which she did not know the purpose. . . . There is probably no person living in this country who has such complete control over the political tradition of England as the Sovereign herself. . . . May she still continue a reign which has been distinguished by public duty and private virtue."

Maliciously, the *Daily Telegraph,* a supporter of Gladstone, took out of context Disraeli's badly chosen phrase, "morally and physically incapacitated," and trumpeted that Disraeli had publicly conceded that Victoria was unfit to govern. Disraeli rushed off an apologetic letter to the Queen through Dr. Jenner, but Victoria remained deeply offended. Yet the words were largely accurate. The moral authority of the English monarchy seemed not to have survived Albert. But for a few echoes, mainly personal outbursts, the last episode of national importance in which that moral authority had been registered was the Prince Consort's intervention in the *Trent* affair, just before he died. Victoria's decade of malaise and drift had left little to the empty throne beyond its almost defunct ceremonial dimension. "Disraeli has done her & the country a left-handed service . . . ," Gladstone wrote to Granville. "The right aim is to keep her up to work. . . ."

Meanwhile, Jenner and the other Court physicians fell silent about the Queen's affliction, but for a signed letter to the editors of the *Lancet* and the *British Medical Journal* (published in both on November 4, 1871), in which Jenner denied that Victoria's revaccination "many months" before had been responsible. He blamed the rumors on anti-vaccination cranks.* All the while, however, Victoria remained very ill with what she called, on September 11, the day her bandages were removed, "almost a *third* illness." In late September she was still feverish and exhausted, and in great pain from swelling of both legs and the left ankle and foot. There was still "violent" pain in her right shoulder and she was "quite unable" to move her right hand. As late as October 18 she

---

*Jenner's protection of his reputation, enhanced by his treating Albert in his last illness, and his care of the Queen, was triumphantly successful. At his death in 1898—he was eighty-five—he left an estate of over £300,000.

was writing in her diary (via dictation to Beatrice), "A most dreadful night of agonising pain. No sedative did any good. I only got some sleep between five and eight this morning. Felt much exhausted in awaking, but there was no fever and the pain was less. Had my feet and hands bandaged. My utter helplessness is a bitter trial, not even being able to feed myself. . . . Was unable all day hardly to eat anything." Still, her right hand had recovered at least enough that she could again begin to affix her initials to papers that continued to come in the familiar red boxes. "Was able to sign," she added, "which is a great thing."

The "rheumatic gout" or rheumatic arthritis—as it affected her hands as well as her feet—was a consequence of the earlier infection, but could have been considered by the Queen's doctors as a separate ailment. Even had Jenner known fully what he was doing, to have offered more information during the Queen's illness would have alarmed the nation without explaining away her long years of malaise, for which he was chief apologist. Merely announcing the fact of serious and undefined illness, from which the Queen was recovering, suggested a physical breakdown that could have been the result of overwork. It was a picture of events that the press and the people—for a time—accepted. Only on November 22 did Victoria feel herself that she was "returning to ordinary life." But since her life was ordinarily so reclusive (especially at Balmoral), and her doctors so circumspect, no one outside her immediate circle knew that she had remained agonizingly ill long after she was declared well.

The Queen's physical breakdown had silenced, with embarrassment, many of her most outspoken republican critics. Unrepentant, however, Sir Charles Dilke continued to go after the Queen as not worth the nation's investment in her establishment of homes, yachts, functionaries, horses, and guards. A Liberal M.P. for Chelsea, as a boy Dilke had first encountered the Queen in Hyde Park, when he was walking with his father, a friend of the Prince Consort. Victoria had stroked his head. "I suppose I stroked it the wrong way," she remarked in his republican heyday.

Tabbed as a future Cabinet member, Dilke had been selected the year before, at twenty-seven, to second the Loyal Address to the Crown in the formalities opening Parliament in February 1870. He had since done his arithmetic, and in a speech at Newcastle-on-Tyne on November 6, 1871, entitled "Representation and Royalty," he ticked off the costs to the nation—nearly a million pounds a year, he estimated—of the "waste, corruption and inefficiency" of the monarchy. The Queen fired off a protest to Gladstone about his young colleague's "gross misstatements and fabrications, injurious to the credit of the Queen, and injurious to the Monarchy. . . ." But Gladstone, always the idealist, had already upheld, at the Lord Mayor's banquet in London on November 9, the right of any Englishman to speak out "without any limit at all" on matters relating to "the institutions under which we live." If Dilke helped to propel the Queen into doing her duty, the Prime Minister may have felt that was an additional bonus.

While the controversy over Dilke's criticism kept newspapers busy (the contrite *Times* called the allegations "recklessness bordering on criminality"), the Prince of Wales was resting from the exertions of a pheasant shoot at the estate of the Earl of Londesborough. The Scarborough region had long been famous for its salubrious waters, and Londesborough Lodge, overlooking the bay, shared the questionable benefits of its spa location. It was, the *British Medical Journal* confessed afterwards, "the worst drained town in England," as became apparent to the playboy Earl's guests, even the Earl himself, when they quickly came down with diarrhea. Returning to Sandringham for his thirtieth birthday, the Prince of Wales was incubating typhoid fever.

A bulletin issued over the signatures of Sir William Jenner and three other physicians from the Prince's home in Norfolk on November 24 blandly announced the illness of the heir to the Throne, adding, "There are no unfavourable symptoms." It did not take long memories, however, for the nation to recall Prince Albert's decline and death, allegedly from typhoid. Quick to capitalize upon a sensation, and penitent after the Queen's serious illness, newspapers rushed out special editions to meet the demands of a public that had never really warmed to republicans. The Royal Family hurried to Sandringham. Even the Queen arrived, although still wan and weak, making demands upon the small guest space available that forced the eviction of lesser eminences to nearby inns and country houses. What appeared most ominous to a sensation-hungry press was that the Prince's fever was likely to crest (it had already reached 104 degrees) on December 14. "It is now ten years tomorrow," the *Pall Mall Gazette* editorialized, "since the Prince Consort died of a similar affliction. As long as the world lasts there will be superstition in it, and however foolish the feeling, there is real anxiety about tomorrow." With sanctimonious sincerity, Gladstone wrote to the Queen that he would not "mock the sorrow of this moment by assurances which . . . must seem so poor and hollow; but he earnestly commends the sufferer and the afflicted round him, most of all the Mother and the Wife, to Him alone who is able either to heal or to console, and who turns into mercies the darkest of all His dispensations." Loyal prayers emanated from pulpits everywhere in the Isles where only weeks before their occupants had privately deplored the Prince of Wales's immorality and uselessness. Newspapers published solemn leaders mawkishly noting the awesome date and the likelihood of the Heir's death. At his bedside, Princess Alexandra, Princess Alice (who had earlier tended her father), and the Queen gathered in the sickroom for the end, Victoria recalling, "Alice and I said to one another in tears, 'There can be no hope.' I went up to the bed and took hold of his poor hand, kissing it and stroking his arm. He turned round and looked wildly at me saying, 'Who are you?' and then 'It's Mama.' 'Dear child,' I replied. Later he said, 'It is so kind of you to come,' which shows he knew me, which was most comforting to me."

Throughout December, wherever "God Save the Queen" was sung, weeping audiences added "God Bless the Prince of Wales." *Reynolds' Newspaper,* claiming that the Prince's condition had never been anything but "purposely exaggerated," described the event as "a sham panic got up for the occasion to serve a political end." Still, republicanism was all but dead, Lord Henry Lennox, the witty younger son of the Duke of Richmond and M.P. for Chichester, telling Disraeli, "What a sell for Dilke this illness has been!" The *Daily Telegraph,* having three months earlier quoted Disraeli gleefully on the Queen's failure to reign, now declared piously, "When we put the Throne of England away in the British Museum, we will, please God, have a nobler reason than that it costs us a million sterling; that is to say, sevenpence three farthings apiece." Suddenly Victoria and her family were a bargain.

A few days after the Prince of Wales was declared out of danger, his personal physician, Dr. William Gull, was awarded a baronetcy, to universal amens. "Had *my* Prince had the same treatment as the Prince of Wales," the Queen said privately, nursing some new skepticism about Albert's medical care, "he might not have died."

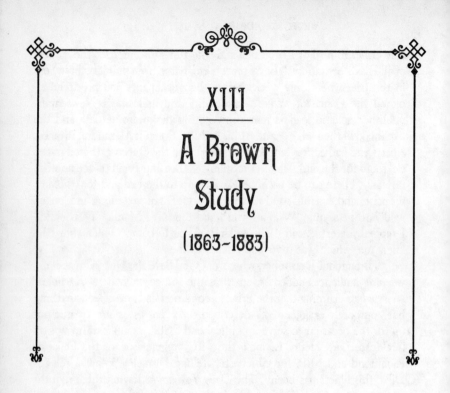

XIII

A Brown Study

(1863-1883)

"The real secret about John Brown and the Queen," William Rossetti wrote in his diary in 1870, on the authority of a visiting spiritualist, Signor Damiani, "is that Brown is a powerful medium, through whom Prince Albert's spirit communicates with the Queen: hence Brown remains closeted with her alone sometimes for hours together." The period was one of intense interest in the occult, and William's brother, Dante Gabriel, whose wife died only a few months after the Prince Consort, had resorted to mediums to make contact with her shade. It was easier, although totally erroneous, to explain John Brown's relationship with Victoria in that context, and rumor reflected such apparent logic.

There was, moreover, a connection with Albert. Brown had been his favorite gillie at Balmoral, and had often been chosen by the Prince to look after the Queen's safety as well as to perform a variety of out-of-doors tasks. When the widowed Queen traveled to Germany in the summer of 1862, and decided to take her own pony chaise, Brown was in charge of it. The next year, when she suffered a series of carriage mishaps, it was Brown who saved her from serious injury when her coachman drove her into a ditch in the darkness, and who seized a runaway horse. He seemed to emerge when needed, and in 1863—the Queen was forty-four—Brown was a rough but shrewd Scot of thirty-nine who liked his whiskey, looked good in a kilt, and was addicted to homely, outspoken observations that ignored rank and status. Albert had enjoyed his company, and had indulged him in the license permitted only to an intimate servant.

When the Queen's physician, Dr. Jenner, wanted, in October 1864, to keep her riding through the winter, Victoria protested that in her "weak and nervous" state a strange groom would not do. Sir Charles Phipps sent for John Brown to lead the Queen's pony, Flora. His duties quickly expanded beyond Flora, and early in February 1865 Victoria determined to keep Brown with her, writing in her journal that he would remain "permanently" and "make himself useful in other ways . . . as he is so dependable." The next day she prepared a memorandum describing his position. He would be in charge of her safety on horses and in carriages, and would continue caring for her outdoors garb and supervising her dogs (petty tasks he would soon relinquish). As "the Queen's Highland Servant," Brown would take orders from her alone.

On March 1, 1865, Victoria was beginning to break her seclusion in token fashion. Hosting a reception for the diplomatic corps, she was put off by the peevish behavior of the Prussian ambassador, and quoted Brown about him in a letter to her daughter in Berlin, perhaps preparing Vicky for an announcement likely to be received badly. "Brown's observation about a cross person seems to me very applicable here: it can't be very pleasant for a person themselves to be always cross." It was "so true and so original. His observations upon everything he sees and hears here are excellent and many show how superior in feeling, sense and judgment he is to the servants here! The talking and indiscretion shocks him."

That Brown was so tactless as to gossip to the Queen was hardly less shocking to the Crown Princess of Prussia than was her mother's enthusiastic approval. A month later, the Queen revealed to Vicky that Brown "entirely and permanently" had become her personal "out of doors" servant. "He comes to my room after breakfast and luncheon to get his orders—and everything is always right; he is so quiet, has such an excellent head and memory, and is besides so devoted, and attached and clever and so wonderfully able to interpret one's wishes. He is a real treasure to me now, and I only wish higher people had his sense and discretion, and that I had as good a maid." His rank and pay (£120 a year), she added cautiously, would be below that of Rudolf Löhlein, Albert's personal servant, still in Victoria's household. "It is an excellent arrangement, and I feel I have here and always in the house a good devoted soul . . . whose only object and interest is my service, and God knows how I want so much to be taken care of."

Exactly how she was being taken care of became the subject of intense and widespread gossip in June 1865, much of it as a result of Edwin Landseer's painting of the Queen on her horse, as led by the curly-haired, kilted Brown. In close intimacy with both as he worked, he passed on what Lord Stanley described in his diary as "strange and disagreeable stories . . . probably not justifying the suspicion to which they lead. The Queen has taken a fancy to a certain Scotch servant, by name Brown: will have no one else to wait upon her, makes him drive her out alone in a pony carriage, walk with, rather than after her, gives orders through him to the equerries, allows him access to her such as no one else has, and in various ways distinguishes him beyond what is customary or fitting in that position." The affair had "become a joke through[out] Windsor, where H.M. is talked of as 'Mrs. Brown': and if it lasts the joke will grow into a scandal." Stanley blamed "eccentricity, solitude, and the impossibility of hearing an honest opinion."

By October, Stanley was worrying how much longer the subject could be kept out of the newspapers. "The man is admitted to her confidence in a way that no one else is, and orders sent through him to persons of higher rank, which alone is enough to create jealousy. The Queen has repelled all friendship with subjects as beneath her dignity, and is not on good terms with any of her family, hence it is impossible that she should be warned of what is being said about her. . . ."

In the years of the Queen's drift into public disfavor, republican sentiment viewed no throne as an improvement upon an empty one. While increasingly the butt of cruel jokes in the popular press about his alleged power over the invisible sovereign, Brown was a bulwark for Victoria. He worked seven-day weeks and would take no leave. His entire waking life was bound up with his service. In mid-December 1865, he attended the Queen as she paid her respects at the "dear Mausoleum" in Frogmore on the fourth anniversary of Albert's death. Then he came to her room for his usual orders, tears rolling down his cheeks. "I didn't like to see ye at Frogmore this morning. I felt for ye," he said, "to see ye coming there with ye daughters and your husband lying there—marriage on one side and death on the other; no, I didn't like to see it; I felt sorry for ye; I know so well what your feeling must be—ye who had been so happy. There is no more pleasure for you, poor Queen, and I feel for ye but what can I do though for ye? I could die for ye."

The Queen would praise his devotion. Brown's simple tenderness was "peculiarly touching," she wrote to Vicky, in the person of a "strong, hardy man, a child of the mountains." Wishing Princess Helena joy after the announcement of her engagement, Brown had added, "Only one thing; I hope you'll never forget the good Queen." The Princess saw nothing touching in his remark, only the rudeness of a servant who did not know his place. When Prince Sigismund, Vicky's youngest son, died, giving the Queen new cause for her grief, Brown came forward—she told Vicky—and announced, "I wish to take care of my dear good mistress till I die. You'll never have an honester servant."

In her journal (as we know now only from her quoting it in a private letter) she added, "I took his dear kind hand and I said I hoped he might long be spared to comfort me and he answered, 'But we all must die.' "

"Afterwards," she added, "so often I told him [that] no one loved him more than I did or had a better friend than me: and he answered 'Nor you—than me. No one loves you more.' " The transparent sincerity suggests a mother and her oversized, and somewhat simple, foster son rather than noble mistress and lowborn lover. Brown's utter personal loyalty was unlike anything else in the Queen's experience. In an earlier, less civilized age he would have killed for her as readily as he carried her tea tray.

Victoria's relations with her Scottish servants were a world removed from her formal and fussy English manners. The close quarters of the original Balmoral residence had made ornate dignities impossible, and life in Highland Scotland was always less ceremonial and rule-ridden than in the public glare of English settings, even Osborne. As a result, her children and grandchildren were expected to demonstrate equal informality. The future Grand Duke Ernest Ludwig of Hesse, one of Princess Alice's sons, recalled that Victoria was always "lenient" with servants, even at Windsor. "Her idea was that when people were well-bred and well-educated, they should know better than to make mistakes. But she would always forgive humble people, whatever they did. When I was a boy, I used to stay with her in Scotland, and the first thing she told me to do was to go and see the servants and gillies I had known the year before."

The Duke of Connaught (Victoria's third son, Prince Arthur) remembered in his late seventies—he lived to be ninety-two—that when he arrived at Balmoral, "before anything else" he was sent to shake hands with the servants. He also remembered a man who looked after the lamps at Windsor Castle, in his later years such a drunkard that officials urged the Queen to authorize his dismissal. One day he fell down a flight of stairs with a lighted lamp, causing a small fire. Finally, it seemed, he had brought about his ruin; but when the report of the episode was placed before the Queen, her son recalled, she only wrote "poor man" in the margin.

The Queen's older children detested her permissive attitude toward servants, particularly toward Brown, and his open, doglike devotion. Princess Alice recognized that he was "an honest and really faithful servant," yet resented Brown's ability to discuss anything whatever with the Queen, while she and her sisters and brothers were told that the perpetually grieving widow could not have subjects brought to her that might be unduly exciting. They were also unhappy about Brown's knowledge of their affairs—duly carried to the Queen—which suggested an informal intelligence network of servants loyal to the Highlander. The Queen once told the Princess of Wales that she was sorry that a ball at the Wales' estate at Abergeldie had not been a success—Brown, Victoria confessed, had found that out.

Servants were not above confiding information to Brown when information meant a modicum of power, because they knew that the Highlander's recommendation for a job, or a promotion, meant more than that of princes. When he spoke, courtiers often cringed, or scattered. Once, asked how many in the Queen's Household could share her pew at Crathie without inconveniencing her when she took the Sacrament, he snarled, "She had better have a place all to herself without all this hombogging." The church at Crathie required his special vigilance. According to *The World* of November 18, 1874, "an enterprising gentleman" secreted himself behind the door of the center gallery to get a closer look at the Queen, "and having accomplished his purpose, departed whistling triumphantly. He bragged of his exploit, and had an imitator the next Sunday. But the tale had reached the ears of the burly John Brown, who, watching his opportunity, . . . flattened the second aspirant between the door and the wall."

Ceremony meant little to him where the Queen's interests were involved. He once horrified a director of the Great Western Railway by striding into a car occupied by the Prince of Wales and his family and announcing—he was only quoting Victoria's words, as if he were an extension of her person—"The Queen wants the boys in her carriage." It is unlikely, too, that the Heir to the Throne ever forgot Brown's injunction, overheard by the servants, "Ye'll no' see your Royal mither till five o'clock!"

Vicky's own attitude became clear when young Princess Charlotte, her daughter, was asked, on a visit, "Say how de do to Brown, my dear." When she did, her grandmother added, "Now go and shake hands with Brown." "No," insisted Charlotte. "Mama says I ought not to be too familiar with servants." When Princess Louise married the Marquess of Lorne in 1871, Brown took up a collection among the staff for a present and himself contributed thirty guineas—a substantial part of his annual salary (then £320), and far more than higher ranks. (Ponsonby, the Private Secretary, gave ten guineas.) Nevertheless, Louise told Ponsonby when they discussed her future servants, "I won't have an absurd man in a kilt following *me* everywhere." When another of the children, Prince Alfred, refused to shake hands with Brown some months after a quarrel at Balmoral, the Queen asked Ponsonby to investigate, and to see that the Prince and Brown met on friendly terms. Only, said Alfred—now captain of a cruiser, the *Galatea*—if Ponsonby was present as a witness, as was the custom in the navy. Victoria was irate with the most arrogant of her sons. "This is not a ship, and I won't have naval discipline introduced here." When the men met, however, the Private Secretary was present, and put some of the exchange into a letter to his wife:

BROWN: Am I right, Sir, in thinking that you are annoyed with something I have done in the past? If so, please tell me, for it is most painful that any of Her Majesty's children should be angry with me.

PRINCE ALFRED: It's nothing that you have done in the past. But I must confess that I was surprised at the extraordinary language you used at the gillies' ball last May.

BROWN: Her Majesty put the whole arrangements for the ball into my hands. . . . At first I did not know that it was Your Royal Highness who had stopped the music, and I was very angry and lost my temper. I cannot think it possible that I used any nasty words, but if Your Royal Highness says so then it must have been so, and I must humbly ask your forgiveness.

As they parted, the Prince announced that he was satisfied with the outcome. "I'm quite satisfied, too," said Brown, refusing to accept the idea of inferiority. And indeed he regarded himself—in the view of out-raged observers—as inferior to no one but the Sovereign. Yet it was Victoria's command that he obey no one but her.

Sometimes, it seemed to the Court, the instructions took a different direction. In what might be called the Great Smoking Row, at Balmoral,* Brown complained to the Queen about being kept up too late at night by royal smokers, considering how early he had to be up to serve her. All the princes smoked, as had their father, and the royal sons-in-law were even heavier smokers than all but the cigar-addicted Prince of Wales. The simplest solution might have been to eliminate the room in question from Brown's surveillance. Instead, Victoria minuted her equerry, Lord Charles Fitzroy, to "simply mention to Prince [Christian of Schleswig-Holstein, Helena's husband] *without* giving it as a *direct order* that the Queen felt it *necessary* for the sake of the *servants . . .* that the smoking rooms should be closed . . . by 12 o'clock—not later." Everyone involved knew the origin of the order. "Do you smoke?" Oscar Wilde's Lady Bracknell asks John Worthing, the wealthy suitor for her daughter's hand. When he confesses uncomfortably that he does, she replies imperturbably, "Good! A man should always have an occupation of some kind." For all but one of the Queen's sons-in-law, little other occupation was open. If Brown heard of their unhappiness, it made little difference. Everyone at Court was aware of Victoria's intolerance of smoking, and once, as her royal sons-in-law were reclining in front of the fireplace at Windsor and smoking up the chimney, a servant came to the door and informed them that her Majesty had detected the infraction of the rules. Brown, they were sure, had told her.

In March 1866, repeating more of the gossip about Brown, Lord Stanley was convinced that although the suspicions had no foundation, the Queen's behavior was giving them credibility. "Long solitary rides, in secluded parts of the park: constant attendance upon her in her room: private messages sent by him to persons of rank: avoidance of observation

---

*At Osborne in 1866 the Queen added a smoking room to the Household Wing. It had no access directly into the house, which meant walking through the rain at times to use it.

while he is leading her pony or driving her little carriage: everything shows that she has selected this man for a kind of friendship which is absurd and unbecoming her position. The Princesses—perhaps wisely—make a joke of the matter, and talk of him as 'Mama's lover.' "

Brown was even less likely to be aware of the press commotion about him than of the family's displeasure, as he was not given to reading. The few political opinions he had appeared to reflect the Queen's franker views. In 1872 he wanted the Government turned out, and was especially unhappy with Gladstone, who was "half a Roman. . . . We canna have a worse lot." When Ponsonby asked him, as eastern Mediterranean affairs again heated up, whether he looked forward to war, he was vehemently negative. "I think it would be awful," he said; "dreadful deal of fighting and at the end no one would be better and a' would be the worse for it."

Brown probably never saw the scandalmongering London weekly *Tomahawk*, particularly the issue of August 10, 1867, which referred to him. A cartoon echoed the impatience of many Englishmen with Brown and with the Queen, and suggested a connection between her servant and her seclusion. In "A Brown Study"—the term in English usage can refer to a daydream—the Crown languishes unused in a glass case, but the

"A Brown Study"—the notorious cartoon in Tomahawk, *August 1867. John Brown is seen musing against a backdrop of a vacant throne and a protesting lion.*

British lion, awakened, is lunging toward a man in Highlander's dress who has his back to an empty throne. Nearly fifty thousand copies of the issue were sold. *Tomahawk* also published a cartoon version of Landseer's portrait of the Queen on horseback, with Brown standing at the reins, under the caption, "All is black that is not Brown."

While such press irresponsibility fed further rumors, nothing changed, except to increase Brown's celebrity. A gentleman in Highland dress, going to a Court function, was once spotted by street boys, who, as the carriage drew in, crowded about it, shouting, " 'Ooray! 'Ere's John Brown!" The occupant shouted back angrily before lowering his window, "I'm no' John Brown: I'm Cameron o'Lochiel!"

Brown's increasing intimacy with Victoria quickly led to scurrilous gossip that she had secretly married her gillie. An anonymous pamphlet entitled "Mrs. John Brown" was circulated, and there were people who believed that if something appeared in print, it had to be true. In that climate, on June 30, 1866, *Punch* published "An Imaginary Dispatch" under a Balmoral dateline, in which the Queen complained to her Ministers about being excluded from foreign affairs. Then it followed the next week with an imaginary *Court Circular*, also from Balmoral:

> Mr. John Brown walked on the Slopes. He subsequently partook of a haggis.
> In the evening, Mr. John Brown was pleased to listen to a bagpipe.
> Mr. John Brown retired early.

Another comic paper, *John o'Groats Journal*, continued the heavy sarcasm in August, suggesting that he had been dismissed "some weeks ago" for heavy drinking, but was likely to achieve "a restoration to power." By October, the *Pall Mall Gazette* was reporting that the British Minister at Berne "has addressed a complaint to the Swiss Federal Council against the *Lausanne Gazette*, on account of an article in that journal containing calumnies against Queen Victoria." Calling attention to yet another report that she had married John Brown was an error in strategy that appalled Henry Ponsonby. If the Queen discovered it (she was again hidden at Balmoral), Ponsonby wrote to his brother Arthur, she would be "angry and wretched." Brown, he suggested, was "conspicuous" because of his Highland dress, but was "only a Servant and nothing more." Yet even Brown's bare knees became a subject of public fun in an anonymous pamphlet, "John Brown's Legs, or Leaves from a Journal in the Low-lands."

It is possible that courtiers who found him domineering beyond his status kept the libel circulating, in hopes of embarrassing the Queen into returning Brown to Balmoral. Since the Highlander had the assignment of carrying messages to and from Victoria, they may have also been behind working him to exhaustion, in vain hopes of having him request reassignment. Such seems possible from the Queen's exasperated plea to Sir Thomas Biddulph, Master of the Household, "that my poor Brown has so much to do that it wd be a *gt* relief if the Equerries did receive a *hint* not to be *constantly* sending for him *at all hours* for trifling messages: he is often *so tired* from being constantly on his legs that he goes to bed with swollen feet and then can't sleep from fatigue!" The pages and ladies were equally to blame, she added, "& it must be put a stop to. . . ."

Brown's visibility became a matter for Government embarrassment. When the Queen announced that she would attend a military review in Hyde Park on July 5, 1867, and would be attended by Brown (in his usual kilts), Ministerial satisfaction at her willingness to be seen as Sovereign was dampened by the expectation of further press gossip about the conspicuous Highlander. The Home Secretary, Gathorne-Hardy, made an unusual Sunday-morning visit to Lord Derby's home on June 30, and while Derby lay in bed nursing his gout and rheumatism, they "had a long talk on the troublesome John Brown. There has been a remonstrance & he is not to be at the Review, but I fear some step which will make things worse in the public view."

The step came quickly. Victoria refused to appear without Brown at her side, which Derby found so "prejudicial" to public perception of the event that he ordered the review "given up." But before the cancellation became public knowledge, news arrived from Mexico that Maximilian, the young emperor imposed unsuccessfully by Napoleon III, had been captured by rebels and executed on June 19. Maximilian's wife was a daughter of Victoria's late uncle, Leopold. The Government seized upon the pathetic news as its cause for calling off the review, but the Queen was not so easily satisfied, writing to her equerry, Lord Charles Fitzroy, without mentioning names, that she "will not be dictated to, or *made* to *alter* what she has found to answer for her comfort." If the Government wanted her, it would have to stomach Brown.

Stomaching Brown was difficult, and would become more exasperating as he rose in the Queen's esteem and in the process acquired more license. He became the one person in her life from whom a fawning hypocrisy was not expected. Helping to secure her bonnet, he could say, "Hoots, then wumman! Can ye no hold yerr head up?" Or, about some wrap that earned his disapproval, "What's this ye've got on today?"

What was coarseness to observers was only disarming to Victoria, and she heard little if anything of such comments as his to the maid-of-honor who asked politely whether he was taking tea to the Queen in his hamper: "Well, no," he said. "She don't much like tea. We tak oot biscuits and speeruts." Nor was she likely to have been told of the outcome of the visit of the mayor of Portsmouth to Osborne, to beseech the Queen to be present at a review of volunteers. Sir Henry Ponsonby had sent in the request, and while he and the mayor sat in the Equerries' Room waiting, Brown poked his head out the door and announced, "The Queen says saretenly not."

When General Henry Gardiner arrived to see the Queen, and shook hands civilly with Brown, asking, "How is the Queen, and what is she saying?" the Highlander demonstrated a sense of humor as well as an unconcern for rank and status. "Well, she just said, 'Here's that damned fellow Gardiner come and he'll be poking his nose into everything.' " That Brown might have been reporting with literal honesty made such remarks even more disconcerting to courtiers and statesmen visiting the Queen.

Stories about Brown's drinking weaknesses were common at Court, but never made any difference to Victoria. Once at Balmoral, when he failed to appear in the box of her carriage, Ponsonby went to Brown's room and found him dead drunk. Without a word to the Queen, the Private Secretary took Brown's place on the box, and Victoria ordered the coachman off without comment. On another occasion, Brown was found helplessly drunk at the Queen's door, and carried off to bed. When Dr. James Reid, who would succeed William Jenner as chief physician to the Court, told the Queen that the combination of strong tobacco and strong drink was proving too much for Brown, who, it was suggested, should give up his favorite Lochnagar whiskey for claret, Victoria bridled at Reid's effrontery in bringing up the unwanted subject. The Highlander was beyond criticism.

At the beginning of 1868, *Leaves from the Journal of Our Life in the Highlands* was published, as edited by Sir Arthur Helps, who corrected the grammar and reduced the underlinings. The book sold twenty thousand copies within a few weeks, and became a best-seller, and the Queen earned more than £4,000 in royalties, which she turned over to charities and gifts "to people who are *not rich.*" Despite the gloom among her children at such widespread reading of their mother's once-private diaries, the largely innocuous extracts from the Albert period, embellished by her own drawings, emphasized her largely middle-class tastes and gave her a visibility that belied her seclusion. They were, Henry Ponsonby's grandson Arthur wrote, "an innocent and rather sentimental picture of purely domestic events, expeditions, family goings and comings, little ceremonies, country scenes, and deaths, births and marriages." In effect, they fleshed out laconic old issues of the *Court Circular* for a public always eager for trivia about how royalty really lived.

Few if any lived the way Victoria did, and she had no intention of deluding her readers. Yet as Arthur Ponsonby observed, it would be possible to pick almost any day recorded in the Queen's Highland journals only by a homely incident or excursion and contrast it with her correspondence for the same day with "some letter to the Prime Minister or the Private Secretary expressing in her most vehement language her desire to interfere in high matters of national importance." Since none of that appeared in *Leaves,* even the most radical of her antagonists were disarmed by her apparent willingness to leave government to her elected officials, while she remained harmlessly in her Scottish retreat. Of course there were other objections—that she was living there uselessly at vast public expense, and possibly not-so-innocently with John Brown. ("What a curious infatuation it was," Gladstone's private secretary Edward Hamilton wrote in his diary.) Yet Brown's early appearances in the journals were hardly more frequent than those of a Grant or a Macdonald, and *Leaves,* full of homely virtues and rural satisfactions, became a public-relations triumph at a time when the Queen needed one. *Punch* carped that the book's chief symbol was the tea tray, although the later chapters suggest more the presence of Brown and his bottle, which helped make the tea palatable. He made the best cup of tea she had ever drunk, she once told him enthusiastically. "Well, it should be, Ma'am," he explained. "I put a grand nip o' whisky in it."

To her public, the Queen was humanized by the friendly circumstances in which she lived, in Scotland, with her servants. That aspect dismayed the Court, but even more indignation arose from Victoria's insistence upon biographical notes on gillies and footmen as if they were gentlemen—suggesting that they were all, Lady Augusta Stanley complained, "on the same footing." (Brown received more than twenty lines, twice that of any other servant.) Still, Victoria knew what she was doing. When she wrote of visiting the lowborn, and even included her sketch of a Scottish baby asleep in its wooden cradle on rockers, her readers knew that she was one of them, if only by adoption. Republicanism, even at its noisiest, as it was to be a few years later, had poor soil in which to grow among the Queen's readership.

For readers of gossip sheets, eager to believe the worst about the famous, especially when they were royalty, Brown continued to furnish a ready source of spice, for he was to accompany Victoria in 1868 on her visit to Switzerland. That she was going abroad at all was considered by her Government as a good thing: she might even be induced to go out in her own country. Rumors surfaced, however, that she was traveling to Lausanne in order to give birth, in secrecy, to Brown's child. (In 1873 a pamphlet would be published by a republican Scot, Alexander Robertson, alleging that the Queen had become the morganatic wife of John Brown, and had borne him a child.*) That in 1868 Victoria was in her fiftieth year made little impression on the gullible; and the visit to Lucerne (rather than Lausanne) was far from secret, given the Queen's entourage and equipage—complete to a wagonette and a Scotch "sociable" (an open four-wheeled carriage with seats facing each other, and a box seat for the coachman) and horses. Brown, Victoria wrote to Vicky that August, sat "in a dicky behind, which has purposely been added, and under which is a box . . . in which go the luncheons, tea baskets, etc." Brown and his brother Archie—another of her gillies—"go about unmolested or noticed in their kilts," Victoria claimed.

The Queen's entourage was difficult not to notice. She had with her three of her children—Louise, Beatrice, and Leopold—as well as secretaries, cooks, maids, menservants, and a chaplain. When Prince Arthur suggested that he might also visit the Pension Wallis, Victoria wrote to dissuade him, "We have no room to spare for a mouse." It would be the Queen's only experience of Switzerland, and one of the rare trips abroad she would make in Brown's lifetime, as he detested foreign travel. "I don't hold," said Brown, "with travelling and racketting about."

Lady Longford, in her biography of Victoria, called that one of his "oddest disservices"—and these were few—to the Queen. "Loathing the

---

*A suit against the pamphleteer was considered, but dropped. As Earl Granville wrote to the Lord Chancellor, "The evils of a discussion on such a subject in a Court of Law, or of an attempt to punish the offender without full discussion appear to me immense."

language, sights and smells himself, he forced her to maintain a strict
Balmoral regimen in Baveno, Mentone, or Cannes. The royal party rarely
set out early, and Brown, imagining Fenians everywhere, refused to stop
during a drive lest a crowd should collect. His own Highland garb made
sure that it did. With folded arms and lowered eyes he sat doggedly
between the Queen and the view. . . . At Baveno the Italian sunshine
pleased him less than ever for he went down with a violent attack of
erysipelas. . . ." From Baveno that spring the royal suite had gone to see
the sights of Milan, but, Ponsonby wrote to his wife, "with Brown on the
box who never raised his head to look at anything," the Queen "saw
nothing . . . I stopped the carriage once and ran back to tell her these were
San Lorenzo's columns. But this stopping of the carriage was coldly
received [by Brown] and a crowd began to assemble to see the Highlander,
so we went on. . . ."

After the Swiss holiday, on which she traveled in well-publicized
pseudonymity as the Countess of Kent, she became more insistent, whatever the complaints, in having Brown conspicuous on her carriage. Even
at Balmoral, Brown's milieu, he was a controversial figure. Victoria had
given him the authority to allocate hunting and fishing times and places
on the Scottish estates, and Brown was alleged by the disappointed to
award himself and his cronies the best conditions. If the weather seemed
unfavorable, or the bag likely to be sparse, one of the visiting Royal
Princes, or sons-in-law, or perhaps the Queen's physician, would be permitted to go out. An example of his opportunities as well as his perceived
importance is preserved on Number 10 Downing Street notepaper in a
message from Disraeli thanking Brown for a "Leviathan" of a Scotch
salmon. "I hope, some day," the Prime Minister wrote, "you may throw
a fly into the humble waters of Hughenden." When it came to new
legislation, Disraeli once joked, "I must first be sure that it would have
the approval of the two J.B.s." He meant, he explained, "John Bull and
John Brown."

"Skittles"—the Mayfair courtesan Catherine Walters, who bedded
many of London's elite, from Lord Hartington to the Prince of Wales—
claimed to Wilfrid Scawen Blunt, one of her lovers, that it was the talk
of Balmoral that Brown was "the Queen's stallion." Her claim to credibility was Sir Joseph Boehm, who told her—she recalled to Blunt many years
after—that he had been commanded to Scotland in 1869–1870 to make
a bust of Brown, and heard then at Balmoral that Victoria, "who had been
passionately in love with her husband, got it into her head that somehow

the Prince's spirit had passed into Brown and four years after her widow-hood, being very unhappy, allowed him all privileges. . . . Boehm saw enough of his familiarities with her to leave no doubt of his being allowed 'every conjugal privilege.' "

Talk there was, and in 1872, Blunt's current mistress, the Rossettian society beauty Georgie Sumner, suggested as much from Scotland, where she had been—as had the Queen—a guest of the Duchess of Sutherland. "The Queen's visit," Georgie joked to Blunt on September 19, "was a great success. I fell in love with John Brown and almost made Her Majesty jealous."

Complaints from the Queen's staff were more about Brown's sweeping Household privileges than any alleged conjugal ones. For a time, Victoria restricted the use of her stables by the Court—except, it appeared, by Brown. Even intervention by the Prince of Wales to Henry Ponsonby had no effect, and it seemed to many that the only solution to Brown's domestic tyranny lay in the hope that tales that he had married were true. A Miss Ocklee, one of the Queen's dressers, was suggested as the likely bride; she often danced with Brown at gillies' balls. When she married someone else in 1873, Brown remained unattached. He also remained above effective criticism; his salary was again raised, and despite his rustic manners and language he was made an esquire. The rank, at the lowest level within the Queen's gift, failed, nevertheless, to protect him from family and courtier conspiracies to get rid of him. When the Queen returned from St. Paul's early in 1872, with Brown sitting behind, as usual, this time (as she wrote to Vicky) "in his very fullest and very handsome full dress," she was announcing, in effect, that Brown was untouchable. Demonstrations of loyalty and enthusiasm were great, causing her to go out again through crowded streets two days later, to take advantage of royalist sentiment in the ebbing tide of republicanism. At the entrance to Buckingham Palace, a seventeen-year-old Fenian, Arthur O'Connor, made his way to the carriage door and pointed a pistol at her. Brown leaped from the rumble and seized the would-be assassin by the throat.

In the aftermath, there were new demonstrations of loyalty, and for a third time in the same week, the Queen rode out to the huzzahs of cheering throngs, the imperturbable Brown surveying things as usual from his box. Determined once again to make her point about her Highland servant, the Queen established a gold "Victoria Faithful Service Medal" for "any very special act of devotion to the Sovereign." Brown received the first; no others were ever awarded.

That Brown was an esquire rather than an ordinary servant, and in a special category all to himself to boot, escaped newcomers to the Court to their peril. When General Sir John McNeill was appointed equerry, he saw no reason to treat the servants any differently from the way he handled his troops. With Brown, he soon found that meant putting his career at hazard. Most intercourse with the Queen—the awkwardness of the system was lost upon her—was by handwritten note or, if Brown was available, by word of mouth through him. At Osborne soon after his arrival, Sir John was brought a message about arranging carriages for the Queen's party. Brown remained standing by the general's writing table until ordered out, McNeill telling him that he would send for him when the authorization was written. Although Brown complied, he also complained without delay to the Queen that Sir John had been overbearing and had shouted at him as if he were a private soldier.

One did that to Brown, the general learned, only once. That evening he received a letter from Victoria asking him if he would like to be transferred to a command in India. He understood that it was not only remote, but a small and minor command indeed, but failed to understand why he was being summarily got rid of. Off he went to Sir Henry Ponsonby, who guessed at the cause, and advised McNeill to reply that he would of course be willing to undertake any assignment Her Majesty was pleased to offer him, but as people would naturally ask why he was so abruptly giving up his post in the Household, he begged that he might be advised what reason he should give.

Since the Queen could hardly furnish the real reason, or any reason, she merely left his response unanswered. He remained an equerry, but for years she never spoke to him; and when after Brown's death she decided to do so again, it was as if no time or circumstance had intervened.

The Queen's esteem for Brown was manifest indirectly, as McNeill discovered, as well as quite openly, more often in token ways that remained personal and private. A book of Scottish dialect verse was inscribed in 1869 "from his true friend VR." A gold watch was an 1875 gift, and a leatherbound Bible "from his faithful friend VRI" in 1878. A sterling silver pipe case with meerschaum pipe was a Christmas gift in 1880; but a Christmas box did not have the special meaning of a gift out of season. The very inscriptions were as much symbolic of the innocence of the relationship as were her other open gestures of affection for Brown. He was also presented by the Queen with a house, "Bal-na-Choile," overlooking the Dee, which she intended for his retirement, but "grace and favour" dwellings were not uncommon.

A New Year's card dated January 1, 1877, could not have been sent by the Queen to her servant had there been any guilt perceived in the relationship. Beneath the picture of a pretty parlor maid were the verses,

> *I send my serving maiden*
> *With New Year letter laden,*
> *Its words will prove*
> *My faith and love*
> *To you my heart's best treasure,*
> *Then smile on her and smile on me*
> *And let your answer loving be,*
> *And give me pleasure.*

Under that the Queen had written,

> *To my best friend J.B.*
> *From his best friend. V.R.I.*

There were similar expressions to her "kind friend" from "his true & devoted one" in 1878, and again in 1879. Perhaps in the convention of manservant and serving maid, there was an element of daydream that Victoria dared not recognize. Victoria's journal entry on her birthday in 1871, at the height of the scurrilous attacks on Brown, again makes clear the straightforward character of Brown's attendance upon her: "My poor old birthday, my 51st! Alone, alone, as it will ever be! But surely my dearest one blesses me."

One of those blessings, the Queen may have thought, was Albert's selection of Brown to be at her side. No two men could have been more different, and she would always refer with longing to the physical beauty she had found in her Prince. Her own feminine charms, such as they were, had long faded, and she knew it. Yet there may have been—despite every purity of motive—a physical delight in the sturdy, kilted Scot who had the task of lifting her on and off her pony, and, when necessary, carrying her from her carriage. Brown was the only man, after Albert, to whose arms she entrusted herself, until Brown himself was gone. He was also the only male with access to the Queen's bedroom—and he rarely bothered to knock. Since the servants knew it, everyone else did.

Although the Queen seldom went to funerals—even those of the mighty, or those of close relatives—in October 1875 she traveled in heavy rain to the house of John Brown's father, to watch from the kitchen while the coffin of old Brown, who had died at eighty-six, was being borne away. "Mr. Campbell, the minister of Crathie, stood in the passage at the door, everyone else standing close outside. As soon as he began his prayer, poor dear old Mrs. Brown came [from next to the fireplace] and stood near me . . . and leant on a chair during the very impressive prayers. . . . When it was over, [John] Brown came over and begged her to go and sit down while they took the coffin away, the brothers bearing it. Every one went out and followed, and we also hurried out and just saw them place the coffin in the hearse, and then we moved on to a hillock, whence we saw the sad procession wending its way sadly down." Then she returned to the house, to comfort the widow with a mourning brooch containing some of her husband's hair (cut off the day before), and she gave lockets to each of the five sons. "We took some whisky and water and cheese, according to the universal Highland custom, and then left," she wrote in her journal, "begging the dear old lady to bear up." Protocol seldom mattered in John Brown's relations with the Queen, and she ignored it just as easily in the privacy of Scotland, where the Browns and others were only less affluent neighbors, and her tenants. The custom in Scotland was for the landlord, in any case, to follow one of his people to the grave.

Among Brown's uses to the Queen was as a bearer of bad tidings, as when her favorite Scots preacher, the Reverend Norman Macleod, died in 1872. "My tears flowed fast," she wrote, "but I . . . thanked good Brown for the very kind way he broke this painful and unexpected news to me." In December 1878 he was even deputed to break the news to the Queen that her daughter Alice, then the Grand Duchess of Hesse, had died of diphtheria, on the very anniversary of the death of Albert. Brown was also sent by Victoria to inquire for her after the sick and dying, his exotic presence manifesting her very special and personal interest. In February 1881 he was sent to Chelsea to inquire about the condition of the dying Thomas Carlyle, only to find that he had come too late.

By then the greying and overweight Queen was no longer the subject of prurient gossip, and Brown's omnipresence was accepted for the watchful care it was. He had long been indispensable to her; now he had become invisible, although he was wearing out in her service. Early in 1883 he insisted upon his seven-days-a-week duties despite chills and fever. Weak from illness, he needed the assistance of another servant, Lockwood, when the Queen, ailing with a swollen knee, had to be carried to her pony chair for a drive. A week earlier, on March 17, as she had noted in her journal, she had "missed the last steps" when going downstairs at Windsor, "and came down violently on one leg." Her knee would never be the same.

A select company had been invited to St. George's Chapel, Windsor, for a Palm Sunday performance of Handel's *The Redemption,* which was canceled because of the Queen's indisposition, and it was six days later that Brown served her for the last time. That evening Sir William Jenner was summoned to Windsor to treat Brown, and by the next morning the crimson streptococcal inflammation of erysipelas had appeared on one side of his face, accompanied by high fever. The Queen's journal as we have it noted only that he had had a bad night. "Vexed that Brown could not attend me, not being at all well. . . ." The next day Brown was delirious, but Victoria seems not to have been told. Using a cane, and the added support of Lockwood, she attended the christening of Prince Leopold's daughter in the private chapel at Windsor, and listened later to a Guards band play the "Alice of Albany" waltz in honor of her new granddaughter. That afternoon, Princess Beatrice took Brown's place in walking beside the pony chair.

By Tuesday, March 29, Brown had lapsed into a coma, and that evening at 10:40 he died. James Reid signed the death certificate as "Erysipelas, 4 days." Leopold came to her dressing room "and broke the dreadful news to me that my good, faithful Brown had passed away early this morning. Am terribly upset by this loss, which removes one who was so devoted and attached to my service and who did so much for my personal comfort. It is the loss not only of a servant, but of a real friend."

The journal entry appears as transcribed by Princess Beatrice; there is no way of knowing what Victoria actually wrote, which may have been more emotional. What is known is how she reacted elsewhere. The same day she lamented to her grandson Prince George of Wales (Albert Edward's second son), "I have lost my *dearest best* friend whom no one in *this World* can *ever* replace." And she urged him to *"never forget* your poor sorrowing Grandmama's *best & truest* friend." To the wife of Brown's brother Hugh, Jessie McHardy Brown, she wrote in a rare personal letter, "Weep with me for we all have lost the best, the truest heart that ever beat. . . . As for me, my grief is unbounded, dreadful, & I know not how to bear it, or how to believe it possible. . . . Dear, dear John— my dearest best friend to whom I could say everything & who always protected me so kindly and who thought of everything—was well and strong and hearty not 3 or 4 days before." Because of his interest in her, she thought, he never took "proper care" of himself, but now he was among the elect, "blessing us and pitying us while we weep." The "excellent upright warmhearted strong John" was gone, she concluded to Jessie Brown on a note of self-pity. "You have your husband—your support, but I have no strong arm now." To Vicky's eldest daughter, the Queen—her grandmother—explained that "for 18 years & ½," Brown "never left me for a day."

The *Court Circular* observed that the "melancholy event" had "caused the deepest regret to the Queen and all the members of the Royal Household." Her wreath sent to the obsequies in Scotland, and placed on Brown's coffin, was "A tribute of loving, grateful, and everlasting friendship and affection from his truest, best, and most faithful friend Victoria R. & I."

The obituary in *The Times* was largely the Queen's own composition, however couched in bland *Times*-ese. Certainly few servants have ever had most of a *Times* column devoted to their biographies, a third of which quoted Victoria's long reference in *Leaves*. "By those in the employment of Her Majesty he was much respected," it added, "being ever ready in his official and private capacity to perform an act of kindness for any one in need of his assistance." There was "Deep regret . . . felt on Deeside. . . . There he was widely known and widely respected. He was loved among his own people, and they regarded his good fortune as an honour reflected upon them." *The World* saw "nothing remarkable in the man himself," but recognized how highly prized to persons of high station, "beset by such a multitude of satellites and flatterers," were "the few of whose integrity and disinterested loyalty they are convinced." "A serious blow to the Sovereign," Brown's death was "like the removal of a familiar object on which the eye has rested and mind has leant during many years." Even that was more regret than was registered among the Queen's children.

To Vicky, the Queen had written of the "terrible blow which . . . has crushed me." The letter was full of ironic echoes of Albert's last days, as Victoria described Brown's end. "Sir William Jenner who knew him well and is never over-sanguine or ever misleads you told me that . . . I need not be so much alarmed. . . . An hour after, all was over . . . ! The shock—the blow, the blank, the constant missing at every turn of the one strong, powerful reliable arm and head almost stunned me and I am truly overwhelmed."

Vicky responded with "loving sympathy" but only added that she was sure that her mother missed someone who had served her faithfully for many years. And she pleaded neuralgia as a reason for not writing more. The Queen followed with a batch of obituary articles, which Vicky suggested gave her mother "pleasure" as "evidence . . . of kindly feeling." Victoria failed to understand an apparently uncaring reaction to what was to her an Albertine catastrophe. What had been a devoted but uncouth and overly familiar servant in the perspective of others had been, to her, "my dearest best friend." Her sorrow was uncontrollable, and as often occurred to her at times of severe stress, she lost the use of her legs. It had happened just after Albert died, and again in 1871 at the height of public criticism of her seclusion. Even after the swelling in her damaged knee had receded, she was unable to walk without help and felt "tied to my chair." Nearly a year after Brown's death she could not stand unaided "beyond a very few minutes," according to the *Court Circular* of January 21, 1884. Her lameness had added to her sorrow, for she had been unable to visit Brown as he lay dying. "I feel so stunned and bewildered and this anguish that comes over me like a wave every now and then through the day or at night is terrible!" she confided to Vicky. "He protected me so, was so powerful and strong—that I felt so safe! And now all is gone in this world. . . ."

All Vicky could do (and even that was beyond the efforts made by the other children) was to express regret at her mother's *"abattement."* She was sure that "dearest Beatrice" was "a great comfort" in the circumstances. Even that seemed less unfeeling than the message from the Prime Minister, Gladstone, who commiserated over the loss of "Mr. J. Brown," whom he identified as a "domestic" in her service. "Your Majesty may be able to select a good and efficient successor," he went on, "though it may be too much to hope that anyone, however capable, could at once fill the void."

Preoccupied with grief and physical disability, the Queen instructed Ponsonby to bar all male members of her Household from her table. "How can I see people at dinner in the evening?" she asked. "I can't go walking about all night holding on to the back of a chair." Because she often had to be carried about, she insisted on keeping her movements secret. The result was a new spate of rumors that her mind had given way. In truth she had become singleminded, as after Albert's death, in her determination to memorialize someone who had meant more to her than even she realized. Sir Joseph Boehm was recruited to create a statue of Brown for

Balmoral, bareheaded and in Highlander garb. Lord Tennyson was asked to prepare an inscription—a couplet that made up in its reflection of Victoria's feelings for its weaknesses as poetry:

> *Friend more than Servant, Loyal, Truthful, Brave,*
> *Self less than Duty, even to the Grave.*

The Queen commanded that Brown's room in the Clarence Tower at Windsor, in which he died, should be left as in his lifetime. Further, she ordered that a flower be placed on Brown's pillow every day; and perhaps because she never issued any further instructions, the practice continued until her own death.

On March 31 she thanked Gathorne-Hardy for his sympathy note, expressing "in broken words her sorrow," and several weeks later, when he met Disraeli's onetime secretary and confidant Lord Rowton (Montagu Corry), Gathorne-Hardy learned that her condition was still "morbid." Rowton had been to Osborne, to which the Queen had repaired, and found her "doing her public duties but dwelling for ever on [Brown's] merits, projecting statue monuments, keeping his room & things as they are, and all as she did for Prince Albert. It will be lamentable if she fulfills her intentions & will do much harm in the country."

Early in May, speculation arose in the London press about a Brown diary "which . . . will need a considerable amount of editing," and *The World* reported that Sir Theodore Martin had demonstrated his "sagacity and independence" by turning down the suggestion that he write a biography of Brown. The proposal seemed to the Queen's Ministers blessedly aborted; they could now turn to other problems, such as the Sovereign's renewed and intensified seclusion. Unwilling to be seen crippled, newspapers reported, she traveled to Osborne in "unexampled privacy." Only indispensable Court staff were allowed to see her leave Windsor, where "a sort of stage has been erected in the hall of the Castle, so that the Queen's wheel-chair can be brought to the door on a level with the carriage." She was then lifted onto her train, and again onto the deck of the *Alberta*. When she went to Balmoral later in the spring, no timetables were issued, and the public was kept from the railway platforms when her train passed. Even her usual carriage ride from Ballater Station to Balmoral was rerouted to evade crowds. (At Balmoral, tenants' and servants' balls were banned for the remainder of the year.)

The wheelchair became a permanent part of Victoria's day-to-day existence. She never again walked more than short distances without the aid of a stick, or supported by a servant. Outdoors she moved about on her pony cart.

Having long planned a continuation volume of *Leaves*, the Queen determined after Brown's death that it would not only be a record of her widowhood as she lived it in the Highlands but, in effect, also a testimonial to a second and implicit widowhood. With Sir Arthur Helps dead, she turned for assistance to Miss Murray MacGregor, who had been useful earlier in preparing a work in which Victoria had a hand, *Highlanders of Scotland*. Princess Beatrice volunteered to design the cover.

From rumor based upon the private edition came speculation that the book would be "to a large extent a biography of the Queen's faithful attendant." That was not the case, but *More Leaves*, published in February 1884, was dedicated to "My loyal highlanders and especially to the memory of my devoted personal attendant and faithful friend John Brown." Among its eight portraits were one of John Grant, head keeper at Balmoral, who had died at seventy in 1879, at a cottage given to him by the Queen near the castle, and another of John Brown. Of the first printing of ten thousand, Mudie's rental libraries took 1,500 for their subscribers, and new editions of five thousand copies each were quickly ordered.

Brown seemed to appear on every page, often in highly personal references, such as the Queen's distress at finding that "poor Brown's legs had been dreadfully cut by the edge of his wet kilt . . . just at the back of the knee." Gladstone thought that the book was "innocence itself," but the Queen's children were horrified at her indiscretions, which they could only refer to indirectly. The Prince of Wales was "indignant" and "disgusted," and complained that he had been omitted altogether (presumably in favor of Brown); Victoria responded acidly that he had been mentioned five times, and would have appeared more often in her pages had he visited her more. The gutter press revived rumors of Brown's enrichment in the Queen's service; in fact, he had left no will, and only £6,816—largely in three bank deposits. It was a substantial sum for someone of the servant class, but he had been well paid and spent little on himself in thirty-five years in service. His personal effects were valued in an inventory filed at Aberdeen at £379 19s 6d.

Since little of Victoria's private affairs remained private very long, a parodist for *Life* produced, for its March 24, 1884, issue, a good-humored mock journal entry suggesting Victoria's naive dependence upon the ever-honest Brown. In it one can detect a sly hint of the Court panic over Brown's own diary, and apprehension about even publishing *More Leaves*.

APRIL 10TH.—I sent for Brown, and read him this journal for a year. He sat with closed eyes, nodding his head whenever I came to a favorite passage. He then said that he did not think any distinguished woman had ever written anything like it. I chided Brown for flattery, but he assured me it was honest truth. I will read it to Mr. Gladstone.

APRIL 12TH.—Mr. Gladstone called. I read it to him.

APRIL 13TH.—Mr. Gladstone is very ill.

APRIL 14TH.—I wanted to read nineteen more chapters of my journal to Brown, but he said he really could not think of letting me tire myself. Said he would take the book and read it in his study. . . .

MAY 7TH.—Mr. Tennyson called. . . . I read him some of my journal.

MAY 8TH.—Brown says Mr. Tennyson is quite ill. I wanted to read some of my journal to Brown, but he said it was very enervating for an author to read her own work. I find this literary life indeed wearisome, and I sometimes wonder how Mr. Tennyson stands it. It killed poor Mr. Disraeli. I suppose it will kill me too some day.

MAY 9TH.—I spoke to Brown about publishing the journal. He said if I did it would create a sensation. To know the working of the sovereign's heart, and see just how much interest she takes in the affairs of the nation, which is so spendthrift in her honour, is a boon for the people. Brown says it will show them just what kind of ruler they have. Brown is right. I will publish the book.

From Vicky came fears that her mother's subjects would misunderstand *More Leaves*. The Queen—almost certainly she was not shown *Life* —demolished that argument with the contention that after reigning for forty-five years she knew her people and what they would like, and that truthful publication disarmed "false biographies." She might even have safely included more about her active involvement with the Highland people than she did, but, because of her public insistence on her prerogatives, few even in her circle realized how innately shy and modest she was. Intimacy was not easy for her, and she maintained a decorous distance even between herself and her closest ladies-in-waiting. With local Scotswomen, wives and mothers of her servants, she felt unfettered. Princess Marie Louise, wife of Victoria's son Alfred, whom she married in 1874, remembered the unhappy day at Balmoral when two children were drowned in a stream, and Victoria joined the wives of the gillies on the bank and waited with them until the bodies were recovered. There was also the time when Princess Beatrice was five, and had gone with the Queen to visit the wife of one of the gillies, and had asked, "Have you a baby in long clothes?"

"No, Princess."

"Do you think you could have one by the next time I come?"

"No, Princess," said the woman, realizing that the Queen and her family would be back at Balmoral in two or three months.

"Well," said Beatrice, used to having her way, "you can think about it, anyway."

Prompted by the references to Brown in *More Leaves*, Swinburne put poetry aside in a letter to Georgiana Burne-Jones, wife of the artist Sir Edward Burne-Jones, and joked about "the forthcoming tragic drama founded on Her Majesty's new volume, which is about to appear in Paris. . . ." And he proceeded to invent a smirking scenario, in French, *Sir Brown*, a play in seven acts and forty-nine scenes, with the opening act entitled "La Mort du Mari"—the death of the husband. Brown enters Osborne House in Highlander's costume and embraces the Queen:

LA REINE: *C'est fini?*
BROWN: *Tu l'as dit. Mais embrasse-moi donc aussi, toi, ma reine!*
LA REINE: *Mon Johny! Mon Jack adoré! Je vais donc enfin être toute à toi!*

At the close, Swinburne wrote, the Prince of Wales avenges his father, and Brown, "stabbed to the heart, expires at the feet of his accomplice, who is spared on condition of taking a vow to appear no more in public—and the Prince exclaims as the curtain falls—

"Dors en paix, ô mon père! Tu m'avais donné la vie—je te donne la vengeance!""

To the echoes of *Hamlet*, Swinburne added suggestions of *Richard III* in shutting up the royal children in the Tower, and some deliberately garbled history involving George II, Bolingbroke, the elder Pitt, and Nell Gwynn. Victoria would have appreciated none of it.

On the heels of the popular success of *More Leaves*, which the Queen fully expected, she sent to Ponsonby, on February 23, 1884, a parcel with a covering note announcing that she had been engaged on the enclosed "little memoir" of John Brown. She had reached 1865, but constant interruptions made it necessary that she secure some help. Her intention was to publish for private circulation only, and to include extracts from Brown's diaries. Her interest in having the life written was no secret, as she had approached Sir Theodore Martin. But when he wriggled uneasily out of it, the Queen had employed Miss MacGregor to do some ghost-editing—"striking out all the unnecessary repetition," the Queen explained to Sir Henry.

Ponsonby recognized the explosive potential of the parcel, and suggested two clergymen who knew about "authorship" as readers. The Queen's acid response was that "Sir Henry has not said if he liked the extracts. . . ." Not only had Ponsonby not liked them at all; he quailed at the idea of any further publicity to the Brown relationship. After further study of the problem, he wrote to the Queen that her story would be of interest to "all who knew Brown" but that he had misgivings as to whether "this record of Your Majesty's innermost and most sacred feelings" should be published. The world at large would not understand the nature of such a relationship, and the reaction might cause unnecessary pain to the Queen.

Two further notes from Victoria followed on March 2, one of them asking for return of the manuscript, so that she could show it to Lord Rowton. With misgivings, Ponsonby passed it on to Rowton, reminding her once more of the possibility that "people in general might convert into other meanings and take up in a spirit which was not intended" much that she had written. Rowton quickly and privately concurred, and pressed for "delay in any form." No one whom Sir Henry consulted had any doubts that, like her earlier literary efforts, it should be confined, if let loose at all, to a limited audience.

News about the book somehow turned up in *The World*, to the horror of Ponsonby, who warned the Queen unhappily that publication might "attract remarks of an unfavourable nature," but it took the new Dean of Windsor, Randall Davidson, at risk of his career, to declare that printing of the book in any form was undesirable. Casting about for a way to tell her that, he used his receipt of a presentation copy of *More Leaves* to suggest that more of the Queen's "gracious confidences so frankly given" would be undesirable.

Exceedingly angry at his presumption, Victoria informed him that she would do as she pleased, and Davidson again put his career at risk with an even stronger letter. Through Lady Jane Ely, she asked the Dean to withdraw his remarks, or at least to apologize for the pain he had caused her. He would apologize for the pain, he responded, "but as to the suggested book . . . I must adhere to everything that I have said." And he offered to resign. Crossly, the Queen announced that she would not attend Sunday service if the Dean officiated, and a substitute cleric was found. Then she sent for Davidson, told him that she appreciated people who had the courage to contradict her, and that she accepted his judgment. "My belief is," he said later, "that she liked and trusted best those who occasionally incurred her wrath."

After escorting Victoria to the simple grave in Crathie churchyard, with its "wreaths from Princesses, Empresses & Ladies in Waiting," Ponsonby mused that Brown had been "the only person who could fight and make the Queen do what she did not wish." Later there would be, for a brief moment in 1884, Randall Davidson. Quietly, Victoria turned over her manuscript, and Brown's diary, to Sir Henry, who even more quietly burned them. By then the first anniversary of Brown's death had come, and on March 27, 1884, the Queen wrote in her own diary, "I cannot cease lamenting." Whether or not the relieved Prince of Wales knew of Davidson's role in the affair, when he became King he made the Dean his Archbishop of Canterbury.

Brown hardly needed a biography to secure his fame. Anything portable was soon carried from graveside by the curious—fragments of wreaths, labels, flowers. Carriages plying the Ballater-to-Braemar route made regular stops of ten minutes at Crathie to see the tombstone. In summer, tourists visited it daily. "You ought to charge a shilling a head," Viscount Bridport, one of the Queen's lords-in-waiting, said to the minister's wife. Even Gladstone, on a rare visit to Balmoral, asked to be shown the hallowed ground.

One of Gladstone's Ministers, Lord Carlingford, found the Queen's conversation at Balmoral unnerving when Brown's name was brought up in contexts that suggested Albert. "This infatuation is wonderful. It is painfully absurd to hear his name pronounced when one would expect another!" By the time he visited in 1885, the bronze statue of Brown executed by Boehm stood on a pedestal only two hundred yards northwest of the Balmoral Castle. In the churchyard at Crathie the gravestone included, at the Queen's request, the words:

> That friend on whose fidelity you count, that friend given to you by circumstance over which you have no control, was God's own gift.

Brown so memorialized was a presence palpable to few other than Victoria. General Sir John Clayton Powell, Master of the Queen's Household since 1866, Carlingford reported, "gets on better since John Brown's disappearance from the scene. He was all powerful—no servant had a chance of promotion except through him, and he favoured no man who didn't like his glass. . . . Some of the courtiers were full of attentions to J.B., gave him presents, etc.—and he despised them for it. He was however unwearied and devoted in his attentions to the Queen." As evidenced by the bank books and the paltry baubles left by John Brown, his reputation was more fearsome than the facts of his life. His legendary insolence was often only ignorance of appropriate behavior. He seduced no women, accepted no bribes, lived for no one but the Queen. When her cousin the Duke of Cambridge lost his trusted steward, the Queen wrote to him that she understood that his steward had also been a friend, and, "Indeed such a loss is often more than those of one's nearest and dearest, for a faithful servant is so identified with all your feelings, wants, wishes, and habits as really to be *part* of your *existence* and *cannot* be replaced."

"If he had been a more ambitious man," the Prince of Wales's own comptroller, Sir William Knollys, said of Brown, "there is no doubt I suppose, he might have meddled in more important matters. I presume all the Family will rejoice at his death, but I think very probably they are shortsighted."

XIV

Faery Queen

(1872–1880)

On New Year's Day, 1872, Victoria was still at snow-covered Sandringham, where Bertie was recovering very slowly. "May our Heavenly Father restore him," she prayed in her journal, "and let this heavy trial be for his good in every way!" She had already requested Gladstone to prepare a public thanksgiving, and he had recommended St. Paul's as the site, "in conformity with unbroken usage." It seemed churlish for her to complain that the cavernous Wren masterpiece was "a most dreary, dingy, melancholy and undevotional church." Even more unhappily, she objected that the very event she had ordered was likely to be "pomp and show" unworthy of the solemn occasion, and that "a long fatiguing Service" was out of the question.

Eager to display the Sovereign to the public, Gladstone would have accepted any terms, and almost any date. Victoria chose February 27— close enough to the opening of Parliament to enable her to evade that occasion. Besides, the Prince of Wales needed all the recuperation time he could get to ready himself, and everyone needed better weather. Victoria even offered to throw in another appearance the same week— a Court reception. But while she claimed that she was still weak herself from a serious illness and could do no more, she announced that at Easter she would hurry incognito across the Channel to Baden, to visit Princess Hohenlohe.

Conscientiously imperceptive about such matters, Gladstone complained about the possible effect on the public of her absence "during the very important portion of the Session of Parliament," and Philip Guedalla in his *The Queen and Mr. Gladstone* emphasizes the apparent irresponsibility by describing the visit as to "a relation." Most of her journey was planned for Parliament's Easter recess; a Minister of State with access to the telegraphs would accompany her; and the "relation" was her dying sister Feodora, now mourning the loss of her youngest daughter to scarlet fever. The Queen had sent a consoling letter and with it the inevitable nineteenth-century memento of the dead, a locket for a cutting of the deceased's hair. "I'm glad you saw Victor," Feodora wrote, "he could tell you that I am not ill." But what her son, Count Gleichen, told the Queen was very different. She feared that she might never see Feo again, and would allow nothing to keep her from Baden in March.

Returning to Osborne, and her red boxes, Victoria worked at overseeing her Government. After some hard and unpopular decisions it was increasingly in trouble in Parliament, and needed the political lift of a spectacle for the masses. Yet there was considerable question as to whether the Prince of Wales would be up to his own public rebirth. A week before the ceremonies he was still weak and bedridden, his left leg swollen and useless. Victoria warned Gladstone that she was uncertain whether her son could manage the excitement and fatigue of a long journey through London, yet she was determined to make it a good show. The people had wanted her to display herself more. Well, then, she would insist upon an open carriage, as February weather in London was nothing to her—hardly more than a Balmoral summer. The Prince of Wales could be scarved to the ears, or more, if necessary.

Wearing a black silk dress and jacket trimmed with miniver, and a bonnet with a white feather, she rode in an open landau drawn by six horses, sitting next to the Prince, who looked wan and walked (when he had to) with a decided limp. Seven royal carriages preceded them down the Mall to Trafalgar Square. At Temple Bar, after waving to the enthusiastic crowds, she took Bertie's hand in hers, raised it aloft, then brought it down and kissed it. The Prince lifted his hat to acknowledge the cheers, and the procession continued on to St. Paul's, which they reached by one o'clock. A large banner read, "I was glad when they said unto me, I will go into the House of the Lord."

They were back at Buckingham Palace at twenty minutes to four, exhilarated by what Victoria called the "wonderful demonstration of loyalty and affection, from the very highest to the lowest." She may have wondered about the Ministerial fuss over her alleged unpopularity. During her convalescence the Queen had read two books about the horrors and excesses of the Paris Commune, and such news of the Republic's agonies as had reached England had already dampened the ardor of irresolute radicals. Further, had the successive life-threatening illnesses of the Queen and the Prince of Wales been part of a calculated strategy, they could not have been improved upon as a means of rescuing the monarchy from opprobrium and reversing the drift toward republicanism. Albert Edward was no better a future king when he recovered; nor was Victoria, but for the closing days of February, a more accessible queen. All that was needed to seal the revival of esteem for Victoria and the Throne, after the illnesses and the vast parade and the mammoth Thanksgiving Service, was a failed assassination attempt, and that act of the impromptu melodrama also arrived, as if on cue.

Still ebullient two days later, Leap Day, the Queen called for her open landau and, with her sons Arthur and Leopold, and Jane Churchill as lady-in-waiting, drove around Hyde Park and Regent's Park, returning by Constitution Hill. There, at the Garden Entrance to Buckingham Palace, as Brown had dismounted to lower the steps, someone squeezed next to her and brushed a pistol against her cheek. Clutching Lady Jane Churchill, she cried out, "Save me!" Brown seized the weak-minded Arthur O'Connor, whose unloaded pistol clattered to the ground. His object, it turned out when he was searched, was to have the Queen sign a petition asking for the release of Fenian prisoners. The result, however, was very different. Londoners thronged palace entrances that evening and all the next day, signing their names to outpourings of gratitude for the Queen's deliverance. To John Delane of *The Times*, the Duchess of Sutherland—Mistress of the Robes—wrote that the Queen remained as much in shock as if the pistol had been loaded. "It is unfortunate that the Queen has always the idea that what has been attempted will be succeeded in some day, and that she will be shot." But Victoria's un-popularity was at an end.

There remained the continuing problem of some occupation for the Prince of Wales, a matter that occupied the Prince's Household, Colonel Ponsonby, and Gladstone and his Cabinet much of the year, with Victoria vetoing all recommendations. Meanwhile, Bertie and Alexandra embarked upon a three-month convalescence in the Mediterranean, the Prince having suggested, before their departure, possibilities in the army and in a cycle of attachments to government departments to learn their functions. Gladstone was willing to accept almost any arrangement that was likely to improve the Prince's capacity to reign. "The Prince of Wales," he would say privately, "knows everything except what is written in books."

For the Queen, the army option was out. Bertie loved uniforms, and wore them with éclat: his military skills ended there. His learning government business in any regimen seemed to her unpromising; he had no interest in reading anything but the racing results. Still, Gladstone saw the Prince's new visibility as an opportunity to press for his education into some aspect of governing. Hundreds of pages of memoranda and letters passed between Gladstone and his aides, and the Queen, without any effect. She had lifted Bertie's hand at Temple Bar, but upon cooler reflection she still saw no kingly quality in him. "She thinks the monarchy will last her time," Princess Alice told Ponsonby, "and it is no use thinking what will come after if the principal person himself does not, and so she lets the torrent come on."

As the unwanted pressure on her mounted, the Queen and her entourage, including Beatrice and Leopold, departed for Baden, crossing the Channel late in March and entraining through a sullen France still occupied at key transit points by Prussian soldiers. In order to spare Feo's waning strength, Victoria had rented the Villa Delmar at Baden to house the royal party, and visited sparingly with her sister. Feo's fireplaces were few, but Victoria found the heat everywhere in Baden stifling. (Very likely she had a slightly higher body temperature than normal, which would account for her lifelong impatience with what others might have considered barely adequate warmth.) Persevering, she took tea with Feo daily, visited other eminences there for the waters, experimented with a "vapour bath" herself (she did not go back), and went shopping incognito, at least in theory. (All her luggage, whether she traveled as Countess of Kent or

Duchess of Balmoral, was labeled "Queen of England.") When she left, it was with Waldmann, a dachshund, who would be with Victoria until 1881, when he earned a granite gravestone with his name at Balmoral.

On the morning of April 6, the sisters parted for the last time, Feodora promising to send a quilt she had worked for Victoria, and had nearly finished. (It went off in May.) The next day Prince Leopold's eighteenth birthday was celebrated on board the *Victoria and Albert*, although he had aggravated his hemophilia, but the Queen preferred to blame it on his "overdoing his standing in London—that evil-doing place which I perceive makes everyone ill." Nearly her first news on return from Germany was O'Connor's one-year sentence. The result, she warned Gladstone, is that the system of justice was "making it *almost impossible* for her to go about in public,—or *at all in London.*" Gladstone explained unpersuasively that before sentencing the prisoner had sincerely repented his act. By year's end, after much pressure from the Queen, the Prime Minister arranged for O'Connor's "emigration to a distant country provided only it be one favourable to his health."

As the year wore on, Victoria became increasingly depressed. It was difficult, she explained to the Princess Royal, to be Sovereign and mother of a large family. She had little joy in her children, and less pleasure in contending with Gladstone's government, which seemed interested in Irish affairs, Church affairs, and economies in every department, from the army and navy to the British Museum, where, Ponsonby would note, the Chancellor of the Exchequer, Sir Robert Lowe, would urge the curators and librarians to use half-sheets of paper. This was not the expansive England in which the Queen thought she lived. "I feel so disheartened," she confessed to Vicky. "I should like to retire quietly to a cottage in the hills and rest and see almost no one. As long as my health and strength will bear it—I will go on—but I often fear I shall not be able for many [more] years (if I live). If only our dear Bertie was fit to replace me!"

Her last days eased only by chloral and morphine, Feodora died in September. For the Queen, Lady Augusta and Dean Stanley went to Baden. "I stand so alone now," Victoria wrote in her journal from Balmoral. No one left alive now, she thought, "could really help me." In December came the death, long expected, of Disraeli's aged wife, Mary Anne. Victoria, who yearned for his return to office, rushed her "heart-felt sympathy . . . in this his first hour of desolation." In January, ex-Emperor Napoleon III died after kidney surgery. He had, Victoria thought, "borne his terrible misfortunes with meekness, dignity, and patience. . . . I could

[not] but think of the wonderful position he had, after being a poor, insignificant exile. . . ."

She was glad to see Gladstone's Parliamentary majorities whittled down to nothing, but when he offered to resign—the Queen had asked him in March, hopefully, "What would Mr. Gladstone call a too small majority?"—Disraeli refused to accept office without a general election to confirm his mandate. Gladstone preferred to hang on, while complaining, at sixty-four, of deafness and difficulty with his eyes, and suggesting his eagerness to retire from politics. His Government limped through 1873, Gladstone even having to take over the Exchequer after a Post Office scandal that did little to keep the Liberals afloat. In the Cabinet shuffle, Gladstone perversely moved Acton Smee Ayrton, a Liberal M.P., from the post of Minister of Works, where he served with the Queen's most reluctant assent, to that of Judge Advocate, prompting Victoria's astonishment at even the possibility of her "personal contact with such a man!" Any relationship, it was agreed after some stalling by Gladstone, would have to be in writing only. Ayrton "could not help regretting," he had told a Radical audience on December 4, 1866, "that when the [Reformist] assemblage was in one of her Majesty's parks and in front of her palace, she should not have . . . enjoyed the gratifying spectacle of looking down upon her loyal people. He must confess he thought it was one of the duties of Royalty to show a feeling of sympathy for the living as well as an affectionate reverence for the memory of the dead." The Queen would never forget. Even Gladstone, so quick to forgive, thought the remarks "indecorous and unjust," but without Ayrton's supporters he did not have sufficient votes to survive in the Commons. Ponsonby, usually Gladstone's staunch defender to the Queen, saw him as "earnestly mad," and Lord Granville calculated the temperature of the Prime Minister's relationship with Victoria correctly when he passed Gladstone a note during a Cabinet meeting in July 1873, which asked, "Which do you and Mrs. Gladstone dislike the least—to dine with the Queen on Wednesday at Windsor, or go down for a Saturday and Sunday to Osborne?" Gladstone preferred the shorter exposure.

To the last, he brought a manic intensity to every proposal, never realizing how abrasive was the "cumbrous" style (in Disraeli's description) in which he communicated with the Queen. It was so complicated, Dizzy wrote to Lady Bradford, "so wanting in melody and harmony," that it gave him a headache. (Victoria once asked Sir Arthur Helps to boil down a lengthy and turgid Gladstonian memorandum into something intelligi-

*"The Two Augurs"—John
Tenniel, in* Punch,
*February 8, 1873,
showing Disraeli and
Gladstone squaring off.*

ble.) Gladstone saw his problems with the Queen differently. "Since the
death of the Prince Consort, the Court (properly so-called) had virtually
dropped out of existence. . . . My way [of "advising the Sovereign"]
. . . was absolutely blocked by Her Majesty." The carefully reasoned
prolixity of his arguments, which he hoped that she would excuse on
grounds of his anxiety for the well-being of the Throne, induced only
fatigue. Although her post-Albert malaise was fading, she would exhibit
little of her real vitality for Gladstone.

A refreshing distraction for the Queen came early in 1873 at Chislehurst. She paid a sympathy visit to Eugénie, and rediscovered the now
fatherless Prince Imperial, pale and sad-eyed, and not yet sixteen. Two
weeks later, on March 6, Louis Napoleon came to lunch at Windsor, and
Victoria found a surrogate son and a new interest. Prince Napoleon, the
son of the first Napoleon's brother Jérôme, who briefly had been King of
Westphalia, wanted to take the boy away from his mother after the
funeral, to use the heir to the lost throne as a symbol around which to
rally the monarchist faction in France. To Victoria's relief, Eugénie
resisted. "Such charming manners—reminding me much of his father yet
he is like her too," the Queen wrote to Vicky after the Windsor visit.
"The tears come to his eyes whenever he speaks of the Emperor."

Victoria arranged for his schooling at the Royal Military Academy, Woolwich, as a Gentleman Cadet. She kept her eye on him through the decade as he matured into a thin-mustached, handsome young man. According to Henry Ponsonby, young Louis Napoleon's final examination at Woolwich before joining the Royal Artillery "was perfectly fair and he passed nearly at the top of the list. He was not first in French. . . . He very seldom talked much of his prospects in France and when he did it was usually in chaff. Still it was evident that he always hoped to return. . . ."

While Gladstone thrived personally on Irish political controversy, his party did not, but it limped on; and the Queen became more outgoing as the Liberals faltered. In April she ceremonially opened Victoria Park in Hackney, traveling in a procession of carriages, Beatrice at her side ("she is the last [daughter] I have, and I could not live without her"). They went along the Euston Road past the grand new Midland Railway (St. Pancras) Station, and into Islington, Bethnal Green, and beyond— "through the poorest and worst parts of London," she explained to Vicky, where "the population [density] really is fearful." After war and revolution across the Channel, and the violent overthrow of kings and princes, that "nothing could go off better or the enthusiasm be greater" for her exposure to the people, despite "no escort," pleased her. "It was a splendid day. In few countries could such a sight be seen." The continuing English affection for monarchy remained a safety valve for discontent.

The next occasion she offered Gladstone, on her accession day (her thirty-sixth), June 20, 1873, was a formal, colorful greeting of the Shah of Persia at Windsor—Beefeaters, bands, bells ringing, cannons booming. The Queen gave him a luncheon, spoke with him in French, and politely pretended not to see the Shah's struggles with a knife and fork, or his drinking water out of the spout of a teapot. Afterwards, she knew, as she wrote to Vicky, he would have a lamb roasted in his room, he and his attendants, sitting on the floor, pulling it to pieces with their fingers. In April, when Gladstone had pressed her to invite the Shah, he had coupled the request with the penurious warning that any costs involved in a state visit to Buckingham Palace would be her own. It was "not bad policy all things considered," he explained to Granville, "that [the Shah] should come & she should pay something: it will tend to keep Londoners content to see the Palace used, & at the Queen's charge." But having taken the precaution, on diplomatic advice, not to have the Shah overnight at Windsor, and unwilling to insult him by forcing him to look for London lodgings, the Queen now asked the Government for funds to restore the suite he used at Buckingham Palace. Victoria seemed always to encounter in Gladstone what she regarded as a misguided frugality.

There had been other problems associated with the Shah's visit. He had been given a military review in Windsor Great Park, and the Queen was furious when her instructions to have Castle Hill lined with troops were disregarded. Ponsonby had to scurry to locate a motley collection of Life Guards and men from the Guard of Honour to suggest a military presence. After the usual exchange of ribbons and medals, Henry Labou-chère, M.P. and proprietor of *Truth*, would complain that the Shah's Garter had cost the nation £548 9s 4d, and was only a "species of millinery." "Labby" did not understand the practicality of "Orders." Exchanges of gifts by heads of state and other high dignitaries were costly, but caused a rapid erosion of rapport if not made. What better way to save expenses, as well as the brain-racking problem of what to give, than to make a king or a count happy with the Grand Cross of some Order?

Having read her Highlands book—he had ordered it translated into Persian—the Shah told Victoria that he was eager to see Scotland. (She did not invite him to Balmoral.) From the Shah she received two baubles. He decorated her personally, and (she noted in her journal) "my cap was rather in danger, but the Grand Vizier came to the rescue, as well as Lenchen and Louise." Whatever the panoply, the Queen wore her widow's cap.

Victoria responded badly, at first, to the great family event of the year. "The murder is out!" she put it, when Prince Alfred, who could have passed for a black-bearded Romanov, announced his engagement to the Czar's only daughter, Marie. Affie's affairs with English ladies—and oth-ers—had so distressed the Queen that she had been about to recant her earlier hostility to a match with his cousin Frederika of Hanover. Earlier she had resisted his contention for the uneasy throne of Greece because it would have required his adherence to the Byzantine Church. Now he would be married in Greek rites anyway (although in the Russian Ortho-dox version), and abroad. She envisaged bearded priests with scapular crosses in residence at Clarence House, and feared that the Duke of Edinburgh "will be ready to be quite a humble servant of Russia."

Having been troubled by the Princess Royal's unhappy situation in Germany, Victoria dreaded another dynastic marriage where she per-ceived even less affinity with England and English ways. Her passionate dislike of Russia was intensified by the refusal of Marie's parents to permit a visit to Balmoral before the marriage. When, under pressure, they relented, suggesting that Marie meet the Queen in Cologne, Victoria fussed to Lord Granville, whose "mild, purring tone" exasperated her, about "Asiatic ideas of their rank." She would not agree to it. But Marie seemed to be a "treasure," and the marriage in January 1874, in St. Petersburg (Victoria did not go), proved neither political nor divisive on religious grounds. It was the first royal break with Anglicanism since 1688, she worried to Vicky. If it led to more, they might have to "pack up" and call back the Stuarts. Yet, when the "sad, sad anniversary" of her sister's death came in September, the Queen felt pained that none of her children would visit Feodora's last resting place—although she was herself unwilling to leave Balmoral. "Were it a Catholic family," she fumed to Vicky, "they would go from any distance."

At home, even High Anglicanism remained too close to the Vatican for her, and one of the Queen's last long lectures to Gladstone was on his alleged leanings toward Roman ritual. When he called for her to dissolve Parliament, and knew that the overdue elections would force him out of office, it was to the Queen's considerable relief, as well as his own.

By mid-February the ballots counted indicated that the majority against the Government would continue to increase, and the Queen pressed Gladstone for his resignation. On February 17 he arrived at Windsor to bargain for baronetcies and other "Dissolution Honours" he wanted for his associates. Victoria, eager for release from him, accepted everything, then asked what he wanted for himself. "Oh, nothing!" he protested, claiming that his condemnation by the country as registered in the election left him unwilling to accept any personal reward. In reality, Gladstone was confident that he would be back, and wanted no earldom that would confine him to the Lords. The Queen, not fathoming his motives, found the self-denial "very disinterested on his part."

On February 20, 1874, at six in the evening, he returned his Ministry's seals of office to Windsor. The meeting was awkward and stiff, as Gladstone knew how glad Victoria was to see him go. She expressed perfunctory concern for his health, offered her hand, and said good-bye. His exit had not been made easier by Disraeli's earlier appearance, at a quarter to three, to discuss appointments, after which he had knelt, kissed hands, and announced, "I pledge my troth to the kindest of *Mistresses.*"

Beginning his second Ministry at seventy, Disraeli appeared extraordinarily old. His dyed hair was startlingly black against the pallor of his wrinkled face, and he seemed wispy and shrunken; but to the Queen he was immense with vigor. His dark eyes flashed; his manners were courtly, as of old; and he was not Gladstone. However loyal to the Queen, Ponsonby preferred the policies of the Liberals, and the blunt if unattractive honesty of Disraeli's predecessor. "It seems to me," he wrote to his wife about the new Prime Minister, "that he communicates nothing except boundless professions of love and loyalty and if called on to write more says he is ill." Disraeli had indeed campaigned largely on the negative program that Gladstone must go. He had no specific legislation in mind, and was not physically up to the demands of the dynamic leadership he had promised the electorate. The result, given his desire to charm the Queen into behaving more queenly, was her opportunity to use him to gain ends impossible under Gladstone. Sir Thomas Biddulph, Keeper of the Privy Purse, saw Disraeli as "a perfect slave to the Queen," and it appeared that way early in his Ministry, when she pushed him into supporting a Public Worship Regulation Bill aimed at purging the Anglican Church of Romish practice. She would have delayed pressing the matter until the next year, because of the "inconvenience and difficulty" it would cause for the new Government, she explained, but that was "impossible" because of the "dangerous" tendencies in the country. The battle proved more difficult than Disraeli expected, as Gladstone returned to fight it with all his elaborate eloquence, which the Queen observed was "not surprising." Pressing her Prime Minister, she telegraphed, "Pray show that you are in earnest and determined to pass this Bill and not to be deterred by threats of delay."

In the Commons, Disraeli needed all his legislative skills to "put down Ritualism"—not, he assured both parties, when practiced by Roman Catholics, whose doctrines and ceremonies he was prepared to treat with reverence. What he objected to was "Mass in masquerade." The Queen's bill was carried, yet Ponsonby saw the Prime Minister as "clever and bright in sparkling repartee but indolent and worn out." What he had was a vision of grandeur for England that may have seemed, to Victoria, Albertine. Had he come with an agenda for accomplishing that vision, he would have had an easier time, but his very posture in the Queen's presence, and his written professions of devotion, conjured up for her a vision of monarchy no longer congruent with external realities. She would rise to her opportunities with the Royal Titles Bill of 1876 and with her pro-Turkish stance when the "Eastern Question" was simmering. It could hardly be said that "Dizzy" manipulated Victoria; rather, his style lifted the Queen into using her position as seemed no longer possible, and the effects would reverberate through the rest of her reign.

"Is there not just a risk," Derby, his Foreign Minister, cautioned Disraeli on May 6, 1874, less than two months into their Ministry, "of encouraging her in too large ideas of her personal power, and too great indifference to what the public expects? I only ask; it is for you to judge." What the "chief" may have sought for Victoria was something of the activist role for her as Queen that had eluded his predecessor. Where Gladstone lectured her at length, Disraeli, as Ponsonby put it, had "a wonderful talent for writing in an amusing tone while seizing the points of an argument." Where Gladstone was, to Victoria, a Romish religious fanatic, Disraeli, who cared nothing for theology or ritual, usually followed the Queen's wishes on Church appointments and practice, and got his way on domestic legislation. While Gladstone withheld from the Queen much of the burgeoning traffic of government dispatches, Disraeli forwarded just enough red boxes to offer her the illusion of being fully informed, and made up for the paucity of paper with witty, novelistic summaries of Cabinet and Parliamentary business. And while both Gladstone and Disraeli wrote books and articles, it was Disraeli who prefaced a discussion by saying, "We authors, Ma'am. . . ."

One key to the Queen's affections was the memory of Albert. As Disraeli's government came to power, the volumes of the Prince Consort's life were emerging, and Henry Reeve's multivolume edition of Charles Greville's diaries was beginning to appear. Victoria considered the diaries "nasty," "scurrilous," and "disloyal." Yet, she noted in her journal, the accounts were "in many ways . . . very full of truth" and even "wonderfully exact." To Sir Arthur Helps she sent a letter that she intended for Reeve, an editor on the staff of *The Times,* accusing him of degrading royalty in the characterization of her uncles. "Not at all," Reeve countered, knowing that his words would get back to Victoria; "it elevates it, by the contrast it offers between the present and the defunct state of affairs."

When the Queen appealed to the Prime Minister to "censure" the diary as "totally unreliable"—when she knew, as did Disraeli, that it was not—he agreed that publication of Greville was ill-judged. Then he observed that the contrast between Theodore Martin's *Life of the Prince Consort* "and a too notorious publication is striking. . . . After the turbulent and callous malignity of the *Greville Memoirs,* one feels as if an angel had passed through the chamber. He may be invisible, but one feels, as it were, the rustling of his wings." Reading between the lines of Greville in her Swiss hotel on their honeymoon, Minny Thackeray offered her husband, Leslie Stephen, an uninhibited interpretation: "Poor old Queen, what a time the Prince must have had with her."

To his confidants, such as Selina, Lady Bradford, whose only fault to the widowered Disraeli was that she had a husband, the Prime Minister called Victoria the "Faery Queen." The antique Spenserian allusion was exactly right. He and the Queen were enacting an elaborate epic for two. Both understood the rules. A queenly Queen was useful for Disraeli; a courtly lover in the antique tradition gave new zest to Victoria's days. Both knew that he was a gouty, wrinkled seventy, and dyed his hair; both knew that she was short and stout and, in Victoria's own words (to the Princess Royal), had an "ugly old face." When he visited Balmoral in September 1874, and had to be treated there by Dr. Jenner for bronchitis, he was able to write to Lady Bradford, "This morning the Queen paid me a visit in my bedchamber. What do you think of that?" In audience she bade him sit, although at first he demurred. (Later he would tactfully replace his chair against a wall.) "He lives only for Her," he insisted, "and works only for Her, and without Her all is lost."

Once, at dinner at Balmoral that September, the Duchess of Edinburgh—Prince Alfred's wife, Marie—asked the Queen whether she had read Disraeli's last novel, *Lothair*. Victoria answered—"with happy promptitude," Disraeli confided archly to Lady Bradford—"that she was the first person who had read it. Then the Duchess asked her Gracious Majesty, whether she did not think Theodora a divine character; the Queen looked a little perplexed and grave. It wd. have been embarrassing, had the Dss. not gone on, rattling away. . . ." Victoria had been presented with a copy—"Your Majesty is head of the literary profession," its author had once told her—but that she had promptly read it was as much hyperbole as was Disraeli's coquetry. Extravagance, Victoria had understood—almost, on that occasion, to her entrapment—was part of the code of courtly love, and belonged to an age when fiction in a relationship, rather than being discreditable, only enhanced it.

As Disraeli confessed to Matthew Arnold, "Everyone likes flattery; and when you come to Royalty you should lay it on with a trowel." He could only describe his reception by the Queen, he once confided, "by telling you that I really thought she was going to embrace me. She was wreathed in smiles, and, as she tattled, glided about the room like a bird." But the result, in 1875 alone, was the Trade Union Act (and a supplementary bill); the Public Health Act; a Factory Act, to protect women and children; an Artisans Dwellings Act, to replace slum housing; a Sale of Food and Drugs Act, to safeguard the consumer; and an Agricultural Holdings Act, to begin the process of protecting the tenant farmer. Despite the dominance of Property in the Tory party, Disraeli understood where the electorate was expanding. The Queen raised no objections. She preferred to have Gladstone at Hawarden than at Downing Street. Like Disraeli himself, she did not bother with the details.

It helped Disraeli that the Queen was more interested in Church appointments than anything else in the first sessions of his Ministry, but she was never in thrall to her Prime Minister. Her aspirations often became his priorities, especially in foreign affairs. Even so, she was no less stubborn than with Gladstone about disruption of her personal schedule, which—whatever the diplomatic cost—seemed as fixed as the calendar. Thus the visit of the Czar—the Duchess of Edinburgh's father—in May 1874 nearly foundered on the apparent incivility of the Queen in abandoning Alexander II for Balmoral. The new Prime Minister had to stake his personal relationship with her on extracting a change in her plans, which she consented to "for Mr. Disraeli's sake and as a return for his great kindness." The bonds of amity with Russia were tenuous, and the Queen and Disraeli warily exchanged expressions of friendship with Alexander at a grand fête at Windsor. The Czar was gracious, Disraeli told Lady Chesterfield, but he saw in Alexander's "sad" face what he guessed was "the loneliness of despotism, or the fear of violent death." In 1881 the Czar would be assassinated.

When Disraeli returned to Downing Street, Great Britain seemed, abroad, globally sprawling but less than great as an imperial power, having declined to interfere in German domination of western Europe or Russian domination of eastern Europe and central Asia. Relations with the United States had been mismanaged from the time of the Civil War, and there was colonial disorder in Africa. The jewel in Victoria's crown, India, was lightly regarded, and the new, shorter route to it through the Suez Canal, opened in 1869, was controlled by other powers. Much of the retrenchment was deliberate Gladstonian policy, which was inward-looking and without pretensions to *gloire.* None of that suited the Queen, but under Gladstone, imperial ambitions gave way to domestic priorities. For his part, the Irish could legislate for Ireland, and the Boers could have South Africa. Britain had to put its house in order at home.

Victoria had other ideas, and as usual they had a personal origin. The unification of Germany under Prussia had made her daughter Vicky a future empress (Kaiserin) rather than a queen, and the marriage of Affie to the daughter of a Czar (emperor) had given both precedence over the Queen's other children. Further, Vicky might, when crowned, have precedence over her mother, only a Queen. Few in Britain considered the titles anything other than parallel, but the Queen was anxious about her dignity. Further, since the end of the Indian Mutiny, with its political consolidation and the appointment of a Viceroy, she had been considered there as Empress, although the title had no statutory validity. Now she wanted Imperial rank, even if it was only a semantic quibble.

Unintentionally, Disraeli revived Victoria's ambitions by reemphasizing imperial interests discouraged by Gladstone. Meanwhile, the red dispatch boxes passed between them happily, and the Queen added to the traffic other kinds of boxes—wooden ones of fresh flowers from Osborne and Balmoral. One, early in 1875, from Osborne House, contained two bouquets of primroses and one of snowdrops. His rapture over the primroses, favorites too of the Prince Consort's, gave rise to the understanding that the primrose was the flower associated with Disraeli himself. In his letters he conjured up a Queen Titania, "who had been gathering flowers with her Court in a soft and sea-girt isle, and had sent me some blossoms which, according to the legend, had deprived the recipient of his senses."

The Queen's catalogue of wants burgeoned with Disraeli's blandishments. If he played the connoisseur of flattery, savoring his relationship with the Sovereign as the unlikeliest of dreams come true, Victoria would enjoy her opportunities to be a queen, rather than a somewhat delinquent student in Gladstone's classroom. An imperial title only sat atop her requests, which ranged down the scale to minor services for her ladies and favorite clergymen. After ten hours in the House on an April evening in 1875, Disraeli returned to Whitehall Gardens to find Victoria's latest shipment of primroses from her Majesty's "Faery Isle" across the Solent, and a new patronage list. "Were he your Majesty's Grand Vizier," he sighed in his response, "instead of your Majesty's Prime Minister, he should be content to pass his remaining years in accomplishing everything your Majesty wished; but, alas! it is not so. . . ."

Disraeli was happy when the Queen exhausted her indignation over events she knew were out of his control. The previous May she had been furious when Lady Churchill's dressing case and jewels were stolen from an Albemarle Street hotel, and when Lady Waterpark lost all her jewels. "Two of my ladies!" the Queen expostulated to Disraeli. "The police must be very inefficient. It is a disgrace to the country!" Then there was the "awful" and "distressing" case of Colonel Valentine Baker of the Tenth Hussars, a friend of the Prince of Wales, who attempted to fondle a young governess traveling alone on the Portsmouth line of the South Western Railway. She escaped outside onto the step of the railway car, to which she clung for five miles until she was noticed. Baker was dismissed from the army and went into the Turkish service, where he became known as Baker Pasha. His older brother, Sir Samuel Baker, the African explorer, another friend of the Prince, had married happily but scandalously beneath him, and the Queen recalled how often she had reminded Bertie about the inconvenience to the Throne of such friends. Then the widowed Lady Clifden, one of her former ladies-in-waiting, threw herself away on a "not very recommendable" officer much younger than herself.

Even more frustrating for the Queen—she was even aboard when it happened—was her yacht *Alberta*'s collision in the Solent with the schooner *Mistletoe*. The *Alberta*'s captain was the Queen's nephew, Prince Ernest Leopold Victor of Leiningen. Gingerly, the Prime Minister stepped aside to let an embarrassing inquest take its course. Two on the *Mistletoe* were drowned, but an Admiralty court of inquiry, two coroner's inquests, and a jury at Winchester all failed to reach a verdict, although it seemed clear that the Queen's vessel had been going too fast and using inadequate lookouts. "No blame," she wrote to Vicky, "can I feel sure be attached to my people on board the *Alberta.*" None was, but the Queen found "the low Portsmouth people" disgraceful for suggesting any culpability. By 1881 Prince Ernest was a vice-admiral.

Victoria's chief concern remained Bertie, and a junket he proposed to make, with Disraeli's approbation, to India. Getting the Prince of Wales out of England for six months, under supervision, seemed to the Prime Minister worth the price, even if the political gains were small. The Prince might even learn something about the Empire. The Queen relented, under the condition that the government would pay for it. "Our young Hal," Disraeli told Derby, his Foreign Minister, "has not a shilling . . . and must not move about India in a *mesquin* manner." Neither the Queen nor the Prince wanted Alexandra to accompany him, and Derby agreed, not only because of the complications of protocol among Indian maharajahs, whose consorts counted for little, but because (he told Disraeli) " 'Hal' is sure to get into scrapes with women whether she goes or not, and they will be considered more excusable in her absence."

Since the Prince planned to take a large party, and inevitably had to exchange lavish gifts with his hosts, Disraeli managed to persuade Parliament to approve the expenditure of £112,500 by the Admiralty and the Treasury, and the Viceroy's government offered another £100,000. It appeared to be an embarrassment for Victoria, as newspapers (except *The Times)* attacked the Prince for making up his party not of experts on the subcontinent but of playboy friends of whom his mother disapproved. Disraeli promised the Queen that he would warn them all against "larks." Meanwhile, *Reynolds' Newspaper* questioned the value of using tax revenues to send someone interested in little more than "pig-sticking and women" to India, and the radical orator Charles Bradlaugh told sixty thousand cheering protesters in Hyde Park that rather than complain about the future king's trip to India, most Englishmen, concerned about his capacities, "indeed . . . would speed him on a longer journey than that."

Refused permission to accompany her husband, the Princess of Wales announced that she would take the children to her parents in Denmark. That put Disraeli into another quandary with the Queen. Foiled about her son's holiday at state expense, she claimed the right to prevent a future sovereign—her grandchild—from leaving the country. Her Ministers suggested that it was a privilege she should not choose to exercise. Victoria gave way with a reluctance that did not endear her further to her daughter-in-law.

The Prince of Wales left on HMS *Serapis,* a specially converted troopship, on a route that would take his party to Athens and then through the Suez Canal, since 1869 the shortest route to India. He was resplendent in his new field marshal's uniform—an unearned rank to which his mother had raised him on his last birthday. Despite the expertise of his tailor, however, he looked less than military, bearing fourteen stone twelve (208 pounds) on his five feet seven inches.

On his thirty-fourth birthday, November 8, 1875, the *Serapis* entered Bombay harbor, first port of call in a progress that succeeded, to Disraeli's relief, because of the Prince's zest for activity. He wrote letters to his mother about his crowded schedule, and she dispatched telegrams urging him to be careful about his health. He also slaughtered sufficient game, from elephants to wild pigs, to stock a very large zoo. But the chief successes of the trip would come in unexpected ways. He had wide press coverage, and had called attention to India in ways that would be useful to the Crown. And he had made a very public passage through the Suez Canal.

Ailing, and occupied more than he cared to be with the problems of Turkey, the feudal and mismanaged empire that lay astride Britain's route to India, Disraeli had nevertheless kept a constant exchange of dispatches on the "Sick Man of Europe" in motion to and from the Queen in 1875. From the beginning of his Ministry he had attempted to buy the French-owned shares in the Canal, since four-fifths of its traffic was British, and it cut many days off the Cape route to India. Although French Syndicates would not sell, early in November Disraeli learned that the Khedive of Egypt, nominally under the suzerainty of Turkey, was nearly bankrupt and was eager to sell or mortgage his 176,000 shares, nearly half the total. Secretly, Disraeli made a bid for them, and the French, realizing that it was impolitic to hold a monopoly over an international waterway, stood aside. With Parliament not sitting, Disraeli—having asked and received the Queen's permission (which he did not need) to strike a bargain—used his friendship with Baron Lionel de Rothschild to have the banking firm raise the £4 million needed. On November 24, 1875, he wrote exultantly to Victoria, as if presenting her with a personal gift, "It is just settled; you have it, Madam. The French Government has been out-generaled."

What she had was the Khedive's interest—not quite a majority stake —and not, in any physical sense, the Canal; and he was less than honest about the alleged victory, although the purchase did forestall any possible occupation of Egypt by France. Derby was more candid in a speech at Edinburgh, to the annoyance of Victoria, who complained that her Foreign Minister had "tried to pour as much cold water as he could on the great success." She preferred Disraeli's fantasy. "The Faery is in ecstasies about 'this great and important event,'" he wrote to Lady Bradford. However described, it was a flamboyant and popular foreign-policy coup, although when the Commons would debate authorizing repayment to the Rothschilds, Disraeli's longtime Liberal adversary, Sir Robert Lowe, objected to the two-and-a-half-percent interest fee.

What Victoria appreciated most about the Suez success, she explained to Disraeli, was that it was "a blow against Bismarck." The reference, he confided to Lady Bradford, was to Bismarck's "insolent declarations that England had ceased to be a political power." From India, the Prince of Wales telegraphed his congratulations. If he and his mother agreed on anything, it was that Britain should play a larger role in world affairs than under Gladstonian retrenchment. The eastern Mediterranean trembled under an unstable peace, but Derby, like Gladstone, preferred no English initiative. Disraeli, prodded by the Queen, was forced to intrude into what became known as the "Eastern Question." Turkey's inept and harsh handling of its subject Slavic peoples in the Balkans seemed more the business of Britain after the Suez purchase than before, and the *Dreikaiserbund*—an informal linkage of the interests of the emperors of Germany, Austria, and Russia—seemed eager to push Turkey out of "Christian" Europe and pick up the pieces. Britain's traditional interest was to permit no power on the Continent to become dominant.

Early in 1876, guessing that her timing was opportune, Victoria announced to Disraeli that she intended to open Parliament in person on February 8. Since Albert's death she had done so only when she wanted something from the two Houses, and again this was the case. As early as January 1873 she had questioned Ponsonby, "I am an Empress & in common conversation am sometimes called Empress of India. Why have I never officially assumed the title?" Presented with the request before he could become elated over the Queen's appearance in Parliament, Disraeli cautioned her that he would not mention a revised Royal Style in her Majesty's gracious opening speech—only a paragraph on the Prince of Wales's visit to India. His first soundings had been negative. Englishmen —especially Gladstonian Liberals—felt that there was no more grand title than Queen of England, and saw no connection between empty social precedence and European politics. Disraeli foresaw a distasteful fight and did not have the stomach for it; but he felt obligated to the Queen to press her case.

A tumultuous throng greeted the Queen outside Parliament. Her Prime Minister could barely enter the House, and in thanking her for her appearance he suggested "what an immense influence your Majesty's occasional presence can produce." Yet he found objections to the Suez purchase bill, which produced carping criticism from Gladstone and Lowe, and additional trouble about the Queen's proposed title. Debate was acrimonious and lengthy. Lowe even warned that adding the label *Empress* did not contemplate the possibility of losing India someday. "The right honorable gentleman is a prophet," said Disraeli, "but he is always a prophet of evil."

Complaints about the bill dragged on, and George Meredith wrote to the Liberal politician John Morley late in March that he fancied Disraeli was "heartily sick of the task his Imperial mistress imposed on him at a moment when he did not know the English people so well." Radicalism, Morley thought, would "have nothing to regret in the passing of the Bill," as it would be a stimulus to political reform. Then Lowe announced his "conviction that at least two previous Ministers have entirely refused to have anything to do with such a change. More pliant persons have now been found, and I have no doubt the thing will be done." The effect on the House was electric.

Although he was Lowe's closest political colleague, Gladstone repudiated the charge that he had been approached by Victoria. On May 2, Disraeli rose, stung by the suggestion that he was a pliant Prime Minister. Had there been, he asked, any "unconstitutional and personal influence of the Sovereign?" He could answer for the late Earl of Derby, Disraeli said; and Gladstone had answered for himself. That left—he ignored himself—only old Earl Russell and the venerated Palmerston. To end Lowe's calumnies he asked leave to introduce the Sovereign's name in debate. Then he read a message from the Queen claiming "not the slightest foundation" for the "calumnious gossip," which Disraeli deplored had come "from the mouth of a Privy Councillor, and one of Her Majesty's late Cabinet Ministers."

On May 5, Disraeli reported to Lady Bradford, "Lowe appeared in a white sheet last night, holding a taper of repentance." To her sister, Lady Chesterfield, he added, "He is in the mud, and there I leave him." Lowe was finished as a political power. By a large majority, Victoria was authorized to sign herself "Queen and Empress." Latinizing the terms in the traditional fashion, she began closing her letters with "Victoria R. & I."

The new Style did nothing to discourage a callousness of behavior that might be excused in an earlier day as regal. At best it was an insensitivity that found her at one moment consoling a crofter's widow at Crathie, and at another being boorish to a Duke in his own home. When it came to her tenants in Scotland, or retainers from her Household, privilege took another form than it did with the lesser nobility—and all nobility was lesser. In February she had gone to the Deanery at Westminster to look in on the last hours of her dear friend Augusta, once one of her ladies, then sat with the grieving husband, Dr. Stanley. In September she visited, with a retinue, the manor house of Inverary, residence of the Duke and Duchess of Argyll, parents of her daughter Louise's husband, Lord Lorne. At Balmoral, as in her other homes, the Queen insisted on four separate dinner servings—for the Queen's party, for her Household, for the Upper Servants, and for the Lower Servants. At Inverary the Queen insisted on the same hierarchy of dinners. The Duke and Duchess

"NEW CROWNS FOR OLD ONES!"

(ALADDIN adapted.)

were not always invited to the royal dinner in their own house, although Victoria came into the drawing room for "ten minutes or so" (according to Ponsonby) to shed her presence upon those who had not broken bread with her.

Another privilege that the Queen claimed was a veto power over the education of her heir after Bertie. By 1876 the time had come to send his sons to school. Both she and Bertie had agreed upon Wellington College; but the Reverend John Dalton, their tutor, warned that neither Prince Albert Victor, heir to the throne after his father, nor Prince George was up to the standards of a respectable school. "Eddy" seemed slow-witted, while George was only a slow learner. Alexandra and Bertie suggested that the boys go off together as naval cadets at Dartmouth. The Queen insisted that Eddy had to go to school; George might train on the *Britannia.* Sadly, Dalton warned, "Prince Albert Victor requires the stimulus of Prince George's company to induce him to work at all. . . . Difficult as the education of Prince Albert Victor is now, it would be doubly or trebly so if Prince George were to leave him. . . ." The Queen gave in, agonizing over the future of the monarchy with such successors in store as her eldest son and grandson.

Among the Queen's other concerns was the deterioration in health of her Prime Minister. Enfeebled by chronic bronchitis and gout, and smoking heavily although he confessed that his cigarettes were "poison," Disraeli struggled to run his Ministry from one sickbed after another. To the Queen he suggested wearily that he either resign the premiership to Derby, or retain it but ease the strain by going to the Lords, leaving leadership of the Commons to someone else, perhaps Gathorne-Hardy or Stafford Northcote. Victoria did not want to lose Disraeli as her Prime Minister, especially to the passive and isolationist Derby, who did not share her violent anti-Russian sentiments. The nation was seething with partisanship over the Eastern Question. Even the Queen wondered to Disraeli why he failed to deplore Turkish atrocities against Christians in Bulgaria. Only the punishment and dismemberment of the immoral Ottoman Empire, the Liberal press suggested, would solve the problem. That solution, Victoria understood, would strengthen Russia. At her request, Disraeli had to remain, an outcome he very likely expected and indirectly sought.

On August 11, 1876, he made his last speech in the Commons, a reply to charges that he had played down the extent of Turkish atrocities. The next day, newspapers reported that he had been made Earl of Beaconsfield and Viscount of Hughenden. *Punch* published a cartoon with the caption "New crowns for old ones!" showing Disraeli, in vizier's garb, offering an Imperial crown to Victoria in exchange for his peer's headgear. Whatever his title, he remained responsible for Britain's policies in the East; and he viewed the Balkans as Turkey's Ireland, a problem of diverse customs and religions to be solved internally. He also saw only strong, large nations as capable of acting as bulwarks against Russian expansionism, and was certain that puny new peninsular states carved from Turkey would be easy morsels for the Czar.

Gladstone's visions eschewed realpolitik for Christian ethics as he saw them, and if charges of moral blindness weakened Disraeli's Ministry, so much the better. Having resigned his leadership of the Liberals to spend more time in "The Temple of Peace," as he christened his study at Hawarden, writing theological tracts and translating from the Greek, Gladstone nevertheless gave three hectic days to drafting a pamphlet entitled "The Bulgarian Horrors and the Question of the East." Published on September 6, it sold 240,000 copies by the end of the month. Filled with his crafty combination of political opportunism and moral eloquence, and his quirky, biblically cadenced catalogues of facts, speculations, allegations, and absurdities, it worked its spell by emphasizing Slavic aspirations and Turkish misrule while evading the implications of a *Dreikaiserbund*, every feature of which had to have been morally and politically abhorrent to him. Disraeli railed at Gladstone as "Tartuffe from the beginning." The Queen called his actions "most reprehensible and mischievous." When Princess Louise defended her father-in-law, the Duke of Argyll, an outspoken Gladstonian, the Queen responded that "irreparable mischief" had been done "in encouraging Russia . . . to think we shall *never* fight or resist their encroachments and arrogance." It was the old Woman Warrior, pressing her Government to stand firm, and seeing herself—and indeed there were parallels—faced with a second Crimea. Yet Lord Salisbury, who was doing most of the shuttling between European capitals as Disraeli's negotiator, and Lord Derby at the Foreign Office, were unwilling to be drawn into a war on Turkey's side against Russia. Victoria had once insisted that involvement in war reflect a compelling national interest. Now her hostility toward Russia and her hatred of Gladstone combined in open belligerence that left the ailing Disraeli nearly isolated in his own Cabinet.

On October 18, 1876, the Queen had written to him that she hoped it was "no inconvenience" to Disraeli for her to be—as usual on her clockwork calendar—at Glassalt Shiel on Loch Muich in such strained times, as it took only an hour and a quarter to send messages there from Balmoral (itself, she failed to add, remote). With a meeting of interested powers about to convene at Constantinople in hopes of pressing Turkey into peaceable concessions, Disraeli assured Victoria that it was no inconvenience to have her far away. From Balmoral, however, for the first time since Albert's death, she went to Windsor to spend the holiday season, to be closer to Whitehall. Russia's mobilization was unconcealed, and just after Christmas the Queen sent for Gathorne-Hardy, then at the War Office.

"The Queen," he noted in his diary on October 29, "was very well & affable, strongly Anti Russ[ia] & still more Anti Gladstone. She spoke of him with horror, of his consorting with a Russian female spy, about wh. there is much gossip. . . ." The "spy" was Olga Novikov, wife of a member of the Russian General Staff, whom Gladstone had escorted from the platform on December 8 at a public rally on the Eastern Question. Compared with the extreme sentiments of other speakers—the Radical historian Edward Freeman wondered whether Disraeli would "fight to uphold the independence and integrity of Sodom"—Gladstone was moderate. On that evening, according to Earl Cairns, the Lord Chancellor,

Gladstone also dined with Mrs. Thistlethwaite, the most notorious of his "rescued women," and Count Peter Shuvalov, the Russian Ambassador, who congratulated him on his "grand triumph" at the meeting. Almost certainly Victoria knew about that, too. Whether or not she thought that Gladstone believed in a Czarist crusade against Islamic oppressors of Christians, she saw other, unsavory sides of "the People's William."

On January 1, 1877, the Queen was proclaimed Empress of India at a *durbar* in Delhi stage-managed by Lord Lytton, whom Disraeli called "our poetical Viceroy." A minor poet, he was the diplomat son of Disraeli's old friend Edward Bulwer-Lytton. Victoria celebrated the occasion in advance by sending Disraeli a large Christmas card signed "V.R. et I." —*Victoria Regina et Imperatrix*—and on New Year's Day she startled her guests, including Disraeli, at a celebratory dinner at Windsor, by wearing masses of jewels—large pearls and irregular uncut stones—given to her by Indian princes and maharajahs. Colorful though they were, Hamilton noted, on the Queen's short, chunky figure they were incongruous. If nothing else, the unusual display indicated how much the Royal Titles Bill had meant to her. She wrote to Lytton to tell him that she had worn her Indian gems, including the Star of India, but not to inform the princes which ones, "for fear of creating jealousy." One collection, she confessed, was "not very convenient" and needed alteration.

Windsor was otherwise unpleasant for Victoria. Once she had marked its associations with Albert's death, on December 14, she preferred to leave for Osborne. Winter rains had flooded the Thames above Windsor, and even left the meadows underwater, yet Osborne was ruled out because there was "scarlet fever, or measles" in the Household there. At Windsor itself, Disraeli had come and fallen ill, complicating her schedule. Only at the end of January could she escape to Osborne. From there she sent the Order of the Garter to her grandson Willy in Berlin for his eighteenth birthday. In effect it was another decoration for nothing, but underlying the family loyalty was concern for Germany's role in the European explosion that she felt might come. Neutrality in Berlin was better than a real—as opposed to a paper—*Dreikaiserbund*.

With a peace faction and a war faction competing for the Czar's attention in St. Petersburg, as the Queen knew from a visit by General Ignatyev, Russian Minister to Turkey, she kept urging firmness upon Derby and Disraeli. "Mawkish sentimentality" for the Russians, she warned, "for people who hardly deserve the name of real Christians," would ignore the "great interests" of England. The aging and ill Disraeli, having revived Victoria's interest in using not only her perquisites but her dormant—and even vanished—powers, was under Titania's spell.

As the Colonial Minister, Lord Carnarvon, who would be a Cabinet casualty at the end of the year, would describe it, Disraeli "was no longer able to control the force which he had called into being." On March 27 the Prime Minister made the two-hour carriage ride to Windsor—with closed windows to avoid worsening his bronchitis—for a long session with the Queen, who exhorted him to keep the Cabinet firm, and offered the carrot of a royal visit to Hughenden Manor. A few days later came another carrot. She asked that he permit his portrait to be painted for her by Heinrich von Angeli, a favorite of Vicky's, who was returning to England. "It would only be the head, and as he is wonderfully quick he would require but very few sittings. Lord Beaconsfield's career is one of the most remarkable in the Annals of the Empire, and none of her Ministers have ever shown *her* more consideration and kindness than he has!" Who was now wooing whom was clear indeed.

On April 21, 1877, Russian troops crossed the Turkish frontier. The moral issue now became a military matter, the unspoken one of the balance of power on the Continent and the voiced concern of the safety of the British route to India. London quickly extracted assurances from St. Petersburg that international waterways would be respected, which Disraeli took to mean that the Russians would stop short of Constantinople and the Straits. Victoria thought she knew better, having received her own private intelligence. In an extraordinary letter, Captain Arthur Balfour Haig, a thirty-seven-year-old Royal Engineers officer, claimed to the Queen that he had learned of far-reaching Russian duplicity. Victoria was always ready to believe in Russian chicanery, and prepared a broadside for Disraeli. But first she responded to Haig from Windsor on May 13, "Would you object if I told the Prime Minister . . . I *knew* from a *certain source* . . . I *cd. not divulge*—that *Russia* has *determined* to have Constantinople, knew it would take us 6 weeks to send men to Gallipoli—and that *they* intended to be *there by the middle of Aug.*—then to come to terms with England and *offer us Egypt!*" In a postscript she added, with further italics, "You need *not* fear that your name shall *ever* be known to any one—and I am *very* grateful for your patriotic feelings and devotion to your Sovereign and country."

The assurance was vital. Haig was equerry to her second son, the Russophile Duke of Edinburgh, very likely the captain's inadvertent source.

Fully intending to be more than a ceremonial sovereign, Victoria attempted to push Disraeli from his perch of inaction, not realizing how isolated her Prime Minister was in his own Cabinet, with Derby leading a group stubbornly opposed to any involvement on Turkey's behalf that might lead to war. Of this harried time Disraeli wrote, "The Queen writes every day and telegraphs every hour." He had authorized a warning to Russia on May 6, and an evasive response arrived only on June 8, enough to satisfy Derby, but not Victoria.

Indignant, the Queen recalled the Crimea to Derby, when the Government had responded, in her view, too little and too late. "In this country feeling is much divided," he explained to her; "but Lord Derby believes that a war not forced on us by necessity and self defence would be unpopular. . . ." He remembered, he added, the Crimean War. Although then a young man, he was in the Cabinet just afterwards, at thirty-two. He had never seen, he reminded her—and she needed no reminders of the Tower rumors—"so near an approach to a really revolutionary condition of public feeling as after the first failures and disasters of that struggle."

Victoria showed the letter to Disraeli, who had not seen it and was perilously close to a break with Derby. Disraeli called it "deplorable." A few days later, June 19, responding to the Princess Royal's pleas from Berlin to keep out of war—the Queen had already told her that Gladstone was a "madman"—Victoria insisted that she indeed hoped to keep the peace. "But I am sure you would not wish Great Britain to eat humble pie to those horrible, deceitful, cruel Russians! I will not be the Sovereign to submit to that!"

The Queen had every intention of using whatever moral authority remained to the Throne to see that Britain had leverage in the crisis appropriate to its position as she saw it. Again and again she exhorted Disraeli to take "a firm, bold line" before British prestige had evaporated and the Russians were before Constantinople. If events came to that, "then the Government would be fearfully blamed and the Queen so humiliated that she thinks she would abdicate at once. Be bold!" To Victoria this may have been more than rhetoric. She assumed that politicians of both parties preferred her to the prospect of Bertie.

Because the Queen saw Ponsonby as too Liberal in his views, whatever his loyalty to her personally, and Disraeli understood that the chief members of his Cabinet would not support the Queen's militancy, an unusual arrangement bypassed both official channels that anxious spring and summer. A lady-in-waiting, Jane Ely, became a courier for both of them, and young Prince Leopold was given a key to the red boxes, "as one of your Majesty's private secretaries," Disraeli put it, in order to give the situation some quasi-official status.

The Russian advance was swift until Osman Pasha held in mid-July at Plevna. At Windsor in July—events had induced her to remain there longer than at any other time since Albert's death—the Queen remained for nearly an hour after dinner with Gathorne-Hardy, "hot against yielding to Russia, [and] wished that the 'wild & wicked' Gladstone would go away for the benefit of his health, [so] that we could take some overt step." She was also incensed at Derby for "his cool allusions to Turkey being 'rolled up' . . . & She 'wd have liked to shake him.'"

The Victoria who at times thought herself a Boadicea was not new to Disraeli. He could recall her Crimean War and Sepoy Mutiny attitudes, and since he had returned as her First Minister in 1874 she had signaled her tastes in anecdote if not art by purchasing Lady Butler's canvas *The Roll Call (Calling the Roll after an Engagement, Crimea)*. At the Royal Academy annual, Elizabeth Thompson, a young woman in her twenties soon to marry a peripatetic Anglo-Irish general, Sir William Francis Butler, had created a sensation with the muted realistic browns and greys of worn bearskins and Grenadier gabardines, and the drama of wounded and exhausted soldiers attempting to file into ranks in the Russian snows. The Queen, hearing about it—it caught what would become her favorite martial theme of splendor amid pain—had the canvas abstracted to Buckingham Palace overnight. When the exhibition ended, she acquired the canvas, making Miss Thompson's reputation as the artist of Imperial pride and confirming Victoria's Imperial faith. Her Ministers might waver, but not the Queen.

On July 29, Disraeli's First Lord of the Admiralty, Ward Hunt, died suddenly. After offering the post unsuccessfully to Viscount Sandon, the efficient M.P. for Liverpool who was in effect, if not title, the Minister of Education, Disraeli suggested to the Queen William Henry Smith, the bookstalls proprietor. He had been effective in the subcabinet job of Secretary of the Treasury. Smith had good judgment, Disraeli persuaded, and was "a first-rate man of business. . . . He is purely a man of the middle class and the appointment wd. no doubt be popular." On August 4 the Queen replied that she was prepared to agree if necessary, but that she feared "it may *not please* the Navy in which Service so many of the *highest rank* serve, & who claim to be equal to the Army

—if a man of the Middle Class is placed above them in that very high Post. . . ." She suggested two others.

Disraeli likened Smith to the Home Secretary, Richard Assheton Cross, of whom he knew she approved, and predicted that he would bring "vigilance & vigor" as well as "conciliatory manners" to the job. The Queen gave in, but admonished, Smith must not "lord it over the Navy . . . & must not *act* the Lord High Admiral which is offensive to the Service." Smith would prove a strong appointment as well as the inspiration for Gilbert and Sullivan's "Ruler of the Queen's Navee" in *H.M.S. Pinafore* two years later.

Although Disraeli remained in poor health through the summer and early autumn, a drumfire of telegrams and notes to Hughenden kept him vigilant to the Queen's views. She was for intervention if Russia failed to withdraw, rather than "falling into a miserable cotton-spinning milk and water, peace-at-any-price policy which the Queen will not submit to." On July 21 he had induced the Cabinet to agree to declare war if Russia occupied and kept Constantinople. Undercutting him, Derby sent Henry Layard, his ambassador in Constantinople, protestations of British neutrality. "It maddens the Queen," she told Disraeli, "to feel that all our efforts are being destroyed by the Minister who ought to carry them out." Derby's delays, as Russia advanced in the Balkans, precipitated a summons to Balmoral for Gathorne-Hardy, Disraeli's lungs being unable to contend with Scottish weather. Military forecasts were that the Turks might winter at Plevna, and her watchword, she told Gathorne-Hardy, was "No second campaign."

To the Queen, Gladstone was as much the enemy as the Czar. To Gathorne-Hardy, Victoria recalled her impressions of a younger—and even then fanatical—Gladstone's attempts to impose his will upon the Prince Consort. Then, Gladstone "had shewn temper with him & 'almost foamed.' She had to say that 'She wd. not do so & so' & then Mr. G. wd. say then I must cease to ask." How much embroidery there was to the tale is unclear, but the remark attributed to Gladstone was characteristic of him. The Faery had a wand of iron.

Suffering, probably, from Bright's disease (nephritis) as well as bronchitis and asthma, Disraeli remained at Hughenden Manor, his domestic program dormant, his foreign policies in the hands of contending Ministers, with the hesitant interventionists under pressure from the Queen. She preferred the resignation of the peace-at-any-price Ministers, as well as the political consequences, rather than indecision, and had no idea how ill Disraeli actually was, as she had never seen him any other way since his second Ministry had begun. Her own physicians as well as Bertie's Sir William Gull had dosed him with useless medications. Inevitably, Disraeli remained bound to Hughenden, which, she wrote to him, was "a very difficult place to communicate with"—although it was near London, which Balmoral and its barely accessible environs were not. She could not understand how British public opinion had been taken in by tales of Turkish barbarity as if there were none on the other side, in addition to which the Russians were known, she observed, for their "slow killing by imprisonment and exile to Siberia."

On December 10, the Turks at Plevna crumbled, and Disraeli determined to put the military on a war footing regardless of misgivings in the Cabinet. The Queen reminded him that people were now getting "alarmed" about Russia, and were turning more sympathetic toward the Turks, "who are defending their home and hearth." Further, "England will *never* stand (not to speak of her Sovereign) to become subservient to Russia, for she would then *fall down* from her high position and become a second-rate Power!" Lady Salisbury reported that Victoria "had lost control of herself, badgers her Ministers and pushes them towards war." Yet she was attuned to the public mood, as echoing her attitude was the music-hall boast,

> We don't want to fight, but, by Jingo, if we do,
> We've got the ships, we've got the men, we've got the money too.
> We've fought the Bear before
> And while Britons shall be true
> The Russians shall not have Constantinople.

Although Constantinople was a word to conjure with, if not to rhyme, the song helped forge a mood rather than to reflect it. It was the moment for the Queen to back her embattled Prime Minister by the promised occasion of her presence. On December 15, she, Beatrice, Ponsonby, and a lord-in-waiting, Colonel du Plat, went by train from Windsor to High Wycombe (a trip of about forty minutes), and thence by open landau, drawn by four horses, to Hughenden. The Earl of Beaconsfield, with his private secretary, Montagu Corry, greeted the Queen at the thronged, beflagged station, and led the Queen's party to Hughenden Manor in another carriage. In the Italian garden, Victoria and Beatrice each planted a tree; then the Prime Minister and the Queen talked politics in the library before luncheon, Victoria urging him "strongly" to "bring things to an issue." By three-thirty it was all over, and Victoria was on her way back to High Wycombe station, where she and Disraeli parted. The afternoon had been short, yet an occasion. It rallied Disraeli's forces and plucked up his nerve. Gladstone's tame historian, Freeman, wrote of the Queen's "going ostentatiously to eat with Disraeli in his ghetto." Not since dining with Melbourne at Brocket had the Queen visited her Prime Minister.

On the eighteenth, the Queen had some of the Cabinet to dinner at Windsor, including Disraeli and his newest Minister, W. H. Smith. Disraeli reassured him, "I am going there myself, and you can, if you like, accompany me; as it is sometimes awkward to be alone on the first occasion. With regard to costume: the usual evening dress, except you must wear breeches." Dinner was at nine, and after a single glass of wine at dessert the Queen rose and everyone left the table, enabling Victoria to chat individually with her guests—"with the freedom of an ordinary lady," Smith wrote to his wife. Such encounters were the rare times when the Queen used the first-person pronoun with representatives of her Government. Exchanges in writing were very different. Henry Ponsonby, who served a quarter of a century as her Private Secretary, received only one letter in which she used *I*—a sympathy letter on the death of his mother. Only personal matters, on very rare occasions, could elicit a royal first-person-singular pronoun from the Queen.

Again at Christmas and the New Year, the Queen remained at Windsor; the prayer in her journal asks that her country's "honour and dignity" be upheld in 1878, and that Russia's "wicked aggression, ambition, and duplicity" be checked. The only respite from concerns about the East came at Osborne, on January 14, when Professor Alexander Graham Bell visited to demonstrate his telephone, which left Victoria unimpressed ("it was rather faint"). But the next year, commercial service was under way in London. She was more interested in a preventive occupation of Gallipoli if the Russians refused an armistice. Victoria was even suggesting names to reconstitute the Cabinet after the expected pacifist defections. Yet on January 26, the British flotilla off Constantinople was ordered away, and Derby and Carnarvon (the Colonial Minister) withdrew their resignations. A few months later Carnarvon would confide to Gladstone how Disraeli would open a Cabinet meeting with a communication from the Queen "urging us very strongly to stand by the principle . . . that any advance on Constantinople would free us from neutrality." Gladstone considered such political interference with the Cabinet as unconstitutional, and an "outrage." It was a paradox that the Queen visible to the public was not the one who administered wiggings to her Ministers but the reclusive widow who went for carriage rides in the Highlands with her ladies. *Leaves* had furnished her with an apolitical shield.

Eschewing the temptation to use stronger language, Victoria described the "countermanding of the Fleet" to Disraeli only as "most unfortunate." The Turkish plight remained desperate, but Disraeli understood that the Russians planned to accept a truce once they had taken Adrianople. Although the signing took place there on January 31, Victoria was not appeased.

"Oh, if the Queen were a man," she had written to Disraeli heatedly on January 10, 1878, "she would like to go and give those horrid Russians whose word one cannot trust such a beating!" Cancellation of the Dardanelles intervention foreclosed that opportunity, although the Queen had employed every device she had to keep her Prime Minister in a warlike mood. "I don't want to bribe myself," he explained to Lady Bradford when he turned down Victoria's offer of the Garter. Events appeared to be going badly. Derby returned sullenly to the Cabinet, apparently after drinking heavily. Montagu Corry, a steadying influence on Disraeli, collapsed with overwork. Lord Carnarvon, who had not returned to the Cabinet after all, leaked to the press Derby's second attempt at resignation. Speaking at Oxford, Gladstone confessed openly that since his return to active campaigning his chief object had been to "counterwork as well as I could what I believe to be the purpose of Lord Beaconsfield."

"The mask has fallen," Disraeli wrote to Lady Bradford. Beneath the "pious Xtian" was a "vindictive fiend." That the armistice was quickly broken by the Russians, as the Queen expected, strengthened her hand with Disraeli, as did Derby's exit. With war fever in Britain increasing, three times in February the navy was ordered to steam to Constantinople. Apparently because of a confusion of objectives, each time the orders were withdrawn. Faced with imminent collapse, and unable to count upon London, the Turks signed an abject peace treaty with Russia at San Stefano, details of which only reached Disraeli on March 23. The clauses left Turkey only a finger in Europe across the Dardanelles; they created, in an enlarged Bulgaria, a Russian satellite extending to the Aegean Sea, and ceded to Russia fifty miles of Turkish Black Sea coast. Confident of support in Austria and Germany, the Russians called for a congress in Berlin to afford the great powers an opportunity to ratify the *diktat.*

The Queen was outraged; Disraeli was in a quandary. Added embarrassment surfaced because one of the navy's ships in a fleet with some reason labeled timid, the *Sultan*, was commanded by Prince Alfred, a Russophile since his marriage to the Czar's daughter; and Alfred had invited aboard Prince Alexander of Battenberg, the Russian choice for the throne of the proposed Greater Bulgaria. Furious, the Queen wanted her son reprimanded and prevented from going home with his ship so that he would not infect her other children, primarily Prince Arthur. If he received a formal reprimand, Alfred announced, he would request a Court of Enquiry. Faced with the embarrassment, Admiral Hornby, who discovered that the Prince of Battenberg had boarded in a German uniform, not a Russian one, sent the Duke of Edinburgh "a private and friendly letter." The Queen, Disraeli complained to his First Lord of the Admiralty, "has been left entirely unsupported."

Other problems kept Victoria in a whirl of Russophobia. She assured Gathorne-Hardy that Derby's "telltale wife . . . made known what was spoken in the Cabinet in St. Petersburg." Lord Salisbury, newly moved up from the India Office to Derby's Foreign Office, expected to head British interests at the Berlin congress, but Disraeli intended to go as well, to furnish the delegation with appropriate clout. Victoria objected that he was "far from strong." The Prince of Wales argued that only Disraeli's presence would prove "that we were really in earnest."

"His health and life are of immense value to me & the country," she objected, "& should on no account be risked. Berlin is decidedly too far." Still, Disraeli wanted to go, seeing the opportunity as his last major bow. Only he could deal with Bismarck, he insisted, playing upon her distrust of the Iron Chancellor.

Bismarck and Disraeli had not met for sixteen years. At first Bismarck, as host and president of the congress, managed its business. His method, Disraeli wrote to the Queen, was that "all questions are publicly introduced and then privately settled." In private, Disraeli could challenge Bismarck's domination, and it helped to have a bellicose Queen at his back, a nation stirred by war fever behind her (a mob had broken the windows at Gladstone's London home, which left no doubt of English feelings), and a fleet still off Constantinople. He did not want Turkey emasculated in Europe and Asia, and ripe for plucking, and he wanted Britain's routes to Asia unthreatened. At one point, when it seemed that

Bismarck and the Russian envoy, Count Shuvalov, would not yield, Disraeli ordered his special train made ready for the departure of the British mission. Suspicious of a bluff, Bismarck rushed over, and found everyone packing. He gave in. *"Der alte Jude is der Mann,"* he said afterwards.

Disraeli returned with what he wanted, plus the plum of Cyprus, astride Britain's eastern Mediterranean sea routes. For the island—and with it as a base—he promised Turkey to defend her interests, a pledge that largely kept the peace in that region for a generation. Lord John Russell had made a famous speech in September 1853, on the eve of the Crimean War, in which he said, "If peace cannot be maintained with honour, it is no longer peace." Now Disraeli recalled it. "Lord Salisbury and I have brought you back peace—but a peace I hope with honour."

Exultantly awaiting his return, the Queen sent Ponsonby on July 16 to present Disraeli with her personal letter of congratulations and a bouquet of her flowers. Henry Cust, an M.P. for Grantham, stopped Ponsonby in Downing Street and remarked in awe about Disraeli, "They say he is to have an equestrian statue opposite George IV." The Prime Minister—in a long white coat—arrived in an open carriage with Salisbury, Lady Abergavenny, and Lady Northcote. Ponsonby handed him the letter and the flowers, shouting above the din of the crowd in Whitehall, "From the Queen!" They went inside and Disraeli wrote a few lines of thanks to Victoria.

Exhausted and suffering badly from asthma, Disraeli nevertheless voyaged to Osborne on July 20 to see the Queen, confident that Parliament would approve the Berlin treaty, and proposed that her son-in-law, Lord Lorne, go to Canada as Governor General. Other family matters had already begun to preoccupy Victoria. She now counted upon her hemophiliac youngest son, Leopold, to continue as unofficial private secretary. He was not only useful to her, but the arrangement kept him close, and she feared for his susceptibility to injury and infection. When he announced that he preferred Paris and even London to dull Osborne and dreary Balmoral, and would no longer accompany her to such places, the Queen declared her displeasure. Her other children were warned to force Leopold to do his duty, which meant living entirely for her service. In particular, the Prince of Wales—denied the dispatch boxes to which his youngest brother was privileged—was to exclude Leopold from dinners, balls, parties, and racing. "He must be made to feel that such conduct to a mother and Sovereign cannot be tolerated."

Now Disraeli wanted to take Louise from her, and send the Princess across the sea—a signal distinction for Lorne, but a long parting from the Queen. Lorne was eager, and accepted. On the other hand, "for public and private reasons" (as Disraeli put it to the First Lord of the Admiralty), the Queen wanted to keep her son Alfred, still at sea in Turkish waters, as far from England as possible. She urged that "some hard work" be furnished for him "away from home."

Providentially, just as Alfred was threatening to resign from the navy, his brother-in-law came up with what became a solution, proposing that as Governor General he arrive in Canada in a "Queen's ship." It put an end to what the Earl of Beaconsfield described to Smith as "a disagreeable correspondence" with Prince Alfred, who was assigned to captain the *Black Prince* to Canada. Then the steamship line that ran the passenger vessel *Sarmatian,* a more comfortable and reliable ship, offered it for the royal couple, and Lorne accepted, throwing the Queen into a fury. At Balmoral she found out about it from the newspapers, and telegraphed indignantly to know "the meaning of this report." Early in October, Smith assured her that the *Black Prince,* "properly handled, as she certainly would be by H.R.H. the Duke of Edinburgh," would be "perfectly safe for the duty on which it is proposed to send her."

Only after appeals from Alfred's pregnant wife, then in Coburg (where the Duke was heir apparent), did the Queen stop looking for further assignments for her son, requesting the First Lord late in December to promote him to rear admiral before disbanding his crew.

Another worry was the Duke of Connaught's sudden engagement to Princess Louise Margaret, daughter of Prince Fritz Carl of Prussia and his estranged wife, Marianne. Victoria disliked the "overbearing" parents, was embarrassed by their broken home, and disapproved of Louise's "bad teeth" and "ugly" nose and mouth. Besides, Arthur was "so good" that he had no reason to marry at all. Soon, however, the Princess was "dear Louischen," and the Queen's only concern—she wrote to Vicky—was that Louise and Arthur "drove down alone together to Frogmore," unchaperoned. The times were changing, but Victoria's clock in most matters had stopped in 1861.

Victoria found further frustration in the education of her grandchildren Eddy and George. She complained to W. H. Smith that they would become "perfect strangers" to her if they continued training as midshipmen, the elder in any case a misfit in the navy, the younger tied to his companionship. For the First Lord, it was another of his royal burdens.

A further family distraction was the death, in English exile, of Victoria's cousin George of Hanover, the blind ex-king, and her discovering herself as executrix on behalf of his son Ernest, who now called himself by his grandfather's title, Duke of Cumberland. Even that was as nothing compared to her distress when, at Darmstadt, Princess Alice's children came down with diphtheria, and—early in December—having exhausted herself with their care, Alice (now Grand Duchess of Hesse) took to bed herself. It is difficult to recall how malevolent and widespread that contagious bacterial disease of the throat once was. Nearly half of its victims, mostly children, did not recover.

Torn with anxiety, Victoria sent Sir William Jenner to oversee Alice's care, but on December 14, 1878, Alice died. She was thirty-five. As the Queen had done almost every year since Albert's death, she had spent the evening of the fourteenth in the Blue Room at Windsor, where, this time, she prayed for Alice's recovery. The next morning Brown came with two telegrams preparing her for the third and final one.

To a granddaughter the Queen wrote, "That this dear, talented . . . tender-hearted . . . sweet child, who behaved so admirably during her dear father's illness, and afterwards, in supporting me in every possible way, should be called back to her father on this very anniversary of his death, seems almost incredible and most mysterious." Vicky, Alice's older sister, wrote a pathetic letter to her mother that went on for twenty-four pages. Her father-in-law, the German Emperor, had refused to permit her or Fritz to attend the funeral "for fear of infection."

Despite her heartfelt outcry, Victoria was becoming almost inured to death, and did not permit mourning to mar the wedding of Arthur and Louise, or to cancel her holiday (as the Countess of Balmoral) to Baveno on Lago Maggiore. At Emperor William's insistence, however, the wedding had to be delayed until the close of Lent, a religious scruple that the Queen could not understand. "A marriage," she told Vicky, "is no amusement but a solemn act." At the wedding in March, however, she abandoned mourning and wore a long white veil, and her Koh-i-noor Diamond, even though another cause for crêpe had appeared. Vicky's youngest—and favorite—son, Waldemar, had died suddenly—also of diphtheria. It was, she wrote to Vicky, "a terrible affliction." Having paid the rent in advance, the Queen went to Baveno as planned.

Disabled by illness that kept him most days under his own roof, Disraeli had seldom seen his royal mistress during the winter months of 1879. "So great a Sovereign as your Majesty," he apologized, "should not have a sick Minister." Even now, five years into an administration suffering from its leader's slackening of the reins, he offered no hint of resignation. His Cabinet was too preoccupied by South African disasters, the Zulus in Natal having routed a British force and inflicted thousands of casualties, including nearly six hundred dead. Reinforcements had to be sent, and Louis Napoleon, the Prince Imperial, now twenty-three, insisted upon going. Disraeli was opposed on political grounds—any attention paid to the young man would offend the French government. With the connivance of the army chief, the Duke of Cambridge, the matter was arranged anyway by the Queen and Eugénie.

"I am quite mystified about that little abortion, the Prince Imperial," Disraeli wrote with exasperation to Lord Salisbury on February 28, 1879. "I thought we had agreed not to sanction his adventure? Instead of that he has royal audiences previous to departure, . . . and is attended to the station by Whiskerandos himself,* the very general who was to conquer Constantinople. . . . What am I to say on this? H.M. knows my little sympathy with the Buonapartes."

Technically, Louis Napoleon went out only as an observer, but, Disraeli told Lady Chesterfield, "I fear . . . that some indiscreet friends, in very high places, gave him privately letters to Ld. Chelmsford, begging that General to place the Prince on his staff." On June 1 the Prince, on a reconnaissance with several companions who fled, was ambushed. Unable to remount his badly frightened horse, he was speared by Zulu *assegais*.

With no cable as yet to South Africa, the news was slow to reach London. On the afternoon of June 19, Disraeli heard of it at the opening of an exhibition at the Grosvenor Gallery. "This is terrible news," he said. "Yes," said G. W. E. Russell, an M. P., "and I am afraid that the French will accuse our people of having deserted him and left him to his fate."

"I am not so sure they will be wrong," Disraeli agreed. "Well! My conscience is clear. I did all that I could to stop his going. But what can you do when you have to deal with two obstinate women!"

In France, among royalists, Anglophobia surfaced to blame Victoria for exploding hopes of a new Napoleonic era. Just old enough to read the newspapers in 1879, Edmond Rostand would later write a play, *Napoleon IV*, charging that young Louis had been ambushed with the connivance of Queen Victoria.

The Queen received the alarming message from Brown. There was

*Lord Napier, who had commanded the British forces never used in Turkey.

bad news, he said. "The young French Prince is killed." In shock, she could not accept what she had heard, and asked Brown to repeat it several times. Then Beatrice came in with the telegram in her hand. "Oh!" she said, "the Prince Imperial is killed." Putting her hands to her head she cried, "No, no! It cannot, cannot be true! It can't be!"

"Dear Beatrice, crying very much, as I did too, gave me the telegram. We sent for Jane Ely, who was in the house when he was born, and was so devoted to him; and he was so good! Oh, it is too, too awful! The more one thinks of it the worse it is. . . ."

There were some anguished hours at Balmoral, she wrote: "It was dawning and little sleep did I get. . . . Beatrice so distressed; everyone quite stunned. . . . Had a bad, restless night, haunted by this awful event, seeing those horrid Zulus constantly before me and thinking of the poor Empress who did not yet know."

Nearly crippled by gout later in the month, Disraeli went nevertheless to Windsor, where the Queen spent an hour and a half "on the one subject which seems greatly to have affected her." He may not have realized how important young Louis Napoleon had been to the Queen. Of her own four sons, only Arthur was not a disappointment. The Prince Imperial was almost the son she never had, and indeed almost a son-in-law. While the Queen had been vainly promoting a Deceased Wife's Sister Marriage Act in order to arrange for Alice's widowered husband, the Grand Duke of Hesse-Darmstadt, to marry Beatrice, her youngest daughter apparently had other ideas. At twenty-one, she still possessed a youthful charm that would fade quickly, but remains best visualized in Sir Joseph Noel Paton's flattering oval portrait, Beatrice's long hair flowing, her right hand grasped by the widow-weeded Victoria. Still "Baby" to the Queen, she nevertheless knew her own mind, and saw no place for Louis of Hesse-Darmstadt in her future.

No religious scruple was involved although the Church of England had long opposed marriages to a deceased wife's sister, impelling bereaved lovers to go to Switzerland or Norway to evade the law, and causing such "illegal" couples to be socially shunned in England. Despite a petition to Parliament, at the Queen's request, from Bertie, the bill had failed in May; Disraeli had been unable to get it through the Lords with the bishops against it. The law remained unrepealed until 1907. Even had it passed, it was unlikely that Beatrice would have rushed into a union with a brother-in-law old enough to be her father, and with four children. She as well as Eugénie seemed discreetly interested in a match with the Prince

Imperial, despite the religious difficulty involved. After all, Alfred had already married in Russian Orthodox ceremonies.

However jealously the Queen supervised her youngest daughter, there were ways for Beatrice to evade her infirm mother, who (despite unconcealed affection for the Prince) would have had to weather diplomatic and religious objections to such a match. Now it could never happen.

Louis Napoleon had written a will before he sailed. Its sixth clause declared his "profound gratitude" to the Queen "and all the Royal Family." If that was intended as recognition of an unrevealed attachment—as he knew only Beatrice and the Prince of Wales—one can read it that way. It is a thin thread indeed, but for the evidence that Beatrice left in her mother's journals of their affection for the Prince Imperial and their profound grief at his death. Court gossip, however, connected him with Beatrice, fixing as one of his reasons for going to Africa his need to prove himself, through his deeds, as acceptable to the British public.

The remains arrived in England three weeks after the catastrophe, and two of the longest journal entries of the Queen describe her attendance at the removal of the body from Camden Place on July 12, and the funeral at the Catholic Church at Chislehurst on July 17. To Lady Chesterfield, Disraeli wrote, "I have just got a telegram from the Queen who has returned to Windsor and who seems highly pleased at all that occurred at Chislehurst this morning. I hope the French Government will be as joyful. In my mind, nothing could be more injudicious than the whole affair." In the rain, Victoria had gone to the funeral with Beatrice (and the usual suite of attendants), to view the magnificent casket into which the hideously ravaged body had been transferred. Only the few who formally identified the remains knew that the crude embalming attempted in South Africa had failed.

The Queen's four sons were pallbearers, and the obsequies were conducted, in the presence of Her Majesty, by Cardinal Manning. Beatrice remained kneeling so long that a bishop sent his assistant to request her to rise. Victoria's attendance was itself unprecedented.

The ceremony, the Queen wrote, was "a fearfully thrilling, affecting moment." Eugénie did not attend, learning only from the volleys of musketry fired by the Gentleman Cadets that it was all over. Then she received the Queen and Beatrice in a small, darkened room and kissed them both, saying, *"Je vous remercie, Madame, pour toutes vos bontés."* "This is the end," Victoria wrote, "of all that was once so splendid and brilliant, and of one who promised to be a blessing not only to his country, but to the world." And she mourned him in private, and was hot-tempered in public, about the military in Natal, whom she blamed for irresponsibility in the Prince's death. When a court-martial found that charges against one officer were not sustained by the evidence, she scrawled across the report *"unpunished"* and "uncensured." Gathorne-Hardy "pointed out to her that this wd. not do and she quite agreed as to the inexpediency of it. . . ."

The Queen consoled herself with reports that the Zulu attackers had behaved "mercifully" by severing two of the Prince Imperial's arteries so that he bled rapidly to death without further suffering, even sewing up the slashes in his jacket, and taking nothing but his watch—"to see what was inside."

Shortly afterward, Eugénie commissioned Richard Belt to execute a bust of the Prince, and when Victoria asked to see it, the sculptor took it to Windsor. The Empress had already expressed approval, but Victoria demurred. "There is one point in the mouth which is not accurate," she insisted. "I will show you what I mean if someone will bring me a gentleman's hat." One was found, and the Queen placed it on her head, observing, "When the Prince Imperial bowed to a lady he raised his hat in this way, and parted his lips like this." Then she returned the hat and declared, "There, Mr. Belt; that is how the Prince Imperial looked." Belt expressed his gratitude and promised amends.

At her London studio, Lady Butler had just finished pinning a seven-foot sheet of brown paper to an old canvas, and with a piece of charcoal and another of white chalk she had begun sketching the outlines of what would become the cavalry charge in *Scotland For Ever,* when Sir Henry Ponsonby called. He had been instructed to inquire whether she would paint a picture for her Majesty. Sensing what the Queen had in mind, Elizabeth Butler "proposed . . . the finding of the dead Prince Imperial and the bearing of his body from the scene of his heroic death on the lances of the Seventeenth Lancers. Her Majesty sent me word that she approved. . . . Then I got a message to say that the Queen thought it better not to paint the subject."

Better an event with less personal pain, Lady Butler understood. She thought instead of the battle for control of Natal, at Rorke's Drift, by the Twenty-fourth Regiment, afterwards the South Wales Borderers. At Portsmouth, where the regiment was now quartered, they reenacted, in uniform, their exploit. To represent the Zulus, she first resorted to "dark masses rather swallowed up in the shade," but a friend found a "sort of Zulu as model from a show in London."

During the picture's progress the Queen asked that it be brought to her at Windsor. The canvas was sent ahead, and in the Waterloo Gallery, Lady Butler saw it in the distance being examined by Disraeli and an associate. As they left, Victoria entered, with Leopold, Beatrice, and several ladies. "The Queen came up to me and placed her plump little hand in mine after I had curtseyed, and I was counselled to give Her Majesty the description of every figure. She spoke very kindly . . . and showed so much emotion that I thought her all too kind, shrinking now and then as I spoke of the wounds, etc. She told me how [in 1874] she had found my [future] husband lying at Netley Hospital after [the] Ashanti [wars in West Africa], apparently near his end, and spoke with warmth of his services in that campaign. She did not leave until I had explained every figure, even the most distant. She knew all by name for I had managed to show, in that scuffle, all the V.C.'s and other conspicuous actors in the drama. . . ."

The Queen purchased the Prince Imperial substitute, *The Defence of Rorke's Drift.* It became, Elizabeth Butler learned, a favorite of Victoria's. "One day . . . , wishing to show it to some friends, the twilight deepening, she showed so much appreciation that she took a pair of candlesticks and held them up at the full stretch of her arms to light the picture. I like to see in my mind's eye that Rembrandtesque effect."

General Sir Evelyn Wood, a V.C. in the Crimea and now knighted for his exploits in Zululand, escorted Eugénie to Natal in 1880 to see the place where her son had fallen, erecting there a large stone cross sent by Victoria. Afterward, he was invited to Balmoral to report on the trip, and returned £3,600 of the £5,000 she had given him to cover his expenses. She also invited the chief heroes of Rorke's Drift to Balmoral, Lieutenant John R. M. Chard and Lieutenant Gonville Bromhead, both of whom had been jumped in rank and awarded V.C.s. Chard came, and was given a gold signet ring as well. Bromhead, on leave, had gone fishing in Ireland and never saw his invitation until the date had passed. Victoria was deaf to his apologies. He was not reinvited. Another V.C. went to Captain Lord William L. D. Beresford, for rescuing, under fire, a fallen sergeant, but when he was commanded to Windsor to receive his medal he wrote to the Queen that he could not accept it unless the man who had accompanied him shared in the award. The next *Gazette* listed a V.C. to Sergeant Edmund O'Toole.

The death of Louis Napoleon raised for the Queen further questions about British unpreparedness in South Africa, and the Government's need to raise tax revenues for the military. "One great lesson is again taught us," she wrote to Disraeli, "but it is never followed: NEVER *let the Army and Navy* DOWN *so low* as *to be obliged* to go to *great expense* in a hurry." It had happened before, she observed, in the Crimean War. "We were *not* prepared. . . . If *we are* to *maintain* our position as a *first-rate* Power . . . we must, with our Indian Empire and large Colonies, be *prepared* for *attacks and wars, somewhere or other,* CONTINUALLY. And the *true economy* will be *to be always ready.* Lord Beaconsfield can do his country the greatest service by repeating this again and again, and by *seeing it carried out.* It will *prevent war.* "

The resurgent Woman Warrior appeared more energetic than her Prime Minister, but he complained to Lady Bradford that as long as the military remained a plaything of the aristocracy it would be inefficient regardless of the cannons and the cruisers. "The Horse Guards will ruin this country, unless there is a Prime Minister who will have his way, and that cannot be counted upon." And, recalling the case of the Prince Imperial, which symbolized to him that interference with the professionalism of the military, "You cannot get a Secretary of War to resist the cousin of the Sovereign. . . . I tremble when I think what may be the fate of this country if, as is not unlikely, a great struggle occur, with the Duke of Cambridge's [choice of] generals."

Fifteen years later the Duke was still in command, leaving a gap between the Queen's principles and her practice. He had held his position since 1856 and would hang on to it for thirty-nine years, commuting to the War Office from his town house in Queen Street, where he lived with his morganatic wife, Mrs. FitzGeorge, a onetime actress, or from his other house in Chesham Street, where he kept his mistress, Mrs. Beauclerk. He had been a colonel at nineteen, Commander-in-Chief at thirty-seven. He represented the Crown, he once wrote to his cousin Victoria in 1858; if his office were abolished, "the Army becomes a Parliamentary Army and would become dangerous to the State." Labouchère of *Truth* described him as standing at the head of his troops, "his drawn salary in his hand." With such posts in the military establishment in the possession of birth and privilege, there was a danger to the state, but not the one that George of Cambridge saw.

There were, as there always are, exceptions. Victoria's nephew Count Gleichen—Prince Victor of Hohenlohe-Langenburg—became an admiral on his merits before retiring to become a professional sculptor. And Victoria's own son Arthur—a dedicated soldier—would write to her in 1879 that he did not want to be named a general without having been a colonel: "Up to now I have worked my way up through every grade, from Lieutenant-Colonel, and I should not wish to skip the rank. . . ."

The Zulu war and an equally unpopular war on the African frontier, combined with poor economic conditions at home, foreshadowed the end of Disraeli's long Ministry. Ill as he was, he would hang on if he could, and pressed the Queen to open Parliament in person, in state "as splendid as might be convenient to your Majesty," to help revive the appeal of the Government. Sounding much like the Gladstone of old, he exhorted that "the splendour of Royalty delights the people." Sending his draft Speech from the Throne, he also noted the completion of Theodore Martin's five-volume *Life of the Prince Consort,* and agreed that a knighthood was in order. Soon he would have to think about parting honors for his outgoing Government, as Gladstone was gaining support, and staunchly anticolonialist. "Remember the rights of the savage, as we call him," Gladstone declared at Dalkeith, and he decried the "Empress of India" title as "theatrical bombast and folly." Still, a by-election at Southwark in February gave the Conservatives a large victory, which encouraged the Queen about prospects after a dissolution. On the same day, February 14, 1880, Disraeli sent the Queen from Downing Street a message in vintage form:

> He wishes he could repose on a sunny bank, like young Valentine in the pretty picture that fell from a rosy cloud this morn—but the reverie of the happy youth would be rather different from his. Valentine would dream of the future, and youthful loves, and all under the inspiration of a beautiful clime! Lord Beaconsfield, no longer in the sunset, but the twilight of existence, must encounter a life of anxiety and toil; but this, too, has its romance, when he remembers that he labours for the most gracious of beings!

He could not have sent *her* a valentine, but he could respond to her own.

Dissolution of Parliament, which Disraeli had wanted to put off until autumn, in hopes of better times, took place early in March. He had telegraphed to Windsor for a meeting to explain that the longer they waited, the worse it was likely to go for the Conservative cause. The farmers in particular were experiencing bad times, and the result was likely to be contagious. "I came back very bad from Windsor," he wrote to Lady Bradford on February 28. "I believe [it is] the consequence of having to pace so often that terrible corridor—the Palace of the Winds. . . ."

The campaign was bitter. As Earl Granville explained to the Queen, "Lord Beaconsfield and Mr. Gladstone are men of extraordinary ability; they dislike each other more than is usual among public men. Of no other politician Lord Beaconsfield would have said in public, that his conduct was worse than those who committed the Bulgarian atrocities. He has a power of saying in two words that which drives a person of Mr. Gladstone's peculiar temperament into a great state of excitement." Gladstone was not opposing the Queen, Granville explained, little realizing how much Disraeli's Russophobic policies were Victoria's.

After dissolution, the Queen went to Baden for the confirmation of two of her motherless grandchildren. Disraeli had tried to send W. H. Smith as Minister-in-Residence, and he pleaded, given the electoral situation, to be replaced by an "ornamental peer." Sir Michael Hicks Beach went instead, and when he asked Disraeli for advice on handling his assignment he was told, "First of all, remember she is a woman." From Baden, Victoria wrote to Vicky realistically about election prospects, "People ignorant and unreasoning think a change of Government will give them a good harvest and restore commerce. . . ." It was during her two weeks there that she learned of the Liberal landslide. "Your Majesty," Disraeli telegraphed to her on April 7, "must not be unnecessarily hurried or agitated at this moment. . . . I take the responsibility on myself."

The Queen answered from Baden the same day in a first-person message, "What your loss to me as a Minister would be, it is impossible to estimate. But I trust you will always remain my friend, to whom I can turn and on whom I can rely. Hope you will come to Windsor in the forenoon on Sunday, and stop all day, and dine and sleep." Before that Sunday she mulled over the alternatives to Gladstone, including abdication—she informed Ponsonby—"rather than send for or have any *communication* with that *half-mad firebrand* who wd. soon ruin everything & be a *Dictator.* Others but herself *may submit* to his democratic rule, but *not the Queen.*" His campaign had demonstrated, she charged, "a most unpardonable & personal hatred to Ld. B. who had restored England to the position she had lost under Mr. G's Gov't."

Although Disraeli knew that it was forever—as brief as that span seemed in the allowance left to him—the Queen hoped that his loss "would only be for a short time." His relations with her, he telegraphed back, "were his chief, he might almost say his only happiness & interest in this world," and she conferred upon him in return the privilege of writing to her in the first person, for "when we correspond, which I hope we shall on many a *private* subject & without anyone being astonished or offended, & even more without anyone knowing about it—I hope it will be in this more easy form. . . . You must not think it is a real parting. I shall always let you know how I am & what I am doing, & you must promise me to let me hear from & about you." And she proposed—she had done so once before—to bestow a peerage on his nephew and heir, Coningsby, who was thirteen. Again Disraeli refused: it had not been earned.

Disraeli wound up his business, sometimes beset by "pesterers of the 11th hour," more often with matters of transition from power, and left Downing Street for the last time on April 25, two days before a farewell audience with the Queen. After that she had to be consoled largely with reminders of his presence, writing to him on May 4 that she rejoiced "to see you looking down from the *wall* after dinner," and still preferred to think that "what has happened is only a horrid dream."

Such exchanges continued to bypass Ponsonby, who the Queen knew would deplore them. From his beloved Hughenden, Disraeli put the best face on his unaccustomed private life. In the spring and summer, when Parliament usually met, he had experienced little of his country seat. Now he wrote to Victoria on June 14, 1880, that after going up to London to cast a vote in the Lords, he would return the next day. "I cannot resist the fascination of the voice of the cuckoo, so mysterious and sultry, the wood-pigeons' cooing, and the sweetness and splendour of the May-blossom. Deign, Gracious Lady, to pardon this weakness (remembering that I never was before in the country in this month) of your Majesty's ever grateful and devoted Beaconsfield."

On three occasions later in the year he stayed at Windsor, and continued to exchange letters with Victoria, usually avoiding politics. On March 1, 1881, he dined at Windsor for the last time, the Queen having no sense of Disraeli's rapid decline. He made, in fact, a major foreign-policy speech in the Lords soon after. Three weeks later a March chill developed into bronchitis, and Disraeli's weak lungs could not respond. Bedridden at the end of the month, he wrote his last letter to the Queen, a shaky penciled note concluding that he was her "prostrate but devoted —B." She pressed her own doctors to see him for a second opinion on his treatment; but Disraeli's own physician, Dr. Joseph Kidd, was a homeopath, which created a problem of medical etiquette among more traditional practitioners. Finally a specialist in chest diseases, Dr. Richard Quain, was induced to visit Disraeli out of loyalty to the Queen. The case, as the patient himself knew, proved beyond medicine.

After hints from the Queen, Disraeli was asked whether he might like to be visited by her Majesty. "No, it is better not," he said. "She would only ask me to take a message to Albert." She sent him flowers from Windsor, and before leaving for Osborne on April 5 she wrote a last letter to him, with instructions that if he was not well enough to read it himself, it should be read to him. Disraeli held it for a moment, then observed, "This letter ought to be read to me by a Privy Councillor." And Lord Barrington, who was one, did so.

The struggle to breathe ended on April 19. He half lifted himself from his pillow to say something; the lips moved but made no sound. Then he sank back. There were no last words.

"As he lived so he died—all display without reality or genuineness," said Gladstone privately. "The Queen feels quite bowed down with this misfortune," she confided to Ponsonby. To Montagu Corry, now Lord Rowton, designated one of Disraeli's executors, the Queen wrote sadly, "Never had I *so* kind and devoted a Minister and very few such devoted friends. . . . My poor faithful Brown was quite overcome when he had to tell me. His sad and tearful face had too plainly told that a heavy blow had fallen."

Unable to say her farewell to Disraeli with the others, Victoria went to Hughenden on April 30, from Windsor. Flowers, including her primroses, still remained from the funeral. "Then we walked down to the vault," she wrote in her journal, "which had been opened purposely for me to see. . . . Could hardly realise it all, it seemed too sad, and so cheerless. I placed a wreath of china flowers." Then, under her portrait, she took tea in the library, just as she had in 1877—only this time with Disraeli's shade. "I seem to hear his voice, and the impassioned, eager way he described everything."

In Hughenden Church, Victoria had a marble monument erected, "placed by his grateful and affectionate Sovereign and friend, Victoria R.I." The "I" was Disraeli's gift. The last line of the inscription was a quotation she had chosen from Proverbs, "Kings love him that speaketh right."

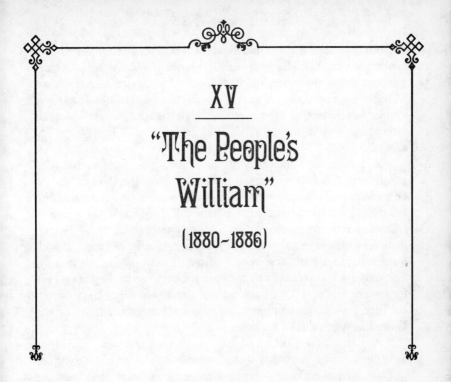

XV

"The People's William"

(1880–1886)

"To me," the Queen wrote to Vicky early in May 1880, " 'the people's William' is a most disagreeable person —half-crazy, and so excited—(though he has been respectful and proper in his manner and professes devotion) to deal with." She found it difficult to reconcile his professed awe for her office and person with what she saw as his demagoguery on the hustings and his selecting revolutionaries for the Cabinet. Gladstone needed the votes of his Radical wing, and Victoria was forced to accept Charles Dilke and Joseph Chamberlain, both of whom had expressed republican sentiments, in the Government. As a matter of pride, she insisted on their assurances of good behavior, and it took two letters before she felt that Dilke had apologized sufficiently for his sins of the early 1870s.

Even Gladstone registered with an apology. Among his outbursts in the campaign for his Midlothian seat, he had falsely quoted the Emperor of Austria as hoping that Disraeli would win. The Queen insisted that Gladstone retract his charge directly to Francis Joseph. After that purely symbolic act of deference, she had to accept him once more as Prime Minister since he would not serve under anyone else. Happy to make way for him was the elected Liberal leader, the greybearded, sad-eyed Marquis of Hartington (later the eighth Duke of Devonshire)—"Harty Tarty" to Disraeli.

A believer in a merely symbolic monarchy as the foundation of government, Gladstone regretted to Ponsonby that the Liberals were to be contending with an activist Queen. Eager, when she had retreated into self-pitying seclusion, to have her more visible, they had not welcomed a Disraelian intrusive sovereign. That, Gladstone confided, in an increasingly democratic age, threatened the institution itself. "My day," he said, "is drawing to a close, and when a man gets worn out he gets gloomy. Formerly I saw no reason why monarchy should not have gone on here for hundreds of years, but I confess that the way in which the monarch has been brought to the front in political and foreign affairs by the late Government has shaken my confidence."

Any hopes the Queen had for a more accommodating Gladstone were put to rest immediately by his pressing within days of taking office to make Sir Robert Lowe—the most tactless objector in the Commons to the Royal Titles Bill—a viscount. To the Queen's objections, Gladstone tirelessly furnished rebuttals. Eventually she yielded. She trusted, she told Gladstone unhopefully, "that her readiness to do so may be reciprocated by him on other occasions."

Then Gladstone—"the people's William"—proposed to balance his budget on the backs of the lower classes by a new tax on beer. Realizing that she was helpless, Victoria chastised him sadly. "The richer classes who drink wine and who are not in any way restricted in their indulgence, can well afford to pay for wine. But the poor can ill afford any additional tax on what in many parts is about their only beverage." She also thought she was being a friend of the poor in objecting to improvements in elementary education—which was already "of too high a standard, & useless in consequence." To educate the lower classes for joblessness, and increase their misery by unrealistically raising their expectations, struck her as immoral. It was a perspective worthy of Melbourne.

None of the preliminaries to the second Gladstone Ministry suggested that he and the Queen would get on any better than before. By mid-July she was writing to Vicky, "Everything is going as badly as can be and I feel thoroughly disgusted and humiliated." At seventy, Gladstone was hard of hearing. It was also a strategic disability that manifested itself in a deafness of every kind when it came to the Queen's views. He began each communication with the formulaic "Mr. Gladstone presents his humble duty to your Majesty," but there the humility ended. If he did not get his way, he pressed again and again and again, until the Queen gave in—if not entirely, out of pride, at least enough for Gladstone to assume a mandate of sorts.

To Earl Granville, leader of the Liberals in the Lords, and Foreign Secretary, the Queen wrote on August 8 a heavily underlined, emotional letter that she asked him to show to Gladstone and the Cabinet:

> She is *seriously* alarmed at the *extreme Radicals* being at all cajoled by the present Government, and she must tell Lord Granville that she thinks the moderate Members of the Government *ought* to do *all* to obtain the *support* of their *moderate Whig* supporters *instead* of courting the support of the *extreme Party.* She *knows* that the Opposition would give them *every support,* in resisting any policy which *strikes* at the *root and existence* of the Constitution and Monarchy. The Queen herself can *never* have *any confidence* in the men who encourage *reform* for the *sake of alteration and pulling down what exists* and what is *essential* to the *stability* of a Constitutional Monarchy. A *Democratic Monarchy* . . . she will not *consent to belong to. Others* must be found *if* that is to be, and she *thinks* we are on a dangerous and doubtful slope which may become too rapid for us to stop, when it is too late.
>
> The Queen is all for *improvement* and *moderate reform of abuses,* but not merely for *alteration's and reform's sake.* . . .

To Gladstone, the problem was that the Queen had been spoiled by Disraeli. "He has over-educated the said pupil a little," the Prime Minister explained irreverently to Granville. Even more nastily, when she objected to Radicals in undersecretaryships, Gladstone circulated a memo to several Ministers, along with a copy of a royal protest, with the comment, "I think this intolerable. It is by courtesy only that these appointments are made known to H.M." Her Majesty, however, considered it a royal right to know, and to object to the objectionable. After one audience he noted, "She is as ever perfect in her courtesy but as to confidence she now holds me at arm's length." It was obtuse of him to have failed to notice that distance widening over two decades. Disraeli had once joked that one needed a separate Ministry merely to deal with the Queen; now Gladstone, walking at Hawarden one day with Lord Rosebery, exclaimed that the Queen alone was enough to kill a man. Victoria would put it another way to Ponsonby, her conduit to the Cabinet: "The Queen must complain bitterly of the want of respect and consideration of her views (which her experience of 45 years might and ought to be regarded on the part of the Government . . .). She feels hurt and indignant."

In November, after months of difficulties with the new Government, the Queen again aired her feelings to Ponsonby, whom she knew to be a Gladstone admirer. Her *"never personally* liking" the Prime Minister, she explained, came from "the feeling of gr^t *displeasure* for the gr^t harm he did *when out* of office w^h told against the late Gov^t and brought all the present difficulties upon us: and this feeling must be lasting. L^d G[ranville] does no good praising the Queen for being civil which she w^d be sure to do on acc^t of Mr. G[ladstone]'s *position* as it is her duty to be so." In no way did Gladstone's political perspectives coincide with her own, and he regretted that her power to influence policy had been exaggerated by Disraeli. "The realm suffers from your Majesty's reserve," he had written to her from retirement, only encouraging her outspokenness to Gladstone and his Ministers. She was for coercive measures to put down turbulence in Ireland, and for maintaining a strong presence in the colonies rather than what she described as "wretched peace" and "murder . . . openly preached."

The first Anglo-Boer war began in December 1880 in the Transvaal, which the British had annexed in 1877, over taxes that the resentful Dutchmen refused to pay. In colonial matters, Gladstone preferred withdrawal to coercion. His Speech from the Throne for Victoria mentioned another example—a proposed evacuation of the southern Afghan town of Kandahar.* Overlooking the North West Frontier, the region seemed crucial to what Rudyard Kipling was to call the Great Game, that contest for strategic position atop the borders of the Indian subcontinent. The stakes were wedges of Asia from the Himalayas to the Persian Gulf, and would keep the Russians and the British suspicious of each other's motives and moves into the twentieth century.

At a Privy Council meeting early in the new year at Osborne, the Queen objected. She even delayed opening the Council until the mem-

*Now also spelled Quandahar.

bers present could receive an answer from the absent Gladstone to her telegram appealing for "anything short of a positive declaration." On grounds of both Liberal policy and constitutional practice, there was to be, his Ministers agreed with Gladstone, "simple and unreserved approval by the Queen of the Speech to be delivered from the Throne in Her name." Embarrassed by the blunt language, Privy Councillors could not face the Queen's gaze. "I spoke to no one," she reported in her journal, "and the Ministers tumbled over each other going out."

To Victoria the tiff was tactless; to Gladstone it was another matter of principle, and at the Queen's insistence he relented only in a letter in which he "humbly" agreed that if circumstances altered adversely, the Government would reconsider Kandahar. It would not take long for the expansiveness that she felt under Disraeli to evaporate under the "G.O.M."—the Liberals' "Grand Old Man."

Colonial withdrawals, the Queen worried, could become contagious. "We must not give way to Boer demands," she wrote to Gladstone on March 11, after an embarrassing British defeat—and retreat—at Majuba on February 26. Nevertheless, the Government gave the Transvaal qualified independence in August 1881 rather than attempt to retake the territory. Only in domestic matters, it appeared to Victoria, was Gladstone uncompromising, although even there she found an exception. For all his hostility to the House of Lords, which he claimed was an anachronism in a democratic society, he preferred the old aristocracy in his Cabinets, and he sought peerages for his followers at every opportunity. There was little effort made to disguise such honors ideologically as attempts to pare down the Tory majority. He even confessed in a letter to the Queen on August 23, 1881, that since her accession the vast majority of peerages had been granted under pressure from Liberal Prime Ministers. Victoria hoped to see an end to it, and Gladstone volunteered insincerely it might never again "fall to his lot, personally" to recommend additions to the Lords.

At Balmoral a month later, the Queen learned that the American President, James Garfield, who had been shot by a disappointed office seeker early in July, had succumbed; as with Mrs. Lincoln, she cabled a message to Lucretia Garfield: "Words cannot express the deep sympathy I feel with you at this terrible moment. May God support you and comfort you as He alone can!" Her own loss, a husband who had been king without a crown, had been, she may well have thought, the greater. Perhaps Albert could have contended more successfully with Gladstone. All she could do, as her actions suggested in Gladstone's second year of office, was to restrain what she saw as his demagoguery. "The times are serious," she warned before a banquet at Leeds, where he was to speak. "Let me express a hope that you will be very cautious." When she commented on a particularly explosive remark, his dismissive thanks to her Majesty "for the free expression of opinion, on the speech made by him . . ." was a brusque rejection.

With nothing seemingly going well, and Gladstone's views, rather than her own, enjoying broad popular support, Victoria received some unearned assistance from what was to be the last assassination attempt directed at her. Murderers of American Presidents seemed to have better aim. This time, as she left her train at Windsor on March 2, 1882, returning from a rare stay at Buckingham Palace, she heard a sharp sound that seemed to her merely a locomotive noise. Then she saw "people rushing about and a man being violently hustled. . . ." There had been a shot.

Having missed, Roderick Maclean was immediately set upon by Eton boys armed with umbrellas. Three days later the Queen received nine hundred Etonians in the Quadrangle at Windsor, singling out for her special thanks the two who had kept Maclean from a second shot. Gladstone observed erroneously that all her seven assassins had been madmen without political motive. Although Maclean, too, was later pronounced insane, Victoria worried about further attempts by Irish radicals, and went to the "dear Mausoleum" to pray at Albert's tomb for her continued preservation. Meanwhile, letters and telegrams poured into Windsor congratulating her on her latest escape. "Anything like the enthusiasm, loyalty, sympathy and affection shown me is not to be described. It is worth being shot at to see how much one is loved."

At Mentone in April—the Riviera was a favorite retreat for Leopold, who suffered from the English chill—Victoria helped her youngest son celebrate his twenty-ninth birthday. Rumor was that she was also going to cross the border into Italy, to see her old drawing master, Edward Lear, at San Remo. Giorgio Cocali, Lear's favorite pastry cook, the story went, had been working for two days and nights baking quantities of macaroons, for "it is known that the Queen of England eats macaroon cakes continually, and she also insists on her suite doing the same." People gathered outside Lear's gate to wait for her, but she did not come. Protocol problems in crossing the frontier precluded a visit, but not long after, the

Princess Royal arrived unexpectedly with her husband—while Lear was sitting at dinner.

At Mentone, Leopold's uncertain health made the Queen anxious, but despite the hemophilia that kept him, in her description, "lame and shaky," he announced that he had found a wife. The young woman (she had been his mother's suggestion) was Princess Helen of Waldeck, twenty-one years old and tough-minded, and under no illusions about the Duke of Albany's prospects for long life. Her prospects otherwise were small. Leopold had wanted a title matching those of his elder brothers, and Victoria observed that anyone might be a Duke, but few could be Royal Princes. Her grant of a dukedom came with the proviso that in her own homes he remained Prince Leopold.

The marriage was solemnized at the Chapel Royal, Windsor, on April 27, 1882. The Queen wore white lace over her usual black, as well as a white veil. As a wedding gift she gave Claremont to Leopold and Helen. She had purchased the estate from the heirs of her uncle for whom Leopold was named. Ten months later, to her surprise, the couple presented her with a granddaughter; she had assumed that the Prince's frailty would preclude that.

A week after the wedding, the Queen made a Royal Progress to High Beech in east London, threading through enormous and enthusiastic crowds apparently without anxiety about assassination attempts, to open Epping Forest as a London park. At dinner on her return to Windsor, Henry Ponsonby handed her a telegram from Dublin. Lord Frederick Cavendish, the new Chief Secretary for Ireland, and Thomas Burke, his Under-Secretary, had been stabbed by Fenians in Phoenix Park. Another telegram later that evening reported that both had died. Cavendish had been married to Gladstone's niece, Lucy.

On May 2, four days earlier, Gladstone had ordered the release from prison of three Radical Irish M.P.s, one of them Charles Stewart Parnell, on grounds that the gesture "would tend to peace and security in Ireland," and reduce the "No Rent" agitation against absentee landlords. (It would tend also, Gladstone knew, to secure Parnell's bloc of votes in the Commons.)

When the Queen heard of Parnell's parole, she telegraphed to Gladstone, as his private secretary, Edward Hamilton, noted, "in a great state of mind on the presumption that it could not be true. It was just one of those stupid omissions to [not] give her information which she has a distinct right to have." What Hamilton did not realize was that not giving the Queen information was already the Prime Minister's established, if unwritten, policy. Since Victoria opposed every move that Gladstone wanted to make regarding Ireland, he had kept her uninformed. It had been his lax policies that had led to the violence, Victoria thought. "Surely," she noted in her journal, "his eyes must be opened now." She wanted effective coercion, seeing nationalism everywhere as something that would go away if firmly discouraged.

Relationships with Gladstone on every level and every subject were bitter beneath the polite formulas in which communications were couched, whether the business was Ireland, or Africa, or the appointment of a bishop. Then, too, the subject of Gladstone's "night walks" was again —in the words of Hamilton's diary—"noised over London." Reportedly, Gladstone and a streetwalker were seen "walking arm-in-arm" near the Duke of York's column in Waterloo Place. To Hamilton, Gladstone did not deny that something of the sort had taken place, suggesting "that he would really give up these night encounters." Although the Queen invited the Gladstones to Prince Leopold's wedding—she could hardly do otherwise—her "unfriendly disposition towards him" prompted him to tell his wife (so Catherine told Hamilton), "She will never be happy till She has hounded me out of office."

The early 1880s saw worldwide confrontations between nationalism and colonialism that put the Queen and her Cabinet on opposite sides. To Victoria, who had acquired Palmerston's perspectives after long years of being his adversary, power in the world came from possessions. To Gladstone, only moral and spiritual power counted, as the cannons could not go off by themselves. A later entry in the Queen's journal about the Gladstone Ministry reflected her impatience with decisions made on the basis of moral principles or budget figures or domestic strategies: "It is to me inconceivable that a handful of men sitting in a room in London, the greater part knowing little about Egypt, should pretend to say whether there is danger or not."

On August 14, 1882, a human specimen of the colonial dilemma came calling at Osborne House. Cetewayo, king of the Zulus, had been captured after the defeat of his primitively equipped army, and brought to England to be impressed by English might. Also, Gladstone wanted to make a case for the chieftain's restoration. At fifty-two, Cetewayo considered himself "an old man." He was tall and broad, and wore, to be received by the Queen, what she called "a hideous black frock coat and trousers" over a colorful native tunic. Through the British Administrator in Zululand, Mr. Shepstone, Cetewayo and his companions exchanged commonplaces with the Queen, the Zulu chieftain proud of having learned the names of Victoria's daughters Helena, Louise, and Beatrice, who were in the curious audience. Then Captain Arthur Bigge, new Assistant Secretary to Ponsonby, ushered the Zulus out, right hands raised above their heads in a farewell salute. (Bigge had known the Prince Imperial at Woolwich and in Africa; his addition to the Household had followed his reporting to the Queen on Louis Napoleon's last days.) By the next January, in accordance with Liberal principles, Cetewayo was back upon his precarious throne.

By that time, Egypt had replaced southern Africa as flashpoint. A Colonel Arabi, exploiting discontent over heavy foreign debts incurred by the Khedive, had led a coup and ceased payments to European bondholders, largely French and English. In Alexandria, Europeans were being killed in riots, and Arabi Pasha was mounting guns at the harbor approaches; republican France hesitated to intervene in what was seen as a nationalist convulsion. With British interests to protect—and Christians "murdered with impunity," Victoria reminded Gladstone—the Government decided, reluctantly, to put down Arabi. A popular war was in the offing, and even the Prince of Wales volunteered to go.

The possibility that the portly and unmilitary Bertie, forty-one and heir to the Throne, might venture abroad, to unhealthy climes where even the environs of officers' clubs concealed unpredictable hazards, horrified the Queen. The Prince of Wales had already enlisted the support of his uncle, the Duke of Cambridge, and claimed that of the commanding general in Egypt, Sir Garnet Wolseley, but for once Gladstone agreed with Victoria. Frustrated, the Prince declared that he would go anyway, with all his equerries—as if he were fielding his private little army—and if that was refused, he would resign his commission as a field marshal (given to him largely for the uniform) and go as a civilian. Wolseley and his staff, the Queen telegraphed Gladstone, "earnestly hope H.R.H. will not go."

Ponsonby communicated the refusal in his most courtly language, observing to the Prince that the Queen hoped that the impossible but "gallant offer" would become generally known, and the next day (July 31, 1882) Granville repeated the consolatory adjective in representing the Cabinet's views to the Prince of Wales. More subtle was his qualifying word *almost:*

Her Majesty, I may almost say, fully agreed with Your Royal Highness's desires to be of use, warmly appreciated the gallant wish to see service, and was proud that the Prince of Wales should not shrink from sharing the dangers and privations of her troops.

But, on the other hand, the imperative demands of public duty compelled Her Majesty to point out the grave difficulties, and inconvenience, of such a proceeding; and, having been advised by the Government, as well as by several leaders of the Opposition, that it would be inexpedient and most unwise, considering Your Royal Highness's rank and position, to join the expedition as a spectator, and impossible for Your Royal Highness to be attached to it on duty, the Queen finally and conclusively decided that it was necessary to ask Your Royal Highness to abandon the idea.

That evening the disappointed Prince turned up nevertheless at the farewell dinner that he was hosting at the Marlborough Club for twenty-three officers in the Household Cavalry. He had hoped to sail with them. Instead, the family was represented in Egypt by the Duke of Connaught, commanding a Guards brigade. At thirty-two a legitimate if very young major general, Prince Arthur would be on the field at Tel-el-Kebir on September 13, when the motley army of Arabi Pasha was smashed. The Queen communicated her pride to Wolseley that Arthur was "worthy of his own dear father" and of the "great godfather" whose name he bore, the Duke of Wellington.

A reluctant empire builder, Gladstone was for immediate withdrawal from Egypt. The Queen reminded him of "the *unfortunate result* of the haste with which our Troops were brought back from Zululand & South Africa, & the consequent loss of prestige w^h ensued in the Transvaal. This s^d be a warning to us in the *present instance.*" Gladstone recorded "another fidgety Telegram from Balmoral," and credited her with seeing only "*one* side of a question." Victoria's "resolute attempts to disturb & impede the reduction of the army in Egypt," he wrote to Lord Hartington "are (to use a plain word) intolerable," and "almost as unconstitutional as they are irrational."

The troops—most of them—came home from Egypt in November 1882, and the Queen reviewed them in St. James's Park, close to Buckingham Palace, on November 18—an unclouded, sunny day. "My heart was in my mouth," she confided to Vicky, "as my darling Arthur rode past at the head of the brave men he led into action—and looking so like darling, beloved Papa." In a separate ceremony that day she gave the lean, drooping-mustached Arthur the Order of the Bath (Military Division).

A few days later there was a second parade. The crisp day was colorful with Indian and Guards uniforms, flags, and bands. "I gave away 330 medals," she told Vicky, "pinning a good many on the officers and men and giving the others into their hands." Her proudest moment came when she pinned the Egyptian Campaign medal on Arthur's breast. Last in order of rank came three Maltese and a number of Indians, "on all of whom I pinned the medal, but, I fear, pricked one. Some of the Indians held out their swords for me to touch, as is their custom. I liked to be able to look at them close by, such fine men, and some of them so handsome. I stood on the fine Turkish carpet which had belonged to Arabi, and which had been taken out of his tent, after Tel-el-Kebir. Arthur slept on it that memorable night, and gave it [to] me."

Beyond the colorful and self-congratulatory façade, the two days of ceremonies signaled that Gladstone was making good his intention to reduce British military presence abroad. To make matters worse, from the Queen's standpoint, he put the Tory renegade Lord Derby—a deserter from Disraeli's "Eastern Question" Cabinet—at the head of the India Office. Derby had just made a speech in Manchester, the theme of which was "Let Egypt take care of itself." To have him oversee the jewel in her Crown was too much. Derby's political philosophy, as she had already described it to Vicky, was "Do nothing—keep out of everything—and shut yourself up." She would rather see Dilke in the Cabinet than Derby, she told Gladstone on December 14. Deaf to the outburst, he replied the next day, "It gratifies me much to say that Lord Derby at once conforms to Your Majesty's desire. I have proposed him accordingly to come to Windsor tomorrow and be sworn in as Secretary for the Colonies." Since the Queen had objected to India, Gladstone stubbornly put him at the head of the Ministry that Derby most wanted to see reduced in responsibility.

It would be "painful" to receive Derby, she telegraphed, but she was powerless under Gladstone's relentless pressure. "He cannot expect a cordial reception, but it is a great thing he does not go to [the] India [Office]," she conceded. The "retrograde course" for the colonies—her accusation to Gladstone on December 22—was, she thought, because the Prime Minister "loved" France and Russia; indeed, one of his aims was to avoid antagonizing Russia in the Middle East, another to satisfy France that the occupation of Egypt was only temporary.

Only Gladstone's ill health, and his relative inactivity in the first months of 1883, kept relations with Victoria from worsening further, after which she went into near-seclusion herself on the sudden death of John Brown.

If what Gathorne-Hardy called in his diary "the morbid condition of the Queen in respect to John Brown" was then the most poorly kept secret in Britain, a second was Gladstone's conduct of his Government, in the Queen's name, as if the Queen did not exist. On April 4, 1883, *The World* denounced the Prime Minister for making "no pretense" of consulting Victoria, although her "knowledge and experience" were without parallel and she was "a woman of an exceptionally gifted order." While she was "habitually consulted" by Disraeli, *The World* reminded readers, Gladstone had "an imperfect disposition to reap the harvest of the Queen's knowledge." The Cabinet seemed in every way to separate itself from identification with the monarchy, as if that institution were only a historical technicality. In a deliberately tactless speech, Joseph Chamberlain, President of the Board of Trade in Gladstone's Cabinet and its leading Radical, referred to the Conservative opposition (in effect, the Queen's party) as representative of the class "who toil not, neither do they spin." (The dapper, monocled Chamberlain, from a prosperous Birmingham manufacturing family, looked always like a representative of the other side.) Taking exception to the charge, the Queen complained to Gladstone that it was offensive to the Crown, and set class against class, and the Prime Minister's secretary, Edward Hamilton, confessed in his diary that it was "certainly not judicious." All that Gladstone did was to confess to Victoria—three months late—that he was "sorry," that his sight no longer permitted him to read "the small type of newspapers," and that he had, accordingly, missed the speech. Chamberlain, whom Gladstone disliked, was too popular among the newly enfranchised electorate and too successful a Party fund-raiser, to put down.

As the Queen realized, Gladstone's excuse was nonsense; and she asked him "to take some steps to mark her displeasure as well as that of the Govt." He lightly rapped the ambitious Chamberlain's knuckles for the "inconvenient results" of his remarks, and the Queen finally had to accept whatever satisfaction she could. She was determined to reduce Chamberlain's influence on the reform bill, which was aimed at redistributing seats in the Commons to give the swollen—and Radical—cities more of their share of seats, and the relatively dwindling and conservative counties less. Calling attention to the Member from Birmingham's alleged irresponsibility helped, as did keeping him the bad boy in Gladstone's school of politics. "The people's William" had promised such a bill in his campaign, and the Queen knew that in some form it was inevitable.

At Osborne in August, the Queen gave an audience to Tennyson as one invalid to another. The poet was shaky on his legs, failing in sight, and more shaggy in hair and beard than ever. Again she told him what a comfort *In Memoriam* "had always been"—she had probably turned to it again when Brown died—and Tennyson shared her feelings about the "darkened" state of the world. Not realizing how truly isolated and alone the Queen felt, Tennyson said, on bidding her good-bye, "You are so alone on that terrible height. I have only a year or two more to live, but I am happy to do anything for you I can."

Tennyson had nine more years of life, adorned with a peerage granted the next month. Paradoxically, the request came in a letter from Gladstone to the Queen that otherwise enraged her even more than had Chamberlain's fiery Birmingham speech. On the *Pembroke Castle,* a passenger liner owned by Sir Donald Currie, on which he had taken a number of the elite for a private cruise, Gladstone had met Tennyson, fresh from Osborne. Their conversation reawakened ideas of honors for the Poet Laureate, who earlier had refused a baronetcy from Disraeli. What he wanted was something that might ennoble his sons after him. From the ship, Gladstone wrote to the Queen.

While happily granting the peerage, Victoria rebuked the Prime Minister for junketing across the North Sea to Denmark and Norway on a quasi-royal progress, and dining with kings and princes, without conforming to the law that required formal leave for the Prime Minister to set foot on foreign soil. More than a breach of etiquette, it suggested a naïve approach to the conduct of foreign relations that the Queen felt would never have occurred to the statesmanlike Lord Beaconsfield. While the excursion continued, the Foreign Secretary, Lord Granville, heard from Victoria, who considered Gladstone's oft-repeated veneration for the Throne insincere at best. "Her unfeigned astonishment at Mr. Gladstone's want of *all knowledge,* apparently, of what is due to the Sovereign he serves," she wrote, was almost beyond words, and she demanded an apology for "this escapade." Gathorne-Hardy observed in his diary that he was amused by Lord Bridport's description of her Majesty's views of Gladstone's junket. "She did not say she wished he was not coming back but evidently was not anxious that his voice should."

Privately, to Granville, Gladstone confided that he was "angry" at her tone, which was "for the first time—somewhat unmannerly." As usual, however, he made his apologies while intending to go on doing what he pleased. His excuse, he explained to the Queen with disarming candor, was that "increasing weariness of mind, under public cares for which he feels himself less and less fitted, may have blunted the faculty of anticipation with which he was never very largely endowed." That blunted "faculty of anticipation" would soon lead to further problems.

Gladstone unburdened himself to his private secretary, blaming the Queen's hostility on his immense popularity among the masses, whom he would tell, "All the world over, I will back the masses against the classes," and "You cannot fight against the future. Time is on our side." Newspapers reported that crowds had gathered at every railway station along his route to the docks, shouting "Gladstone!" Never able to resist making some pungent political statement anywhere an audience gathered, "the people's William" often earned further royal rejoinders. "She feels, as he puts it," Ponsonby wrote, "aggrieved at the undue reverence shewn to an old man of whom the public are being constantly reminded, and who goes on working for them beyond the allotted time, while H.M. is, owing to the life she leads, withdrawn from view. Hence comes a dislocation of the natural and just balance of popular interest. Mr. G. is quite right. (But how can it be otherwise when the Queen never shows herself—never resides for above two nights in the year in the capital, declines to open Parliament, avoids all state occasions, and sees next to no one?) What he wraps up in guarded and considerate language is (to put it bluntly) *jealousy*. She can't bear to see the large type which heads the columns of newspapers by 'Mr. Gladstone's movements,' while down below is in small type the Court Circular."

On matters that Gladstone felt were unimportant, or that directly affected the Court, he continued to ask the Queen's pleasure. One of those was the tunneling under London parks for a new section of underground railway. Since Buckingham Palace was nearby, although not directly affected, Bertram Mitford (later Lord Redesdale), in charge of the Office of Works, was sent to Balmoral, arriving on November 12. It was cold and a heavy snow was falling. At the castle was a note from Henry Ponsonby: "Please go to your room, order tea and make yourself comfortable. We are off to a picnic."

Eventually Ponsonby returned, looking frozen, and huddled by Mitford's fire until dinner. The party at the table—as usual, with Beatrice—

was small. Mitford waited for an opportunity to bring up his subject. None came, as the talk revolved about the Queen's recollections. After dinner, in the drawing room, each guest had the usual little audience with Victoria, and Mitford, aware that decorum required that the Queen initiate the subjects for conversation, found no way to allude to the underground railway. It was, he recalled, as if he were "an invited guest instead of a mere official on duty."

The next morning—he was to leave at midday—the Duchess of Roxburghe brought him a signed copy of the large illustrated edition of the Highlands journal and told him when the Queen expected to see him upon his business. When he met her, she noted in her journal, he explained "a plan of tunnelling under the Parks, from Westminster, . . . which would enable Parliament Street to be widened. I said I would only give my consent on the condition that no air-holes, or smoke, or noise, should come near the Palace, or the former be seen in the Parks." Then she added, Mitford recalled, "But I so seldom go to London now that I hardly feel as if I had the right to express an opinion."

Mitford was gallant. "I only wish, Madam, that we at the Office of Works oftener had the opportunity of profiting by Your Majesty's advice." The tunneling scheme was approved.

In all four seasons of the year, Balmoral was notorious for its chill, which Victoria found one of its charms. "All doctors," Victoria insisted, "say that heat is unwholesome but cold wholesome." More and more as she grew older, she was drawn in winter to the Mediterranean sun; yet her antipathy to fires remained. Once at Osborne, warned that the Queen was coming to pay a visit, the Ponsonby family, housed on the estate, hurried to remove (in buckets) all traces of the drawing-room fire, then opened the windows to freshen the air. Ponsonby recalled a discussion at Balmoral, involving the Queen and Princess Beatrice, "as to whether if you were condemned to one or the other you would rather live at the Equator or the North Pole." Long-suffering, Beatrice chose the Equator.

Events near the Equator continued to add to the Queen's frustrations with the Gladstone regime. In November 1883 she recorded in her journal that Granville, the Foreign Secretary, was a "very weak reed to lean upon" with respect to African affairs, and that he and Gladstone had advised the Khedive, now a British ward, to give up the Sudan, which was only impoverishing him, and let the "interior country" south of Aswan go to the various religious and nationalist factions that wanted it and would fight for it. In the early weeks of 1884, Gladstone agreed to further intervention only to evacuate the garrison at the Sudanese capital of Khartoum. General Charles "Chinese" Gordon, who had fought in Africa and the Far East, and knew the Sudan, was then, at fifty, a half-pay officer about to enlist in the service of Leopold II and go to the Congo. Instead, he was reactivated to return to Khartoum—but only to withdraw the British forces and leave the land to the followers of Mohammed Ahmed, the "Mahdi," a religious reformer turned warrior chief.

Granville had been scathing in private over the Queen's anxieties to secure her colonies, suggesting to Gladstone that she ask Eugénie "whether she now thinks she was right in urging her Husband to undertake the Mexican . . . War." Everyone but Gordon understood that the general's mission, after a series of ambushes and other slaughters had further reduced the wavering Western presence, was a strictly limited undertaking. Granville, who promoted the idea of using Gordon, pointed out to Gladstone that the general had "an immense name in Egypt" and was "popular at home," but had "a small bee in his bonnet." Gladstone was familiar with bees in bonnets, but Sir Evelyn Baring (later Lord Cromer), his proconsul in Cairo, cautioned the Foreign Office, "A man who habitually consults the Prophet Isaiah when he is in a difficulty is not apt to obey the orders of any one."

The warning went unheeded. Messages to Baring from Gordon as he moved south were disconcertingly God-obsessed. "We are pianos," he wrote on blank telegraph forms that became his diary, "events play on us. Gladstone is no more important in the events of life than we are; the importance is, how he acts when played on." How Gladstone acted when played upon by Gordon (or God, as the concepts somehow fused) became apparent when the general determined not to extricate the Khartoum garrison, but to extirpate the Mahdi. "Clearly," Gladstone said later, "we made a mistake, great but greatly excusable; the cause was insufficient knowledge of the man, whom we rather took on trust from the public impressions, & from newspaper accounts. . . ."

Victoria registered her anxiety early. "The Queen trembles for General Gordon's safety. If anything befalls *him*," she warned Gladstone, "the result will be awful." The Prime Minister was more concerned about the prospects of his new Reform Bill to extend the franchise. As soon as it was questioned by the Opposition, the radical faction among the Liberals became what the Queen called "noisy demagogues" in attacking the House of Lords. A bastion of privilege to Dilke and Chamberlain, the Lords was the representative of "the true feeling of the country" to

Victoria. Passions on both issues—Gordon and Reform—rose through the year. Gordon was quickly seen as overriding his (in Gladstone's words to the Queen) "pacific mission," and Radicals in his Government similarly overrode the Prime Minister.

With Gordon soon mired in the Sudan, the Queen proposed sending additional forces. Gladstone disapproved, writing bluntly that the general would be supported "to the full extent which national interests will permit." When she presented the Prime Minister (there was no choice but to do so) with her new *More Leaves from a Journal of a Life in the Highlands,* she was careful, Edward Hamilton observed, "not to commit herself to any expressions of even the mildest luke-warmness." She simply wrote "To Mr. Gladstone from the Queen." Elsewhere she confided how much political intent there had been in publishing the book. "I have always been fully aware of what I was doing," she assured Vicky, who worried, as did Bertie, that *More Leaves* was an incautious gesture, "and [I] know perfectly well what my people like and appreciate and that is home life and simplicity. I know the good, the great good, it did in '68 and now again."

With both Sudanese matters and the new Reform Bill escaping from what little control the Queen had over them, she needed no new family problems. There was further talk, however, of the Prince of Wales's financial and personal indiscretions. His supporters in Parliament suggested bailing him out of his new debts by claiming that the "retirement from public life" of the Queen put him to "material expenses" in her place. Gladstone discussed the matter with Hamilton, and noted the danger of a Parliamentary committee of inquiry if the matter was raised as proposed legislation. "They would probably find," Gladstone thought, "a total absence of economical management of his affairs. . . ."

Three days after the Queen telegraphed to Lord Hartington that Gordon, now surrounded at Khartoum, was "in danger," and that the Government was "bound to try and save him," Prince Leopold died suddenly at Cannes. He had gone south for some sun and warmth. (Pregnant with their second child, Princess Helen had remained in England.) Victoria had realized that her "bright, clever son, who has so many times recovered from such fearful illnesses, and from various small accidents," as she put it in her journal on March 28, would someday suffer a final and fatal hemorrhage. Nevertheless, she felt crushed. "To lose another dear child, . . . and one who was so gifted, and such a help to me, is too dreadful!"

The Prince of Wales went to Cannes to accompany the body to England. At Leopold's testamentary request, he was buried in St. George's Chapel, where he had been married. ("I should have liked the Mausoleum," Victoria wrote.) For the press, she wrote a rare public letter, for the first time in the first person, expressing her thanks for the sympathy manifested toward her.

Late in April, despite mourning, the Queen went to Darmstadt for the marriage of her granddaughter, Alice's Victoria, to Louis of Battenberg, her granddaughter's cousin. "These poor children have been like my own since their darling mother's death," she told Vicky, "and I feel like an old hen when her ducklings go on the water."

Although Hesse was no longer a meaningful political entity, the occasion was stylish and elaborate, with a surprise at the close. According to Count Friedrich von Holstein, who sent his diary leaves to his cousin, Ida von Stülpnagel, so that they could not be found in his possession to prejudice his ambassadorial career, the Queen arrived already aware of the widowered Grand Duke Louis's involvement with a beauteous Russian mistress, Alexandra Kolomine, divorced wife of a diplomat and known for "unusually sordid" earlier affairs. "The person most infuriated," Holstein wrote, "is the Queen of England who wanted to marry the widower to her youngest daughter, Beatrice." And he went on to describe Victoria's long efforts to secure through Parliament a "Princess Beatrice's bill."

The shy, inexperienced Beatrice had no interest in the bride's father, but—in her behalf—Victoria did, until the Grand Duke secretly married Alexandra Kolomine, then announced the fact before the guests at his daughter's wedding had left Hesse. On May 3, Henry Ponsonby wrote to his wife that the Queen was reported to be "in the tantrums." In public all was quiet, but the Grand Duke remained under siege no less than Gordon in Khartoum. In June, Hermann Sahl, retired German Secretary to the Queen, wrote to Ponsonby from Darmstadt, "You will be glad to hear that *substantially* the untying of the morganatic knot is now accomplished, and by degrees the *formal* severance will be pronounced by a Court of Law convened for this purpose." Alexandra had been bought off for 500,000 marks (then £25,000). Who furnished the money is unknown, but it may well have been Victoria.

Beatrice knew the time was unripe for mentioning it, but the two weddings had been a success from her standpoint. She had evaded a match with Grand Duke Louis, and she had met a brother of the bridegroom. Her mother was to learn about it when the Hessian storms lifted.

"In the last few days," Count Holstein wrote on May 7, 1884, "I have heard some remarkable details of the way the Queen of England alarmed and tyrannized over her family in Darmstadt. A quarter of an hour before dinner . . . she would say which of the royal personages was to dine with her. The rest of them ate elsewhere. She completely ignored the attendants of the various princes and princesses." Her son-in-law Frederick William ("Our Crown Prince") "did not dare" to present to her his adjutants, and when Vicky, her daughter, presented her ladies, "the Queen did not even raise her eyes, and there was no question of her addressing even a single word to them." Since her rage at Grand Duke Louis affected every moment of her stay at Darmstadt, whenever she absented herself, Holstein observed, the effect was "like an ascension to heaven" for everyone else.

Given the hostility to the Queen from every Bismarck appointee, the testimony is suspect, yet Holstein's reactions were meant for his secret diary. He had asked, he added, whether the secret of the Queen's authority lay in her personality. On the contrary, he quoted his unidentified English source, Victoria was "an undersized creature, almost as broad as she was long, who looked like a cook, had a bluish-red face and was more or less mentally deranged." She was "very rich," his hostile source told him, and was likely to enjoy her wealth "for many years to come, unless the effects of alcohol prevent it."

Once the Queen returned home, and the Grand Duke had given in, her attitude returned to pure sweetness. "Dear Louis is so really good," she wrote to Vicky on May 15, "and has such a chivalrous feeling toward Countess Czapaska"—Alexandra's name before her first marriage—"but his eyes were opened and he knows that others believe the worst of her. He cannot bear to hear her violently abused . . . for if a man is much attracted to a woman and thinks she is attached to him . . . he cannot in a day hate her. That conviction of her depravity must come gradually." The annulment was signed on June 3.

Less satisfactory was the conclusion of another Darmstadt romance. Vicky's daughter Victoria Moretta considered herself engaged to Prince Alexander of Battenberg, another of the four attractive brothers from Hesse-Nassau, on the River Eder. Supported by his uncle, the Czar, with whom he had since fallen out when he declined to be a puppet, "Sandro" had become Prince (in effect, king) of Bulgaria. Vicky's elderly father-in-law, the German Emperor, and her eldest son, Willy, a future Emperor himself, refused to recognize the morganatic Battenberg princelings as *von Geblüt* royalty, while Bismarck recommended not offending the Czar. The marriage was forbidden, and Vicky labeled the decision as further persecution from the Prussian element in Berlin, which looked on her as little more than an English subversive. Letters would fly back and forth between the Queen and her daughter for months, until Fritz refused to appeal over the head of his upstart son to the doddering William I. To Victoria the German mania for blood purity was "a little like about animals." Because of the aborted "Bulgarian marriage," Prince Willy told Herbert Bismarck, son of the Chancellor, in October 1885, "the old hag" would not see him and his brother Prince Heinrich when they came to Sandringham as guests of their Uncle Bertie.

Late in May the Queen walked in public without assistance (but for a cane) for the first time in years, traversing the platform at Perth to breakfast at the station when her saloon car halted for nearly an hour en route to Balmoral. Even crossing a narrow walkway was a public triumph. She did not repeat the performance very often, and more and more permitted herself to be seen in a wheelchair. Her problems with mobility, combined with the death of Brown, had caused her to give up regular attendance at Crathie Kirk and at Whippingham Church, and to employ a chaplain for private services. Tourists in Scotland and on the Isle of Wight were disappointed, as gaping at her on a Sunday had become an event.

With her new causes for grief, Balmoral had become an even duller place, and attendees at royal dinners struggled to relieve the solemnity when the Queen was preoccupied and silent. After Vicky sent her a pamphlet on the housing of the working classes, the subject became one for discussion at dinner, and the Queen sent Gladstone a letter suggesting that better housing was a question of more importance than others—she very likely meant the new Reform Bill—being considered by the Government. At her table an earnest clergyman, describing the slum overcrowding in the East End of London, observed that in one house he visited, seven had to sleep in one bed. "Had I been one of them," said the Queen, "I would have slept on the floor."

For days at Balmoral or Osborne the Queen was often unseen, sending messages, on matters great and small, on notepaper, and eating privately or with Beatrice or a lady-in-waiting. If the courtier to whom the message was carried was unavailable, a chastising followed. One Sunday morning, Ponsonby and his assistant, Fleetwood Edwards, were both out briefly to church when a note from the Queen was delivered. A four-page reprimand from Victoria followed, requiring that Sir Henry and Major Edwards arrange never to be out *"at the same time."* Yet they had little of importance to communicate, or to receive, given Gladstone's exclusion of the Queen from major decisions.

An opportunity to become involved on the domestic scene occurred when the Lords defeated Gladstone's Reform Bill on July 9, 1884. It appeared that the Lords itself might become the victim of its own intransigence. "End them or mend them," was the Radicals' cry. The Queen urged Gladstone "to *restrain, as he can,* some of his wild colleagues and followers," but restraint largely required Conservative compromise. The Queen, in what now would be called a damage-control operation, set about converting Disraeli's successor as Tory leader, the balding, black-bearded Robert Cecil, third Marquess of Salisbury, to Reform. It was the beginning of what would be her last long and intimate association with a major politician. To the young George Curzon, Salisbury was "that strange powerful inscrutable and brilliant obstructive deadweight," and indeed he and his debonair nephew and private secretary, Arthur Balfour, had threatened to obstruct franchise reform as long as possible. To avoid further conflicts between the two Houses, without humiliation for the Lords, Victoria intervened personally. Di-

"Visiting Grandmama"—
Willy and the Queen in
Punch, *August 3, 1889.*

rectly and through such Tory intermediaries as Disraeli's old crony, Lord Rowton, she sought a moderate position that would preserve what she explained to Gladstone was a necessary "balance of power," a "restraining power." Although it took until November, accommodation succeeded, Conservatives being won over by a number of redistricting boundary changes in their favor. There was little help from Gladstone's Radical wing. From Balmoral on October 11, 1884, the Queen wrote to Gladstone that although her "task of conciliation" was not made easier by "the strong expressions used by [his] Ministers," she was *so much* impressed by the importance of the issue at stake that she has persevered in her endeavors and has obtained from the Leaders of the Opposition an expression of their readiness to negociate . . . in the hope that this *may* lead to a compromise. . . ."

Even Gladstone saw Victoria's efforts as averting "a great public mischief." Once compromise on all issues was settled, on November 27, 1884, he telegraphed to the Queen at Windsor, "Points of substance all settled this afternoon. Only form remains. Humbly congratulate." For the first time in their joint relations, Gladstone may have fully meant what his words communicated. Victoria responded, "I gladly and thankfully return your telegram. To be able to be of use is all I care to live for now."

The new legislation put agricultural laborers, the only large class of males still excluded from the franchise, on the rolls, and further extended the franchise in the cities, although the right to vote still depended upon the ownership or occupation of property. The bill also made most voting units single-member districts with roughly equal populations. Pleased with the outcome, Gladstone followed his cipher telegram with a letter praising "that wise, gracious, and steady exercise of influence on Your Majesty's part. . . ."

Soon relations with "the old sinner," as the Queen called him privately (to Vicky), were as they always had been, but for the moment there was shared bliss in the fact that the system of constitutional monarchy still worked. That system, however, under normal conditions left the Queen with little more than ritual, often only ceremony invoking her name and ignoring her person.

In the new, brief atmosphere of sweetness and mutual congratulation, the Queen wrote to Gladstone suggesting—as Edward Hamilton summed it up—that "it would please the old centenarian [Sir Moses] Montefiore and likewise the Jewish community at large, if the Baronetcy were extended to the great-nephew." Sir Moses had no closer male heirs. Victoria had first met him nearly sixty years earlier, at Ramsgate. He was now one hundred years old. He was, she wrote Gladstone "an excellent man, charitable to the highest degree & universally respected." The Prime Minister had his colleagues investigate, and found that Montefiore, like Disraeli, had no desire to pass his title on to someone who had not earned it.

The disappointment was small, as was the intended deed. What concerned the Queen more—even alarmed her—was the continued siege of Khartoum by the Mahdi. As the new year of 1884 opened, Gordon appeared to be running out of provisions. Troops had finally been sent to relieve him, but, the Queen feared, too late. Her grandson Willy sent her a military plan he had devised for the relief of Gordon, but Victoria failed to acknowledge it, perhaps feeling that it was an intrusion into a purely British matter. Willy was offended. Finally, at a battle early in January, a relief column at Abu Klea on the Nile, led by Lieutenant Colonel Frederick Burnaby, pushed the Mahdi's forces aside, but at the cost of Burnaby's life. He fell, the Queen reminded Gladstone, "with his face to the foe—the death a true soldier always courts, & which the Queen—as a Soldier's daughter & Mother—cannot but admire!"

Bending the Constitution, the Queen telegraphed directly to Burnaby's superior, Lord Wolseley, triggering a political complaint from the Marquis of Hartington at the War Office. To Ponsonby, but meant for Hartington, she fired back that she "always *has* telegraphed direct to her Generals, and *always will* do so, as they value *that* and don't care near so much for a mere official message. . . . But she thinks Lord Hartington's letter *very officious* and *impertinent* in *tone*. The Queen *has* the *right* to telegraph congratulations and enquiries *to any* one, and won't stand dictation. She *won't* be a *machine* but the Liberals always wish to make her *feel* THAT, and she *won't accept it.*"

Ponsonby laundered Victoria's language to Hartington to "I am commanded by the Queen to observe that her Majesty has always been in the habit of telegraphing in her own name to the General commanding a force which has achieved a victory. But she regrets that in the case of Abu Klea she omitted to telegraph the message simultaneously to you." In March, the Queen would bypass officialdom by writing instead to Lady Wolseley that the Government was "more incorrigible than ever," and that her husband should "use strong language . . . and even threaten to resign if he does not receive strong support and liberty of action." A few weeks later she would write similarly to Wolseley himself, closing with the usual words guaranteed to preserve a sensitive message: "The Queen would ask Lord Wolseley to destroy this letter as it is so very confidential. . . ."

Liberty of action was the last thing that Gladstone wanted of the military, having seen where Gordon had put him. Abu Klea should have been unnecessary. He humbly shared in her Majesty's "strong sense of the high military qualities displayed alike by the commanders and the men of Your Majesty's army," but he did not like the cost of opposing nationalism where it existed, or seeking "annexations intended to forestall the colonising efforts of other countries." Then came news, on February 5, of the fall of Gordon's famished garrison when an advance detachment from Lord Wolseley's relief force was within sight of the town. Gordon was dead. Later, Lord Cromer would write that the Wolseley expedition was "sanctioned too late," because Gladstone had refused to believe that it was needed.

At Osborne Cottage, Mary Ponsonby was startled by the unannounced appearance of a black figure—the Queen—announcing in a choked voice, "Gordon is dead!" Seething with humiliation and fury, Victoria fired off identical telegrams to Gladstone, Granville, and Hartington. Gladstone and Hartington had been staying at Holker with Hartington's father, the Duke of Devonshire. On his way back to London, the Prime Minister was handed the message, composed in haste and anger, and obviously not ciphered. "These news from Khartoum are frightful, and to think that all this might have been prevented and many precious lives saved by earlier action is too fearful."

Uncoded, and available to anyone along the telegraph line, it was as blunt a public rebuke as Victoria could devise. With the nation in gloom, as every day of the siege had added to Gordon's image as hero—Gladstone replied with dignified rage, and at four-page length, beginning by noting that he had "the honour this day to receive Your Majesty's Telegram *en clair*, relating to the deplorable intelligence received this day. . . ." He expected "abundant wrath and indignation" from the country, but insisted that "our proper business was the protection of Egypt, that it was never in military danger from the Mahdi." The error, he insisted, lay in being there. Then he kept an engagement to go to the theater; and when the press reproached him for it, he said that the War Office had yet to confirm Gordon's death. For a time, music-hall performers sang a song reversing the "G.O.M." initials associated with Gladstone to "M.O.G." —Murderer of Gordon:

> *The M.O.G., when his life ebbs out,*
> *Will ride in a fiery chariot,*
> *And sit in state*
> *On a red-hot plate*
> *Between Pilate and Judas Iscariot.*

To the general's sister, Augusta (Gordon was not the marrying kind, and preferred street urchins), the Queen wrote letters of sympathy that took broad swipes at her Government. "That the promises of support were not fulfilled," she railed on February 17, "—which I so frequently and constantly pressed on those who asked him to go—is to me *grief inexpressible!* Indeed, it made me ill! My heart bleeds for you. . . ." In 1888 two letters from Victoria to Miss Gordon were published in *The Times,* on the same day (March 7) that they were to appear in a book of the general's correspondence, and Liberal-leaning newspapers took the Queen's permission to print her "delirious" and "hysterical" letters as further implicit condemnation of Gladstone. Outraged, Algernon Swinburne took time from his versifying to write to the *St. James's Gazette* defending "the noble and womanly words of indignant sympathy," but the letter was not published.

Gladstone had no alternative (other than leaving office) but to go to Parliament on February 19 and announce that the Government had determined to use all necessary resources to crush the Mahdi. The whole idea was so repellent that he neglected even to say a kind word for "Chinese" Gordon, the madman who had trapped him in the Sudan. A vote of censure in the Commons lost by only fourteen votes, and "the people's William" considered—but rejected—resignation. "The culpability of this miserable Government with the motto 'Too Late' is wicked and dreadful," the Queen wrote to Vicky. "On their heads rests the precious blood of Gordon and thousands! Imagine my feelings—though my conscience is clean! I warned, urged without ceasing, all in vain."

Even private joys failed to ease the Queen's ire. When she announced Princess Beatrice's forthcoming marriage to Prince Henry ("Liko") of Battenberg, a union exactly right for the last daughter, whom her mother wanted to keep at home, Victoria complained to Gladstone's lieutenant, Lord Carlingford, "that some of her Ministers have not written to congratulate [her]." Nor had the German royal house, which remained rigid on matters of blood. Vicky's own "naughty foolish sons," the Queen told her daughter, followed the mean-spirited Hohenzollern line, but "if the Queen of England thinks a person good enough for her daughter what have other people got to say?"

The cool courtship was exactly what the Queen wanted. "There is no kissing, etc. (which Beatrice dislikes)," she confided to Vicky. It was important that Beatrice not become so romantic as to want a love nest apart from the Queen's residence. Painfully shy, and aware of her plain features, Beatrice knew exactly how much of a love match she had made; yet like many such unions, it succeeded better than couplings predicated on tender love. If the pair had a passion for anything at the start, it was tobacco. Liko chain-smoked cigars, and Beatrice—when apart from her mother—chain-smoked cigarettes. Victoria could not have been unaware. Smoking had become, for some women, a feminist statement.

On the twenty-first birthday of her grandson Prince Albert Victor, and then on the twentieth of his brother, Prince George, she found little to celebrate. Eddy showed no signs of future kingliness, and Victoria heard from the Duke of Cambridge, a ready defender of privilege, that the Prince loved uniforms, but was "an inveterate and incurable dawdler, never ready, never there." Realizing that Prince George, too, had his father for a model, she warned him, as a birthday greeting, "As for betting or anything of that kind, no end of young and older men have been ruined, parents' hearts broken and great names and Titles dragged in the dirt."

For the most part the Queen seemed permissive toward her grand-children, largely because there was little else she could do; but Bertie's sons, only a heartbeat or two from the Throne, were different. She worried that Albert Victor, the eldest, was too "languid," yet she hoped he might grow into responsibility. Even Bertie showed signs of maturity at forty-four. As for the other grandchildren, and now great-grandchildren, she was overwhelmed by their numbers, and by the personal financial burdens many of them represented, as Parliament saw no reason to have children out of the line of succession live on public largesse. The Prince of Wales's brood seemed enough, and Henry Labouchère's parody of the National Anthem in *Truth* reflected popular attitudes:

> *Grandchildren not a few,*
> *With great-grandchildren too,*
> *She blest has been.*
> *We've been their sureties,*
> *Paid them gratuities,*

Pensions, annuities,
God save the Queen!

Although her grandchildren were already dismayingly numerous, Victoria was unhappy about the likelihood that Louise would have no family. After a sleigh overturned in Canada, and she was dragged by the hair and lost most of an ear, the Princess sought medical treatment in England, hid the hurt beneath her hair, and did not return to Ottawa. When Lord Lorne, for whom the Queen had real affection, gave up his post to come home, there was no longer a marriage, although they would continue to be seen together in the Queen's presence. After their wedding, neither had ever appeared interested in the other. The accident had only furnished a dramatic ending to a relationship that was already over.

The motherless children of Princess Alice were Victoria's special concern. They spent much time with her, Princess Victoria of Battenberg even traveling to Windsor for the birth of her first child; and late in February 1885, the Queen put all other cares aside to sit by her granddaughter from seven in the morning until labor ended at five in the afternoon. Always seeking omens, the Queen found one in that the new baby, a daughter, had been born in the same bed as her mother. The child, named Alice, would become the mother of the consort to Elizabeth II, Prince Philip, and thus grandmother to a likely future king of England.

However maddening and upsetting external events were to Victoria early in 1885, they had the impact of hurrying Gladstone out of office. Outrage over a series of bombings that caused minor damage in the Tower, Westminster Hall, and the Commons had the result of derailing the greater democratization being pushed by Chamberlain. The Queen was full of warnings to her Ministers about Radical excesses encouraging more violence. With Egypt and the Sudan claiming much of the press's attention, and abuse heaped upon Gladstone into mid-March, the Queen happily held a drawing-room at Buckingham Palace—"at which She remained a whole hour!" Edward Hamilton noted. She was walking and standing more firmly, with a cane, and at Osborne had walked a mile, a vigor that would not last very long. When things went her way, her physical condition often improved, just as when they did not, some of her physical functions deteriorated.

The next day, March 19, Victoria sent to Gladstone, in Hamilton's description, "letters written by an officer in India and by the wife of another officer. They are of course written in an alarmist tone. It is a pity that such communications should come into Her hands. . . . By better authorities the condition of India is thought to be specially favourable." But it was not, and letters had already been exchanged that week between Windsor and Downing Street about Russian designs in Afghanistan. The menace to India seemed real, with Russian agents instigating the Afghans to attack the British and the Indians. Prince Arthur was given a divisional command and sent to Pindi, which involved the Queen even more, and she taxed Gladstone to get over his pro-Russian sympathies and to see the threat as Russian, rather than as a mere Afghan frontier dispute in poorly charted territory.

Even Gladstone saw the possibility of war; and from Aix-les-Bains in the alpine Haute-Savoie, where the Queen had gone with her usual huge entourage, she applauded the Government's firmer measures. By May, a boundary commission had been agreed upon with Russia to defuse the situation. Having salvaged English dignity, Gladstone searched again for ways to extricate the army from the Sudan, leaving that territory to the Mahdi by default. "The Queen . . . cannot resign if matters go ill," she wrote to Hartington, "and her heart bleeds to see such short-sighted humiliating policy pursued, which lowers her country throughout the world." Each retreat from responsibility, she warned, would lead to having to send troops back again. Leaving it to Ponsonby to formulate some appropriate language, she asked him, "Can the G.O.M. not be roused to some sense of honour?"

Eager to turn to issues from which India and Egypt had distracted him, Gladstone took up Irish local government, and the perennial problem of the Prince of Wales. The Queen could do little but fume at tampering with the Irish status quo, but she had much to say about giving Bertie a greater role in political and ceremonial affairs. She would decide, she told Gladstone, what Cabinet papers the Prince would see or not see; and she would decide what levees might be suitable for his appearance. "Admission of the Prince, at his time of life, to an interior knowledge of affairs," Gladstone pleaded through Ponsonby, "appears to me very judicious and desirable. . . ." All that resulted was the Queen's tolerance—by not rejecting the idea—of the Prince of Wales's joining a Royal Commission on Housing for the Working Classes. He may have had little to do with the final report, but its mention of the previously unmentionable—that slum conditions fostered rape, incest, and illegitimacy—stirred the nation's conscience and led eventually to the Housing of the Working Classes Act of 1890, the foundation of later British housing law. That the

Prince of Wales signed the report was a public-relations coup for the Commission.

Under strain from the Dilke and Chamberlain factions of the party, and from Irish members, Gladstone's Liberal coalition began breaking up in May 1885—"fresh internal Ministerial bothers," Edward Hamilton called the situation. The Queen was surprised when she learned, at Balmoral on June 9, 1885—there was still frost on the ground—that the Government had been defeated by twelve votes on the budget. A telegram offered Gladstone's resignation. Although increases in Conservative voting strength required a general election, Victoria was unsure that the Liberals could really be kept from further office, but she announced herself ready to accept the Government's resignation, and sent for Lord Salisbury.

With Ascot so close to the Castle, she was reluctant to return to Windsor during the noise and bustle of racing season. Negotiations for the new Government began in the isolation of Balmoral, Salisbury having to conduct his business with London by telegram. Soon she was confronted with Gladstone's shopping list of parting peerages, baronetcies, Garter nominees, and Privy Council recommendations, twenty-four in all. At seventy-five, he wrote to Lord Carlingford, "he cannot perceive or confidently anticipate any state of facts which could change his long cherished desire and purpose to withdraw at the end of the present Parliament from active participation in politics."

Even pleas from the Prince of Wales that her absence weakened the position of the Throne failed to move her. "She forgets," Edward Hamilton wrote in his diary on June 12, "that there is another Palace to which She might come, and which would be more convenient than even Windsor—Buckingham Palace. Never did a Sovereign throw away such a chance. No more popular or graceful act could have been done than if She had ordered her special train the moment She heard of the crisis and come straight to London."

Abbreviating her Balmoral holiday with ill-tempered reluctance, the Queen hastened south belatedly on June 16. "She has given out," Hamilton wrote, "that Ministerial crises must not happen again in Ascot weeks and during Balmoral times." In London the interregnum dragged on, as Salisbury tried to form a Cabinet without a majority, and with too many applicants. After being out so long, Hamilton wrote, "the desire for office among the Tories is not merely an appetite or hunger; a real famine prevails."

At one o'clock on the afternoon of June 24, a Wednesday, Gladstone went to Windsor to deliver his Ministerial Seals. He would not accept for himself the repeatedly offered earldom, but one of his proposed peerages was for Sir Nathaniel Rothschild, M.P. for Aylesbury, whose father, Lionel, had died a commoner in 1879. (All five sons of Mayer Amschel Rothschild were barons of the Austrian Empire, but Lionel, as a British subject, was simultaneously a commoner.) Eleven years before, the Queen had turned down a peerage for Lionel, long an M.P. for the City, because he was a Jew. As Edward Hamilton wrote afterward, "She made little or no difficulty; she had overcome the strong scruples she entertained respecting the proposal when Mr. G. made it during his First Administration."

As they bowed out, the Queen shook hands formally with Hartington and Granville but pointedly not with Gladstone. Humbly he asked if he might kiss her hand—the correct thing in the circumstances. She offered her fingers. Recognizing the fragility of the Tory Ministry to come, and suspicious of Gladstone's determination to retire, Victoria was glumly certain that she would see "the people's William" in the same setting again.

The Salisbury Ministry that followed passed like a brief phrase in a long polemical paragraph by Gladstone. Long troubled by throat problems, the "G.O.M." largely kept silent from his front seat on the Opposition benches. Optimistically, the Queen even wrote to him that she "trusts Mr. Gladstone is recovering from the hoarseness with which he has been troubled for so many months, and takes this opportunity of expressing a hope that he will spare himself from speaking in public meetings for some time to come."

For Victoria, the event of the year outside politics was Beatrice's marriage. At twenty-eight—Prince Henry of Battenberg was twenty-seven—Beatrice added a footnote to history by being the first royal bride to be married in a parish church—Whippingham, at Osborne, on July 23, 1885. The unimportance of the bridegroom, and the distance from the Throne of the bride, made a quiet wedding possible. There were some absentees. Vicky and her husband could not come because German royalty were forbidden to recognize the match. The church was small, and the wedding luncheon was served on the lawn at Osborne House.

The description of the ceremony in *Truth* was in Labouchère's inimitable style:

The Prince of Wales seemed ill at ease and out of sorts; so also did the Queen, who looked exceedingly cross. . . . The bride looked very flushed and rather nervous. . . . Decided absence of beauty among the group of bridesmaids. . . . The Archbishop (Dr. Benson) introduced a novelty at the end of the service—to the horror of the congregation, who by this time were tired to death and longing for luncheon—in the shape of an address by himself. . . . The Queen had consented to this innovation on condition that the homily should not exceed two or three sentences, and it only occupied a few minutes; but Her Majesty commenced to tap her foot in a very ominous way and the Prince of Wales was evidently fidgety and eager for the ceremony to end. . . . The Queen, who had become more cheerful and amiable [after the service], followed with the Prince of Wales, who seemed sulky and did not appear to respond with any enthusiasm to his mother's observations. . . . The Grand Duke of Hesse looks old and haggard. . . . The Duke of Edinburgh looked even more sour and supercilious than usual and the sullen expression which has become habitual to the Duchess appeared to be accentuated for the occasion. . . . Princess Louise looked well but has a very flighty manner. Lord Lorne was in tartans, but certainly looked very common. . . . Prince George of Wales seemed thoroughly well pleased with himself. He is a very ordinary looking lad but apparently has more go about him than his brother. . . .

The Queen's elevating Liko to Royal Highness furnished him status valid only within her dominions. Since he was of no political or dynastic consequence, her giving him the Order of the Garter further displeased her less privileged sons-in-law, who thought the Bath was sufficient. The Queen ignored every variety of family rumpus involving Prince Henry, and enjoyed the support and continued companionship of "Baby," which his residence with Victoria meant. Even on her honeymoon Beatrice was away from her mother only two days, and then only at a villa at nearby Ryde, never leaving the island. On her marriage she received the same settlement as had her sisters (except Vicky), Parliament voting a dowry of £30,000 and an annuity of £8,000.

"A happier-looking couple could seldom be seen kneeling at the altar together. It was very touching," the Queen insisted in her journal. To Vicky she wrote that she bore up until the couple's departure—"then fairly gave way. I remained quietly upstairs and when I heard the cheering and 'God Save the Queen' I stopped my ears and cried bitterly." She was sixty-six, and twenty-five years a widow. She had seen the last of her nine children married—and two of them were already dead.

The new government had come to precarious power just as the new Reform legislation had extended the franchise. A General Election in November and December found Lord Rosebery, Lord Privy Seal in the previous Gladstone Cabinet and a coming man among the Liberals—even Victoria liked him—exhorting his disunited party to shelter under the "Gladstone umbrella." Although still bothered by chronic hoarseness, Gladstone appealed for a clear majority independent of the Irish vote. "How can Mr. Gladstone," the Queen complained to Henry Ponsonby in an interoffice note from Balmoral, "at 76 with a broken voice stand again?"

Even as the acrimonious campaign closed, she remained hopeful, noting in her journal on December 2 that as a result of Reform, "The Counties go against the Government, but the Radicals are generally beaten in the Boroughs." (To her, all Liberals were Radicals.) Unfortunately for stability, the 334 Liberals elected—there were 250 Conservatives—were less than a majority because of 86 Irish Home Rulers. "Things must [not] and can not return to what they were, for it would be UTTER ruin to the country and to Europe," she wrote to Salisbury, hopeful that he could form a ruling coalition of moderates. "The country at large is not Radical and we want the best and *strongest* men to join."

To various men of power in both parties, whom she called "moderate, loyal, and *really patriotic* men, who have the safety and well-being of the Empire and Throne at heart," the Queen appealed in the waning days of December to join forces to keep the Government from falling again into "the reckless hands of Mr. Gladstone." She enlisted the Marchioness of Ely as well as Henry Ponsonby to write additional appeals, but Ponsonby finally had to bring the chilly reality to the Queen. "He hears that Mr. Gladstone is very anxious to resume office," the Private Secretary wrote, "and that as long as this is the case no other Liberal Minister would have a chance of forming a party to govern."

The newspapers spoke of the Salisbury Government as if it were finished, but Salisbury hung on at the Queen's insistence, hoping to make common cause with the Irish Members and keep Gladstone out. All that Victoria's intervention accomplished was to delay the inevitable, and expose her powerlessness. She even offered to make the supreme sacrifice for Salisbury: she would open Parliament in person, hoping that the gesture would place a royal imprimatur upon his Government.

The occasion, on January 21, 1886, was Victoria's final Parliamentary appearance, and she spared nothing to keep Gladstone out. "It was one of the grandest sights I have ever seen," wrote the future Lady Monkswell, whose husband, Robert Collier (he would become the second Lord Monkswell later in the year), had lost his seat for Chatham the month before.

> Four rows of ladies on either side of the House of Lords, all in their best clothes, feathers & diamonds: the whole of the floor of the House packed as tight as they could sit with peers in their robes, one mass of scarlet, ermine & gold. Besides these a good number of Judges & Bishops & Officers: the Prince of Wales, & Dukes of Edinburgh, Connaught & Cambridge in exceedingly gay uniforms. I sat for nearly two mortal hours on that broad bench without a back before the trumpets sounded, & the little black robed Queen came in. She had a little diamond crown on the very top of her head, ermine on her dress, & a great many diamonds. She folded the robes of state around her & sat quite still till the Commons rushed in with their usual tumult. I saw her smile rather at that. Then she handed the speech to the Lord Chancellor who stood on her right, & he read it. Princess Beatrice, in red velvet, stood close to her on her right & Prince Albert Victor on her left. It took about 3 minutes to read the speech, then she walked out & it was over. Prince Albert Victor supported her down the steps of the Throne.

For those who yearned for spectacle, the Queen's presence had provided it. Yet her failure to address Parliament herself, although the speech was hardly more than a page, with the words even composed by the very Ministry she was attempting, by her presence, to save, suggested that her heart was not in it. She had conceded the outcome.

There were a few more desperate efforts to stave off Gladstone. From Osborne a week later, as she was attempting to negotiate alternatives, she telegraphed to Salisbury to urge him not to resign "on a triviality." She thought of a coalition under Hartington, in which Salisbury might serve. Then she suggested that the clever George Joachim Goschen, who at fifty-five had served in several Liberal Cabinets but had earned the respect of the Tories, might put together a Ministry dedicated to forestalling Home Rule for Ireland. Goschen was, the Queen told Salisbury, "an independent man."

Both Houses adjourned on January 28. "The Queen does not the least care [who knows it] but rather wishes," she told Ponsonby, "[that] it sh^d be known that she has the gre[ate]st possible disinclination to take this half crazy & really in so many ways ridiculous old man—for the sake of the country." The next morning Lord Salisbury resigned, advising the Queen to send for Gladstone. Ponsonby crossed the Solent at the Queen's instructions, reaching London late in the day. Gladstone had been waiting for a summons, but the only caller had been Lord Rosebery, who found him reading a book that may have suggested parallels with his present problems—*The Court of Louis XIV.* He was just resting, he said, having tired himself out drafting answers to possible objections from the Queen: she might ask him to renounce Home Rule as a condition of office, while his chief aim on resuming it was to settle the Irish question.

Taking care not to leave Carlton House Terrace all day, Gladstone entertained political associates at dinner. One of them, G. W. E. Russell, recalled Gladstone's impatience. "It begins to look," the old man remarked, "as if the Government meant after all to ignore the vote of the House of Commons, and go on. All I can say is that, if they do, the Crown will be placed in a worse position than it has ever occupied in my lifetime."

Ponsonby's first call was upon Lord Salisbury at Downing Street, where he found a telegram from the Queen instructing him to call upon Goschen. He was not at home, but had just written to her stressing the urgency of sending for Gladstone, for there would be immense sympathy in the country for him if he was ignored longer. Ponsonby sat chatting with Mrs. Goschen until nearly midnight, when her husband arrived and stressed again the need to have Gladstone in Downing Street, if only to prove that his medicine was no cure.

Ponsonby reached Gladstone's house at 12:15 A.M., just as he was going to bed. He was seventy-seven, and it had been a long day. Ponsonby was brief, and his lines well-rehearsed. The Queen had not sent for Gladstone earlier, because he "had so often expressed the wish to retire," but she now wished to know whether he was willing to undertake the strain of forming a new Government.

"Matters have changed since then," said Gladstone. Had Sir Henry brought a formal letter from the Queen?

No, he confessed; it went without saying that Victoria was reluctant to prepare one.

No matter, Gladstone rushed to say; he was "satisfied with this verbal summons." Then he climbed the stairs and went to bed.

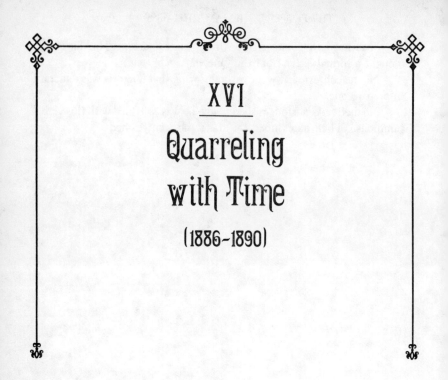

XVI

Quarreling with Time

(1886–1890)

On Monday, February 1, 1886, Gladstone left Waterloo Station at 9:30 A.M. to catch a boat from Gosport to Cowes. A special steamer brought him to Osborne before lunch, to kiss hands and begin discussions on taking office. The Queen thought that he looked "very pale, when he first came in, and there was a momentary pause, and he sighed deeply." Victoria had to sit perilously close to the G.O.M.'s flaring white sidewhiskers to make herself heard. "I remarked," she noted, "that he had undertaken a great deal, to which he replied he had, and felt the seriousness of it." He was, she thought, "dreadfully agitated and nervous." He was always uneasy in her presence. Beneath her formal banalities remained an icy dislike.

Determined to get off to a good start, Gladstone confided that as the Queen wanted, he had kept Granville from the Foreign Office, but had to offer the Colonial Secretaryship instead. They took up Ireland, which

Gladstone insisted was the primary national problem, and "he might fail, it was 49 to 1, that he would, but he intended to try." He stayed to lunch and continued discussions afterwards, observing that he had to give Chamberlain, "who would not be dangerous," a major post, but would not offer one to Dilke. To Victoria, Gladstone seemed less radical, although "intensely in earnest, almost fanatically so, in his belief that he is sacrificing himself for Ireland." Just as earnestly he asked the Queen "not to send him unpleasant letters at night as it prevented his sleeping." Then he left for London, reaching Waterloo at 7:45; and after a late dinner he spent the rest of the long evening in political discussions and interviews with prospective appointees.

As she did with great regularity, and with highly dubious constitutional judgment, the Queen sent a report of her discussions to Salisbury. Afterwards, she secretly kept the Opposition informed on Government moves, even sending him copies of letters from Liberal Ministers, and of her own replies to Gladstone. Officially she and Salisbury parted on February 6, a Saturday, with exchanges of remembrances—among them a bronze bust from her, and a portrait of him by Watts for the Queen. By then the Cabinet had been settled, and a crisscross of passages to and from Osborne had formalized the Government. Victoria had no interest in making things easier for the new appointees by receiving them at Windsor. A letter to one of Gladstone's private secretaries, Horace Seymour, described the chaos created. "The Solent," Henry Ponsonby wrote, "is covered with steamers carrying Ministers hither and luncheons are prepared in various rooms for such as must go at 2, at 2.30 and at 3. The Queen's yacht *Elfin* has gone to look for some of them at Portsmouth. The Queen's launch *Louise* is searching about Cowes Harbour for others. The Queen's yacht *Alberta* has gone to Southampton for the Duchess of Edinburgh. So our Navy is well employed."

For a few weeks Victoria was content with the new Ministry because prominent in it was the smooth-shaven, smooth-talking young Lord Rosebery, at thirty-nine the Foreign Secretary. To the Queen, he was the rising man among the Liberals. That he had married Hannah Rothschild did not hurt his prospects; rather, it enabled him the better to afford his earldom. Besides, Lady Rosebery disliked Gladstone, who she privately said would "never understand a man, still less a woman." Victoria went so far as to send Gladstone a report card on Rosebery, giving him high marks for "firmness & tact; doing remarkably well."

Firmness was one quality she found wanting in Gladstone administrations. On February 8 the Queen missed it once more, when a demonstration in Trafalgar Square by the unemployed ended in violence. After inflammatory speeches from Socialists H. M. Hyndman, John Burns, and H. H. Champion, many who had massed in the square poured into Pall Mall, St. James's Street, and Piccadilly, then through Mayfair and into Hyde Park. Mobs stoned the windows of posh gentlemen's clubs and ladies' shops, and lingered in some places to indulge in a little looting. Police reserves rushed to the scene were sent, in error, to the Mall rather than to Pall Mall.

Victoria railed at Gladstone for having permitted another "humiliating" episode, embarrassing abroad as well as at home. It was, she told him, "a *momentary* triumph of socialism," and "steps, and very *strong ones,*" were needed to prevent a repetition of the "disgrace to the capital." Gladstone confessed to "the keenest pain and regret," but insisted upon "the general efficiency of that admirable force, the London police."

To the Home Secretary, H. C. Erskine Childers (whom the Queen had kept from the War Office because he was too reform-minded for the Duke of Cambridge), Victoria suggested through Ponsonby that she believed, "strictly speaking, a public meeting in Trafalgar Square is illegal," and proposed that Childers forbid "tumultuous assemblages in that place." When the Government meekly followed the Queen's suggestion, it eliminated a safety valve for discontent, and opened the way for several years of defiant "Free Speech" demonstrations. By the time her ban was finally considered dead, it had helped to revitalize the Socialist movement in England. It was not one of Victoria's shining moments, but change was accepted by her more grudgingly than by others who had less to conserve.

Her quarrel with Time continued when, early in March, the Radical campaign to reduce the power of the House of Lords resumed. The "wretched" Henry Labouchère, the Queen complained, had been seditious enough without Gladstone's crafty supporting speech in ostensible reply. What "Labby" had urged, Gladstone hastened to explain, was only "that the more unworthy members . . . could be expelled," and that the House of Lords could be liberalized only through "a large infusion of Life Peers." Gladstone saw both possibilities as reasonable if the Lords was to survive at all, but the Queen responded with a lengthy defense of the hereditary peerage, and of the independence of the upper House as a check upon the excesses of the vote-dependent Commons. Gladstone humbly thanked Victoria "for condescending to suggest the points in which his speech on Mr. Labouchère's motion appeared to be deficient."

Ponsonby, too, warned "that the feeling against the House of Lords was increasing and that some Reform must take place if the Institution was to remain." She asked who (among respectable politicians) wanted to alter the Lords. He first identified the Earl of Elgin's brother, Robert Preston, who was M.P. for County Fife. "Everyone knows he is a radical," said Victoria.

"Lord W[illiam George Spencer Scott] Compton," Ponsonby offered. M.P. for South-West Warwickshire, he would be the sixth Marquess of Northampton.

"He is the same."

"Lord Wolmer," said Ponsonby. William Waldegrave Palmer, then Viscount Wolmer, was Liberal Unionist Whip, and later the second Earl of Selborne.

"Really! I wonder what Lord Salisbury says." Wolmer was Salisbury's son-in-law.

"Albert Grey," Ponsonby added, referring to the future fourth Earl Grey, then M.P. for Tyneside and a future Governor General of Canada.

"Impossible!" snapped Victoria.

Gladstone's Ministry was too divided to handle the range of difficult and controversial subjects he wanted taken up; yet the G.O.M. felt he had little time. He had already told the Queen that Ireland was his first priority, and modernization of the Lords gave way to that on April 8, 1886, when he introduced his Home Rule Bill in the Commons. Reginald Brett (the second Viscount Esher), a Liberal M.P. until 1885, as well as private secretary to the Marquess of Hartington (who was hostile to Home Rule), saw Gladstone as "plunging about in it, like a child in a tub." He thought he had an impressive array of supporters among the Liberal elite, among them Earl Spencer, Lord President of the Council and former Lord Lieutenant of Ireland, and once a member of Albert's Household. Spencer had been vilified in Ireland for the repression following the Cavendish murder, and had become a convert to Home Rule (*"pervert* I think I ought to say," was the Queen's judgment). Gladstone thought that Chamberlain was also on his side, but the Member from Birmingham was not called "Jumping Joe" for nothing. Despite the Prime Minister's flow of oratory about an Ireland standing "at your bar, expectant, hopeful, almost suppliant, . . . [asking for] a blessed oblivion of the past," Chamberlain and others expected Gladstone to *examine* rather than *introduce* Home Rule, and on that semantic difference festering rivalries and grievances surfaced.

Gladstone spoke for three and a half hours. He was, he thought, divinely inspired. Home Rule was moral, and it was Christian, even if it split his party. Many Liberals felt that their seats were at risk if they supported a separate Parliament in Dublin; others used the bill as an excuse to desert the old man for potential new leaders. In the weeks of debate that followed, Hartington, Chamberlain, Bright, and others separated themselves from the Prime Minister, who had no intention of giving up his fight, even if it cost him the Government.

In the cold late spring, with morning frost still on the ground at eleven, the Queen left Windsor early on May 4, the day after Gladstone's newest manifesto maintaining his position on an Irish Parliament, to open the Colonial and Indian Exhibition at South Kensington. Her procession went in state from Paddington Station, passing noisy and excited crowds. Planned during the pre-Gladstone months, the Exhibition stood for everything Gladstone disliked about colonial involvement—exoticism, exploitation, public expense, and the exaltation of the misnamed White Man's Burden. There was an Indian Hall, and a facsimile Bazaar, and exhibits from Australia, Africa, and other red-tinted swatches of the globe. For the public, few of whom had ever traveled more than a handful of miles beyond their homes, the event offered a glimpse of Imperial England across the seas. For Victoria, it was a tactile introduction to the Empire she would never see, a trip into her Imperial fantasies. "We passed," she wrote,

> between rows, two or three deep, of Indians of all kinds, in the richest brightest costumes, all connected with the Exhibition and its exhibits, including the workmen. There were Parsees in white, with curious black glazed head gear, and numbers in turbans of every shade. We were warmly greeted, with salaams, an old man of 100 held out a carpet for me to touch, and others held out their hands with pieces of money in them for me to touch. Then along past the entrance to "Old London," to the Australian Colonies (Central Avenue), and so on into the Albert Hall, through a sort of subterranean passage. . . . Excepting some very high towering trophies one could see nothing, on account of the masses of people standing on either side. . . . Everything seemed beautifully arranged and the people all looked much pleased. Bands stationed at different points played as we walked along. How pleased my darling husband would have been at the whole thing, and who knows but that his pure bright spirit looks down upon his poor little wife, his chil-

dren and children's children, with pleasure, on the development of his work! The walk was very long and fatiguing, though very interesting. Bertie kindly helped me up and down the steps, whenever we came to any.

The Queen's favorite walking stick was exactly right for her progress through the Exhibition. It was made from what was reputed to be a branch of an oak planted by Charles II, on which was fixed a miniature Indian idol, part of the loot from Seringapatam, acquired when the fortress in Mysore was captured by Lord Cornwallis in 1792. The cane symbolically merged Queen and Empress.

At the Albert Hall, an ode for the occasion by Tennyson, with music by Sir Arthur Sullivan, was sung, with a solo by Emma Albani. An Address to the Queen was read by the Prince of Wales, and she replied briefly, after which Bertie kissed her hand. Memories welled up about the Great Exhibition of 1851, the crest of her life with Albert, as she noted in her journal. "What thoughts of my darling husband came into my mind, who was the originator of the idea of [such] an exhibition, an idea fraught with such fearful difficulties and carried through against such fearful odds!"

There were speeches, prayers, hymns, and finally "Rule Britannia," sung with fervor. No one inside the Hall was a convert to Gladstone's doctrine of diminishing Empire. Then the Queen's party left, Victoria curtseying to the cheering crowd. She was at Buckingham Palace for lunch by 1:30—one of her rare uses of the residence.

Fewer and fewer people seemed to be swallowing Gladstone's strong medicine for English ills, colonial and internal, as the Queen found further confirmed two days later. A message arrived from Lord Salisbury, in response to one from the Queen in which she had enclosed a letter from George Goschen, a moderate Liberal, suggesting that Gladstone's Ministry could not survive its divisions much longer. On the sixth, also, Gladstone visited Buckingham Palace before she left for Windsor. "I . . . urged," she noted in her journal, "the advisability of Mr. Gladstone's trying to alter his course, and to have several governing bodies for Ireland, but he said this was impossible. . . ."

Once Gladstone took his leave, she wrote to him in a further effort to head off a costly division in the House. She could *only* see danger," she warned, adding that she wrote "with pain, as she always *wishes to be able* to give her Prime Minister her *full support,* but it is impossible to do so when the Union of the Empire is in danger of disintegration and serious disturbance." Even so, she acknowledged, he was "solely actuated by the belief that he is doing what is best not only for Ireland but for the whole Empire."

The next week, continuing a crowded schedule of activities involving a largely covert employment of wheelchairs, Victoria took a train to Liverpool to open an International Exhibition of Navigation and Commerce. She was well aware that she was in her fiftieth year as Sovereign, and that her Golden Jubilee was only twelve months away. The round of ceremonial visits tested her ability to cope with a Jubilee Year, and likely popular response. On both counts, Liverpool was a success. Despite heavy rain, crowds were enormous. Liverpudlians went mad with delight at their Queen, who proceeded in an open landau in wind and rain through sopping city streets, past the formations of the trades and guilds with their wet and drooping banners and devices.

At the presentation of the Address, the City Recorder, Charles Henry Hopwood, Q.C., at the expense of his wig, silk gown, and new white silk stockings, hung on, in the gale, to the casket containing the parchment. In drenching rain, under umbrellas and waterproofs, the royal party made its way to the statues of Victoria and Albert that the Queen had not seen before, having last been in Liverpool in 1851. Then, at the Albert Docks on the Mersey, now "rough and angry," she boarded a ferry through a covered passage, "though . . . the bridge was so slanting and the cloth which covered it so wet and slippery." The only shelter aboard was a tiny cabin into which only the Queen and Beatrice could squeeze. Seeing almost nothing while rain sloshed down the windows, they steamed past the oceangoing liners that ran the Liverpool–New York route. Tea was taken "somewhat under difficulties" in the cramped cabin, the ritual as well as the refreshment being too vital to postpone. As they left the Cloughton ferry, a gilded iron crown, dislodged by the gale, toppled heavily from a flagstaff. No one was injured, and the party went on to see the beginning of a fireworks display that somehow went off despite the hostile weather.

By seven, the Queen was back at Windsor, "quite bewildered and my head aching from the incessant perfect roar of cheering." It had all been "touching and gratifying." She now knew that despite renegade peers in the Lords, radicals in the Commons, rabble-rousers in the parks and squares, and ragging in the popular press, she had become a national institution. Any concerns about 1887 had vanished.

For her sixty-seventh birthday, Victoria invited Madame Wilhelmina Clauss-Szárvady to Windsor. A pupil of Robert Schumann, she had often been invited by Prince Albert, and the Queen, who lived much among her memories, asked the veteran pianist, now, like Victoria, many times a grandmother, to play a sonata by Scarlatti that she had played for the royal couple thirty years before. Like so much else that now occupied the Queen, the appearance was an informal rehearsal for the Jubilee, the singling out of symbolic people and places, the trial-run trips, presentations, and openings, the testing of physical stamina and personal popularity. She had J. E. Boehm come to Windsor to make a medallion portrait for the new coinage in gold, silver, and bronze, to be issued during the Jubilee year of 1887. She also had him fashion a small bust of her in marble, which she wanted to present to the composer Franz Liszt. Then seventy-six, Liszt was at Windsor in early April, sixty-two years after his first visit, when Prince Esterhazy had taken him, at fourteen, in a post-chaise to play for "the greatest gentleman in Europe," George IV. Now his white hair fell in thick masses over his shoulders, and his gnarled fingers could no longer fly over the keys. The Queen reminded him that he had played for her two years after her marriage, and again at the Beethoven festival in Bonn.

She had not seen Liszt when, ten years earlier, he accompanied his son-in-law, Richard Wagner, only as far as Paddington Station, where Wagner and Cosima and the conductor Sir William Cusins entrained to Windsor for an audience, on May 17, 1877. "After luncheon," the Queen then noted in her journal, "the great composer Wagner, about whom the people in Germany are really a little mad, was brought into the corridor by Mr. Cusins. I had seen him with dearest Albert in '55, when he directed at the Philharmonic Concert. He has grown old and stout, and has a clever, but not pleasing countenance. . . . I expressed my regret at having been unable to be present at one of his concerts." She did not say, but he undoubtedly knew, that she had not attended a public concert since Albert's death. Wagner's private opinion of her was even less flattering than the Queen's of him. On January 18, 1880, according to Cosima's diary, he told her of his "annoyance with the queen, the silly old frump, for failing to abdicate and thereby condemning the Prince of Wales to an absurd existence; in earlier times, he said, sons became their mothers' guardians when they came of age."

Liszt was more courtly. Also, he had something he could do beyond uttering, as Wagner had done, expressions of insincere gratitude for being permitted in the Sovereign's presence. At the grand piano in the Red

The Descendants of Victoria

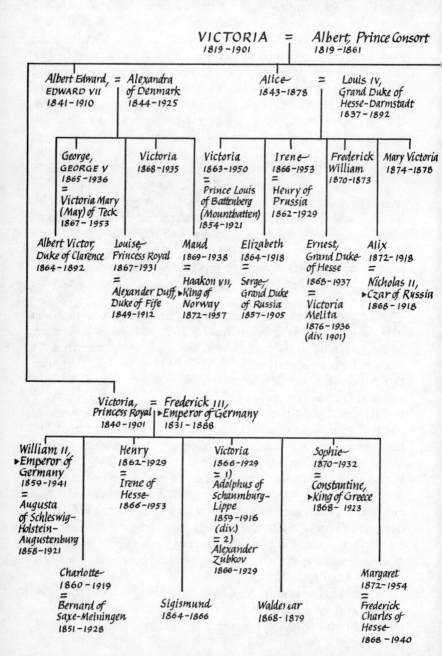

VICTORIA = Albert, Prince Consort
1819–1901   1819–1861

Albert Edward, = Alexandra of Denmark
EDWARD VII   1844–1925
1841–1910

Alice = Louis IV, Grand Duke of Hesse-Darmstadt
1843–1878   1837–1892

George, GEORGE V 1865–1936 = Victoria Mary (May) of Teck 1867–1953

Victoria 1868–1935

Victoria 1863–1950 = Prince Louis of Battenberg (Mountbatten) 1854–1921

Irene 1866–1953 = Henry of Prussia 1862–1929

Frederick William 1870–1873

Mary Victoria 1874–1878

Albert Victor, Duke of Clarence 1864–1892

Louise, Princess Royal 1867–1931 = Alexander Duff, Duke of Fife 1849–1912

Maud 1869–1938 = Haakon VII, King of Norway 1872–1957

Elizabeth 1864–1918 = Serge, Grand Duke of Russia 1857–1905

Ernest, Grand Duke of Hesse 1868–1937 = Victoria Melita 1876–1936 (div. 1901)

Alix 1872–1918 = Nicholas II, Czar of Russia 1868–1918

Victoria, Princess Royal 1840–1901 = Frederick III, Emperor of Germany 1831–1888

William II, Emperor of Germany 1859–1941 = Augusta of Schleswig-Holstein-Augustenburg 1858–1921

Henry 1862–1929 = Irene of Hesse 1866–1953

Victoria 1866–1929 = 1) Adolphus of Schaumburg-Lippe 1859–1916 (div.) = 2) Alexander Zubkov 1866–1929

Sophie 1870–1932 = Constantine, King of Greece 1868–1923

Charlotte 1860–1919 = Bernard of Saxe-Meiningen 1851–1928

Sigismund 1864–1866

Waldemar 1868–1879

Margaret 1872–1954 = Frederick Charles of Hesse 1868–1940

Their Marriages into the Royal Houses of Europe

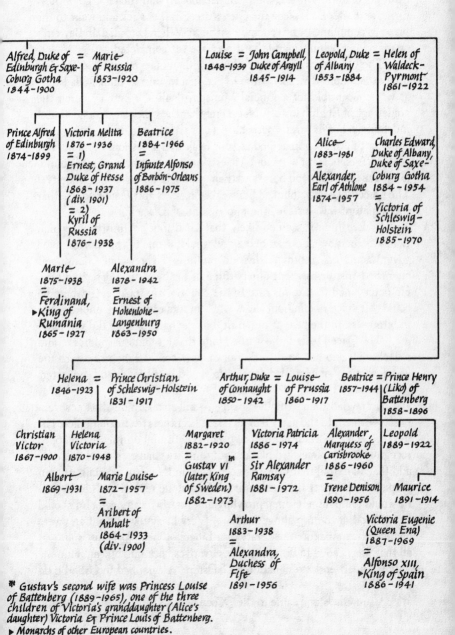

Alfred, Duke of Edinburgh & Saxe-Coburg Gotha 1844–1900 = Marie of Russia 1853–1920

Louise 1848–1939 = John Campbell, Duke of Argyll 1845–1914

Leopold, Duke of Albany 1853–1884 = Helen of Waldeck-Pyrmont 1861–1922

Prince Alfred of Edinburgh 1874–1899

Victoria Melita 1876–1936 = 1) Ernest, Grand Duke of Hesse 1868–1937 (div. 1901) = 2) Kyril of Russia 1876–1938

Beatrice 1884–1966 = Infante Alfonso of Borbón-Orleans 1886–1975

Alice 1883–1981 = Alexander, Earl of Athlone 1874–1957

Charles Edward, Duke of Albany, Duke of Saxe-Coburg Gotha 1884–1954 = Victoria of Schleswig-Holstein 1885–1970

Marie 1875–1938 = Ferdinand, ►King of Rumania 1865–1927

Alexandra 1878–1942 = Ernest of Hohenlohe-Langenburg 1863–1950

Helena 1846–1923 = Prince Christian of Schleswig-Holstein 1831–1917

Arthur, Duke of Connaught 1850–1942 = Louise of Prussia 1860–1917

Beatrice 1857–1944 = Prince Henry (Liko) of Battenberg 1858–1896

Christian Victor 1867–1900

Helena Victoria 1870–1948

Margaret 1882–1920 = Gustav VI * (later, King of Sweden) 1882–1973

Victoria Patricia 1886–1974 = Sir Alexander Ramsay 1881–1972

Alexander, Marquess of Carisbrooke 1886–1960 = Irene Denison 1890–1956

Leopold 1889–1922

Albert 1869–1931

Marie Louise 1872–1957 = Aribert of Anhalt 1864–1933 (div. 1900)

Arthur 1883–1938 = Alexandra, Duchess of Fife 1891–1956

Maurice 1891–1914

Victoria Eugenie (Queen Ena) 1887–1969 = Alfonso XIII, ►King of Spain 1886–1941

* Gustav's second wife was Princess Louise of Battenberg (1889–1965), one of the three children of Victoria's granddaughter (Alice's daughter) Victoria & Prince Louis of Battenberg.
► Monarchs of other European countries.

Drawing Room at Windsor, Liszt played, at Victoria's request, music from his oratorio *The Legend of St. Elizabeth,* and then a Chopin nocturne, and after each piece the Queen arose on her stick and went to the piano to compliment the venerable virtuoso. When Liszt died in Bayreuth on July 31, Boehm's marble bust was not yet completed.

The Queen's mail began to bulge with Jubilee messages. "The last fifty years," Lord Rosebery wrote to her, in a manner as unlike Gladstone as was conceivable for a Liberal Minister, "will . . . be considered the golden age of English history. Not merely has the Empire extended almost indefinitely; but its several parts have a close relation to each other, which could not have been imagined at your Majesty's accession. . . . This vast progress is coincident with your Majesty's reign, and these infinite dominions have their common bond and their symbol of union in your Majesty." The Queen may have blinked her weakening eyes and wondered whether the signature was, instead, the ghostly one of Disraeli.

By late June it seemed likely that Gladstone's Ministry, in which Lord Rosebery was Foreign Secretary, would be one of the shortest-lived governments on record. A division on June 9 threw out Gladstone's cherished Irish legislation, ninety-three of his own party deserting him. He determined to take his case to the country. He spoke everywhere he could, his voice holding out, he wrote, "in a marvellous manner. I went in bitterness, in the heat of my spirit, but the hand of the Lord was upon me." The Queen feared, she warned him, that his "unusual addresses and speeches . . . do not tend to a dispassionate consideration of a measure which so many of Mr. Gladstone's wisest and best friends and supporters feel bound to oppose."

Even Gladstone's "night-stalking"—still an obsession of his at seventy-six—came into the party debate about his fitness for further office. His own secretary, Edward Hamilton, pleaded with him on July 13, 1886, to recognize a conspiracy "to blacken your private character. . . . I will only add that I am told that your traducers have in their pay a certain woman prepared to support their calumnies." Gladstone replied on July 16 that he would cease his nocturnal prowling, but for "two cases, which I should have liked not to drop altogether. . . ." Very likely few votes if any were changed by innuendo; the reality of a Liberal–Liberal Unionist split was all that was needed to bring the Conservatives back into office. "Humble duty Cabinet tender resignation," Gladstone telegraphed to Osborne on July 20.

Again Gladstone came to the Queen with a Christmas list of parting peerages. Exasperated, she reminded him that there had been "extensive promotions to his followers" only months before. Sailing to Osborne to give up his Government's seals for the third time, he pondered what to say. Evading as usual the real issues, they somehow, once more, discussed education for the masses, and Gladstone found himself agreeing with the Queen that more education than a person could use was a mistake, encouraging futile aspirations. Although he may have accepted the Queen's point of view in order to get the distasteful ordeal over with, Gladstone was a landed proprietor with 2,500 people living and working on a Welsh estate of seven thousand acres that included a working coal mine. In 1890 he would tell his tenants that he thought the arrangement was "the best and most wholesome system"—hardly a radical point of view, and certainly closer to Victoria's *noblesse oblige* than to the principles of many of his followers. He led a party divided against itself and held together only by the glue of his personality.

Neither he nor the Queen mentioned Ireland, although she suggested that he refrain, at least for a time, from public utterances that might "encourage violence." He had written, she knew, emotional letters to his loyalists who had lost their seats—"monstrous, wicked, socialistic letters," she told Vicky. "For long I stood up for his Motives, but now they are clearly actuated by Vanity, ambition & malice & shew signs of madness."

Pale and trembling, he took his leave. In his diary he suggested madness elsewhere—that Victoria had become "seriously warped" after 1874—the year his long Ministry had ended and Disraeli had assumed office. "To me, personally," he added, "it is a great relief, including in this sensation my painful relations with the Queen, who will have a like feeling." Neither he nor Victoria expected to see the other in the same situation again.

When the Queen visited Liverpool in May, the hardly secret machinations to defeat Home Rule and drive Gladstone out followed her. She had been her unconstitutional self again, encouraging a coalition of Tories and Liberal Unionists, and using members of her Household to carry openly subversive messages. "There is one vital point wh she hopes Lord Salisbury, Lord Hartington & Mr. Goschen will *fully consider* & wh must *not* be *tolerated*," she warned Salisbury. "It is the Withdrawal of the Bill, [only] for Mr. Gladstone to bring it forward again next year. . . . Pray advise me how to protect agst such a fearful danger & *possibility* & consult *together* HOW this contingency can be stopped." Victoria was following the Disraelian advice that overreaching served to stretch her diminished powers. Now Disraeli's Tory successor, Salisbury, a satisfactorily patrician Cecil, once again arrived at Osborne, on August 3, an hour after Gladstone's Cabinet had steamed away in the other direction.

On August 17 the Queen convened the first Privy Council under the new Ministry. "The Queen looked very well & cheerful," Gathorne-Hardy, now Lord President of the Council, noted in his journal. "Lady Ely told me she was another person & found Salisbury's tone & way with her most acceptable. The riddance of the other [is] itself a great relief." Two weeks later, on August 30, Gathorne-Hardy was at Windsor for dinner with the Queen and a dozen others, including Prince Willy and Prince Henry, who, at Gathorne-Hardy's ear, was "very indignant at the treatment of his brother." Victoria was angrier than ever over the Prussian snubbing of the Battenberg brothers, especially Berlin's support for Czarist efforts to unseat Prince Alexander. Once the Czar's choice for Prince of Bulgaria, he had defeated attempts to undermine his government, until he was captured and forced to abdicate.

The Queen supported intervention to restore Alexander, who briefly, in September, managed a brief return to Sofia but then barely escaped with his life. No other nation would back him, he was seen as a pawn in larger struggles. "The Queen," Gathorne-Hardy wrote on September 7, "[was] athirst for England's glory [and] cannot bear to see her diplomacy scorned and intervention coldly disdained by the Great European Powers who have made some scandalous bargain." He was seeing only one dimension of the matter. Victoria had dreams of her granddaughter becoming a queen; now the prince who represented the route to that unsteady throne would never be king.

On December 8, 1886, the exiled Sandro arrived in England. He was handsome, dashing, and homeless, and Louise told her mother that he reminded her of "Papa." Victoria agreed, although his only resemblance lay in being a German princeling without occupation. Alexander still hoped to marry young Victoria Moretta some day, he insisted; but Vicky knew, and soon would tell the Queen, that Sandro had been interested only as long as the marriage seemed politically useful. Once the match was worth nothing, he did not care who knew that his real interest was Fräulein Loisinger, an actress. He married her in 1888, called himself thereafter Count Hastenau, and died at thirty-six in 1893.

Although the fortunes of the Battenbergs distracted Victoria through the waning months of 1886, anticipations of the Jubilee year occupied much of her time. In November she explored privately the largest indoor arena she had entered since the heady days of the Crystal Palace. The new, electric-lit Olympia, in West Kensington, usually seated nine thousand spectators, yet the Queen sat alone, but for her attendants, at the National Agricultural Show, advertised as "instructive" and "devoid of one single element of vulgarity." Even Beatrice was missing from the entourage, for on November 23 she had given birth to a son, her first child and a Battenberg.

The Queen would visit the Olympia again in November 1889, this time with the Prince of Wales, to see P. T. Barnum's spectacle, *Nero, or The Burning of Rome,* which ran one hundred nights and had a cast of 1,240 performers and almost as many animals. A private performance was impossible, but she sat in a box apart from the throng. Barnum himself appeared, driving around the three rings of the circus in an open carriage drawn by two horses, calling out to the audience, "I suppose you've come to see Barnum, didn't you? Wa-al, I'm Mr. Barnum." When his leading clown, Robert Edmund Sherwood, pranced out before the Queen, pantomimed the cleaning of his hands, and then broadly offered one to the Queen to shake, as he did to others in his audience every other day, Barnum was beside himself with despair over the breach of etiquette, "jumping around like a chicken on a hot griddle," Sherwood remembered. Still, Victoria graciously took the clown's hand, and the crowd exploded with applause. Barnum forbade an encore. "If you go on again," he said, "how do I know you won't invite her to dinner?" The old impresario was seventy-nine. It was his last encounter with the Queen.

Electric lighting, such as the Queen experienced at the Olympia, was not new to her. Gradually through the 1880s, public places in London, like the British Museum, were installing electricity, which was still erratic and apt to sputter out. There were days when, the arc-lighting having failed, the great domed Reading Room was closed abruptly and patrons sent away. The Round Tower at Windsor would be illuminated for the Jubilee, and in 1888 the Crimson Drawing Room was wired and electric lamps connected. One of the workmen, however, suffered an electric shock in the operation, and Victoria ordered the power turned off. Only ten years later, when even middle-class homes were being electrified, did she permit one chandelier to be converted into an "electrolier." Her more "modern" children could not wait for that. In February 1889, Beatrice and Liko had electric lighting installed in their own apartments.

The Ministry that stewarded England into the Jubilee year was not quite the same as the one the Queen had welcomed at Osborne only months before. One of its younger stars, Lord Randolph Churchill, had been the Tory Chancellor of the Exchequer. The post was often a launching platform for future Prime Ministers, and Churchill, a descendant of the Dukes of Marlborough, had the ancestry as well as the ability to go far. In the witty manner of Disraeli he had written to the Queen explaining Commons matters, and on September 22 she had replied with gratitude for his "regular and full and interesting reports . . . ," and saw "much skill and judgment in his leadership." His excitability had become more pronounced, although not in his relations with her; but she was concerned about how his passion for rigid economies would affect her Civil List.

What triggered Churchill's departure proved to be something else. At dinner with the Queen on December 21, 1886, he discussed the budget estimates for the armed forces as if he had accepted them, and then blamed the alleged excesses as his reason for leaving the Government. "That very night in my House," the Queen fumed to Vicky, "on Windsor paper he deliberately wrote his resignation & sent it to Lord Salisbury." When Salisbury refused to accept it as final, Churchill sent a second and more intemperate letter. Politicians—and the Queen—assumed that the clever and ambitious Lord Randolph was staking out a position from which to challenge his party's leadership.

He may have intended that, but his behavior seemed not that of a sane man, and proved to be one of the early symptoms of the brain deterioration that brought Churchill's career to an untimely end. Whether it was tertiary syphilis, as believed, or a brain tumor, the end was agonizing, embarrassing, and prolonged. He was unprincipled and unreliable, she warned Bertie, who was one of his friends; and early in 1888 she reminded him, "Pray don't correspond with him, for he really is not to be trusted and is very indiscreet, and his power and talents are greatly overrated." George Goschen, grandson of a Leipzig publisher and son of a London banker, took over the Exchequer post from Churchill, and became the leading Liberal Unionist in the Tory Cabinet.

A different kind of loss from the Cabinet was the former Foreign Secretary, Stafford Northcote, once Gladstone's private secretary. Less than two years earlier he had become the Earl of Iddesleigh. "He fainted at the top of the stairs, at Downing Street," Victoria noted in her journal on January 12, 1887, "and died in twenty minutes! . . . I felt quite bewildered and stunned. . . ." Northcote, at sixty-nine, had been only a year older than Victoria. Salisbury took on the added duty himself. Then

Sir Michael Hicks Beach, Chief Secretary for Ireland, had to step down because of failing eyesight. "This is dreadful," Victoria wrote in her journal on March 2. But, she added, "Lord Salisbury has named his clever and agreeable nephew [Arthur Balfour] as the person fittest to succeed . . . and I was just going to make the same suggestion."

With the approach of spring, the Queen began her Jubilee appearances and progresses, going to Birmingham on March 23. "The reception," she estimated, "was as good as at Liverpool, but I think that, while there were not such ragged people as we saw there, there were at Birmingham more *generally* poor and rough ones. . . . What was very remarkable was that in that very Radical place, amongst such a very rough population, the enthusiasms and loyalty should have been so great." Some of the ceremonial appearances she might have made in a less crowded year were assigned to other members of the Royal Family—since then a familiar use of the monarchical machinery, and a justification for its existence. Always jealous of her status and privileges, the Queen saw no one as a legitimate substitute for herself. Ponsonby was instructed that at Jubilee ceremonies, and "always" thereafter, her children were to insert "my dear Mother" into their speeches to validate the authority under which they appeared —"it should never be omitted when they represent her."

"The Queen's Jubilee"—Judge, *June 4, 1887, pointing to the panoply and the poverty.*

With the major ceremonials set for May and June, Victoria took her usual holiday, going to Cannes and Aix-les-Bains, and exploring the gorge of the Grande Chartreuse, where she visited the cloisters of the Carthusian monks who were famed for the liqueur that bore the name of the place. The Grand Prieur Général, "a stout, burly, rosy-cheeked man, wearing spectacles," took the Queen's party on a tour of the monastery, which even she found cold. (Although it was April 23, and a hot sun glared, snow still covered shady areas.) All the monks wore white cowls over shaven heads, and while the principal functionaries wandered freely —one turned out to be a former Russian general who had been attached to the London embassy—there were also younger, enclosed monks. Victoria expressed interest in them—attractive young men always interested her—and she was escorted to a cell where, she was told, she would find a young *"compatriote."* At the cell, the Grand Prieur unlocked the door, which led into two tiny rooms,

and the young inmate immediately appeared, kneeling down and kissing my hand, and saying, "I am proud to be a subject of your Majesty." The first little room looked comfortable enough, and he had flowers in it. The other contained his bed and two little recesses, in one of which stood a small altar, where he said he performed his devotions and said his prayers. In the other deeper recess, with a small window, is the study, containing his books. I remarked how young he looked, and he answered, "I am 23," and that he had been five years in the Grande Chartreuse, having entered at 18! I asked if he was contented, and he replied without hesitation, "I am very happy." He is very good-looking and tall, with rather a delicate complexion and a beautiful, saintly, almost rapt expression. When we left the cell and were going along the corridor, the Général said I had seen that the young man was quite content, to which I replied that it was a pleasure to see people contented, as it was so often not the case.

As I felt very tired, I asked not to go up any more stairs, and we turned back and went down again. The Général expressed his regret at our visit being so short, but excepting the Refectory and kitchen we had seen everything of real interest. He walked across with us to the Hôtellerie des Dames. . . . Here two very friendly Sisters, sort of Soeurs de Charité, welcomed us. Refreshments were prepared in a big room, and here the Général took leave of us, but the Procureur remained. He offered me wine, but I asked for some of their liqueur, and by mistake he gave me some of the strongest. Got home, much satisfied with our expedition, at eight. Rather tired.

Ceremonials, addresses, and progresses resumed on the Queen's return, but a telegram received at Windsor in May blighted the festivities at the start. Two eminent German throat surgeons had examined Crown Prince Frederick on the eighteenth and advised removing a growth in his throat "from the outside, a most alarming remedy." The family as well as the physicians wanted Dr. Morell Mackenzie, the leading throat specialist in England, to examine Fritz. Victoria's own Dr. James Reid went to Harley Street to press him to go, and Mackenzie spent much of the months that followed in attendance on the Crown Prince. Beneath the Jubilee excitement the Queen would mask an anxiety more profound than her experience at Sandringham, when Bertie had seemed to be dying, or at Windsor, when Albert had struggled through his final illness, for the period of grave concern would drag out for thirteen months.

Early in the agony, the Queen was set upon by Bismarck's diplomats to enlist her support in separating the Crown Princess from her Court Chamberlain, Götz, Count von Seckendorff. Whatever her own relationships with servants of far lower class, Victoria nevertheless deplored the long-standing *cavalier servente* position of the Count in Vicky's court. Loyal and devoted, the gaunt, dour Seckendorff caused talk by his protectiveness and his propinquity. Yet Vicky needed someone like the Count in political and social situations in which her husband, once an active general, could not always be close at hand, and when, for ceremonial reasons, they were often in different places at the same time. Now, with Fritz's withdrawal into invalidism, she needed the Count more than ever, but Bismarck feared the Count's influence even more than that of her mother.

Earlier, to Ponsonby, Victoria had deplored the constant, concerned presence of the Count. Persistent rumors had long pointed to him as Vicky's lover, hardly more likely than a royal romance between Victoria and John Brown. Why, the Queen once asked Ponsonby, nevertheless, had Vicky taken Seckendorff, while on a visit to Balmoral, up Craig Lochnagar? She never had any of her own gentlemen accompany her alone on such expeditions. Off to Osborne went Bismarck's emissary Hugo von Radolinski, in an effort to detach Seckendorff from Vicky. The Count now seemed Morell Mackenzie's chief support in the Crown Prince's entourage—and Mackenzie's passive treatment, while unlikely to make Fritz well, might keep him alive longer than would drastic throat surgery. "I flattered her terribly," Count Radolinski wrote to Count Holstein about "Mama." He told the Queen "that she was the only person to whose wishes her daughter paid regard. She smiled sweetly like a blushing girl and was really completely charming. For three days in succession she invited me to dine with her with an intimate group. . . . I am very satisfied with my campaign."

Despite the optimistic report, typical of the self-delusion of spies and conspirators, Radolinski, who followed Fritz's entourage everywhere, had no success whatever with the Queen or anyone else. Events were simply out of Victoria's control, as they were out of Count Radolinski's; and the Queen in any case preferred the comforting diagnosis of Mackenzie, however false her instincts told her it was, to the horrors she knew lay ahead. Hoary-bearded and parchment-pale, and clad in dress white, Fritz seemed almost his own ghost, haunting the Jubilee proceedings with a mute dignity.

Among her most melancholy forebodings was the certainty of an early and lengthy reign for Prince Willy, who appeared to have inherited every unfortunate Hohenzollern trait and few if any of the redeeming ones. By November 9 there was no longer any way to postpone the truth, and Mackenzie telegraphed from Germany that cancer had been confirmed. "My darling has got a fate before him which I hardly dare think of," Vicky confided to her mother, but the Queen convinced herself that the situation was "not quite devoid of hope." Prince Willy knew better—as he had already known—and Mackenzie belatedly made it clear that he could see (in the Queen's words) "simply palliatives to prolong life." The German doctors wanted to operate, on the chance of recovery. Acrimony embittered each consultation, as Vicky and Fritz preferred the "English" treatment to the Prussian one.

Fritz himself was only told on the eleventh of November. "The dream of his life," Vicky had written pathetically to the Queen, "was to have a son who should be something of what our beloved Papa was, a real grandson of his in soul and intellect. . . . One must learn to abandon dreams and to take things as they come. . . ." There had been little rapport between father and son in the formative years, as Willy struggled under the harsh regimen meant to compensate for his withered left arm. He had grown haughty and arrogant, and despised what he considered the soft, un-Prussian liberalism of the Crown Prince, who had long been intellectually dominated by the strident Anglomania of his wife. Possibly Willy yearned for an idealized, iron-willed father figure, finding that only momentarily when his father received the expected death sentence from his doctors. "Standing upright, unbowed, looking the speaker straight in the eye," Willy wrote to his former tutor, Georg Ernst Hinzpeter, "he received the announcement. Without a tremor or the slightest movement he thanked them for their care and attention, and dismissed them; dumb and astonished they departed from the hero, still engrossed with his character, as he showed himself the true Hohenzollern and great soldier. . . . What a man!" But the dying man was now of little further consequence to Willy, who behaved in public as in private as if he were already Kaiser. To his intimate friend Philipp Eulenburg he referred to Queen Victoria as "the Empress of Hindustan" and to his mother and sisters as "the English colony," while the doctors treating his father were "Jewish louts" and "Satan's bones." Neither Willy's grandfather nor his father could live much longer. "It is a terrible state of affairs," Victoria told her journal, "and I am haunted by it."

On January 4, 1888, the Queen went by pony cart to Osborne Cottage to visit Mary Ponsonby for a firsthand report from San Remo. Mrs. Ponsonby had visited Vicky, who had taken her husband to winter under a Mediterranean sun. The Queen's journal for the day evidences the juxtaposition of reality and unreality that made her life bearable. Mrs. Ponsonby, the Queen wrote, "said poor dear Vicky's trials, difficulties, and anxieties were terrible. Fritz's state was certainly far more satisfactory at present. Had my daily Hindustani lesson."

The Hindustani lesson was the responsibility of Abdul Karim, who had dried the Queen's Jubilee signatures and waited at table. Ambitious and proud, he complained that the work was beneath him. At home in Agra he had been a *munshi*—a clerk. He claimed that made him a professional—a scribe who, in a largely illiterate population, composed letters for those who could afford his fee. Learning the rudiments of Hindustani, the Queen quickly convinced herself, might give her a greater sensitivity toward her subjects in the subcontinent, and Abdul Karim had his duties shifted to occasional lessons for Victoria, and large blocks of leisure time. He was given a raise from the Privy Purse, and was authorized to send for his dependents.

The acquisition of Indian servants, with whom the Queen chatted as informally as she did with her gillies at Balmoral, created new theological doubts for her. Never passionate about points of doctrine, she found her faith more and more limited, beyond ethical teachings, to the existence of a Hereafter in which her soul would be reunited with Albert and others whose memories she cherished. To Gathorne-Hardy, one evening at Balmoral, she asked searching questions about Gladstone's religious beliefs, and expressed her doubts about a Trinity. "She then spoke of her Mahomedan servants, their strictness, non belief in the possibility of a Son of God, [but] with a reverence for Jesus. I am afraid or rather I ought to say without fear I was not sympathetic except in acknowledging an obedience in them wh. Xtians fail, but I am afraid that she is not strong or right in theology & knows but little while she thinks her vague ideas [are] a religion. . . . She has a horror of evangelical religion. . . ."

Although Victoria continued to delude herself that Fritz was not dying of throat cancer, on February 11, Dr. Ernst von Bergmann hastened to San Remo to perform a tracheotomy on the Crown Prince to relieve the blockage in his throat. After the surgery, Fritz breathed, but with difficulty, and only through a silver cannula. Morell Mackenzie telegraphed to Dr. Reid, for the Queen's information, that the tube was unsatisfactory; and at San Remo he argued with the German doctors that the cannula irritated the Prince's trachea and caused constant bleeding. In the weeks that followed, the Queen instructed Mackenzie to take over the case, and he did, inserting his own tube and insisting, on March 6, on a public declaration from the other physicians that he was in charge, that there were "no differences of opinion," and that there was no certainty "that the malady is likely soon to take a dangerous turn."

To protect his reputation, Mackenzie wanted German backing, yet he already had received confirmation on March 4 from German pathologists, in Mackenzie's own words, "that the morbid process was of a cancerous nature." That week the aged William I, Fritz's father, lay dying. On March 8, word came to San Remo that the end was near, and on the next day the Emperor, ninety-one, was dead. Had Fritz been declared unfit to reign because of disabling illness, he and Vicky worried, although there was no constitutional reason for their fears, he might have been passed over in favor of his own son. Willy, ambitious for a regency, had been playing what Victoria called "a double game" with Bismarck. With Mackenzie's untruths attested to by all the attending medical men, including the professors from Prussia, Fritz was able to succeed, although not rule. While his Household gathered in the drawing room of the San Remo villa, the new Emperor Frederick III, unable to speak, sat at a small table and drafted the announcement of his own accession. Then he wrote another memorandum investing his Empress, Victoria, with the Order of the Black Eagle—the German equivalent of the Garter. A third note, to Mackenzie, thanked him "for having made me live long enough to recompense the valiant courage of my wife." Then, gathering strength from the emotion of the event, he drafted a telegram to Queen Victoria: "At this moment of deep emotion and sorrow at the news of my father's death, my feelings of devoted affection to you prompt me, on succeeding to the throne, to repeat to you my sincere and earnest desire for a close and lasting friendship between our two nations." The Queen found the sentiments "beautiful" and put the telegram in her journal.

Determined to reign, Frederick III left San Remo at nine the next morning, in full uniform, in a special train for Berlin, arriving thirty-six hours later in whirling snow. Sir Edward Malet, the British Ambassador, reported to Victoria seeing the new Emperor at Charlottenburg Castle walking erect and proud. The Prince of Wales, there for the old Emperor's funeral, told her that the Emperor Frederick "had a hunted, anxious expression, which was very distressing to see."

Mackenzie remained in attendance, reporting regularly to the Queen, who had determined to return from her now-regular early spring holiday in the south by way of Charlottenburg. She wanted to see Fritz once more, and to see her daughter as Empress. There might not be much time. "My OWN dear Empress Victoria it does seem an impossible dream," she wrote breathlessly to Vicky, "may God bless her! You know *how* little I care for rank or Titles—but I cannot *deny* that *after all* has been done & said, I am *thankful & proud* that dear Fritz & you shd have come to the Throne."

After a memorial service at Windsor for the late Emperor, on March 16, the Queen left for Italy. In Florence, Sidney Peel remembered, crowds filled the piazza, coming to gaze at the repaired façade of the Duomo. One spring day in 1888 while Peel was there, policemen cleared a path through the throng for a small carriage. It was Victoria, in her pony cart, which went everywhere with her, now almost an extension of her failing legs. She ordered the carriage stopped, fumbled in her corsage, and drew out a locket that she held up to the Duomo. Peel afterwards asked a lady-in-waiting about the curious ceremony, and was told that the Queen often held up a miniature of the Prince Consort, in blue enamel and pearls, to show him something that he had missed in his earthly life. Clearly, the lady-in-waiting observed, Albert had told Victoria of his youthful visit to Florence, and she thought it would interest him to see how the Duomo looked after restoration.

The Queen's train took her north in April, through Bologna and the Brenner Pass into Austria. At Innsbruck the train halted for a greeting on the platform from Emperor Francis Joseph. Fifty-eight and with a broad white beard, he was in full uniform in the broiling sun. Like Victoria, he had succeeded an uncle at eighteen. She had not seen him since her visit to Coburg in 1863, when he had made the journey north for the dedication of a memorial to Albert.

In a room at the station "full of flowers," which probably aggravated the Queen's "sick headache," they sat down "à quatre" to lunch, Beatrice and Liko having accompanied Victoria on each leg of the journey. She could eat "next to nothing," but was impressed that Francis Joseph had traveled seventeen hours from Vienna to see her, which made his professions of amity between their countries meaningful. Russia, he told the Queen, was "incomprehensible." She could not agree more, and the leave-taking was "very affectionate."

At Munich the train stopped for a greeting by the Queen Mother of Bavaria, still in mourning for the mad King Ludwig. Wagner's patron had drowned himself two years before. The younger son, King Otto, Victoria noted, was equally mad, and the kingdom, in any case ruled largely from Berlin, was under a regent. At Regensburg the train stopped again, for the Queen to dine, after which she sat up late into the night, "full of anxiety for the next day."

For the Charlottenburg portion of the trip, Lord Salisbury begged, she should have a Minister in Residence: the German leadership, prompted by Bismarck, had been upset at the Queen's visit, assuming a dominance over Vicky that would result in Victoria's manipulating the German throne. Victoria refused, insisting that she was making a private visit. She found Fritz in bed, but Mackenzie claimed his patient was improving. At the Schloss in Berlin she paid a condolence call on the aged Empress Augusta, going up alone in a tiny pre-electric elevator to find her onetime friend and confidante "quite crumpled up and deathly pale, really rather a ghastly sight. . . . One hand is paralyzed and the other shakes very much." Shrunken and silent, Augusta was eighty-seven.

The next day, April 25, Prince Bismarck (as he had become under William I) came for an audience with the Queen. Nervously he asked Major Bigge whether Victoria would be standing or sitting, and how he was to behave. Just after noon, Vicky brought the burly Bismarck in. The tiny Queen shook his hand and asked him to sit. He brought up Fritz's illness. "I thought him not looking so ill . . . ," she told Bismarck without confidence. Then she expressed satisfaction that there was no talk of a regency. He assured her that there would be none. "Even if he thought it necessary, which he did not, he would not have the heart to propose it." She asked him to stand by Vicky, which he promised insincerely that he would. "Hers," he said, "was a hard fate." Worried about Willy as Emperor, Victoria emphasized his inexperience, especially his not having traveled anywhere but England. (At the least, she had sent Bertie on one junket after another.) Bismarck was unconcerned; should Willy "be thrown into the water," the Chancellor said, "he would be able to swim."

On April 26, having kissed Fritz, pale and mute, and urged him to visit her "when he was stronger," Victoria left for England. On the platform, the Empress struggled with her emotions. "Dear Vicky came into the railway carriage, and I kissed her again and again. She . . . finally broke down, and it was terrible to see her standing there in tears, while the train moved slowly off, and to think of all she was suffering and might have to go through. My poor poor child, what would I not do to help her in her hard lot!" The power struggle soon to come would be no struggle at all. Once Vicky lost Fritz, she lost everything.

Frederick's difficulties increased daily, each morning bringing closer the dreaded finding that there was no further way to feed him, or to assist his breathing. On June 14, 1888, Victoria received a telegram at Balmoral from Mackenzie that pneumonia had developed, and the Emperor was sinking. She telegraphed Willy that she was "so troubled about poor dear Mama. Do all you can, as I asked you [when in Berlin], to help her at this terrible time of dreadful trial and grief. God help us!" The next day it was over. Frederick III had reigned ninety-nine days.

"I am broken-hearted," the Queen telegraphed to Willy, at twenty-nine now the Emperor William II. "Help and do all you can for your poor dear Mother and try to follow in your best, noblest, and kindest of father's footsteps."

Before the month was out, the Queen knew from Bertie's trip to Berlin to represent her at the funeral, that Bismarck was "untrue and heartless," and Willy unreliable. On paper, however, Willy was the affectionate son and grandson, writing to his "Dearest Grandmama" about his widowed mother that he was "doing my uttermost to fulfill her desires." He would then travel to meet with the Czar, "which will be of good effect for the peace of Europe." He hoped also to confer with other monarchs "to look out for dangers which threaten the monarchical principle from democratical and republican parties in all parts of the world." Victoria found it "sickening" to see Willy already going to banquets and reviews, and traveling about in state as Emperor, only weeks after his father's death. Two generations removed from him and worlds apart in upbringing, she paralleled her grandson only in the determination to make their Queen-Empress and Emperor-King titles meaningful. But Victoria had grudgingly accepted the erosion of power, and made the best of her perquisites and the little authority that remained. Willy embraced the authoritarian rule that Bismarck had preserved and enhanced for William I.

Dr. Morell Mackenzie billed Victoria £12,000 for his thirteen months' attendance upon the Emperor Frederick. Mackenzie had sacrificed his entire practice, in which he would have earned upwards of £15,000 a year. Attacked by the German medical establishment for failing to permit surgery when it might have helped his patient (or killed him sooner), he wrote a backbiting book about the case in his own defense, but never recovered his reputation or his practice. Mackenzie died in 1892, at fifty-five.

German affairs continued to dominate the Queen's year. Willy began to complain through his ambassador about not being treated appropriately to his rank, and about British hostility to German aspirations in Europe and abroad. To Lord Salisbury on October 15, 1888, Victoria unburdened herself. She and the Prince of Wales, she explained,

> have always been very intimate with our grandson and nephew, and to pretend that he is to be treated *in private* as well as in public as "his Imperial Majesty" is *perfect madness!* He has been treated just as we should have treated his beloved father and even grandfather, and as the Queen *herself* was always treated by her dear uncle King Leopold. *If* he has *such* notions, he [had] better *never* come *here*.
>
> The Queen will not swallow this affront.
>
> . . . All this shows a very unhealthy and unnatural state of mind; and he *must* be made to feel that his grandmother and uncle will not stand such insolence. The Prince of Wales must *not* submit to such treatment.

As regards the political relations of the two Governments, the

Queen quite agrees that that should not be affected (if possible) by these miserable personal quarrels; but the Queen much *fears* that, with such a hot-headed, conceited, and wrongheaded young man, devoid of all feeling, this may at ANY moment become *impossible*.

The wife of an English diplomat in Berlin recorded that the Germans "all say that the English royal family never treat the Emperor William as a sovereign but like a little boy." There was some truth in the observation, as Victoria had reigned too long to be able to visualize her grandson, who seemed only yesterday to have been in swaddling clothes, as an emperor already more than ten years older than she had been herself when she acquired her crown. Her concern about Willy's cranky arrogance became obsessive. Vicky appealed to be permitted to visit, as an escape from alleged ill treatment by "Bismarck and his son," and by Willy himself. "It makes my blood boil!" the Queen told her journal. To Gathorne-Hardy she confided that Willy's treatment of the Empress was "abominable," and that he "seemed to think of himself as in some supernatural position."

There were other distractions. Abdul returned home to India on leave, suspending the Queen's Hindustani lessons; but she was mesmerized by the "Whitechapel murders" attributed later to an uncaught "Jack the Ripper." The Home Secretary, Henry Matthews (later Viscount Llandaff), and the Prime Minister received notes from Victoria about investigating the murders. The messages suggested the methods of her fictional contemporary, Sherlock Holmes, who first appeared in a story in 1890. Since the killer's victims were largely ladies of the evening, the Queen asked Matthews, "Has any investigation been made as to the number of single men occupying rooms to themselves?" And, she observed, "The murderer's clothes must be saturated with blood and must be kept somewhere." She also wondered whether "all cattle boats and passenger boats" had been checked for a fleeing killer, and whether there was sufficient "surveillance at night." Persistent rumors, probably kept from the Queen, pointed to Prince Eddy as the East End predator. A later allegation named his family's physician, Sir William Gull. No convincing suspect was ever found, and Jack the Ripper seems too strenuous a role for the languid Duke.

On November 19, Vicky arrived in England, met at the dock by a party including the Queen, the Duke of Cambridge, and the German ambassador, Count Hatzfeldt. The Queen was alarmed by the sympathetic crowds that had gathered in London, and by the flags displayed, worrying that Vicky would find both an affront to her mourning. Her daughter, in a heavy black veil and blind with weeping, saw nothing. It was two days before her forty-eighth birthday, and her life was effectively over.

Vicky stayed well into the new year. As 1889 arrived at Osborne, the Queen noted, no one sat up to celebrate its arrival. She dismissed protests from the Prime Minister that the former Empress's presence as a near-exile kept relations between Britain and Germany uneasy. When Vicky returned in February, however, the Government entertained feelers from Count Herbert Bismarck, Foreign Minister and the Chancellor's son, for a state visit that would enable Victoria to receive her grandson as Emperor.

On the day that Vicky was to leave for Germany, February 26, 1889, the Queen held an immense drawing-room just after noon. Aristocratic London had been invited, to bid the Empress farewell. Lady Monkswell noted in her diary that it snowed at "intervals of half an hour" and that she had "a most miserable long wait in the brougham in Buckingham Palace Road getting colder & colder." Afterwards—again the press had complained about the hazards to womanhood of a palace reception—the Queen revised her style edict to permit high-necked dresses at Windsor and Buckingham Palace functions. Once the last guests backed their way out, the Empress Frederick—as she preferred to be known—followed them. A month later the Queen herself left England, this time taking her spring holiday at Biarritz and San Sebastian. Crossing the border into Spain, she met the Queen Regent and the young Queen Christina, and heard a choir sing "God Save the Queen" in Basque. Nearly seventy, Victoria was now more an institution than a sovereign. Whitehall and Westminster functioned as always, with only the *Court Circular* recognizing her absence.

In many ways she only played at being Queen, creating, for example, Abdul Karim as her *Munshi,* or Indian Secretary, on his return from leave, and giving him the task of answering correspondence from India that required only form responses. As sensitive about his status as was the Emperor of Germany, Karim continually created problems that the Queen ignored or decided in his favor, his presence poisoning the atmosphere wherever he accompanied her. And he went with her almost everywhere. Since age and frailty and distance had prevented her from going to India, she would have her own India—the Queen's *Munshi,* for one, and an ornate Durbar Room added to Osborne House to display her burgeoning collection of Indian crafts, furniture and curios.

That the Queen altered Albert's design for Osborne was itself remarkable. She abhorred change. The functionaries in her Household who oversaw the furniture and furnishings in her homes were careful to replace worn hangings, carpeting, and upholstery with close facsimiles of the discarded materials, to avoid having any change come to her notice. The Earl of Crawford noted in his diary that even at Buckingham Palace, "which is only occupied six or seven times a year, . . . there are naturally many things lying about on tables, chairs and on the floor—books, for instance, shawls, and old envelopes. These are carefully picked up; numbered, catalogued, inventoried; chalkmarks are made upon the carpets, pins stuck on to chairs. When the Queen is next expected everything is replaced with scrupulous care." At hallowed Osborne, the Queen accommodated herself to the idea of altering the Prince Consort's architectural concept by employing the firm of Cubitt, Albert's original contractor, to build the oversized annex, its high-ceilinged main room thirty feet by sixty feet, with suites above for Beatrice and Liko, and for a Minister-in-Attendance.

Although popular belief credits John Lockwood Kipling, keeper of the museum at Lahore, and father of the more famous Rudyard, with the interior design of the Durbar Room, it was one of his pupils at the Mayo School of Industrial Art, Bhai Ram Singh, who planned and supervised the elaborate white-and-gold fretwork interior. While Victoria resisted the future at Windsor, she ordered electricity installed to light the Durbar Room, and the rest of the building as well, although she preferred not to use it herself. A battery-house near the servants' barracks, with gas generator, furnished the power. The trophies from India—the subcontinent was itself a trophy—had to be visible, and the Queen's sight was no longer what it had been.

At a theatrical entertainment staged at great expense by the Prince of Wales at Sandringham, the Queen brought her *Munshi*. When she arrived the day before, April 25, 1889, it was her first visit to Sandringham since December 1871, when Bertie had seemed to be dying of typhoid fever. Having reconciled himself to the frustrations of waiting out his turn as sovereign, and having received an additional £36,000 annually from Parliament for his children (with even Gladstone concurring), he was entertaining in style, maintaining his mistresses, and somehow—since the Jubilee—satisfying his mother that the Empire might someday be safe in his hands. The contrast to Willy in Germany—the Prince's nephew—had done much to improve Bertie in the Queen's eyes. He seemed solicitous of his mother and circumspect about his private life, which for the moment he no longer lived in public; he had official access to the Queen's red boxes, and demonstrated an aptitude for foreign affairs. At forty-seven he was becoming kingly.

As host at Sandringham, the Prince of Wales had furnished seating in the ballroom for nearly three hundred guests, from royalty to neighbors, servants, and tenants. Abdul Karim, having risen from *khidmatgar* (waiter) to *Munshi,* refused to sit with the servants. His dignity affronted, he retreated to his room. Afterwards, the Queen insisted that he was part of the Household. Although members of the Household rejected his pretensions as groundless, they were forced to sit with him at dinners, through vast silences created by his presence. He boasted, to no response, of his own growing establishment (he had clerks under him now), and Arthur Bigge appealed to Ponsonby, his superior, "Don't you think it well to resist these moves upwards?" But at the Braemar games in 1890, on the Queen's instructions, he was placed among the gentry. The Duke of Connaught spoke angrily to Ponsonby about it, but the Private Secretary, now grown venerable and white-bearded in the Queen's service, suggested that it would be better not to mention the matter. Karim became, in 1892, the *Munshi Hafiz* Abdul Karim, appeared in the *Court Circular,* and was given a furnished residence at Osborne, at which people claiming to be his wife and various aunts stayed, stimulating colorful rumors that enlivened an otherwise drab Household. Dr. Reid claimed that every time a Mrs. Karim fell ill, a different tongue was put out for him to examine.

That Reid himself was called upon to attend the *Munshi's* extended family was indicative of Victoria's relationship with her newest favorite, who in 1889 was still a young man in his late twenties. The medical staff available to the Queen was enormous, and Reid, since Jenner's retirement in the early 1880s, had been chief physician to the Queen in a Household medical department that in 1889 consisted of three Court physicians, ten honorary physicians, two paid surgeons, three honorary surgeons, three *accoucheurs,* two oculists, one children's doctor, four honorary palace doctors, one dentist, and nine apothecaries.

Black-bearded and resplendent in white turban and gold-threaded belt and sash, the *Munshi* appeared to the unwary as a resident Maharajah, and articles began to appear in the popular press questioning his place. The attacks, the Queen told Ponsonby, were *"low* and really outrageous."

Questioning his antecedents, she insisted, was "quite out of place," as she had known archbishops who were sons of butchers and grocers, and peers "who ran about barefoot as children." (He had claimed his father was a doctor, but investigation proved him to be a prison apothecary.) Ignoring the facts, she went on, "Abdul's father saw good and honourable service as a Dr. . . . The Queen is so sorry for the poor Munshi's sensitive feelings."

To assuage his pain at social snubs, she offered him an additional house, at Balmoral, where he installed a spouse. "I have just been to see the Munshi's wife (by Royal command)," a young maid-of-honor to the Queen wrote.

> She is fat and not uncomely, a delicate shade of chocolate and gorgeously attired, rings on her fingers, rings on her nose, a pocket mirror set in turquoises on her thumb and every feasible part of her person hung with chains and bracelets and ear-rings, a rose-pink veil on her head bordered with heavy gold and splendid silk and satin swathings round her person. She speaks English in a limited manner and declares she likes the cold. The house surrounded by a twenty foot palisade, the door opening of itself, the white figure emerging silently from a near chamber, all seemed so un-English, so essentially Oriental that we could hardly believe we were within a hundred yards of this Castle.

The Sandringham performance that the *Munshi* had boycotted had featured Henry Irving and Ellen Terry in one of their box-office successes, *The Bells*, adapted from the French melodrama *Le Juif Polonais*, followed by the trial scene from *The Merchant of Venice*, in which Irving played Shylock and Ellen Terry played Portia. Afterwards the Queen spoke to the pair, Irving impressing her as "very gentleman like, and she, very pleasing and handsome." She could not have been unaware of their offstage relationship, or of Ellen Terry's illegitimate children, but that earlier individual named Victoria who had inhabited the Queen's form was gone, transformed by time. Now at Balmoral, she and some of her ladies smoked cigarettes outdoors to keep the gnats away—but that, to her thinking, was hygienic.

However belatedly, Victoria was widening her experience even in other ways, as is suggested by some of the exotic visitors to Windsor. One, who came to dinner on May 5 and remained the night, was a squat, bushy-bearded "Professor Arminius Vambery," a Hungarian scholar-gypsy of about fifty-five, who had traveled through central Asia disguised as a dervish. Vambery, expert in Moslem lore and fluent in the regional languages, knew the rulers of Turkey, Persia, and Afghanistan, and the fierce local khans and caliphs. "Mama was very much interested in making his acquaintance," the Prince of Wales had written to Vicky; and the Queen had first met him at Sandringham when she visited for Irving's performance. Vambery limped next to Victoria in Bertie's park, keeping pace with her donkey cart; answering her questions, he was amazed at her knowledge of details, and of "the strange Oriental names," even her pronouncing them correctly, "a rare thing in a European, especially in a lady." Her memory for matters discussed by Asiatics who visited at Court was capacious; also, the *Munshi* may have done his job better than his detractors knew. Vambery even claimed, the Queen noted in her journal, that he knew "the poor brokenhearted Emperor and Empress of Austria and poor Rudolf." Only a few weeks had passed since the notorious suicide at Mayerling of the Archduke Rudolf, the heir to the throne.

Victoria followed up the encounter; someone with Vambery's knowledge of the land corridors to India was worth talking to. At Windsor, having entered his birthdate in the royal birthday book, a requirement for guests, he was escorted to his apartment in one of the round towers. "As I gazed at the lovely landscape," he wrote, "with the Thames winding in and out among the trees, and remembered the ideas I had formed of this royal castle when I read Shakespeare, I was deeply moved by the wonderful change in my position. If someone had told me in the days gone by that I, who was then living in the poorest circumstances, and even suffering hunger, should one day be the honoured guest of the Queen of England and Empress of India at Windsor, that men in high position would lead me through the ancient halls, show me the royal treasures, and that I should sit next but two to the Queen at table, I should in spite of my lively imagination, have thought him a fool. . . ." Looking at his reflection in his mirror, the self-styled professor, forty years removed from a small Jewish village near Budapest, declared to himself, *"Haschele Wamberger, das hast Du gut gemacht!"*

Victoria was seventy on May 24, 1889. At Windsor, "Drino"—Beatrice's eldest son, Alexander—brought flowers to her bedroom and said, "Many happy returns, Gangan." It seemed very far away from the "bright happy" birthdays that had ended in 1861. Nearly every day was an anniversary of the death of someone close to her—that of Fritz on June

15 now the closest and most terrible. When her last aunt, the Duchess of Cambridge, died, the Queen hastened to London to see the body laid out at St. James's Palace—"looking so peaceful & at rest—& free fm all suffering! She looked so nice—with a white cap tied under her chin, her head just a little turned to one side wh gave such a look of comfort—her hands folded over her breast—& a little crucifix wh dear Alix had brought her . . . in her hands."

The Queen made an exception and went to the funeral at Kew Church. "I was never at any funeral (in England) nor at any Royal one —but only my own poor darling Child's, 5 years ago & this is the *only* other one I shall!" she wrote to Vicky. Yet she had gone not only to Prince Leopold's obsequies, and to the Prince Imperial's, but to tenants' funerals at Balmoral, these apparently not being relevant to the Queen's count. "Aunt Cambridge," she added, was "the *last* above me! . . . George & I are *now* the *old ones* & we must feel that!"

The Emperor William was careful to schedule his visit to begin after the first anniversary of his father's death. On the very anniversary day, his sister, Princess Victoria of Prussia, was visiting the Queen. Disconsolate over her loss of "Sandro" Battenberg and an abortive attachment to the Russian Grand Duke Alexander ("the 2nd failure," Queen Victoria called it), she was sent for before going to bed at Balmoral on the dreaded evening of June 15. "Grandmama," she wrote to her mother, ". . . took me in her arms, & kissed me over & over again—we could but cry together in silence." The Queen had found an acceptable way to weep for the dream that failed.

Since the Emperor was sailing directly to the Isle of Wight, a proposal was made to the Queen to send some Yeomen of the Guard to Cowes to grace the reception. From Henry Ponsonby came an impatient answer: "The Queen says she is damned if the Beefeaters shall leave London." But in preparation for Willy's visit, the Queen gave him the rank of a British admiral, so that he could wear the coveted uniform at a review at Spithead. In accepting, he signed himself "Ever your most affectionate and devoted Grandson," and to the British ambassador in Berlin he confided that his grandmother's gift made him "quite giddy. I feel something like Macbeth must have felt when he was suddenly received by the witches with the cry of 'All hail, who are Thane of Glamis and of Cawdor too.'" That Macbeth was an ambitious usurper who came to a bad end was lost upon him. After the Shah of Persia in July, Willy came in August, resplendent as an Admiral of the Fleet. To improve the occasion, the Queen gave Prince Henry, Willy's brother, the Order of the Garter. As family they breakfasted as well as took dinner in the tent at Osborne, her favorite place because of the crisp air. All was cordial, and Willy afterwards sent a thank-you for "your unbounded love and kindness to me."

A further message of gratitude from Berlin had an ominous suggestion. Parliament had just voted millions for seventy new vessels. Willy, who would now "watch every phase" of Royal Navy warship development, "knowing that the British ironclads, coupled with mine and my army, are the strongest guarantees of peace," was taking note. German arms were, in the Emperor's view, a personal plaything; and he loved races, especially arms races.

If anything in 1889 showed that age and infirmity had not kept the Queen from her dispatch boxes, and that she wanted to be kept informed, it was the commutation of the death sentence of twenty-four-year-old Florence Maybrick, who had poisoned her husband. A life sentence was not enough for a husband-killer, the Queen complained to Mr. Matthews. The Home Secretary responded that he had consulted with eminent legal authorities, who agreed that the arsenic administered may not have been sufficient to have caused Maybrick's death—the reason for a reduction in the charge to attempted murder. To Ponsonby, the Queen penned a note: "Would Sir Henry thank Mr. Matthews, and say that the only regret she feels about the decision is that so wicked a woman should escape by a mere legal quibble!" Florence Maybrick would survive the Queen by forty years.

The Queen's mail bulged with trivia, but her bureaucracy kept much of it from her, as unworthy of her interest or attention. Crank correspondence on religion was one of her peeves, and had raised her short temper when she had been in mourning for Albert. After that she was shown little of it, but in 1890 the self-styled General of the Salvation Army, William Booth, sent her his book, its title a parody on English intervention in Africa, *In Darkest England.* The social welfare and self-help schemes it outlined to relieve unemployment, overcrowding, and poverty were fixed to an Evangelical fulcrum. Delicately, Ponsonby brought the book to Victoria.

Booth was securing a great deal of press attention, and his Army was gaining converts. The Queen could not be left behind, but she was also, by coronation oath, Defender of a different Faith. She could not, she had Ponsonby write to Booth, express an opinion on the details of his programs, "but understanding that your object is to alleviate misery and suffering, her Majesty cordially wishes you every success in the undertaking you have originated." Booth sent the letter to *The Times,* which, after authorization from the Court, printed it. The outcome was exactly the way the Queen wanted it. The Established Church was unthreatened by the exchange; the Salvation Army and its missionaries were happy; Victoria had appeared socially responsible.

Another army—her own—was a continuing problem. The Queen's red boxes had long been filled with complaints about the Duke of Cambridge's obsolescent but tenacious hand in the War Office; in 1890 the objections surfaced in detail in the report of a Parliamentary commission. The Duke was 70 and represented a bygone era in military outlook; his personal interference in appointments had made it difficult for merit to be rewarded over social status and family ties. He had inherited his title and powers from the Duke of Wellington, and had used them to block reforms. The Queen considered the charges "reckless" and wanted no change, retaining the power for the Sovereign of naming the Commander-in-Chief, as she put it to Ponsonby, to "hand down to her son and grandson her crown unimpaired." Being a lady of remarkable stubbornness, she could postpone, although she could not prevent, the future.

Similarly, she could do nothing about the Foreign Office's attempts to heal boundary disputes in Africa with France and Germany by judicious swaps of distant land. In one surprising exchange, the British relinquished Heligoland, a strategic bit of rock and sand in the North Sea close to the German coast, in order to secure their borders in East Africa. In turn, Germany relinquished Zanzibar. The Queen was furious. "Giving up what one has is always a bad thing," she objected to Salisbury; the philosophy was consistent throughout her years as Sovereign.

Africa interested the Queen far less than India did, especially after memories of the Prince Imperial began to fade, but in 1890 she received Henry Morton Stanley for a second time. She had not liked him when, on September 9, 1872, she wrote, from Windsor, "I have this evening seen a Mr. Stanley, who discovered [David] Livingstone, a determined, ugly, little man—with a strong American twang." The explorer and journalist was then thirty-one. On May 7, 1890, again at Windsor, he was invited to dinner by the Queen, and according to Countess Battersea, again he did not "look at all distinguished," but was all the more celebrated as an adventurer, and as the author of *In Darkest Africa.* "We were all invited," Countess Battersea wrote, "to take our places behind the Royal Family in one of the spacious and beautiful rooms, where a map of Africa, illustrating Stanley's perilous journeys, was exposed for our view. A very interesting lecture was given by the traveller. . . . At the close, a little coal-black youth was taken up to the Queen by the lecturer and formally presented. Her Majesty smiled graciously and extended her hand; the boy grasped it and wrung it warmly, perhaps rather severely, for I noticed that the Queen seemed not merely astonished, but uncomfortably so. . . . But the boy went smilingly and serenely away from the dignified presence of Her Majesty, not knowing how he had transgressed the ordinary conventions of Court etiquette."

Forgiven later for having taught the African boy to shake hands American-style, and re-naturalized as a British subject (he had been born in Denbigh), Stanley was knighted by the Queen in 1899.

When it came to small personal matters, the Queen could still prevail. For the 1890 Durbar at Delhi, she requested a grant of land in Agra for the *Munshi,* and select places at the Durbar for the *Munshi* and his father. Reluctantly, Lord Lansdowne agreed to accommodate the *Munshi,* but his father had no status and remained ineligible, despite entreaties from Windsor. Bigger plums also evaded her, but she persisted. She was also trying to force her son Arthur, the Duke of Connaught, upon the Government as Commander-in-Chief in India, a transparent move to put him in line to succeed her cousin George as army chief. The ploy did not work. She might award a uniform, but not an office.

As the Queen's authority faded, her reputation paradoxically increased. While W. T. Stead was writing in his *Pall Mall Gazette* about the public complaint "that it has too little Monarchy for its money," it had received, since the Jubilee, much more of Victoria than all but a few people remembered. She was the only sovereign most Britons then alive had ever known, and everyone realized that few years remained to her. The result was a massive turnout to see Victoria wherever there was any advance word of an appearance. On June 27, 1890, for example, she had gone to Kensal Green Cemetery from Paddington Station in a closed carriage to pay her respects at the grave of the Marchioness of Ely, who had been one of her few close friends and long a member of the Household. "There were crowds out," she wrote in her journal; "we could not understand why, and thought something must be going [on], but it turned out it was only to see me. . . . Unfortunately, there were such crowds that the privacy of my visit was quite spoilt; still, I felt glad so many bore witness to this act of regard and love paid to my beloved friend."

For Victoria, whatever was fixed and immutable was as she wanted it, and whatever she wanted to do agreeably filled her life, regardless of the inconvenience to others. She was Queen. That her own privacy discomfited others was of little concern. In the days of her mourning for Albert she had ordered naval guns that could be faintly heard at Osborne stilled. In later years she regularly telegraphed objections to the authorities who filled the Solent with the distant echoes of cannon. When the City of London Artillery Volunteers practiced with seven-inch guns at Southsea Castle across the water, she ordered the firing stopped immediately. Artillery practice anywhere in the vicinity of Spithead and Portsmouth was likely to be halted when she was in residence ten miles away. For "the defence of 'Old England,' " *Truth* trumpeted, the Queen should cease the discouragement of military readiness by her "peremptory stoppage." The Queen paid no heed to Henry Labouchère's paper.

More and more, Victoria used a walking stick in public. After the Sultan of Zanzibar saw her lean on one, he inquired of the Court whether she would accept, "as a birthday present," a crutch-handled stick. Ponsonby replied affirmatively—if not "too heavy or costly," and scaled to the Queen's height at thirty-four and a half inches. Neither lameness nor age kept the Queen from what she wanted to do. Like her Osborne stays, her Balmoral retreats began and ended with clockwork regularity, and she thrived on the sameness and dullness of the regimen. Young Marie Adeane recalled going thirty-four miles to the Linn of Dee in November in a jolting, open carriage. "It was dull and we got quite chilly sitting bolt upright in one position but the Queen was . . . not a bit tired and brisk as a bee. . . ." The next day the Queen went for a "tremendous climb" to the Prince Consort's cairn—no trouble for her in the pony chair, but Marie, as a maid-of-honor, had to walk by the side of the cart, uphill. Victoria never noticed such impositions; nor did she concern herself with the monotony of waiting indoors, with nothing to do, by ladies and lords who were subject to her infrequent calls. As Miss Adeane wrote in June 1890, again from Balmoral, the life "in waiting" was "utterly dull, often limited to having dinner with the Queen on alternate nights," and with "*no* duties to perform to occupy our minds and the weather is horribly cold and wet. . . . We just exist from meal to meal and do our best to kill time."

Even with the Household physically available, the Queen seldom talked to anyone other than at tea or meals, quite content with her red boxes, or to daydream alone with her memories. Communication, as always, was by note. "The Queen is very reasonable when you can get at her," Marie Adeane would write in 1891, "but the odious practice of doing everything through a third person makes endless difficulties and misunderstandings."

Despite their dreary sameness, royal invitations to dinner were coveted, for if the Queen was in a good mood, memorable stories flowed from her fund of reminiscence, and others rushed to seize the conversational threads. Eligibility, however, remained severely restricted. Dr. James Reid, who had been appointed a resident physician in 1881, succeeding Jenner, found himself, as a professional employee, excluded from the Queen's table. Since ladies and gentlemen of the Household were nonetheless free to be his guests at a less dismal dinner—Reid had a repertoire of jokes that seemed not to stale—the Queen found that some of her invitees were often unavailable. "I hear Dr. Reid has dinner parties!" she confessed finally, and brought an end to the competition by having him at the Household table. Reid would even garner a baronetcy in 1897, and in 1899 he married a former maid-of-honor, Susan Baring, a niece of Lady Ponsonby.

After years at Victoria's table, Reid complained, he found himself "excited about small things which when he got away he didn't care a damn for." A Minister-in-Attendance in the 1890s saw life at Balmoral as "like a convent. We meet at meals . . . and when we have finished, each is off to his cell." Little had changed from the Queen's earliest years at Windsor. The ghost of Greville would have recognized the setting.

Even the most lugubrious entertainment became an event for the starved Household. On October 11, 1890, the Queen recorded, "After dinner, the other ladies and gentlemen joined us in the Drawing-room, and we pushed the furniture back and had a nice little impromptu dance, Curtis's band being so *entraînant.* We had a quadrille, in which I danced with [Prince] Eddy!!" One visualizes the silent agony of the pleasure-loving Eddy, mired in chill Balmoral, dancing—ever so slowly—with his tiny, stout, lame, black-swaddled grandmother. For a moment, Victoria was back in 1840.

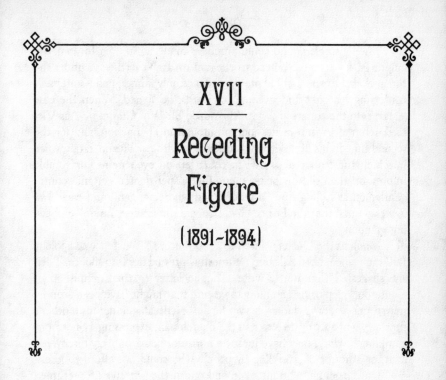

XVII

Receding Figure

(1891-1894)

$\mathbb{T}$he Tranby Croft scandal, early in 1891, once again collapsed the Queen's hopes for the Prince of Wales's metamorphosis into a model monarch. Equally agonizing was the prospect that the Tories were on their way out again, and that Gladstone, feeble physically but still a Pied Piper when he began to speak, would once more be back to kiss hands. At Balmoral in October 1890 the Queen had confided to Gathorne-Hardy that she did not know "how she could send for a man over eighty to form a Govt., a man who in 1880 told her that he had only one more year of political life." Even so, by-elections in which Liberals gained seats portended more of Gladstone.

The first of the Queen's embarrassments in 1891 emanated from the Yorkshire country house of Tranby Croft, where the Prince of Wales, playing baccarat with his friends, became involved in the exposure of a crony who was cheating. With a private income of £80,000 a year at a time when a single pound could purchase an elegant dinner for two, the culprit hardly seemed to need to cheat at cards. Nevertheless, under the threat that the others would preserve silence only if he signed a statement confessing his guilt and swearing off cards, he signed. When the case leaked into the papers anyway, "the horrid Sir Wm Cumming," as Victoria referred to him in her journal, brought a libel action, and for the second time in his life, Bertie was called as a witness. The uncertain voice in which the Prince answered in court left an even more unfavorable impression than did his being there. One paper quoted certain country gentlemen as calling him "a wastrel and whoremonger," and even *The Times* wished that the Prince "had signed a similar declaration" eschewing gambling.

Much as the Queen wanted to get on record "in defence or apology for" the Prince, Lord Salisbury "earnestly" pressed her into silence. Then she suggested that Bertie write a public letter to the Archbishop of Canterbury deploring gambling, a gesture that might have been seen by newspaper readers as ludicrous; yet he did, eventually, under his mother's pressure, write a private letter to the churchman, expressing a "horror of gambling," which may have meant a horror of being publicly discovered at it, or a horror of gambling by people who could not afford to lose.

Duleep Singh, who flitted in and out of the Queen's life, returned to make matters awkward for her. Her first souvenir of India, still pensioned by the state as a displaced maharajah, he had aged badly into his middle fifties. Now poor, portly, and promiscuous, he lived on borrowed money and dallied with showgirl camp followers. Victoria had helped arrange his marriage, and was godmother to his first son, Victor. Like Freddie, the second son, Victor hunted girls and game. Now cut socially, the elder Singh needed absolution from the Queen. He came to her during her spring holiday on the Riviera in March, Marie Adeane wrote, "to beg the Queen's forgiveness for all his misdeeds. The Queen said he was quite calm at first then wept bitterly imploring forgiveness and finally when she stroked his hand recovered his equanimity." Miss Adeane was outraged at Duleep Singh's intrusion and the Queen's permissiveness. "I believe he is a monster of the deepest dye and is treated far better than he deserves." But Bertie, nearly the same age, had also been less than discreet, and the Queen could not dismiss a onetime surrogate son with a standard of morality she would not apply to the Prince of Wales.

On Duleep Singh's death in 1893, she wrote to Victor about how handsome and charming she had once considered his father, and how "painful" the separation had been. She did not mention Polly Ash, a dancer at the Alhambra, to whom the debt-ridden ex-maharajah had not long before given an allowance of £3,000 a year. Rather, she sent a wreath for the coffin and remained "always your affectionate friend & Godmother, Victoria R & I." In the Durbar Wing corridor remained the marble bust of Duleep Singh by Marochetti and the idealized full-length portrait by Winterhalter, done in 1854, when young Duleep was sixteen.

With Bertie continuing to be a subject of scandal as a result of amours so public that the bedroom doors might just as well have been left open, the embarrassed Alexandra spent much time away from him and even abroad. She had long played her expected public role of consort to the future king, and did so with dignity, although she told her mother-in-law frankly, "It is no pleasure being a Queen." Privately, she had long ceased sharing a bedroom with her husband, who was satisfied that she had provided sufficient heirs. For his other needs he preferred warm, voluptuous women to the cold, gaunt Alix.

Since the Prince of Wales was often away, and usually without her, she determined to intrude into the matrimonial futures of her sons, realizing that something had to be done soon. The managerial Victoria was bound, otherwise, to begin the search, as Eddy would be king after

"The rare, the rather awful visits of Albert Edward, Prince of Wales, to Windsor Castle"—Max Beerbohm, from Things Old and New.

his father, and required a queen. At twenty-seven he had an honorary LL.D. from Cambridge and numerous orders, honors, and titles, but the Duke of Clarence and Avondale—Prince Albert Victor—seemed listless about everything but the sensual life. He had a reputation for taciturnity, but only because he had nothing to say. He could barely read, had inherited deafness from his mother, and had a drooping, vacant face that some women—and perhaps some men—found attractive. Little of his actual life was known to Victoria, but she did know that under the pleasant, gentle manner he affected for her lay almost nothing, and that a woman of character might not be the making of him, but might at least prop him up.

With so many granddaughters in need of husbands, she no longer worried about the hazards of consanguinity, and had ideas of marrying him to one of Alice's daughters. Princess Alix of Hesse, however, the Queen soon explained to Vicky, insisted "that if she is *forced* she will do it," but under no other circumstances would she marry Eddy. It showed "great strength of character," her grandmother confessed, for the girl was refusing "the greatest position there is."

Would-be wives could not have been unaware of Prince Eddy's reputation. Sharing his life would have been a considerable hardship, even for a future Queen of England. He drank heavily and chain-smoked Turkish cigarettes; he was treated for gonorrhea and possibly for syphilis; he had gout, although he was a young man; and an actress claimed that her baby was his. His manly enthusiasms extended from the hunt to the boudoir, and in 1889 may have extended also to a homosexual brothel in Cleveland Street, patronized by Lord Arthur Somerset, manager of the Prince of Wales's stables. Princess Margaret, daughter of the Dowager Empress and sister of Emperor Willy, was Victoria's choice, but was too plain for Eddy, and he quashed the suggestion. Besides, he announced that he wanted as his bride the daughter of the Comte de Paris, a grandson of King Louis-Philippe, and pretender to the French throne. Hélène Louise, nineteen, was a devout Roman Catholic. She was interested, however, in being Queen of England, and as a biographer of Eddy's mother has put it, the languid Prince "fell victim to those members of either sex who encouraged him. For expediency's sake he could put on a good act and give an impression of being in love."

Although Victoria issued a warning that Hélène was constitutionally ineligible, with Alexandra's blessing, Eddy proposed and was accepted. The conspirators arrived at Balmoral on a brilliant August day in 1890 while the Queen was working outdoors as usual on her dispatch boxes, and claimed her attention for their declaration of love. Victoria was enchanted, and assumed that the matter of Hélène's religion would be disposed of—a small price to be Queen. For the Comte the price was too high, and Hélène was ordered home. Flexible as always, Eddy transferred his ardor to Lady Sybil St. Clair Erskine—which Victoria announced would not do. By January 1891, a slightly more distant cousin than Margaret was put on show at Sandringham. Princess May was the daughter of Princess Mary Adelaide, Duchess of Teck, the Queen's first cousin, and sister to the Duke of Cambridge. May was fair, stately, and nearly twenty-four. She had all but given up hope of finding a suitable husband. Eddy was not the prince of her dreams, but he would be king, and her parents were wild with excitement over the possibility. "Fat Mary"— May's mother—was the most popular "royal" in the kingdom. She was everyone's choice, after the Queen, to preside at ritual openings, dedications, and celebrations. For Victoria, however, her jollity was oppressive, and Mary had seldom been a royal guest.

Calling for current photographs, the Queen pronounced Princess May to be as unlike her mother as was possible, which was good, and even more unlike her swarthy father, Francis, Duke of Teck, which was better. In October the tension finally terminated with a summons to Balmoral for May and her brother Adolphus. The eccentric Duke and his Duchess were not invited. (They had been to Balmoral once, in 1868.) Their children took the night train to Aberdeen on November 4, 1891, transferring to Ballater, to visit "Aunt Queen" themselves. Victoria wanted an unhindered inspection, and kept Bertie, Alix, and Eddy away as well.

For Bertie, busy weekends with a new infatuation, his "Darling Daisy" Brooke, the future Countess of Warwick, it was a relief not to have to vegetate among the unheated fireplaces and intermittent snow. He had spent a difficult year, as the Tranby Croft case did not come to trial until early in June. The early months, rife with scandal about Bertie and the ladies, and Bertie and his gambling gentlemen, exasperated the Queen, as did his heir's failed search for a spouse. Eddy's "education and future have been a matter of some considerable anxiety to us, and the difficulty of rousing him is very great," the Prince of Wales explained to his mother. "A good sensible wife with some considerable character is what he needs most, but where is she to be found?"

While the Queen considered the limited alternatives, she went through the motions of being Sovereign. The President of the Local Government Board, Richmond Ritchie, reported to her at Osborne that there were three hundred fewer paupers recorded in London in 1890 than in 1889, although the general distress was still great. (It was likely that death, rather than prosperity, had improved the statistics.) She permitted Sir Arthur Sullivan to dedicate his grand but boring opera *Ivanhoe* to her; it was first performed on January 31, 1891, and forgotten in a few years. She gave an audience at Windsor to the diamond-mining entrepreneur Cecil Rhodes, Prime Minister of the Cape Colony, and listened at length to his prophecies. "He said," the Queen noted in her journal on February 24, "Great Britain was the only country fit to colonize, no other nation succeeded. He hoped in time to see the British rule extend from the Cape to Egypt. He thought everything would be arranged and the difficulties got over." Privately the Queen agreed that other colonial nations had failed to pick up the White Man's Burden, meanly exploiting the natives everywhere the British flag did not fly. Her own cousin, Leopold II of Belgium, who controlled the Congo as a private fiefdom, was the most vicious of the European landlords, with a reputation so notorious that people wondered why she was willing to see him when he came to London.

Two days later, at Portsmouth, she launched a warship, declaring— her only words—"Success to the *Royal Arthur,* " and also christened the *Royal Sovereign,* grateful for the modern device of an electric button that broke the bottles of wine for her. She remembered, in Albert's day, christening the *Marlborough,* "which was rather an unfortunate occasion, as she stuck, would not slide down, and almost heeled over!"

With Salisbury still at Downing Street, and little for the Queen to exercise herself over, she filled her time with domestic pursuits, including theatrical entertainments, Court-generated and professional. Neither mourning nor etiquette entered into the Queen's insistence that plays, musical or otherwise, be brought to her at great expense. Nor were security or privacy concerns involved, as when she wanted to, she would go to see Buffalo Bill or P. T. Barnum in a London hall seating thousands; yet she refused to visit Covent Garden for opera, the Albert Hall for concerts, the Savoy Theatre for Gilbert and Sullivan operetta, or any of the dozens of theaters and recital halls in the West End. The excuse that she would not go as a widow where she had once gone with Albert was hollow and empty. Neither the Savoy nor the Albert Hall had existed in Albert's time, any more than had Earl's Court or the Olympia.*

To suit the Queen's convenience, at Windsor's Waterloo Gallery on March 6, 1891, she and the Household were spectators at a D'Oyly Carte production of *The Gondoliers*. Royalty sat in the first row. A fortnight later the Gallery housed the melodrama *A Pair of Spectacles*, starring actor-manager John Hare.

Often, too, there were concerts and recitals, usually arranged by Signor Paolo Tosti, a popular singer and composer who was *persona gratissima* with the Queen. Her tastes ranged from Tosti's own sentimental songs to Wagnerian arias, and from English singers and instrumentalists like Ben Davies, Kennerley Rumford, Leonard Borwick, and Clara Butt, to such Continental performers as the brothers De Reszke, Emma Albani, Marie Brema, and Francesco Tamagno. The Master of the Household in the 1890s, Edward Pelham-Clinton, would arrange for gifts, honoraria, and special trains from London for the productions, the construction of scenery and preparation of costumes, and supper after the performances. With so many performers egomaniacal or eccentric, the logistic and diplomatic problems were enormous. There were always special needs, and extra attentions had to be paid to oversensitive artists who felt like itinerant musicians unless the Queen treated them like nobility. Then there was Marie Janotha, who placed a device on the piano to keep away the evil eye, and who knelt at the Queen's feet before she played.

When entertainers had to be brought to Balmoral, the investment might have underwritten a major London production, although sometimes less than a dozen gathered in the drawing room after dinner. "I sat by the Queen," Lady Lytton noted in her diary after one private concert, "and her manner to the radiant artists was perfect . . . and each did extra well. Gounod's *Ave Maria* with [violinist Johannes] Wolff and Albani was perfect. Albani received a sapphire bracelet . . . and the gentlemen will each receive something and all their expenses *paid*. The Household supped with the artists and guests and it was very merry." The group, which included young Clara Butt, then twenty-two, and other singers and instrumentalists,

---

*In June 1892, although in mourning for a grandson and a son-in-law, she asked Ponsonby to arrange for her to see "privately" the Olympia extravaganza *Venice*, which included a reproduction of a segment of the Grand Canal. "In the day of course & it is not a theatre or a play & it will be 5 months & ½ after her dear grandson's death & 3½ after her dear son-in-law's & she w^d like very much to see it."

had been on a tour of Scotland, but sometimes they came from London on royal command, and were compensated accordingly.

By 1896 the Queen was also entertained by exhibitions of "cinematographie"—very badly done, Marie Adeane would note. After tea, daily, Victoria continued her Hindustani lessons with the *Munshi*, both spoken and written. Some weeks were varied further by a foreign guest—the Sultan of Zanzibar, the King of Belgium, the German Emperor and his small children (but his annual visits were becoming tiresome to the Queen and exhausting to protocol-harried officials). With the calendar, her abode changed, the Windsor weeks of the schedule normally being reserved for state guests.

At the time of the wedding of a daughter of Princess Helena (Princess Christian of Schleswig-Holstein), at Windsor in July, the Queen was noticed as having adopted something new—or almost new. Lady Monkswell saw her in an open carriage drawn by two horses, and watched men walking by take off their hats as she passed. "She wore a *hat*, the like of which I remember 35 years ago, with a large black & also a white feather in it. So gay for an old lady of 72." Victoria had not put away the Jubilee bonnet and the widow's cap for good, nor even bought new clothes; but she seemed determined—within her limits of discretion—to enjoy what was left of her reign.

On August 19, 1891, the Prince of Wales's private secretary, Sir Francis Knollys, wrote a letter to Sir Henry Ponsonby that arrived while the Queen was entertaining representatives of a visiting French fleet at Osborne. Princess Alexandra, he reported, had suggested to her son Albert Victor that he gain some useful experience by visits to the Continent and the colonies, and that he marry Princess May (given the Queen's approval) in the spring. The Duke of Clarence had agreed only to the marriage. "I think the preliminaries are pretty well settled," Knollys went on, "but do you suppose Princess May will make any resistance? I do not anticipate any real opposition on Prince Eddy's part if he is properly managed."

Eddy had returned from a trip to India in May 1890 looking thin and yellow beneath his doe-like eyes and waxed, turned-up cavalry mustache. His long neck, always encased in high collars, seemed even longer, and more than ever his appearance emphasized his nickname, "Collars-and-Cuffs." Travel did not agree with him, and there were doubts whether marriage would be any help either. After the three days of receptions for French officers and sailors, most of the events—after a sunny morning on the nineteenth—having been slogged through in deluges of rain, the

Queen turned her attention to Prince Eddy. Despite the weather, her Durbar Room had been a success for a grand dinner of the captains of the French warships, and the naval review had proceeded despite the downpour. Pageantry exposed ships and travel at their best, and Victoria may have thought again, in such circumstances, of the Prince of Wales's letter to her about her lethargic, unstable grandson: "The real reason why we thought visits to certain Colonies were desirable was because the voyages would be longer."

The Queen understood. No one had been informing her officially about Prince Eddy's delinquencies, but she understood that marriage to a woman of strict character was urgent. "I ask again *who* it is tells the Queen these things?" Knollys queried Ponsonby in December after Victoria had written to Princess Alexandra about Eddy's "dissipated life." By then, however, the marriage had been arranged. Eddy's betrothal was state business—"for the good of the country," as Knollys put it to Ponsonby. Other state matters were, in her opinion, not as urgent, although death had cost her one of her most dedicated public servants, William Henry Smith. He had refused honors while in her Cabinet. She would ennoble his widow.

The future of the monarchy, Victoria felt—should it somehow survive Bertie—lay in a young woman who could be more guardian than wife for Bertie's heir. She also had to look like a queen. May arrived with her brother just after noon on November 5, 1891. "So improved in looks" was the Queen's verdict to Vicky, who had been skeptical about May. Some people, said the Empress Frederick, thought that May was *"oberflächlich"* —shallow. (Vicky still hoped to sacrifice a daughter as bride for Eddy.) After carriage rides in the hills, amateur theatricals indoors in weather even Victoria found "wet & cheerless," and desperate visits to her aunt Beatrice with her brother "Dolly" to smoke cigarettes out of range of Victoria, May understood that she had survived.

The young Tecks returned with a letter to Princess Mary Adelaide that made marriage all but certain, and on December 3 the Prince of Wales wrote to his mother that Eddy had been instructed to propose, and had agreed. That weekend he was already under the same roof with May, at a country house near Luton Hoo, and there the engagement was agreed upon. The next week all of England knew—unofficially, through the gossip telegraph. Only the weekend after, following a visit to Windsor, was the formal announcement made. They were allotted apartments in

St. James's Palace, and the Queen took the couple into the Mausoleum for the ritual posthumous blessing of the Prince Consort.

Victoria followed up the visit with a letter to May rejoicing at "your becoming My Grandchild" and stressing "how much confidence I have in you, to fill worthily the important position to which you are called by your marriage with Eddy." The Queen's delight went beyond what she could safely explain to May. Victoria needed reassurance as the year ended. Eddy's brother, Prince George, had just come through a bout of typhoid fever, the malady that it was believed had carried off his grandfather and had in fact nearly taken his father; his weight had fallen to nine stone (126 pounds), and during the festivities for Eddy, George had been unable to leave his sickroom. The Queen was aware of how fragile the immediate line of succession was. Bertie's daughters seemed to her even weaker than his sons.

Despite all her children and grandchildren, Victoria harbored qualms about the future of her throne. As the year ended, her concerns were reinforced by a shooting accident and by the Christmas issue of a London paper. In a holiday hunting party, Prince Arthur, the Duke of Connaught, had accidentally shot his brother-in-law, Prince Christian, in the head. Helena's husband had to have his eye removed, under chloroform. In London, *Truth* had published a satirical number based upon Emperor William's last visit, inventing his views of the Prince of Wales's behavior at Tranby Croft, and of Bertie's mistresses and their cooperative husbands. To the Queen's embarrassment, the Prince of Wales was in even more public trouble over his women, Lord Charles Beresford having quarreled with him over their rival interest in the beauteous Daisy Brooke. A pamphlet unsubtly titled *Lady River* made the social rounds with the spicy details, and according to *Truth*, all a London hostess had to do was to announce a reading from it to fill her drawing room. Lord Charles demanded an apology from the Prince for being drawn into the publicity and having his wife insulted thereby. The affair boiled over into a delicious December scandal that overshadowed the news of the Duke of Clarence's betrothal.

Incensed, the Queen took the matter to Lord Salisbury to see what could be done to damp down the gossip. Salisbury showed her a memo from Sir Francis Knollys assuring him that the Princess of Wales "supports the Prince in everything connected with the unfortunate affair, and is anxious to do all in her power to assist him." Warnings of immediate and future social opprobrium from the Court—after all, Bertie would someday be King—ended the crossfire of threats, but spoiled the royal Christmases. It was not even safe for the Prince of Wales to be at Sandringham with his angry but formally loyal wife. Withdrawn as usual to Osborne, the Queen hoped that a showy royal wedding would be a helpful public distraction.

On the last day of 1891, the Queen's nephew, Prince Victor of Hohenlohe, who had long called himself Count Gleichen, died suddenly. Victoria had been fond of him, more so, very possibly, than of her own sons. At his graveside on a cold, blustery January day, Prince Eddy, in attendance and careful now for his grandmother's approbation, apparently developed a cold. He went off on a shooting holiday anyway, returning on the afternoon of January 7, 1892, so ill that he went right to bed.

By then, the Tecks had arrived at Sandringham to celebrate Eddy's twenty-eighth birthday, and to discuss the wedding scheduled for February 27. The next morning, however, Eddy was barely able to totter downstairs to examine his presents. May found herself more nurse than fiancée. A screen was set up in Eddy's bedroom over which houseguests could peer, but only Alexandra and May were permitted at the bedside by Dr. Francis Laking, who quickly sent for Dr. W. H. Broadbent, the attending physician to Prince George during his bout of typhoid.

On January 9, Eddy was declared to be suffering from an inflammation of the lungs. Physicians were shy of using the word *pneumonia.* By the twelfth he was "rather worse," although on the eleventh he had been "going on very satisfactorily." On the thirteenth he was delirious, and the next morning, raving nearly to the end, the heir presumptive to the Throne of England died. It was another fateful fourteenth.

Helena brought Victoria the news. "Poor, poor parents," she wrote in her journal; "poor May to have her whole bright future . . . merely a dream! Poor me, in my old age, to see this young promising life cut short!" Warned not to attend the funeral in the January chill, she put Windsor at the disposal of the bereaved parents, and remained at Osborne.* "Gladly would I have given my life for his," Bertie wrote to her, "as I put no value on mine." At St. George's Chapel on January 20, Princess May placed a bridal wreath of orange blossoms on the coffin.

The romantic pathos of the event captured the nation as the life of

*One of the Prince of Wales's equerries, Major General Sir Arthur Ellis, was surprised at examples of the Queen's parsimony at Windsor. "We all admire various little economical thrifty dodges here," he wrote to Ponsonby. "In the W.C.s—NEWSPAPER squares. . . ."

the flaccid Prince never could have. For the moment, everyone preferred to forget how hopelessly wrong Eddy would have been for the lot to which the accident of birth had destined him. A group of miners' widows from Barnsley, for whom the Queen had initiated a fund to relieve their distress in 1866, following a pit cave-in, sent Victoria a letter in which they remembered with gratitude her interest in them as a widow herself, and wishing "it were in our power, dear Lady, to dry up your tears and comfort you, but that we cannot do." They offered their prayers to her and to Eddy's parents and to Princess May as the Queen's "sorrowing subjects."

Princess May was immediately the subject of intense national speculation. Why should she not marry Eddy's brother, and remain in line for her destiny? George was twenty-six and unmarried. "The dear girl looks like a crushed flower, but is resigned & quiet & gentle—it *does* make one so *sad* for her," the Queen wrote. She had no intention of putting pressure on May or on Prince George, but subtle influences would exist anyway. Alexandra and Bertie continued to regard May as a daughter, and Alexandra asked May to continue to call her *Mama*. Twenty-six years before, Alexandra's own sister, Dagmar, had married the Czarevitch Alexander after his brother, the Czarevitch Nicholas, to whom she had been betrothed, died. She was now the Czarina Marie Feodorovna. There were other such precedents, but a decent mourning interval had to pass.

With Albert Victor no longer a possible king, the Queen discreetly asked George whether he would be willing to assume the name of Albert when he came to the Throne. Prince George asked Ponsonby's advice on how to respond. "He would gladly lay down his life for the Queen," the Private Secretary said, "but if she asked him to call himself Thomas he would certainly refuse." Still, the Queen created George Duke of York, extricated him from the seafaring career he had begun to detest, and established a Household to prepare him for the life that he had never contemplated.

In port the new Duke had not lived austerely, keeping mistresses at Southsea and at St. John's Wood. The London lady had been shared with his brother. He also felt he had an understanding of a more chaste sort with Marie ("Missy"), eldest daughter of his uncle, the Duke of Edinburgh, who was only seventeen. Now, with the pressure building for an arrangement with May, he urged Missy's parents to approve an engagement. The influence of the Russian-born Duchess was clearly apparent when the Edinburghs, without consulting their daughter, rejected the suit. Even Victoria was irritated, despite her preference for Princess May, when in June the betrothal of Marie to Crown Prince Ferdinand of Rumania was announced. The Queen wondered at the preference for the heir to a "very insecure" country to the heir of England. On the positive side, she now took it for granted that May had no further rivals.

Victoria had sent a letter to *The Times* and other newspapers, thanking her people for their messages of sympathy upon Prince Eddy's death, and the reaction was that it had been a courteous thing to do. In general, now, people like the Miners' Widows at Barnsley remembered the old Queen's dignity and kindness rather than her less acceptable earlier behavior, and few knew how she lived her private life, for which in any case they were likely to indulge her. Emily Lytton (later Lutyens), then eighteen and the daughter of Victoria's former Viceroy in India, comforted herself about going with her mother and brother to see the Queen at Windsor that it would save her the discomfort of presentation at a drawing-room. With the indifference only a teenage girl could affect, she wrote an elderly friend, "There is a certain amount of interest in seeing the Queen at Windsor, while there is none in seeing her at a drawing-room. She is the only one of the Royal Family for whom I have any respect. From all I have heard of her, in spite of her age and ugliness, she yet looks and behaves like a queen. . . ."

The Queen's domestic problems (Grand Duke Louis of Hesse, her son-in-law, had also died that spring) had dominated the early months of 1892, but the approaching General Election claimed her attention as the year progressed. When Evelyn Baring, proconsul in Egypt, was created Baron Cromer in June, and wrote his thanks to the Queen for "the personal support I received from Her Majesty in the dark Gladstonian days . . . ," Victoria noted on the back of the letter for instruction to Ponsonby, "The Queen will be glad to support him again in *fresh* dark Gladstonian days." She understood that they were approaching. Ireland remained the issue that made or unmade governments, and early in July the Liberals and their allies prevailed, although without a majority for Home Rule. The Queen realized that she would have "that dangerous old fanatic thrust down her throat," and instructed Ponsonby in arranging for the transition to be firm in keeping extremists out of the Cabinet. In the heat of the campaign she had even found one of Rosebery's speeches "almost communistic." "Independent of the real misfortune for the country & Europe," she told the patient Ponsonby from Balmoral, "the idea of a deluded excited man of 82 trying to govern England & her vast Empire with the miserable democrats under him is quite ludicrous. It is a bad joke!" To her journal she confided her unhappiness that the misrepresentations of election rhetoric had toppled an effective Ministry. "These are trying moments and it seems to me a defect in our famed Constitution, to have to part with an admirable Government like Lord Salisbury's for no question of any importance, or any particular reason, merely on account of the number of votes."

Unwilling to send for Gladstone with any urgency, Victoria stalled until she was back at Osborne. "Her hand is forced," she finally confessed to Ponsonby on July 23, while declaring that the incoming Government would be composed of "greedy place seekers who are republicans at heart." A few days later she still could not make up her mind "to send at once for that dreadful old man (not because she has any personal dislike of him) as she utterly loathes his dangerous politics, the language he has held, the way in which he has used every artifice to get in & whom she can neither respect nor trust." Why, she wanted to know, was no other Liberal a potential Prime Minister? Why not Hartington, Granville, or even Rosebery? But no one else would chance trying to form a Government if the G.O.M. wanted the job.

The change came just as the Queen was preparing for yet another visit from her nephew Willy, who loved to sail at Cowes. To ease the ceremonial burden, Victoria had insisted that the royal holiday be considered private. Willy and Henry were even prevailed upon to live on board their yacht. Salisbury's Government resigned in mid-August, and soon packets steamed back and forth from the mainland, ferrying the new and outgoing Ministers. "I shall never forget my last interview as Minister," Gathorne-Hardy, an old Disraeli stalwart, wrote in his diary. Now elevated to Earl of Cranbrook, he accepted the fact that at seventy-eight he had served in his last Cabinet. "Oh, my dear Lord Cranbrook," said the Queen, "I cannot tell you how sorry I am to lose you or part from you." And she burst into tears and held out her hand, "which kneeling down & feeling much affected I kissed expressing my deep gratitude for all her goodness to me in the long past years."

When she recovered her composure the Queen began to talk of Gladstone, now eighty-three, and "how changed he was in appearance, in conversation & manner, very deaf, and shewing feebleness about the mouth." Gathorne-Hardy assumed some exaggeration, but he knew that the G.O.M. was growing frail. She had refused to accept Labouchère in the new Cabinet, the Queen told Hardy, because he would not give up his scurrilous newspaper; and she claimed that she had a letter from Gladstone claiming that he was unaware of Labouchère's connection with *Truth*. Her daughters, Victoria added, said that she should have the letter framed.

Whether or not there could have been such a Gladstone protestation of innocence, it was not of recent date. Ponsonby's preliminary discussions with Gladstone about his Ministers included talk of Labouchère's unwillingness to give up the £10,000 he claimed to earn annually from *Truth*. "Labby" remained out of the Cabinet, and declared to his followers that he would not be muzzled as the price of office.

While there were many of Gladstone's party whom Victoria preferred without portfolio, there was one she wanted in the Cabinet; yet he was reluctant to serve. The Earl of Rosebery's wife had died, to the Queen's distress as well as his own, and more than a year after, he was still withdrawn into his unhappiness and loneliness. Gladstone was willing to have him again as Foreign Secretary; even the Prince of Wales pressed for Rosebery's return. The Queen was sure—it reinforced her liking for Rosebery—"that he did *not* wish to *throw in his lot with these people*, as if he did so now . . . it would naturally ruin his career." At her request, Bertie wrote to Rosebery as an "old friend" to ask him to serve "for the Queen's sake and for that of our great Empire." It was a rare intrusion into her sphere on the Prince's part, but it was at his mother's prompting, arranged through Ponsonby.

Rosebery gave in. A telegram of acceptance arrived, "which is a great thing," the Queen noted in her journal from Osborne, "but we could not think what made him change his mind." She had forgotten that on July 26—more than two weeks had since passed—she asked for Bertie's intervention. Yet the very involvement of the Prince, at a time when his mother's disenchantment with his sleazy personal life seemed profound, was significant. Sooner rather than later, he would be sitting in her place, and she was accommodating herself, and her future Ministers, to that.

On August 18 she took her final leave of the Tory Ministry, then greeted the new one with more satisfaction than she had first counted upon, as Rosebery was present. The next day "Georgie" came to lunch and to have a talk with the Queen. If May came up in conversation, Victoria left that unreported. The Duke of York was about to leave for Heidelberg to study German. Such proficiency, considered essential for the future king, had not been part of his sailor's education.

What most disturbed the Queen about Gladstone's new Cabinet was the threat of modernity. She already knew that the Secretary of War, Henry Campbell-Bannerman, was determined to reform the Duke of

Cambridge right out of the War Office. The old Duke—he was Victoria's age—feared the appointment of Charles Dilke most of all, and preferred "C.B." But "C.B." soon announced himself in favor of promotion by merit rather than by seniority, and of a reorganization of the Guards battalions. The Queen would resist, largely by delaying tactics, almost every move toward practicality and efficiency, and worked to influence Campbell-Bannerman when he was Minister in Residence at Balmoral. His first experience there, he wrote to his wife on October 22, 1892, was "Siberia! Snow all round." And he reported how the Queen's entourage lamented "the dullness." Dinners were "triste enough, everyone half whispering to their neighbor," he reported two days later. Afternoon tea was "the only bright hour of the day & I think they are all so sick of each other they jump at a stranger."

Like others, he likened life at Balmoral, despite the English band that played Viennese and Hungarian airs in the corridor every evening, to a convent, with each occupant returning after meals to his or her cell. Every inhabitant had "a good fire and five new candles each night." Just as electricity had not come to Balmoral, neither had typewriters, although they had been in use in England since about 1880, and for a very few since 1876. The Queen even complained when typewriters were used and their products inflicted upon her. To the patient Sir Henry Ponsonby, every day growing more frail and white-bearded and stooped in Victoria's service, Rosebery appealed from Whitehall, "The Queen dislikes our typewriting. We swarm with typewriters here, and in every embassy, legation and consulate—or most of them. These ingenious machines are paralysed by the Queen's displeasure. We have consequently set ourselves to mend our ways, and I now send you for submission to Her Majesty a specimen which, to my admiring eyes, is rather the print of a family Bible than the faint scratch of a typewriter. Will she deign to smile on it, and so liberate a fettered industry?"

Every typeface was rejected by the Queen, who required that officials submit all business to her in handwritten form. Interoffice exchanges continued by typewriter, but anything meant for Victoria had to be laboriously recopied. Only after Ponsonby was succeeded by Arthur Bigge did a typewriter become part of the equipment of the Private Secretary's office, and even then it had to be used for messages unseen by the Queen.

Having opened with a death that affected the Queen deeply, 1892 closed with another, that of Lord Tennyson in October. What he meant to Victoria can be seen in Emperor Willy's telegraphing his condolences.

Whatever his ambitions and aberrations, he usually remained attuned to his grandmother's feelings; and Anglo-German relations might have been better in his reign had his own sensitivities been more effectively played upon.

A Poet Laureate had to be named to replace Tennyson; the debate would be lengthy and the results unsatisfactory. The two obvious alternatives were impossible, Swinburne for his private life and public notoriety and William Morris as an outspoken Socialist zealot. At Windsor late in November, Gladstone ("very deaf and aged" to the Queen) raised the subject and recommended the fifth-rate William Watson. Victoria suggested that the appointment be "left in abeyance."

Seldom were subjects of any significance discussed by Gladstone and the Queen. If he had anything of importance to convey, he talked (or wrote) to Ponsonby, and when she had something serious to say to the G.O.M. that she did not put in writing, she had Ponsonby do the talking. Gladstone preserved his list of topics introduced by him or the Queen at that November audience:

1. Inquiry for the Queen's health.
2. The fogs of London & Windsor.
3. The Laureateship. W. Watson.
4. The Dowager Duchess of Sutherland . . .
5. The Roumanian Marriage . . .
6. Lord Acton: not yet personally known to the Queen.
7. Condition of Lady Kimberley.
8. Has Mrs. Gladstone still a nephew who is a master at Eton?
9. Dean Wellesley . . .
10. The Dean of Peterborough.
11. Health of the Bp. of Rochester.
12. Agricultural distress (H.M. seemed half inclined to lay it upon "large importations").
13. Commission thereupon (not desired).

"These," Gladstone noted, "are all or nearly all of the topics of conversation introduced at the audience tonight. From them can be gathered in some degree the terms of confidence between H.M. and her Prime Minister." Most of his audiences were, he thought, "a sham." To her, *he* was a sham. They differed upon almost every point, and the Queen found Gladstone as a person, however devoted others were to him, sanctimonious and repellent. His world was legally and ethically complicated; hers was one of simple values and simple choices. Like "Chinese" Gordon, whom Gladstone considered his opposite, he was God-obsessed and possessed of an original and quirky morality. He was a Tory, Balfour joked, in everything but essentials.

Although most matters now brought to the Queen were unimportant and ceremonial, a Minister she received other than the G.O.M. was likely to find her gaze penetrating and her grasp of issues formidable. Campbell-Bannerman "felt like a little boy talking to his grandmother." Her few contemporaries brought her the most pleasure. Empress Eugénie now lived at Farnborough Hill, having found Chislehurst unbearable after her son's death; Victoria visited her on December 1 with a small group of attendants—eight, excluding servants, with Beatrice (and Liko) inevitably in the party.

The way that Victoria and Eugénie responded to each other, Mary Ponsonby recalled, was "perfect." Each had good reason to be jealous of the other. Even as she aged, Eugénie remained statuesque and beautiful, appearing elegant in any surroundings and in whatever dress. A widow without wealth or status, an exile, with her only son dead, her life was empty of the Queen's success and status and trappings. Yet to the squat, lame, unhandsome Victoria, whom age had treated badly, Eugénie was what an empress in some ideal world might be, and the Queen admired her the more for her quiet courage in adversity. Victoria had taken Eugénie in at the nadir of her fortunes, and against the wishes of her Foreign Office, and continued to treat her as an equal. Their mutual affection was unfeigned and unhidden.

In her journal, the Queen noted that Eugénie was "wonderfully well. The cure at Bath has made her quite active again. If I only could become so too! But unfortunately I cannot stand baths!" Baths meant heat, and for Victoria that was intolerable. Later in the month, when one of her ladies read from the newspapers to the Queen, who, even when her sight had been better, never read the papers herself, one of the accounts she listened to concerned financial scandals in France. "Secretaries and Deputies" in the unstable Republic were involved. "Oh!" she noted in her journal, "if only the dear Prince Imperial were alive, he would be on the throne now, I am convinced."

A positive encounter with modernity occurred on December 3, when the impresario Sir Augustus Harris brought his Covent Garden production of *Carmen* to the Waterloo Gallery at Windsor. The touches of raw realism, muted by the music (which the Queen "knew well") and made exotic by the colorful costumes, failed to offend. Zélie de Lussan, who played Carmen, acted, the Queen thought, "with a *coquetterie* and impudence, accompanied by grace," that was "never vulgar."

At Christmas, Victoria learned, Prince George of Wales sent Princess May a brooch, and May replied on the twenty-eighth, "We can only trust that 1893 will be a happier year for us than 1892." Both signals were clear. When the Queen noted in her journal at Osborne on the last day of 1892, "I can hardly dare to look forward to the New Year," she already knew that there was at least one satisfactory event in store. After tea, she went downstairs in the lift to watch the dress rehearsal of the next Court theatrical.

In another time and place, the Queen's informal impresario of theatricals, Alick Yorke, a groom-in-waiting, might have been described, one of his later relations wrote, as "an elderly pansy, though . . . no breath of scandal ever passed his way." The trials of Oscar Wilde that exposed homosexuality in England even more than did the Cleveland Street affair (much hushed up at high levels), were not to come until 1895. Ten years earlier, Labouchère's Criminal Law Amendment Act, among other strictures, proposed making "gross indecencies" between members of the same sex a punishable offense. When the bill was presented to the Queen for her scrutiny, she allegedly read a provision as implicitly recognizing the existence of such behavior between females. "Women don't do such things," she is reputed to have said; and rather than explain otherwise, her Ministers altered the bill to refer only to males. Another version of the same account has lesbianism excluded because no one was willing to explain it to Victoria. Very likely both stories belong in the same category with George Washington and the cherry tree. The Queen's informal intelligence network, as with Gladstone's very different proclivities, kept her well informed, despite literary and social taboos affecting a variety of sexual "indecencies." Victoria may have been conservative in many social matters, but she had lived too long and was far too inquisitive to have remained an innocent.

However closely the plump, black-mustached Alick Yorke fit the cliché description of the fey 1890s aesthete, brandishing huge blossoms in his buttonhole, large jeweled rings and stickpins, extravagant suits and a cloud of scent about him, the Queen chose not to notice. He was useful, and he was amusing. That others in the Household dreaded each banal theatrical either because they would have to perform in it, or because they would have to watch it, never occurred to her. That her Chamberlain's Office, in her behalf, ran up huge bills to import London artists and productions made the domestic entertainments seem a bargain, but not to the players dragooned into them, from the imperturbable Henry Ponsonby to a "faint hearted" young maid-of-honor, as Marie Adeane described herself when pushed onstage.

The inmates of the royal residences were relieved when the entertainment was furnished by someone else, as with the Covent Garden *Carmen*, or Henry Irving's production of Tennyson's blank-verse *Becket*, which the Queen commanded to Windsor on March 18, 1893. While *Carmen* was somehow passable, Victoria advised Ponsonby that she was "rather alarmed at hearing from the P^{ce} of Wales & P^{ce} George that there is some very strong language (disagreeable & coarse rather) in *Becket* w^h must be somewhat changed for performance *here*. . . . P^{rss} Louise says some *scenes* or perhaps *one* are very *awkward*. . . . The Queen hates anything of that sort." When Ponsonby confessed that he saw nothing "very objectionable," the Queen suggested cutting or modifying "some few things in the scenes between Rosamund & Queen Eleanor & Fitzurse." Perhaps a reference to a "lewd caress" was cut, or Rosamund's reference to promiscuity was too close to certain well-known royal behavior to be described in the presence of her guests:

> *I have heard of such that range from love to love*
> *Like the wild beast—if you can call it love.*
> *I have heard of such—yea, even among those*
> *Who sit on thrones. . . .*

Although the Prince of Wales sat in the audience next to the Queen, Alexandra did not come. The long play lasted until midnight, after which Victoria received Irving and Ellen Terry, "and told them how pleased I was." She would confirm that opinion two years later when, on the morning of July 18, 1895, Irving took the train from Paddington to Windsor to be knighted—the first of his profession so recognized. As Victoria touched the sword to Irving's shoulder, she added "I am so very, very pleased" to the traditional ceremonial words.

Also with the Queen at *Becket*, along with the ubiquitous Beatrice and Liko, was the Empress Frederick, who was spending the spring at Osborne. Seeing her mother now once a year at most, she realized more than those who saw Victoria daily how much she had aged. She hardly walked at all now, and complained that no glasses enabled her to see a printed page, and that people talked too softly. When she drove into Hyde Park from Buckingham Palace on the last day of February, she was pleased at the "immense and most loyal demonstrative crowds," forgetting at first that she had not shown herself in two years.

She had been Queen so long that when scholars attempted to write lives of her late Prime Ministers—and there had now been twelve of them, excluding the seemingly immortal Gladstone—recourse had to be made to the Queen's papers, which she had made available only for a biography of Albert. On February 15, 1893, *The World* reported that Sir Arthur Gordon had been given access to her private library at Buckingham Palace for a book on his father, the fourth Earl of Aberdeen. She was a historical resource herself, but etiquette forbade interviewing her.

The Queen also knew that her hold upon history was often a means of clinging to the shards of power left to the Throne. When Gladstone introduced, along with his Home Rule measures, a minor Welsh Suspensory Bill that the G.O.M. did not "sufficiently explain," she wrote to him that he had "led her to suppose that it was only a Bill for suspending claims founded in vested Church interests in certain districts in Wales, [whereas it] was, as Mr. [H. H.] Asquith [the Home Secretary] admitted, the first step towards the disestablishment and disendowment of the Church of England." She charged that the measure, in reality, was directed "against the whole Church," and she asked Gladstone to "pause before taking so disastrous a step as to attempt to disestablish part of the English Church, of which she is the head; and of which she always thought Mr. Gladstone a loyal member."

The Prime Minister sent her a detailed argument of his own about the "quasi-national claims" of Wales, and then forwarded her letter to Asquith with the derisive comment, "The Queen's studies have not yet carried her out of the delusive belief that she is still by law the 'head' of the Church of England." The Home Secretary introduced the bill, but it was later dropped, and Victoria felt that the act of shelving it was a rare Gladstone recognition of defeat.

Late in March, Victoria went to Florence for her holiday in the sun, but first paid a rare visit to an artist's studio. Alfred Gilbert had been commissioned to sculpt a sarcophagus for the tomb of the Duke of Clarence, and had designed a model (now at the Victoria and Albert Museum) of a sworded, recumbent figure in military dress, an angel above his head bending forward to place upon the Prince's handsome brow an unearned wreath of laurel. Less reverent elements in the press had scoffed at the military funeral for the languid, unmilitary Eddy. Gilbert was adding his own hyperbolic touches, and the Queen was satisfied.

A disciple of J. E. Boehm, and designer of the *Eros* statue in Piccadilly Circus, only just completed, Gilbert was the natural inheritor of royal favor. Boehm, Sculptor in Ordinary to the Queen, had executed much of the memorial statuary to the departed great, from Disraeli to the Duke of Kent, Victoria's father. In his later years Victoria had soured somewhat on his work, possibly because Princess Louise, who had all but separated from her husband, not only studied under Boehm, but seemed to find other kinds of consolation in his company. She had never found that solace with Lorne, whose sexual interests inclined toward handsome guardsmen.

The Jubilee coinage that the Queen had approved after Boehm gave it his imprimatur suddenly lost its appeal, and she had announced to the Chancellor of the Exchequer, George Goschen, in September 1889, that she disliked it "very much" and wanted it replaced. A year later, while shifting heavy busts in his studio in the Fulham Road, Boehm, then fifty-six, collapsed. Princess Louise was with him, and he died in her arms. His last important work was a statue of the Emperor Frederick commissioned by his Empress, to be unveiled on December 15, 1890. Boehm died two days earlier, and in her shock the Queen forgot her differences with him and remembered him as "kind and obliging," and "one of the greatest sculptors of the day."

His protégé, Sir Alfred Gilbert, probably a more sensitive artist, would have problems finishing the Clarence memorial and other commissions, and went bankrupt, fleeing the country in 1901. Eventually he was persuaded back, at seventy-two, in 1926, to complete the last of the saints and angels.

In Florence in 1893, Victoria pursued sculpture of a less cloying sort, going on an orgy of gallery-hopping by pony cart, wheelchair, and— leaning on her walking stick—by foot. Crowds saw her at the Pitti Palace, the Uffizi, Santa Maria Novella, and the Annunziata; but what made her happiest of all was the weather. It was, she wrote to Gladstone on April 12, "splendid, always sunshine and blue sky. . . . They have had snow for six weeks here!" Walburga, Lady Paget, a close friend of the Empress Frederick, saw the Queen, "very tottery on her legs," and walking with a stick. Getting her in and out of her conveyance was a complicated operation. "The Queen generally keeps her own carriage waiting for an hour," Lady Paget noted in her diary. "At last she came out, after an infinity of rugs, shawls, parasols and drawing material had preceded her. Carpeted steps were pushed near the carriage and a grey-headed Highlander on one side and a lemon-turbaned Indian on the other, lifted the old lady into the large landau. The stalwart Highlander closed the door of the carriage after the other ladies had got in, whilst the Indian, with his delicate brown hands, pulled the Queen's gauze veil over her face. In her young and bell-like voice she then called out: 'To the Ponte Vecchio.' She was in black with a round white felt hat."

On May 10, when the Queen was back in London, the news went about that Victoria's veil had fallen off, a rare mishap for her entourage. The occasion was the opening, in state, of the Imperial Institute in South Kensington, another stage in the fulfillment of Albert's dream. Beneath the veil, *The Star* reported, the Queen evidenced a "cheerful healthy countenance," and her subjects "were not lacking in their warmth." One of *The Star*'s team of reporters who had written musical criticism as "Corno di Bassetto" noted that the band played "respectable tunes," not the "low" ones "to which democracy marches when it takes the floor in Hyde Park." Then he went on to unfamiliar material, describing the Queen "in black with jet beads," helped up the steps by her eldest sons. Everyone was affected, he wrote, and even "the *Star* man WEEPS WITH LOYALTY."

The Prince of Wales read the address to the Sovereign, "but without much artistic turn for the platform. He needs a course of practice in Hyde Park under Mr. John Burns's tuition to drive his style home. When he has done, the Queen, [speaking] seated, shows him the proper way to do it. There is not an actress on the English stage who could have done it better—tone, style, all are of the best."* The *Star* man's artistic instincts were half serious—he felt the pity of it all "that so able an artist should be wasted on a throne." The Queen, he noted, "resorts to her spectacles" now and then, and the ceremonies over, including Sir Arthur Sullivan's "new march, not so very new either," Victoria "using her walking-stick a little, is helped down the steps." At ground level "she starts gaily off to shake hands with Indian princes like the Honourable Samuel Slumkey at the Eatanswill election [in Dickens's *Pickwick Papers*]. A wave of bob-

---

*The memory of the occasion remained with Bernard Shaw. Thirty years later he wrote, in a letter to Cecil Lewis (June 24, 1924), "Queen Victoria had a beautiful voice and first rate delivery at an age when she could not have played any part on the stage presentably except the nurse in *Romeo and Juliet.*"

bing, curtsying and salaaming passes down the banks [of spectators] as she flows through them. . . . The band plays the march from [Meyerbeer's] 'Le Prophète.' . . ."

On May 16, at Windsor, the Queen announced at a Privy Council, a week before her seventy-fourth birthday, what almost everyone already knew. Prince George of Wales, heir presumptive after his father, was engaged to Princess Victoria Mary of Teck. Early in February, *The Observer* had telegraphed Sir Henry Ponsonby to ask whether it was true that the engagement would be made public on February 11. He telegraphed back from Osborne, "Thanks for the information I had not heard it before and cannot find out any one in this house who has." A memo from the Queen commented, "Excellent answer. Pray show it the P. of Wales & let the Queen have copies."

The pressure on the young couple was unrelenting. At the Duke of Fife's country house near London—the Duchess was Prince George's sister Louise—Princess May visited on May 2 to see the Fifes' new baby, Princess Maud. "Now, Georgie," said Louise, "don't you think you ought to take May into the garden to look at the frogs in the pond?" George had been on the Continent—after Heidelberg, in Athens and Rome. Beside the pond, he proposed and was accepted. "We telegraphed to all the relations," May remembered.

The afternoon before the wedding, Victoria arrived at Buckingham Palace for a garden party in honor of Prince George and his bride. Five thousand guests had been invited to Marlborough House, where, on the Prince of Wales's spacious lawns, marquees had been erected under which royalties and commoners strolled, and in which refreshments were served. Victoria had her own private tea tent, where guests were received—and quickly dispatched—from five-thirty until a quarter to seven: ambassadors, Indian princes, foreign dignitaries. According to her journal, the Prime Minister and his wife "were brought up to speak to me," but Gladstone may have first tottered in unannounced, as a story that emanated from a Household official was that when the Queen first noticed the old man, she snapped, "Does Mr. Gladstone think it is a public tent?"

The wedding took place in London at the Chapel Royal of St. James's Palace on July 6, 1893, a hot, cloudless day. The crowds reminded the Queen of the Jubilee. Early in the morning, while still in bed at Buckingham Palace, she "heard the distant hum of the people." For the drive to the chapel with Mary of Teck in the new glass State Coach drawn by four "creams," the Queen wore her wedding veil over her usual black, and a small coronet. Through an error in logistics, the Queen's coach took the short route down the Mall and arrived first. There was only one gentleman usher to greet her. Princess Mary Adelaide looked about and saw an empty room to the left of the chapel, and suggested that her cousin wait there. Then she started up the aisle herself toward the altar, with her lady-in-attendance, Miss Thesiger, following. Suddenly Miss Thesiger felt a tug upon her skirt, and a voice announcing, "I am going first." It was the Queen, hurrying along on her stick. For once, Victoria said afterward, "it was very amusing to see everyone else come in." She "could not help remember that I had stood, where May did, fifty-three years ago, and dear Vicky thirty-five years ago, and that the dear ones, who stood where Georgie did, were gone from us!"

The Duke and Duchess of York returned from their honeymoon on July 31, going to Osborne to the Queen. "Very fine day," she began her journal. "Breakfast as usual in the tent." The green-fringed tent, like a large parasol, was the usual location for Victoria's breakfasts and lunches in good weather. The setting hardly differed now from year to year. Turbaned Indian servants would stand impassively on guard, often sharing duties with kilted Highlanders. One or more of the Queen's dogs napped beside her on the grass. One of her daughters, usually Beatrice, but sometimes Helena or Louise, would be in attendance along with a maid-of-honor or lady-in-waiting. Seldom would more than one daughter be present at table. They had never liked each other, and time had not healed their jealousies and rivalries. Often a granddaughter or two—one was almost always visiting—shared the Queen's hospitality, and everyone ate from dishes and utensils that gleamed with gold.

Sometimes she would invite a female guest to share her pony chair and rattle slowly around the grounds. Often they would go into nearby villages, and when she left her own property she would be escorted by a carriage or two from the Household. Outriders would keep a discreet distance. Then it was back to the tent to her red boxes, with a lady-in-waiting to read for her, or a princess, and everyone else but her impassive Indian or Highland attendants would quietly withdraw until summoned. Others "in waiting" waited indoors. Household attendants not on call, and guests, could wander the island, gaze out at the glittering waters of the Solent, or return to their rooms or their resident cottages. One told the time of year by the inclination of the sun or the drop in temperature.

At dinner a band played, and more guests were at table. On the day of the newlyweds' arrival, the Durbar Room was used. It was ablaze with electric light and with the jewels of the women, including Princess May's new necklace of diamonds—a gift from the Queen—and a tiara on her upswept hair. The Prince of Wales wore an admiral's uniform, military dress being popular among the Queen's men, whether earned or honorific.

On August 23 the Queen's second son, Alfred, acquired another wardrobe of uniforms, and the dukedom of Coburg. Although politically emasculated by German unification, Saxe-Coburg-Gotha survived, and the childless Ernest had long designated the Duke of Edinburgh, his eldest nephew but for the ineligible Prince of Wales, as his successor. Victoria marveled that her son "was now the reigning Duke, a foreign sovereign!! My head was full. . . ." There would be battles in Parliament over the continuation of the Duke's annuity, and Victoria telegraphed to Gladstone to have "his friends" oppose "that frightful Mr. Labouchère's motion." Gladstone did.

The G.O.M. was less eager to advance the cause of the Queen's third son, Arthur, but Campbell-Bannerman assured him that the Duke of Connaught, despite his backing from the Queen and her cousin George, still the ostensible chief of the Army, was the best candidate for the command at Aldershot. Victoria looked on the post as a vestibule to the Duke of Cambridge's job. "C.B." hoped to extricate it from the family when he could. To her cousin, the Queen wrote afterward that she was "grateful . . . for not allowing my dear Arthur's just claim to be disregarded to suit other people's whims and fancies." The army remained one of the last bastions of royal influence.

As usual, the Queen went to Balmoral for the autumn months, and it was there that Miss (later Dame) Ethel Smyth, composer, feminist, and lesbian, had an audience. Empress Eugénie was staying at Birkhall, one of the Balmoral houses, at Victoria's invitation, and had the composer as her guest. When, at the stroke of three, the Queen's carriage arrived at the edge of the garden, Miss Smyth, then thirty-five, tweedy and square-jawed, remembered, there were few of the French entourage to be seen. Victoria "had the greatest horror of coming across stray people." But for Eugénie and her attendant, Madame Arcos, and the footmen, "it might have been a deserted house."

It was a stormy afternoon like so many at that season in Scotland. Although the footmen waited until the last moment to unroll the red carpet, it was "sopping wet before the august visitors had time to set foot on it." The Queen had arrived with Princess Louise and Lady Ampthill, and once all were appropriately seated with the Empress, Miss Smyth was beckoned into "the Presence."

Seated on an ordinary cane chair was "a wee little old lady, . . . on her head a close white straw hat, tied under her chin with a black rib-bon. . . . I should have been terrified but for the wonderful, blue, childlike eyes, and the sweetest, most entrancing smile I have ever seen. . . ." The interview was short, made difficult by the rush of the raging wind and rain; yet Ethel was asked to sing over the din. Guessing the Queen's tastes, she tried several German songs. "You ought to hear her sing her Mass," Eugénie then hinted. "Whereupon," Ethel Smyth recalled, "I performed the *Benedictus* and the *Sanctus* after the manner of composers, which means singing the chorus as well as the solo parts, and trumpeting forth orchestral effects as best you can. . . ."

It was "a noisy proceeding in a small room," but the Queen liked it, and suggested that the Empress bring her guest to Balmoral. The com-mand indeed came, and at dinner Miss Smyth said, in her awe, little or nothing at the table, and marched with the others afterward to the drawing room for a few words with the Queen. Unaware of the rules, and seeing her friend Eugénie in the sanctum reserved for Victoria, she stum-bled in uninvited, and was gently led back by Princess Helena. On the tartan hearth rug she then timidly awaited her turn, was reintroduced by Princess Louise, remembered nothing of her exchange with the Queen, and "somehow or other . . . backed away into the obscurity from which I should never have emerged." But then Victoria said, "Now let us hear some more of your Mass." This time there was a grand piano, and seated at it, with the Queen and Empress on her right and left, and groups of royalty and courtiers in the near distance, Ethel Smyth began. When the *Sanctus* seemed a success, she went on to the *Gloria,* and thumped at the keys and pedals as she sang in a manner to make the absence of orchestra and chorus "scarcely missed." Lost momentarily in her music, Miss Smyth had forgotten that she was playing for the Queen. Then she remembered —but applause rang out and she was grateful.

One of the most formidable and intimidating females of her time, Ethel Smyth was awed by the reputation of an unprepossessing lady of seventy-four who knew how to summon up a dignity commensurate with her rank. Quickly and blessedly, departure time came, and after the Queen said a goodnight to Miss Smyth, and a hope "that we shall see you at Windsor," she watched the ritual of leave-taking for the sovereign and the ex-sovereign. While the others stood rigid, "the Queen motioned the

Empress to pass before her; this the Empress gracefully declined to do. Then they curtsied low to each other. The movement of the Queen, crippled though she was, was amazingly easy and dignified; but the Empress, who was then sixty-seven, made such an exquisite sweep down to the floor and up again, all in one gesture, that I can only liken it to a flower bent and released by the wind. Then they passed *together* out of the door, practically shoulder to shoulder; but I believe . . . that on such occasions the visiting Sovereign is permitted to permit the home Sovereign to lag about one inch behind."

Even Balmoral was not a time capsule in which events were frozen, although it seemed there that little ever visibly changed. Well aware of events at home and abroad, the Queen directed a blizzard of telegrams and memoranda to Whitehall on domestic matters and on the increase in tensions abroad, the Empire challenging and in challenge at a dozen colonial borders and frontiers. Again, she wanted the navy strengthened, but Liberal leaders discouraged any thought of increased taxation. Sir William Harcourt wrote to the Queen smugly that an Opposition motion on the navy "is in fact a vote of want of confidence in the Government. This will be easily defeated."

In her name Henry Ponsonby sent a response that she was "sorry that you fear a discussion on the safety of the Empire, and so convert a question which creates anxiety among all parties, I had hoped including yours, into a political dispute." Partisan disputes were, in fact, increasing, as the Tories sensed the numbering of days of Gladstone's Government, and probed for weak spots. When it came to political sensitivities, however, no one had a longer memory than the G.O.M., or held a political grudge longer. As a result, early in the new year of 1894, when the Queen proposed to raise the Marquess of Lansdowne a step in the peerage on his retirement as Viceroy of India, Gladstone, vindictive to his Opposition, ungraciously demurred, despite the precedents for the honor. "Politics never have had to do with such a thing before," the Queen exploded, but Gladstone was already in Biarritz, having taken leave on medical grounds. He responded on January 17 from his refuge on the Bay of Biscay with a long letter, encyclopedic in its detail, in which he found two distant exceptions from the general practice, in the Ministries of Peel and Palmerston. The Sovereign, he conceded, was the "fountain of honour," but the Viceroy was responsible for administrative acts, and it was "also true that the Sovereign is the fountain of law"—and responsible to it.

Although Gladstone would not budge on his Government's powers, he observed that the Queen would soon be getting new leadership. His Ministry had been limping along without him anyway, and even when he returned, he seemed in no condition to carry on. To Ponsonby on February 14, 1894, he confided that his sight was failing, and had even deteriorated during his holiday abroad. Ten days later he announced his resignation and retirement from politics on grounds of failing health. He was annoyed that even his Secretary for India, the Earl of Kimberley, had disapproved of his obduracy about Lansdowne, and that his own party accepted "mad" naval budget estimates more in the direction that the Queen wanted than as he had recommended. Although eager to see him go at last, Victoria was perturbed that the news was all over London before it reached her at Osborne.

In Gladstone's absence, more than the Lansdowne matter had disturbed her, and not all of the problems could be blamed upon the G.O.M. An anarchist attempt to blow up the Greenwich Observatory had failed, and the French tailor who was to place the bomb, Martial Bourdin, had blown himself up instead; but his funeral became an opportunity that the Queen deplored for a demonstration by sympathetic groups on the Left. Gladstone had pressed for the appointment as Canon of Westminster of Basil Wilberforce, son of the famous bishop who had known Victoria as a child; but Wilberforce was an outspoken advocate of total abstinence from alcoholic drink, which the Queen found "an impossibility," and she did not want the Abbey pulpit to be used to preach impractical doctrine. And both Bertie and Emperor Willy were soliciting her, directly and indirectly, for something for which she was unarguably the fount of honor, additional honorific military titles that included new fancy dress. Bertie had been offered a colonelcy in Willy's Dragoon Guards, and was expected in turn to lobby his mother for an army rank for the Emperor, who, Bertie argued, "should he [now] attend a Review, would . . . be obliged to mount a horse in Admiral's garb." Suffering since early December from pain in her legs, and even more immobile than usual, the Queen had little tolerance for trivial vanities. To Ponsonby she called it "fishing for uniforms" and "a hateful business," and labeled Willy "a spoiled child." It took relentless pressure, but by the end of April, when she was to go to Coburg to see Alfred installed as reigning Duke, and could not help but meet Willy as Emperor, she gave in. The Emperor William became honorary colonel-in-chief of the First Royals, and could wear the traditional red coat he so much wanted. The Queen was impatient with his arrested adolescence.

On the evening of February 28, Gladstone, eighty-four, came to Windsor to discuss the transition. His hooded eyes and beaky nose under a nearly bare skull, and his gaunt face, the flesh now fallen away, gave him the appearance of an aged eagle. Hobbling in, frail and trembling, he first remained standing, despite the Queen's entreaties, but she "made him sit down." Victoria considered the deference feigned and absurd. After four Ministries, their cordial dislike of each other had hardened into mutual detestation. Gladstone had served in Parliament for sixty-one years, since Victoria was a princess still uncertain of her prospects. Refusing to pretend in a pretty speech, she told him only that she had received his letter and was sorry "for the cause of his resignation" rather than for his exit from the Government. Both had altered much over the years, going through most of Shakespeare's Seven Ages, but neither could see much of the evidence, as both suffered from failing vision, and Gladstone muttered something about his blindness having "greatly increased since he had been at Biarritz." Then, the Queen recorded, "he talked of some of the honours for his friends, but not many," and was ushered out.

Unlike Victoria, Cabinet members the next day were choked with tears when Gladstone formally announced his decision. Unwilling to seem moved, he privately called his Ministers "blubbering," and went on to the Commons to make what few realized was his final speech, as it was a caustic attack upon the House of Lords rather than a recognizable valedictory. Then he went to Downing Street to begin packing his belongings.

On March 2, the Queen invited the Gladstones to Windsor for dinner and to spend the night, more perhaps because it was the appropriate thing to do than because she wanted to see "the people's William" again. One can imagine that few words were spoken. The next morning Mrs. Gladstone asked to see the Queen after their separate breakfasts. "She was very much upset, poor thing," Victoria wrote, "and asked to be allowed to speak, as her husband 'could not speak.' This was to say, which she did with many tears, that whatever his errors might have been, 'his devotion to your Majesty and the Crown are very great.' She repeated this twice, and begged me to allow her to tell him that I believed it, which I did; for I am convinced it is the case, though at times his actions might have made it difficult to believe. She spoke of former days, and how long she had known me and dearest Albert. I kissed her when she left."

That afternoon, after a brief Privy Council session with the Queen, and before leaving Windsor, Gladstone wrote a letter of formal resignation, attributing his retirement to increasing deafness and encroaching cataracts. "His desire to make this surrender [of office] is accompanied," he assured her, "with a grateful sense of the condescending kindnesses which Your Majesty has graciously shown him on so many occasions during the various periods for which he has had the honour to serve Your Majesty." Then he placed it in a red dispatch box and carried it himself to his last audience. He may have permitted himself the thought that now the Queen might finally show some emotion. While she glanced, unseeing, at his letter, he observed that it was painful to depart, but that it was best for the Empire that there should be someone at the head of Government "who could look into everything, and attend to and watch over it all." His colleagues, he promised, would "act loyally" under any Prime Minister she might choose.

Ignoring, as usual, serious business with him, the Queen discussed the competence of their oculists (she had been unable to secure spectacles that worked for her), thanked him for helping to continue Affie's annuity as Duke of Coburg, and added a final gracious word about Mrs. Gladstone, whom she sincerely admired. He waited for something further about his remarkable periods of stewardship as Prime Minister, but there was nothing. "He then kissed my hand," she wrote, "and left."

A brief note from Victoria the same day accepted the resignation and wished him "peace & quiet with his excellent & devoted wife in health & happiness." Only "a kind and generous farewell from Ponsonby," Gladstone said ruefully, filled for him "the place of a farewell from my Sovereign." To the Archbishop of Canterbury, Victoria was unsentimental about her Prime Minister's departure. "Mr. Gladstone has gone out," she said with a laugh, "disappeared all in a moment. His last two Ministries have been failures. Indeed, his last three. Mr. Gladstone takes up one or two things—and then nothing else interests him. He cares nothing for foreign affairs, which are always essential to England. . . . He will not attend to any suggestions but his own mind's. He does not care what you say. . . . It makes no difference. He only says 'Is that so? Really?' "

Gladstone's own assessment went into a secret memorandum he left among his papers, recalling a ride on muleback in Sicily in 1838. "The beast was wholly inaccessible to notes of kindness by voice or hand," but "its undemonstrative unsympathetic service was not inefficiently performed. . . . I had been on the back of the beast for many scores of hours, [and] it had done me no wrong; it had rendered me much valuable service, but . . . I could not get up the smallest shred of feeling for the brute, I could neither love it nor like it. . . . What that Sicilian mule was to me, I have been to the Queen. . . ."

The old adversaries met only once more, at Cannes on March 22, 1897. Gladstone, now eighty-eight, found the seventy-eight-year-old Queen "decidedly kind, such as I had not seen for a good while before my final resignation; and she gave me her hand . . . , which had never happened with me during all my life." After a few minutes' exchange of generalities, they parted for the last time. Later in the year, when Gladstone died, the Queen's epitaph in her journal was gentle. "Heard at breakfast time," she wrote at Windsor on May 19, 1898, "that poor Mr. Gladstone, who had been hopelessly ill for some time and had suffered severely, had passed away quite peacefully this morning at five. He was very clever and full of ideas for the advancement of the country, always most loyal to me personally, and ready to do anything for the Royal Family; but alas! I am sure involuntarily, he did at times a good deal of harm. He had a wonderful power of speaking and carrying the masses with him."

In a letter to the Empress Frederick, the Queen expressed herself more strongly, refusing to agree with newspaper obituaries—or Vicky— that Gladstone was "a great Englishman." He was "clever," she admitted, but he "set class against class," and "never tried to keep up the honour and prestige of Gt. Britain." And she would not forgive his abandoning Gordon and his giving away the Transvaal or that he "destroyed the Irish Guards." As for his personal relations with her, she was willing to be more charitable, and carried that feeling over into a handwritten, nearly illegible note to Catherine Gladstone expressing her sympathy. "No wife was ever so devoted as you were," she concluded, "and the loss of the one object of your life is irreparable."

A telegram to Mrs. Gladstone from Balmoral followed on May 28, the day of the funeral at Westminster Abbey. "My thoughts are much with you today," it began, "when your dear husband is laid to rest." She instructed that the text appear as part of the *Court Circular,* but it was printed by *The Times* on May 31 in an adjacent column. In it Victoria acknowledged Gladstone as "one of the most distinguished statesmen of my reign. I shall ever gratefully remember his devotion and zeal in all that concerned my personal welfare and that of my family." As always, Victoria was scrupulously accurate. She could not say the same thing about his politics.

At the Abbey, the Prince of Wales and the Duke of York, both future kings, acted as honorary pallbearers, and after the oaken coffin was lowered, each kissed Catherine Gladstone's hand. The Queen reacted with unconcealed irritation. She would make no false claims about the relationship, and rejected what looked to her like a stagey suggestion that it had been better than it was. Victoria remained unforgiving, even in the finality of the grave.

XVIII

Metamorphosis

(1894~1897)

At Buckingham Palace on March 5, 1894, the Earl of Rosebery kissed hands as Prime Minister. The Queen was delighted with his Cabinet, and by Rosebery's proposing an immediate increase in the navy budget. The G.O.M.'s son Herbert was to be First Commissioner of Works—a safe enough post, whatever its suggestion that the baneful influence of "the people's William" persisted. Even Rosebery's continuing H. H. Asquith as Home Secretary did not disturb her, although she often found Asquith's energy misapplied, and his new marriage a mistake. In a facetious postscript to a memo to the Private Secretary in February, Asquith had noted his forthcoming marriage to the very model of a modern miss, the flamboyant Margot Tennant. Then he added, "Have I to ask the Queen's consent?" "How curious," she minuted to Ponsonby, *"that* he sh^d ask if my consent is required to his marriage.

If this *was* required the Queen w^d not give it as she thinks she is most unfit for a C. Minister's wife."

"Unteachable and splendid," Asquith would describe the ambitious Margot. Victoria might have cited her as the example of what was wrong with education for women, a practice the Queen considered as pernicious as the campaign to give them the vote. Overeducation remained a preoccupation of the Queen. She told the historian James Bryce, now in Rosebery's Cabinet and responsible for education, that it was crucial to have people realize "that to be labourers and house-servants was as good and necessary as being clerks, and that the duty of supporting and helping their parents ought to be inculcated into the children's minds, not merely educating them for *themselves.*" Democracy bewildered the Queen. It interfered with her hopes to hand down to posterity the system that had worked so well for her class. That the system had not worked very well for others was outside her concerns. The new mobility that enabled many to escape the predestination of class and birth was to her a discouragingly disintegrating thread in the national fabric.

With the new Ministry in place, Victoria went off on her spring holiday to Florence, arriving just in time to learn from home of the defeat of the Government by two votes on an anti–House of Lords motion, adroitly brought to a vote by Henry Labouchère while many Members were absent from the House. The embarrassment was reversed, but it left the Queen feeling—not altogether unhappily—that Rosebery would not be in office very long. He was no better than Gladstone, she realized when she read Rosebery's words on the debate. The Peers, he contended, "represent nothing" because "they are not deputed or chosen by any interest, body, or class to represent them. It may be true, as your Majesty says, that they often represent the true feeling of the country . . . but that can scarcely be the case at present, when the country has chosen a Liberal House of Commons to represent it, while nine-tenths of the House of Lords are opposed to that party."

The Queen preferred most things to remain as they were, and recognized only with reluctance that the world moved. Had she been able, she might have arrested all change in the year of the Crystal Palace. Yet even that realization of Albert's dream was itself the symbol of accelerated change in every aspect of life. The paradox of change within the illusion of Old World stability was to be dramatized in Coburg in April, where she went from Florence to see Affie as reigning Duke. A sentimental throwback to the days of Albert and Ernest, Coburg appeared little different except that a railway cut helpfully through the pocket principality. The "dear old Festung" remained, and the picturesque Schloss Ehrenburg; also the gingerbread houses. Yet Coburg was an anachronism—a picture postcard with political direction from Berlin.

Change appeared all about the Queen. When she returned, and stopped at Manchester en route to Balmoral, some things only *looked* the same. At Albert Square, where the Lord Mayor presented an Address, there was "a statue of dearest Albert under a canopy, in the style of Sir W. Scott's monument in Edinburgh and like the Hyde Park one [of the Prince]." The new emerged when she steamed to the Mode Wheel Docks in her waiting yacht, and declared the new canal and docks open "by opening the large lock with an electric wire attached to hydraulic machinery," which in turn automatically caused a salute to be fired. All the events at which she was a presiding symbol were now somehow linked to a force called electricity, which, when she was young, was familiar only as a mysterious and unstable phenomenon in the stormy sky. Even the steam locomotive had been unknown when she was born, and what had been an unruly iron beast when she was a child had transformed Britain, and had even made possible the distant poles of her hideaways at Osborne and Balmoral, a seclusion from which she had belatedly emerged.

Now past seventy-five, Victoria could look ahead with confidence to a material prosperity for her Empire that seemed without end; she could also see continuity for her royal line into the fourth generation. On June 23, 1894, slightly less than a year after the Duke and Duchess of York were married, a son was born to them. Destined to be a king, he was, in the Queen's journal, a "fine, strong-looking child," and she recorded no disappointment that Edward Albert Christian George Andrew Patrick David did not include *Victor* among his names.* "What joy! What a blessing!" she wrote. In the country that elation was eclipsed by an explosion at the Albion Colliery, Cilfynydd, Wales, which entombed 260 men and boys. The next day brought another distraction, the assassination of Sadi Carnot, president of France. In the Commons on June 25, Sir William Harcourt moved a vote of condolence with the French people; three days later he moved an address of congratulation to the Queen on the birth of the royal infant.

*The Prince preferred *David*, but while King, until his abdication to marry the American divorcée he loved, he called himself Edward VIII.

On the first occasion, Keir Hardie, once a miner himself, asked whether the House would also offer sympathy to the relatives of victims of the mine disaster. "Oh, no," said Sir William. "I can dispose of that now by saying that the House does sympathize with these poor people."

Hardie attempted anyway to add a miners' sympathy amendment, but was ruled out of order. When the congratulatory motion came up on the twenty-eighth, he spoke against it, "in the interests," he explained, "of the dignity of the House, and in protest against the Leader of the House of Commons declining to take official cognisance of the terrible colliery accident in South Wales." Shouted down for allegedly having made a vulgar attack on the Queen, Hardie was deserted by the membership, including his few Labour colleagues. The incident gave him a reputation as an extremist that would dog him for decades, and it demonstrated the sentimental affection for Victoria that now withstood even the smug obtuseness of those who represented her Government.

On returning to Windsor the Queen received two young Europeans whose fates were to change the world far more than would the new baby. The heir to the Austro-Hungarian throne, Archduke Francis Ferdinand, thirty years later, on June 28, 1914, would be the victim at Sarajevo of a solitary anarchist. The chief adversaries in the war his death precipitated, bringing down what was left of Victoria's world, were to be her grandsons George and Willy.

On that sunny, cloudless day in early summer, the Czarevitch Nicholas was also visiting, with his bride-to-be, Princess Alix of Hesse, the Queen's grandchild. His angular features and black spade beard made "Nicky" a mirror image of the royal infant's father, Prince George. In Siberian captivity in 1918, Nicholas and his Czarina were murdered along with their children by Communist revolutionaries whose ascendancy the Great War had made possible.

At Aldershot, where the Queen took Nicholas by train on July 11 to see how British military preparedness was accomplished, she was saddened by memories of Albert. "The whole place was so much a creation of my darling husband . . . that every spot seems to be full of memories." She took a turn around the grounds in her low-slung pony chair that went with her everywhere, an extension of her increasingly useless legs, and found the plantings Albert had planned, rhododendrons and evergreens, "wonderfully . . . high and thick."

Victoria was back at Windsor on July 13 to vent her feelings to the Earl of Rosebery about legislation she felt was needed, and legislation she could do without. With its reputation for civil liberties, England—London in particular—had long been a haven for European revolutionaries. Since the Greenwich Observatory outrage, which had killed only its perpetrator, Victoria had been pressing for restrictions upon the ability of "these monstrous anarchists and assassins to live here and hatch their horrible plots in our country." The Liberal position, Rosebery explained, was of "police supervision" without abrogating "our ancient position as regards asylum."

The Queen also saw the wrong kind of progress in the rise in inheritance taxes. The new Death Rates, she argued, would affect the stability of property, with a father unable to transmit land to a son. It was "wrong in principle and will have such disastrous effects." Rosebery admitted that he was "himself inclined to take a somewhat gloomy view of its effects on the class to which he himself belongs." Yet he saw its necessity, and suggested averting the "severer effects" of the law by transferring property in one's lifetime, and "by greater simplicity in living." Neither suggestion appeased the Queen.

As the future ruler of Imperial Russia left with his bride, who had made the grandest match of any of the Queen's grandchildren, it seemed appropriate that foreign affairs should become Victoria's major preoccupation in the closing months of 1894. Japan had designs upon Chinese ports not already occupied by European trading powers, and the Queen wanted pressure put on Tokyo. There were tensions between France and Belgium over the future of the Congo, and with Germany as well, which did not want the British to acquire territory that might link Cairo with the Cape, as was Cecil Rhodes's dream. Further, the Boers in the Transvaal had denied a political role to "alien" white residents, largely English, and these had petitioned the Queen for assistance. Unhelpfully, Emperor William had written to her proudly of a new increase in his army, the better, he explained, to inhibit any threat from Russia, where the dying Czar was unable to control events. "Alicky," Victoria now knew, would soon be Czarina.

Even in the Household, major change was afoot. Sir John Cowell, Master of the Household, died suddenly in August. Victoria was "thunderstruck." Lord Edward Pelham-Clinton was asked to replace him, but he pleaded poor health. She asked him to try the job out for six months, and he remained into the next reign. A Household official, however, paid dearly for his perquisites. The Queen, although aware that Ponsonby was failing, persistently badgered him about what she called his small handwriting and pale ink. Her sight was weakening badly, Sir Henry realized. Since he knew that she would not accept that fact, he laboriously furnished larger and larger copy in the darkest ink he could find. Nothing worked, while her own handwriting was also deteriorating. "I must make some coup d'etat to get away," the exasperated Ponsonby wrote to his wife from dreary Balmoral.

Since the Liberal majority was still planning to weaken the powers of the Lords, the Queen sent for her Minister-in-Residence, Henry Campbell-Bannerman, to lecture him on the "subversive" character of the change. She took the proposals personally. It was "cruel," she complained, "that after all her long reign at her age, with her many cares," she should have to oppose a principle more appropriate to a "President" than to her. Exercised about the fate of the Lords, she called "C.B." to an audience at the late hour of seven o'clock on November 7, 1894. However unusual that occasion, her journal says little about it other than that after tea she had "some conversation . . . on the vexed question of the House of Lords." In Campbell-Bannerman's lengthy notes are Victoria's observations that the Commons was now "too strong," that it included "shocking people . . . who would sweep everything away," and that "all the better classes" were alarmed. She would not concede that the challenge to the hereditary principle, and to her conservative view of politics, was coming from a majority of people rather than from a noisy rabble of "Irish Members" and "destructives."

On January 1, 1895, Edward Hamilton predicted in his diary that the new year was "pretty certain to see a change of Government . . . about half-way—probably on some unforeseen contingency." The first change, however, came in the Household. In January 1894, responding to rumors about his health, Ponsonby had written a jocular note to Spencer Ponsonby-Fane, a cousin who worked in the Lord Chamberlain's Office: "I immediately sent to inquire after myself and the answer was Never was better." At sixty-nine he had perceptibly slowed down, and caused the Queen anxiety when, even with her faded vision, she perceived changes in his handwriting that suggested trouble ahead. On January 7, 1895, the stroke she saw coming occurred. His right arm and leg were paralyzed, and his speech impaired. He lay listlessly in his cottage at Osborne, and the Queen, in a businesslike memorandum, divided his duties between Colonel Arthur Bigge (Private Secretary) and Sir Fleetwood Edwards (Privy Purse).

Rosebery's government was some solace to Victoria, as it meant less attention to Irish Home Rule and to reform of the Lords. At Windsor in February, Sir Mountstuart Grant Duff, a retired colonial administrator and diplomat, saw little change in the Queen except for her increasing immobility. He did not realize how little she was able to see through the veil of her cataracts, and how she made up for it in other ways. "After dinner the usual circle is formed," he wrote on February 26, 1895, ". . . The Queen is prevented by her lameness from moving more than she can help, and her guests are led up to her while she remains seated; but I do not remember seeing her so animated, and her voice struck me as unusually strong."

In March the Prime Minister became ill, and was incapacitated for two months. The Queen slowed Government business still more by going on her usual spring holiday, this time to the Riviera, where she and a huge entourage stayed at the modest and misnamed Grand Hotel in Cimiez, a mile northeast of Nice, where there had long been an English colony. One of her Household officials, in advance of the trip, showed her a list of the Indian, English, and Scots attendants she planned to take, and a list of the Royal Princesses and their suites accompanying her, and asked, in the interests of economy, whether any could be dispensed with. Victoria insisted that she needed every one, even though many had nothing whatever to do.

After Aix-les-Bains, the Queen had gone in successive springs to Florence, Biarritz, Grasse, and Hyères, but had not found a site in which to settle down. Her experience of Aix-les-Bains had been a happy one, and she had purchased land in the vicinity on which to build a country house. Haute-Savoie combined the Alpine qualities of Balmoral with the mild atmosphere of Osborne. Before having the first stone laid, Victoria wanted to have the authorities make some changes in the roads, to preserve her privacy. She was prepared to pay liberally for the work, but when local landowners objected, the Queen sold the property.

When she left for good, it was with a souvenir. On one of her carriage drives—she usually took two daily, before and after lunch—she saw, on the edge of the Lac de Bourget, a farmer approaching slowly in a cart drawn by a gaunt white donkey. She stopped her carriage and asked if the donkey was for sale. He had paid a hundred francs* for him, said the farmer—"and he was cheap at the price."

"I will give you two hundred," she offered. "Will you take it?"

*A little more than £3—or $15 at the time.

Suspicious of foreigners, the farmer hesitated, then agreed. "You can buy two donkeys with that," Victoria assured him, while an attendant counted out the notes. Jaquot pulled her cart thereafter on Riviera holidays, as well as at Osborne, where he was shipped with her pony chair and furniture.

The Grand Hotel at Cimiez was rented for the Queen complete, for five weeks, at a cost of fifty thousand francs. The economic benefits to the area in having the Queen and her suite spend her francs impelled the authorities to improve the roads. Victoria shipped her favorite items to supplement the hotel's less sumptuous furnishings. For her own table, her own linen and plates and utensils went everywhere, as well as English bacon and sausages, which, with fried fish and eggs, were at every royal breakfast.

Meals and carriage drives were the highlights of her days abroad. A French chef, M. Ferry, and his staff prepared most dinners, each with her favorite soup, *crème de volaille* (she also liked her chicken soup clear and jellied); and she usually had her Indian cook prepare an additional dish. Except for visiting village fairs and religious festivals, she preferred her drives to be in the direction of lonely places away from the towns. Unless the rain daunted Jaquot, she would merely put up her umbrella and have the donkey plod along as if the sun were shining, the royal entourage following in loyal misery.

The telegraph ensured that she was never out of touch with London, and she knew when she returned that it was to battle once more in behalf of her cousin George. Writing to her in early May, the Duke of Cambridge explained to her what she already knew—that if he did not retire voluntarily, he would be forced out. Colonel Bigge was deputed to explore the alternatives with the War Office, and found that there was no longer any way that the old Duke could keep his seat warm for Prince Arthur —that the Duke of Connaught might have a chance at the top job five years hence, but only after "some other General has held it for a term." To Bigge, whom she knighted on May 24, her birthday honors occasion, the Queen confided that "tho' it had been the dream of her life" to see her son succeed the Duke of Cambridge, she "would not now press it." Nevertheless, she wanted to retain the power of appointment to prevent the office from becoming a "Parliamentary" one.

Rosebery reassured her that there was still a chance for the nearly egg-bald Arthur, and Victoria agreed to the "sacrifice." The Duke, however, refused to be dislodged, pointing to his thirty-nine years as Commander-in-Chief and his robust health. At that point, Campbell-

Bannerman lost patience, and Bigge had to report to the Queen that further delay would create embarrassment for everyone. From Balmoral she telegraphed, with her usual acute intelligence about goings-on at Whitehall, "It is most urgent that the arrangements about C.-in-C. should be complied with forthwith, as I hear a Ministerial crisis is expected at the end of this month. Mr. C.-B. *must* settle it. Think Duke wrong not to have retired some years ago, and that it is undignified to cling to office. End of October or beginning of November should be the term."

The Duke's mulishness persisted into June, as he was determined to extract whatever he could get in honors and emoluments as the price of his exit. There was no way he could be unseated by the Government, he insisted: he had a Royal Warrant as his "security." Also, he wanted a pension, which the Queen, in a memo to Bigge, called "preposterous." He already had £14,000 a year from public funds, plus a house free of rent and taxes. In the end the Duke was ejected, and "C.B." paid him a fulsomely insincere tribute in the Commons. Still, the episode became an excuse for the Opposition to topple the Government. Returning from Balmoral to Windsor on June 21, Victoria heard with surprise when her train stopped at Carlisle that the Government had been defeated on the matter "of George's retirement. Did not quite see that this would cause a crisis."

The crisis arose from something far more trivial. Rosebery's Ministry had been defeated on a motion to reduce the salary of the Secretary of State for War by £100, in effect condemning Campbell-Bannerman for permitting the army's supply of small-arms ammunition to run short. With the heirs of Gladstone split between Rosebery and Sir William Harcourt, Chancellor of the Exchequer, Liberal majorities had been dwindling. Harcourt, an imperious six-feet-four, was a Plantagenet by birth, yet leader in the Commons because of Rosebery's earldom. At sixty-eight he had seen his last opportunity to be Prime Minister vanish when Rosebery was named. Sir William picked up the pieces as chairman of the post-election Party. With many Members absent for the snap vote, the Government lost by seven votes—"a *chance* blow," Harcourt wrote to Rosebery without disappointment, "but in my opinion a fatal one."

From Windsor the Queen telegraphed Rosebery that if he resigned, she would not accept the decision. It was a strange turnabout, as Rosebery's Liberals were largely Gladstone's appointees. For the first time as Queen she was beginning to understand that even a Prime Minister she liked need not share her views. Two weeks later, the Reverend Randall

Davidson, then Bishop of Rochester, and an old friend, dined two evenings with Victoria and came away after "a good bit of talk" with the impression that the Queen was "not specially happy at the change in government. In her heart I think she *personally* likes Rosebery, Bannerman, Spencer and Fowler better than their successors." On the evening of June 22, Rosebery tendered his resignation, telling the Queen that it was "an immense relief to give up his office."

The formalities of beginning Lord Salisbury's third Ministry were hurried, as Victoria was expecting a state guest. The Shahzada (Prince) Nasrulla Khan of Afghanistan arrived laden with "a splendid casket" containing a letter from his father, the Ameer, and "forty fine shawls and eight hundred rugs." As a mark of her favor, the Queen showed him the Mausoleum. After that, she retreated to Osborne, where she enjoyed her outdoor breakfasts under the striped tent, and summoned up her reserves of patience for Emperor Willy's annual summer visit. That meant dinners in the Durbar Room, with elaborately insincere toasts by the Queen and the Emperor, and concerts by the string band of the Royal Marine Artillery and the German band of Willy's Marines. One of the Emperor's party—he enjoyed having members of his entourage indulge in adolescent behavior—was "Uncle Hermann" Salzmann, a painter of sea scenes, who sang loudly, each time the Queen's entrance required it, *"Gott seefe der Queenchen ein."* "God Soap the Little Queen" amused his master. Did Victoria know? She never seemed to lack informants.

With relief when the Emperor again left Cowes, the Queen returned to her beloved tent. Hunched over her red boxes, she attempted to read the increasingly indistinct correspondence.

By October, at Balmoral, the Queen was having the hymns sung in her private Sunday chapel services, Lady Lytton noted in her diary, "written out very large for her, and [even] then [she] uses a magnifying glass." Empress Eugénie was visiting, from the house nearby that Victoria had made available to her and her suite. Lady Lytton noted that Victoria always called Eugénie *"ma chere soeur."*

Always with the Queen was a cluster of fidgety princesses—daughters and granddaughters eager to do more than go to church or lunch, or to help read what even Victoria's double glasses could not clarify. At one dinner, on October 16, at which Prince Henry of Battenberg was at the Queen's side, she complained, in a Scots accent she fell into at Balmoral, "I *a* do*a*nt know why the candles give no*a* light now, it is so *daark.*"

Since the Queen resisted cataract surgery, a gamble that could cost her what sight she had, Sir James Reid had consulted Professor Hermann Pagenstecher of Wiesbaden, whom the Queen considered "one of the greatest oculists in Europe." On August 24, he had traveled to Osborne to examine her. Pagenstecher, fifty-one, had been an ophthalmic surgeon at the London Eye Hospital from 1872 to 1880, and was author of the *Atlas of the Pathological Anatomy of the Eyeball.* In 1889 he had successfully treated Princess Helena, whose guest he now was on his English visits. Unable, despite his large reputation, to persuade the Queen to chance his knife, Pagenstecher prescribed belladonna to temporarily dilate the pupils and disperse the film.

In November the Queen and her entourage learned of trouble for the Government in the Ashanti country, where King Prempeh of Kumasi was raiding the Gold Coast for slaves. The Ashanti wars of the 1870s had largely pacified the foreshore, where the British had been trading for two centuries. There, also, General Garnet Wolseley had made his reputation and his fortune (through a grant of £20,000 from a grateful Parliament). The Imperial sway, however, did not extend very far inland from Accra. Wolseley, now Lord Wolseley and Commander-in-Chief in place of the Duke of Cambridge (the Queen had preferred Sir Redvers Buller, who had fought in Natal), was sending a new expedition into the turbulent Ashanti bush.

Bored with his life as an elevated gentleman-in-waiting, Liko— Prince Henry of Battenberg—craved escape from his women's world, where his chief accomplishments had been to father Princess Beatrice's Alexander, Ena, Leopold, and Maurice, and to persuade the Queen to permit smoking rooms at Balmoral and Osborne, where there was little else for him to do. On November 17, the Queen wrote, Liko told her "that he seriously wishes to go on the Ashanti expedition, and I told him it would never do."

Realizing that he might have no further opportunity to break free, he went directly to Wolseley and Lansdowne at the War Office, and was provisionally accepted. Then he returned to Beatrice, and to the Queen. He was a soldier, he insisted. His brothers had been trained to be soldiers, and while his three brothers had been on active service, that had been denied him. The Queen sent Dr. Reid to talk him out of it, emphasizing the unhealthy climate of equatorial west Africa, but Liko insisted that although the climate "no doubt was bad . . . with care he might be able to avoid fever, and the campaign was likely to be short." Victoria let him go.

"Took tea with Beatrice and Liko," Victoria wrote on December 6, at Windsor, "and directly afterwards he came to wish me good-bye, and was much upset, knelt down and kissed my hand and I embraced him. He said he went, not out of a wish for adventure, but because he felt it was right." Beatrice came in "sadly," and then they left together for Aldershot, the staging point for the party. "I could think of little else but this sad parting. God grant that dear Liko may be brought back safe to us!" Perhaps she should have added to her prayer Butcher, his manservant, who in immemorial tradition went with his master.

It was a period of partings. On November 21, Henry Ponsonby died, and five days later he was buried at Osborne. The Queen did not attend the funeral, but a month later she went to Whippingham churchyard to place a wreath on the grave. Beatrice, now without Liko, was with her. Prince Henry had just landed in Africa.

Victoria had waited to return to the Isle of Wight until her Albertine ritual of mid-December had passed. "I ended the day as I had begun it," she wrote on December 14, 1895, "by going to the dear sacred Blue room." It was her thirty-fourth marking of the "terrible anniversary," but this time, at least, there was a compensatory event. In her dressing room that morning she found telegrams informing her that a second son had been born to the Duke and Duchess of York. "Georgie's first feeling was regret that this dear child should be born on such a sad day. I have a feeling it may be a blessing for the dear little boy, and may be looked upon as a gift from God!" There was no question but that her great-grandson would be named Albert, though he would choose, thirty-nine years later, to be called George VI.

On December 27, Liko joined the main column of the British force marching inland toward Kumasi. The heat was intense, and men collapsed as the column moved north. At the same time, far to the southeast, on the frontier of the Transvaal Republic, technically under the suzerainty of the Queen, but ruled by Boer settlers claiming allegiance only to President Paul Kruger, a motley military force had gathered under a mild-looking physician, Dr. Leander Starr Jameson. He had abandoned medicine to administer Cecil Rhodes's eponymous fiefdom to the north —also technically under Victoria's suzerainty. Rhodesia, however, did not have a seemingly endless reef of gold, as existed beneath the Witwatersrand, on the western edge of Kruger's boomtown of Johannesburg. Rhodes's hardly covert aim, expressed personally to the Queen, who had made him a Privy Councillor, was to reincorporate into the Empire the landlocked highlands, rich in gold and diamonds, and to protect his investments there, and those of his financier friends. As Prime Minister of the Cape Colony, he could not stage the strike as an official act, but he would accept in the Queen's name a new regime of British-led opportunists and adventurers. The *Uitlanders* had exploited the land and transformed the indigent pastoral state, but the Afrikaans-speaking population was no more interested in giving political rights to outsiders than they were in granting civil rights to the black tribes whose land they had taken and whom both white populations regarded as little more than beasts of burden.

Messages streamed back and forth between London, Cape Town, and Johannesburg. The incursion was postponed, canceled, rescheduled. On December 29, Jameson's men crossed the unmarked border, and on New Year's Day 1896, they were almost within sight of the mounds of gold tailings. In "Jo'burg," however, no rising had materialized. On the morning of January 2, 1896, surrounded and out of ammunition, the frustrated raiders ran up their white flag at Doornkop, northwest of the city. Embarrassed, the Cape Prime Minister had to resign, claiming that Jameson had "ruined" him. Less chagrined was the cocky new Poet Laureate, Alfred Austin, whom Salisbury had pressed upon the Queen on December 22 for her list of New Year honors. In jingling rhyme he produced a spirited boast that reflected the public mood more than the Queen's umbrage. It was intended as a "rescue," not a "raid," he claimed, and if it was "wrong," he was not "scared by a scolding name," or by "points of law":

> *When men of our own blood pray us*
> *To ride to their kinfolk's aid,*
> *Not Heaven itself shall stay us. . . .*

Victoria was not amused; nor was she pleased by the fact that her High Commissioner at the Cape, Sir Hercules Robinson, had to plead for the captives' release. Even more exasperating was Emperor Willy's telegram of congratulations to Kruger. The Prince of Wales pressed the Queen to condemn the message from Berlin as an unfriendly act, and Beatrice read to her a flurry of anti-German telegrams and messages. ("My sight is so bad," Victoria dictated to her daughter, "and I have not yet succeeded in getting spectacles to suit.") The "affair" in the Transvaal was at best "very unfortunate," but she heard "satisfactory accounts" from elsewhere in Africa, largely from the newspapers. In the Gold Coast, so Beatrice read to her, "the native Chiefs . . . were greatly excited and surprised when Sir Francis [Scott] introduced Liko, 'who had married the Queen's daughter.' . . . The papers also say that Liko has been made Military Secretary to the General." It was curious that Victoria's information had to come from the London press.

With Dr. Jameson in prison in Johannesburg, the Queen wrote to her errant grandson in Berlin as "your Grandmother to whom you have always shown so much affection and of whose example you have always spoken with so much respect," that his "unfriendly" letter, "which I feel sure it is not intended to be," had left "a very painful impression here." From the Foreign Ministry in Berlin, Georg Count von Münster wrote to Count Holstein on January 13 in a letter marked "very confidential and private" that "our Kaiser" only "saw the surface of things" and sent his telegram "without realizing in advance that it was a match to set fire to an accumulation of inflammatory material." German assistance had indeed been wooed by Kruger, and given the state of English imperialistic feeling, even war was not beyond possibility, with Germany drawn in. "The Queen and the men in control," Münster assured Holstein, "are too level-headed for that," but if a firebrand should catch public attention, "then the nation in its present temper would follow him." Already, he thought, the English Admiralty had been provided with pretexts to further strengthen the fleet, but he thought that "this was done less against us than against America, for the conflict can break out at any moment."

If there were not enough colonial brushfires in Africa and Asia at the moment for the British, there was another in South America, a boundary dispute between Venezuela and British Guiana, about which President Grover Cleveland had threatened to invoke the Monroe Doctrine and involve the United States militarily on Venezuela's side. "So much to do," the Queen wrote in her journal, "and my troublesome eyes make everything much more difficult."

As army chief, Viscount Wolseley warned Victoria that it was important to extricate Jameson's men from Boer detention, as there were "excellent officers with them, . . . [and] they would be a loss to your Majesty's army. Sooner or later the Transvaal must be an English province." Everything, he added, was going well for the Ashanti force. "I find that the newspapers receive earlier and better news than we do. . . . I had a good account of the voyage to the Gold Coast, and of how much Prince Henry had done. . . ." The general expected his troops to be in Kumasi in a few days.

The release of the Jameson party to British authority, on the expectation of their punishment, came quickly. The Queen wrote to Kruger—a message prepared by Joseph Chamberlain, the Colonial Secretary—that his generous act would "conduce to the peace of South Africa." Rumor had it that while in England eleven years before on a Boer mission, the burly, spade-bearded "Oom Paul" Kruger had been invited to tea with the Queen. Unversed in etiquette, or deliberately rebellious, Kruger, then fifty-two, allegedly had refused on presentation to bow to the Sovereign, as he bowed only to God. Further, he had poured his coffee into his saucer to cool it, forcing her Majesty, so as not to embarrass him, to follow suit. In fact, nothing of the sort had happened, as he had never met the Queen. Yet there was a Boer belligerence that Kruger personified. In that very year of 1885, when there was a scarcity of flour and a British duty had been imposed upon imported Australian flour, raising the price of everyone's staple, Kruger said, *"Ja, as julle wil Ourna se brood eet, dan moet julle daar voor betaal!"*—"Yes, if you want to eat Grandma's bread, then you must pay for it!"

With her long memory, the Queen went back to the year before Kruger's visit and suggested that her Prime Minister determine Britain's actual legal rights in the Transvaal, especially since the German Ambassador had questioned her suzerainty. If his "Law Officers . . . consider Convention of 1884 did not invalidate preamble of 1881," she telegraphed to Salisbury from Osborne, "you will stoutly maintain that position. . . ." Salisbury was forced to reply that the Earl of Derby, Gladstone's Colonial Secretary, "almost surrenders the position" in a letter to Kruger. Suzerainty in any case meant little more than a scrap of paper recognizing the Queen.

On January 10, the day of Victoria's exchange with Salisbury, a telegram to Princess Beatrice from General Scott arrived: "Prince Henry is suffering from fever, slight, but sufficient to prevent going on to the front." Victoria telegraphed for further news, and found that Butcher had remained with Liko. He and a medical officer were taking the Prince to a hospital ship, the HMS *Blonde.* To the Prince of Wales, in an exchange on Emperor Willy's "impetuousness" and "conceit," the Queen added the news of Liko's malaria, which had caused him to "venture . . . back to the ship this morning. It is a terrible disappointment for him, but we heard this morning that the fever is declining, so perhaps he may yet go back. It is a terrible trial for darling Beatrice. . . ."

Reassuring telegrams followed. Liko had "slept well, has taken nourishment this morning, symptoms show great improvement, is able to undertake journey." Later in the day came another telegram. The Prince had reached Manso, just inland from the port of Sekondi. "This has given great joy to dear Beatrice," Victoria wrote in her journal, "who has been in such cruel suspense." A few days later, the party arrived at the military hospital at the Cape Coast. "Have been very ill," read a telegram over the Prince's name, "but thanks to the unceasing care of Dr. Hilliard and Butcher, I have safely arrived here."

In reality, Liko was so low that the *Blonde* weighed anchor immediately for Madeira. Offshore of Sierra Leone, on the evening of January 20, Liko died. On January 22 the telegram that Victoria and Beatrice anxiously awaited, and that they expected would bring news of the Prince's safe arrival in Madeira, brought instead word of his death. Arthur carried the dreaded message to the Queen's dressing room door before she had arisen for the day. Beatrice followed him in. "The life has gone out of me," she said, her voice trembling. At thirty-eight, she was now widowed even earlier than her mother had been; and she would be a widow even longer—fifty years.

To Victoria also it was a "terrible blow." She did not know whether she could even commit the fact to paper. "What will become of my poor child?" she wondered. The answer to that, something that perhaps she could not yet confess even to herself, was that she would have her "Baby" back. "There is such grief in the house. . . . Went over to Beatrice's room and sat a little while with her; she is . . . so piteous in her misery. What have we not all lost in beloved, noble Liko, who has died in his wish to serve his country! He was our help, the bright sunshine of our home. My heart aches for my darling child. . . . It seems as though the years '61 and '62 had returned. . . ."

On February 3, 1896, Prince Henry's body, preserved in rum in a makeshift tank constructed from biscuit tins, arrived in Portsmouth on the HMS *Blenheim* and was transferred to a more seemly coffin. Unable to go to Madeira to be with her husband for his convalescence, Beatrice went instead to Portsmouth to accompany his remains. The crossing to the Isle of Wight was made on the *Alberta*, and the next afternoon Victoria was at the pier with Beatrice's children and a party of attendants. When the Queen saw Beatrice on board, she was "entirely veiled in black, standing at the head of the coffin." The scene was "terribly affecting and pathetic, on a beautiful evening all lit up by a glorious setting sun. I was completely overcome when I placed my wreath."

Liko was buried at Whippingham Church the next day. The Queen summoned Sir Alfred Gilbert to design a memorial, and sent a letter to the papers to thank "my people" for their expressions of sympathy and sorrow. Liko had been Governor of the Isle of Wight, and of Carisbrooke Castle. Victoria transferred the largely honorific titles to his widow.

On February 13, Beatrice left with her children for Cimiez, where Victor Cazalet had offered his Villa Liserb. (Cazalet had business interests in Brasil—as its citizens spelled it—and his Riviera hideaway roughly suggested that, backwards.) She "hoped to have more courage to go on" when they met again, she told her mother. The Duchess of Teck, in a letter from Osborne on February 9—she had gone there for the funeral —reported that Princess Louise had *"froissé"* (hurt)* the bereaved Beatrice "terribly by calmly announcing, that *she* (Louise) was Liko's *confidante* & Beatrice nothing to him, indicating by a *shrug* of the *shoulders!"* How much of a euphemism the term *confidante* was can only be guessed. Louise's frustrations had long been less than secret, especially since Boehm's death in 1890. Almost certainly the outburst did not occur in Victoria's presence, but there was little that went on in her Household that could be kept from her. There were too many witnesses. The Queen felt as alone as she had ever been.

A bust of Liko was commissioned by Victoria for a niche at Frogmore, and her world went on much as before, punctuated by regular visits to the friendly ghosts from her past who peopled the "dear Mausoleum." Ascending the dozen stone steps had long been difficult for the Queen, but at the top the doors opened into her still, special world. From the entrance one could see, recumbent high upon the massive sarcophagus of Aberdeen granite, Marochetti's marble effigy of Albert, under which his body had rested since 1868. The unfilled space at his side, Victoria consoled herself each time, was her own. The Prince Consort would rest at her right hand through all eternity.

Despite the black winged angels at the base of the block, the effect upon the Queen was cheerful. The mosaic floor of the central octagon was bright and colorful, as were the stained-glass windows, trompe-l'oeil mo-

---

*The Duchess wrote *"frisséd"*—either in excitement or in bad French.

saic walls, and the brilliant gold stars on the domed blue ceiling. Many of those closest to her in life were now there, at least symbolically. Some were actually buried beneath the green lawn to the rear. In a smaller mausoleum across the stream were the remains of her mother, and an upright marble statue so lifelike that the lace on the Duchess's gown seemed almost real. At the base Victoria had placed, with an extremity of feeling that had surfaced only after her mother's death, the avowal, "Her children rise up and call her blessed." Between the two structures was a monument to the Queen's good friend Augusta Bruce Stanley.

Inside the larger tomb Victoria would revisit not only Albert, but the daughter who had cared for him in his last days, Alice. In the wing to the left was Boehm's reclining marble figure of the princess, with her child, also dead of diphtheria, in her arms. Then there were busts of Alice's husband, Grand Duke Louis, and the newest one, of Liko. The Queen could move on to a bust of her son Leopold, and a standing group by William Theed of Albert and herself in purported Anglo-Saxon costume, the Prince's knees exposed, as in kilts. Finally, in the ambulatory to her right, was a standing, heroic statue of the tragic Emperor Frederick, her son-in-law, in military garb, with Iron Cross at his neck, Garter on his chest, and sword in hand.

His German decoration and aspect mirrored the ambience of the mausoleum. Above the many biblical quotations in English, and discreetly placed above eye level, were others in German. With only one exception, everyone interred or remembered under the starry dome was German, or married to a German. Even the structure itself was Coburg-inspired, and designed, in Albert's lifetime, by his artistic adviser, Ludwig Gruner of Dresden.

To another sensibility the effigies and epigraphs might have been pathetic reminders of past sorrows; to Victoria her family lived again as she, with her aides, and almost always with Beatrice, now a mourner herself, paused at each monument in turn and renewed old associations, the sculptor's work responding to her touch when her eyes no longer perceived the nuances of form. Perhaps she also reached low for a bronze tablet on a wall in the right wing, the only memorial not family in the mausoleum and erected at her instructions and with her own inscription, in 1883. "In loving and grateful remembrance," it read, "of John Brown the faithful and devoted personal attendant and friend of Queen Victoria whom he constantly accompanied here. These words are insribed by Her whom he served so devotedly for thirty-three years."

In the half-light below an ornamental urn the sentiments would have been difficult to read, even by a visitor whose sight was more acute than the Queen's. Victoria may never have realized that a word in the inscription was misspelled. That her stubby fingers could feel down far enough to recognize John Brown's name in the bosom of her family was enough. That her surviving family knew of the flaw in the lettering seems certain, and that it was never corrected suggests their silent small revenge upon the despised gillie. Unaware, Victoria would leave Frogmore renewed in spirit, ready to confront whatever lay ahead for another day.

With the family once again plunged into mourning and turmoil, there was at least an excuse to defer the annual visit of Emperor Willy, who looked forward to the summer regatta at Cowes. The real cause, which no one needed to spell out, was the Kruger telegram. Although Victoria had accepted Willy's explanation that he had meant no offense, he was not invited again until 1899. On Sunday, February 23, Bishop Davidson came from his new seat at Winchester to preach in the Chapel at Windsor, and made his sermon on the subject of how to accept sorrow. Prince Henry's death was only indirectly referred to, yet it was the reason for summoning Davidson. Victoria told Lady Lytton that she was disappointed. Not everyone saw Liko's death as a national loss, although to the Queen he had been the chief masculine presence. That role now fell to the balding, heavy-mustached Arthur Bigge, although he was only Household.

With Beatrice away, other family members kept the Queen company, which meant a more elaborate table and, once the prescribed month of mourning had passed, the reappearance of a band at formal dinners. On one occasion old Sir Lyndoch Gardiner, who was Senior Equerry, but over eighty and failing in memory, forgot to summon the band. He would have to resign, he lamented. It was past five, and Windsor had, at the Queen's insistence, remained without telephones. Ordering a groom to gallop to Windsor Great Park, Frederick (Fritz) Ponsonby, Sir Henry's son, now Bigge's assistant, sent a message to the Second Life Guards to rush some sort of band, which required rounding up men who were off duty in town. Yet there was no way to get them to the terrace once dinner had been served. Ponsonby arranged for ladders from the castle fire brigade, so that the band members could scale them and be in their places without disrupting Victoria's dinner. When she arrived at 8:45, late as usual, on the arm of an Indian attendant, there was still no band and no "God Save the Queen."

Ponsonby recalled his certainty that he had failed. "The despondent look on General Gardiner's face made me wretched. But as I sat down I saw through the window dark figures climbing onto the small terrace, and before the Queen had a mouthful of soup the band struck up an overture. . . . But of course the Queen noticed the absence of the National Anthem—she always noticed everything." The next day the old general received a crisp note that the band was to play the National Anthem whenever she came in to dinner.

Whether it was a result of pressure from Ponsonby or because she wanted news sooner than it could come by telegram, Victoria had telephones installed at Windsor in the summer of 1896, with private lines to the post office and railway station in town, and to Marlborough House and Buckingham Palace in London. It would become easier to summon a band.

Late in March, she went off to the Riviera with her hundred attendants, again nearly filling the Grand, in Cimiez. As usual, Victoria brought her own bed, bedclothes, and bedchamber servants; her own carriage, coachmen, and outriders; her wheelchair, with kilted and turbaned attendants to propel her about; her mobile hospital, with doctors, dentists, oculists, nurses, and medical equipment (yet Sir James Reid, who examined her every morning at nine-thirty, would not see her other than fully clothed until her very last illness).

Beatrice, who had been staying nearby, "in patient resignation," rejoined her mother, further swelling the entourage, and doubling the sadness. Despite the sunny weather, the Queen wrote to Lord Salisbury, "A heavy cloud overhangs our poor house everywhere." Soon Salisbury— who owned a villa nearby in Beaulieu—was himself in Cimiez, consulting with the Queen and snatching some sun for himself. Thereafter in person and later by letter and telegram, Victoria belabored him and Joseph Chamberlain with advice about sticking to their Imperial guns in Africa and elsewhere. For Chamberlain it was not unwelcome interference; he sensed that the Queen was attuned to the national mood, and his own.

The Queen's mail was not all official, in the familiar red boxes. With two secretaries to read and dispatch her correspondence, she first went through her boxes, then turned to the family mail and the bundles of letters from supplicants. When she was in France, these took a Gallic turn. After handling the usual governmental mail, her responses sent by telegram, in code, she had her secretaries, usually ladies-in-waiting, separate the obsequious, crafty, silly, and blatantly begging letters from the few she intended to take seriously. There were requests from French correspondents for English postage stamps, or for her autograph. One asked that she pay a boy's fees at a Bordeaux grammar school. Another, from Lorraine, asked for a bicycle. Some offered to sell her things, including a red, white, and blue cat; others begged for items of clothing. Often, correspondents sent the objects they intended to sell to the Queen, asking for money or the return of the merchandise. Many letters came from self-styled inventors, who wanted the Queen's assistance or patronage for perfecting contrivances that seemed more fiction than science, and another batch regularly came from poets who had work they wished to dedicate to the Queen, or for which they wanted a fee. One Frenchman wanted "an order for . . . first-class champagne" for his verses; another threatened suicide "if Your Majesty does not lend an ear to my entreaty." Then there were the authentic madmen. One *Comte* wanted her assistance to "replace" him on the throne of Egypt; another, from Oran, in Algeria, and addressed to "Madam and Dear Mother," asked her "to give a little thought to me, your son, whom you abandoned in India." Such letters were seldom answered, but they brightened French holidays for her bored staff, otherwise faced with visions of unexciting dinners and dull donkey-cart excursions.

When Victoria returned early in May, the presence of the mourning Beatrice kept the Household in gloom, and on May 27 the gloom was transferred overnight to Balmoral. Back in waiting, Marie Adeane—now Marie Mallet, as she had married Arthur Balfour's secretary, Bernard Mallet—recalled spending the first three hours north from Windsor, as the train jolted along, reading the newspapers to the Queen, with "dressers and pages tumbling in and out opening and shutting windows, changing capes and caps," and carrying in, to cool the saloon car, "a huge foot-bath full of ice."

The month of June opened Victoria's sixtieth year on the throne, and papers wondered about a celebration in 1897, and what such a Jubilee might be called. Some also speculated—even hoped—that the Queen might use the occasion to retire in favor of her son. Courtiers were careful to keep that delicate matter from her ears; it was no problem to keep such things from her eyes. After the first Sunday service at Balmoral, at which the Reverend Cameron Lees preached on widowhood, and the Queen "cried a great deal" (although she had commanded the subject), Marie Mallet wrote to her husband that the evening before she had read—"slightly bowdlerized"—a *Spectator* article on the Queen to Her Majesty.

Reacting to the piece, Victoria confided to Marie that she "always *disliked* politics and does not consider them a woman's province but that the Prince Consort forced her to take an interest in them even to her disgust, and that since he died she has tried to keep up the interest for his sake. This is very touching."

It was untrue. There had been occasions when she resented the intrusion of politics, but her activism had not been generated by loyalty to Albert's shade. The article, the Queen concluded to Marie, was "sensible and loyal, but the *Spectator* has often been the reverse and at one time I never allowed it to come into my room."

On September 23, 1896, the Queen had reigned longer, by one day, than any other English sovereign. She had wanted no celebration until she completed sixty years the following June, but congratulatory messages arrived from everywhere in the Empire. Largely through the initiative of Joseph Chamberlain, the idea began to take shape that the 1897 Jubilee should be a celebration of Imperial Britain. Restricting foreign guests to Colonial heads and representatives, rather than kings and emperors and princes, eased the problems of protocol, and eliminated those of housing Crowned Heads. It also seemed to foreclose any ceremonial burdens beyond the aged Queen's capacities, and appealed to the expansionist and self-congratulatory mood of her subjects. Months of searching for a name for the event that would capture imaginations came up only with flat or impossible tags, until Bigge suggested "Diamond Jubilee." Across his note, in blue chalk, the Queen wrote "Appd V R I."

Apart from spontaneous and premature celebrations of the Jubilee, the major events of the fading year were a visit from the young Czar and his Czarina—Victoria worried about their possible assassination by anarchists—and the victories of Bertie's horse *Persimmon* at Newmarket and at the Derby. To Lady Lytton, Victoria confided that she didn't like the Derby win—such successes only encouraged gambling by others, "and the Prince Consort was so against it. . . . But it makes the Prince [of Wales] happy and is perhaps a better excitement than others." There was no need to spell out what the "others" were.

For the Court, Marie Mallet mourned, there was no excitement— only "intense monotony." From dreary Balmoral she wrote that there seemed "a curious charm to our beloved Sovereign in doing the same thing on the same day year after year." Possibly the most sensational event in Marie's cycle of waiting was the annual visit to Crathie Church on November 5 "to wreathe the tombs of the various Browns; H. M. got out of her [pony] chair and laid a bunch of fresh flowers on John Brown's grave with her own hands. The Prince Consort [at Frogmore] and the Highland tenants share this unique honour; it is really very curious. . . ."

In Scotland, a foretaste of the twentieth century arrived in the person of a Mr. Downey, who photographed the Queen and her family, she wrote in her journal, "by the new cinematograph process, which makes moving pictures by winding off a reel of films. We were walking up and down, and the children jumping about." When Christmas came, the Queen, faithful to her calendar, was back at Osborne, where Salisbury visited to discuss candidates for New Year's honors. She approved a peerage for Sir Joseph Lister, to whom she may have owed her life in 1871, but it was difficult to look back, for she only saw, closer at hand, the loss of Liko. It was better to look toward the new Jubilee.

The official celebration, suggested by her son Arthur as 1897 began, was to be "an open-air *Te Deum* in front of St. Paul's." The Queen, immobile and half blind, would sit in her carriage while whatever happened went on about her. With the first anniversary of Prince Henry's death approaching, the Court withheld plans from the Queen until a discreet interval had passed, but as the date drew near, heads of state of other countries began asking permission to attend, or to send "congratulatory Embassies," and it became necessary to decide on a format. For Victoria, Sir Arthur Bigge wrote to the Prime Minister formally asking that sovereigns be discouraged on grounds of the unavailability of appropriate hospitality on the Queen's part. The Chief Rabbi asked Lord Salisbury about a common time for public services of Thanksgiving, and Bigge suggested Sunday, June 20. The Queen scrawled a note under a memo. "Quite approve. 11 should be the hour."

The chief problem in making the Jubilee, except for the extravaganza before St. Paul's, an Imperial celebration, Lord George Hamilton (Secretary for India) pointed out to the Queen, was that many of "the best native Chiefs" would find it difficult to leave their lands. The Empire was extensive, but it was not quiet. Nor was the rest of the world placid, with further war in the Balkans again threatening, and unrest elsewhere. The Queen registered her anxieties, even intervening through her Minister in Copenhagen to the King of Denmark, attempting to persuade his son, who ruled Greece, not to challenge Turkey over the island of Crete. Victoria was taking what was, in England, an unpopular side, but a pragmatic one. In April, Greece invaded—and lost.

Almost as important to the Queen as the Jubilee, and world affairs, was the welfare of her *Munshi* and his friends. For several years there had been continual skirmishing between the Queen and the Court over perquisites for Abdul Karim, from places at dinner to places in government. At one point Fritz Ponsonby wrote to the Viceroy in India, "I have now got to think it lucky that the *Munshi*'s sweeper does not dine with us." In the early months of 1895 she had pressed Salisbury for a diplomatic post in Turkey for the *Munshi*'s friend Rafiüddin Ahmed, and the campaign continued into 1897. In December 1892, the turbaned and bearded Ahmed, who claimed to be a barrister and had since insinuated himself further into the Court, was described in a headnote to an article he had published in *The Strand* as "an eminent Indian scholar." That he had published the contribution at all owed to the good offices of the *Munshi*, who had furnished him, thanks to the Queen's assistance, with copies she had made of two pages from her diary where, under the *Munshi*'s tutelage, she had written her entries in both Hindustani and English.

"The Queen's Hindustani Diary" was a revelation strangely entrusted to the fawning Ahmed, who could have sold the proprietor of *The Strand*, Sir George Newnes, for his issue that included the Sherlock Holmes adventure "Silver Blaze," anything in which the Queen had a hand. The facsimiles of journal leaves—all that suggest the real thing,

A page from the Queen's diary, in Hindustani and English, on January 14, 1892, the day of the death of Prince Eddy, the Duke of Clarence. Strand Magazine, *December 1894.*

since Beatrice's pyre—were padded out with photographs of Ahmed and the increasingly plump *Munshi,* a signed photograph of the Queen, presented to the author at Christmas 1891, and the most cloying paragraphs of praise that had ever been printed about her in an English magazine.

Although the piece also suggested that Ahmed had been honored by conversations in Constantinople with the Sultan of Turkey, and was a potential emissary from the Queen to any number of Moslem potentates, her Ministers considered Ahmed at best a seller of whatever secrets he would extract. Finally, Salisbury disposed of Ahmed by asserting that he would "gladly employ him if a suitable opportunity occurred. But he . . . has unfortunately met with indications of the [racial] prejudice that exists in your Majesty's services. . . ." By claiming her views, and his impotence, he thought he had got himself off the hook.

On March 11, 1897, the Queen left once more for the Riviera, taking a slow train (it stopped for her meals) south, and halting at Paris for a visit to her saloon car by François-Félix Faure, the President of France. In Cimiez she had the Duke of Cambridge for lunch, and then the Emperor of Austria, whom she pleased by asking him to call her, familiarly, *Du.* This time her huge entourage lodged at a large new hotel that had been built in front of the Grand, shutting off its view of the sea. It was the Excelsior, which in her honor became the Excelsior Regina, although so many dukes and princes populated the Riviera that Salisbury joked that one had a choice between royalty in the winter and mosquitoes in the summer.

The *Munshi* was on the Queen's list to make the trip, which meant that he would be dining with the Household. He was not on the train. Ponsonby, Bigge, Reid, and others talked Harriet Phipps, senior maid-of-honor and the Queen's personal secretary, into asking Victoria to drop Abdul Karim from the travel roster. The Queen's rage was unlike anything since Albert's day. She swept everything atop her desk onto the floor, and declared that nothing would keep her *Munshi—Le Munchy* to the French press—from France. Gently intervening, Salisbury, who claimed to know France because he kept a holiday villa there, persuaded her that the French were "odd" and might misunderstand the *Munshi*'s position. To avoid any chance that they might be rude to him, he came separately, and immediately invited Rafiüddin Ahmed to join him. That was too much for the Household. Without asking the Queen, Bigge and Ponsonby sent Ahmed packing, giving him forty-eight hours to go. From Cimiez they bombarded Indian officials with telegrams seeking hostile information on *Le Munchy* and on Rafiüddin Ahmed, hoping to find that both could be labeled security risks.

Neither proved to have a record, even of indiscretion, and Victoria, finding out later about the inquiry, promised to ban Ahmed—as a "meddler"—from her houses, but still pressed for his employment. As for the *Munshi,* the Queen assured Salisbury that Abdul Karim "does not read English fluently enough to be able to read anything of importance"—a declaration that protected him but cast doubt upon any value he had for her. He helped her, she declared, "to read words which she cannot read." Although her energy was flagging, it would never falter where the *Munshi* was concerned. To improve his social position, he would receive a Jubilee medal and a minor honor that put several letters after his name; and she would impose him upon visiting Moslem dignitaries. But Ahmed was gone. "All is quiet & satisfactory now," the Queen wrote to Lord Salisbury on December 27, 1898, "excepting that the injured individual cannot get over it."

While on the Riviera the Queen visited Empress Eugénie, who had a villa at Cap Martin, and early in the evening of April 22, a few days after Easter Sunday, Victoria was visited by Sarah Bernhardt. She was also staying at the Excelsior Regina, and had been invited to perform. Victoria had not seen the great tragedienne on the London stage, but a delicious and probably apocryphal story survives from her performance in Sardou's *Cleopatra* at Covent Garden in 1892. At the close, she stabbed the slave who had brought her tidings of Mark Antony's defeat at Actium, and stormed and raved and wrecked some of the scenery in her frenzy. Finally, as the curtain fell, she collapsed in a convulsive, shuddering heap. When the applause died down, a British matron was heard to say to her neighbor, "How different, how very different, from the home life of our own dear Queen!"

Not only was the Queen's Court very different from that of the tempestuous Egyptian, although she still could summon up a rage or two, as over the *Munshi;* her world was very different from that of Madame Bernhardt, who at best might be said in terms of the time to have been morally lax. No longer did Victoria make a fuss over such things. Life was too short to live by self-denial, and the Queen was eager to see a Bernhardt performance. The half-hour, three-character playlet was *Jean Marie,* by André Theuriet.* Victoria found it "extremely touching," with acting

*Mistranscribed in all versions of the Queen's journal as Adrien Fleuriet.

that was "quite marvellous, so pathetic and full of feeling . . . tears rolling down her cheeks. . . . The story is much the same as that of *Auld Robin Grey.*"

Afterwards Lady Lytton, who had known Sarah Bernhardt through her writer-husband, introduced the actors to the Queen, an encounter that may have surprised the Empress Frederick, who had written to her daughter Sophie—Victoria's granddaughter—in 1893 that although Sarah Bernhardt was "an extraordinary actress from all I have heard, I hope you did not make her acquaintance, as alas no *lady* can, she is so very bad, and has an awful reputation."

Deciding that it was an event to commemorate in the Queen's Birthday Book, Fritz Ponsonby took down the huge volume and asked Madame Bernhardt to add her name and the date of her birthday. Everywhere the Queen went, the current book went with her, although she could no longer read it; "On occasion," Ponsonby recalled, "it had been mistaken for the Bible." The actress startled him by kneeling on the floor to write, and filling up an entire page with *"Le plus beau jour de ma vie,"* and adding her name with a flourish.

"I felt I had done my duty nobly and when a message came . . . asking me whether I had got Sarah Bernhardt's signature I sent the book in with pride for the Queen to see." It was the wrong book. Victoria had a special volume for performing artists, and besides, the Queen was "much put out" by Madame Bernhardt's taking up a whole page. In any case, he was to find her and get her name in the right book. It meant purchasing a ticket that evening for *La Tosca,* and waiting for an interval. Between the acts, he rushed to the dressing rooms and explained his errand—that he had been commanded by *La Reine d'Angleterre* to secure a signature in a royal book that he described as *"plus intime."* After some scurrying about for a property inkstand, which consumed an entire interval, the dressing room attendants, one of whom Ponsonby took to be the lover of the moment, produced pen and ink. Ponsonby tried to snatch the book away before Madame Bernhardt could read the other names. *"Un moment que ça sèche,"* she said, pretending that the signature was not yet dry, and glanced at what other names she could. They were mere performers, while the other book was for dignitaries. "She handed back the book to me with a shrug of the shoulders."

War between Greece and Turkey over Crete continued while the Queen was abroad, and the situation of the Greeks became increasingly desperate as their intervention was turned back. When Victoria returned, she attempted to enlist other European powers to help pull the warring sides apart. By marriage and by blood, the Greek royal family was on both sides related to her. Increasingly she had become grandmother to Europe. "Germany, or rather William, behaves too shamefully," she had written from Cimiez on April 21; and from Windsor on May 8 she added, "Received a rude answer from William, sent *en clair,* whilst my telegram was in cypher." She had used that badgering device—about Gordon—to get at Gladstone. On May 13 she recorded "another grandiloquent telegram, also *en clair,* from William." To the German ambassador in London, Paul von Hatzfeldt, Count Holstein wrote that "the Kaiser needed some sort of success in foreign affairs to strengthen his popularity at home," and that when William read a parallel comment in another letter, he commented, "Well, really, I have a certain amount of that already."

The Queen's "poor old birthday again came round," she wrote on May 24. She was seventy-eight. The event "seems sadder each year," and her "great lameness" made her feel "how age is creeping on." The next day Leopold II of Belgium came with "a most splendid erection of orchids, one can hardly call it a bouquet, which he had brought from Belgium." She knew his reputation, but he knew how to be ingratiating. Although she had turned away other heads of state who wanted to come to Jubilee Day, she invited him and his youngest daughter, Princess Clementina.

On June 3, 1897, Friedrich Hirschhorn, a Kimberley diamond merchant, incorporated at Elands Drift, in Cape Colony, the Diamond Jubilee Company, Ltd., to search for diamonds and other minerals, mine them, and "dispose of the same." On the other side of the continent, at the boomtown of Pilgrim's Rest in the eastern Transvaal, the Jubilee Mine was opened to dig and pan for gold. Everywhere in the colonies, the Jubilee tag was being applied to places and things with even more gusto than in 1887, and remote locations in the Empire were beginning to celebrate their tenuous linkages to a tiny, stout old woman in London. In the South African novelist C. Louis Leipoldt's autobiographical novel *Stormwrack*—Leipoldt was seventeen in 1897, and a witness to the Jubilee—the inhabitants of a mixed English-Afrikaans village in the northern Cape, based upon Clanwilliam, argue whether to celebrate the event. Old Doremus van Aard, in a flashback scene, recalls to young Andrew Quakerley that it is a "better time now [than under the old Company] that we are under the rule of our good sovereign lady, Alexandrina Victoria—God bless the woman." Annually, the Dutch and English mark the Queen's birthday loyally, and the village's "oldest inhabitant could not remember that the anniversary festivities of Her Most Gracious Majesty Queen Alexandrina Victoria—for it was the custom to give the Queen her full name—had ever been omitted."

Whether to celebrate the Diamond Jubilee—Andrew Quakerley is now seventy-seven—is a different matter. In 1887 the village planted a commemorative orange tree, now buried in windswept sand, its surrounding fence dilapidated. Political feelings over the Transvaal have divided the community, but the Magistrate convenes a meeting anyway to determine what, if anything, should be done to honor the Queen. Hendrik van Aard, Doremus's son, is an old man, burly, big-boned, and an elder of the church, and above the murmuring he is heard to ask to speak.

"Friends," he says, peering under his steel-rimmed spectacles, ". . . I look back for sixty years, and I mind me how as a small boy my father told me that we had a woman to reign over us. I mind me how he told me that there were folk who feared that a woman's rule would not be strong enough. . . . We have none of us seen her, . . . but we know what she looks like, and we know that she is a Christian woman, God fearing, a decent body who has ruled wisely and well."

He knows, he adds sternly, that there are people as dissatisfied in 1897 as those who in 1837 worried about the lack of a king. He wants no talk of politics to mar the occasion. "Let them leave us if they want to have no part in honouring a lady to whom our respect and our loyalty are due not only because she is our rightful, God-appointed sovereign, but also because she is a woman who through years of tribulation and sorrow has been a good woman."

A middle-aged, bearded man, Gideon Ras, shoulders his way forward and claims the floor. "We have no obligation towards the Queen," he insists. ". . . We owe more to our old President [Kruger], and . . . if we are true Afrikanders, true to our tradition, our race, our religion, and the customs of our great Pioneers, who led us out of the wilderness of English oppression . . . , we should honour Oom Paul and not Queen Victoria!"

In the end, a committee is formed to prepare an Address, in English and Dutch, "to be delivered in a locally made wooden casket enclosed in a leather cover elaborately tooled and gilded." On Jubilee Night, the village is illuminated; church and lodge groups parade in the square, and an old muzzle-loader is fired by native constables; prayers are led in English and Dutch; "God Save the Queen" is sung; and three hurrahs are shouted. In the crowds, and in private dinners afterward in which the Queen is toasted, older villagers point out to the more militant younger ones "that Alexandrina Victoria could hardly be held responsible for whatever had been committed by [Joseph] Chamberlain." As one on-looker writes to a friend in Cape Town, loyalty to England had little to do with the commemoration. "For sixty years our people have considered the Queen as a personality standing outside politics. Of their personal loyalty, in so far as she is the personification of authority, there can be no question. . . . But I can tell you that in this Transvaal business most of our people are in sympathy with the Transvaal."

As if validating that premise, the people of the Witwatersrand erected a bronze monument to Her Most Gracious Majesty, recognizing a reign "memorable not only for its length of years" but for "closer unity between the Motherland and the Colonies."

Everywhere in the Empire there were similar effusions of loyalty for the symbolic Victoria, most of them less qualified than in the tinderbox of the Transvaal. Few anywhere now encountered the real Victoria, yet few homes in Britain or among expatriates in the Empire were without some representation of the youthful or the aged Queen—on calendars, oleographs, cabinet photos, Jubilee mugs, commemorative plates—and on every postage stamp of the millions printed and posted since 1840. There was even a four-by-three-foot portrait of Her Most Gracious Majesty the Queen printed by B. Israel in London, having taken, the caption read, four years and seven months to execute, and that told the story of her life in 173,000 words, all of them wound round and round to fashion a reasonable likeness.

An angle of vision not furnished by the paeans and the portraits was ventured by Bernard Shaw in a paragraph of a play review:

Think of the young lady of seventy years ago, systematically and piously lied to by parents, governesses, clergymen, servants, every-body. . . . Surely every shop-window picture of "the girl Queen" of 1837 must tempt the Queen of 1897 to jump out of her carriage and write up under it, "Please remember that there is not a woman earning twenty-four shillings a week as a clerk today who is not ten times better educated than this unfortunate girl was when the crown dropped on her head, and left her to reign by her mother wit and the advice of a parcel of men who to this day have not sense enough to manage a Jubilee, let alone an Empire, without offending everybody." Depend on it, seventy-eight years cannot be lived through without finding out things that queens do not mention in Adelphi melodramas.

For most of her subjects, the Queen had already metamorphosed, through age and remoteness from the reality of their lives, into myth. Few could recall another sovereign. Emily Ampthill, who had traveled from Scotland with the Queen in her luxurious royal carriage, recalled the veneration in which the Queen was now viewed, her earlier seclusion and self-indulgence forgotten. Unable to sleep as the first light of morning leaked into her windows—it was about four—Lady Ampthill raised the blind and was surprised to see people along the tracks. "The hedge or palings which protect the railroad marked a continuous line of people who had tramped across country to witness the passage of the train—people who knew that they could not see their beloved Queen, but who were glad to see the train which carried her along. In remote districts the people were thin in numbers—in the more populous counties sometimes thirty, forty deep—all this on a dark threatening grey morning."

As the train continued steadily on, "the men took off their hats and the women held up a handkerchief or sometimes kissed their hands: in no case did anybody raise a cheer, for the Queen's rest is valued by her subjects." In such fashion did humble folk celebrate Victoria's Jubilee— saluting the onrushing royal train in full recognition that there could be no reciprocal acknowledgment. It was a loyalty and devotion at odds with pressures in Parliament for democracy and reform. Balancing continuity and change was the constant concern of her Governments. The Queen represented continuity.

The great day of celebration spilled over into several ceremonies. On June 20, the Windsor phase began. With all her surviving children present, and Beatrice out of mourning and all in white, the Queen went to a service in St. George's Chapel. Then she visited Albert's tomb, "and remained sitting there some little time." The next morning, after breakfast with Vicky and Lenchen, she drove to Windsor Station. "It has always been clear to the female subjects of the Queen," Lady Monkswell wrote in her diary on the great day that followed, "that her 'mantles' were made in the year *one.*" She was amused to hear from her friend Mrs. Cox that Victoria purchased her garments in Windsor, having things sent to the castle for inspection. Mrs. Cayley, wife of a Windsor clothier, had said unhappily to Mrs. Cox, "Oh Ma'am, I could have cried to see Her Majesty start for the Jubilee in her second-best 'mantle'—after all the beautiful things I had sent her." The Queen, Lady Monkswell thought, had a "frugal mind." Perhaps it was in some sense a middle-class one, but it kept her, in at least a small way, in tune with her people. Once out of the sooty station and on the train, Her Majesty extracted the "best" mantle from a box, and changed.

From Paddington, crowds lined the streets all the way to Buckingham Palace. Victoria noted passing under a "lovely" arch with the motto "Our hearts thy Throne." At the palace, until she escaped into the garden for tea, she sat in her wheelchair to receive addresses from foreign princes and ambassadors, and greetings from a variety of relations and relations-by-marriage, many also foreign nobility—even her own son, now the Duke of Coburg. For dinner with the foreign dignitaries she was dressed in a gold-embroidered gown made for her in India, and she wore diamonds in her cap. Afterwards the ballroom was "very full and dreadfully hot, and the [electric] light very inefficient." It was after eleven when she was finally wheeled back to her room, exhausted. "There was a great deal of noise in the streets, and we were told that many were sleeping out in the parks."

June 22 was the "never-to-be-forgotten day," decreed as a special Bank Holiday. Wooden stands were erected everywhere in the line of progress to and from St. Paul's. Whitehall, the National Gallery, Charing Cross Station, St. Martin's-in-the-Fields, and smart hotels in the Strand vanished behind them. The population of the city had tripled, to nearly four million, since Coronation crowds had swarmed into London from the country and from abroad to see the new Queen. Thousands were already in the streets by seven in the morning. The week before had been cold and rainy; even the great day dawned dull and grey, but troops in scarlet and bearskins, coming and going, kept the atmosphere agitated, as did the peddlers who hawked souvenir Jubilee pennants, flags, programs, balloons, mugs, pictures, place mats, noisemakers, and fireworks.

By the time the Queen was dressed and had breakfasted with her daughters, the colonial troops, with their bands, had passed the palace. Then came the home forces, whom she watched from her balcony before going to press an electric button that touched off a telegraphic message to the Empire: "From my heart I thank my beloved people. God bless them!" Then she was helped into her state landau, drawn by eight creams, with the Princess of Wales and Lenchen sitting opposite, and the Prince of Wales and the Duke of Cambridge, stubborn and sturdy at seventy-eight, mounted on horseback, on either side. Prince Arthur, a field marshal and chief of the arrangements for the procession, followed.

The royal party had left at 11:15, with Vicky in a separate carriage pulled by four black horses caparisoned in red. Her rank as Empress prevented her from sitting opposite her mother with her back to the horses, and the Queen had to sit alone. The pace was slow, but that gave time for the sun to emerge, lighting up the ornaments and the finery, the flowers and the loyal inscriptions. The orderliness of the crowds matched the regularity of the procession. There were more police marching than patrolling, more soldiers stepping smartly than standing guard. There was an earnestness about the enthusiasm, appropriate to the veneration of a grandmotherly sovereign, and as many tears as cheers. Representing her own generation were the Chelsea Pensioners in their red Royal Hospital uniforms, who had special seats, as did the Lords and Commons. At one place in a reserved stand were grizzled survivors of the Light Brigade charge at Balaclava, in the Crimea; and many schools had arranged for their own scaffolding and seats. Letitia Whitty, six years old, was there with her father. Eighty-nine years later she remembered, "I wouldn't wave at that ugly woman."

At Temple Bar in the Strand—the Queen missed Temple Bar itself, removed in 1878 to expand the street—was the Lord Mayor in full robes and chain, to present his sword, which the Queen touched. Then he mounted his white horse and, the Queen noted, "galloped past bareheaded, carrying the sword, accompanied by his Sheriffs." What Victoria did not know was that the Lord Mayor, a man of the City rather than an experienced horseman, had been handicapped by his robes and sword, and unable to control his mount; when its canter had become unexpectedly a gallop, the Lord Mayor's ceremonial hat had flown off. By the time he arrived at St. Paul's, well ahead of the Queen, his horse had resumed its slow gait and the Lord Mayor his hat. The appreciative throng at the Cathedral steps cheered his resumption of dignity.

At the entrance to St. Paul's, the Queen's carriage paused before the masses of spectators, drawn-up Colonial troops in colorful uniforms, bishops in their copes, and Royal Princes. A *Te Deum* was sung, followed by the Lord's Prayer, a special Jubilee prayer, a benediction, and a lusty singing by everyone within hearing of the "Old Hundredth." This time the hymn had new words for the Jubilee:

In years to come, whate'er may be,
'Mid joy or sorrow, good or ill,
May she, O Lord, Thy goodness see,
Keep and defend and guide her still.

Grant her Thy peace, long may she reign.
And when at length Thy call shall come,
If so Thy will be, free from pain.
Take her to Thine eternal home.

Victoria may not have noted any difference in the thundered words from the thousands of renderings she had heard over the years. Her journal records only the fact of the "Old Hundredth," but it was the Jubilee version about "a virtuous reign, a life sincere," with reference to her "length of days," that was being sung everywhere in the Empire at the same hour on the same day. The Queen wept, wiped her eyes, and then thanked the Archbishop of Canterbury and the Bishop of London for their service of Thanksgiving.

The next day the *Daily Mail,* describing the service at St. Paul's, announced that the Mother of the Empire had gone to do homage to the One Being "MORE MAJESTIC THAN SHE"—"as if to imply," James Morris later wrote, "that she was merely reporting the state of the imperial garrison to her superior officer. War, empire and religion were inextricably related in the public mind." It implied even more. To many of her subjects, although her powers were only symbolic, the remote figure in the carriage was the most important individual in the world.

To waves of cheering, the Queen continued on to the Mansion House, where the Lord Mayor dismounted, presumably with relief, and the Lady Mayoress presented her with a silver basket of orchids. The procession moved south over London Bridge, lined with troops and closed to pedestrians, and along Borough Road in South London, where the poorest onlookers lived. Again the crowds were orderly and enthusiastic, the lampposts decorated with bunches of flowers. Crossing back over Westminster Bridge and past the Houses of Parliament, the carriages reentered the Mall and completed the six-mile circuit in the hottest hours of what had become a sultry day. In her carriage, the Queen opened a long-handled black lace parasol, lined with white, given to her for the occasion by Lady Lytton's uncle, Charles Villiers, who had been in the House of Commons since Victoria was a princess of sixteen. He was now ninety-five.

Back "home" at a quarter of two, the Queen rested until tea, and later attended a large family dinner, having herself wheeled back to her room at eleven. "There were illuminations," she noted in her journal, "which we did not see, but could hear a great deal of cheering and singing." She was elated by the success of the day. "No one ever," she claimed, ". . . has met with such an ovation as was given to me." But the Jubilee summer was far from over. There were hundreds of Addresses and thousands of gifts, and a special day had been set aside for Addresses from the Houses of Lords and Commons, and from local governments.

In four separate ceremonies in the "hot and dark" ballroom at Buckingham Palace the next afternoon, Victoria received the Lords, the Members of Commons, the chairmen of County Councils, and then four hundred Mayors and—the Scots equivalent—Provosts, each with an Address. Unable, she noted, to read "without spectacles or a magnifier," she said only a few words in return each time, and handed the presenters an official written answer. When she left the Palace at five-thirty for Paddington, and Windsor, the throngs were as great as ever. The wooden stands were now filled with schoolchildren to give them their special opportunity. At Hyde Park Corner, a Guard of Honor was paraded, and Addresses were presented by Lord Londonderry for the School Board; the Bishop of London, Mandell Creighton, for the Church Schools; Cardinal Vaughan on behalf of the Roman Catholic children; Lord Rothschild for Jewish children; and still others for Wesleyan children and nondenominational schools. From Paddington to Slough she had tea in the train; then she disembarked to more throngs and Addresses, including one from Lord Rothschild as Lord Lieutenant of Buckinghamshire. He had apparently rushed to her train from Hyde Park Corner, and dashed to the platform before she emerged for his greeting. Then she continued to Eton for still another Address, and to Windsor Bridge for yet another, from the Thames Conservancy. At the foot of Castle Hill the final Address from the Mayor and Corporation of Windsor was delivered under her Jubilee statue of 1887, and a choir sang "God Save the Queen"; then thousands of schoolchildren who lined the road to the castle sang. It was eight when she returned wearily to the castle.

On the twenty-eighth, after some rest built into her schedule, the Queen left again for London for a huge garden party on the grounds of Buckingham Palace. There were foreign royalty and royal relatives, stage personalities like Henry Irving and Ellen Terry, concert artists like Emma Albani and Paolo Tosti. With her eldest daughter at her side (it was an informal occasion), and later her daughter-in-law, Alix, to order the coachman when to halt—as someone had to be the Queen's eyes—she traveled along the lawns in a victoria* at a slow walk, drawn by two greys, and preceded by an outrider on an old grey. "She went all round the garden," Lady Monkswell wrote, "everybody crowding round & curtseying. . . . She was bowing and looking very happy. . . . She then went & sat in a large tent banked up with flowers; it was wide open—all the front—& her faithful subjects could see her taking tea & having her toast buttered by the Indian servant. . . . Lord Lathom [the Lord Chamberlain] was taking in the Indians & other distinguished people, & I saw some come out with photographs in their hands."

When Victoria emerged, she was assisted into her landau for the trip back to Paddington Station. "Got back to Windsor at eight, very tired," she wrote.

The Jubilee was not yet over. Before the colonial troops representing the Empire returned home, they were brought to Windsor on July 2, where they were drawn up for the Queen. Lord Roberts and Lord Methuen walked alongside her carriage and identified each contingent. She stopped, curious, despite fading sight, at "the Sikhs from India, the Hong-Kong Police from China, and the Houssas from West Africa. . . . One of the English officers and a native one had known Liko, and the latter was called up for me to speak to him." The troops marched past, saluting, and afterwards an officer and a noncommissioned officer from each unit were brought to the Queen. She tried out the *Munshi*'s Hindustani on some of the Sikhs, "who were fine, handsome men." Before leaving, she asked Lord Roberts, "will you tell the officers and men what a great pleasure it has been to me to see so many of my subjects from the different Colonies here to-day? I hope they will all return here some day, and I wish them happiness and all prosperity." He shouted her message to the troops.

The next day, a Saturday, Victoria went out of her way to be the monarch she could be. The reception of Members of the House of Commons at Buckingham Palace on June 23, the second of the four large groups rapidly shuttled in and out, had been mismanaged, and had gone badly. "Not half the Lords or a quarter of the Commons," Lady Monkswell estimated, "even saw the Queen. They all went home very much displeased, & there were nasty remarks in the radical papers. They were

*A low, light, four-wheeled carriage with a seat for two and a perch for a coachman.

enjoying their grievance to the uttermost when it was announced that the Queen would receive the faithful Commons, their wives & daughters at Windsor! Such a thing as a Garden Party at Windsor has not taken place in my lifetime. This takes the wind entirely out of the sails of the discontented; every one of them that can walk will go—even perhaps some of the Irish—& the Queen will be more popular than ever."

On the broad lawn under the castle terrace, the people's elected representatives swarmed, with their ladies, around the groaning buffet tables. Again the Queen, in a small carriage, mixed with the milling politicians. "Drove about slowly amongst my guests and spoke to some. Some of the Labour Members were presented, which I heard afterwards gratified them very much." The Labourites were a new, third, party, and represented, she understood, a direction in which England might move after she was gone. She had resisted the future in many ways, but the gesture showed her settling for a truce with it.

"We scarcely expected," David Lindsay, Conservative Member from a Lancashire district, wrote in his diary, "that the Queen would entertain us so royally at Windsor; for the trouble, worry and also the expense cannot have been small." The twenty-six-year-old M.P., in his first term from a seat that was traditionally family-held (later he would be the twenty-seventh Earl of Crawford), was impressed not only by the gesture, but by the special effort that Victoria made to link herself to oncoming change. "We turned up in the hundreds, including two [Irish] Nationalists whom the Queen asked to be presented to her. She was looking very well, very young and very happy. She stayed a long time among her faithful commons, scores of whom, including plenty of Radicals and not a few Labour members were brought up to her carriage: we had a free run of the castle, perfect weather, ample refreshments: bands, a thousand chairs and finally Imperial tobacco. It was magnificent. . . ."

Lindsay was especially pleased by the Duke of Portland, who, dressed in the Windsor uniform "and looking like a subpostmaster," received a tip of a two-shilling piece from an M.P. With the run of the Castle, M.P.s peered at the treasures. One of them, James Caldwell, a Scot, after going through the priceless Old Masters and magnificent *objets d'art* with his sister, decided that what he liked best was "the silver key with which Her Majesty opened the Glasgow waterworks." James Jacoby, a Derbyshire Liberal, announced to other Radicals of his persuasion after a thorough sampling of the Windsor champagne, "If the Prince of Wales wants his

Civil List increased I am ready to support his application tomorrow." He invited Lindsay to join him in another iced champagne. Frank Lockwood, Gladstone's last Solicitor-General, after what seemed a lengthy tête-à-tête with the Queen, while others clustered nearby, was asked what Her Majesty had said to him. "You may rest assured, my dear," he told his daughter, "that nothing passed between us which your mother would have blushed to hear."

Reaction to the affair was all Victoria might have wished. Arthur Balfour wrote of his "immense pleasure" at its success. "It not only wiped out all recollections of the *contretemps* of the preceding week, but afforded a degree of satisfaction which could never have arisen from the presentation of an Address. . . ." To Sir Arthur Bigge, accompanying a letter of thanks to the Queen, Sir William Harcourt, leading the Opposition, wrote that the affair had been *"right royally* done: everything most handsomely provided, and great courtesy to the guests from the Court and Household. It was a happy thought happily executed, and has given great satisfaction and will do great good in all ways." To the Queen herself he offered the gratitude of the Liberal Members for the "gracious and magnificent reception. . . . It was impossible that any greater reward should have been bestowed for their loyal and devoted attachment to your Majesty's Person and Throne." He spoke of "thoughtful kindness," of a "noble entertainment," and a recollection "always [to] be treasured in their grateful memories," but never realized that at least half the reason for the joy in the event was that it was shared by wives and daughters who had no role in the bungled Buckingham Palace ceremonial. Had the original event gone off properly, it would have eliminated families from a far grander spectacle at Windsor, the last likely blaze of Victorian self-congratulation.

A veteran of several Gladstone Cabinets and in effect, still, an adversary, Harcourt was no less magnetized by the mood of the occasion than the others, confessing his "gladness that the Queen should have been able so well to support the immense fatigue of this memorable celebration," and he hoped that "her life may still for years be spared to those who look up to her with reverence and affection."

On July 6 she received the Special United States Envoy to the Jubilee—later the ambassador—Whitelaw Reid, who told her that Americans were "much attached" to her, and spoke of her as "the good Queen." For a final time, the next day she received the fifteen colonial premiers, whom she swore in as Privy Councillors, and awarded Jubilee medals. In turn, they each presented her with "Addresses in most beautiful caskets." Then Mrs. Mary Chamberlain, spouse of the architect of the Imperial mood, presented their wives.

A typical day at the close of the festivities was July 8, 1897. Presentations began in the Grand Reception Room at Windsor at three in the afternoon. Each deputation assembled separately nearby just before the ceremony, and was escorted into the Queen's presence to find her seated and awaiting them. A Court chamberlain had already explained the rigid procedures for the ceremony. The presenter read the Address, kissed Her Majesty's plump, beringed hand, and kissed it again on receiving her reply. The mover and seconder of the Address were presented, and each in turn kissed Her Majesty's hand. Then the deputation retired to the Garter Room, just vacated by the previous presenting group, "and thence, as soon as practicable," the instructions went, anticipating the traffic of numerous deputations, through the Waterloo Chamber and the Guards Chamber to St. George's Hall, where refreshments were served. With the deputations each including a hundred or more participants, many of the Queen's subjects could then say that they had been in her presence, and had drunk to her health under her roof. Afterwards, the happy groups massed on the station platform at Windsor for the train to Paddington.

Despite the elaborate arrangements to keep the Queen little more than a visible eminence at each Jubilee event, each occasion was taxing. Many Addresses were delivered instead to the Prince of Wales, acting in her name, although each presenter he received recognized the second-class status of the event despite the realization that the burly, now grey-bearded Prince was soon to be king. At St. James's Palace on one day alone —July 21—he spent the entire day receiving, separately, forty-one presenting bodies, including the Royal Astronomical Society, the Royal College of Physicians, the Society of Architects, the Coroners' Society, several universities, a dozen religious groups including the YMCA, and town and city councils from Glasgow to the south of England.

Requests to be received by the Queen had come from every kind of organization and governmental unit at home and in the colonies, all fielded first by the Home Secretary, Sir Matthew Ridley. Not all of them could be disposed of with a substitute. The Deputies of some Protestant Dissenting bodies—ranging from Presbyterian and Baptist to the Society of Friends—had the legal "right of personal approach to the Sovereign," to protect their civil rights, and they claimed it. So did the nation's most prestigious body of scientists, the Royal Society. All those whose claims were validated were bunched together on July 15 to meet the Queen and present Addresses, each group limited to a deputation of twenty. It closed Victoria's involvement in the Jubilee, which at first was to encompass a single day, and a quarter of an hour at the steps of St. Paul's, and had instead continued for nearly a month. When the Queen ceased her Jubilee appearances altogether, Bertie continued to stand in for her.

In many ways the Diamond Jubilee had completed the metamorphosis of a stout, lame, nearly blind little lady in a bonnet, now nearly eighty, into legend. Those permitted into her paradoxically august presence, rendered more regal by setting and circumstance, understood that the chances of another such occasion were as remote as the planets. She was likely to be seen again only in portraits adorning drawing rooms and public offices, and on her postage stamps.

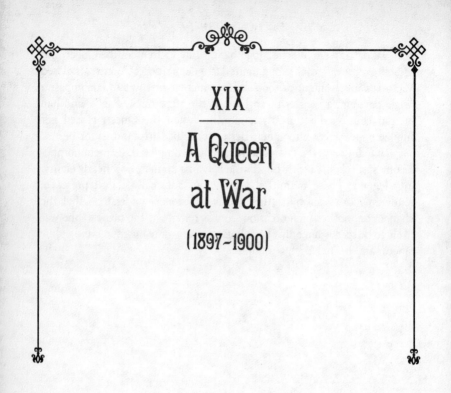

XIX

A Queen
at War

(1897-1900)

On October 25, 1897, the Queen prepared a directive for her own funeral. She wanted a minimum of pomp, not even the traditional "Dead March" from Handel's *Saul,* and white-and-gold draperies rather than mausoleum black. As titular head of the armed forces she commanded a military funeral complete with flower-banked gun carriage drawn by eight horses—"not black ones," she decreed. Not only the *Munshi,* but her German secretaries were to have places in the line of march. What had become known as Victorian mourning was not meant for Victoria herself.

Precipitating the directive was the final illness of Princess Mary Adelaide of Teck. As she lay helpless, only days before her death on October 27, her family became aware that she had left no will and no instructions for her funeral. Her cousin Victoria made sure that no vagueness remained about what to do in the event of her own demise.

Apart from the deterioration of aging, and a stiffened lame knee that prevented her from kneeling at divine services, the Queen's health remained good. She still had a splendid appetite. At Balmoral in October, Lady Lytton recorded a tea at which, after two scones, two pieces of toast, and several biscuits, Victoria conceded, "I am afraid I must not have any more." Frugality had nothing to do with it, although only a few weeks later, Arthur Bigge and Fleetwood Edwards, having begun a campaign to reduce excessive Household expenditures, confronted the Queen diplomatically with a list of excesses. "Then I must tell my maid my bed *cannot* be mended for the present," Victoria said. Annual repairs to Buckingham Palace and Windsor Castle alone cost an alarming £40,000, but Arthur Balfour assured the Queen, so his secretary, Bernard Mallet, reported, "that she ought have no anxiety on such matters and . . . never deny herself what she wanted." Victoria, according to Mallet, "said it was very good for her to have to deny herself things. Once she thought to economize by having fewer different kinds of bread at breakfast!"

It was clear from the bed and bread episodes that Victoria was now old. Aging seemed apparent, too, in her passionate stubbornness. After the Duke and Duchess of York had made a popular visit to Ireland, the National Conservative Union pressed for a royal residence there, something the Queen had long opposed for the Duke's father. Sir Michael Hicks Beach promised to find the funds, and Lord Cadogan visited the Duke, who promised to live in Ireland for a period each year. No one had asked Victoria. On November 17 she gave the plan an unequivocal *no*, insisting that the climate was unhealthy. She had said that before, and would not be swayed. There was little she could do with Parliament, but when it came to the Royal Family her powers seemed absolute.

In attempting to prepare himself for his future role, the Duke of York managed to get into difficulty with his grandmother in yet another way. When she found that he was reading Walter Bagehot's economic essays, she was displeased that he was studying such a "radical" writer. She had read more radical books herself, or at least had portions read to her, one of them Henry George's *Progress and Poverty,* published in the 1880s, which she described to the Reverend Stewart Headlam as "difficult." But Bagehot, in his influential *The English Constitution,* its royal purple binding notwithstanding, had validated the reduced powers of the monarchy since the first Reform Bill. Published in 1867, with a supplement added in 1879, it had dismissed the industrious Victoria as "a retired widow," a description that fit her in 1867 but became less and less valid.

The Queen's memory remained long. In conversation at Windsor in December she recalled her boredom, at sixteen, when she had first heard *The Messiah* at York Minster. All other oratorios, she thought, were even worse. The nineteenth-century fashion for long and lugubrious religious works moved her not at all. She enjoyed hymns and anthems, and both Sir Arthur Sullivan and Sir Villiers Stanford composed new ones for the usual December 14 service at the Mausoleum at Frogmore. While she went through the traditional motions at Osborne most years, for Victoria the Christmas season had lost its savor after December 14, 1861. Under the Household tree in the Durbar Room on Christmas Eve, with the Royal Princesses (except for the absent Vicky) around her, the Queen gave her presents to family and retainers. In addition to gifts ranging from silver spoons to inexpensive trinkets, each received a German gingerbread man, a custom by which she continued to recall Albert. Then the Queen was wheeled about to examine her own presents. Dinner followed, complete to boar's head on the sideboard, a baron of beef, and her annual woodcock pie from the Lord Lieutenant of Ireland.

As the New Year of 1898 approached, Bernard Mallet noted in his diary, the Queen "spoke pathetically and for the first time of her old age, blindness and lameness, of her losses [by death] . . . which had saddened this great Jubilee year, for which, nevertheless, she was thankful. Who can help doing all they can to make happy her last years! I feel it is a great privilege. . . ."

To ease the evening of her reign, courtiers undertook assignments for her that seemed quixotic but made her feel useful. One was the confidential mission upon which she sent Sir Theodore Martin, biographer of the Prince Consort. He visited editors of leading London newspapers and weeklies to urge them to soften their offensive tone toward Germany and William II. Gross bad taste thrived on both sides. Willy hoped, in particular, that the Queen would stop the publication of *Punch*.

Anything that could contribute to the softening of invective, Victoria thought, might make the German press less strident and the German leadership less belligerent. Martin returned on January 14 with promises of a more conciliatory temper from ten publications. Even *Punch* promised to be less "mischievous." Yet he realized that political and commercial tensions would bestir the London press even if the Emperor's abrasive talk, and the boastfulness of the German press, could be brought under control. The civility would not last long, but the effort demonstrated the Queen's continued exercise of her powers through the prestige of the

Throne. That esteem had been low when she let it be so, but since Disraeli, and especially since the first Jubilee, she understood that the occupant and the Throne were one and the same.

One of the Government's colonial priorities had been the retaking of territories Gladstone had let go after Gordon's death. There was little the Queen could do but applaud; however, at Osborne in February she told Surgeon-Major-General William Nash, commander of the Royal Victoria Hospital at nearby Netley, and a veteran of the Egyptian campaigns, that she would find the funds to furnish "extra good wooden legs for the men who had lost them."

When she next visited Netley, in May, she was, in what had become her expected way, an example to the invalided, arriving energetically in her wheelchair and moving briskly up and down the corridors saying a few sympathetic words to each patient, recalling those she had seen on past inspections, and pinning decorations on an Aberdeen piper and a Dorset lance corporal. On the wall in the lower corridor was an engraving representing her first visit, decades earlier. In the picture she was bending over the bed of a wounded soldier from the Crimea, with Albert and their two sons standing close by. Two days later, on May 16, she reviewed at Windsor, from her wheelchair, 105 veterans of the Crimea and the Indian Mutiny, brought from a soldiers' home in Bristol. Their ages ranged from sixty to eighty-five, but they were all on their feet for a salute, after which they were escorted indoors for refreshments.

There seemed no end to the wars that were the price of maintaining colonies, as Victoria had learned once again at about the time she left in March for some Cimiez sun. More fighting in faraway places appeared likely, and she was less than eager to be drawn in. After compelling Britain to back away from a border dispute with Venezuela, the United States was continuing to behave like an imperialistic bully, this time threatening to humble Spain in Cuba and the Philippines. The Queen Regent of Spain lamented to Victoria her country's impotence and the world's indifference. From Cimiez, Victoria inquired of Salisbury what might be done, and the Prime Minister warily offered nothing but sympathy. When, just as cautiously, he disclaimed for his Government any desire to keep Russia out of the Manchurian coastal city of Port Arthur since there were British port protectorates nearby, the Queen found solace in the stance. The world, she wrote to the Prime Minister on March 27, 1898, "should not have the impression that we will not let anyone but ourselves have anything, while at the same time we must secure our rights and influence." That was not much help to weak colonial nations such as Spain. The pathetic Queen Regent remained a "poor thing" whose plight Victoria deplored, and shrugged off.

On April 13, the President of France, François-Félix Faure, paid a private visit to the Queen at the Excelsior Regina Hotel. Although he was a head of state, Victoria was reluctant to treat the president of a republic as a sovereign. She arranged instead for Bertie, who was nearby at Cannes, to meet him in the hotel lobby, and positioned the three Royal Princesses at the top of the stairs. "I stood at the door of the drawing-room," Victoria wrote, "and asked him to sit down. He was very courteous and amiable, with a charming manner, so *grand seigneur* and not at all *parvenu*. He avoided all politics. . . ."

Fritz Ponsonby recalled the encounter as going far less smoothly. At first seeing no one but Household staff to greet him (the Prince of Wales not having arrived in time), Faure "kept his hat on to imply that the visit had not properly begun. . . . The President was then conducted upstairs, and the Prince of Wales came hurrying out as if he were late. It was only then that the President took his hat off." Of course Bertie *was* late, and Faure was protective of his dignity.

The quarter of an hour with the Queen was private, while others in Victoria's circle talked with Faure's "two gentlemen," who were then presented. Departing, Ponsonby recalled, the President "kissed the Queen's hand and said goodbye. This he did very well and the Queen stood up with the help of her stick and said some polite remarks about the beauties of France."

So many royal personages and other European elite spent each season on the Riviera that the Queen held almost constant court there each March and April. One day it was Leopold II of Belgium, who seemed to Fritz Ponsonby "very nervous and frightened of her and sat twisting his hands like a schoolboy. It was curious that she should like him, because his morals were notorious, but the Queen seemed to overlook this." Another guest in 1898 was young Queen Wilhelmina of the Netherlands, then eighteen. One sovereign she did not want to see, since the Kruger telegram, was her grandson William II. She would have been even more displeased had she known how he had received her campaign to reduce Anglo-German tensions, as he professed to be "astonished" by the "lull" in attacks from the British press. "In a private inquiry," he later wrote, "I found out that H. M. the Queen herself through a friend . . . had sent word to the British Papers that she wished this ignoble and false game to cease. This is the land of the 'free Press'!" When the tenth anniversary of Frederick III's death came on June 15, 1898, the Queen "regretted" her son-in-law's loss "more and more," seeing it "as quite a calamity for the whole of Europe."

From Molde, in Norway, on July 12, William telegraphed his grandmother that he had just inspected the *Raleigh*, flagship of a training squadron visiting the port, and found the ship in "first-rate order." He was glad to be able "to spend some hours with so many charming brother officers." The yacht *Hohenzollern* was in Norwegian waters because the Queen had not invited Willy to Cowes. His hint was clear.

Dapper, white-coated naval officers in their gold-braided summer finest, exchanging social visits, represented only the sunnier side of a seaborne career. "The accounts of the Spanish-American war are dreadful," Victoria had written in her journal six days earlier. "The Spanish Fleet has been destroyed and the Admiral taken prisoner." In the Sudan, Kitchener's forces were boating up the steamy Nile toward Khartoum, and the Cabinet had decided to her satisfaction "that any other flag in that valley should be removed"—a reference to a token French presence at Fashoda that might bode further trouble. There were problems, too, on other frontiers in Asia and Africa, and concessions would have been fatal to any Ministry in London. As Lord Salisbury explained to the Queen, "British public opinion is [not] always right in this attitude of mind; but, when the public is excited on the subject as they are now, it is too strong to be resisted. . . ."

In the interest of maintaining British influence in East Africa, the Queen, at Osborne on August 8, spoke into a large horn device to record a phonographic message to the Emperor Menelik of Ethiopia, wishing for "friendship between our two Empires." Sending the cylinder with the message, and a phonograph upon which to play it, was calculated to impress the monarch of one of Africa's most backward independent nations. The recording, the Queen commanded, "will be sealed up; and destroyed after he has received the message." It was the first time that modern technology had linked heads of state in such fashion.

In the diaries of her contemporaries, that voice still echoes. Her new Clerk of the Privy Council, Sir Almeric Fitzroy, remembered his first Council, and encountering "the shrivelled octogenarian figure . . . with the habitual dignity that belongs to her, and a clearness of articulation that is startling in its melodious resonance." The contrast of voice and the vessel from which it issued struck him that late October day in 1898:

"Shortly after the bow with which I was dismissed Her Majesty retired, and as she left the room on the arm of her Indian attendant, she appeared to have shrunk into something infinitesimally small and old."

The Council had been convened at Balmoral, and the Queen had paid a rare visit to Crathie Church. Recognizing the venerable royal presence, the minister petitioned the Almighty for her in a curious Psalmist Scots that "as the Queen became an auld woman she might put on the new man, and in all righteous causes stand before her people like a he-goat upon the mountains." A silent amen must have come from the figure in the wheelchair.

The great event of the waning year was the victory at Omdurman, early in September, and the retaking of Khartoum. Gratified in particular by "the memorial service where poor Gordon met his cruel fate," the Queen telegraphed to Sir Herbert Kitchener her congratulations and the offer of a peerage. Soon the general was back in Britain to receive his honors, and on October 31 he visited Victoria, who, by the inexorable dictation of her calendar, had removed to Balmoral.

Dinner conversation with ladies was awkward for Kitchener, who had little experience of them and at forty-eight was a solitary, saturnine bachelor. Victoria was not slow to fill in the silences, however, as she was eager to tell the liberator of Khartoum how she had upbraided and embarrassed Gladstone after Gordon's death by her telegram *en clair*. Monopolizing the conversation (one did not interrupt the Queen), she went on about what was a favorite subject. At a rare pause, Kitchener seized his opportunity. The capture of Omdurman, he confessed, left him greatly inconvenienced by having two thousand Sudanese women on his hands. Princess Beatrice asked what they were like, which briefly baffled Kitchener. "Very much like all women," he said, finally; "they talked a great deal." The royal ladies had no idea how ruthless Kitchener was, and would continue to be, to civilians trapped by his wars.

The day before, so Victoria learned in late November, Colonel Harrington, her representative in Abyssinia, had delivered her phonograph message to King Menelik, and had the cylinder played. "The message was received with ceremony by the King, and after it was delivered, an artillery salute was fired, the King standing to show his respect for the honour paid him." Queen Taitou recognized a reference to herself and exclaimed, "She says my name!" He was also informed, Harrington wrote to the Prime Minister, who relayed the report to Balmoral, "that the King took the opportunity of again listening to her Majesty's message several times, and expressed his surprise that her Majesty's voice at her age should be so firm and distinct. . . . The cylinder was then returned to me and immediately broken into pieces as promised. . . ." Victoria's voice was duly lost to history.

On returning to Windsor later in the month, Victoria learned about South African conditions from her Governor at the Cape, Sir Alfred Milner, who predicted that the Boers "were not likely to be[have] any better." Then it was Lord Kitchener's turn for a second visit, on December 3, before returning to Africa. From the Queen the general received a parting gift that would have been highly unlikely only a few years earlier. "Gave him," she noted in her journal, "a cigarette case with my monogram, with which he seemed much pleased."

Earlier the same day she had gone by train with Kitchener and Princess Beatrice to revisit the military hospital at Netley, and rolled in her wheelchair through the wards while those invalids who could stand rose to attention. There were Indian frontier veterans and Sudanese casualties, to two of whom—a sergeant and a private—she gave medals. A lieutenant, she noticed, "was lying on an ambulance stretcher covered with a quilt I had worked." Almost certainly he did not know it, as Victoria did not want her handiwork prized as something apart. Before leaving, she noted, she was "shown the Röntgen Ray apparatus"—her first encounter with the X-ray. In her eightieth year, she found the artifacts of a new world becoming unavoidable.

A New Year's letter from Emperor Willy suggested strongly his desire to heal the rift with his "Most Beloved Grandmama." He was planning, she already knew from her ambassador in Berlin, Sir Frank Lascelles, to hold a Gold Cup yacht race at Kiel in honor of her eightieth birthday, and obviously hoped to be at Cowes later in 1899. The state of Europe, he contended, was bad—but for Germany and Britain, which had allegedly mutual interests. But he was not reassuring about disarmament replacing Anglo-German weapons competition. How an inch of armor plating on a British warship was to be equated to a rifle battalion in the Tyrol, he confessed to Victoria, he could not imagine. Russia, he thought, was "on the brink of a collapse," a forecast that was premature by nearly two decades. And France was riven by "corruption and injustice."

One of the Queen's visitors in November had been the Russian foreign minister, Prince Lobanoff, and his wife, who were at lunch at Windsor with Eugénie and with the novelist Mrs. Humphry Ward; the Dreyfus case was mentioned, despite the Queen's unspoken rule that political matters not be taken up at her table. The Russians "shook us all very much," Marie Mallet noted, "by saying that no injustice towards the Jew is possible. They *all* ought to be exterminated." Princess Lobanoff added, "Jews! What are they? Little heaps of dirt and rags, how can anyone speak to them?" Marie wondered, "What would they say if she met the Rothschilds at dinner?" No reaction of the Queen survives, but her dislike of Russia and things Russian remained steadfast.

As for France, Victoria was exercised about the meanness of spirit that the Dreyfus affair exposed in a nation whose land and people she loved. With French press criticism of British expansionism in Africa further increased since the Tricolor was taken down in the Sudan, she considered foregoing her annual stay on the Riviera, which fattened French pocketbooks. Soon her ambassador in Paris, Sir Edmund Monson, was under siege, and urged her to go as usual, as a gesture of continuing goodwill. As the old year ended, she kept her options open.

The Queen's life was now circumscribed as much by the dead as by the living. She would not leave Windsor in December before marking the anniversary of Albert's death by a visit to the Mausoleum, and she would not leave Osborne in January before the memorial service for Prince Henry. Meanwhile, officials in France and England worked to ease her concerns as well as her conscience about returning to the Riviera in March. She worried about a possible rightist coup by the generals and colonels who had cashiered Captain Dreyfus; and she continued to feel awkward about giving the implicit approbation of her presence in Cimiez to a nation that approved of the way Dreyfus had been framed.

President Faure assured Monson, he reported to the Queen, "that the excitement caused by the Dreyfus case has been greatly exaggerated," and the "internal situation . . . misunderstood abroad," but he confessed to doubts on both counts. Salisbury, a Francophile, dismissed Monson's concerns to Sir Arthur Bigge, assuring him, indifferently, "There are revolutions and revolutions." Further, he did not feel that tampering with the French courts or imprisoning "a certain number of Jews" need cause the Queen to "take any notice." Still, "if she were nervous, she could always, with her horses, find herself on the other side of the [Italian] frontier in two hours." He preferred that to canceling the visit, and suggested "no precautions except perhaps taking a suite of rooms at Bordighera in the name of one of the Ladies-in-Waiting." A "bad revolution," however, was "likely to be accompanied by an immediate peril of war," and that, he thought, might "entirely alter the position of the Royal party." It was an astonishing position for the Queen's Minister to take.

When Emperor Willy's fortieth birthday arrived on January 27, 1899, all she could add to the melancholy fact in her journal was, "I wish he were more prudent and less impulsive at such an age!" Still, she sent him a congratulatory message, and he responded effusively, "I fully understand how extraordinary the fact must seem to you that the tiny, weeny little brat you often had in your arms and dear Grandpapa swung about in a napkin has reached the forties! Just the half of your prosperous and successful life! It is full of unceasing work, and animated with my untiring trials to emulate such grand example as you set us all."

What William did not say was that he was working tirelessly to isolate Britain from other European nations by alleging to their heads of state that British interests on the Continent and abroad were at odds with their own. Victoria wrote privately to the Czar, "I am afraid that William may go and tell things against us to you, just as he does about you to us. If so, pray tell me openly and confidentially. It is so important that we should understand each other and that such mischievous and unstraightforward proceedings should be put a stop to."

Early in February, young Prince Alfred, the Duke of Coburg's only son, dying of tuberculosis aggravated by venereal disease, shot himself. The Queen knew of his indiscreet life; it seemed to go with the duchy. In her journal he was "a poor dear boy," but her concern was more for the succession. The ostensible heir to the toy state was the Duke of Connaught. There was also Arthur's son, the Queen thought, "and failing him Charlie," Leopold's son and the young Duke of Albany.

Although President Faure died suddenly in mid-February, there was no succession crisis in France. Emile Loubet, who had been premier in 1892, was elected President by the Chamber of Deputies, which pleased Victoria. "He is said," she noted on February 18, "to be an honest respectable man, and not to have taken any violent Dreyfus part." More than that, he was known to favor settlement, and he quickly appointed René Waldeck-Rousseau to form a Ministry to resolve the case that had divided French society. Loubet would discover that more easily promised than done, but it made the Queen's Cimiez stay less anxious.

While in France, Victoria saw Affie, who came from Coburg to discuss the succession. She knew that he had an unmentionable malady. Neither referred to it, but they urged Arthur to stake a claim for himself and his son. When he did, however, Emperor William demanded that Arthur leave his British uniform behind him and enter the German army, take up his principal residence in Germany, and have his son educated there. He could not "pose as a German prince" and still hold a British command. The Queen's ambassador in Berlin dismissed the Emperor's hostility as "ill-humour." William had not been invited to visit England for the Queen's eightieth birthday in May. Also, the division of the islands of Samoa he saw as not to Germany's advantage, although Samoa was "a hairpin to England compared to the thousands of square miles she is annexing right and left unopposed every year." Coburg remained unresolved.

From Omdurman, Lord Kitchener wrote to the Queen that the bones of the Mahdi had been found. He first thought of sending the prize to the College of Surgeons in London, but had second thoughts and saw to their burial in a Moslem cemetery. Victoria was relieved. She disapproved, she wrote to Kitchener, of the "destruction of the poor body of a man who, whether he was very bad and cruel, after all was a *man* of a certain *importance*—that it savours, in the Queen's opinion, too much of the Middle Ages not to allow his remains to be buried in private. . . ." When the Reverend Edgar Sheppard, Sub-Dean of the Chapel Royal, discovered that not all of the Mahdi had been as reverently interred as Victoria assumed—his skull had been turned into an ink-pot—he kept the information to himself.

Her reunion at Cimiez with Vicky was more pathetic than either was willing to confess to the other. The Empress Frederick was slowly dying from inoperable cancer of the spine. She appeared wasted, but would admit nothing. Eugénie knew, and had offered Vicky her villa at Cap Martin. It made possible the memorable sight of three royal widows—the two empresses walking on each side of Victoria's donkey cart, Vicky sustained by morphine and a stubborn determination to outlive her mother. She was fifty-eight.

When the Queen left France, she sent a message of thanks to President Loubet for his nation's hospitality, and Loubet telegraphed to Windsor his appreciation. Victoria wanted no wedges driven between Britain and other nations through Willy's meddling, and the bread-and-butter note was her contribution to amity. At Windsor she spoke with Prince Arthur about the Coburg succession, and Willy's "tiresome interference." Neither the Duke of Connaught nor his son planned to meet German objections, and the Queen was prepared to let "Charlie Albany" become a German—as was his mother in any case—in order to be a reigning duke. (He would take his Germanism very seriously; living into the Hitler era, he became a Nazi.)

Since May 24 was the Queen's eightieth birthday, she put off her trip to Balmoral until the event was appropriately marked. She did not want Emperor William and his family at Windsor, and had made that clear by inviting him instead to Cowes. Willy responded with a long Anglophobic list of accusations against England, largely blaming Lord Salisbury, for "disdainful" treatment of Germany. He was grieved about the gulf between Britain and Germany over so many matters. A "pleasure trip" was impossible, he claimed, because of German public opinion.

Victoria sent the letter to Salisbury, who disposed of each allegation to her satisfaction. She then admonished William, somewhat ungrammatically, "I doubt whether any sovereign ever wrote in such terms to another Sovereign, and that Sovereign his own Grandmother, about their Prime Minister." Enclosed was a copy of Salisbury's detailed rejection of each complaint to show William that he was "under a misapprehension," and a reminder that her invitation had not been to the races at Cowes but to her home at Osborne, and that she was "always your affectionate Grandmother, V.R.I." Taken aback, William accepted the spurned invitation, and would come in November.

The Queen's eightieth birthday was celebrated in relative quiet, although everywhere she now went, her presence brought out tens of thousands. Even her going to Paddington Station attracted crowds reminiscent of the Jubilees. At Windsor on May 24 she received delegations, Addresses, and gifts, including eighty roses from the First Life Guards; in her pony cart she viewed a march-past of Scots Guards, with Arthur at their head as colonel-in-chief. Afterwards, she drove across the Long Walk to the Mausoleum, where she placed flowers "at the foot of the dear tomb. How much my dear Albert would have rejoiced to see all these marks of love and loyalty!"

After a family dinner she sat in the first row, in the Waterloo Gallery, to view the first and third acts of Wagner's *Lohengrin*, "enchanted" by "the most glorious composition, so poetic, so dramatic, and one might almost say, religious in feeling and full of sadness, pathos, and tenderness." The de Reszke brothers' singing was "beyond praise." She had grown up in the *bel canto* world of Rossini and Donizetti; now she had experienced the new musical theater of Wagner and Puccini.

Victoria arrived at Balmoral on May 27. There was still frost on the ground, yet daylight lasted until nine in the evening. The natural light was a relief to the Queen, as the new electric lighting everywhere at Balmoral created more glare for her than visibility. Dr. Pagenstecher had visited her at Windsor and again dilated her eyes, but the effect was only to permit her to see, temporarily, around her cloudy cataracts. With her vision so poor, she was dependent entirely on being read to, sometimes by her ladies, but more frequently, when the matter seemed confidential, by Princess Beatrice, who was often in a hurry to get the uninteresting matter over with, and made mistakes or skipped lines, which caused the Queen confusion. Marie Mallet, who, as Extra Bedchamber Woman, did some of the reading and correspondence, thought that Beatrice deserved "shaking," but the Princess had been trapped for years in a role in which she found herself increasingly impatient.

To assist Victoria in reading, as her spectacles were of little use, Fritz Ponsonby had experimented with blacker and blacker ink, and oversized writing, but nothing worked; she was now unable to distinguish faces clearly enough to identify people before they spoke to her. She began, too, to mistake some people for long-dead relatives, which was not a matter of failing vision but failing memory. On one occasion in June 1899 a dinner guest was Paul Cambon, the French ambassador. The Queen, who had the seating list in advance, assumed that as senior envoy he would be seated on her left. The Master of the Household had erred, however, and placed him on her right. Her practice was to begin to talk to the least interesting of her guests on either side, so that she could devote her time largely to the other. Thinking, then, that Cambon was the Italian ambassador, Count Deym, she asked, "Where is your King now?"

Cambon realized that the Queen had mistaken him for his Italian colleague. With unhesitating tact, he placed the King on his yacht, and continued on, describing his last meeting with his Majesty. As it became more obviously painful to drag out the masquerade, Victoria understood her error. Afterwards she summoned the unfortunate Household official to berate him for embarrassing her.

Nothing of the blunder appeared in the Queen's journal, where she referred to Cambon as "a most agreeable well-informed man with large views"—in part, perhaps, a compliment to his knowledge of Italian matters. She was far more interested in his opinions of the Dreyfus case, as the government had arranged for a retrial, and at Balmoral the Queen had called it "great news." Now, in July at Windsor, Cambon spoke in terms the Queen approved of the *"misérable affaire de Dreyfus,"* and how he thought that feeling in France had changed. To Victoria he predicted an acquittal, and thought that "the whole affair had arisen from the fact of his being a Jew," and that Dreyfus was "intelligent and clever," but unlikable. *"Il était la victime de son caractère,"* the Queen quoted Cambon as saying.

On September 9, 1899, she "heard the news of poor Dreyfus' fresh condemnation by five votes to two. . . . After having been so splendidly defended . . . , it is dreadful that it should have been in vain. Everyone is greatly excited and distressed about it." She sent a telegram to her Prime Minister, saying, "I am too horrified for words at this monstrous horrible sentence against this poor martyr Dreyfus. If only all Europe would express its horror and indignation! I trust there will be a severe retribution. V.R.I." Salisbury agreed with her "burning indignation." Not since her message to Gladstone about Gordon had she sent an uncoded telegram on a sensitive matter. When the text of a similar telegram to her ambassador leaked out in Paris, as she intended it would, there was outrage from the rightist press about her meddling, and vicious caricatures appeared of a corpulent, beak-nosed, and witchlike Queen. Even so, her public intervention as the most influential reigning monarch can only have assisted President Loubet—as perhaps Victoria hoped it would—to free Captain Dreyfus.

On September 20, Ambassador Monson, whom she had asked for all possible information, reported to her that Dreyfus had been "liberated." There was to be more legal action—it took until 1906 before the captain's honor was restored—but at least his sentence had been remitted and he was not returned to the notorious penal colony of Devil's Island. "Meanwhile," Sir Edmund Monson wrote to the Queen on October 1, "the French newspapers have found in the Transvaal an opportunity for retaliating upon England for the freedom with which the English Press criticised proceedings at the Rennes Court-Martial."

In May, just before her birthday, the Queen had received a document signed by thousands of "British Subjects resident in British South Africa" asking for her help in redressing the grievances of the 21,684 signers of a petition to her from the Transvaal Uitlanders. The non-Boer population claimed that there was no freedom of the press, nor of public meeting, that they were often arbitrarily jailed, and that they were overtaxed but had no voting representation in the government. All were violations of the Convention of 1881 by which Gladstone shed the colony. The Cape Colony residents now backed the Uitlander petition, alleging that the Transvaal regime was "a source of unrest, insecurity, and injury to business, throughout Your Majesty's South African possessions." Then came messages from Natal that troops were needed to protect that frontier against attack from the Boers, and reinforcements were sent both from England and from India. The Queen had supported the move; she wanted no national humiliation. The only news from Africa that was not gloomy was that her agent in Abyssinia, Colonel Harrington, had arrived at Osborne in August with a return phonograph message from Emperor Menelik and Empress Taitou, which she had listened to through a large horn-shaped speaker and found "very curious."

As the late summer of 1899 faded into autumn, events caused the Queen to dwell less on her family problems and her physical handicaps, despite constant reminders of both. One letter read to her by Princess Beatrice suggested that the Queen might get about more efficiently if she wore a tight leather jacket to which a balloon could be affixed, and she could float rather than walk. It was an unfunny reminder of her increasing dependence. When Fritz Ponsonby wanted to marry, she had forced him to delay the wedding for three years, as she needed him close, and wanted no wife to be in the way; she also took it badly when Sir James Reid became engaged to one of her maids-of-honor, for no one seemed more necessary, and she had long assumed that the doctor would remain a bachelor and go everywhere with her.

Impending war made it impossible to think so much of her own person. The dour backwardness of Boer behavior contributed to her sense of just national purpose. In the face of apparently legitimate grievances from her subjects in Afrikaaner country, she had no idea how much the war had been sought by Alfred Milner and Cecil Rhodes in South Africa, and by that onetime radical republican who was her Secretary for the Colonies, Joseph Chamberlain. Boer intransigence was what they required as *casus belli*, and President Kruger was playing into their hands.

Late in August the German ambassador in London, Paul von Hatzfeldt, had written to Count Holstein that he did not believe that war would come "unless they have gone mad in Pretoria." Kruger's insistence that Britain renounce its largely meaningless suzerainty was "doing Chamberlain the greatest favour." The ambassador assumed that Chamberlain would find different pretexts to retake the Transvaal if the Uitlander one were settled, "until he has achieved his aim." Limited in what she read by what was read to her, and restricted in whom she saw by who was permitted into her presence, the Queen knew nothing of the political strategies of her Ministers at home or abroad to reabsorb the Boer states. The Duchess of Buccleuch once told the Queen that she had met Rhodes at a dinner party in London, but had not wanted him to be introduced to her, as she had heard that he disliked all women and was sometimes very rude to them. "Oh, I don't think that can be so," said the Queen, "because he was very civil to me when he came here." Rhodes had prophesied to her a Cape-to-Cairo colony, and she knew of his hand in the Jameson Raid; but he had seemed to her more enthusiast than conspirator.

The Boers, Salisbury reported on September 29, remained "obstinate." Further, he told the Queen, "It is impossible to avoid believing that the Boers really aim at setting up a South African Republic consisting of the Transvaal, the Orange Free State, and your Majesty's [Cape] Colony." While sending out General Sir Redvers Buller, with troops that increased her forces in South Africa to 70,000 men, "the largest number *ever* sent from the United Kingdom for any war," Viscount Wolseley assured the Queen blandly on October 4, 1899, that "I still cling to the idea that in the end we shall have no serious fighting." Before sailing, Buller had an audience with the Queen at Balmoral on October 5. She found him "blunt" and "straightforward." It was no disadvantage to Victoria's confidence in his leadership that his mother was a Howard and a niece of the Duke of Norfolk.

Soon afterward, Chamberlain transmitted to the Queen the text of what he described as an "ultimatum" from Kruger that she found "astounding," and that appeared to mean war. It demanded the withdrawal of all troops landed at the Cape since June 1, and of all troops from the Transvaal-Natal frontier, and the return of all forces on the high seas intended for South African service. If no satisfactory reply was received by five on the morning of October 11, Kruger would consider that equivalent to a declaration of war. "In the face of this attack," said Lord Rosebery, speaking for the Liberals, "the nation will, I doubt not, close its ranks and relegate party controversy to a more convenient season."

At Balmoral, Victoria visited her guard of Gordon Highlanders, which was about to embark for South Africa. "I drove down the line," she wrote; "they marched past and re-formed. . . . I addressed them a few parting words as follows: 'I desire to wish you Godspeed. May God protect you! I am confident that you will always do your duty and will ever maintain the high reputation of the Gordon Highlanders.' The men then gave three cheers." She shook hands with the captain of the guard and spoke to the two lieutenants, and "felt quite a lump in my throat as we drove away. . . . I thought of how those remarkably fine men might not all return." Characteristically, she then telegraphed Salisbury, who had proposed to pay for the war by adding a penny per pound to the income tax, and sixpence to the price of a pint of beer, that she did not want the burden of taxation to "fall upon the working classes." Salisbury put off the proposal for future consideration.

In Germany, newspapers were noisily anti-British, describing Imperial England as a wicked giant, and printing abusive caricatures of the Queen. In South Africa, however, Britain appeared anything but fearsome. Kruger's aim had been to strike before the enemy forces had been augmented, and he did. The British press published a litany of retreats and disasters. Suddenly again the Woman Warrior, Victoria seemed rejuvenated by each setback, and when, as in 1854, two archbishops proposed a national "Day of Humiliation," she told Fritz Ponsonby that she objected to ordering people to pray for anything. "Let them pray," she said; "I hope and trust they will do so, but it should be without any order from me." Yet the first months of the war were days of repeated humiliations. "The Queen," Fritz Ponsonby recalled, "would often break down and cry at the long lists of casualties—at least we thought them long in those days; she seemed impatient for victory and unable to understand why the British Army did not have one great victory and put an end to the war."

Unfamiliar names became part of press vocabulary—Nicholson's Nek, Ladysmith, Lombard's Kop, Sannah's Post, Dewetsdorp, Reddersberg, Kroonstaad. At Nicholson's Nek an entire battalion and a battery of artillery surrendered. Ladysmith was isolated and besieged. "I suppose we could not expect to have no reverses," she told Ponsonby, who brought the bad news, "but we must win, [even] if the whole Army has to go out."

The war was exactly a month old when the Queen emerged from her railway carriage at Windsor Station after more than seventeen hours' travel overnight from Balmoral. It was not quite nine in the morning. At a quarter to one she was off in a carriage with Beatrice and with Emily Ampthill to the Spital Barracks, to inspect three squadrons of the Household Cavalry about to leave for South Africa. After she accepted their salutes, driving down the line, the soldiers re-formed around the carriage so that she could address them, and in a voice as clear as ever, she took leave of "you, who have always served near me . . . before you start on your long voyage to a distant part of my Empire, in whose defence your comrades are now so nobly fighting." Then Colonel Nield introduced his officers, one of whom was Princess May's brother, Dolly Teck. When the men were asked to give her three cheers before she departed, "they gave many more and would hardly stop."

The Times marveled at her "physical stamina," and praised her "habitual subordination of ordinary personal comfort to ceremonial requirements." It was becoming habitual, but there were many in Victoria's entourage who could remember when she refused to change her schedule even when a Government fell. Now there would be many more leave-takings, and, soon, returnings of the wounded. The Queen was at many, showing no public signs of fatigue. In private, she gave way to her exhaustion. After one long day, with the prospect of a Privy Council session the next morning, she dined at 9:15, then afterwards fell asleep twice while talking to Lord Balfour of Burleigh, "much to his consternation," Almeric Fitzroy noted. Awakening, she excused herself "with great candour on the score of her long drive," and continued, "with great animation," her condemnation of Sir William Harcourt's speeches as "unpatriotic and disloyal."

Questioning either the methods or the morality of the war led to quick accusations of being "pro-Boer." Both concerns, nevertheless, were openly voiced, and the ineptitude of British planning and tactics agonized and embarrassed the Queen. The army was incompetently led, pinch-penny equipped, and meagerly supplied. At one point late in October the Queen's speech closing the short session of Parliament had to be altered at the last moment, before formal submission to her, by substituting "the splendid qualities displayed by our soldiers" for "the victories won."

The Queen was not always on the move. She was, after all, eighty. Yet soon she was back at Windsor Station, with a large party, en route to Bristol to open the Royal Convalescent Hospital, traveling most of a day in a jolting railway carriage in order to spend two hours—from two to four o'clock—proceeding through beflagged streets and visiting the military hospital. The daughter of a local vicar had written to tell her of a blind and paralyzed invalid, Robert Caines, whose house was on the route she was to take, and the Queen had her carriage slowed at the spot so that the old man could at least hear her pass. Afterward she sent him a £5 note, assuming that it would be of more use than her photograph. Going and returning, her train was slowed in populated places to give people an opportunity to see the Queen at her window.

On November 20, Emperor William and his family paid their postponed visit to Windsor, at a time when Victoria had to rely more upon herself to handle a state guest than ever before. Lady Salisbury, who had been hopelessly ill, died that afternoon. Since Lord Salisbury held the Foreign Office portfolio, and was two advisers in one, she had to handle her grandson largely by herself, although Arthur Balfour, as representative of his uncle, had a session with the Emperor. That the visit had come off at all was a result of a political settlement, a few months earlier, of claims to various Pacific island groups, in which Britain withdrew from Samoa, leaving the islands to be divided between Germany and the United States. Britain acquired Tonga instead; and Germany was permitted to purchase the Caroline Islands from Spain, which no longer saw any use for them after losing the Philippines. Germany was stretching out as a colonial power, and William was finding more reason to expand his navy.

Despite embarrassments in Natal, which might have given William cause for secret joy, he could see in Britain the massive resources that would eventually overwhelm the Boers. On November 25, 1899, the day before the Emperor left Windsor for Sandringham, news arrived from Egypt that Sir Reginald Wingate had defeated the Khalifa and his Dervish army, leaving many of them dead on the field. "This, I hope, means the end of Mahdism," Victoria wrote, "and I think it is far the best way it could end." Emperor William was suitably impressed. To his staff he exclaimed grandly, before the Round Tower at Windsor, "From this Tower the world is ruled!"

The Queen knew better than William that all was not well. Some towns in Natal held out grimly. The British appeared blundering and often foolish. Buller, with an army to relieve Ladysmith, retreated and advanced, and retreated again. Newspaper hoardings splashed "Buller Across the Tugela [River]," then "Buller Re-crosses the Tugela." Everywhere he was rechristened "Sir Reverse." The American expatriate artist James Whistler, fervently pro-Boer, when informed that the general had boasted that he had retreated without losing a man, a flag, or a cannon, added to a guest at one of his famous breakfasts, "Yes, or a minute." When an English friend claimed that the cream of British manhood had gone to South Africa, Whistler retorted, "Whipped cream!" With defeats came the unsentimental realization that jingoism was not enough; this was best summed up in an unsentimental portrayal of the British soldier by the unofficial poet laureate of the Empire, Rudyard Kipling:

*When you've shouted "Rule Britannia," when you've sung "God Save
   the Queen,"
When you've finished killing Kruger with your mouth,
Will you kindly drop a shilling in my little tambourine
   For a gentleman in kharki ordered south?
He's an absent minded beggar, and his weaknesses are great—
   But we and Paul must take him as we find him—
He is out on active service, wiping something off a slate—
   And he's left a lot of little things behind him!
   Duke's son—cook's son—son of a hundred kings—
   (Fifty thousand horse and foot going to Table Bay!)
Each of 'em doing his country's work
   (and who's to look after their things?)
Pass the hat for your credit's sake, and pay—pay—pay!*

Recited in music halls, the poem raised large sums for relief of
families desperate on the low soldiers' pay, or dependent upon meager
widows' pensions.

The Queen sought a symbolic present to send to the troops for
Christmas as something special from her. Soon, ships were bringing every
soldier in the field a flat tin box of chocolate with the Queen's head
embossed on the lid, a profile that Kipling pictured as her troops might
have:

> *'Ave you 'eard of the Widow of Windsor
>   With a hairy gold crown on 'er 'ead?
> She 'as ships on the foam—she 'as millions at 'ome,
>   An' she pays us poor beggars in red.*

Every soldier in South Africa and in transports on the high seas was
to receive such as a box, bound in red, white, and blue ribbon, and had
to sign a receipt for it. A hundred thousand slabs of chocolate went
south,* and legends grew about their efficacy. Some soldiers would not
touch a morsel, determined to take the sacred gifts home. Sean O'Casey's
brother Tom returned to Dublin, "the Queen's coloured box of chocolate
in his kit-bag still full of the sweetmeat, for what soldier could chocolate given by a Queen?"

More than one box was reputed to have stopped a bullet. An authen-

*Belatedly, the tins were distributed in mid-January

tic example was sent to the Queen by the medical officer treating Private James Humphrey of the Royal Lancasters on February 28, 1900. The forwarding note from the military hospital at Frere explained that the box had been in the soldier's haversack. The bullet had gone through it and lodged in the chocolate rather than in Private Humphrey's spleen. Bigge suggested that the Queen "would doubtless wish another box be sent to Private Humphrey."

The gift was highly prized—a rare if not unique contact, the troops felt, with her Majesty. Men refused £5—two months' pay for a private soldier—for the Queen's chocolate. On visits to hospitals, Victoria carried additional tin boxes, and one legless soldier declared gallantly, "I would rather lose a limb than not get that!" Widows and bereaved mothers were often sent the boxes together with the personal effects of a soldier buried far from home.

Victoria interested herself in every way in which she might play a role in the war. On December 4, 1899, she received the largely American volunteers staffing the hospital ship *Maine*, outfitted with American funds. The vessel itself was on loan from a Baltimore shipping company, and the entire project was the brainchild of the American-born widow of Lord Randolph Churchill, Jennie. The medical staff was invited to Windsor for a luncheon with Princess Helena, whose son Christian was eager to join the war. Then they were presented to the Queen, who thanked them for their "kindness in coming over to take care of my men." Two days later, Jennie Churchill was invited to "dine and sleep" at Windsor. Victoria worried to her, "I think the surgeons look very young."

"All the more energetic, therefore," said Jennie, in an uninhibited American rejoinder. It was easy to forget the polite trailing "Ma'am" when for two weeks she had agonized over her son Winston, a correspondent for the *Morning Post.* He was a prisoner of the Boers, who had overturned and seized a poorly defended armored train. The misfortune would be the beginning of his celebrity, as he soon managed to escape, and write about it. Absorbed in preparations to get the *Maine* off to South Africa, Lady Churchill could not give much time to anxiety about her son. The expected American-flag status of her ship had been denied by Washington, and she had to appeal hurriedly to the Duke of Connaught, an old friend, to secure a Union Jack instead. On December 16 he presented the flag in person, in the Queen's name, a Union Jack with a red cross on a white ground in the center. "Never before," said the Duke innocently as the flag was run up, "has a ship sailed under the combined flags of the Union Jack and the Stars and Stripes. . . ." Jennie could not confess that they had no authority to fly the Stars and Stripes, and had it run up anyway. On Christmas Day the ship moved out in heavy fog, to cheers from a dockside throng the volunteers could not see.

During what became known as Black Week—December 10 through 15, 1899—British forces suffered extraordinary casualties. Yet Ladysmith was still unrelieved, Buller having been routed while trying a frontal assault up the railway line. The Queen learned of the multiple disasters when she went to breakfast on December 16 and was handed "a very unsatisfactory telegram" received by the War Office from Buller. He reported severe casualties and heavy fire from the enemy; and while he boasted that the enemy had suffered heavy losses, his forces had "not seen a dead Boer." Buller estimated that they had faced a force of 20,000 men in that sector alone, although the entire population of the Transvaal, including women and children, was only 85,000.

Visiting Windsor on December 18, Arthur Balfour was despondent. "Please understand," said Victoria, "that there is no one depressed in *this* house; we are not interested in the possibilities of defeat; they do not exist." She decided not to go to Osborne for Christmas, in order to be more accessible to her Ministers. From Berlin came a confused holiday greeting from Willy, about "Peace and goodwill among men," and about how "the British aristocracy have shown the world that they know how to die doing their duty, like the other gentlemen!"

Because of the newspaper publicity about its fourteen-year-old bugler, one of Buller's regiments that had marched to its slaughter became particularly admired by Victoria. General Arthur Fitzroy Hart, commanding the Dublin Fusiliers, had failed to send out scouts, knew nothing of what lay ahead for his troops, and, despite a hail of musketry, had kept them in textbook-tight ranks. Ordered to the rear because of his youth, Arthur Dunn had disobeyed and remained with his company; when its forward ranks crumpled, he panicked, and raising his bugle, he sounded an advance. Men fixed bayonets, and charged blindly into the Tugela, about ten feet deep at that point. Some drowned; others who swam across were cut down by Boer fire on the other side. A few swam back and saved themselves, including Bugler Dunn, who was wounded in the arm and chest and lost his bugle. Invalided home, the boy became a hero because the country needed one, and perhaps because he was too young to be court-martialed. At Portsmouth he was lifted to the shoulders of the delirious crowd, and he was taken to Osborne to meet the Queen, who presented him, to national joy, with a new silver bugle. She described him in her journal as "a nice-looking, modest boy." One of the first heroes of the war, he was responsible for many of the Dublin Fusiliers' 216 casualties at Colenso.

Two days before Christmas, Lord Roberts of Kandahar, V.C., sixty-seven, military hero of Afghan and other colonial wars, and army chief in Ireland, left for South Africa to take charge of the faltering operation. Prince Arthur—his senior as a field marshal—pleaded to go as second-in-command, but was not permitted, on the technicality that he could not waive his rank. The Prince of Wales saw Roberts off. His ship was the *Dunottar Castle,* which earlier had carried Buller to South Africa. Bertie reported to his mother "a dense and unmanageable crowd, with danger of being squashed." Roberts, standing on deck, wore an unmilitary black coat and top hat, which he raised to acknowledge the crowd on the dock. *The Times* described him as a "little, vigorous, resolute, sorrowful man in deep mourning." The day before he had visited the Queen, who wrote in her journal, "He knelt down and kissed my hand. I said how much I felt for him. He could only answer, 'I cannot speak of *that,* but I can speak of anything else.' "

Roberts's only son, Frederick, had died of wounds suffered at Colenso the week before, and even the Boer General "Piet" Joubert had telegraphed his sympathy to the young officer's parents. So had Victoria, who had received a response from Dublin, "Our loss is grievous, but our boy died the death he would have chosen." Lieutenant Roberts had been shot from his saddle while foolhardily trying to rescue some of Buller's abandoned big guns. He became the first posthumous Victoria Cross. Seven V.C.s were awarded for mad attempts to retrieve the ten abandoned naval guns, the first heavy artillery lost by any British force in a century. Although only living soldiers could then earn the Victoria Cross, a convenient fiction explained that Buller had recommended the V.C. for young Roberts before he died, and the Queen sent a message to Lansdowne at the War Office, "Would wish to have it, so that I may hand it to Lady Roberts myself."

On the day after Christmas—Boxing Day—Victoria, still at Windsor, gave a tea under a large, trinket-decorated tree, perhaps the first to be lighted by electric lights, to the wives of Windsor troops serving in South Africa. Then, she wrote, the "children trooped in, and after looking at the tree they all sat down to tea at two very long tables, below the tree. Everyone helped to serve them, including my family, old and young, and my ladies and gentlemen. I was rolled up and down round the tables, after which I went away for a short while to have my own tea, returning when the tree was beginning to be stripped, handing myself many of the things to the wives and dear little children. . . . It was a very touching sight, when one thinks of the poor husbands and fathers, who are all away, and some of whom may not return."

On December 28, two days later, she received thanks from Kitchener, then en route to South Africa, for being given the assignment as deputy to Roberts. The Duke of Connaught—at her insistence—took Roberts's post in Dublin. By New Year's Eve she was finally at Osborne, summing up in her journal the "very eventful, and in many ways sad, year." On New Year's Day 1900 she telegraphed good wishes to the blundering Sir Redvers Buller, a signal of her stubborn backing in his adversity. Roberts arrived in Cape Town on January 10, with Kitchener, to replace Buller as overall commander, but Buller stayed on.

At Osborne on January 22, the Queen saw Joseph Chamberlain, whom she had called Gladstone's "evil genius" in 1882 and "a dreadful socialist" in 1885. Now they appeared to think alike, and he assured her "that he had done everything in the world to prevent the war, but that it had come, for come it must have in the future, it was better that it should have been now, before the numbers of the enemy were still greater." He was certain that "the back of the war will be broken if we can relieve Ladysmith." Four days later she had a telegram from Buller that his forces had abandoned Spion Kop, with two hundred killed and three hundred wounded, including Major General E. R. P. Woodgate, in command. A few days later she learned that the dead included twenty-two officers, and she expressed horror to Lansdowne at the "terrible list of casualties." Wolseley, who also visited her, claimed—unknowingly echoing Emperor William—that the severe toll in officers "proves that the gentlemen to whom the Queen gives Commissions in the Army realise the privileges of their position as gentlemen, and accept the responsibilities inseparable from that position."

Fortunately for her agonized state of mind—Victoria was having trouble sleeping—what she was told erred on the low side. There were at least 1,700 dead, wounded, and missing, and the stench of the unburied corpses in the African heat quickly drove the Boers from the strategic prominence they had won.

Across the continent, other British enclaves were under siege. In the center, south of the Vaal River, Kimberley was isolated; near Ladysmith, in the east, Mafeking was surrounded, although a siege by Boer standards involved Sabbatarian cessations of shelling on Sundays, and a half-hour evening stand-down at five-thirty for coffee. On February 2 the mayor of Mafeking sent a telegram of devotion and resolve to Victoria to mark the hundredth day of the siege. On the sixteenth she received news of the relief of Kimberley, which seemed the first break in the cycle of despair, and a sign that the masses of troops rushed to South Africa, however badly trained, were having some numerical impact. Emperor William offered his reaction to the Kimberley news, which the Queen could not possibly misinterpret. "How happy Mr. Rhodes will be!" Willy telegraphed slyly. Cecil Rhodes had been in the besieged town throughout its ordeal, but that may not have been what William meant at all.

Victoria now nodded off a great deal, making sleep at night more difficult, and further increasing her tendency to doze her days away. "My evening task is now no light one," Marie Mallet wrote from Osborne on February 4; "the Queen sleeps soundly and yet adjures me to keep her awake, even shake her if necessary, this I cannot bring myself to do, so I read and rustle the paper and wriggle on my chair and drop my fan and do all in my power to rouse my Sovereign, but she would be so much better off in bed and so should I!" A few days later, on an afternoon drive, the Queen sat with her back to the horses, "so funny," Marie thought, "to be out of the wind." Victoria had never before sat in such an unqueenly position, but as Marie had realized on returning to her lady-in-waiting cycle after a six months' absence, "she has changed since I was here last and looks so much older and feebler that my heart rather sinks." In the carriage, she and the Duchess of Roxburghe "made feverish efforts to keep the conversation alive but the Queen slept peacefully on my shoulder and was hard to rouse."

On one morning early in Marie Mallet's round of duty, she went with the Queen to Whippingham Church for "a gloomy little funeral service in honour of poor Prince Henry's burial day. These reiterated services are very tiring but I really think the Queen enjoys them; at any rate they are the only lodestones that draw her within the precincts of a church!"

Back at Windsor, as the Queen was preparing to leave, on the morning of February 27, for the military hospital at Netley, news arrived from Lord Roberts. General "Piet" Cronjé, surrounded, starving, and cut off at Paardeberg, and bombarded with heavy weapons for which he had no response, had surrendered with his six thousand men, women, and children. Dressed like the farmer he was, the hulking, black-bearded

Cronjé contrasted sharply with the tiny, khaki-clad, white-mustached Roberts, five-foot-three. "You have made a gallant defence, sir," said Roberts.

While there was consternation in Pretoria, where churches had held special services to pray for the garrison at Paardeberg, Roberts telegraphed the Queen that he thought it was "satisfactory" that the first good news of the war had occurred "on the anniversary of Majuba." (Majuba had been the scene of the last battle of the first Anglo-Boer war, where on February 26, 1881, British regular soldiers had been defeated by Transvaal farmers one-sixth their numbers, and Gladstone in London had decided that it was best to settle for nominal suzerainty and evacuation.) When, two days later, Ladysmith was relieved, Buller having finally crossed the Tugela, it appeared that Boer resistance was cracking.

The news came as the Queen was preparing for an Investiture at Windsor, with the Duke of York assisting. "Georgie," she wrote, stood at her side and assisted her with the decorations—"and I used his sword for the few knighthoods." The message from Ladysmith identified a Dundonald regiment, from County Down; Wolseley recommended that some appropriate gesture toward Ireland was in order—that it would have "a magical effect upon that sentimental and imaginative race all over the world." For "the Queen's initiative," he proposed that all Irish regiments be authorized to wear a shamrock in future years on St. Patrick's Day. "Every year," he pointed out, "Irish Members of Parliament make much capital out of the fact that Irish regiments are not allowed to wear . . . a national emblem."

Victoria approved, and also directed that a regiment of Irish Guards be formed. In time for St. Patrick's Day, the War Office issued an order authorizing the wearing of the shamrock, much as the Welsh Fusiliers wore the leek on St. David's Day. Both ideas led to a third and more far-reaching one for the Queen. On March 2, 1900, Prince Arthur had visited from Ireland. He was the logical person to whom to propose an Irish Guards unit, and he added the further suggestion that a visit to Ireland might substitute for the Queen's annual trip to the south. In the altered wartime perspective, the unhappy island suddenly seemed the opportune place for her to be. No one before had dared raise the matter with the Queen that the French or Italian Riviera would be inappropriate for her while the nation was bleeding, and Europe was lacking in sympathy; yet her Household had prudently delayed arranging for a Mediterranean holiday.

"THE GRACIOUS QUEEN"

"The Gracious Queen"—an 1899 French poster attacking Victoria. Hovering in the background is Joseph Chamberlain, her apparent manipulator.

The Italians were every bit as offensive to the Queen as the Germans and the French. A caricature in *Il Fischietto* pictured a hugely fat *"Sainte Reine"* with an explosive temper, and *L'Asino* showed her in a tentlike uniform with a cannon slung on her back. In the German *Kladderadatsch*, a fat Victoria in widow's black let a bulldog loose on an innocent Boer maiden, and *Lustige Blätter* showed an immensely rotund queen, in black, assisted by a monocled Joseph Chamberlain, coloring more of a map in British red. In Austria, *Rumoristische Blätter* caricatured a bulging-eyed Victoria pulling in a Lilliputian Paul Kruger on a string, while *Kikeriki* put her in admiral's uniform accepting the obeisance of tiny black natives, and also in widow's weeds tearfully drinking "Ladysmith" English bitter. *Weekblad voor Nederland* showed her at a sink, vainly trying to wash the blood of the dead and wounded from her hands, while a top-hatted Death (a monocled Joseph Chamberlain) looks on smilingly, and *La Réforme* in Belgium, calling her *Grandmaman*, pictured her in a cannon-laden chariot labeled with the motto of the Order of the Garter, *Honi soit qui mal y pense*—Evil be to him who thinks evil. From St. Petersburg to Lisbon, the Continent was hostile to the war against the Boers, and a bloated and repellent Victoria bore the brunt of the cartoonists' wrath. Since she saw only what was put before her, she knew nothing of their brutality, but a

Europe whipped to that kind of anti-British frenzy remained no place for her to holiday.

Within days, plans for a royal visit to Dublin were under way. Although the Queen was largely bound to a wheelchair or a carriage, and there were concerns for her safety, the war had spurred her into rejecting invalidism for symbolism. Accordingly, almost as if it were a trial run for Ireland, Victoria ventured upon a Royal Progress from Windsor into London, and thence into the City, on March 8, to express as best she could her appreciation to the City of London for raising a remarkable force for the war, the City of London Imperial Volunteers. Its uniforms and equipment, all but its rifles, were paid for out of a Mansion House fund to which the public had subscribed £100,000. It had been a direct outcome of Black Week, and had been outfitted and trained so rapidly that the first units were already on troopships bound for Durban. For the first time, a British Army unit—a battery of artillery, a battalion of infantry, and two companies of mounted infantry, 1,550 men in all—was officered without the qualification that the leadership consist of gentlemen, and manned without the qualification that they be otherwise. All ranks included professionals—barristers, architects, civil servants, schoolmasters. The CIV augured the future.

From Paddington to Buckingham Palace, and from the palace to Blackfriars, where the Lord Mayor, in full regalia, waited with his aldermen, the crowds were of Jubilee magnitude. Helena and Beatrice sat opposite the Queen in her carriage, which the Lord Mayor, Sir Alfred Newton, approached in order that Victoria could thank him "for all the City has done."

The next day she went out again, the Princess of Wales replacing Helena this time. Traveling west rather than east, as far as Hyde Park and Exhibition Road, Victoria gave crowds an opportunity to celebrate what most assumed was the beginning of the end of the war; and on the morning of March 10 she drove out in her carriage onto the palace lawn to see off two battalions of Guards, whom she wished Godspeed. Then, without changing carriages, she departed for Paddington and Windsor.

To the Queen, Roberts forecast that the Orange Free State was "rapidly settling down," and he thought that the Transvaal "will probably hold out," but could not last much longer. Also seeing the end near, Emperor William offered his "friendly intervention" to restore peace—in effect, to salvage the two Boer republics. "Please convey to the Emperor," she telegraphed to Sir Frank Lascelles in Berlin, "that my whole nation is with me in a fixed determination to see this war through without intervention. The time for, and the terms of, peace must be left for our decision, and my country, which is suffering from so heavy a sacrifice of precious lives, will resist all interference." The Prince of Wales's private secretary, Sir Francis Knollys, thought that the message was "worthy of Queen Elizabeth."

Victoria went off again by train from Windsor on March 22, this time via Waterloo Station, to Woolwich Arsenal, where twenty thousand men were working to produce munitions. A half-holiday was declared, and the workmen "cheered so tremendously that it quite drowned out the band playing *God Save the Queen.*" Two miles farther was the Herbert Hospital, the route "crowded with a dense mass of cheering and shouting people." The route was full of symbols, including "the little house in which General Gordon was born, and the statue of the Prince Imperial, just outside the Military Academy [at Sandhurst]." Wheeled through the corridors lined with convalescent wounded, she struggled to see, through her dim eyes, every man. In the wards she maneuvered up to each bed, so that she could speak to each of the bedridden casualties. To some she gave flowers, and asked where they had received their wounds, learning that several had been "in that dreadful affair at Colenso," and that others had arrived only days before. It was four miles back to Waterloo Station, over Blackheath, past the Fever Hospital, the Naval School for Boys, and the Crippled Children's Home, all of them fronted by deafeningly enthusiastic crowds. Victoria was back at Windsor at seven, "somewhat fatigued." She was only two months short of eighty-one. Someone else of similar age, as blind and as crippled as the Queen, might have been pardoned for indulging in some self-pity in the privacy of an invalid's parlor. She had done so herself thirty years and more earlier, when she was physically far more sound.

On April 1, Victoria telegraphed a message of "confidence and admiration" to Colonel Robert Baden-Powell, commanding the troops at besieged Mafeking. Cut off from most ways of sending and receiving news, Mafeking often relied on a powerful heliograph. In the town, to keep up confidence, Baden-Powell (he claimed it was his staff) had stamps printed, his head replacing the Queen's. When Victoria found out about it later, despite her pride in the defiance of Mafeking, she was annoyed.

Just before she left for Ireland, she asked the Colonial Office to do something about the flood of visitors to South Africa who got in the way of the war. Officials still marveled at her way of finding out what they did not want her to know, but she talked to everyone she could about the war, including wounded serving soldiers, who were innocent of deception. Her ladies seemed to have their own sources of information. While the shooting went on, Cooks was organizing tours of now-quiet battlefields; families were visiting hospitals and graves; and an "unusual number of ladies," Chamberlain told Milner on the Queen's instructions, seemed to have inconvenienced Cape Town although they had (as Milner confessed) "no particular call or business." In effect they did have, but they were not what Victoria wanted there, and she deplored "the hysterical spirit" they brought with them. As General John Maxwell put it decorously, "every hole and corner is crammed with ladies who alternate squabbling among themselves with the washing of officers' faces."

The Queen's disapproval embarrassed Roberts, as his wife Nora and their two daughters were then en route to join him at Bloemfontein, and he had looked the other way when other officers' ladies arrived and took up valuable space and resources. His women, he wrote to the Queen, were needed for hospital work. "I understand that Your Majesty does not approve of ladies coming out to South Africa from mere curiosity," the uxorious Roberts explained. "I am forbidding any to enter the Orange Free State, except those who have a son or husband in hospital or whose husband is likely to be quartered in Bloemfontein for some time." His regulation, Victoria must have realized, was a deliberately leaky vessel. General Maxwell confided to his wife that Lady Roberts wastefully went on to Pretoria in a special armored train, "and as Kitchener says, she has represented nearly 500 tons of supplies. . . ." Whatever Victoria knew about the conduct of the war, which was often disgraceful—hospital inadequacies in South Africa were reminiscent of the Crimea—she also knew that even her moral authority, which was all the authority she had, was further limited by layers of bureaucracy and miles of ocean.

It was not the Queen's war, but she threw her ebbing strength into it. As disabled as some of her soldiers invalided home, she visited units about to sail for the war, and she greeted them again on their return; she wrote and telegraphed encouragement to her generals and their units in the field; she visited hospitals and convalescent homes, unafraid of encountering gruesome casualties, and she personally decorated the maimed. She defended indefensible military decisions and the incompetent officers who made them, rather than impede the conduct of the war by calling them into question; to correct abuses and improve efficiency, she berated, nevertheless, the bureaucratic shortcomings and inadequacies she found out about; she was equally concerned about considerate treatment of the enemy, and of such innocents caught in the crossfire as the Zulus. What the Queen could do, she did. It was no coincidence that she became the embodiment of the national spirit.

That spring—summer, below the Equator, would be the South African winter—she sent to Lord Roberts scarves of khaki Berlin wool with VRI crocheted on each, which she had made herself, to be given to private soldiers from the colonies as her personal acknowledgment of the services of the Colonials. Not until August did she hear of the results. "There was the greatest competition to become the fortunate possessors of these scarves," he wrote. Further, with troops "widely scattered and so constantly on the move," it was difficult to locate the most deserving. He had chosen four privates—from Canada, Australia, New Zealand, and Cape Colony. The Canadian recipient, he noted, although "unanimously elected by his comrades in Roberts's Horse as the man most worthy to receive the scarf," turned out to be an American volunteer. "I decided that his nationality need not be considered a deterrence."

Victoria disembarked in Dublin on April 4, carrying bunches of shamrocks. Her bonnet and parasol were embroidered with silver shamrocks. She had not been in Ireland since the disastrous visit in 1861, just before Albert's death, when she and the Prince Consort had traveled to observe Bertie's development as a soldier. Afterwards, she had given a statue of Albert to Dublin, but the mayor and the Corporation of Dublin refused to accept it, and the Queen had a very long memory. Without the war, there would have been no further visit. Now she chose to forget the rebuff and to remember instead the valor of her Irish troops. In turn, Dubliners hung banners, she noted in her journal, which read, "Blest for ever is she who relied / On Erin's honour and Erin's pride," and "In her a thousand virtues closed / As Mother, Wife, and Queen."

She settled down in the Viceregal Lodge with a modest establishment for three weeks, while the Viceroy, Earl Cadogan, moved with his family to Dublin Castle. What followed was a routine of long progresses every afternoon, in bunting-decked streets filled with cheering throngs. The Queen, Mary Ponsonby recalled, thought that her workload was twice as great as on her last visit, when she was only half her present age. She "thoroughly believed the Irish loved her," and was delighted by the gaiety of the people. Hospitals, schools, convents, and factories were among the destinations of her drives; and she visited the Dublin Zoo in her donkey chair, which itself drew crowds. For security, police cyclists in plain clothes preceded and followed her carriages at discreet distances, and there were no incidents. Official visitors and events filled most evenings, and she had dinner with Cardinal Logue and other Roman Catholic clerics; but the high moment for her—she remembered the bumbling Bertie as an officer trainee—was a review of troops in Phoenix Park conducted with precision by another son, Field Marshal the Duke of Connaught.

Even across the Irish Sea there was no way to keep the war from mind, as messages arrived several times daily from the Cape, and she was apprised also of the embarrassment created by the publication by the War Office of dispatches from the debacle at Spion Kop. The revelations, she telegraphed Salisbury, "will ruin the discipline of the Army." Serving soldiers, however, not only had little access to London newspapers; most could not read them.

In the midst of the Cabinet frenzy, the Queen, on April 26, steamed for Holyhead, and home. "I own I am very tired," she wrote. All told, in a reign of nearly sixty-four years, she spent almost seven years in Scotland but only five weeks in Ireland.

Whatever War Office controversy remained in early May about lifting the lid on the lapses in generalship in South Africa was blotted out on the nineteenth by news of the relief of Mafeking. The eruption of violent and boisterous enthusiasm all over England was so great as to put the participle *mafficking* into the language. The mass hysteria would not be matched until Armistice Day in 1918. The Queen had been scheduled to visit Wellington College, where Beatrice's son "Drino" was a student. Her route became a flood of frenzied emotion. "The people are quite mad with delight," she wrote in her journal, "and London is said to be indescribable." In the aftermath, her eighty-first birthday was not forgotten, but became less an occasion than birthdays of earlier years. Within the month the troops who had been singing "Marching to Pretoria" had indeed occupied it, and Paul Kruger had fled in a railway carriage into an unoccupied area of the Transvaal.

Victoria was now too weary to appreciate the hysteria of victory, and had seen it come—if it had come, as the fighting had not ended—at far greater cost than expected. When a message dated June 11 arrived at the War Office from Lord Roberts suggesting that the pedestal in Pretoria intended for an unfinished statue of President Kruger be used instead for one of her Majesty, for which the army in South Africa might subscribe funds, she was not pleased. Her comment at the bottom of the telegram, which Lansdowne had transmitted to Windsor, politely accepted the suggestion as "gratifying," but observed that it was "premature." Not so to Roberts, who predicted—erroneously—to the Queen on June 21 that "by the time your Majesty receives this letter the enemy ought to have been driven into a small corner, a measure which will, I trust, result in a general submission."

From Africa, too, came another message from Emperor Menelik of Ethiopia, whose earlier contacts with the Queen had been by phonograph cylinder. This time the Emperor thanked her for the horses and hunting dogs she had sent, and agreed to permit his southern frontier to be marked wherever her Majesty would "settle it." Empress Taitou appreciated Victoria's picture "because I knew that I will never have the chance of seeing your Majesty in person, . . . my heart's wish. . . ." She had received the little dog that the Queen had sent. "He was a very nice little dog, but death took him from me." Such exchanges between monarchs suggest an age vastly simpler and more remote than the year 1900, yet at almost the same time the Queen could listen to speeches at a mayoral banquet in Liverpool on the telephone while dining at home. Innocence and simplicity, cynicism and complexity, still coexisted.

Family matters involving grandchildren and great-grandchildren now seldom occupied the Queen; there were too many of them and they were far-flung. But on June 25, 1900, her granddaughter Victoria—Alice's daughter—gave birth to her last child, a son, at Frogmore House, in the Home Park at Windsor. The Queen, close by, took more interest than usual, and asked before the child was born that it should "bear my name of whatever sex it may be." The Battenbergs suggested Victor for the future Earl Mountbatten of Burma, but the Queen pressed for Albert as well. In the end, he was christened Louis Francis Albert Victor Nicholas, and was called by none of them. His parents preferred Dickie.

At the Queen's last presence at a christening, she insisted upon holding Dickie throughout the ceremony. As he thrashed about, he knocked off her spectacles, and while still at the font he entangled an arm in the veil of her cap. "He is a beautiful large child and behaved very well," she commented forbearingly in her journal on July 17.

Between the birth and the christening, the Queen had given her last garden party, for five thousand people, on the lawns of Buckingham Palace. As she had done three years before, she twice toured the grounds with Princess Alix in an open carriage, this time drawn by two small white horses; and other royal personages followed her on foot in what Victoria called "the most broiling heat." Distracted by other matters, she went through the motions of appearing without pretending much interest. There was chaos in Peking, where a rebellion seemed in progress, fomented by the Dowager Empress. Inhabitants of foreign legations were being taken prisoner or slaughtered; the British compound was under siege, but holding out; and an international force had been proceeding north from Tientsin to attempt a rescue. She felt "quite miserable, horror-struck," she told her journal. Meanwhile, Boer counterattacks and guerrilla warfare in the Transvaal continued, and Roberts confessed, "I wish I could tell your Majesty that the war was likely to end soon, but at present the Boers seem inclined to hold out." That unhappy fact was brought home to the Queen with regularity. On July 18 a once-handsome officer, Captain E. B. Towse of the Gordon Highlanders, was led by his wife into the Queen's presence to have a Victoria Cross pinned to his tunic. A Boer bullet had extracted his eyes.

At Osborne, the Queen's clock appeared to be running down. Her digestion was "becoming defective," Marie Mallet thought. "If only she would follow a diet and live on Benger's Food and chicken all would be well but she clings to roast beef and ices! . . . Sir James [Reid] has at last persuaded her to try Benger's and she likes it and now to his horror, instead of substituting it for other foods she adds it to her already copious meals. . . ." Benger's Food, a wheat-flour-based additive containing enzymes to aid digestion, was mixed as a paste into hot milk. It proved no solution for Victoria, Marie noted. "Of course when she devours a huge chocolate ice followed by a couple of apricots washed down with ice water, [the Queen] . . . ought to expect a dig from the indigestion fiend."

Victoria's nights as well as her days continued troubled. She often could not fall asleep until nearly dawn, and complained of back pain. There were too many worries besides those of her own aching body. Since Black Week, and even earlier, she had often broken down and cried at the long list of casualties, and wept privately in her own bed as she lay sleepless. She worried about Vicky, who was too ill to visit, but would write little about it. Late in July her fears about Affie were confirmed when a coded telegram about his condition was first withheld from her, and finally its contents read. The Duke of Coburg had incurable cancer of the throat and tongue. "Affie," she assured herself, "is quite ignorant of the danger. . . ."

Six days later, on July 31, she was told of her son's death. Marie Mallet found the Queen looking "crushed and sad," and Princess Beatrice, her chief prop, "dreadfully self-absorbed and unsympathetic." In her journal, Victoria confided, "I think they should never have withheld the truth from me as long as they did. . . . I pray God to help me to be patient. . . ." The next day she saw "Tino"—Constantine, Duke of Sparta, and Vicky's son-in-law—who had arrived with the Prince of Wales. "Alas!" she added, "he did not give a good account of dear Vicky." The Queen had lived too long.

XX

Mourning for Victoria

(1900–1901)

Through the late summer and early autumn the Queen's journal describes "wretched" days and "restless" nights. When Albert's birthday again came around on August 26, she seemed to feel closer to him than before. "How I remember the happy day it used to be, and preparing presents for him, which he would like! I thought much of the birthday spent at the dear lovely Rosenau in '45, when I so enjoyed being there, and where now his poor dear son [Affie], of whom he was so proud, has breathed his last."

Early in September the siege of Peking was broken, and the British forces relieved. With that favorable outcome and the prospect of peace in the Transvaal, Lord Salisbury asked the Queen to dissolve Parliament so that new elections might furnish a more solid mandate. As the campaign proceeded, Lord Wolseley's retirement as Commander-in-Chief of the army loomed, and Salisbury pressed for the popular Lord Roberts to replace him. After his services in South Africa, the Prime Minister contended, no other choice was possible.

At Balmoral, Victoria met in a strategy session with Bertie and Arthur to attempt some move that would make her dream for Arthur possible. It was her last serious effort to exert some personal authority in the decision process. She was surprised, she wrote to Salisbury, that the Duke of Connaught was not proposed. His experience and service had long qualified him. "Please remember," she added, "all that occurred when he was so anxious to go to South Africa, and you assured me that his being prevented doing so by the Government would not injure his chances of succeeding Lord Wolseley. I also naturally wish to see him at the head of the Army during my lifetime."

There was no chance of a reversal, as she and Arthur both knew. Royal authority known to her uncles had disappeared with the first Reform Bill, when she was only thirteen, and five years away from becoming queen. Her long reign had witnessed further erosion of power, to which she had contributed in the years of deliberate seclusion which she had allowed to last too long. On September 28, Salisbury pointed to the "very democratic spirit" which was the impetus for reforms, even in the military, and how "the moment would be singularly inappropriate" for a backward step.

In her disappointment, the Queen wrote to Lord Roberts from Balmoral, deploring the "indifferent success" of even the best of her generals, as it was "painful to see how this guerrilla warfare still continues." Arthur had been prevented from leading troops in South Africa. She was hinting unsubtly that he could have improved on what had been, and could not do worse in the top job than other officers not handicapped by the accident of high birth and the unrelenting democratic spirit.

Parliamentary elections in October—the Khaki Election, as it was called—went as expected, and Salisbury returned with an increased majority. His continuation at Downing Street was taken for granted, but the formalities had to be complied with. As the Queen's surrogate, Sir Arthur Bigge took the overnight train to London to conduct Cabinet discussions. Since the release of the Spion Kop dispatches, Victoria had been eager to see Lord Lansdowne leave the War Office, and had greeted warmly his pre-election hints about retirement. Bigge, however, came back with the news that the Secretary for War had, instead, been promoted. Eager to divest himself of his extra portfolio, Salisbury had conferred the Foreign Office upon Lansdowne. All the Queen could do was to note her misgiv-

*Queen Victoria at 80. Lithograph done by
William Nicholson, 1899.*

ings. Power, even persuasive power, had largely vanished. She was too frail
and too old.

So much had the Queen's hold slipped that two of her ladies-in-
waiting about to take up their duties had to make the journey to Scotland
by third class, as no one had made arrangements for them. Marie Mallet
frugally took a cheap ticket and made herself "cosy" overnight with
pillows and rugs. Accommodating officials at King's Cross Station passed
her luggage free, although she had twice the allowable weight.

At Aberdeen Station she met Edith Lytton, who traveled the rest of
the way with her "very comfortably." They recognized the change in the
Queen when they saw her again on October 24. "She has grown so thin
and there is a distressing look of pain and weariness on her face; it makes
me very sad." For weeks Victoria had suffered from poor appetite, and
was noticeably gaunt. Usually a tonic for her, Balmoral was no help in the
fading months of 1900. Lord James of Hereford, as Minister-in-Attendance, found her much altered from his last encounter. "The Queen had
lost much flesh, and had shrunk so as to appear about one-half of the
person she had been. Her spirits, too, had left her. . . ." Her disappointments had been many. The toll of South Africa had been very great, and
had not yet ended for her. On October 27 a telegram at Balmoral alerted

her that Helena's son, Prince Christian Victor, who had survived military service in India, the Sudan, the Ashanti country, and the Transvaal, had come down with malaria, just on the verge of returning home. Two days later it was enteric fever, and a later telegram that day announced his death. He was thirty-three. "Lenchen," she thought, "so worshipped this son. . . . Again and again the terrible thought of this fresh blow and irreparable loss brought tears to my eyes." When not alone Victoria made, Marie thought, "heroic efforts to be cheerful but her face in repose is terribly sad; I do not want to live to be very old; the penalties are too great."

The Queen's nights were now "fair" at best. "The sitting through meals, unable to eat anything," she confessed, "is most trying." On November 11, she wrote, "Had a shocking night, and no draught could make me sleep, as pain kept me awake. Felt very tired and unwell when I got up. . . . Could do nothing for the whole morning. Rested and slept a little." Yet she told Marie one melancholy evening broken only by fresh telegrams and messages about "Prince Christle," that after Albert's death she "wished to die, but *now* I wish to live and do what I can for my country and those I love." Somehow she still managed to snap back with a resiliency that amazed those around her now disquieted by her lapses into somnolence and wavering memory. The Privy Council sat on November 12, Almeric Fitzroy recalled, and "when the transfer of seals incidental to the changes in the Cabinet took place, her memory guided us through the mazes of a somewhat intricate transaction whereon official records were dumb, and the recollection of Ministers a blank."

Even so, with the Queen's slipping hold, Household affairs, like Marie's travel arrangements to Scotland, were breaking down. The footmen, Marie observed, "smell of whisky and are never prompt to answer the bell," and each dinner was "more like a badly arranged picnic." Only the Queen failed to notice. One evening in November she ordered nothing but a small dish of noodles, "and it was entirely forgotten, so she had nothing." Victoria was hardly even aware that the *Munshi* had returned, after a year's absence in India. She had requested that the Viceroy, Lord Curzon, look after him there, and Curzon had duly reported meeting the *Munshi*'s father, his son having then been ill. "Why the plague did not carry him off I cannot think," Marie wrote to her husband; "it might [then] have done one good deed!"

In the aftermath of Prince Christian Victor's death, the Household had returned to Windsor, making Victoria's last stay at Balmoral her shortest one. The clockwork calendar by which she had functioned was itself faltering. Sir James Reid still saw her every morning, listened to her complaints of back pain and sleepless nights, and urged her to eat her breakfast eggs. She still kept to something of a routine of official audiences, seeing Lord Salisbury about changes in the Cabinet, and receiving a delegation of Anglican nuns who had lived through the siege of Mafeking. In mid-November the new Cabinet kissed hands, and she received a delegation of one hundred invalided colonial troops who had served in South Africa. Returning to Windsor and involving herself with business, rather than isolating herself with family grief at Balmoral, had been salutary, and in a strong voice she welcomed the soldiers, thanked them for their "loyal and devoted services," and wished them well on their return home. One, she noted in her journal, was "an old Australian chaplain, who lost his leg by the bite of a mad horse." At her side he named the different regiments to which the men belonged, as she could no longer make out their insignia.

Another visitor was Sir Redvers Buller, who confessed that he had not expected the war to last so long. The Queen loyally assured him he had done his best. Then the Prince of Wales arrived, and he talked with his mother "for some time," almost certainly, among other things, about the dying Empress Frederick, to whom Bertie was devoted. Vicky's sixtieth birthday was November 21, 1900. Her condition, the Queen knew, was "heartbreaking," although no one offered any details. She sent Beatrice across the Channel to Kronberg, where Vicky had already been bedridden, in constant pain, for two months. Beatrice's report on December 11, as recorded in the Queen's journal, must mask even greater agony than described, the Empress "not much altered in face . . . but terribly ailing and suffering," with reading her only occupation "as she cannot use her hands." The lines are recorded without comment.

On November 29 Victoria inspected troops in a makeshift way, reviewing the First Life Guards, returned from the Cape, from a carriage in an archway of the castle. It was a year, she noted in her still-clear voice, since she had bade them farewell. "Alas!" she concluded, "the joy at your safe return is clouded over by the memory of sad losses of many a valuable life, which I, in common with you all, have to deplore." The next day, again in a carriage, accompanied by a daughter and a granddaughter, she watched a march-past of 240 Canadian troops, to whom she wished "a safe and happy return to your homes." The Canadian officers dined with her afterwards, and found her feeling low about the death of her grandson.

Reginald Brett (he had succeeded as the second Viscount Esher in 1899) thought that she was "unwell . . . *a beaucoup baissé.*" Yet, as they were escorted out, the Canadian adjutant said, with emotion, "I could die for her!" Something of her legendary aura had remained in what was to be her last review.

In early December her attention was taken up with the retirement of Lord Wolseley, and his replacement at the War Office by Lord Roberts, who had fallen from his horse in South Africa and broken his arm, delaying his return. Kitchener was to take over at the Cape. Her usual barrage of memoranda, often signed in her behalf by someone else, concealed the gravity of her decline. Nevertheless, that was becoming more difficult to hide. A conspiracy of silence prevailed, and when the Brazilian ambassador came to Windsor to present his credentials and had to leave without doing so, the awkward fact went unreported.

Seized by another attack of aphasia—these had become frequent but not talked of—the Queen could not receive visitors, but her Household continued to schedule appearances, and was even planning another removal en masse to Cimiez in March, problems with France having been resolved. Among her visitors now, however, was Bertie's doctor, Sir Francis Laking, who urged that she get over her "squeamishness" about food, and take "a little milk and whisky" as a stimulant several times a day.

A semblance of public appearances was essential, if only for the *Court Circular,* and on the twelfth, Beatrice and May took her in a carriage to the nearby Windsor Town Hall to purchase gifts at a sale of Irish needlework. Arriving before the public opening, Victoria was wheeled around to each stall, and the ladies—most of whom she knew—were presented to her. On the always terrible fourteenth, so full of memories, she drove with Beatrice and May, and several granddaughters, down the hill to the Mausoleum, for a noon service conducted by her old friend the Bishop of Winchester, Randall Davidson. As always, December 14 was the hinge in her schedule, after which—the year before was a wartime exception—she crossed the Solent for Christmas. The journey appeared no different from dozens of earlier trips to Osborne. In her comfortable saloon car she was accompanied by Jane Churchill; the royal yacht at Gosport was under steam, waiting to cross to Trinity Pier. Yet the effort so prostrated the Queen that Lady Churchill remarked to her maid that Victoria appeared to be "a dying woman."

For days she did little but sleep fitfully, recalling hazily two afternoon drives with a granddaughter, and "a dinner in the room where we usually breakfast." Bedridden, she knew little of what was going on about her, although she learned that dispatches from South Africa suggested that the pace of pacification had been "unsatisfactory, the Boers being terribly active all over the country." She telegraphed a Christmas message to troops still mired in the veld.

Her nights remained restless and her days uncomfortable. She ate little, and a breakfast she "really liked" was an event to be noted. The holiday season, for myriad reasons, she found "terribly sad." A family Christmas tree stood, forlornly for her, in the gaudy Durbar Room, and she was wheeled in to see it on Christmas Eve, one of the most unfestive that she could remember. Even the traditional candles seemed dim. "I felt very melancholy," she noted in her journal, "because I see so badly." There were more reasons than that—the casualty lists, including Prince Christle; her physical malaise; and the sudden illness of Jane Churchill, whose son had to be sent for across a stormy Solent.

Christmas Day itself, despite the presence of children and grandchildren, and a menu of *crème d'orge à l'Américaine, filets de sole panés sauce Ravigote, celestines à la Noël,* roast beef, plum pudding, and *éclairs au chocolat,* as well as the usual sideboard of woodcock pie, game pie, and boar's head, none of which Victoria (who "dined" alone in her room) could eat, was further devastated by the news, brought by Sir James Reid, that Lady Churchill had died. She had been one of the few remaining people whose associations went back to the happy days with Albert. Jane's son, Victor—Lord Churchill—visited the Queen the next day, and thanked her for the fifty years of association with his mother that had been the most important thing in her life. In her journal, for weeks now dictated to her granddaughter "Thora" (Helena's daughter, Princess Helena Victoria), Victoria wrote, "I could scarcely speak."

Windy, stormy nights at year's end added to the Queen's sleeplessness. By day she was "low and sad," dwelling upon Lady Churchill's passing. Despite gale winds, her body had been moved to the mainland on the twenty-eighth. A letter from the dying but still thoughtful Vicky, enclosing a reading glass as a Christmas gift, only supplemented the Queen's sorrows. Responding to the brave gesture, but now beyond reading, she dictated a note that confided her own poor health, "but nothing to cause you alarm. . . .I have been able to get out a little most days." Some afternoons, weather permitting, Victoria was still attempting brief carriage rides, her only activity, and on December 29 she noted in her diary that she had "managed to eat a little cold beef, which is the first I have had for weeks, and I really enjoyed [it]." Her appetite was so feeble that its occasional return was something to record. On the last day of the year, Prince Louis of Battenberg, a navy captain and the husband of the Queen's granddaughter Victoria of Hesse, arrived to secure her signature as new trustee for her "private money." After reports from South Africa that continued "not very good" and a supper of Benger's Food, she fell asleep and missed the opening of the twentieth century.

Attempting to remain active, on New Year's Day 1901 she went in a carriage with her son Arthur and granddaughter Thora to visit the Soldier's Home on the island, and said a few words to the convalescent wounded. She was glad to hear the next day that Lord Roberts had finally arrived, direct from South Africa, his arm still in a sling. She saw him in the drawing room at five, the occasion prompting a burst of her obstinate vitality. Tiny and frail, Roberts was one of the few men with whom she conducted business who was nearly her size. Nearly forty-two years earlier she had seen him for the first time, and pinned on his breast a Victoria Cross. He kissed her hand, and spoke warmly of the dead "Christle." On December 11, on the way home, he had made the trip to Colenso to see his son's grave, and the place where he had fallen. "It was murder," he had told his guide.

What he said to the Queen about the episode is unknown. In her journal Victoria records giving Roberts the Garter, the only time in her reign that a general (outside of her family) was so honored. "I also told him I was going to confer an earldom on him, with the remainder to his daughter"—there being no son to inherit the title. He presented his staff, including his six Indian orderlies, of whom Victoria remarked, characteristically, "such fine-looking men."

The Queen was "now much better," Sir James wrote to Marie Mallet on January 4; ". . . she now causes me no present anxiety. How far she may still improve it is impossible to say at her age; but I hope she may continue her invalid habits for some time longer, and so give herself every chance."

The *Court Circular* continued to report daily that the Queen "drove out" with one of her ladies, or with a princess, mornings and afternoons; some of the excursions may have existed only on paper. For weeks the weather had been murky at best, and generally worse; and the failing Queen's world—even after another visit by Dr. Pagenstecher—had become a blur of dimly perceived impressions. On the eleventh, a Saturday, not only was Victoria supposed to have driven out in the morning, but according to the record, she saw her Secretary for the Colonies, Joseph Chamberlain, that afternoon. The *Court Circular,* however, noted only that he had arrived on the eleventh and left on the twelfth, without mentioning an audience, a highly unusual circumstance. Again on January 15, the *Circular* noted that Lord Roberts had "terminated his visit to the Queen," and that Victoria "drove out" in the afternoon with Helena and Beatrice. Yet no audience was mentioned. The field marshal had arrived, found the Queen feeble and confused in mind, and left circumspectly. Very likely Chamberlain also found Victoria befuddled.

On the evening of Roberts's abortive audience, no one was summoned by the Queen to prepare a journal paragraph for the day. The night before, her journal entry had been dictated to Princess Helena; it was the last.

On the fifteenth, in hopes of enjoying some afternoon sunshine, the Queen had been lifted into her carriage, her widowed daughter-in-law Marie of Coburg accompanying her. The weather remained poor, and the outing was cut short. On a drive in the winter gloom not many years before, shortly after Liko's death, Lady Errol had said soothingly to Victoria, "We will all meet in Abraham's bosom."

"I will not meet Abraham," the Queen had contended, and the entry in her diary for the day includes the complaint, "Dear Leila, not at all consolatory in moments of trouble." Now her ladies were saying much the same thing when she spoke of "being united with my beloved Albert very soon." She still refused to receive Abraham.

The Prince of Wales would have understood. He was said to have joked, none too privately, that his mother was reluctant to go to heaven because there the angels would precede her.

Without attempting to consult the Queen, Household officials notified the proprietor of the Excelsior Regina Hotel that her Majesty would not be returning to Cimiez in March. A cancellation payment of £800 was forwarded.

On the sixteenth, Victoria was too feeble to rise from her bed. Sir James Reid observed what he described as signs of "cerebral exhaustion" and right-side facial paralysis, which gradually faded although her speech seemed slurred. He decided that it was time to advise her secretariat formally that she was seriously ill, as there was bureaucratic machinery to be set in motion in such circumstances. Yet even on that Wednesday she had at least one dispatch read to her, for she instructed Sir Frank Lascelles in Berlin respectfully to decline an honor for himself offered by her grandson Willy. On the day before she had announced her decision to assign a grace-and-favor residence to Sir James Reid and his wife near the Round Tower at Windsor. When her doctor had married Susan Baring, the Queen had been furious; now she seemed aware that it was urgent to have him close by at all times. He was to move in as soon as the Court again assembled at the castle.

The first rumors of the Queen's illness appeared in the London papers on Thursday, January 17, although the *Court Circular* reported— possibly a fiction—that the Queen had again "driven out" the day before. The next day, however, the *Circular* reported activity only from Marl-borough House and York House, fueling speculation and concern. No news was not good news, and fresh rumors prompted a belated bulletin from Osborne on Saturday, under the caption, "The Health of the Queen." Victoria, it announced, "has not lately been in her usual health, and is unable for the present to take her customary drives. The Queen during the past year has had a great strain upon her powers, which has rather told upon her Majesty's nervous system. It has, therefore, been thought advisable by her Majesty's physicians that the Queen should . . . abstain for the present from transacting business." What the bulletin did not say was that the Queen, already weakened by insomnia and impaired nutrition, had suffered a series of small strokes. Her memory flickered, as did her sight, and she had to be told who was present at her bedside.

A heart specialist, Sir Thomas Barlow, was called from London, although the Queen had no history of cardiac problems, and late on Friday, the eighteenth, her children were summoned. The Prince of Wales was scheduled to have dinner with a friend, the beautiful and formidable Agnes Keyser, at her town house at 17 Grosvenor Crescent, which she had turned into a private nursing home for officer casualties. He decided that cancellation would be of no use to anyone, and arrived as expected, starting for Osborne the next morning. At Kronberg, the Empress Frederick, a wasted, bedridden figure herself, was not told. In her last letter from her mother, dated January 6, the Queen had hoped soon to "improve." The Duke of Connaught happened to be in Berlin when recalled, and Emperor William, hearing the dramatic news, left the celebrations of the two-hundredth anniversary of the Hohenzollern dy-nasty in Prussia, to rush with him to England. The Duke arranged for the cruiser *Minerva* to be at Vlissingen to meet William's special train, but when it was late in arriving they chartered a Dutch Royal Mail steamer.

Having learned from his grandmother about the effectiveness of uncoded telegrams, William sent one to the Prince of Wales announcing arrival of the party in London at 6:15 P.M. on Sunday, January 20. As a result the public did not have to be informed officially, for the news raced through the city. Bertie returned to meet his brother and nephew, stopping at Marlborough House on the way to change into Prussian uniform as a courtesy to William. The sight at the railway station would have amused the Queen had she known of it, but she was slipping in and out of consciousness, a frail figure in white, on a great canopied bed, little aware of her surroundings.

At midnight her somnolence seemed so deep that the Bishop of Winchester, who had returned earlier in the day, was sent for, but she rallied, and in the early hours of morning asked Dr. Reid, "Am I better at all?" He told her that she was, and she asked for her white Pomeranian dog, Tutti, who was put on her bed until he was too restless to remain; but by then Victoria had slipped again into sleep.

The Emperor and Prince remained overnight in London, then went to Portsmouth by train. It was now late in the day on Monday. The Princesses and Bishop Davidson were in the room when William approached. "My first wish is not to be in the [lime]light," he said, "and I will return to London if you wish. I should like to see Grandmama before she dies, but if that is impossible I shall quite understand." He kept tactfully in the background, while his uncle, who at fifty-nine had grown bald and hoary-bearded, went into the bedroom first, and watched for the next wakeful moment.

At one point, while Bertie waited, so Princess Louise told Lord Esher, the Queen awakened and said, to no one in particular, "The Prince of Wales will be sorry to hear how ill I am. Do you think he ought to be told?" Although those in the room strained to catch each word, the only others that Louise recalled clearly were Victoria's "I don't want to die yet. There are several things I want to arrange."

It was 12:15 P.M., just after noon on January 22, when the Queen realized that the burly presence by her side was her eldest son. She opened her arms and whispered what would be her last recognizable word, "Bertie." He wept, but she did not know. Davidson returned to the bedside, where she lay quietly, "looking white and thin." During the family's desultory luncheon, the doctors watching for the end perceived a change in her breathing, later described as "paresis of the pulmonary nerves," and called again for the Bishop of Winchester, who came with the Vicar of

Whippingham. Then the family, including William, was sent for, and as they watched around the bed, the clergymen took turns praying aloud. When Davidson recited the last verse of Newman's "Lead Kindly Light," he "noticed" that Victoria was listening, an unlikely possibility.

At four, in the waning winter light, the doctors authorized issuance of a bulletin, "The Queen is slowly sinking." Reid raised her head, supporting it under the pillow, to ease her breathing. On her other side, William rushed to assist with his unwithered right arm, and the two remained uncomfortably at the bedside, neither shifting position for two and a half hours. Her children and grandchildren, each time they thought the end was imminent, called out their own names to her, perhaps hoping to send something of themselves with her into the beyond. At six-thirty, just after Princess May arrived with Arthur and his daughters, the Queen's face, which had been pinched by episodes of paralysis, relaxed and became calm. Ten minutes later the final bulletin of Victoria's reign was issued over the signature of the Minister-in-Residence at Osborne House, Arthur Balfour. It was a single line: "The Queen died peacefully at 6:30." The pressmen at the gate raced, on bicycles and in carriages, for the post office in East Cowes to file their telegrams.

The watch over the body began instantly, with Indian and Scottish attendants of the Queen taking places at the four corners of the deathbed. When the 60th Rifles arrived from Parkhurst Barracks to provide the guard over the coffin, no one knew the procedures. No sovereign had died in sixty-four years. The "historical ignorance, of everyone from top to bottom" on the part of those "who should know something of procedure," Esher deplored, was beyond description. "You would think that the English Monarchy had [not] been buried since the time of Alfred."

The drill book was silent on reversed arms, but Ponsonby, with Sir John McNeill, devised a ceremonial. Then the Duke of Connaught discovered that it was the privilege of the Queen's Company, Grenadier Guards, to keep watch over the dead Sovereign, and a telegram was dispatched, summoning the Guards from Windsor. Meanwhile, a coffin had to be secured, and the Queen's minute instructions carried out.

Later on the evening of the twenty-second, the family gathered around the canopied bed for a final farewell to the wasted figure in white. The next morning, Albert Edward, no longer Prince of Wales, crossed the Solent to attend a Privy Council at St. James's Palace, at which he was to be proclaimed King. The summons delivered by messengers read,

"Levée Dress (Crape left arm)." At Osborne, Alexandra protested that she would not permit anyone to refer to her as Queen until the old Queen was laid in her grave, but in practice she was quickly overruled. Between one and four in the afternoon, Household servants and tenants on the Osborne estates were permitted to see Victoria in the bedroom where she died, and filed in quietly, in small groups. At the same time, the dining room of Osborne House was being stripped of furniture, and the walls hung with crimson drapery, to turn it into a temporary chapel.

In London, *The Times* encouraged readers that the nation could be consoled in its "irreparable loss" by "the well-founded conviction that the Queen has left behind her a worthy successor, who may be trusted to walk in her footsteps." On the other hand, the next edition of *Reynolds'*, the Sunday paper never timid in its treatment of the Prince of Wales, observed that "it cannot be said that the life of the new Sovereign has been altogether edifying." As Margot Asquith put it in her diary, Bertie had devoted "what time he does not spend upon sport and pleasure ungrudgingly to duty." The King's first response to his new role was seen by many as a test of whether he would walk in his mother's path, or set his own course. Once he took the oath from Frederick Temple, Archbishop of Canterbury, he made the answer clear. To the Council and guests he declared, "I have resolved to be known by the name of Edward, which has been borne by six of my ancestors. In doing so, I do not undervalue the name of Albert, which I inherit from my ever-to-be-lamented, great, and wise father, who by universal consent is I think deservedly known by the name of Albert the Good, and I desire that his name should stand alone."

The royal party that had accompanied the King to London, including the Duke of Connaught and the Duke of York—now heir apparent—returned to Osborne House the next afternoon. In the Council Room, members of the Household were all formally presented, and, a cushion having been placed at the King's right arm, they kissed hands. Osborne had been left in the charge of Emperor William for the day and a half that the King and his entourage had been away in London—the only time a German sovereign (without a coordinate British title) had ever ruled, even informally, over any part of England. He had overseen the transformation of the room in which Victoria was to lie in state, and since the Queen had forbidden undertakers, he had even measured his grandmother for her coffin. Long awed by her indomitability, he confided to Bishop Davidson, "I have never been with her without feeling that she was in every sense my Grandmamma and made me love her as such. And yet the minute we began to talk about political things she made me feel we were equals and could speak as Sovereigns."

Despite a useless arm, William would have lifted the Queen into her coffin himself had her sons not insisted upon their rights. To their surprise, Edward and Arthur found that Willy could indeed have accomplished the transfer with his good arm: their mother seemed now little more than linen and lace. The next morning, the body was brought downstairs to the *chapelle*, and the coffin placed on a small dais draped, at Willy's insistence, with a Union Jack. Afterwards he claimed the flag as a trophy, and took it back with him to Berlin.

Banked with flowers, the silver crucifix from above her bed in her hands, and her lace wedding veil and white widow's cap covering her face and hair, the Queen's body, unseen now in the closed coffin, lay in state at Osborne House while funeral preparations went on at Windsor. Velvet royal robes draped the coffin under the Imperial Crown. Eight huge candles lit the room. The strong scent of gardenias made the changing of the guard every hour a real as well as a technical relief for the Grenadiers.

Sunday, January 27, was the Emperor William's birthday. Despite a gale whipping across the Solent, the King's Household, the late Queen's Household, and officials from the German Embassy in London joined the officers of William's yacht—on which he was now quartered—in offering congratulations. There was little else to do. It was even colder and more rainy the next day, but inhabitants from the scattered communities on the Isle of Wight straggled to Osborne House to pay their respects to the Queen.

The hereditary Earl Marshal of England was the fifteenth Duke of Norfolk. In his hands were the funeral arrangements, which Victoria had set out with meticulous detail. As head of the army and as "the daughter of a soldier" she had requested a military funeral. On February 1, finally, a cold but clear day, the coffin, covered by a white and gold pall, was placed in the small royal yacht *Alberta* at Cowes and moved slowly, through an avenue of warships in two rows, to Portsmouth. King Edward, standing on the bridge of a trailing cruiser, noticed the yacht's standard flying at half mast. He inquired why. "The Queen is dead, Sir," he was told.

"The King of England lives," he retorted; and the standard was raised to full height. He was nearly sixty; his best years were behind him;

but he was going to be as much of a king as he could be. A special train, its blinds drawn, took the Queen's body to Victoria Station. In the fields, as the train rumbled slowly east, people knelt. From Victoria to Paddington, the route by gun-carriage was crowded with silent throngs.

A state funeral procession in the days of the horse reverberated with a pomp absent since, a thunder of trampling that intensified the muffled drumbeat, and a flourish of equine trappings that suggested a continuity with history. The Queen's funeral had several other striking aspects. It was a ceremony for a woman sovereign, but not a woman was visible. The kings and princes and generals on horseback, and the marching troops, were accompanied by a half-dozen closed carriages containing the only women in the procession other than the dead Queen—Alexandra and the Princesses, riding unseen. Near the coffin rode Victoria's cousin, George, stubborn and straightbacked, white-whiskered and in field marshal's uniform, defying time. And there was Earl Roberts, the one person, Lady Monkswell thought, that people felt they might cheer in the prevailing solemnity, "so he got a quiet cheer from everybody as he came along." After the coffin came the new King, and with him, on a magnificent white horse, Emperor William. Word of his attentions to the Queen on her deathbed had become general knowledge, and William rode in a rare atmosphere, for him, of English admiration.

Watching from Surrey House, opposite the northeast corner of Hyde Park, Constance Battersea was "impressed by the silence of the streets, the absence of music, the continuous booming of the guns that had almost a fateful sound, then the noise of the horses' hoofs striking the road, the rattle of swords, and the clatter of the stirrups." With Lady Battersea was her mother, a Rothschild daughter now nearly eighty, who remembered "standing in the gallery of St. James's Palace more than sixty years before . . . , watching with many others the triumphal passing by of a radiantly happy young bride—beautiful from happiness—with her chivalrous and handsome husband. . . ." To Lady Battersea, "that small coffin and the two principal riders"—the English and German sovereigns—remained in memory long after the hoofbeats and the drumbeats ceased.

In her funeral instructions, Victoria had written, "I would wish just to say that as a gun-carriage is very rough jolting & noisy, one ought to be properly arranged." Having stood in the chill outside Windsor Station, however, the horses that were to draw the gun-carriage to the castle started up unevenly and snapped their traces. The band, its drums rolling, had already turned the corner, moving uphill. Fritz Ponsonby rushed to tell the King, and Prince Louis of Battenberg said calmly, "If it is impossible to mend the traces you can always get the naval guard of honour to drag the gun-carriage." Since that required rope, the knitted harnesses of the horses were removed, and the communication cord of the funeral train commandeered. And the Queen, who had thought of everything but the frailty of human works, was borne by her bluejackets in an improvised procession of even greater dignity than she had conceived.

A brief service, based on Victoria's instructions, followed in the castle, in St. George's Chapel, where her body remained banked by flowers until Monday, February 4. The "extreme shortness" of the casket containing the Queen's body, Almeric Fitzroy noted in his diary, "struck one with pathetic insistence; almost a child's coffin in shape, so near the centre was its widest point." The committal service in the Mausoleum at Frogmore was the first funeral of a sovereign at Windsor to be held before dark. The winter light was almost gone when the small coffin passed through the doors over which she had ordered placed, in 1862, the words, "*Vale desideratissime.* Farewell most beloved. Here at length I shall rest with thee, with thee in Christ I shall rise again." Faith in a final reunion with her husband was almost the sum of her theology, from his death to her own.

The recumbent white figure executed to the Queen's instructions nearly forty years earlier, to lie side by side with Albert, had been found by the Office of Works. An old laborer at Windsor who had helped wall it up for security in 1863 remembered where it was put. Its placement closed the Queen's story just as she had wanted it. In Marochetti's marble she is forever young, and forever with her Prince.

At Windsor two days after the funeral, Lord Esher had an appointment with Edward VII. "The Indians," he noticed, "—[those] who were there —were wandering about like uneasy spirits. No longer immobile and statuesque, as of yore." The King would soon repatriate them, as well as the *Munshi*, and order a conflagration of the *Munshi's* papers. The Boehm bronze of John Brown was banished to storage, and many memorials of Her Majesty's Highland servant discreetly removed or destroyed. A hoard of elephant tusks, the annual tribute of African chieftains already forgotten, was disposed of, and neglected antiques from George IV's Pavilion at Brighton dragged out and dusted. Victoria's clutter of memorabilia, as well as paintings and statuary in place since Albert had decided upon their location, were moved, less to make way for the King's objects than to replace the atmosphere of 1861 with that of 1901. "Alas!" Queen Alexandra wrote to the dying Empress Frederick on May 14, "during my absence [in Copenhagen] Bertie has had all your beloved Mother's rooms [in Buckingham Palace] dismantled and all her precious things removed."

Change was inevitable and reflected a radically different concept of the world. From Winnipeg, distant even by Canadian standards, Winston Churchill, on a lecture tour capitalizing on his war experiences, wrote to his mother about the King's current favorite, the bosomy Mrs. Alice Keppel, "Will the Keppel be appointed 1st Lady of the Bedchamber?" And the King, confronting 6,600 army commissions that had piled up in the last months of Victoria's life, ordered that his signature be affixed with a rubber stamp—except on commissions of those officers with whose families the Sovereign was personally acquainted. He gave orders for new bathrooms and lavatories in the royal residences, for extension of the telephone systems, for several coach houses to be converted into garages for motorcars. Further, disregarding his mother's will, which asked that Osborne House be kept in the family, he made certain that he would seldom, if ever, have to go there again by presenting the property to the nation for use as a convalescent home for naval officers, and as a Royal Naval College. With zest the balding, greybearded King strolled about rooms and corridors at Windsor and in Buckingham Palace that the Queen for years had traversed only in her wheelchair, pushed by an impassive Indian servant. Now, in his own style, hat on his head, hunting dog at his heels, cigar in his mouth, he represented new forces at work in the Empire. What seemed vulgarity to those who preferred to remember the old Queen was vigor to the generation that had, with impatience, waited to succeed her.

"We grovel before fat Edward—E[dward] the Caresser, as he is privately named," Henry James observed to Oliver Wendell Holmes, Jr. ". . . But I mourn the safe and motherly old middle-class queen, who held the nation warm under the fold of her big, hideous Scotch-plaid shawl and whose duration had been so extraordinarily convenient and beneficent. I felt her death much more than I should have expected; she was a sustaining symbol."

As "an old Victorian," Bernard Shaw, in the centenary year of the Queen's birth, wondered why the makers of statuary had "so horribly guyed" her. "It was part of her personal quality that she was a tiny woman, and our national passion for telling lies on every public subject has led to her being represented as an overgrown monster. The sculptors seem to have assumed that she inspired everything that was ugliest in the feminine fiction of her reign. Take Mrs. Caudle, Mrs. Gamp, Mrs. Prig, Mrs. Proudie, and make a composite statue of them, and you will have a typical memorial of Queen Victoria." Such a representation, he explained, was "pure plastic calumny," for in reality, Queen Victoria was "a little woman with great decision of manner and a beautiful speaking voice. . . . She carried herself extremely well." Yet statues "at every corner" shrieked libels. The graceful recumbent figure in marble that represented the Victoria she wanted remembered had been sealed away, but for a few days each year, in the recesses of Frogmore.

"Lots of people have been asking me to sing Victoria in exelsis," the poet Robert Bridges wrote a friend, "but I find that I have not much feeling for the old Queen; though I can't help going on praying for her at family prayers, which the children observe to me. . . ." Hundreds of soppy verses did appear, with perhaps only two laconic lines in a poem by Ford Madox Ford realistically assessing how the Queen's death was felt, and what it was likely to mean—"A shock, / A change in the beat of the clock. . . ." Even the prostitutes walked London streets dressed in mourning, and crossing sweepers carried crêpe on their brooms. "It seemed," Bridges thought, "as though the keystone had fallen out of the arch of heaven." Yet Victoria's world of simple values and loyalties, and her rigid view of the Crown, had preceded her in death.

In few ways was the Queen herself, but for the association of her name with an age, "Victorian." The prudery and stuffiness associated with her Court were a protective coloration that succeeded only too well in concealing the complex woman who preferred her island hideaway and her Highland retreat to her palace and castle; her bonnet, and then a widow's cap, to a crown; and a donkey cart and, necessarily, a wheelchair, to a throne. She was no more an exemplary mother than she had been an exemplary Queen, although for the most part she was convinced she was both. She had been haughty as well as humble; shallow as well as shrewd; self-indulgent as well as selfless. Her five-foot form was filled with paradoxes that she never reconciled.

Victoria had not presided over the metamorphosis of the monarchy into a publicity-conscious symbolic institution, but it had happened nevertheless. In some ways she had contributed to the change—deliberately as well as by default. The Sovereign's political role had been weakening inexorably. In the end, her linkage with that lengthy transformation, once she had emerged from the shadows of what had seemed full-time widow-hood, had endowed the Throne with a dignity and a purpose that could not have been imagined during the notorious Regency and the disreputable reigns of her uncles.

The long afternoon of her post-Albert seclusion has a melodramatic quality that causes it to linger in memory more tenaciously than the bright Albertine morning and noon, or the spirited post-Jubilee evening. What Victoria had left behind as legacy was the sturdy ceremonial monarchy now ratified by public affection, by a yearning for continuity and tradition, and by the middle-class values that were her own and that remain beneath the fairy-tale veneer of royalty. She became England.

Sources

The standard edition of Queen Victoria's correspondence is A. C. Benson and Viscount Esher, eds., *The Letters of Queen Victoria: A Selection from Her Majesty's Correspondence Between the Years 1837 and 1861* (London: John Murray, 1907). The second series, covering the years 1862–1885, edited by George Earle Buckle, appeared in 1926; the third series, covering 1886–1901, also edited by Buckle, appeared in 1932. Each series appeared in three volumes, and each contains extracts from the Queen's journals as transcribed by Princess Beatrice from the originals, now destroyed. All letters are quoted from this edition except where otherwise cited. Other compilations of material from Victoria's diaries, almost entirely in each case extracted from the nine volumes of correspondence, are Christopher Hibbert, ed., *Queen Victoria in Her Letters and Journals* (London: John Murray, 1984); and Barry St. John Nevill, ed., *Life at the Court of Queen*

Victoria 1861–1901 (Exeter: Webb and Bower, 1984). Additional brief quotations from Victoria's letters and journals are found in the Longford biography and in the unfinished (to 1861) Woodham Smith biography (see notes to Chapter II).

I Jubilee (1887)

The Guy's Hospital campaign is reported in the pages of *Dramatic Review*, June 25, 1887, and earlier in the *Pall Mall Gazette*, December 10, 1886. After a year only £80,000 had been raised. The Queen's concern that Bertie was not fit to replace her appears in a letter to Vicky, June 5, 1872, in the 1871–1878 volume *(Darling Child)* of the Roger Fulford edition of the letters to the Princess Royal (London: Evans, 1976). It is repeated in other forms several times further. Swinburne's letters are quoted from the Cecil Y. Lang edition (New Haven: Yale University Press, 1962). Meredith's letters are quoted from the C. L. Cline edition (Oxford: Oxford University Press, 1970). A. H. Wall, *Fifty Years of a Good Queen's Reign* (1886), was reviewed anonymously by George Bernard Shaw in the *Pall Mall Gazette*, November 16, 1886. Sir John Brunner is quoted from his speech to his constituents in Stephen Koss, *Sir John Brunner, Radical Plutocrat* (Cambridge: Cambridge University Press, 1970). Lord Bute's rejection of Jubilee honors is reported in *Truth*, June 9, 1887, and confirmed (but without naming names) in the Queen's *Letters*, in a diary entry. Winston Churchill is quoted from William Manchester, *The Last Lion* (Boston: Little, Brown, 1983). The Jubilee Addresses to the Queen, with few exceptions, are stored at the Public Record Office, London. A descriptive catalogue of Jubilee gifts was published by Harrison & Sons, London, on November 15, 1887. A copy is in the Public Record Office, Lord Chamberlain's Papers. The snubbing of the Hawaiian Queen and Princess is described in Liliuokalani's memoirs, *Hawaii's Story* (Rutland, Vermont: Tuttle, 1964—reprint of the 1898 edition), and in *Truth.* The menu of the Jubilee luncheon is reproduced in Nevill. Chief Letsie's letter is in Victoria's *Letters;* his history is from the Cape Town State Archives, including the "lice" quotation. Sir Sydney Cockerell's diary is in the British Library; his entry is June 21, 1887. Gathorne-Hardy's comment about the Queen's lame knee is from his diary, June 18, 1887, in Nancy E. Johnson, ed., *The Diary of Gathorne-*

Hardy (Oxford: Oxford University Press, 1981). The Queen's memoranda to Henry Ponsonby are quoted in Arthur Ponsonby, *Henry Ponsonby, Victoria's Private Secretary, His Life from His Letters* (New York: Macmillan, 1943). The gift Irish egg is reported in *The World,* July 6, 1887, which also describes the royal garden party. Whistler's report of his presentation to the Queen is from the *Whistler Journal,* ed. Joseph and Elizabeth Pennell (Philadelphia: Lippincott, 1921). His letter to W. H. Smith on the Spithead etchings is quoted in Katherine Lochman, *The Etchings of Whistler* (New Haven: Yale University Press, 1984). The exchange between the Queen and old Mr. Seely is quoted by Lord Riddell in his *More Pages from My Diary* (London: Country Life Press, 1934). "The Queen's Speech" at the "Charing Cross Parliament" was published in *Our Corner,* August 1887.

II Alexandrina Victoria (1817–1820)

The Duke of Kent's relationship with "Madame de St. Laurent" is exhaustively explored in Mollie Gillen, *The Prince and His Lady* (Toronto: Griffin House, 1970). The 1790 episode of Adelaide Victoire, the Prince's earlier, illegitimate, daughter, is also revealed in Gillen. Background on the Royal Dukes is from Morris Marples, *Wicked Uncles in Love* (London: Michael Joseph, 1972), and Roger Fulford, *The Royal Dukes* (London: Duckworth, 1933). Background details on the Duchess of Kent (Princess of Leiningen) are from Harold A. Albert, *Queen Victoria's Sister* (London: Robert Hale, 1967). Details on Amorbach are from the Royal Geographical Society, London, via Capt. Alan Hanley-Browne. The first volume of Victoria's *Letters* errs in claiming that pre-Napoleonic Leiningen extended "about 252 miles on the left bank of the Rhine"; if it had, the princely state would have been one of the most powerful in Europe. Thomas Creevey's diary is Sir H. Maxwell, ed., *The Creevey Papers* (London: John Murray, 1903). The Duchess's letters to Polyxene von Tubeuf are quoted from Elizabeth Longford, *Queen Victoria* (New York: Harper, 1964). The Duke's financial negotiations with his English backers are admirably detailed in Cecil Woodham Smith, *Queen Victoria, Her Life and Times 1819–1861* (London: Hamish Hamilton, 1972).

III Gilded Cage (1820–1830)

The Duchess of Clarence's commissioning of the sculptor Scoular is from Marples, *Wicked Uncles in Love.* The Duke of Cumberland's letter to George IV on Kent's "little girl" is #790 in A. Aspinall, ed., *The Letters of King George IV* (Cambridge: Cambridge University Press, 1938). (The Duchess of Kent's 1827 letter to the King, and her birthday letter for Victoria a month later, are #1367 and #1389 in the same source; Victoria's reference to "dear uncle king" is from #1405.) Sir Henry Halford's "poor *wishy-washy* thing" comment on the Duchess of Clarence is from Marples. Leopold's loans to his sister Victoire are spelled out in the *Memoirs of Baron Stockmar* (London: Longmans, Green, 1879). Victoria's letter to Vicky on her "unhappy life as a child" is June 9, 1858, in Fulford's first series, *Dearest Child, 1858–1861* (London: Evans, 1964). She refers to the Duchess's saving her baby relics in a letter dated April 10, 1861. Victoria's memoir of childhood, composed in 1872, in manuscript at Windsor, is quoted at length in the first volume of her *Letters.* *The Greville Memoirs* are quoted from the eight-volume edition edited by Henry Reeve (London: Longmans, Green, 1896—described as "a new edition"). Negotiations for the continued support of Kent's ex-mistress are quoted from Gillen, *The Prince and His Lady.*

Victoria's dolls are described and illustrated by Frances H. Low in "Queen Victoria's Dolls," *The Strand* 4 (September 1892); and by Wendy Monk [Trewin], *Puffin Annual* no. 2 (n.d.). Her visit to George IV's Royal Lodge is described by Victoria in reminiscences quoted in her *Letters,* and in Christopher Hibbert, *George IV* (London: Allen Lane, n.d.). Harriet Arbuthnot's report of the little Princess Victoria is from Frances Bamford and the Duke of Wellington, eds., *The Journal of Mrs. Arbuthnot* (London, 1950). "A King for Greece!" is quoted from Clare Jerrold, *The Court of Queen Victoria* (New York: Putnam's, 1912).

IV Royal Pawn (1830–1837)

The circumstances of Prince George of Cumberland's blindness are related in a letter from Princess de Lieven to Lady Cowper, September 15, 1832, in *The Lieven-Palmerston Correspondence, 1828–1856,* translated and edited by Lord Sudley (London: John Murray, 1943). The death of Madame Mongenet is recorded in Gillen, *The Prince and His Lady.* Princess Victoria's first drawing-room appearance is recorded in the *Greville Memoirs* as February 25, 1831. The William IV Coronation imbroglio with the Duchess of Kent is recorded in detail in *The Times*, September 7 and September 10, 1831. The satiric suggestion that Princess Victoria be made the Bishop of Derby, to save the nation allowance money, is reported in John Aston, *When William IV Was King* (New York: D. Appleton, 1896). Victoria's appearance at the Duchess's dinner party on April 17, 1832—the "Miss Guelph" allusion—is in *The Croker Papers*, edited by Bernard Pool (New York: Barnes & Noble, 1967). Victoria's first Progress with the Duchess is detailed in Lady Elizabeth Grosvenor's letters as quoted in Gervas Huxley, *Lady Elizabeth and the Grosvenors* (London and New York: Oxford University Press, 1965). Victoria's reading from *The Dairyman's Daughter* on the Isle of Wight in 1833 is reported in Ian Bradley, *The Call to Seriousness* (New York: Macmillan, 1976). That she was "crushed" under her regimen comes from a letter to King Leopold, July 29, 1845.

William IV's personality emerges in Fulford's *Royal Dukes* and in Philip Ziegler, *King William IV* (New York: Harper & Row, 1973) and in Peter George Patmore, *The Court of Queen Victoria*, which quotes Creevy as well as Oliver Wendell Holmes. Marina Warner, *Queen Victoria's Sketchbooks* (London: Macmillan, 1979), includes drawings of the Princess's opera-going. Greville's comments on Victoria at the races are from the September 15, 1835, entry in his *Diaries*, and King William's birthday comments on Victoria are from the August 30, 1835, entry. His sending Victoria a 200-guinea Broadwood piano for her eighteenth birthday is from Aston, *When William IV Was King.* The King's final illness is graphically detailed in Greville, and Victoria's reactions are from her diary and letters.

That Victoria's doctor, Sir James Clark, had written a thesis on the salubriousness of cold, fresh air, *"De Frigoribus Effectis,"* is reported by Elizabeth Longford in "Queen Victoria's Doctors," in Martin Gilbert, ed., *A Century of Conflict, 1850–1950* (London: Hamish Hamilton, 1966). The false report of Queen Adelaide's pregnancy, and the malicious attribution to Lord Howe, are from a letter dated January 29, 1835, from Lady Cowper to Princess de Lieven.

The cartoon attacking Cumberland, "The Contrast," is reproduced in Lord George Russell's anonymously published *Collections and Recollections* (London and New York: Harper's, 1898). The largely hidden story of Lord Elphinstone's interest in Princess Victoria is reported cryptically in the account of Elphinstone's life in the *Dictionary of National Biography*, and in Longford, *Queen Victoria*. A few corroborative hints appear in Victoria's letters as Queen, and more openly in Robert Browning's letter of June 21, 1861, to Mr. and Mrs. William Wentworth Story, published in Gertrude Reese Hudson, ed., *Browning to His American Friends* (New York: Barnes & Noble, 1965).

V Virgin Queen (1837–1840)

The "Dowager" exchange, Mrs. Stevenson's reports of Windsor and other matters, the Elizabeth on horseback remark, and the description of the Duchess of Sutherland, are from the letters to her sisters in America by Mrs. Sallie Coles Stevenson, wife of the American minister to Great Britain, Andrew Stevenson, and an intimate of many at Court 1837–1841. See Edward Boykin, ed., *Victoria, Albert, and Mrs. Stevenson* (New York: Rinehart, 1957). The original 191 letters are at Duke University.

Victoria's account of her first days as Queen are from her diary and letters. *The Times*'s concerns about Melbourne's influence are described in a leader of June 21, 1837. Melbourne's attitudes are described from his letters and conversation in Philip Ziegler, *Melbourne* (London: Collins, 1976). The confusion of applying feminine tags to royal proclamations and bills is described in Lord George Russell, *Collections and Recollections*. Victoria's conversations with Melbourne on the Sykes-Maclise scandal are quoted from previously unpublished comments in the Queen's journals for February 2, 1839, used to annotate a letter from Charles Dickens to Daniel Maclise, June 2, 1840, in Madeline House and Graham Storey, eds., *The Letters of Charles Dickens*, Pilgrim Edition, vol. 2 (Oxford: Clarendon Press, 1969). Victoria's conversations with Melbourne on *Oliver Twist* are from a journal entry dated December 30, 1838, used to annotate a Dickens letter dated February 13, 1840.

Greville's reports of the new Queen are from his *Diaries;* his description of the near-exclusivity of her attentions for Melbourne come from the entry of December 15, 1838. The "hot sermon" exchange is quoted by Greville on July 23, 1838. The Queen's relations with Lord Palmerston are detailed through 1865 in Brian Connell, *Regina vs. Palmerston: The Correspondence between Queen Victoria and Her Foreign and Prime*

Minister 1837–1865 (New York: Doubleday, 1961). Stockmar's own account of his role in the new reign is from E. von Stockmar, ed., *Memoirs of Baron Stockmar* (London: Longmans, Green, 1873).

Victoria's signed invitations to the coronation are quoted from the invitation to William, Earl of Listowel, and Countess Listowel, dated May 9, 1838, and quoted as item 190 in Maggs's catalogue 1061 (1985). The "Queen-Mother"/"Mother of the Queen" argument in the Commons is quoted in Frances Howes, *Henry Brougham* (New York: St. Martin's Press, 1958). The Queen's being overworked with trivial detail is reported by Croker in his diary entry for August 15, 1837. Disraeli's letter on the Queen's visit to the City, to his sister Sarah, November 14, 1837, is reproduced in J. A. W. Gunn et al., eds., *Benjamin Disraeli Letters* (Toronto and Buffalo: University of Toronto Press, 1982) as is his letter to Sarah, June 21, 1837, on the coronation. John James Ruskin's letter to his wife, Margaret, May 2, 1838, on the Queen's watercolor purchases, is in Van Akin Burd, ed., *The Ruskin Family Letters,* vol. 2 (Ithaca: Cornell University Press, 1973).

Lord William Russell's gossip with Lady Russell on the Flora Hastings affair is from his letter dated April 15, 1839, in Georgiana Blakiston, ed., *Lord William Russell and His Wife* (London: John Murray, 1972). Prince Albert's early letters are from Kurt Jagow, ed., *Letters of the Prince Consort,* translated by E. T. S. Dugdale (London: John Murray, 1938), hereafter referred to as Jagow; and (Sir) Theodore Martin, *The Life of the Prince Consort* (London: Smith, Elder & Co., 1875–1880), hereafter referred to as Martin. Metternich's "eight feet high" slur is quoted by Lord Clarendon in a letter dated April 3, 1861, to the Duchess of Manchester in A. L. Kennedy, ed., *Social and Political Letters to the Duchess of Manchester 1858–1869* (London: John Murray, 1956). Melbourne's warning to Victoria on making Albert King Consort is recalled by Lord George Russell in his *Collections and Recollections.*

VI Royal Husband (1840–1843)

The "Prince Hallbert" street song is quoted by Charles Dickens in a letter of February 1, 1840, to Richard Monckton Milnes (Baron Houghton), in House and Storey, eds., *The Letters of Charles Dickens,* Pilgrim Edition, vol. 2. Albert's precedence problems are described in Victoria (letters and journals), Jagow, and Stockmar, as well as in a lengthy appendix, "The Royal Precedency Question," in Greville. The allegation that Victoria was "a silly child" is from John James Ruskin's letter to his wife, February 13, 1840, in *The Ruskin Family Letters*, vol. 2. Victoria's letter to "Dear Good Victo" about marriage, dated March 9, 1840, from Buckingham Palace, is translated from the German in the G. Michelmore & Co. catalogue, *Two Hundred Extraordinarily Important Books, Autographs and Manuscripts*, London [1925], and is from Pattee Library Special Collections, Penn State. Albert's letters are from Jagow. The Lord Mayor's banquet which Albert left early is described in Fulford, *The Royal Dukes*.

That Victorian doctors were hopelessly confused about women's cycles of fertility between menses is clear from Dr. George H. Napheys, in *The Physical Life of Women* (1869), describing the time "midway between the monthly recurring periods" as safest "for the consummation of marriage." Medicine then assumed that women went into heat as animals did.

Victoria's relations with Palmerston are from their letters and from Kenneth Bourne, *Palmerston: The Early Years* (New York: Macmillan, 1982). The royal couple's visit to portraitist John Lucas is described by Elizabeth Barrett (Browning), in a letter to Mary Russell Mitford, October [14,] 1841, in M. B. Raymond and M. R. Sullivan, eds., *The Letters of Elizabeth Barrett Browning to Mary Russell Mitford* (Waco, Texas: Browning Library & Institute, 1983). Details of the Queen's progress to Scotland are from the Lord Chamberlain's records. Details of Mendelssohn's visits are from his letters to his mother and to Ignaz Moscheles quoted in Felix Moscheles, ed., *Letters of Felix Mendelssohn to Ignaz and Charlotte Moscheles* (Freeport, New York: Books for Libraries Press, 1970). Laurence Housman's *Victoria Regina* was published as "a dramatic biography" in several volumes. "Morning Glory"—the scene after the wedding night—appeared in the first series (London: Cape, 1930); "Leading Strings," on palace economics, appeared in the second series, *The Queen's Progress* (London: Cape, 1932). The anecdote about the Prince's refusal to obey the Queen's summons to return home from a Royal Academy evening appears in S. M. Ellis, ed., *A Mid-Victorian Pepys. The Letters and Memoirs of Sir William Hardman* (London: Cecil Palmer, 1923). Dr. Locock's comments to Mr. Arbuthnot about the Queen's pregnancies are from Lady Longford, "Queen Victoria's Doctors." The Queen's request to Locock to have Albert read to her is from

Sallie Stevenson's letter to her sister Emily Rutherford, December 29, 1840. In the Boykin edition, Dr. Locock's name is misread from Mrs. Stevenson's longhand as "Dr. South." Albert's marital difficulties with Victoria are best described by Robert Rhodes James in *Prince Albert* (New York: Knopf, 1984), from Anson's memoranda and Albert's notes to Victoria, in the Royal Archives.

VII Dual Monarchy (1844–1848)

Victoria's self-portrait at twenty-six is reproduced in Warner, *Queen Victoria's Sketchbooks.* Albert's various comments about the English guaranteed to make him unpopular are described in Roger Fulford, *The Prince Consort* (London: Macmillan, 1945), in his "Home Life" chapter. Greville, Princess Lieven, and Lady Palmerston add gossip on the Queen's alleged unpopularity. Victoria's encounter with Wordsworth is described by Elizabeth Barrett (Browning) to Mary Russell Mitford, May 2, 1845. Edward Lear as drawing master to the Queen is described in Lady Strachey of Sutton Court, ed., *Letters of Edward Lear* (Freeport, New York: Books for Libraries Press, n.d.), originally published in 1907.

Details of Osborne House as well as its furnishings appear in *Osborne House, Isle of Wight* (London: Her Majesty's Stationery Office, 1960), and the Department of the Environment's *Catalogue of the Principal Items on View at Osborne House* (London: Her Majesty's Stationery Office, 1965).

P. T. Barnum's account of his visits to the Queen are in his memoir, *Struggles and Triumphs: Or, Forty Years' Recollections of P. T. Barnum* (1869), as taken from the abridgment by Carl Bode (New York: Penguin, 1981). That "Tom Thumb" (Charles Sherwood Stratton) was three feet, one inch in height rather than a foot smaller, as Barnum advertised him, is proven by Benjamin Moran in S. A. Wallace and F. E. Gillespie, eds., *The Journal of Benjamin Moran*, vol. 1 (Chicago: University of Chicago Press, 1948), hereafter referred to as Moran. Assistant Secretary of the United States Legation in London, Moran measured "Tom Thumb" for his passport application. The Queen's visit to Madame Tussaud's is recounted in John T. Tussaud, *The Romance of Madame Tussaud's* (New York: George H. Doran Co., 1920). The Master of Trinity's response to

Victoria about the polluted Cam is described by Gwen Raverat in *Period Piece: A Cambridge Childhood* (London: Faber, 1952).

The Royal couple's art tastes are examined from the works themselves in the Royal collections and in Benedict Read, *Victorian Sculpture* (New Haven: Yale University Press, 1982), with its wealth of reproductions; Winslow Ames, *Prince Albert and Victorian Taste* (London: Chapman and Hall, 1968), again with a wealth of illustrations; and Dickens's letter on Maclise to Professor Felton, quoted in Thea Holme, *Chelsea* (London: Hamish Hamilton, 1972).

George Eliot's "humbug" comment to John Sibree, Jr., appears in a letter to him dated editorially March 8, 1848, in Gordon S. Haight, ed., *Letters of George Eliot*, vol. 2 (New Haven: Yale University Press, 1954).

VIII The Splendid Misery (1848–1853)

Major sources are Victoria, Martin, Greville, Stockmar, and Connell *(Regina vs. Palmerston)*. The growing-up of the royal children is best described by Victoria herself in her drawings reproduced in Warner. The literature on the Great Exhibition is enormous. One of the best sources was never catalogued—the 1983–1984 Prince Albert exhibition at the Royal College of Art, London. Some idea of it can be gleaned from Hermione Hobhouse's usefully illustrated *Prince Albert: His Life and Work* (London: Hamish Hamilton, 1983), which was sold at the exhibition in lieu of catalogue. The Lord Chamberlain's records provide valuable detail. Read's *Victorian Sculpture* illustrates the art objects of most interest to Victoria and Albert.

George Eliot's positive response to Albert—and "deplorable" one to Victoria—appears in her letter of May 24, 1852, to Mr. and Mrs. Charles Bray, in Haight. Lord Stanley's journals are quoted from John Vincent, ed., *Disraeli, Derby and the Conservative Party: Journals and Memoirs of Edward Henry, Lord Stanley* [afterwards fifteenth Earl of Derby] (New York: Harper & Row, 1978), hereafter referred to as Stanley. *The Times* leader quoted is from the issue of May 2, 1851. Details about "Miser Nield" are from Thea Holme, *Chelsea*.

The story of the Osborne visitor with the deformed foot accosted by the royal children is told by Lord George Russell in *Collections and*

Recollections. Victoria's seasick crossing to Osborne is recalled by Lord Hertford in *The World,* in the "What the World Says" column, February 6, 1884. Her brief visit to Aboyne, en route to Balmoral, is described in the Earl of Bessborough, ed., [*Diary of*] *Charlotte Guest* (London: John Murray, 1950). The building of the cairn to mark the purchase of Balmoral is described by Victoria in her October 11, 1852, entry in *Leaves from the Journal of Our Life in the Highlands* (London: Smith, Elder, 1868).

IX The Woman Warrior (1853–1858)

Major sources remain Victoria, Martin, Greville, Stockmar, and the Palmerston letters, as well as Stanley. Theo Aronson, *Queen Victoria and the Bonapartes* (London: Cassel, 1972), and Jasper Ridley, *Napoleon III and Eugénie* (New York: Viking, 1980), furnish much detail about Victoria's encounters with Louis Napoleon's family here and hereafter. Mary Ponsonby's recollections of Victoria in Paris are from Magdalen Ponsonby, ed., *Mary Ponsonby: A Memoir, Some Letters and a Journal* (London: John Murray, 1927). Count Nieuwerkerke's covert protest at Eugénie's removal of Louvre pictures is described by Edmond and Jules de Goncourt in their December 11, 1866, entry in *Pages from the Goncourt Journal,* translated by Robert Baldick (Oxford: Oxford University Press, 1962). Lady Augusta Stanley (Bruce) is quoted from the Dean of Windsor and Hector Bolitho, eds., *Letters of Lady Augusta Stanley: A Young Lady at Court, 1849–1863* (New York: George H. Doran, 1927). The "fiery little devil" description of Victoria by James Buchanan is from Nathaniel Hawthorne, *The English Notebooks,* ed. Randall Stewart (New York: Russell & Russell, 1962; first published in 1941). Laurence Housman's *Victoria Regina* dramatization is from his "The Popular Voice" scene, in *Gracious Majesty* (New York: Scribner's, 1942).

Victoria's interest in William Mulready's nudes is quoted from Kathryn Moore Heleniak, *William Mulready* (New Haven: Yale University Press, 1980), which includes (plate 147) a reproduction of the male nude drawing purchased for Albert's birthday. Her sittings with Joseph Durham are described in Hawthorne's August 31, 1856, *Notebooks* entry. Her sittings with Gibson are described by Read in *Victorian Sculpture.*

The Queen's relations with the press during the Crimean War are detailed in Alan Hankinson, *Man of Wars: William Russell of "The Times"* (London: Heinemann, 1972), and Arthur Irwin Dasent, *John Thaddeus Delane: Editor of "The Times"* (New York: Scribner's, 1908).

Victoria's first brush with Wagner is described in Martin Gregor-Dellin, *Richard Wagner: His Life, His Work, His Century*, translated by J. Maxwell Brownjohn (New York: Harcourt Brace Jovanovich, 1983). Her attempts to discipline her daughters are recounted by John Ruskin to his father, John James Ruskin, in a letter dated August 30, 1863, in Van Akin Burd, ed., *The Winnington Letters: John Ruskin's Correspondence with Margaret Alexis Bell and the Children at Winnington Hall* (London: Allen and Unwin, 1969).

The Times's leader deploring the aesthetics of the Victoria Cross is from the issue of June 27, 1857. The "no more fun" protest is quoted by Nevill in his introduction to *Life at the Court of Queen Victoria*. He gives no source.

X Albert the Good (1858–1861)

Martin quotes extensively from Albert's diaries, often in German, and details extensively (and perhaps unwittingly) symptoms of the Prince's illness(es) and decline that do not conform to his doctors' later diagnoses. Lady Augusta Bruce's letters describe the younger children growing up, and Albert's last days. Albert's difficulties with Victoria are described by Rhodes James (in his *Prince Albert*) in quotations from Albert's notes to the Queen in the Royal Archives. Details of Albert's earlier health complaints, and evidences of obtuseness on Victoria's part, appear in the first volume of Fulford's edition of her letters to the Princess Royal, *Dearest Child*. Benjamin Moran's diaries are quoted from Moran.

The Queen's confrontation with Prince Victor (later Count Gleichen), her nephew, is best detailed in Harold A. Albert, *Queen Victoria's Sister: The Life and Letters of Princess Feodora* (London: Hale, 1967). A Balmoral country dance is described by Bertram Mitford (Lord Redesdale) in his *Memories* (New York: Dutton, n.d.). Dr. William Baly's death is recalled in *British Medical Journal*, January 26, 1901. Lord Clarendon's and other correspondents' letters to the Duchess of Manchester come from A. L. Kennedy's edition. Lady Paget's recollections of Court life, 1858–1860, are from *Embassies of Other Days, and Further Recollections by Walburga, Lady Paget (Countess Hohenthal),* vol. 1 (New York: George Doran, 1923). Lord Torrington's description of Christmas at Windsor is from Dasent's *Delane.* Victoria's "no more American funerals" is from Moran.

Albert's terminal illness is detailed at length in the many biographies of the Prince, in Victoria's letters and journals, in Martin, and in recollections of courtiers; however, only Daphne Bennett, in *King Without a Crown* (London: Heinemann, 1977), speculates in a one-page appendix that typhoid fails to account for Albert's symptoms, and suggests a "wasting disease." My own survey of the clinical particulars over the years 1858–1861, offered separately to five medical specialists, British and American, has elicited considerable skepticism over the typhoid diagnosis. Chapters 10 and 11 of the present volume describe the particulars and offer alternative diagnoses.

The Woman in White appeared monthly in the magazine *All the Year Round* in 1859–1860, and was published in book form in 1860. The Queen's promise to read it appears in a letter to Vicky, November 3, 1860. I am grateful to William Schupbach for calling the typhoid-typhus incident in the novel to my attention. The "Last Moments" scene was painted imaginatively by an unknown artist, probably Octavius Oakley, and was met with disapproval by the Royal Household. A description of the dramatis personae appears in W. Schupbach, "Last Moments of H.R.H. the Prince Consort," *Medical History* 26 (1982).

XI Victorian Mourning (1861–1866)

The Observer's obituary appeared December 15, 1861. Elizabeth Gaskell's description of London in mourning appeared in her letter to Marianne Gaskell, December 26, 1861, in J. A. V. Chapple and Arthur Pollard, eds., *Letters of Mrs. Gaskell* (Cambridge: Harvard University Press, 1967). Disraeli's reactions are from Stanley; Torrington's from Dasent's *Delane.* Victoria's journals—once the initial shock had receded —are extremely detailed about the aftermath, and she would add even more recollections a decade later. Her letters to Vicky in Fulford's second volume, *Dearest Mama* (London: Hale, 1968), cover her emotional life in 1861–1864 in considerable and seemingly unvarnished detail. The

Duke of Cumberland's mourning for his wife in 1841 as King of Hanover is described in *Royal Dukes*.

Victoria's reaction ("twaddle") to Bishop Davidson is reported by him in G. K. A. Bell, *Randall Davidson* (London: Oxford University Press, 1938). Dr. Clark's imaginative diagnosis to the Queen about Albert's cause of death (overstrained heart) is quoted by Lady Longford in "Queen Victoria's Doctors." Clarendon's judgment of Holland and Clark ("old women"), and dismissal of Jenner's competence, is in a letter to the Duchess of Manchester. The Queen's own note in the Royal Archives, November 7, 1877, quoting Jenner that no one can diagnose typhoid at first, is from "Queen Victoria's Doctors."

Victoria's relationship with Tennyson from 1862 to Tennyson's death a generation later is detailed in Hope Dyson and Charles Tennyson, eds., *Dear and Honoured Lady, the Correspondence Between Victoria and Alfred Tennyson* (Rutherford: Fairleigh Dickinson University Press, [1971]). The Queen's financial situation following Albert's death is examined in a letter from Sir Charles Phipps to the Lord Chamberlain, Viscount Sydney, January 17, 1862, and other documents in the Lord Chamberlain's records, in Vera Watson, ed., *A Queen at Home. An Intimate Account of the Social and Domestic Life at Queen Victoria's Court* (London: W. H. Allen, 1952). Martin adds supporting details, declaring that the Prince left *"absolutely no fortune."*

The Queen's interest in memorializing Albert is described contemporaneously by Torrington to Delane in Dasent, by Lord Clarendon in letters to the Duchess of Manchester, by Charles Dickens in his letters, and—in illustrative detail—in Read's *Victorian Sculpture*. Lord Derby's interview with the Queen in June 1862 is in Stanley; Disraeli's touching speech in the Commons on the Prince, and Victoria's response, is from Sarah Bradford, *Disraeli* (London: Weidenfeld & Nicolson, 1982). Gladstone's post-Albert relations with the Queen are from Philip Magnus, *Gladstone: A Biography* (New York: Dutton, 1954). The Queen's *Album Consolatium* (2 vols.) is British Library Add. MSS. 62089/90. Her letter to General Grey thanking him for verses translated for her first wedding anniversary after Albert's death is dated February 10, 1862, and quoted as item S-1142 in *The Collector* (Walter Benjamin, Inc.), No. 910 (1985).

The handbill satirically announcing the Queen's retirement is from Stanley, as is Bertie's retort to his mother on smoking. The Queen's unsigned declaration in *The Times* about her handling Court duties was published April 6, 1864.

The Queen's letter to the Prince of Wales about naming his second son George is quoted from Kenneth Rose, *King George V* (New York: Knopf, 1984). Her recollection of the invasion of her privacy in Coburg when there to unveil an Albert memorial was made to Gathorne Gathorne-Hardy and quoted in his journal entry for January 4, 1867.

XII Victoria Adrift (1866–1872)

Victoria's presentation copy of the biography of Albert to Duleep Singh is described as item 149 in the Paul Richards catalogue 202, 1985. Quotations from the volume, particularly its introductions, are from *The Early Years of His Royal Highness the Prince Consort,* compiled, under the direction of Her Majesty the Queen, by Lieutenant-General the Hon. C. Grey (London: Smith, Elder, 1867). Quotations from the diary of Gathorne-Hardy are from the Nancy E. Johnson edition. Extracts from the letters of Lady Augusta Bruce (now Stanley) are from the Dean of Windsor and Hector Bolitho, eds., *Later Letters of Lady Augusta Stanley 1864–1876* (London: Cape, 1929). Carlyle's reaction to meeting the Queen appears in Fred Kaplan, *Thomas Carlyle: A Biography* (Ithaca: Cornell University Press, 1983). The Queen's reactions to her meetings with Dickens and with the Carlyle party appear in her journals, as does her response to news of Dickens's death.

W. E. Gladstone's sexual peculiarities are dealt with by Richard Shannon in *Gladstone,* vol. 1 (London: Hamish Hamilton, 1982), and in M. R. D. Foot and H. C. G. Matthew, eds., *The Gladstone Diaries* (Oxford: Clarendon Press, 1968–1978), published as of this writing only through 1868 although a footnote allusion to a later entry attributes Gladstone's "battle between inclination and duty" allusion to seeking out women of the streets to a diary entry for October 18, 1869. Details of Mrs. Thistlethwaite's early life are also from notes in the *Diaries.* Gladstone's correspondence with Lord Granville is published as *The Political Correspondence of Mr. Gladstone and Lord Granville,* ed. Agatha Ramm (London: Royal Historical Society, 1952). Derby and Disraeli, except where noted, are quoted from Stanley's diaries. The Marquess of Salisbury's "Jew adventurer" line is quoted from Bradford's *Disraeli.* Princess Feodora's letters to Victoria are from *Queen Victoria's Sister.* The *Pall Mall Gazette* attack on the Queen's drawing-rooms is from the March 29,

1871, issue. The *PMG*'s "An Inauspicious Event" attack on the Prince of Wales is from the April 11, 1871, issue.

The first reference to the Queen's illness is her August 4, 1871, allusion to a possible insect sting (Journals, Royal Archives, furnished by Oliver Everett, Librarian). The *British Medical Journal*'s report of September 16, 1871, on the Queen's illness, with little additional data, appears in the *PMG* on September 14, 1871. (*BMJ* was released several days in advance of its date.) The *Daily News*'s apology to the Queen is on September 15. That Jenner's medical memoranda to the press were often composed or dictated by the Queen herself is proven by Royal Archives documents such as L 25/65, in which Victoria refers unclinically to her "nervous temperature." Lady Longford notes this in "Queen Victoria's Doctors." Jenner's anonymous defense of the Queen appeared in the *Lancet*, August 19, 1871, and an identical report to the *BMJ*'s account of her illness appeared on September 16, "The Health of the Queen." His letter to the editor denying that revaccination had anything to do with her illness appeared in both *Lancet* and *BMJ* on November 4, 1871. Medical surmises are based on consultations with British and American physicians and pathologists on the basis of medical data released and the Queen's description, in her journals and letters, of her illness, its acute phase, and her slow recovery.

XIII A Brown Study (1863–1883)

W. M. Rossetti's diary entry is June 20, 1870, in Odette Bornand, ed., *The Diary of W. M. Rossetti, 1870–1873* (Oxford: Clarendon Press, 1977). The basic book on the Brown relationship is Tom Cullen, *The Empress Brown: The Story of a Royal Friendship* (London: Bodley Head, 1969). Its conclusions are, despite the title, unsensational. Stanley's private notes are from his diary. W. S. Blunt's diary on Skittles's tales is quoted from Angela Lambert, *Unquiet Souls* (New York: Harper, 1984), with additional details on Georgie Sumner's gossip from Lady Longford's biography of Blunt, *A Pilgrimage of Passion* (New York: Knopf, 1980). The disciplining of General McNeill is related by Sir Frederick Ponsonby (later Lord Syonsby) in *Recollections of Three Reigns* (New York: Dutton, 1952). Brown's behavior abroad and his dialogue with Prince Alfred are described by Henry Ponsonby in letters to his wife in Arthur Ponsonby's *Henry Ponsonby, Queen Victoria's Private Secretary* (London: Macmillan, 1942). Swinburne described his "La Mort du Mari" in a letter, March 3, 1884, to Georgiana [Burne] Jones, in Cecil Lang, ed., *The Swinburne Letters*, vol. 2 (Oxford: Oxford University Press, 1959).

The Queen's letters to and from Vicky are in successive volumes of the Fulford-edited correspondence. The "No one loves you more" dialogue is from *Your Dear Letter*, the 1865–1870 correspondence. The private letter completing the episode, written by the Queen to a Brown relation after John Brown's death, is in Cullen's *Empress Brown*. Duke Ernest Ludwig and Prince Arthur are quoted on the Queen's attitude about behavior by superiors toward servants by Hector Bolitho, from conversation with them, in *My Restless Years* (London: Max Parrish, 1962). Victoria's intolerance of smoking, and a servant's discovering a violation at Windsor for her, is described in an unsigned column in *Hawk*, July 31, 1888. Many stories of Brown's arrogance ("biscuits and speeruts" . . . "saretenly not" . . .) are told from Henry Ponsonby's recollection in Arthur Ponsonby's memoir. Brown's protection of the Queen at Crathie is described in *The World*, November 18, 1874, and the story of Cameron of Lochiel appeared in *The World*, April 4, 1883.

The report of Brown's death in *The Times*, liberally quoting the Queen, appeared on March 29, 1883. Press speculation about her biography of Brown appeared in "The Queen's New Book," *The World*, January 30, 1884. Further details are furnished in *Henry Ponsonby* and in Bishop Davidson's memoir. Gathorne-Hardy's diary references on the subject appear on April 27, 1883, in the Johnson edition. *Lord Carlingford's Journal*, ed. A. B. Cooke and J. A. Vincent (London: Oxford University Press, 1971), May 30, 1883, refers to Cowell's managing the Household at Balmoral without Brown's interference, in the aftermath of Brown's death. In an entry of October 9, 1895, Marie Mallet, in *Life with Queen Victoria: Marie Mallet's Letters from Court, 1887–1901*, ed. Victor Mallet (London: John Murray, 1968), describes the Queen's presence at a Brown family funeral a dozen years after Brown's death.

XIV Faery Queen (1872–1880)

Correspondence with Princess Feodora is from *Queen Victoria's Sister*. Particulars of the Queen's last visit to her are from Victoria's journals and the *Later Letters* of Lady Stanley (Bruce). Disraeli's correspondence is from G. E. Buckle and W. F. Monypenny, *The Life of Benjamin Disraeli, Earl of Beaconsfield* (London: John Murray, 1929); Robert Blake, *Disraeli* (New York: St. Martin's Press, 1966); Bradford; and the Marquis of Zetland, ed., *The Letters of Disraeli to Lady Bradford and Lady Chesterfield* (London: Benn, 1929). Disraeli's appearance in 1874 is described by Bertram Mitford in *Memories*. Disraeli's relations with the Queen are also described by Henry Ponsonby, not an admirer, in his son's memoir and in the Queen's letters and journals. The Queen's letter to Captain Haig is from item 162 in Autographia (1986), San Rafael, California, quoted from a three-page autograph letter signed on black-bordered stationery. Haig's identification is from army lists at the National Army Museum, London. Victoria's correspondence with Gladstone during this period is in Philip Guedalla, ed., *The Queen and Mr. Gladstone* (London: Hodder and Stoughton, 1933), and from *The Political Correspondence of Mr. Gladstone and Lord Granville*.

The Queen's waning power is described in Frank Hardie, *The Political Influence of Queen Victoria* (London: Oxford University Press, 1935), and in Walter Bagehot, *The English Constitution*, 2nd edition (London: Kegan Paul, 1879). Gathorne-Hardy's diary is from Johnson. W. H. Smith's correspondence with Disraeli and with the Queen is from his biography by Viscount Chilston, *W. H. Smith* (Toronto: University of Toronto Press, 1965). The Queen's letter to Princess Victoria of Hesse on Alice's death is from Richard Hough, ed., *Advice to a Grand-Daughter* (London: Heinemann, 1975). *"Der alte Jude . . ."* is from Mitford, *Memories*. Prince Arthur's letter to his mother asking that he be permitted to work himself up through each military grade is quoted in his *DNB* entry. Controversies over the education of Bertie's and Alexandra's sons are described in David Duff, *Alexandra: Princess and Queen* (London: Collins, 1980).

Minny Thackeray's comment to Leslie Stephen on the Albert-Victoria relationship as seen from the biography of the Prince Consort is from Noel Annan, *Leslie Stephen: The Godless Victorian* (London: Weidenfeld & Nicolson, 1985).

The Prince Imperial's relations with the Royal Family, his demise, and the aftershocks, are described in Disraeli's letters, the Mitford memoir, E. E. P. Tisdall, *The Prince Imperial* (London: Jarrolds, 1959), and Ridley, *Napoleon III and Eugénie*, as well as the Queen's journals. Elizabeth Butler's reminiscences are in her *Autobiography* (Boston: Houghton Mifflin, 1925). Additional details about the Zulu wars come from Donald R. Morris, *The Washing of the Spears* (New York: Simon and Schuster, 1965). The oval portrait of Beatrice and the Queen, attributed by Christie's to Sir Joseph Noel Paton, was sold to the National Portrait Gallery in July 1985.

XV "The People's William" (1880–1886)

Gladstone's correspondence with Victoria is from Guedalla, *The Queen and Mr. Gladstone*. The Queen's letters to Vicky are (through 1885) from the fifth volume of the Fulford series, *Beloved Mama* (London: Evans, 1981). The Queen and Edward Lear in 1882—the rumored visit to San Remo—is reported in Vivien Noakes, *Edward Lear* (Boston: Houghton Mifflin, 1969). Cetewayo's visit is described in the Lord Chamberlain's papers, in the Queen's journals, and in Morris, *The Washing of the Spears*. Gathorne-Hardy's diary extracts are from his published *Diary*. Extracts from the diaries of Sir Edward Hamilton are from Dudley W. R. Bahlman, ed., *The Diary of Sir Edward Walter Hamilton*, 2 vols. (Oxford: Clarendon Press, 1972).

"The Queen and Her Ministers" appeared anonymously in *The World* on April 4, 1883. Mitford's broaching the London underground railway scheme to the Queen is described in his *Memories*. Extracts from the diaries of Count Holstein are from Norman Rich and M. H. Fisher, eds., *The Holstein Papers*, vol. 2, *The Diaries* (Cambridge: Cambridge University Press, 1967). The "North Pole" story is from *Henry Ponsonby;* the earnest clergyman on East End overcrowding is from F. Ponsonby, *Recollections of Three Reigns*. Extracts from Lord Carlingford's diaries are from his published *Journal.* The Queen's warning to Prince George on gambling is quoted from Kenneth Rose, *King George V.*

Extracts from Lady Monkswell's diaries are from the published text, *A Victorian Diarist: Extracts from the Journals of Mary, Lady Monkswell. 1875–1895*, vol. 1, ed. E. C. F. Collier (London: John Murray, 1944).

Material on Prince William (later William II) is from Lamar Cecil, "History as Family Chronicle: Kaiser Wilhelm II and the Dynastic Roots of the Anglo-German Antagonism," in John C. G. Röhl and Nicolaus Sombart, eds., *Kaiser Wilhelm II—New Interpretations* (Cambridge: Cambridge University Press, 1982). The Queen's letters to Miss Gordon were published on the leader page of *The Times* on March 7, 1888. Swinburne's then-unpublished letter in their defense is dated March 29, 1888, and appears in the Lang edition of his *Letters*. The dramatic events leading to Gladstone's being offered Downing Street yet again are described hour by hour in A. B. Cooke and John Vincent, *The Governing Passion: Cabinet Government and Party Politics in Britain 1885–86* (London: Harvester Press, 1974).

XVI Quarreling with Time (1886–1890)

Post-1886 letters exchanged between the Queen and Vicky are from Sir Frederick Ponsonby, ed., *The Letters of the Empress Frederick* (London: Macmillan & Co., 1929). Details about Dr. Morell Mackenzie are from R. Scott Stevenson, *Morell Mackenzie: The Story of a Victorian Tragedy* (London: Heinemann Medical Books, 1946). Harold Nicolson's locket tale is recounted in an unpublished portion of his diary for February 2, 1942, where he reports Sidney Peel's recollection of the incident as a boy in Florence. Nigel Nicolson has kindly furnished a photocopy of the diary page, which includes more details than the published entry in vol. 3 of the *Diaries* (ed. N. Nicolson), which describes the incident via a letter to Vita. Wagner's complaint to Cosima about Victoria's failure to abdicate in favor of her son is reported by Martin Gregor-Dellin in *Richard Wagner*.

Prince William's description of hearing the news from his father of Frederick's mortal illness is quoted from William's letter to Hinzpeter, November 11, 1887, in Thomas A. Kohut, "Kaiser Wilhelm II and His Parents: An Inquiry into the Psychological Roots of German Policy Towards England Before the First World War," in Röhl and Sombart (see notes to chapter 15). The Queen's long description of the Grand Chartreuse is in her journals. "Morality Old and New" was an unsigned leader in *The World*, December 15, 1886. Gladstone's relations with the Queen come largely from *The Governing Passion* and from Edward Hamilton's

Diaries. Ponsonby's remark about the crowded Solent is from a letter to Horatio Seymour, misdated in the memoir of Ponsonby. Gladstone's "child in a tub" relish of the Home Rule uproar is quoted from Reginald Brett (Lord Esher) in Joyce Marlow's *The Oak and the Ivy: An Intimate Biography of William and Catherine Gladstone* (Garden City: Doubleday, 1977).

The Queen's invitation to Madame Svárady to play at Windsor is reported in *The World*, May 26, 1886. Lady Battersea's appearance at Windsor in 1886 is reported in her *Reminiscences* (London: Macmillan and Co., Ltd., 1923). Edward Hamilton reports his plea to Gladstone to give up night-stalking in his *Diaries.* Gathorne-Hardy's recollections are from his *Diaries.* "Arminius Vambery's" encounters with the Queen are reported from his papers and her journals in Lory Alder and Richard Dalby, *The Dervish of Windsor Castle. The Life of Arminius Vambery* (London: Bachman & Turner, 1979). The Queen's Salvation Army letter, conveyed through Henry Ponsonby, was dated November 17, 1890, from Balmoral. It was published in *The Times* three days later.

The various critical and satirical remarks about the Queen by Prince (then King) William and his entourage are quoted by John C. G. Röhl in "The Emperor's New Clothes: A Character Sketch of Kaiser Wilhelm II," in Röhl and Sombart. Hugo von Radolinski's letter to Count Holstein from the yacht *Victoria and Albert,* dated July 20, 1887, is quoted from the *Holstein Papers.* The Medical Department of Her Majesty's Household in 1889 is listed in the Lord Chamberlain's Papers (Public Record Office). David Lindsay's observation about the scrupulous placement and replacement of the Queen's things is from *The Crawford Papers: The Journals of David Lindsay Twenty-seventh Earl of Crawford and Tenth Earl of Balcarres 1871–1940 During the Years 1892 to 1940,* ed. John Vincent (Manchester: Manchester University Press, 1984). Crawford also reports Lady Ampthill's story of the royal train.

The Queen's refusal to bring Beefeaters to Cowes to greet Emperor William is told by Almeric Fitzroy in his *Memoirs of Sir Almeric Fitzroy* (London: Hutchinson & Co., [1920]). Princess Victoria of Prussia's visit to her grandmother on the first anniversary of Frederick III's death is related in her letter to Vicky dated June 15, 1889, in James Pope-Hennessy, ed., *Queen Victoria at Windsor and Balmoral: Letters from Her Grand-daughter Princess Victoria of Prussia June 1889* (London: Allen & Unwin, 1959). The Queen's last visit to a Barnum show is described in Irving Wallace, *The Fabulous Showman* (New York: Knopf, 1959). Lady

Battersea's *Memoirs* are the source of details of Henry M. Stanley's 1890 visit to Windsor. Countess Blucher's memoir, *Embassies of Other Days*, is the source of the allegation that the British Royal Family treated William like the little boy they remembered. Additional correspondence on William's treatment as Prince and as Emperor is in *Henry Ponsonby*, and the Queen's own *Letters*.

Gathorne-Hardy's concerns about the Queen's theology are in his diary entry for September 10, 1888. Lady Monkswell's *Diary* describes the Empress Frederick's last drawing-room at Buckingham Palace. That the Empress's treatment by her son was "abominable" is quoted by Gathorne-Hardy, November 18, 1888, from conversation with the Queen. Dr. James Reid's comments about paying house calls on the *Munshi*'s family is from *Henry Ponsonby*. The attack upon the Queen for silencing artillery practice in the Solent is part of an unsigned article in *Truth*, July 31, 1890.

XVII Receding Figure (1891–1894)

Gathorne-Hardy's conversations with the Queen are taken from his *Diary*. Her arrangements for concerts at Windsor, Osborne, and Balmoral are described by Frederick Ponsonby in *Recollections of Three Reigns*. Duleep Singh's children are described from memory by Victor Mallet in his notes to *Life with Queen Victoria*. The Duke of Clarence's failings are detailed in chapter 8 of James Pope-Hennessy's *Queen Mary*. Lady Monkswell's description of the Queen's hat is from her *Diary*. The Queen's utilizing the Prince of Wales as conduit to Lord Rosebery to pressure Rosebery into the Foreign Ministry is seen in her memorandum of July 26, 1892, to her Private Secretary in *Henry Ponsonby*. Campbell-Bannerman's description of a conversation with the Queen as "like a little boy talking to his grandmother" is from *Recollections of Three Reigns*. Gladstone's list of trivia which had been the substance of a long conversation with Victoria is reproduced in Guedalla's *The Queen and Mr. Gladstone*. Rosebery's appeal to Ponsonby about the Queen's spurning typewritten messages is quoted in Rose's *King George V*. Campbell-Bannerman's description of Balmoral is from his biography by John Wilson, *C.B.: The Life of Sir Henry Campbell-Bannerman* (New York: St. Martin's Press, 1973). Cromer's "dark Gladstonian days" message to Victoria was dated from Cairo June 28, 1892; Victoria's response, on the reverse side, is from

Henry Ponsonby. Lady Emily Luytens (then Lytton) recalled her visit to the Queen in *A Blessed Girl* (London: Hart-Davis, 1953). General Sir Arthur Ellis's complaint about "NEWSPAPER squares" in the Windsor toilets, dated January 22, 1892, is in *Henry Ponsonby.* Ethel Smyth's reminiscence is *Streaks of Life,* quoted in Mrs. C. S. Peel, *A Hundred Wonderful Years* (London: Bodley Head, 1926). The Queen's continuing battle to secure posts for Prince Arthur is described in *C.B.* The Queen's opening the Imperial Institute is described at length in *The Star,* May 10, 1893. Bernard Shaw notes in his *Diaries* (University Park: Penn State Press, 1986), ed. S. Weintraub, which reporting assignment was his.

The description of the Queen, in Florence, entering her carriage, is from Lady Paget's *Embassies of Other Days,* and refers to April 1893. Her appeal to be able to see the spectacle *Venice* at the Olympia is in *Henry Ponsonby.* Details about Boehm and Gilbert are from *Victorian Sculpture* and from Richard Dorment's *Alfred Gilbert* (New Haven: Yale University Press, 1985), and the Queen's letters and journals. Marie Mallet's description of Natalie Janotha is from her diary, published as *Life with Queen Victoria.* Discussion of compensation to visiting artists is also in Mallet. Shaw's letter to Cecil Lewis on Victoria's beautiful voice in the aging body is dated June 24, 1924, in D. Laurence, ed., *Collected Letters of Bernard Shaw,* vol. 3 (New York: Viking, 1985). The Queen's request to Prince George to change his name to Albert is reported in *Recollections of Three Reigns.*

XVIII Metamorphosis (1894–1897)

The Queen's Scotch accent, used automatically at Balmoral with the servants, is described by Lady Lytton in Mary Lutyens, ed., *Lady Lytton's Court Diary, 1895–1899* (London: Hart-Davis, 1961). She also notes the visits of Dr. Pagenstecher through January 1901. Sir M. E. Grant Duff kept voluminous diaries. The volume utilized here is *Notes from a Diary 1892–1895* (London: John Murray, 1904). Frederick Ponsonby describes his search for the *Munshi*'s father, a prison apothecary, in *Recollections of Three Reigns.* The dislodging of the Duke of Cambridge is chronicled in the Queen's letters and journals and in Campbell-Bannerman's biography, *C.B.,* particularly chapters 12 through 17. George von Münster's letter to Holstein on the Kaiser's inflammatory behavior is dated January

16, 1896, in the *Holstein Papers*. The Kaiser's lackey Hermann Salzmann is quoted in Röhl and Nicolaus.

"Oom Paul" Kruger's visit to England and the apocryphal stories that grew up around the visit relative to the Queen are examined and dismissed in John Fisher, *Paul Kruger: His Life and Times* (London: Secker and Warburg, 1974), and in Johnannes Meintjes, *President Paul Kruger* (London: Cassell, 1974). The "Grandma's bread" quotation is from Manfred Nathan, *Paul Kruger* (Durban: The Knox Publishing Co., 1941).

The affair of the missing band at Windsor is described in *Recollections of Three Reigns*. Lady Monkswell's recollections after 1894 are in E. C. F. Collier, ed., *A Victorian Diarist: Later Extracts from the Journals of Mary, Lady Monkswell, 1895–1909* (London: John Murray, 1946). The Queen's home life and life at Cimiez is taken largely from her journals and from the diaries of Marie Mallet and Edith Lytton. The Bernhardt performance is from Lady Lytton and Frederick Ponsonby. "Queen Victoria as I Knew Her," by Xavier Paoli of the French *Sûreté Générale*, appeared in *Harper's Weekly*, July 12, 1913.

The Jubilee, as described in C. Louis Leipoldt's *Stormwrack* (published 1980), is taken from the corrected typescript in the Leipoldt Papers, University of Cape Town Library. The "Hymn for the Diamond Jubilee" is taken from a copy in the State Archives, Cape Town. The Jubilee portrait of the Queen drawn in words is in the possession of Professor Gunnar Sorelius, University of Uppsala, Sweden, in whose office I saw it. Bureaucratic details of Jubilee presentations, memorials, etc., are from the Lord Chamberlain's Papers in the Public Records Office, London. David Lindsay's diary extracts are from his *The Crawford Papers*. Letitia Whitty's childhood remembrance of the Jubilee is from "The Royal Couple Drops In," *Time*, November 18, 1985. That the Queen approved the "Diamond" designation in faint blue chalk appears in Lady Longford's *Queen Victoria*. Some of the Jubilee gifts are described from the Victoria and Albert Museum, where they are displayed. The *Daily Mail's* "More Majestic than She" is from J. Morris, *Heaven's Command: An Imperial Progress* (New York: Harcourt Brace Jovanovich, 1973).

XIX A Queen at War (1897–1900)

Almeric Fitzroy's diary extracts are from the *Memoirs of Sir Almeric Fitzroy*. That the Queen found Henry George's *Progress and Poverty* "difficult" is from F. G. Bettany, *Stewart Headlam* (London: John Murray, 1926). Headlam was once a Court chaplain. That the Queen once complained to Prince George about his reading Bagehot is from Lord Riddell's *More Pages from My Diary*. Extracts from Lord Esher's journals and letters, here and in Chapter XX, are from Maurice V. Brett, ed., *Journals and Letters of Reginald Viscount Esher*, vol. 1, 1870–1903 (London: Ivor Nicholson & Watson, 1934). The Queen on bed-mending is from Mallet. Her food-economizing is from Lytton.

The Lobanoffs' visit to Windsor is from Mallet; Bernard Mallet's diary is the source of Kitchener's visit to Balmoral, along with Frederick Ponsonby's *Recollections*. William II's impulsiveness is described by Holstein on May 31, 1898, to Paul von Hatzfeldt, in *Holstein Papers*. Félix Faure's visit to the Queen at Cimiez is in Ponsonby's *Recollections*. The three empresses in Cimiez are described by Daphne Bennett in *Vicky*.

Byron Farwell in *The Great Boer War* (London: A. Lane, 1976) details some of the circumstances of the Queen's chocolates; Victoria's letters and journals add further details; Tom O'Casey's experience is described in Sean O'Casey's memoir, *Drums Under the Windows* (New York: Macmillan, 1956). The Duchess of Buccleuch's story about Cecil Rhodes was told to Frederick Ponsonby in *Recollections*. The Queen's anger at the marriage of her maid-of-honor, Susan Baring, to Dr. James Reid, is told by Lady Lytton, who also reports the suggestion in the Queen's mail that she be attached to a balloon for better mobility.

The Mahdi's metamorphosis into an ink-pot was later confided by Sheppard to his son, Canon "Dick" Sheppard, who told Laurence Housman in February 1933. (From Housman's papers via Katherine Lyon Mix to S.W.)

The petition to the Queen from her South African subjects is from the copy in the University of Cape Town Libraries. The Queen's Dreyfus sympathies are reported by Mallet and Lytton, and in the Queen's own letters and journals. Her mistaking M. Cambon for the Italian ambassador is reported by Frederick Ponsonby and supplemented by the Queen's journals. Ponsonby also goes into detail about the Court bureaucracy's attempts to assist the Queen to overcome the sight handicap. Electric light at Balmoral is described by Lady Lytton (it did not help the Queen).

Victoria's Christmas for local families of Boer War soldiers at Windsor is described in the anonymously published *Notebooks of a Spinster Lady, 1878–1903* (New York: Cassell, 1919). Jennie Churchill's memoir, which includes her visit to Windsor, is *Reminiscences of Lady Randolph Churchill* (New York: Century, 1908).

Boer War particulars are from the Queen's diaries and letters, from Byron Farwell, and from Thomas Pakenham, *The Boer War* (New York: Random House, 1979). The Queen's behavior at the christening of the future Earl Mountbatten is from Philip Ziegler, *Mountbatten* (New York: Knopf, 1985). Political cartoons attacking Britain, and the Queen in person, over the Boer War are reproduced in *John Bull sur la Sellette* (Paris: Librarie J. Strauss, 1900), the copy used here from Pattee Library Special Collections (Pennsylvania State University).

XX Mourning for Victoria (1900–1901)

The Queen's failing health is reported in Mallet, Lytton, Fitzroy, Esher, the *Court Circulars* (discreetly, but even there, omissions are significant), and the Queen's own letters and journals. The *Lancet's* medical report on the Queen's death appeared on January 26, 1901, the same date as that in the *British Medical Journal.* Both are clearly by the same hand, very likely Sir James Reid. The Queen's refusal to meet Abraham is from Princess Marie Louise's *My Memories of Six Reigns* (London: Evans, 1956).

The comment by William II about his love for Victoria was made to Bishop Davidson and appears in his biography. Robert Bridges's comment (to Lionel Muirhead, April 12, 1901) appears in Donald E. Stanford, *The Selected Letters of Robert Bridges,* vol. 1 (Newark: University of Delaware Press, 1983). Winston Churchill's letter to his mother from Canada is quoted by Ralph Martin in his *Jennie,* vol. 1 (New York: Prentice-Hall, 1969). Grant Duff describes "Levée Dress (Crape left arm)" in his *Notes from a Diary.* That King Edward VII removed his mother's Indian servants as well as their traces, and expunged most traces of Brown, appears in Lytton, Esher, and all biographies of the King. The remark by Alexandra (to Vicky) about the King's expunging Victorian memorabilia is in Duff's *Alexandra.* That the Marochetti marble had to be searched for is described by Esher. Extracts from Lord Edward Pelham-Clinton's diaries are from St. John Nevill's edition. Lady Battersea's memory of the funeral is from her *Reminiscences;* Mary Monkswell's from her *Diary.* Problems with the horses drawing the coffin at Windsor are described by Frederick Ponsonby. Henry James's letter on the Queen and her successor is to Clare and Clara Benedict, January 22, 1901, in Leon Edel, ed., *Henry James Letters,* vol. 4 (Cambridge: Harvard University Press, 1984). Bernard Shaw's "The Ugliest Statue in London" was published in *Arts Gazette,* May 31, 1919.

Acknowledgments

$\mathcal{M}$y thanks go, first of all, to the friend and publisher who proposed that after many books on Victorian figures I should attempt a life of the paramount Victorian herself.

Researching a life of Queen Victoria is such a monumental task that listing the authorities to be consulted is alone almost enough to daunt the biographer. In the preceding source notes I do not cite every past scholar upon whom I have leaned, as the notes would have become longer than the book. I have touched upon the essentials, particularly where recent decades of scholarship, especially the exhumation of contemporary diaries, letters, and journals, have altered our perspectives significantly. Here, however, I would like to note my gratitude to many scholars and writers, living and dead, whose labors have made this biography possible, including (to be sure, some will be inadvertently missed), Theo Aronson, Georgina Battiscombe, Daphne Bennett, A. C. Benson, E. F. Benson, Hector H.

Bolitho, Gordon Brook-Shepherd, James Brough, George Earl Buckle, Agnes Carey, Algernon Cecil, Brian Connell, Egon Caesar Count Corti, Dormer Creston, Tom Cullen, A. W. Dasent, David Duff, Hope Dyson, Viscount Esher, E. P. Evelyn, Sir Roger Fulford, Charles Grey, Philip Guedalla, Alan Hardy, Christopher Hibbert, Hermione Hobhouse, Kurt Jagow, Robert Rhodes James, Clare Jerrold, Lady Elizabeth Longford, Mary Lutyens, Sir Philip Magnus, Victor Mallet, Dorothy Marshall, Sir Theodore Martin, Bertram Mitford (Lord Redesdale), James (Jan) Morris, Barry St. John Nevill, Alison Plowden, Arthur Ponsonby, Frederick Ponsonby, Magdalen Ponsonby, James Pope-Hennessy, Gwen Raverat, John Raymond, Kinley E. Roby, Dame Ethel Smyth, Baron E. Stockmar, G. Lytton Strachey, E. E. P. Tisdall, W. W. Tulloch, A. H. Wall, Tyler Whittle, Cecil Woodham-Smith, Kenneth Young, and Philip Ziegler.

Those to whom I owe specific debts of gratitude for assistance performed during the research and writing of this *Victoria* are John Burnside, M.D., Harry P. Clark, Louis Crompton, Frances Dimond, Jenny Emrys-Roberts, Kenyon Emrys-Roberts, Meyrick Emrys-Roberts, M.D., Oliver Everett, Patrick Garland, Joseph Glick, Alan Hanley-Browne, Eileen Hanley-Browne, John Hargleroad, M.D., Bridget Henisch, Heinz Henisch, Charles W. Mann, Jr., Keith Mantz, M.D., Nancy McCall, James Milholland, Jr., Katherine Lyon Mix, Nigel Nicolson, Robin Price, John Röhl, Shirley Rader, Judith Rayback, Jacqueline Rogers, Ulrich Ruch, Minerva Schwalb, Jeffrey Senior, D.M.D., Tom Smith, Peter Stansky, Alfred Triolo, Rodelle Weintraub, and Philip Winsor.

Institutions and archives essential to my research have been the Barbican Library, London; the British Library and its Newspaper Library; Guildhall Library of the City of London; the London School of Economics and Political Science and its Library; the Pattee Library, The Pennsylvania State University; the Public Record Office, London; Rutgers University Library; the State Archives, Cape Town; Surveyor of the Queen's Pictures; University of Cape Town Library; the Victoria and Albert Museum; the Wellcome Institute for the History of Medicine; and Windsor Castle, the Library.

I wish to acknowledge also the gracious permission of Her Majesty Queen Elizabeth II for the republication of material from the Royal Archives which is subject to copyright. For quotations utilized from the correspondence between Victoria and the Princess Royal, edited by Sir Roger Fulford, *Dearest Mama, Dearest Child, Darling Child, Beloved Mama,* and *Your Dear Letter,* I am also grateful to Bell & Hyman, publishers.

Index